The Palgrave Handbook of Peacebuilding in Africa

Tony Karbo • Kudrat Virk
Editors

The Palgrave Handbook of Peacebuilding in Africa

palgrave
macmillan

CENTRE FOR
CONFLICT
RESOLUTION

Editors
Tony Karbo
N'Zarama Centre for Peacebuilding
Abidjan, Côte d'Ivoire

Kudrat Virk
Centre for Conflict Resolution
Cape Town, South Africa

ISBN 978-3-319-62201-9 ISBN 978-3-319-62202-6 (eBook)
https://doi.org/10.1007/978-3-319-62202-6

Library of Congress Control Number: 2017959586

Cover design by Samantha Johnson

Printed on acid-free paper

This Palgrave Macmillan imprint is published by Springer Nature
The registered company is Springer International Publishing AG
The registered company address is: Gewerbestrasse 11, 6330 Cham, Switzerland

This book is dedicated to the memory of Ali A. Mazrui (1933–2014), Founding Director of the Institute of Global Cultural Studies at Binghamton University, State University of New York; Boutros Boutros-Ghali (1922–2016), former United Nations Secretary-General; and Margaret Vogt (1950–2014), former Special Representative of the United Nations Secretary-General to the Central African Republic, all three trailblazers and courageous champions of the quest for a Pax Africana.

Foreword: Three Prophets of *Pax Africana*

This book is one of the first comprehensive assessments of Africa's security architecture over the last three post-Cold War decades, authored primarily by eminent African scholars and practitioners, joined by equally eminent colleagues from beyond the continent.

It is thus fitting that the volume honours three Prophets of *Pax Africana*: Kenya's Ali Mazrui, Egypt's Boutros Boutros-Ghali, and Nigeria's Margaret Vogt, who joined the ranks of the ancestors in the Hereafter that Mazrui had described as "after Africa", in 2014 (Mazrui and Vogt) and 2016 (Boutros-Ghali). 2017 was the golden jubilee of the publication of Ali Mazrui's *Towards a Pax Africana: A Study of Ideology and Ambition*. This volume opens with a chapter from this seminal book explaining the concept of *Pax Africana*. Through this idea, Mazrui called for Africans to create and consolidate peace on their continent through their own exertions. His idea of "continental jurisdiction" was a sort of "Monroe doctrine" that urged outsiders to stay out of the continent and let Africans resolve their own disputes themselves. In the related idea of "racial sovereignty," Mazrui argued that inter-African interventions by brotherly outside states were more legitimate than those of outsiders. But, the question that the Kenyan posed five decades ago has still not been answered: "Who will keep the peace in Africa now that the colonial powers are departing?"

Mazrui was the foremost African public intellectual of the last five decades, and indefatigably promoted African unity, also serving on two Organisation of African Unity (OAU) eminent panels on reparations, and on transforming the continental body into the African Union (AU). He often identified poor governance and external intervention as the roots of Africa's conflicts, noting that Africa's soldiers—including those like Uganda's Idi Amin and Liberia's Samuel Doe whom he termed *lumpenmilitariats*—were no more successful than civilian autocrats at the socio-economic transformation of their countries. Mazrui often talked of the African state as a political refugee: desperate and bewildered and in need of external rescue. He also often bemoaned the negative impact of ethnicity in African politics. One of the contemporary causes of the disappearance of *Pax Africana* has been the violent extremism that has wracked Africa, from the Sahel to Somalia, in a perversion of Mazrui's notion of an African "warrior tradition".

Even more than he focused attention on Africa's domestic travails, Mazrui identified the pernicious role of external actors such as the United States (US), Russia, and France during, and in some cases, after the Cold War, as having contributed enormously to Africa's continuing conflicts. He consistently criticised *Pax Americana*'s "war on terror", as well as *Pax Gallica*'s continuing neo-colonial interventions on the continent, urging instead that actual and potential regional hegemons like Nigeria, South Africa, Egypt, the Democratic Republic of the Congo (DRC), and Ethiopia seek to assume a "gate-keeping" role to keep Africa free of external meddlers: these are all topics covered in this book.

Egyptian scholar-diplomat, Boutros Boutros-Ghali—our second Prophet of *Pax Africana*—served as the first African United Nations (UN) Secretary-General between 1992 and 1996. Having obtained a doctorate in international law from the Sorbonne in Paris and taught at Cairo University for 28 years, he was the most intellectually accomplished Secretary-General in the history of the post. During his tenure, Boutros-Ghali sought to play the role of "the Pope on the East River", bluntly condemning the double standards of powerful Western powers in selectively authorising UN interventions in "rich men's wars" in the Balkans, while ignoring Africa's "orphan conflicts".

Boutros-Ghali's enduring legacy to *Pax Africana* will be *An Agenda for Peace*: a landmark document published in 1992 on the tools and techniques of conflict prevention, peacemaking, peacekeeping, and peacebuilding for a post–Cold War era. This document still remains an indispensable guide for contemporary conflict management efforts. This volume's chapters are, in fact, framed around these four themes, and the multi-dimensional peacebuilding operations and international criminal tribunals pioneered during this era are also examined in detail in these chapters.

Our final Prophet of *Pax Africana* is Nigerian scholar-practitioner, Margaret Vogt, who like Mazrui, has a chapter in this book. She was a pan-African peacemaker and scholar-diplomat who contributed tremendously to Africa's evolving security architecture. Vogt led the team of experts that crafted a security mechanism for the Organisation of African Unity in the early 1990s, which subsequently sought to manage conflicts across the continent. She also pushed the OAU and the AU to make more efforts to involve women in African peacemaking and peacebuilding initiatives.

While helping to establish the OAU's security mechanism, she led another team of experts to devise a security mechanism for the Economic Community of West African States (ECOWAS). This was the first such sub-regional mechanism on the continent, and built on the lessons of the organisation's peacekeeping missions in Liberia and Sierra Leone in the 1990s. Vogt had, in fact, co-edited one of the earliest books on the ECOWAS Ceasefire Monitoring

Group (ECOMOG) mission in Liberia in 1992; another on Nigeria's historical peacekeeping role in 1993; and a two-volume comparative study of peacekeeping in Chad and Liberia in 1996.

She spent the last 15 years of her life working for the cause of peace at the United Nations, also serving as *chef de cabinet* at the AU Commission. She was the deputy Special Representative of the UN Political Office for Somalia, and Special Representative of the UN Integrated Peacebuilding Office in the Central African Republic (CAR). All of these experiences have been captured in her rich chapter in this volume which seeks to bridge the gap between theory and praxis.

It is to these three Prophets of *Pax Africana* that this book is dedicated, and the framing of the volume has benefitted immensely from their theoretical and practical insights.

Institute for Pan-African Thought and Conversation
University of Johannesburg
Johannesburg, South Africa

Adekeye Adebajo

Acknowledgements

Half a century ago, the late Kenyan scholar Ali Mazrui—one of Africa's foremost public intellectuals—published his seminal 1967 work, *Towards a Pax Africana: A Study of Ideology and Ambition*, in which he eloquently laid out the idea of African ownership of African peace and security as the logical conclusion of the continent's struggle for independence from colonial rule. Transforming this ambition of an African-owned peace into a lived truth remains an ongoing quest, reflected in the endeavours of the African Union (AU)—successor to the Organisation of African Unity (OAU)—to realise anew an effective African peace and security architecture, to serve as the foundation of a prosperous and peaceful continent where over 1.2 billion African citizens can thrive and live together in dignity. Against the backdrop of wide-sweeping changes in the global order and of a resurgent pan-African outlook, this book seeks to contribute to the search for that "new" *Pax Africana*. We are immensely grateful to the University of Chicago Press, the Orion Publishing Group, and Kim Forde-Mazrui, the executor of his father's estate, for permission to reprint Mazrui's original articulation of the concept of *Pax Africana*, which lies at the intellectual heart of this volume. We would like as well to thank all the contributing authors—a diverse group of scholars, policymakers, and practitioners, including several in the vanguard of peacebuilding in Africa—for sharing their experiences and insights on the pages of this volume, and for their patience and perseverance in bringing it to fruition.

This project was initiated by the Centre for Conflict Resolution (CCR) in Cape Town, South Africa, with a view to assessing the progress being made by, and supporting the efforts of, the AU and Africa's regional economic communities (RECs) towards making, keeping, and building peace on the continent. Our debt to CCR for its initiative is profound. We thus owe a wealth of gratitude to all the staff at the Centre, both past and present, for their indispensable support in the completion of this work. Particular thanks are due to Adekeye Adebajo, former Executive Director of CCR (2003–2016), under whose leadership this project was conceived, for his invaluable guidance and unflagging commitment to achieving its goals. We would like further to acknowledge the main funders of the Centre's Africa Programme over the years: the governments of Denmark, Finland, the Netherlands, Norway, and Sweden.

A special word of thanks must go to participants at a CCR seminar, held in August 2013, for their invaluable feedback on early drafts of many of the contributions to this volume, as it also must to the three anonymous peer reviewers for their useful suggestions for further strengthening the draft manuscript. We are grateful as well to Jason Cook, for his meticulous copy-editing, and to Lisa Kleinholz, for her able indexing of the final manuscript.

Finally, it has been a pleasure to work with Anca Pusca, Anne Schult, Katelyn Zingg, and their colleagues at Palgrave Macmillan. We hope that this book will provoke debate on critical questions in the field of peace and security in Africa, while encouraging bold and innovative thinking on tackling the challenges that the continent continues to face in its quest for a just and sustainable African-owned peace.

August 2017

Tony Karbo
Kudrat Virk

Contents

List of Acronyms

ABC	Abyei Boundaries Commission
ACC	Anti-Corruption Commission (Sierra Leone)
ACCORD	African Centre for the Constructive Resolution of Disputes (South Africa)
ACHPR	African Commission on Human and Peoples' Rights
ACIRC	African Capacity for Immediate Response to Crises
ACJHR	African Court of Justice and Human Rights
ACPP	African Conflict Prevention Pool (Britain)
ACUNS	Academic Council on the United Nations System
ADDR	Amnesty, Disarmament, Demobilisation, and Rehabilitation programme (Nigeria)
AERC	African Economic Research Consortium
AfCHPR	African Court on Human and Peoples' Rights
AfDB	African Development Bank
AFISMA	African-led International Support Mission in Mali
AFRC	Armed Forces Revolutionary Council (Sierra Leone)
AGA	African Governance Architecture
AGOA	African Growth and Opportunity Act (US)
AGS	American Graduate School (France)
ALC	African Leadership Centre
AMIB	African Union Mission in Burundi
AMIS	African Union Mission in Sudan
AMISOM	African Union Mission in Somalia
AMU	Arab Maghreb Union
ANC	African National Congress (South Africa)
APC	All People's Congress (Sierra Leone)
APC	armoured personnel carrier
APRM	African Peer Review Mechanism
APSA	African Peace and Security Architecture
AQIM	Al-Qaeda in the Islamic Maghreb

ARS	Alliance for the Re-Liberation of Somalia
ARV	anti-retroviral
ASF	African Standby Force
AU	African Union
AWD	African Women's Decade
AWDF	African Women's Development Fund
BDEAC	*Banque de Développement des Etats de l'Afrique Centrale*
BDOHP	British Diplomatic Oral History Programme
BINUB	United Nations Integrated Office in Burundi
BINUCA	United Nations Integrated Peacebuilding Support Office in the Central African Republic
BIPSOT	Bangladesh Institute of Peace Support Operations Training
BMATT	British Military Assistance Training Team
BRICS	Brazil, Russia, India, China, and South Africa
CAR	Central African Republic
CCR	Centre for Conflict Resolution (South Africa)
CCSSP	Commonwealth Community Safety and Security Project
CDF	Civil Defence Forces (Sierra Leone)
CDP	Congress for Democracy and Progress (Burkina Faso)
CDSP	Common Defence and Security Policy (AU)
CEDAW	Convention on the Elimination of All Forms of Discrimination Against Women
CEN-SAD	Community of Sahel-Saharan States
CEWS	Continental Early Warning System
CFA	*Communauté Financière Africaine*
CGHR	Centre of Governance and Human Rights (University of Cambridge)
CIA	Central Intelligence Agency (US)
CIC	Center on International Cooperation (New York University)
CIMIC	civil-military cooperation
CISU	Central Intelligence and Security Unit (Sierra Leone)
CLAs	Community Liaison Assistants
CMA	Coordination of Movements of the Azawad
CNN	Cable News Network
CODESRIA	Council for the Development of Social Science Research in Africa
COE	contingent-owned equipment
COMESA	Common Market for Eastern and Southern Africa
COS	Special Operations Command (France)
CPA	Comprehensive Peace Agreement (Sudan–South Sudan)
CPDTF	Commonwealth Police Development Task Force
CSCPF	Continental Structural Conflict Prevention Framework
CSIS	Center for Strategic and International Studies (US)

CSSDCA	Conference on Security, Stability, Development, and Cooperation in Africa
CSVA	Country Structural Vulnerability Assessment
CSW	Commission on the Status of Women (UN)
CUNPK	Centre for United Nations Peacekeeping (India)
CUNY	City University of New York
DAC	Development Assistance Committee (OECD)
DCAF	Geneva Centre for the Democratic Control of Armed Forces
DDR	disarmament, demobilisation, and re-integration
DFID	Department for International Development (Britain)
DGSE	Directorate-General for External Security (France)
DISECS	district security committees (Sierra Leone)
DPA	Department of Political Affairs (UN)
DPKO	Department of Peacekeeping Operations (UN)
DRC	Democratic Republic of the Congo
EAC	East African Community
EALA	East African Legislative Assembly
EASBRICOM	Eastern Africa Standby Brigade Coordination Mechanism
EASBRIG	Eastern Africa Standby Brigade
EASF	Eastern Africa Standby Force
EASFCOM	Eastern Africa Standby Force Coordination Mechanism
EASSI	Eastern African Sub-Regional Support Initiative for the Advancement of Women
ECCAS	Economic Community of Central African States
ECCASBRIG	ECCAS Brigade
ECDPM	European Centre for Development Policy Management (Netherlands)
ECHA	Executive Committee on Humanitarian Affairs (UN)
ECOBRIG	ECOWAS Brigade
ECOMOG	ECOWAS Ceasefire Monitoring Group
ECOSOC	Economic and Social Council (UN)
ECOWAS	Economic Community of West African States
ECPA	Executive Committee on Peace and Security (UN)
EEC	European Economic Community
EPA	economic partnership agreement
EU	European Union
EUFOR	EU Force
EURORECAMP	European Reinforcement of African Capacities to Maintain Peace
FAO	Food and Agriculture Organisation
FAS	Femmes Africa Solidarité (Senegal)
FDI	foreign direct investment
FGS	Federal Government of Somalia
FIB	Force Intervention Brigade

FLS	Frontline States
FNL	National Forces of Liberation (Burundi)
FOMAC	Central African Multinational Force
FRELIMO	Mozambique Liberation Front
G-20	Group of 20
GDP	gross domestic product
GER	Gender Equity and Reconciliation
GFW	Global Fund for Women
GIA	Armed Islamic Group of Algeria
GIMAC	Gender Is My Agenda Campaign
GRIPS	National Graduate Institute for Policy Studies (Japan)
HDI	Human Development Index
IAPTC	International Association of Peacekeeping Training Centres
ICAR	Institute for Conflict Analysis and Resolution (US)
ICC	International Criminal Court
ICC-OTP	International Criminal Court–Office of the Prosecutor
ICG	International Crisis Group
ICGLR	International Conference on the Great Lakes Region
ICISS	International Commission on Intervention and State Sovereignty
ICJ	International Court of Justice
ICRC	International Committee of the Red Cross
ICTR	International Criminal Tribunal for Rwanda
ICTY	International Criminal Tribunal for the Former Yugoslavia
IDP	internally displaced person
IDRC	International Development Research Centre (Canada)
IEC	Independent Electoral Commission (South Africa)
IFI	international financial institution
IGAD	Intergovernmental Authority on Development
IGASOM	IGAD Peace Support Mission in Somalia
IGD	Institute for Global Dialogue (South Africa)
ILO	International Labour Organisation
IMATT	International Military Assistance Training Team
IMF	International Monetary Fund
IMTD	Institute for Multi-Track Diplomacy
IPI	International Peace Institute (US)
IPLG	Institute of Peace, Leadership, and Governance (Africa University)
IRAPP	IGAD Regional HIV and AIDS Partnership Program
ISIS	Islamic State of Iraq and al-Sham (also Islamic State of Iraq and Syria)
Isis-WICCE	Isis-Women's International Cross Cultural Exchange (Uganda)
ISR	intelligence, surveillance, and reconnaissance aircraft

ISS	Institute for Security Studies (South Africa)
JSDP	Justice Sector Development Programme (Sierra Leone)
KNDR	Kenya National Dialogue and Reconciliation process
KPTJ	Kenyans for Peace, Truth, and Justice
LPA	Lagos Plan of Action
LPI	Life and Peace Institute (Sweden)
LPRC	Liberia Petroleum Refinery Corporation
LRA	Lord's Resistance Army
LSE	London School of Economics and Political Science
M23	March 23 Movement (DRC)
MAPROBU	African Prevention and Protection Mission in Burundi
MDG	Millennium Development Goal
MICOPAX	Mission for the Consolidation of Peace in the Central African Republic
MINURCA	United Nations Mission in the Central African Republic
MINURCAT	United Nations Mission in the Central African Republic and Chad
MINURSO	United Nations Mission for the Referendum in Western Sahara
MINUSCA	United Nations Multidimensional Integrated Stabilisation Mission in the Central African Republic
MINUSMA	United Nations Multidimensional Integrated Stabilisation Mission in Mali
MINUSTAH	United Nations Stabilisation Mission in Haiti
MISCA	African-led International Support Mission to the Central African Republic
MIT	Massachusetts Institute of Technology (US)
MNLA	National Movement for the Liberation of Azawad
MOCC	Military Operational Coordination Committee (AU)
MODAT	Ministry of Defence Advisory Team
MONUC	United Nations Organisation Mission in the Democratic Republic of the Congo
MONUSCO	United Nations Organisation Stabilisation Mission in the Democratic Republic of the Congo
MOU	memorandum of understanding
MPLA	Popular Movement for the Liberation of Angola
MSU	Mediation Support Unit (UN)
MUJAO	Movement for Unity and Jihad in West Africa
NAM	Non-Aligned Movement
NAP	National Action Plan
NASBRIG	North African Standby Brigade
NATO	North Atlantic Treaty Organisation
NCP	N'Zarama Centre for Peacebuilding (Côte d'Ivoire)
NEPAD	New Partnership for Africa's Development
NGO	non-governmental organisation

NOCAL	National Oil Company of Liberia
NPFL	National Patriotic Front of Liberia
NSA	National Security Agency (Sierra Leone)
NYASA	New York African(a) Studies Association
NYU	New York University
OAU	Organisation of African Unity
OCHA	Office for the Coordination of Humanitarian Affairs (UN)
ODI	Overseas Development Institute (Britain)
ODM	Orange Democratic Movement (Kenya)
OECD	Organisation for Economic Cooperation and Development
OFOESA	Office for Field Operations and External Support Activities (UN)
OHCHR	Office of the High Commissioner for Human Rights (UN)
OIC	Organisation of Islamic Cooperation
OIOS	Office of Internal Oversight Services (UN)
ONGC	Oil and Natural Gas Corporation (India)
ONS	Office of National Security (Sierra Leone)
ONUB	United Nations Operation in Burundi
ONUC	United Nations Operation in the Congo
ONUMUZ	United Nations Operation in Mozambique
OPDSC	Organ on Politics, Defence, and Security Cooperation (SADC)
ORCI	Office for Research and the Collection of Information (UN)
OSD	Operational Support Division (Sierra Leone)
P-1	permanent one member of the UN Security Council (US)
P-2	permanent two members of the UN Security Council (China and Russia)
P-3	permanent three members of the UN Security Council (Britain, France, US)
P-4	permanent four members of the UN Security Council (Britain, France, Russia, US)
P-5	permanent five members of the UN Security Council (Britain, China, France, Russia, US)
PBC	Peacebuilding Commission (UN)
PBSO	Peacebuilding Support Office (UN)
PLANELM	Planning Element
PNU	Party of National Unity (Kenya)
PROSECS	provincial security committees (Sierra Leone)
PRSP	poverty reduction strategy paper
PSC	Peace and Security Council (AU)
PSD	Peace and Security Department (AU)
R2P	responsibility to protect
RAP	Regional Action Plan

RCD	Rally for Congolese Democracy
REC	regional economic community
RECAMP	Reinforcement of African Capacities to Maintain Peace
RENAMO	Mozambique National Resistance
RPF	Rwandan Patriotic Front
RSLAF	Republic of Sierra Leone Armed Forces
RUF	Revolutionary United Front (Sierra Leone)
SA	Service Action (DGSE)
SAAPS	South African Association of Political Studies
SADC	Southern African Development Community
SADC SF	SADC Standby Force
SADCBRIG	SADC Brigade
SADCC	Southern African Development Coordination Conference
SADRA	Southern African Development and Reconstruction Agency
SAIIA	South African Institute of International Affairs
SANDF	South African National Defence Force
SAP	structural adjustment programme
SARW	Southern Africa Resource Watch
SCSL	Special Court for Sierra Leone
SDG	Sustainable Development Goal
SDGEA	Solemn Declaration on Gender Equality in Africa
SEA	sexual exploitation and abuse
SGBV	sexual and gender-based violence
SHIRBRIGG	Standby High-Readiness Brigade
SILSEP	Sierra Leone Security Sector Reform Programme
SIPA	School of International and Public Affairs (Columbia University)
SIPO	Strategic Indicative Plan of the Organ (I and II) (SADC)
SLP	Sierra Leone Police
SNA	Somali National Army
SOF	Special Operations Forces (France)
SOFA	status-of-forces agreement
SPLM/A	Sudan People's Liberation Movement/Army
SSD	Special Security Division (Sierra Leone)
SSR	security sector reform
STI	sexually transmitted infection
SWAPO	South West Africa People's Organisation
TCC	troop-contributing country
TFG	Transitional Federal Government (Somalia)
TRC	Truth and Reconciliation Commission (Liberia)
UFDR	Union of Democratic Forces for Unity (CAR)
UIC	Union of Islamic Courts (Somalia)
UK	United Kingdom
UKZN	University of KwaZulu-Natal (South Africa)

UN	United Nations
UNAIDS	Joint UN Programme on HIV/AIDS
UNAMID	African Union–United Nations Hybrid Operation in Darfur
UNAMIR	United Nations Assistance Mission for Rwanda
UNAMSIL	United Nations Mission in Sierra Leone
UNAVEM	United Nations Angola Verification Mission
UNDOF	United Nations Disengagement Observer Force
UNDP	United Nations Development Programme
UNECA	United Nations Economic Commission for Africa
UNEF	United Nations Emergency Force (I and II)
UNEP	United Nations Environment Programme
UNESCO	United Nations Educational, Scientific, and Cultural Organisation
UNFICYP	United Nations Peacekeeping Force in Cyprus
UNFPA	United Nations Population Fund
UNHCR	United Nations High Commissioner for Refugees
UNICEF	United Nations Children's Fund
UNIDIR	United Nations Institute for Disarmament Research
UNIFIL	United Nations Interim Force in Lebanon
UNIIMOG	United Nations Iran-Iraq Military Observer Group
UNISFA	United Nations Interim Security Force for Abyei
UNITA	National Union for the Total Independence of Angola
UNITAF	Unified Task Force
UNMEE	United Nations Mission in Ethiopia and Eritrea
UNMIL	United Nations Mission in Liberia
UNMIK	United Nations Interim Administration Mission in Kosovo
UNMISS	United Nations Mission in South Sudan
UNMOGIP	United Nations Military Observer Group in India and Pakistan
UNOAU	United Nations Office to the African Union
UNOCI	United Nations Operation in Côte d'Ivoire
UNOM	United Nations Office in Mali
UNOMIL	United Nations Observer Mission in Liberia
UNON	United Nations Office in Nairobi
UNOSOM	United Nations Operation in Somalia (I and II)
UNPOS	United Nations Political Office for Somalia
UNSC	United Nations Security Council
UNSOA	United Nations Support Office for the African Union Mission in Somalia
UNSOM	United Nations Assistance Mission in Somalia
UNSOS	United Nations Support Office in Somalia
UNTAC	United Nations Transitional Authority in Cambodia
UNTAG	United Nations Transition Assistance Group
UNTSO	United Nations Truce Supervision Organisation

UPEACE	University of Peace
US	United States
USAID	United States Agency for International Development
VCCT	Voluntary Confidential Counselling and Testing
WAHO	West African Health Organisation
WEF	World Economic Forum
WIDER	World Institute for Development Economics Research
Wits	University of the Witwatersrand (South Africa)
WSR	Women's Situation Room
ZANU-PF	Zimbabwe African National Union–Patriotic Front

List of Figures

List of Tables

PART I

The Theory and Practice of *Pax Africana*

CHAPTER 1

Introduction: Towards a New *Pax Africana*

Tony Karbo

> *[T]he peace of* Africa *is to be assured by the exertions of* Africans *themselves. The idea of a "Pax Africana" is the specifically military aspect of the principle of continental jurisdiction.*
>
> Ali A. Mazrui, *Towards a Pax Africana*

Peace and stability have been elusive for most of Africa's post-colonial experience. The problems associated with violence in Africa have a long history, but since the end of the Cold War (1945–1990), the nature and dynamics of conflicts have changed. Most conflicts since the end of the Cold War have been internal, caused primarily by ethnic (identity), economic, political, and demographic reasons (see also Deng in this volume). Meanwhile, the continent's abundance of large deposits of natural resources has ignited a new search for spheres of influence by former colonial powers, such as Britain and France, and in recent years, emerging powers, like India and China, have also entered the fray. Since 2000, Africa, through its continental and regional organisations, has made significant progress in its efforts to address the problems associated with violent conflict. The African Union (AU) has developed legal and institutional frameworks to guide and promote democratic governance, peace and security, and socio-economic development on the continent. These include: the 2000 Constitutive Act of the AU; the 2002 Protocol Relating to the Establishment of the Peace and Security Council (PSC); and the 2007 African Charter on Democracy, Elections, and Governance. Generally speaking, African states have made notable progress towards greater democratisation, peace, and human security, which merits acknowledgement. This has been reflected in, among other things, the holding of regular elections, the end of several major conflicts (such as in Angola, Liberia, Mozambique, and Sierra Leone), and the acceleration of economic growth. However, this progress has been slow and

T. Karbo (✉)
N'Zarama Centre for Peacebuilding, Abidjan, Côte d'Ivoire

T. Karbo, K. Virk (eds.), *The Palgrave Handbook of Peacebuilding in Africa*, https://doi.org/10.1007/978-3-319-62202-6_1

fragile,[1] with the AU continuing to grapple with challenges in the implementation of its various legal and policy instruments, as well as institutional weaknesses.[2]

A lethal combination of weak and fledgling states with inherited problems, pervasive poverty, and fragile economies that remain largely dependent on former colonial powers, along with a complex web of inherent contradictions within the African state, have contributed to the plethora of violent conflicts that have plagued the continent since independence (see also Omeje in this volume). From West Africa (Côte d'Ivoire, Guinea, Guinea-Bissau, Liberia, Sierra Leone); to the Horn of Africa (Djibouti, Eritrea, Ethiopia, Somalia); to Eastern Africa (Kenya, South Sudan, Uganda); to the Great Lakes region (Burundi, the Democratic Republic of the Congo [DRC], Rwanda); to North Africa (Algeria, Egypt, Libya, Tunisia); and to Southern Africa (Angola, Lesotho, Mozambique, Zimbabwe), the African state has not been able completely to shake off the vestiges of colonialism. The wars since the end of the Cold War have been devastating, leading to the loss of thousands of lives—not including the estimated 800,000 people killed during the 1994 Rwandan genocide[3]—with many more displaced and rendered refugees outside their countries. For example, about 70,000 people were killed and 2.6 million displaced during the conflict in Sierra Leone from 1991 to 2002,[4] while around 250,000 people lost their lives in Liberia's civil war between 1989 and 2003.[5] Thus, while most African countries at independence had expectations of stability, peace, and socio-economic development, what several newly independent states experienced instead were massive outbreaks of violence on a scale and magnitude that had hitherto not been experienced on the continent.

The late Kenyan scholar Ali Mazrui in his seminal work *Towards a Pax Africana: A Study of Ideology and Ambition*[6] outlines some of the long-term ideological influences, and indeed consequences, of Africa's imperial experience, but also articulates a concept of "Pax Africana" that lies at the heart of this collection of essays. The ambition of *Pax Africana*, as Mazrui suggests, is an agenda for peace in Africa, with this peace to be guaranteed by Africans themselves. *Pax Africana* is not an idea that seeks to force compliance with principles and norms for a peaceful Africa, but rather to guarantee collective security on the continent by having African countries contribute to the creation and sustenance of that peace. In other words, a *Pax Africana* in Mazrui's view is one in which Africans secure the peace for the continent themselves—with their own material and financial resources. It is about both who participates (nationality) and where the participation occurs (jurisdiction). As Mazrui argues, armaments for Africans should be procured only for protection against imperial powers, and not against each other. Against the backdrop of the Cold War, Mazrui—writing in 1967—also discusses questions related to disarmament, non-violent resistance, security cooperation, and the role of the United Nations (UN) as an enforcer of international peace and security. The fundamental question raised by Mazrui was: Who is responsible for keeping the peace in Africa after all colonial powers would have withdrawn from the continent? And so it remains.

As Nigerian scholar Adekeye Adebajo has observed: "Ali Mazrui ... was one of the earliest analysts to articulate the need for Africans to take on the responsibility of keeping, building and consolidating peace on their own continent."[7] This book seeks to assess progress towards the realisation of this African vision of taking responsibility for the maintenance of peace and security on the continent, as one belonging to all member states of the African Union. More specifically, the volume aims to examine the progress being made in peacemaking, peacekeeping, and peacebuilding by the AU and Africa's regional economic communities (RECs), including the Economic Community of West African States (ECOWAS), the Southern African Development Community (SADC), the Intergovernmental Authority on Development (IGAD), the Arab Maghreb Union (AMU), the East African Community (EAC), and the Economic Community of Central African States (ECCAS). It also seeks to assist these regional bodies in building peace in countries emerging from conflict. Towards that end, the book explores issues related to the prevention, management, and resolution of conflicts; relations between Africa's regional organisations and the UN on matters of peace and security; the role of major powers such as the United States (US), France, and Britain,[8] and their contributions to African peacekeeping efforts; and the regional and international dimensions of challenges related to peacebuilding, state-building, and post-conflict reconstruction on the continent. The book further considers the lessons that can be drawn from UN peacekeeping and peacebuilding experiences in Africa, and how these could inform a more effective division of labour between Africa's fledgling security organisations and the world body.[9]

The Concept of *Pax Africana*

Contrary to expectations, the removal of the imperial yoke—as just mentioned—did not usher in an era of peace, stability, and socio-economic development in Africa. The cost in human life, resulting from combat, as well as the suffering and starvation brought on by war, has been striking, with over 10 million Africans having been killed and about as many made refugees since 1960.[10] The acquisition of political independence also did not significantly change economic relationships between the European colonial powers (such as Britain and France) and their former African colonies, which continued to be dependent on the former through partnerships that can best be described as exploitative. Several decades on, many African countries—for example, Burundi, the Central African Republic (CAR), Guinea-Bissau, Liberia, Madagascar, and Malawi[11]—continue to have large segments of their populations living below the international poverty line of $1.90 a day.[12] Indeed, between 1990 and 2010, Africa excluding North Africa made the least progress in reducing the incidence and intensity of poverty compared to other major regions of the world, failing to meet the UN's Millennium Development Goal (MDG) of eradicating extreme poverty and hunger by 2015.[13] Africa's reliance on primary commodity exports—over 60 per cent of its total to the European Union (EU), as a bloc the continent's largest trade partner, in 2016[14]—also explains, in part, why progress towards socio-economic development and efforts to narrow inequality gaps have been limited on the continent.

In May 1963, the Organisation of African Unity (OAU) was established to champion the independence of African states from the vestiges of colonialism. Its creation, though, was the outcome of a debate between two different interpretations of pan-Africanism.[15] Ghanaian leader Kwame Nkrumah cut a key figure. Having led the successful struggle for Ghana's independence in 1957, Nkrumah embarked on a quest for Africa's liberation from colonialism. He proposed the establishment of an African High Command to spearhead this liberation struggle and to coordinate regional security efforts. Nkrumah strongly believed that Ghana's freedom was incomplete, and would be meaningless, without the rest of the continent also achieving its independence. His proposal for an African High Command was supported by some countries such as Algeria, Egypt, Guinea, Mali, and Morocco (together known as the Casablanca Group). However, others—for example, Liberia, Nigeria, and Senegal—rejected the immediate establishment of an African High Command, and proposed instead a gradualist approach to integration in Africa, while emphasising "the importance of non-interference in the affairs of other African states".[16] Those who favoured this approach, which eventually won out, fell under the umbrella of the Monrovia Group.[17]

As Ghanaian scholar Sam Amoo has noted, "member-states' commitment to the … 'peaceful settlement of disputes by negotiation, mediation, conciliation or arbitration'" was a founding principle of the 1963 OAU Charter. Ever since, "African states have … maintained that conditions of peace and security … constitute the cornerstone upon which African solidarity and cooperation can [and should] be built". The Commission of Mediation, Conciliation, and Arbitration was created "as one of the four principal institutions of the OAU to underscore regional and organizational commitment to peaceful settlement of regional conflicts".[18] However, this mechanism was weak. The commission, as Adebajo has pointed out, "did not have any powers of sanction",[19] and it was constrained by issues related to the sanctity of state sovereignty and territorial integrity. Though weak overall, the OAU—designed as a framework for collective regional security and promoting regional cooperation in Africa—was instrumental in resolving some conflicts. Following independence, many African countries found themselves embroiled in international border disputes inherited from the colonial period. "It is in managing these types of disputes that the OAU … registered some of its most notable successes. In the 1960s and 1970s, for example, the OAU was successful in resolving a number of border disputes, including those between Algeria and Morocco, Mali and Upper Volta (now Burkina Faso), Somalia and Kenya, and Ethiopia and Somalia."[20] Also, with much of the rest of the continent having gained its independence by the mid-1970s, the OAU played an important role in mobilising support at the

UN for the Frontline States (FLS) and liberation movements in Southern Africa in their struggles to end colonialism in Namibia, South Africa, and Zimbabwe.

By the mid-1990s, however, against a backdrop of wider changes, OAU member states recognised that if they were to realise the vision of a *Pax Africana*, something had to be done differently. The fall of the Berlin Wall in 1989 and the subsequent demise of the Soviet Union in 1991 spurred the OAU to devise more effective, continental conflict management mechanisms. The crises that broke out from the 1990s onwards—for example, in Liberia, Sierra Leone, and Somalia—together with the neglect of the continent by the UN and the international community, only lent further impetus to African efforts to create more effective mechanisms for the prevention, management, and resolution of conflicts on their own continent. The OAU's earlier preoccupation with liberation struggles was overtaken by a need to tackle the numerous conflicts that broke out in the wake of the demise of the East-West rivalry between the erstwhile Soviet Union and the United States. Recognising the need, in 1990 the OAU adopted a Declaration on the Political and Socio-Economic Situation in Africa and the Fundamental Changes Taking Place in the World. At the same time, there was recognition as well of the changing nature of conflicts from inter-state to intra-state, "which called for a more dynamic approach, given the African pre-occupations with concepts such as sovereignty and noninterference in the internal affairs of Member States, as enshrined in the OAU Charter".[21] In 1992, Tanzania's Salim Ahmed Salim, then OAU Secretary-General—after extensive consultations—submitted a report on the establishment of a new security mechanism for the organisation. Subsequently, in 1993, African heads of state meeting in Cairo adopted a declaration establishing the OAU Mechanism for Conflict Prevention, Management, and Resolution.

At the turn of the twenty-first century, the OAU embarked upon an ambitious project to transform the organisation into one that would be more responsive to the human development needs of the continent. Some scholars, such as Ethiopia's Solomon Dersso,[22] have argued that the establishment of the African Peace and Security Architecture (APSA) in December 2003,[23] was the most comprehensive step taken (to date) by African leaders towards the achievement of a "new" *Pax Africana*. (See Kuwali in this volume.) But what exactly is this new *Pax Africana*? How important is it for the maintenance of peace and security in Africa? To what extent has the African Union—which replaced the OAU in 2002—succeeded in meeting the ideals of Mazrui's *Pax Africana*? Does the APSA provide the means through which a true *Pax Africana* can be realised?

Mazrui—as mentioned earlier—was among the first to put forward the idea of Africans taking responsibility for the maintenance of peace and security on their own continent. At the time, the idea seemed to echo the aspirations of the founding fathers of the OAU, albeit in a deeper, more profound reconstitution of the OAU's structures and functions. At the close of the 1990s, the OAU began a process of transformation into the African Union, which was completed in July 2002 in the South African port city of Durban. The impetus for the establishment of the AU was the result of several factors, including proliferation of violent internal conflicts in the wake of the end of the Cold War. The African economic and development agenda had earlier culminated in the 1980 Lagos Plan of Action and 1991 Abuja Treaty, and a desire to accelerate the regional integration process through the establishment, in the first instance, of a common market, a central bank, a monetary union, as well as a pan-African parliament. The metamorphosis of the OAU into the AU sought to build a partnership between African governments and all segments of civil society; combat the scourge of conflicts on the continent; and promote and protect human rights, consolidate democratic institutions and culture, and ensure "good governance" and the rule of law.[24] The transformation thus went far beyond a mere change in name; rather it sought to articulate a fundamental paradigmatic shift in policy regarding the maintenance of peace and security in Africa and to craft a deliberate response to the violent intra-state conflicts engulfing large parts of the continent. A key objective of the AU is to integrate Africa into a prosperous and peaceful continent, an Africa "driven by its own citizens and representing a dynamic force in [the] global arena".[25] This reflects the formation of an ambitious plan to undertake anew the creation of a *Pax Africana*.

In Mazrui's view, for a *Pax Africana* to be realised, a national police force is required to maintain law and order within national boundaries, with all African countries taking responsibility for securing peace and stability on the continent. To reiterate, this does not imply the imposition of peace on other nation-states as much as it describes the nationality and continental limits of their jurisdiction. For Mazrui, "*Pax Africana* asserts that the peace of *Africa* is to be assured by the exertions of *Africans* themselves", and refers to "the specifically military aspect of the principle of continental jurisdiction".[26] Furthermore, Mazrui's idea of *Pax Africana* views the UN primarily as an instrument for bringing about disarmament or as an additional armed entity capable of forcing combatants apart. The idea also presupposes the existence of a front for mobilising forces to protect international peace. As early as 1961, leaders including Tanzania's Julius Nyerere and Ghana's Kwame Nkrumah were calling for all newly independent African states to renounce their massive spending on the procurement of arms, as this money could be better used for improving education, health, and social services; and to focus rather on uniting in the struggle against colonialism. These political visionaries were already, even before the establishment of the OAU, calling for Africans to be the custodians of peace, and for this peace to be under the supervision of African states. To a significant extent, the creation of the African Union as well as the New Partnership for Africa's Development (NEPAD, preceded by the Millennium Africa Recovery Plan, Omega Plan for Africa, and New African Initiative) mark a continuity. The 2000 Constitutive Act of the AU "was an important milestone in the process of creating political continental unity and the African Economic

Community. It was a major achievement of ... African leaders and a triumph for Pan-Africanism".[27] Key figures in the founding of the AU and its institutions included Algeria's Abdelaziz Bouteflika, South Africa's Thabo Mbeki, Nigeria's Olusegun Obasanjo, Libya's Muammar Qaddafi, and Senegal's Abdoulai Wade.

As Mazrui noted, though, in 1967: "A more difficult problem for *Pax Africana* concerns the behaviour of its own instruments of enforcement *internally*. The ultimate instruments of self-pacification in Africa are Africa's own police and armed forces. If the peace is disturbed by ... [an ethnic] insurrection or by corrupt politicians, Africa's armed forces might be called upon to re-establish authority. But what if the peace is disturbed by those armed forces themselves?"[28]

From the OAU to the AU

The search for a peaceful and prosperous Africa remains ongoing, with violent conflict continuing in many parts of the continent despite efforts by the AU to achieve peace and stability. Countries such as Burundi, the CAR, the DRC, Ethiopia, Mali, Somalia, and South Sudan, to name but a few, all continue to experience high levels of violence, with alarming consequences for their populations (mass displacements, refugees, deaths, and insecurity) and for their economies. (On Mali, see Adebajo; on Somalia, see Hirsch, and Mahiga; and on South Sudan, see Deng, all in this volume.) Burundi and the CAR, for example, are among the poorest countries in Africa, with more than 75 per cent and 65 per cent of their respective populations living below the international poverty line ($1.90 a day).[29] Both ranked in the bottom ten of the 2016 Human Development Index (HDI), along with, among others, the DRC, commonly described as one of the world's most long-standing and worst humanitarian crises; and South Sudan, where ongoing violence (since 2013) has displaced over a quarter of the country's population.[30] Consequently, stabilising the continent has been a core goal of both the AU and the UN. The AU has considerable potential as a partner for the UN in Africa, but the partnership faces significant challenges, including differences in their views on peacekeeping and unanswered questions about the role of Africa's RECs.[31] (See, for example, Hirsch, and Gambari in this volume.) Implementation of the African Peace and Security Architecture also has been fraught with practical problems, including a gap between capabilities and expectations, with realities on the ground "falling well short of the ambitious vision and rhetoric contained in its [the AU's] founding documents".[32] (See Kuwali, and Nagar in this volume.)

As British scholar Paul Williams has noted, the AU's "specific vision for conflict management reflects an awareness that the precondition for achieving ... [its] overarching goal [of a peaceful and prosperous Africa] is security and stability on the continent". This vision is outlined in the Union's Constitutive Act of 2000, which "commits AU members to accelerate political and economic integration of the continent, including through the establishment of a common African security and defense policy; to defend the sovereignty, territorial integrity, and independence of its member states; to promote peace, security, and stability throughout Africa; and to encourage democratic principles of good governance, human rights, and sustainable development".[33]

The AU's Constitutive Act and the OAU Charter are, in many ways, not fundamentally different. For example, both place an emphasis on the principles of sovereign equality, non-use of force, and peaceful settlement of disputes, and contain a "general commitment to non-intervention in the affairs of ... member states".[34] What is markedly different, though, is the AU's adoption of "a much more interventionist stance through its legal frameworks and institutions".[35] Its Constitutive Act includes a collective right to intervene in certain circumstances, and in this respect reflects a paradigmatic shift from a rigid understanding of sovereignty as non-intervention that permitted indifference to gross human rights abuses, to a responsibility to protect (R2P) African citizens in extreme cases.[36] Specifically, Article 4(h) of the act gives the AU a right "to intervene in a Member State pursuant to a decision of the Assembly in respect of grave circumstances, namely: war crimes, genocide and crimes against humanity".[37] This for the first time provides a legal basis for intervention by the continental body, and in so doing gives primacy to the rights and interests of Africa's citizens over state-centric principles of sovereignty.[38] In Dersso's words: "Most notably, it revises the understanding and scope of application of the principles of state sovereignty and non-interference."[39]

The new dispensation under the AU thus envisions a robust and more specific role for the continental body in conflict management, in a deliberate reflection of its recognition that, as a minimum precondition for stability and development on the continent, the Union must move away from the traditional principle of non-interference to a more interventionist posture. This more robust role is set out in various legal documents, and interpreted and implemented by a set of inter-related institutions. The Protocol Relating to the Establishment of the Peace and Security Council of the African Union was adopted at the inaugural meeting of the AU Assembly in July 2002 and entered into force in December 2003.[40] In addition to the Peace and Security Council, the African Peace and Security Architecture—the "Africa Union's blue print for the promotion of peace, security and stability in Africa"[41]—includes the Continental Early Warning System (CEWS), the Panel of the Wise, the African Standby Force (ASF), and the Peace Fund (see Kuwali, and Nagar in this volume). Of these institutions, the elected 15-member PSC is (to date) the most structured, with clearly articulated objectives; and bears responsibility for operational and strategic decision-making vis-à-vis "a long list of tasks related to the prevention, management, and resolution of conflict across Africa".[42]

Another major development has been the establishment of the African Governance Architecture (AGA)—a key component of the institutional and legal frameworks that collectively form the new march towards a more responsive Africa. For example, unconstitutional changes of government, a common event on the continent after independence, are now largely a thing of the past.

The AU has demonstrably rejected several coups, including in the CAR (2003), Guinea-Bissau (2003), São Tomé and Príncipe (2003), Togo (2005), Mauritania (2005 and 2008), Guinea (2008), Madagascar (2009), and Niger (2010).[43] Often working through its sub-regional organisations, the AU has condemned the coups and called for the restoration of the legitimately elected governments, and in some cases played a mediating role that led to the return to power of the legitimate government (for example, in Guinea-Bissau in 2003) or to the conduct of elections as a compromise (such as in Kenya in 2007–2008 through IGAD, and in Zimbabwe in 2010 through SADC). (On Kenya, see Wamai in this volume.) It has also become "commonplace for the AU to make public statements in favour of democratic governance".[44] The outcomes of these efforts, however, have been mixed. In some cases, such as Zimbabwe, governments of national unity were negotiated, but the long-term causes of conflict and instability have remained largely unaddressed.[45] In other cases, such as Burundi, opponents of incumbents have been terrorised and silenced through violence.

Furthermore, though Article 4(h) of the AU's Constitutive Act signals a major shift in thinking about sovereignty and non-intervention in the context of gross human rights abuses, it has also posed difficult political and legal questions. Chapter VIII of the United Nations Charter of 1945 deals with the relationship between the UN Security Council and regional arrangements, with Article 53, in particular, noting that "no enforcement action shall be taken under regional arrangements or by regional agencies without the authorization of the Security Council".[46] But as Williams writes:

> [T]he word "intervene" in Article 4(h) implies that the AU Assembly could authorize military force for humanitarian protection purposes without the host government's consent or prior to a UN Security Council (UNSC) resolution—in possible contradiction to Article 53 of the UN Charter. While there is some debate on this matter, the weight of international legal opinion sees humanitarian intervention authorized outside the UNSC as illegal. Probably in recognition of this problem, by 2005 the Roadmap for the Operationalization of the African Standby Force explicitly stated: "The AU will seek UN Security Council authorization of its enforcement actions. Similarly, the [regional economic communities] will seek AU authorization of their interventions."[47]

The AU, compared to its predecessor, the OAU, has an ambitious transformative peace and security agenda that includes more aggressive and robust peace operations and conflict management initiatives. However, 15 years since its creation in 2002, the AU faces major obstacles in achieving its objectives of effectively responding to Africa's conflicts. The challenges are mainly located within three key institutional pillars of the APSA—the Peace and Security Council, the Panel of the Wise, and the African Standby Force (see Kuwali, and Nagar in this volume)—and arise from a number of inter-related factors, including the attempt by the AU to reshape Africa's peace and security architecture at a time when several conflicts were raging across the continent; a dearth in incentives and sanctions appropriate for effectiveness in security operations; and a lack of direction in the discourse regarding AU reform efforts and in broader debates about appropriate relationships between the UN and regional organisations (see Vogt in this volume).[48]

As Williams has noted: "The AU's shortcomings are not [necessarily] fatal."[49] The participation of regional actors in the management of conflicts in their own regions has compelled the UN to cooperate with regional organisations such as the AU.[50] Peace operations such as those undertaken by the AU in Burundi (2003–2004), Sudan's Darfur region (since 2004), Somalia (since 2007), and Mali (2013); and the West African regional organisation ECOWAS in Liberia (1990–1998) and Sierra Leone (1997–1999), provide examples of regional roles in peacekeeping in Africa as either sub-regional (re)engagement, Africa-wide leadership, or collaboration between the UN and the African Union. The AU and its international partners can bolster the Union's conflict management capacity in the short and long terms. The AU Constitutive Act envisages an organisation empowered to play a major role in resolving Africa's armed conflicts. Chapter VIII of the UN Charter envisions a role for regional organisations in conflict management. However, it is not clear how the AU and the UN are to translate this framework into a functional partnership. Despite the positive steps towards the creation of a robust framework for conflict management, conflict resolution, and peacebuilding, it remains unclear how the AU and UN can reconcile different interpretations of the various protocols and statutes that govern peace and security in the international system.[51]

Towards an Understanding of Conflict Prevention, Peacemaking, Peacekeeping, and Peacebuilding

The distinction between the concepts of conflict prevention, peacemaking, peacekeeping, and peacebuilding was popularised by former Egyptian UN Secretary-General Boutros Boutros-Ghali. In 1992, in a report titled *An Agenda for Peace*, Boutros-Ghali suggested to the United Nations an approach to international peace that takes into consideration a proactive rather than reactive posture to violent conflict. Boutros-Ghali suggested that taking a proactive approach would allow the UN and its Department of Peacekeeping Operations to deal with threats to peace and security more quickly and effectively. *An Agenda for Peace* called for the adoption of four major approaches to peace: preventive diplomacy, peacemaking, peacekeeping, and post-conflict peacebuilding.

Embedded in this approach is the assumption that peacebuilding must take place through a developmental lens, with a view to addressing the fundamental root causes and conditions of violent conflict. At the heart of this approach is the call "to address the deepest causes of conflict: economic despair, social injustice and political oppression" and pervasive poverty.[52] So, post-conflict peacebuilding can take the form of concrete projects contributing to social and economic development—for example, in the fields of agriculture, transportation, water and energy resources, education, and culture.[53] *An Agenda for Peace* assumes that successful peacemaking and peacekeeping will lead to post-conflict reconstruction, as long as the root causes of violent conflict are addressed through development.

These new proposals concerning peacemaking, peacekeeping, and peacebuilding in *An Agenda for Peace* faced enormous difficulties due, in part, to the fact that the UN and its organs (such as the Security Council, which is responsible for the maintenance of international peace and security) did not have the capacity to prevent an outbreak of violence in countries such as Somalia, Rwanda, Liberia, and Sierra Leone. The major powers on the UN Security Council, in particular, its permanent five (P-5) members—the US, Russia, Britain, France, and China—were reluctant to make the necessary resources available. To appease the P-5, Boutros-Ghali prepared a supplement to *An Agenda for Peace* in 1995,[54] which became the blueprint for UN peacekeeping operations. The supplement was designed to enhance the effectiveness of peace operations, including through the transfer of decision-making responsibility concerning post-conflict peacebuilding from the Security Council to the General Assembly, to the Secretary-General, and to other UN agencies entrusted with social, economic, human rights, and humanitarian responsibilities. It took ten years for the UN General Assembly to finally approve the establishment of its Peacebuilding Commission, in 2005. The commission was mandated to mobilise resources for post-conflict reconstruction and for the development of long-term strategies for sustainable peace (see Otobo in this volume).

The concepts of conflict prevention, peacemaking, peacekeeping, and peacebuilding have been used by the UN, and more recently by the African Union, to define the means through which peace and security can be attained. For the AU and its Peace and Security Council, these concepts express the parameters and interpretations of the Union's 2000 Constitutive Act, including, in particular, Article 4(h). For the UN, they outline the boundaries and potential interpretations of Chapters VI and VII of its 1945 Charter.[55] Conflict prevention, peacemaking, peacekeeping, and peacebuilding, as well as post-conflict reconstruction and conflict transformation, are all important dimensions of the conflict resolution spectrum. Each plays an important role in rebuilding war-torn societies. This volume seeks to unpack them in different ways, based on both scholarly and practitioner perspectives. The slightly greater attention given to peacekeeping here is merely a practical reflection of the wealth of African practitioner experiences in this area that the volume has been able to bring together. This, in turn, echoes to some extent the centrality of peacekeeping to the African peace and security endeavour.

Outline of the Book

The 25 chapters that make up this volume are organised into six inter-related sections. The first section sets the scene for the rest of the work, focusing on the theory and practice of *Pax Africana*, and comprises this introduction; a reprint of Ali Mazrui's original articulation of *Pax Africana* from his 1967 work on the topic; and two chapters on the AU's institutional architecture for the maintenance of peace and security on the continent. The subsequent four sections are guided by the distinction drawn by Boutros-Ghali between conflict prevention, peacemaking, peacekeeping, and peacebuilding as approaches to generating peace. The second section starts to traverse this spectrum by looking at conflict prevention and peacemaking in Africa. It includes an in-depth consideration of the contested role of the International Criminal Court (ICC) in conflict prevention, and three case studies—Sudan, Kenya, and Somalia—that highlight the challenges, but also potential, of African efforts to make peace on the continent. The third and fourth sections focus on peacekeeping: the military approach to peace that lies at the heart of Mazrui's idea of *Pax Africana*. More specifically, the third section looks at the politics and practice of keeping peace in Africa by the UN Security Council and African regional organisations, including a case study of Mali, while the fourth explores the matic issues such as accountability and the role of HIV/AIDS in, and cinematic portrayals of, peacekeeping on the continent. The fifth section turns to peacebuilding and comprises chapters on the political economy of its practice in Africa, the impact of inequality on it, women and gender, the role of the UN Peacebuilding Commission, and as a case study, the simultaneous processes of peacemaking and peacebuilding in Somalia. The final section looks at the role of key external actors—including the UN, France, Britain, and South Asian troop-contributing countries to UN missions—in the maintenance of peace and security in Africa.

Immediately following this introduction, Mazrui's original 1967 essay on "Towards a Concept of 'Pax Africana'" opens Part I, setting the scene for the discussions in the rest of the volume. His call for the establishment of a continental security arrangement by Africans for Africans is followed by in-depth exploration of the evolving African Peace and Security Architecture, and the African Standby Force (the military aspect of the APSA), being created by the AU, in chapters by Malawian scholar Dan Kuwali and South African scholar Dawn Nagar, respectively. Kuwali, in exploring the role of the APSA in his chapter, highlights the challenges facing Africa and its peace and security institutions. To this end, he argues that the main problem with the APSA is a lack of political will by Africa's leaders to engage in military interventions. Kuwali also argues that Africa generally lacks the capacity to respond rapidly to crises given its heavy reliance—material and financial—on external actors to prop up its capacities to carry out interventions in complex emergencies. To address these and other inherent challenges of the APSA, Kuwali suggests the establishment of robust preventive interventions, and that the AU should actively engage to address the structural sources of violence in Africa.

Dawn Nagar, in her chapter, interrogates African security convergence and the role of the African Standby Force, in particular, as a security outfit that addresses the main question raised by Mazrui regarding the leadership role of Africans in Africa to protect themselves against the imperial powers, and indeed against each other. Nagar asks critical questions regarding the ASF: Is it a panacea to Africa's security problems? Is it emblematic of the new *Pax Africana*? What have the AU and Africa's RECs achieved in their efforts towards security convergence? And what are the main challenges facing the operationalisation of the ASF? Nagar agrees with Kuwali on the vicissitudes of the APSA and the ASF and their capabilities, and the readiness of individual states within the framework of the RECs. She further argues that the peace and security agendas of the RECs have progressed much faster than that of the AU, resulting in a situation that creates tensions between the RECs and the AU. (See also Vogt in this volume.)

Part II of the book turns to conflict prevention and peacemaking efforts in Africa. Establishing appropriate international institutions with legitimacy from the UN can assist in conflict prevention. As suggested by Boutros-Ghali in *An Agenda for Peace*, conflict prevention is an important aspect of building peace in divided societies. Dutch legal scholar Sarah Nouwen, in her chapter, highlights the assumptions that underpin conflict prevention, while drawing out the distinctions between the application of domestic law and that of international law with regard to war crimes and crimes against humanity. For Nouwen, international criminal courts do not need to rely heavily on preventive theories of criminal law but rather to focus on searching for responses to crimes of impunity and crimes against humanity. The ICC as an international *criminal* court has the primary responsibility to respond to *crimes*, and not to conflict. By its nature, argues Nouwen, the ICC can, in some instances, serve only as a deterrent to future crimes, depending on the nature of the outcome and the theory used in the determination of a case. Nouwen shows that, in several instances, both crime and impunity will be consequences of conflict. At times, they could also be conduits to conflict. Yet impunity is usually not caused by a lack of law, but by a lack of enforcement. Nouwen admits that while the ICC can address some specific cases of impunity, it may not be able to deal with other issues related to, for example, economic and patronage crimes (see also Omeje in this volume).

Following Nouwen, South Sudanese scholar-diplomat Francis Deng, in his chapter, lays out the prerequisites and indeed necessary conditions for conflict prevention in divided societies. In a classic contribution to the debates on conflict prevention, Deng points to the imperative of preventing mass violence and related atrocities in Africa by, first and foremost, interrogating, identifying, understanding, and addressing the root causes of conflicts. Focusing on the experiences of Sudan—a country that before its break-up and the subsequent independence of South Sudan in July 2011 was, in many ways, a microcosm of Africa—Deng argues that identity, though malleable and constantly changing, is a primary factor that transcends material considerations, while acknowledging that there is a mutually reinforcing interplay between identity and material considerations. In Deng's analysis, the inequitable distribution of resources, not identity, is the decisive factor in conflict initiation. Deng maintains that a vitally important ingredient of group identity is the "correlative complex of cultural values, institutional structures, and patterns of behaviour associated with the group". Societal divisions based on identity markers depend to a large extent on how national identity is framed.

The conflict prevention and peacemaking efforts of the AU have proven to be fraught with challenges. Interventions in Sudan and South Sudan, and indeed Somalia and the CAR, have thus far produced mixed results. Kenyan scholar Njoki Wamai, in her chapter in this volume, maintains that African-led mediation efforts have produced varying levels of success and failure. In her assessment of the 2008 Kenyan mediation process, Wamai argues that the country's experience provides three lessons and dilemmas for conflict prevention in Africa. First, to be successful, such an intervention must be African-led with adequate resources. Second, the involvement of local civil society actors and their support of the mediation process are important in securing legitimacy from citizens. The composition of civil society must also be an inclusive one (involving women, youth, as well as business leaders, among others) to exert sufficient pressure on the protagonists to reach a negotiated settlement. Third, Wamai suggests that the perceived impartiality of the lead-mediator is an important factor in determining the levels of confidence and trust in the process. At the same time, the experience of the Kenyan mediation process headed by former Ghanaian UN Secretary-General Kofi Annan also revealed the challenges of the liberal peace project. Rather than focusing on transformation, the Kenyan mediation process was keen to reach a political settlement at all costs and occupied itself with appeasing the political elites. This narrow focus, argues Wamai, solicited in the long term an outcome that is not sustainable, as could be seen in the ICC indictment of a sitting president (Uhuru Kenyatta) and deputy president (William Ruto) of Kenya (the charges were later dropped for lack of evidence).

Coming as well from an experiential perspective, former US ambassador and long-time diplomat John Hirsch discusses the prospects of peace in Somalia—a society whose identity has been regarded as homogeneous. Unlike other societies in Africa, Somalia is one of only a few whose identity difference is the clan. In his chapter, Hirsch questions why the Somali conflict has been so protracted, and why the AU and the UN have for so long been unable to resolve the Somali problem with greater success. Hirsch explores the complex politico-cultural relationships that inform the Somali situation and the convoluted conflict dynamics within the greater Horn of Africa and the Gulf of Aden. Hirsch concludes that Somalia has been a real test case for the UN Security Council's evolving relationship with the AU. (See also Mahiga in this volume.)

Part III of the book next explores peacekeeping in Africa with a focus on the political factors that shape peacekeeping interventions. Sierra Leonean scholar-diplomat James Jonah, based in large part on his experiences at the UN, including as a former Under-Secretary-General for Political Affairs, provides a historical perspective on UN peacekeeping. Jonah explores the historical origins of international peacekeeping, noting that the ideas of peacekeeping and progress on disarmament were first mooted by then–US secretary of state

Christian Herter in February 1960, when he proposed a general and complete disarmament in the context of a viable peacekeeping structure. Jonah also notes that the first real test of peacekeeping, as an enforcement action, for the UN was in the Congo crisis of the 1960s. The mission was fraught with challenges and called into question the efficacy of the entire UN peacekeeping enterprise. The Congo experience provoked a virulent attack against then–UN Secretary-General, Sweden's Dag Hammarskjöld, by Soviet premier Nikita Khrushchev, who accused Hammarskjöld of being complicit in the assassination of Congolese leader Patrice Lumumba. The assassination also disillusioned several African states regarding the utility of UN peacekeeping.

The East-West rivalry during the Cold War did not facilitate the successful implementation of the UN peacekeeping agenda, with the US and its Western allies on the Security Council using their veto power to block intended interventions in their spheres of influence. The same was true for the former Soviet Union. Jonah notes that it was only under Mikhail Gorbachev in the mid-1980s that the Soviet Union accepted the UN Secretary-General as the chief administrator of the UN. Jonah, in his chapter, also underscores the UN's heavy reliance on relief and humanitarian assistance, rather than on finding sustainable political solutions to conflicts, that drew much international criticism.

Following Jonah, former Costa Rican diplomat Bruno Stagno Ugarte, in his chapter, looks more closely at the UN Security Council and its experiences with conflicts in Africa. Ugarte posits that the conservative positions held by the Security Council regarding the maintenance of international peace have been put to the test in Africa, with the Council approving more peacekeeping interventions on the continent than for any other region in the world. Ugarte argues that the changes in the frequency and indeed the nature of interventions were precipitated by the rise in the number of inter-state conflicts that many states experienced in Africa after the end of the Cold War and the establishment of regional and sub-regional security structures in Africa (such as ECOWAS and SADC). The successive deployment of missions in different parts of Africa and elsewhere soon overwhelmed the UN Security Council. This situation led the Council to mandate its first ever UN peacekeeping mission to a conflict situation—Liberia—where there were troops from one of Africa's sub-regional organisations—ECOWAS—already deployed to keep the peace. In 1993 the Council mandated the deployment of the UN Observer Mission in Liberia (UNOMIL) to operate simultaneously with the Military Observer Group already deployed by the Economic Community of West African States.

Nigerian scholar-diplomat Ibrahim Gambari, in his chapter, further assesses the responsibility and practice of the 15-member UN Security Council as a partner for African countries, and the role of the AU in the maintenance of peace and security on the continent. For Gambari, the AU-UN partnership remains an unequal and uneasy one. The challenge, argues Gambari, lies in developing the partnership into a more balanced relationship, one based on mutual respect and mutual benefits. Gambari seeks to provide a comprehensive analysis of the politics of peacekeeping based on his more than 25 years of experience with the United Nations, including as joint special representative for, and head of, the AU-UN Hybrid Operation in Darfur (UNAMID) from 2010 to 2012. Gambari highlights the important changes that have taken place in the international system, including the events that led to the Rwandan crisis of 1994 and the genocide that followed, concluding that the UN was ill-prepared to lead peacekeeping missions during this time. Gambari agrees with Deng that the root causes of conflicts and instability, especially where involving economic origins, or deep historical and ethnic antagonisms, did not disappear with the end of the Cold War. Rather, in his view, as in the emblematic case of Rwanda, post–Cold War intra-state conflicts came to exemplify the inability of the Security Council to address them effectively.

The Rwandan tragedy brought into sharp focus the true nature of the UN Security Council as a political institution that functions in concentric circles of interests and relative influence. Gambari argues that unless the membership of the Security Council is reformed and democratised (in terms of its composition and its operational methods) to reflect the economic, demographic, and political realities in the world today, and unless Africa obtains full representation on the body, the Council will continue to safeguard its own narrow interests at the expense of the citizens of the world. Gambari provides us with a sense of hope, though, arguing that despite the challenges in the quest for a *Pax Africana*, the African continent has and will continue to be a major contributor to international peace and security. For him, the deployment of UNAMID in Darfur in 2004 and the AU Mission in Somalia (AMIS) in 2007 demonstrates the need for a change in paradigm from analysis of the African continent as a mere consumer of international peace and security, to a producer of security.

Gambari's exploration of the AU-UN experience in the new *Pax Africana* dovetails well with the contested issue of the imperial French military presence and interventions in former French colonies in Africa. Nigerian scholar Adekeye Adebajo, in his chapter, explores the resurgence of militancy in northern Mali since 2013 and the response of ECOWAS led by Nigeria. Adebajo argues that Nigeria, the regional hegemon in West Africa, offered a rather weak response to the crisis in Mali, while France, using its membership in the UN Security Council, sought to use its Council influence as an instrument to protect its parochial interests in francophone Africa generally, and in Mali and neighbouring Niger specifically. In the case of the peacekeeping mission in 2013 in Mali, Adebajo maintains that France used the UN and the European Union and the leaders of francophone West Africa much more effectively to pursue its interests compared to Nigeria's use of ECOWAS and the AU. Furthermore, while the elimination of the militant threat in northern Mali is in the interest of both African and Western countries, for Adebajo it is interesting that France could launch an old-style neo-colonial intervention into a country in Nigeria's backyard, under the pretext of Paris sending troops to guard uranium mines in neighbouring Niger, without any challenge from Nigeria or indeed ECOWAS as a collective of West African states. The French intervention in Mali exposed some of the other interests at the heart of France's regional role and introduced a new form of colonialism whereby France, without any right, takes over the security of a sovereign nation without being challenged by the state or regional organisations or indeed the international community. Adebajo concludes that in the case of Mali, "*Pax Gallica* (France) decisively trumped *Pax Nigeriana* (Nigeria)".

Ghanian scholar Kwame Akonor opens Part IV of the volume, looking at key themes in peacekeeping, with an examination of crimes committed by peacekeepers. In his chapter, Akonor offers four explanations for limited criminal prosecutions in the wake of abuses—in particular, sexual exploitation and abuse by members serving in peacekeeping operations. These explanations include the institutional structure of UN peacekeeping operations, economic deprivation, variations in cultural and legal systems across troop-contributing countries, and the psychological impact of conflicts on societies. Though there is no perfect solution to dealing with sexual exploitation and abuse by peacekeepers, perhaps the most effective way of holding peacekeepers accountable is to create a culture of accountability in peacekeeping operations. As a way to demonstrate its commitment to its citizens and to promote the concept of a new *Pax Africana*, the AU should allow the African Court on Human and Peoples' Rights to prosecute AU peacekeepers outside their home countries. This, Akonor argues, will put the responsibility squarely on peacekeepers.

In a further exploration of issues related to the accountability of peacekeepers, Uganda's Paul Mulindwa and South Africa's Oscar Siwali in their jointly authored chapter discuss the existing UN and AU policy mechanisms for dealing with the HIV/AIDS pandemic in militaries. Mulindwa and Siwali identify the challenges of policy implementation, and assess the prospects for coordination and better monitoring of infection prevalence rates among peacekeeping troops. They call for peacekeeping missions to create conditions for reduction of the spread of the disease, citing the risky behaviours of peacekeepers and the high turnover rates among peacekeepers as major contributing factors to the spread of the virus. The issue is further complicated, Mulindwa and Siwali argue, by the disparate HIV/AIDS policy frameworks of troop-contributing countries and the UN. For example, the UN encourages testing but has made it a voluntary exercise, while many countries do not even have this requirement. To reduce levels of infection prevalence and new infection rates, Mulindwa and Siwali argue that HIV/AIDS testing should be mandatory in all national militaries. This could be realised through the AU's Common Defence and Security Policy of 2005, and the UN's Department of Peacekeeping Operations.

Meanwhile, the economic pursuits of imperial powers in Africa continue to be at the centre of the way Africa is portrayed to the rest of the world. Hollywood's portrayal of Africa, for example, is couched in economic terms by the making of war movies about Africa for economic gain. Tunisian scholar Ines Mzali, in her chapter in this volume, takes a critical look at Hollywood's portrayal of Africa in movies such as *Black Hawk Down* (2001), *Hotel Rwanda* (2004), and to a lesser extent *Blood Diamond* (2006). Mzali explores how African conflicts and Africans as a people have been depicted in movies on the one hand, and how international peacekeeping interventions have been constructed and presented in movies on the other. Mzali contends that Hollywood's interest in Africa has always been represented through a binary lens of "self" versus "other", suggesting an inherent polarisation in African societies. This bleak view of Africa also continues to be used in political, media, and other cultural representations of war and violence, and shape international perceptions about the continent.

Continuing on Boutros-Ghali's spectrum of approaches to peace, Part V of the book turns to peacebuilding in Africa. Nigerian scholar Kenneth Omeje, in his chapter, argues that violent and predatory economies are a prominent feature in many armed conflicts in Africa and elsewhere around the world. When conflicts end, these politico-economic dispensations do not disappear at the signing of a peace agreement or a ceasefire, but remain and continue to provide resources for belligerent parties to pursue strategic goals in the conflict-affected environment. In Africa, lootable resources (natural resources such as diamonds and gold) continue to provide sources of revenue for disaffected criminal conflict entrepreneurs, peace spoilers, and other actors at the margins of the war-to-peace transition process. Viewed from a political economy perspective, another major practical feature of the war-to-peace transition in Africa is the sharing of the peacebuilding resource dividends to ensure both the survival and the continuity of a fragile governance structure. Approached from a liberal governance perspective, post-conflict peacebuilding in Africa tends to promote the shared interests of African political elites and external free market entrepreneurs.

But rebuilding post-conflict societies requires holistic and innovative approaches to peacebuilding. This need is further emphasised by British scholar Oliver Richmond in his chapter in this volume. As he notes, the post–Cold War era has been marked by a combination of "liberal internationalism, Northern centrism, and a global system of neo-liberalism, interspersed with some relatively authoritarian states", with peacebuilding in Africa tending to be driven by the systemic paradigm rather than be rooted in local contexts. There is some similarity in thinking with Omeje that sustainable peacebuilding must be viewed as an "agency for re-creating international order and maintaining both ... regional and ... global security". Richmond, similarly to Adebajo, also notes that historical inequalities in Africa have persisted, while the inequalities between Northern states (many of them former colonisers) have widened even further around the world. Post-conflict reconstruction and state-building agendas must address these inequalities, as a peacebuilding project based on liberal capitalism and global neo-liberalism underwritten by the industrialised North is no longer sufficient for building just and sustainable peace in Africa.

British scholar Antonia Porter's chapter moves the discussion to the role, in particular, of women and gender in peacebuilding. Porter argues that the proliferation of international, continental, and regional efforts geared towards gender equality, though meaningful, has not been able to dismantle the systems and realities that perpetuate gender inequalities. She takes particular issue with gender and development practitioners' emphasis on reducing gender inequality in political participation through gender quotas, which in almost all cases has not translated to substantive reorganising of power relations, as achieving gender equality in peacebuilding and political decision-making calls for more than a greater numerical representation of women. Similarly, the inclusion of women in some traditionally male-dominated peacekeeping instruments has been undermined by stereotyping the contributions of women in conflict, peacekeeping, and peacebuilding processes. There is some consensus among analysts, as Porter observes, that armed forces, peacekeeping operations, and soldiering are rooted in ideologies that idolise men, misogyny, and conventionally masculine traits as "good soldiering". Instead of institutions, practices, and cultures adapting to accommodate and effectively utilise women and their perspectives, women are pressured into assimilating masculine values and roles, rather than transforming sexist ideologies and practices. The inclusion of women in this fashion dilutes femininity and undermines the purpose of including women in peacekeeping operations, while entrenching problematic masculinities. Furthermore, Porter reiterates that peacebuilding discourses that juxtapose "war" and "peace" ignore the pervasive structural and physical violence women endure in a patriarchal world. For gross gender-based violence during wartime is merely the exacerbation of the everyday violence women experience at home, in the streets, at their workplaces, and in their communities.

Next, Nigerian international civil servant and scholar Ejeviome Eloho Otobo, in his chapter on the UN Peacebuilding Commission, argues that the ability of the commission to provide support to countries on its agenda in ways that link security and development issues is an important feature and strength of the design of the institution. But the Peacebuilding Commission has been bedevilled as much by the definition of its tasks as by the operational details within it. Otobo maintains that the work of the commission is marked by multiple expectations that in themselves are not clearly defined. One such expectation is that its work must be tangible and visible. The question of measuring tangibility and visibility has been debated for many years in the peacebuilding field. For example, argues Otobo, peacebuilding cannot provide in tangible terms its main remit—advocacy, resource mobilisation, and coherence. There is also no value in the level of advocacy the commission provides in programme implementation.

From a praxis-oriented point of view, Tanzanian diplomat Augustine Mahiga, in his chapter, examines the interwoven processes of peacemaking and peacebuilding in Somalia over the past two decades, based largely on his close experience of, and relationship with, the peace process in the country from 2010 to 2013. Following the fall of the military regime of Siad Barre in 1991, multiple efforts to bring peace in Somalia had failed before an IGAD-brokered transitional government was set up at the Mbagathi peace conference in Kenya in 2013. Third-party roles in conflict prevention, resolution, and peacebuilding must be analysed from the point of view of interests. Towards that end,

Mahiga eloquently articulates the reasons why the UN peacekeeping missions and the US-led intervention of the 1990s failed in the context of Somalia. Other regional actors including the Gulf states and the sub-regional organisation IGAD also failed in their early efforts to bring peace to the country. Mahiga discusses the role played by civil society, including women's groups, in local efforts to bring peace to the troubled country. He advocates for the use of multiple processes and strategies, including liberal peace but also national-level peacebuilding strategies, for the generation of sustainable peace and political reconciliation in war-torn societies. This, according to Mahiga, is the way to navigate the delicate balance of multiple interests between local, regional, and international actors in fragile situations.

Part VI turns to the role of external actors. The late Nigerian scholar-diplomat Margaret Vogt, in her experiential narrative, questions the logic of UN and AU partnerships, and advocates for a more coordinated relationship between the two organisations on peace and security matters in Africa. Coordination and collaboration must be comprehensive, including engagement with Africa's regional economic communities. The synergy between AU structures and UN structures in Addis Ababa and New York has yet to be fully exploited and made to bear fruit in both organisations. Vogt cites, for example, the lack of communication not only between entities within AU structures in Addis Ababa, but also between the AU Peace and Security Council and the AU office in New York. This, Vogt argues, has led to a great many missed opportunities in terms of strengthening the AU-UN partnership. In this respect, Vogt seems to agree with Gambari that the new partnership framework for the UN's relations with the AU should be based on the premise that the two organisations need to cooperate more closely to promote an international peace and security agenda that takes into account Africa's daunting political and socio-economic developmental needs. Vogt further argues that within the new framework, the AU and Africa's RECs must align with, and extend the support being provided by, the UN's organs, including the UN Peacebuilding Fund.

American political scientist Douglas Yates, in his review of French interventions in Africa, agrees with Adebajo in asserting that French colonisation has never ended on the continent. Yates reviews the historical and contemporary French involvement in security and other matters (economic, political, and cultural) in Africa, and highlights the role that France continues to play more than 50 years after the independence of many of its former colonies. According to Yates, between 1960 and 2005 France launched some 46 military operations in its former African colonies, excluding clandestine operations that have involved the secret services and special operations. With the help of three case studies—the French interventions in Mali, the Sahel, and the Central African Republic between 2013 and 2016—Yates illustrates the not so obvious rationales for French engagement in peacekeeping missions in francophone Africa: economic and cultural interests. Consequently, French involvement in Africa has overstretched the French military establishment and indeed its resources (material and financial), a situation that has forced the French authorities to drastically reduce budget allocations to their military and therefore military adventures in Africa and elsewhere in the world. Yates argues that if French interventions continue, they may result in the French armed forces being unable to accomplish their peacekeeping goals in Africa, including those of protecting civilians and combating terrorism abroad and at home.

Sierra Leonean–born scholar Ismail Rashid, in his chapter, explores the role of Britain in security sector reform (SSR) in Sierra Leone. Britain, a former colonial power in Sierra Leone (as was France in Mali), utilised a new political engagement in the protracted conflict in the country. While violence continued in the northern parts of the country in 1999, the British government (under Prime Minister Tony Blair) developed a deliberate policy to reform the security sector in Sierra Leone, as part of its involvement in peacebuilding in the country. Two British military operations in 1999 and 2000 helped to stabilise the faltering UN Mission in Sierra Leone (UNAMSIL) and to rescue the 1999 Lomé peace agreement between the government of Sierra Leone and the Revolutionary United Front (RUF) rebel group. The British intervention was lauded as an exemplary achievement in the ethical, security-enhancing, and poverty-minimising Africa policy agenda of the Blair government. Rashid maintains, however, that Britain had been compelled to act by idealist as well as realist reasons. Despite the public pronouncements of the British government about partnership and local ownership of the reforms, several senior Sierra Leonean military officials felt disempowered and lacked ownership of the SSR process. The British and their Sierra Leonean counterparts faced considerable challenges in defining "security" and "development", and in figuring out the precise relationship between the two, especially within the relatively short duration of the SSR process.

In the penultimate chapter of this volume, Indian scholar Kudrat Virk interrogates the different motivations of South Asian countries—among the largest troop-contributing countries—for UN peacekeeping missions in Africa. The fundamental questions posed by Virk are as to why Bangladesh, India, and Pakistan have consistently contributed troops to peace operations in general, and what accounts for the large number of South Asian blue helmets in Africa in particular. Virk contends that the answers to these questions are located in a broad blend of ideological, political, and economic reasons. The mix of, and interplay between, these factors varies, however, among the South Asian trio. Whereas institution-building, for example, has particular importance in the case of Bangladesh, the maintenance of a positive image and influence is more prominent in that of Pakistan as a source of motivation to provide blue helmets. For India, meanwhile, given its status as an emerging power, its larger global ambitions, and its specific interests in Africa, including the continent's abundant resources to drive its economic rise, the country's early idealism has blended with more parochial reasons to sustain its proclivity for peacekeeping. The larger point, for Virk, though, is that Africa itself is not central to the peacekeeping rationales of these three countries, except to some extent India. While African capacities to contribute to peace and security on the continent are growing, the African endeavour still faces significant challenges, and the South Asian contributions of "boots on the ground" remain important. Though there is potential for Africa to learn from the experiences of the South Asian trio, and for the partnership between them to mature, this requires greater initiative and interest all around.

Overall, the contributors to this volume offer arguments and ideas that seek to answer some of the questions that have been posed here with regard to the concept of a new *Pax Africana*, but they also raise more questions. These relate, among other things, to the relationship between the AU and Africa's RECs; the coordination of their integration activities and plans on the continent as they affect aspirations for peace and security; the relationship between the AU and the UN; as well as the balance between the self-interests of individual states, the AU, and Africa's external partners. All together the chapters thus urge a critical reflection on a range of issues affecting the pursuit of a new *Pax Africana*. Peacemaking, peacekeeping, and peacebuilding are not just concepts that are in the public discourse in the corridors of the UN, the AU, and the RECs. They also affect the real lives of people in the conflict-affected countries. The activities conducted for purposes of promoting the objectives of conflict prevention, peacemaking, peacekeeping, and peacebuilding, to succeed, must stress the building of relationships among belligerents and communities affected by violence. In this respect, the quest for a new *Pax Africana* continues. This volume provides a glimpse into why this quest has been so elusive.

Notes

1. *See, for example*, Mo Ibrahim Foundation, *A Decade of African Governance, 2006–2015: 2016 Ibrahim Index of African Governance*, Index Report (Dakar, October 2016).
2. *See* Centre for Conflict Resolution (CCR), *The African Union: Regional and Global Challenges*, Seminar Report no. 53 (Cape Town, August 2016).
3. International Commission on Intervention and State Sovereignty (ICISS), *The Responsibility to Protect: Research, Bibliography, Background—Supplementary Volume to the Report of the International Commission on Intervention and State Sovereignty* (Ottawa: International Development Research Centre, 2001), p. 101.
4. United Nations Development Programme (UNDP), *Evaluation of UNDP Assistance to Conflict-Affected Countries* (New York, 2006), p. 71.
5. David Fickling, "Q&A: Charles Taylor and Liberia's Civil Wars", *The Guardian*, 3 April 2006, https://www.theguardian.com/world/2006/apr/03/westafrica.qanda (accessed 27 July 2017).
6. Ali A. Mazrui, *Towards a Pax Africana: A Study of Ideology and Ambition* (Chicago: University of Chicago Press, 1967).
7. Adekeye Adebajo, "Towards a New *Pax Africana*: Building Peace in Africa", paper prepared for a Trust Africa web discussion on "Building Sustainable Peace", September 2006, http://www.trustafrica.org/en/publications-trust/speaches-and-lectures (accessed 21 December 2016).
8. Britain is used synonymously with the United Kingdom (UK) in this volume.

9. CCR, *Towards a New Pax Africana: Making, Keeping, and Building Peace in Post–Cold War Africa*, Seminar Report no. 46 (Stellenbosch, May 2014), p. 7.
10. Adekeye Adebajo, *The Curse of Berlin: Africa After the Cold War* (New York: Columbia University Press, 2010), p. 32.
11. Based on data from the World Bank's Poverty and Equity Database, http://povertydata.worldbank.org/poverty/region/SSA (accessed 24 July 2017).
12. In 2015, the World Bank updated the international poverty line to $1.90 a day (based on 2011 prices). This was previously $1.25 a day. For more information, *see* World Bank, "FAQs: Global Poverty Line Update", 30 September 2015, http://www.worldbank.org/en/topic/poverty/brief/global-poverty-line-faq (accessed 24 July 2017).
13. United Nations Economic Commission for Africa (UNECA), African Union (AU), African Development Bank (AfDB), and UNDP, *MDG Report 2015: Assessing Progress in Africa Toward the Millennium Development Goals* (Addis Ababa, 2015), pp. 2–4. *See* Richard M. Mkandawire and Mandivamba Rukuni, "Eradicating Extreme Poverty and Hunger (MDG One)", in Charles Mutasa and Mark Paterson (eds.), *Africa and the Millennium Development Goals: Progress, Problems, and Prospects* (Lanham, MD: Rowman and Littlefield, 2015), pp. 107–125.
14. European Commission, Directorate-General for Trade, "European Union, Trade in Goods with Africa (All Countries)", 3 May 2017, http://trade.ec.europa.eu/doclib/docs/2011/january/tradoc_147189.pdf (accessed 24 July 2017). The pattern of Africa's growing trade with the BRICS bloc (Brazil, Russia, India, China, and South Africa) is broadly similar. Kudrat Virk, "The ACP, the EU, and the BRICS: Opportunities on the Horizon or Just a Mirage?", in Annita Montoute and Kudrat Virk (eds.), *The ACP Group and the EU Development Partnership: Beyond the North-South Debate* (New York: Palgrave Macmillan, 2017), p. 326.
15. CCR, *The African Union*, p. 8.
16. Adekeye Adebajo, "Paradise Lost and Found: The African Union and the European Union", in Adekeye Adebajo and Kaye Whiteman (eds.), *The EU and Africa: From Eurafrique to Afro-Europa* (London: Hurst, 2012), p. 50.
17. The Monrovia Group consisted of Ethiopia, Liberia, Libya, Nigeria, Sierra Leone, Somalia, and Togo, and eventually the 12 francophone members of the Brazzaville Group (Benin, Burkina Faso, Cameroon, the Central African Republic [CAR], Chad, Congo-Brazzaville, Côte d'Ivoire, Gabon, Madagascar, Mauritania, Niger, and Senegal). Adebajo, "Paradise Lost and Found", p. 49, and n. 18 on p. 470.
18. Sam G. Amoo, "The OAU and African Conflicts: Past Successes, Present Paralysis, and Future Perspectives", Working Paper no. 5 (Fairfax, VA: Institute for Conflict Analysis and Resolution [ICAR], George Mason University, 1992), p. 1. *See also* Organisation of African Unity (OAU), *OAU Charter* (Addis Ababa, 25 May 1963), http://www.au2002.gov.za/docs/key_oau/oau_charter.pdf (accessed 7 July 2017).
19. Adebajo, "Paradise Lost and Found", p. 51.
20. Monde Muyangwa and Margaret A. Vogt, *An Assessment of the OAU Mechanism for Conflict Prevention, Management, and Resolution, 1993–2000* (New York: International Peace Academy, 2000), p. 5.

21. Sam Ibok, "Conflict Prevention, Management, and Resolution in Africa", 2000, p. 5, www.unpan1.un.org/intradoc/groups/public/documents/cafrad/unpan001836.pdf (accessed 27 July 2017).
22. Solomon Dersso, "The Quest for *Pax Africana*: The Case of the Africa Union's Peace and Security Regime", *African Journal on Conflict Resolution* 12, no. 2 (2012), http://www.ajol.info/index.php/ajcr/article/download/83269/73328 (accessed 19 December 2016).
23. This is the date of entry into force of the 2002 Protocol Relating to the Establishment of the Peace and Security Council of the African Union.
24. "Transforming the Organization of African Unity into the African Union", *Africa Recovery* 15, no. 3 (October 2001), p. 22, http://www.un.org/en/africarenewal/vol15no3/153init2.htm (accessed 27 July 2017).
25. AU Commission, *Strategic Plan 2009–2012*, AU Doc. EX.CL/501 (XV) Rev. 2, 19 May 2009, p. 11.
26. Mazrui, *Towards a Pax Africana*, p. 203.
27. Abdalla Bujra, "Pan-African Political and Economic Visions of Development from the OAU to the AU: From the Lagos Plan of Action (LPA) to the New Partnership for African Development (NEPAD)", Occasional Paper no. 13 (Addis Ababa: Development Policy Management Forum (DPMF), n.d.), p. 17, http://www.bujra.com/documents/Pan-African%20Political%20and%20Economic%20Visions%20of%20Development.pdf (accessed 27 July 2017).
28. Mazrui, *Towards a Pax Africana*, p. 211.
29. Based on data from the World Bank's Poverty and Equity Database.
30. UNDP, *Human Development Report 2016: Human Development for Everyone* (New York, 2016), tab. 1, pp. 200–201; CCR, *Building Peace in South Sudan: Problems, Progress, and Prospects*, Seminar Report no. 57 (Cape Town, June 2017), p. 20; World Bank, "Country Profile: South Sudan", http://data.worldbank.org/country/south-sudan (accessed 24 July 2017).
31. Paul D. Williams, "The African Union's Conflict Management Capabilities", working paper (Washington, DC: Council on Foreign Relations [CFR], October 2011), https://www.cfr.org/report/african-unions-conflict-management-capabilities (accessed 14 November 2016 and 24 July 2017). *See* Paul D. Williams and Arthur Boutellis, "Partnership Peacekeeping: Challenges and Opportunities in the United Nations–African Union Relationship", *African Affairs* 113, no. 451 (2014), pp. 254–278. *See also* Lesley Connolly, "AU-UN Partnership Is a Necessity Not an Option", *Global Peace Operations Review*, 2 June 2016, http://peaceoperationsreview.org/commentary/au-un-partnership-is-a-necessity-not-an-option (accessed 24 July 2017).
32. Williams, "The African Union's Conflict Management Capabilities", p. 1.
33. Williams, "The African Union's Conflict Management Capabilities", p. 3.
34. Williams, "The African Union's Conflict Management Capabilities", p. 3.
35. Tim Murithi, "The African Union's Evolving Role in Peace Operations: The African Union Mission in Burundi, the African Union Mission in Sudan, and the African Union Mission in Somalia", *African Security Review* 17, no. 1 (2010), p. 73. *See* Williams, "The African Union's Conflict Management Capabilities", p. 3.
36. *See* Adekeye Adebajo, Mark Paterson, and Jeremy Sarkin (eds.), "Africa's Responsibility to Protect", special issue, *Global Responsibility to Protect* 2, no. 4 (2010).

37. *Constitutive Act of the African Union* (Lomé, 11 July 2000), art. 4(h).
38. Dersso, "The Quest for *Pax Africana*", p. 28.
39. Dersso, "The Quest for *Pax Africana*", p. 28.
40. Williams, "The African Union's Conflict Management Capabilities", p. 7, and n. 15 on p. 26.
41. AU Commission, Peace and Security Department (PSD), "African Peace and Security Architecture", http://www.peaceau.org/uploads/african-peace-and-security-architecture-apsa-final.pdf (accessed 24 July 2017).
42. Williams, "The African Union's Conflict Management Capabilities", p. 3.
43. Williams, "The African Union's Conflict Management Capabilities", p. 4.
44. Williams, "The African Union's Conflict Management Capabilities", p. 4.
45. On this point, but in the context of a discussion on South Africa's foreign policy, *see* Devon E.A. Curtis, "South Africa's Peacemaking Efforts in Africa: Ideas, Interests, and Influence", in Adekeye Adebajo and Kudrat Virk (eds.), *Foreign Policy in Post-Apartheid South Africa: Security, Diplomacy and Trade* (London: Tauris, 2018), pp. 69–92.
46. *Charter of the United Nations* (San Francisco, CA, 26 June 1945; entry into force 24 October 1945), chap. VIII, art. 53, http://www.un.org/en/sections/un-charter/chapter-viii/index.html (accessed 22 July 2017).
47. Williams, "The African Union's Conflict Management Capabilities", p. 4.
48. Williams, "The African Union's Conflict Management Capabilities", p. 1. *See also* Terry M. Mays, "African Solutions for African Problems: The Changing Face of African-Mandated Peace Operations", *Journal of Conflict Studies* 23, no. 1 (Spring 2003), pp. 106–125.
49. Williams, "The African Union's Conflict Management Capabilities", p. 1.
50. *See, for example,* Connolly, "AU-UN Partnership Is a Necessity Not an Option".
51. Williams, "The African Union's Conflict Management Capabilities", pp. 1–2. *See* Williams and Boutellis, "Partnership Peacekeeping".
52. United Nations, *An Agenda for Peace: Preventive Diplomacy, Peacemaking, and Peace-Keeping*, Report of the Secretary-General Pursuant to the Statement Adopted by the Summit Meeting of the Security Council on 31 January 1992, UN. Doc. A/47/277, 17 June 1992, para. 15.
53. United Nations, *An Agenda for Peace.*
54. United Nations, *Supplement to* An Agenda for Peace: *Position Paper of the Secretary General on the Occasion of the Fiftieth Anniversary of the United Nations*, Report of the Secretary-General on the Work of the Organisation, UN Doc. A/50/60, 25 January 1995.
55. Gabriela Monica Lucuta, "Peacemaking, Peacekeeping, Peacebuilding, and Peace Enforcement in the 21st Century", *Insight on Conflict*, Peace Direct, 25 April 2014, https://www.insightonconflict.org/blog/2014/04/peacemaking-peacekeeping-peacebuilding-peace-enforcement-21st-century (accessed 27 July 2017).

CHAPTER 2

Towards a Concept of "Pax Africana"

Ali A. Mazrui†

Linked with these themes of alignment and military stability after independence is the closely related theme of disarmament. In its modern guise disarmament is either what the Great Powers ask each other to agree to, or what the smaller powers demand of the bigger powers. The summit conference of independent African states which created the Organization of African Unity included in its preoccupations the question of disarmament—and then appealed to the Great Powers to reduce conventional weapons, put an end to the arms race and sign a general and complete disarmament agreement under strict and effective international control.[1]

But disarmament is not necessarily something negotiated and agreed upon between equals. It can be something imposed by the mighty on the weak. In this latter sense "disarmament" of a kind was part of the rationale of imperialism. What this chapter hopes to demonstrate are some of the long-term ideological repercussions in Africa of this aspect of the imperial experience.

Disarmament is normally associated with the ideal of peace. But it has important implications for that other ideal of human dignity. Historically dignity has been more often served by the bearing of arms than by their

Editors' Note: This is a reprint of a chapter from the late Kenyan scholar Ali Mazrui's seminal work, Towards a Pax Africana: A Study of Ideology and Ambition *(Chicago: University of Chicago Press, 1967), in which he lays out the ideal and political relevance of the pursuit of* Pax Africana, *while reflecting on its implications. It is reprinted here with the permission of the University of Chicago Press, the Orion Publishing Group, and the Executor of Ali A. Mazrui's Estate, with minor format changes. The single quotation marks in the original have been changed to double quotation marks, for the sake of consistency with the rest of this volume.*

A.A. Mazrui† (✉)
Institute of Global Cultural Studies, Binghamton University, State University of New York, Binghamton, New York, United States

†Deceased

T. Karbo, K. Virk (eds.), *The Palgrave Handbook of Peacebuilding in Africa*, https://doi.org/10.1007/978-3-319-62202-6_2

renunciation. For many societies there was something rather effeminate or infantile in being "defenceless". Manliness postulated a capacity to defend oneself physically. On this point the Constitution of the United States and the tribal ways of the Kikuyu people have been in accord. The Second Amendment of the American Constitution guarantees "the right of the people to keep and bear arms". And Jomo Kenyatta tells us of the paramount resolution of young Kikuyu boys on being initiated by ancient customs—"We brandish our spear, which is the symbol of our courageous and fighting spirit, never to retreat or abandon our hope, or run away from our comrade."[2]

But imperial rule then came to Africa—and with it came, as we have noted, concepts like that of *Pax Britannica*. V.I. Lenin was later to argue that imperialism was the "monopoly stage of capitalism". What was perhaps more defensible was the thesis that imperialism was a monopoly stage of *warfare*. Nor is this a mere witticism. Implicit in concepts like that of *Pax Britannica* was the idea that the white races had a duty to disarm the rest of mankind. And so when the champions of imperial rule were at their most articulate in its defence, one argument they advanced was that imperialism had given the African, for example, a chance to know what life was like without violence. In 1938 Jomo Kenyatta could therefore complain bitterly in the following terms:

> The European prides himself on having done a great service to the Africans by stopping the "tribal warfares", and says that the Africans ought to thank the strong power that has liberated them from their "constant fear" of being attacked by the neighbouring warlike tribes. But consider the difference between the method and motive employed in the so-called savage tribal warfares and those employed in the modern warfare waged by the "civilized" tribes of Europe, and in which the Africans who have no part in the quarrels are forced to defend so-called democracy.[3]

It is to be remembered that this complaint was made about a *year* before World War II. The preceding world war had been enough to demonstrate Europe's capacity for self-mutilation while still asserting the right to disarm the coloured races except for purpose of fighting Europe's wars. The Third Pan-African Congress held in Lisbon in 1923 was already challenging this doctrine of the white man's exclusive right to initiate war. The Congress first argued the link between Negro dignity and world peace. "In fine, we ask in all the world that black folk be treated as men. We can see no other road to Peace and Progress", the meeting affirmed. It also asserted a connection between Negro dignity and the right to bear arms, though it linked this second assertion with a demand for general disarmament. The reasoning implicit in the demand of the Congress was that if the white man was going to insist that everyone else should be disarmed the white man must also renounce his own weapons. And so this Third Pan-African Congress called for

> World disarmament and the abolition of war; but failing this, and as long as a white folk bear arms against black folk, the right of black to bear arms in their own defence.[4]

In each colony the imperial doctrine of monopoly of warfare merged with a more familiar doctrine in political analysis—the idea that in a political community only the rulers ever have a right to use violence in dealing with citizens. Indeed, political analysts since Weber have sometimes *defined* the state in terms of its "monopoly of the legitimate use of physical force within a given territory".[5]

A variant formulation of this same idea in the West is the ethic that no citizen should "take law into his own hands". This again is an assertion of state-monopoly in certain forms of coercion.

When the colonial power became, to all intents and purposes, "the State" in many parts of Asia and Africa, a doctrinal merger took place between this principle of state-monopoly in physical coercion and the imperial claim of monopoly in warfare. In the total ideology of imperialism the right to *initiate* violence became a prerogative which only civilization and statehood could bestow.[6]

It was in the context of these assumptions that a new doctrine was later born to challenge imperial rule. This is the doctrine of passive resistance which Gandhi came to symbolize. Passive resistance fought against imperialism without challenging either the State's exclusive right to physical coercion or the imperial doctrine of monopoly of warfare. It sought to fight the imposition of *Pax Britannica* on India without violating the principle of peace.

A new conception of the coloured man's dignity grew out of the principle of passive resistance—a dignity not of the soldier and the right to bear arms but a dignity of the martyr and his resistance to the violence of others. The martyrdom of Jesus Christ himself became the martyrdom of a coloured man. Gandhi, for one, preferred to think of Jesus as a fellow Asian and therefore a man of colour himself. Not long before he died, Gandhi had occasion to quote once again the Golden Rule, "Do unto others as you would that they should do unto you." He then went on to ask:

> Or do [the white men] take in vain the name of Him who said this? Have they banished from their hearts the great coloured Asiatic who gave the world the above message? Do they forget that the greatest of the teachers of mankind were all Asiatics and did not possess a white face? These, if descended on earth and went to South Africa, will have to live in segregated areas ... unfit by law to be equals of whites.[7]

Gandhi did not include himself among those great teachers of mankind but Kwame Nkrumah of Ghana was later to pay tribute to him in these terms: "We salute Mahatma Gandhi and we remember, in tribute to him, that it was in South Africa that his method of nonviolence and nonco-operation was first practised".[8]

But Gandhi become more than just the Jesus of Afro-Asian nationalism. In some ways he became almost an antidote to Jesus Christ. Just as Augustine had allied Christianity with a concept of *Pax Romana*, so did Christianity later come to be linked to the whole vision of *Pax Britannica*. In Africa Christianity came to be particularly associated with colonization. In one of his early speeches twenty years ago, Jomo Kenyatta is said to have compressed into a witticism a feeling of disaffection shared by many other nationalists: "The white man came and asked us to shut our eyes and pray. When we opened our eyes it was too late—our land was gone."[9]

Much later Albert Luthuli, himself a devout Christian, came to feel keenly the handicap which the religion had come to experience in the age of nationalism in Africa. Luthuli lamented:

> The average African says the white man is the cause of all his troubles. He does not discriminate between white men and see that some come here for material gain and others come with the message of God.[10]

It was in contexts of this kind of reasoning that Mahatma Gandhi sometimes became a nationalistic antidote to Jesus Christ. The message of Jesus had been used to encourage submission from the natives. That message had not been presented as a call for "non-violent *resistance*" but at best a call for "non-violence". Christianity could even be interpreted to mean "non-resistance"—a coming to terms with the kind of rule God had put the natives under. "My Kingdom is not of this earth"—this declaration came to imply what E.H. Carr called "a boycott of politics".

But Carr was wrong in bracketing Gandhism and Christianity together as "doctrines of non-resistance".[11] What Gandhi provided to Negro nationalism was the element of resistance to the passivity of imperial Christianity. Carr was certainly wrong in extending the description of "boycott of politics" to Gandhism as well as to Christianity. If politics is an activity between groups rather than between individuals, then Gandhism was almost a politicization of Christian doctrine. As Martin Luther King, Jr., the American Negro leader, put it:

> Prior to reading Gandhi I had about concluded that the ethics of Jesus were only effective in individual relationship. The "turn the other cheek" philosophy and the "love your enemies" philosophy were only valid, I felt, when individuals were in conflict with other individuals … Gandhi was probably the first person in history to lift the love ethic of Jesus above mere interaction between individuals to a powerful and effective social force on a large scale. …[12]

The Reverend Dr King came to feel that Gandhism was "the only morally and practically sound method open to oppressed people in their struggle for freedom."[13]

It is, in fact, one of the curious things of history that, outside India itself, the torch of Gandhism came to be passed not to his fellow Asians, but to Negroes both in the New World and in Africa. It is not without significance that the first non-white winners of the Nobel Prize for Peace were Ralph Bunche, Chief Albert Luthuli and Martin Luther King.

Perhaps Gandhi himself would not have been surprised. Quite early in his life he saw non-violent resistance as a method which would be well-suited for the Negro as well as the Indian. In 1924 Gandhi said that if the black people "caught the spirit of the Indian movement their progress must be rapid".[14]

In 1936 Gandhi went even further. And to understand his claim one should perhaps link it up with something which was later said by his disciple, Jawaharlal Nehru. Nehru said: "Reading through history I think the agony of the African continent … has not been equalled anywhere."[15]

To the extent then that the black man had more to be angry about than other men, he would need greater self-discipline than others to be "passive" in his resistance. But by the same token, to the extent that the black man had suffered more than any other, passive but purposeful self-sacrifice for the cause should come easier to him. And to the extent that the black man had more to forgive the rest of the world for, that forgiveness when it came should be all the more weighty. Perhaps in response to adding up these considerations, Gandhi came to the conclusion by 1936 that it was "maybe through the Negroes that the unadulterated message of non-violence will be delivered to the world."[16]

And so it was that in America the torch came to be passed to King. And in South Africa, where Gandhi first experimented with his methods, it passed to Luthuli. In Northern Rhodesia Kenneth Kaunda became a vigorous Gandhian—"I reject absolutely violence in any of its forms as a solution to our problems."[17]

In the Gold Coast Nkrumah had translated *Satyagraha* into a programme of "Positive Action", a programme which he himself defined as "nonco-operation based on the principle of absolute non-violence, as used by Gandhi in India."[18] In 1949 *The Morning Telegraph* of Accra went as far as to call Nkrumah the "Gandhi of Ghana".[19]

African conception of dignity now seemed very different from what was implied by the old ceremonial affirmation of young Kikuyu initiates which Kenyatta once told us about—the glorification of the spear as "the symbol of our courageous and fighting spirit". But these new conceptions of dignity could now also be differentiated from the submissive virtues of early missionary teachings.

Yet one question remained to be answered: could passive resistance survive the attainment of independence? Would Gandhism retain political relevance once its immediate objective of liberation from colonialism was achieved?

It is perhaps not entirely accidental that the two most important Indian contributions to African political thought were the doctrines of non-violence and nonalignment. In a sense they are almost twin-doctrines. Gandhi contributed passive resistance to one school of African thought; Nehru contributed nonalignment to almost all African countries. We have noted how Uganda's President Milton Obote put it in his tribute to Nehru on his death. Obote said: "Nehru will be remembered as a founder of nonalignment. … The new nations of the world owe him a debt of gratitude in this respect."[20]

But how related are the two doctrines in their assumption? For India itself Gandhi's non-violence was a method of seeking freedom, while Nehru's non-alignment came to be a method of seeking peace. And yet nonalignment was, in some ways a translation into foreign policy of some of the moral assumptions which underlay passive resistance in the domestic struggle for India's independence. Gandhi himself once said:

> Free India can have no enemy ... For India to enter into the race for armaments is to court suicide. ... The world is looking for something new and unique from India. ... With the loss of India to non-violence the last hope of the world will be gone. ...[21]

In spite of Gandhi's vision, independent India did not practise abstinence. Gandhian non-violence was not fully translated into a foreign policy. Suspicion of Pakistan in particular was too strong to permit that. And yet of all the countries in the world, India under Nehru came nearest to symbolizing the search for peace. For a crucial decade in the history of Africa and Asia, India was the diplomatic leader of both continents. And in the doctrine of nonalignment she bequeathed to many of the new states a provisional foreign policy for the first few experimental years of their sovereign statehood.

With that policy the wheel of global pacification had come full circle. Asia and Africa had once been colonized partly with a view to imposing peace upon them. But now nonalignment had turned the tables on old concepts like *Pax Britannica*. It was now those who were once colonized that were preaching peace to their former imperial tutors.

As we have noted, the shrine within which this message is preached is now primarily the United Nations. There are many aspects of peace with which the United Nations has tried to grapple. The most idealistic of these is the quest for disarmament. Many of the most important aspects of disarmament are discussed outside the United Nations, though often with its blessing. The eighteen-member Geneva negotiations on disarmament are a case in point. But for Africa it is not the idea of disarming nuclear giants which is of immediate import; it is more modest ventures in military abstinence. And modest issues of disarmament remain directly linked to the work and aspirations of the United Nations.

But what role is envisaged for the UN in this regard? Broadly, two conceptions of the role of the UN in disarmament have been discernible among Africans. The United Nations is conceived either as an instrument for bringing about disarmament or as an additional armed entity capable of forcing combatants apart. Sometimes the old idea of monopoly of violence which imperialism once claimed has, somewhat unrealistically, been urged on to the world body today—a call to the United Nations to become something like *Pax Humana*. On the eve of their independence Tanganyikans discussed precisely such a concept as one hypothetical solution to the new nation's military needs. Joseph Nyerere, brother of the leader of Tanganyika's ruling party, proposed in the

National Assembly in November 1961 that the new independent Tanganyika should consider placing her armies under the United Nations. After all, Tanganyika could not defend herself against a major power. Joseph Nyerere therefore urged that

> as far as military operations against any other country is [*sic*] concerned we would have no right to use our forces at all, except under the orders of a United Nations' command.[22]

Joseph's brother, Julius Nyerere, shared some of the premises but drew a different conclusion. In a speech addressed to a seminar of the World Assembly of Youth in August 1961 Tanganyika's national leader criticized the whole concept of each state in Africa arming itself separately. Given discrepancies in power, it was unlikely that an African state's motive for arming itself was to protect itself against an attack by one of the Great Powers of the world. "If an African state is armed then, realistically, it can only be armed against another African state", Julius Nyerere asserted.[23]

Nyerere might have been overstating his case. But the experience of Somalia's dispute with Ethiopia, Algeria with Morocco, Rwanda with Burundi, Gabon with Congo-Brazzaville, Tshombe's Congo with her neighbours, and even the accusations between Malawi and Tanzania in 1964–5, were soon to lend credibility to that analysis of Julius Nyerere's at the seminar in 1961.[24]

But was Nyerere suggesting that newly-sovereign African states should renounce armaments? His answer for Tanganyika was:

> All that we need with our national boundaries are sufficient police forces for the purpose of maintaining law and order within those boundaries; as far as larger commitments are concerned, these should be on an African basis.[25]

This introduces us to that concept in the rhetoric of general pacification which, to establish historical continuity, we have called *Pax Africana*. But the political ambition implied by this concept is not to impose an African peace on *others*—that would indeed be ambitious. The word "Africana" in this concept describes both the nationality of the peace-makers and the continental limits of their jurisdiction. For *Pax Africana* asserts that the peace of *Africa* is to be assured by the exertions of *Africans* themselves. The idea of a "Pax Africana" is the specifically military aspect of the principle of continental jurisdiction.

For Tanganyika itself the problem was dramatized not at the time that Tanganyika attained her independence, but two years later. On achieving independence Tanganyika did not, after all, renounce armaments for herself. She succumbed to what Janowitz describes as "a universal political conception that a new state requires an army."[26]

But, as we have noted, in January 1964 the army of independent Tanganyika mutinied. And in order to subdue the mutinous soldiers we know that the Tanganyika Government had to ask for the help of British troops. So had the

Governments of Kenya and Uganda. For at least a few weeks the old slogan of *Pax Britannica* received a new lease of life. And British patriotism found a new feeling of global purpose. The British Prime Minister could even afford to indulge in a few benign, I-told-you-so remarks addressed to leaders of former British colonies at large. We might here repeat Sir Alec Douglas-Home's remark at the time:

> I have always pleaded with our African and Asian friends not to push their requests for independence soon. ... I was afraid that they would get their independence before they had the two essential things that are necessary if you are to run a country. One is a police force, loyal to the Government; and another is armed forces, loyal to the elected government of the day. ... This has been proved, of course, beyond doubt now.[27]

But for Tanganyika at any rate reliance on *Pax Britannica* was short-lived. President Nyerere called an emergency meeting of the Organization of African Unity and appealed for help to replace the British troops in Tanganyika with African ones as soon as possible. In effect he was invoking the doctrine of *Pax Africana* as defined above. Nyerere's fellow Africans responded—and it was not long before Nigerian troops replaced British troops in the barracks of Tanganyika. In the meantime Tanganyika set out to create a new and more reliable army for herself.[28]

But it has been in regard to the Congo that the ideal of *Pax Africana* has had a particularly direct political relevance. Let us remind ourselves of the continental context of the Congo's independence. 1960 was the year in which more than fifteen African countries became independent. Never before had so many states become independent in a single year. Nor is that phenomenon ever likely to be repeated in any other year in the future. Among the countries which became independent in that year was, as we know, the Congo. But it was not long before law and order broke down in that country. And so the Congo situation articulated in a particularly eloquent way a question which many others had already asked about the continent as a whole—who was going to keep the peace in Africa now that the imperial powers were withdrawing?

Belgian troops moved into the Congo when law and order broke down. Was there no alternative to imperial peace? Africa was as yet not equipped to assert a *Pax Africana* over itself. Lumumba invited the United Nations—and the rest of Africa was soon to approve of this move for the time being. Better collective police action by the world body than a return to imperial pacification. And so in August 1960, at an All-Africa Conference held in Leopoldville at the behest of Lumumba, a resolution was passed commending the United Nations "for the work it is doing for peace in the Congo by effecting a withdrawal of the Belgian troops of aggression from the entire territory of the Republic of Congo."[29]

As between the old idea of imperial pacification and the new ambition of *Pax Africana* the United Nations temporarily provided a third alternative. And yet it was soon clear that the United Nations as an alternative could never be as self-sufficient as imperial pacification had been and as African self-policing aspired to be. Among the first to insist on some kind of accountability by the United Nations to Africa as a whole was Kwame Nkrumah. In March 1961 Nkrumah argued that

> unless at this juncture the United Nations acts in full consultation with the African States and in accordance with the needs of Africa, the same results will flow from the United Nations' interventions in the Congo as flowed from the intervention of the great powers in African affairs.[30]

Nkrumah discerned a parallel between big power competition in 1960–1 for the control of the Congo and the colonial rivalry which led to the Berlin Conference of 1885. That colonial rivalry of the late nineteenth century was to Nkrumah "the second cold war of those days"—and at the Berlin Conference "the only interested parties not represented were the inhabitants of Africa". Nkrumah warned lest the United Nations should now be converted into a similar "conference", designed to settle the rivalry of the Big Powers of today at the expense of the racial sovereignty of others. What the Ghanaian President was asserting was the dictum that peace in any part of Africa could now only be assured under the supervising eye of the rest of the continent.[31]

The United Nations did try to pacify the Congo under the critical eye not only of Africans but also of others. By the end of 1963 it was clear that the United Nations did not have either the resources or the independence to be an effective substitute for the old Imperial Peace. Towards the middle of 1964 the United Nations therefore withdrew from the Congo.

And yet pacification of the Congo by Africans themselves from internal continental resources was as yet not a practical proposition. It was within this context that the employment of mercenaries by Moise Tshombe became a major issue in inter-African politics.

But what indeed are the implications of white mercenaries for the whole ideal of *Pax Africana*?

From one point of view the employment of mercenaries by an African government should be more consistent with the country's sovereignty than a request to another country, or even to the United Nations, for a loan of troops. By *buying* foreign soldiers for his own use, Tshombe showed, in one sense, greater independence than Lumumba had done when he invited the United Nations to help him out. After all, while Tshombe's mercenaries were presumably answerable to Tshombe who paid them, the troops of the United Nations were never accountable to Patrice Lumumba.

If, then, the purchase of soldiers of fortune by an African government is more of an exercise in sovereignty than the loan of troops answerable to someone else, it should follow that the employment of white mercenaries by Tshombe was more in keeping with *Pax Africana* than either Lumumba's request in 1960 for UN troops or the request of Uganda, Kenya and Tanganyika in 1964 for the loan of British troops.

It could further be argued that the purchase of soldiers from outside was comparable to the purchase of arms and ammunition. Both mercenaries and guns were instruments of warfare. It might be true that Tshombe could only remain in power with the backing of foreign soldiers. But none of the other African governments manufactured their own military equipments either. In any case, one government might remain in power by equipping its *native* army with *foreign* guns. Another might hypothetically have its own "home-made" guns but used by soldiers externally recruited. A third might survive by employing both foreign soldiers and foreign guns. Why, it might be asked, should any one of these be less of a distortion of the balance of forces in a divided country than any of the others?[32]

Consideration of nonalignment might preclude certain forms of military aid. But the purchase of soldiers is more analogous to military *trade*. And the buying of arms, for example, had never been regarded as a compromise of nonalignment.

There was another way in which the ideal of *Pax Africana* might be said to be served by the use of white mercenaries. Future peace in Africa partly depends on minimizing the chances of continuing feuds. Sometimes Tshombe's critics in 1964 seemed to take it for granted that it was better for the Congolese to be killed by fellow Congolese than to be killed by white mercenaries. But it was at least as convincingly arguable that if there was any killing to be done, it was better for the Congo's future that it should be done by foreigners. For this must mean that the Congolese themselves would have fewer atrocities to *forgive each other for*. Tshombe himself might never be forgiven. But from the point of view of the country's future, it might indeed have been a good thing if his *entire* army had consisted of white mercenaries. The Civil War in the Congo would then have been less of a *civil* war. And there would have been fewer Congolese among the casualties of at least the Government side of the war.[33]

By minimizing reasons for future revenge between Congolese themselves, the use of foreigners to commit some of the atrocities might, cynically but truly, be a positive contribution to the realization of future peace.

But there is another side to the issue of mercenaries from the point of view of *Pax Africana*. What mattered about the mercenaries was not simply that they were non-Africans but that there was good reason to suspect them of being fundamentally *anti*-African. Even in the days when Tshombe was employing mercenaries to help detach Katanga from the rest of the Congo, his chosen fields of recruitment were singularly "anti-African" in their reputation. As Nkrumah said to Tshombe in a letter dated as far back as 12 August 1960, "you have assembled in your support … the most determined opponents of African freedom. How can you, as an African, do this?"[34]

Perhaps it was inevitable in the circumstances that Tshombe's most promising field of recruitment of mercenaries should have been the Republic of South Africa. But the participation of white South Africans in an African Civil War had immense symbolic implications for African nationalism at large. Very soon the Congo became the first battleground between Afrikaners and troops from or supported by independent African states. It is true that the Afrikaners were not part of a regular South African army. Nor were they all trained for military service. But if, in spite of that, they could tip the scales in an African civil war, Africa's military vulnerability when confronted with South Africa had wider implications than had originally been supposed. *Pax Africana* was a remote ideal if a few South African adventurers could determine which faction in an African country remained in power.

The symbolic implications of the situation were aggravated by one further consideration. Of all the countries in Africa south of the Sahara, the only one which had the potential to rival South Africa in wealth, and in the power which came with wealth, was in fact the Congo itself. Only the Congo had the requisite combination of territorial size, population and mineral resources to be a possible serious rival to South Africa before the end of the century. And yet here were the fortunes of the Congo being determined by the intervention of amateur soldiers from the land of *apartheid*.

Associated with the problem of *apartheid* is the problem of the remaining colonies in Africa, with particular reference to the lingering Portuguese presence. On the question of methods of liberation a major change has taken place in the ethic of African nationalism. When Ghana attained independence in 1957 without resort to an armed insurrection, Gandhism appeared to have once again been vindicated. Nkrumah, as we have noted, had been a disciple of Gandhi in his methods—and now his country was the first black colony to win independence from Britain. The following year Ghana's capital was the scene of the first All-African Peoples Conference, the Accra conference of December 1958. At that conference one of the major areas of debate was the issue of whether violence should be recognized by the conference as a legitimate instrument of African nationalism. The Algerians—then struggling with the French—put up a spirited case defence of armed insurrection, but black Africa was not fully in agreement. In the end a compromise resolution was agreed on:

> That the All-African Peoples Conference in Accra declares its full support to all fighters for freedom in Africa, to all those who resort to peaceful means of non-violence and civil disobedience as well as to all those who are compelled to retaliate against violence to attain national independence and freedom for the people. Where such retaliation becomes necessary, the Conference condemns all legislations which consider those who fight for their independence and freedom as ordinary criminals.[35]

The solution was a compromise in that it legitimated insurrection only when the colonial regime had become "violent" in its methods. On balance, however, the prevalent mood of the conference was what its Chairman, Tom Mboya, described it—"the December, 1958, Accra Conference resolves to use non-violent positive actions", Mboya observed.[36]

But by the time of the conference at Addis Ababa which set up the Organization of African Unity, Africa's mood regarding violence in the colonies had changed. The Heads of State at the Conference had received a joint memorandum from national liberation movements in the remaining territories. The memorandum had argued the formation of an "African Liberation Bureau" whose functions were to include the following basic ones:

(a) To co-ordinate the struggle for African liberation in all non-independent territories.
(b) To receive, distribute and transport funds and other forms of aid, *including military equipment and personnel*, on behalf of the African liberation movements.[37]

The Heads of the independent States responded with suitable resolutions. Resolution 10 of the conference started by urging the liberation movements themselves to co-ordinate their efforts in a way which would result in a "rational use of the concerted assistance given to them". Resolution 11 established a co-ordinating committee of the Organization of African Unity itself. The committee, which later became known as "the Liberation Committee" or "the Committee of Nine", was made "responsible for harmonizing the assistance from African States and for managing the Special Fund to be set up for that purpose."[38]

Resolution 14 granted refuge on the territories of independent states to nationalists from liberation movements "in order to give them training in all sectors". Finally, there was Resolution 15 which was a decision

> to promote in each State the transit of all material aid and the establishment of a body of volunteers in various fields, with a view to providing the various African national liberation movements with the assistance they need in the various sectors.[39]

But what had happened to the Gandhism which had once animated and inspired many an African nationalist? There were a number of reasons for the greater militancy which the ethic of African nationalism had now assumed. But one important factor in the transformation of Africa's mood was the action taken by India herself over Goa. This was the first instance of a former colony taking direct military action to reject the imperial power from the neighbourhood. It is true that China's role in the old French Indo-China contributed to the humiliation of the French at Dien Bien Phu. But China was never a colony in quite the sense as India and Africa had been. And the victory of the Vietnamese themselves at Dien Bien Phu was in any case substantially a victory of the Vietnamese themselves—much as Algerian independence came to be ultimately attributable to the Algerians themselves. India's military action against the Portuguese regime in Goa was, however, in a class by itself. It was accomplished with ease and confidence. It was a display of Asiatic power against the imperial arrogance of a European country. It was the first case of a former colony appearing to "bully" magnificently one of the oldest Empires that European expansionism had created.

The impact of this event on Africa was greatly accentuated by the fact that Portugal's last Empire was now in Africa itself. Tom Mboya was soon saying in Kenya that he was "strongly in favour" of India's action over Goa. He went on to say that it was disturbing that some Goans in Kenya should still owe allegiance to Portugal. Mr Mboya was emphatic in his assertion that. "No African in Kenya will tolerate any Goan who supports Salazar."[40]

And on the West coast of Africa the man who had once been described as the "Gandhi of Ghana" was, as we have noted, now declaring: "I am most happy about India's annexation of Goa, which I consider long overdue."[41]

This then was the great paradox of India's ideological impact on African nationalism. The same country which had once made African nationalists subscribe to the Gandhian approach to liberation had now set a grand military precedent of armed ejection.

The United Nations in turn was soon to feel the effects of this new militancy in anti-colonialism. There were pressures on the world organization for some kind of military sanctions against Portugal. By the middle of 1965 Tanzania's Second Vice-President, Rashidi Kawawa, was telling a United Nations committee that its functions were the same as those of the Liberation Committee of the Organization of African Unity. It was the twenty-four nation UN Committee on Decolonization that Kawawa bracketed together with the OAU Committee of Nine—and called the "two liberation committees of historic importance in the struggle against colonialism."

The Chairman of the UN Committee, M. Coulibaly of Mali, appeared reluctant to see a UN Committee identified with a neo-military regional body. Mr Coulibaly therefore said that he had always advocated peaceful means—and, with a shrewd diplomatic touch, he went on to praise President Nyerere of Tanzania for supporting "the peaceful achievement of independence in colonial territories".[42]

But by the end of that conference in Dar-es-Salaam Chairman Coulibaly's tone was different. His Committee adopted a resolution on Portuguese territories on 10 June 1965. Commenting on the resolution the following day, Chairman Coulibaly said it would be legitimate for other states to give every form of aid to nationalist movements in Portuguese African countries. Force could legitimately be used in those territories to prevent the Portuguese from using force to suppress nationalist movements. M. Coulibaly added that this was the first time that a UN Committee had directly called for such military support for the African people.[43]

Was the world body, which was originally intended for peace, now being perverted to serve nationalistic ends? It all depended upon the point of departure of one's reasoning. The world as a whole could perhaps best be shielded from the consequences of breaches of the peace in Africa when those breaches were dealt with by Africans themselves. But for as long as a colonial presence lingered on in Africa, such a principle of *Pax Africana* could not encompass the whole continent. For that very reason, nationalists might assume the principle would fall short of complete effectiveness. A *Pax Africana* postulated a triumph of continental jurisdiction, and perhaps of racial sovereignty. The Portuguese presence violated both those principles. A breach of the peace of the kind sanctioned by the UN Committee on Decolonization might therefore be inevitable before a concept of *Pax Africana* could at last assume some meaning. In short, the old idea of imperial pacification had to end before a new African peace could assert itself. It was therefore arguable that the United Nations, if involved in such an undertaking, might conceivably fulfil both the ultimate goal of peace and the immediate cause of African dignity.

A more difficult problem for *Pax Africana* concerns the behaviour of its own instruments of enforcement *internally*. The ultimate instruments of self-pacification in Africa are Africa's own police and armed forces. If the peace is disturbed by a tribal insurrection or by corrupt politicians, Africa's armed forces might be called upon to re-establish authority. But what if the peace is disturbed by those armed forces themselves?

As we have noted, East Africa in 1964 had to invite back a *Pax Britannica* in order to cope with her own mutinous troops. There have been other examples since then of military insubordination in Africa, sometimes directed against military regimes themselves. The painful search for a *Pax Africana* therefore continues. Decolonization might be a necessary condition for it. But it is far from being a sufficient one.

Notes

1. See the collection of speeches and other conference documents, *Addis Ababa Summit*, 1963, *op. cit.*, p. 102.
2. Jomo Kenyatta, *Facing Mount Kenya* (first published 1938) (London: Secker and Warburg, 1959), p. 199. The initiation ceremonies have been simplified since then.
3. *Ibid.*, p. 212.
4. See George Padmore (ed.), *History of the Pan-African Congress*, *op. cit.*, pp. 22–3.
5. See Max Weber, "Politics as a Vocation", H.H. Gerth and C. Wright Mills (eds.), *From Max Weber: Essays in Sociology* (New York: Oxford University Press [Galaxy Book], 1958), pp. 77–8. Gabriel A. Almond has broadened Weber's definition in order to include types of political organization other than the state. See Almond's "Introduction" to Gabriel A. Almond and James S. Coleman (eds.), *The Politics of the Developing Areas* (Princeton: Princeton University Press, 1960), pp. 6–7.
6. See Eric Stokes, *The Political Ideas of English Imperialism*, an Inaugural Lecture given at the University College in Salisbury, Rhodesia (Oxford University Press, 1960), esp. pp. 21–33. See also Ernest Barker, *Ideas and Ideals of the British Empire* (Cambridge: Cambridge University Press, 1941), esp. pp. 61–70; 139–64.

7. *Harijan* (Ahmedabad), 30 June 1946. See also Haridas T. Muzumdar (ed.), *Sermon on the Sea* (Chicago: Universal Publishing Co., 1924).
8. See Speeches, *Positive Action Conference on Peace and Security in Africa*, *op. cit.*, p. 4. Other African leaders who have paid tribute to Gandhi include Jomo Kenyatta, Tom Mboya, Rashidi Kawawa and Kenneth Kaunda. See *Africa Quarterly* (New Delhi), Vol. II, No. 2, July–September 1962. See also Gandhi, *Satyagraha in South Africa*, translated from the Gujarati by Vaiji Govindji Desai (Madras: S. Ganesan, 1926).
9. Kenyatta has felt that the entire interpretation of the Bible as propagated by Europeans was calculated to vindicate the superiority of whiteness over blackness. The forces of evil were "black", the angels "white". In January 1962 Kenyatta called for a reinterpretation of Christianity and for a reversal of symbolism as between those two colours. See *The Guardian* (Manchester), 30 January 1962.
10. Quoted in the *New York Times*, 19 March 1961. See my article, "Africa and the Egyptians' Four Circles", *African Affairs*, *op. cit.*
11. E. H. Carr, *The Twenty-Years Crisis*, *op. cit.*
12. *Stride Towards Freedom*, *op. cit.*, pp. 76–7.
13. *Ibid.*
14. *Young India*, 1924–1926 (Madras: S. Ganesan, 1927), pp. 839–40. Consult also Pyarelal, "Gandhiji and the African Question", *Africa Quarterly*, Vol. II, No. 2, July–September 1962. See as well the selection from Gandhi entitled "Mahatma Gandhi on Freedom in Africa", *Africa Quarterly*, Vol. 1, No. 2, July–September 1961. For a more extensive discussion by Gandhi on non-violence consult Gandhi, *Non-Violence in Peace and War* (2nd ed.) (Ahmedabad: Navajivan Publishing House, 1944).
15. Jawaharlal Nehru, "Portuguese Colonialism: An Anachronism", *Africa Quarterly*, Vol. 1, No. 3, October–December, 1961, p. 9. See also Nehru, "Emergent Africa", *Africa Quarterly*, Vol. 1, No. 1, April–June, 1961, pp. 7–9.
16. *Harijan*, 14 March 1936.
17. See *Black Government* (Lusaka: United Society for Christian Literature, 1960).
18. *Autobiography*, *op. cit.*, p. 92.
19. *The Morning Telegraph*, 27 June 1949.
20. See *Uganda Argus*, 29 May 1964.
21. *Harijan*, 14 October 1939.
22. Tanganyika *Assembly Debates*, Thirty-Sixth Session (sixth meeting), 30 November 1961. Cols. 18, 20.
23. See *The Second Scramble*, *op. cit.*, p. 7.
24. This point is discussed in a different context in my article "Tanzania Versus East Africa: A Case of Unwitting Federal Sabotage", *The Journal of Commonwealth Political Studies*, *op. cit.*
25. *The Second Scramble*, *op. cit.*
26. M. Janowitz, *The Military in the Political Development of New Nations* (Chicago: Chicago University Press, 1964), p. 100.
27. Reported in the *Mombasa Times* (Kenya), 22 February 1964.
28. For Nyerere's sense of "national humiliation" at having had to use non-African troops consult his opening speech to the OAU meeting he had called. For the text of the speech see *East African Standard*, 13 February 1964.
29. See UN Document No. A/PV 860, 18 September 1960, p. 81.

30. Address to the resumed session of the United Nations General Assembly, 7 March 1961. See the edition issued by the Ghana Ministry of Information, p. 8.
31. *Ibid.*
32. In Europe, of course, employing soldiers of fortune used to be a long-established tradition in warfare. One of its remnants today is the idea of Swiss Guards for the Pope. A more operative survival is the French Foreign Legion. A reviewer of Patrick Turnbull's *The Foreign Legion* (London: Heinemann, 1964) said in the East African news magazine, *Reporter*, in January 1965, "The French Foreign Legion, which is now a dwindling force, is basically an army of mercenaries. This is, of course, a dirty word today, although why it should be worse to kill one's fellow men for money than to kill them for nothing is never clearly explained." (*Reporter*, 29 January 1965, p. 7.)
33. All this is *assuming* that the mercenaries would have been no more ruthless in their treatment of their opponents than native troops would have been.
34. Reproduced in Ghana Government's W.P. No. 6/60, p. 8.
35. For resolutions of conference see Colin Legum, *Pan-Africanism*, *op. cit.*, Appendix 22.
36. See Mboya, "Vision of Africa", in *Africa Speaks*, *op. cit.*, pp. 22–3.
37. See *Addis Ababa Summit*, 1963, *op. cit.* The emphasis is mine.
38. The nine members of the Committee appointed were Algeria, Congo (Leopoldville), Ethiopia, Guinea, Nigeria, Senegal, Tanganyika, Uganda and the United Arab Republic. It was decided that the Headquarters of this Liberation Committee was to be Dar-es-Salaam. *Ibid.*, p. 101.
39. *Ibid.*, p. 10.
40. See *Mombasa Times*, 11 January 1962.
41. Speech by Nkrumah. See *Ghana Today*, 21 January 1962. Refer also to Nehru, "Portuguese Colonialism: An Anachronism". Of historical interest also is Gandhi's *Goan Struggle for Freedom* (Ahmedabad: Navajivan Publishing House, 1954, reprint).
42. Radio Tanzania, 31 May 1965. See BBC Monitoring Records, ME/1874/B/3.
43. Radio Tanzania, I June 1965. See BBC Monitoring Records, ME/1883/B/2.

CHAPTER 3

Squaring the Circle: The Role of the African Peace and Security Architecture

Dan Kuwali

The 1993 Continental Mechanism for Conflict Prevention, Management, and Resolution was established by the Organisation of African Unity (OAU) to, among other things, anticipate and prevent conflicts. However, the OAU restricted its efforts to settling border disputes and adjudicating ideological differences resulting from the Cold War. As a response to the ineffectiveness of its predecessor, the legal architects of the African Union (AU)—which replaced the OAU in July 2002—have constructed an impressive array of peace and security institutions that together comprise the African Peace and Security Architecture (APSA). The establishment of the APSA, distinguished by its intervention regime under Article 4(h) of the 2000 AU Constitutive Act, also seeks to get around the problem of paralysis or inaction by the United Nations (UN) Security Council, as during the Rwandan genocide of 1994, by ensuring that the AU can take action in situations where the UN is unwilling or unable to act. (See Ugarte in this volume.) The idea to construct the APSA is in line with the arguments put forward by former UN Secretary-General Boutros Boutros-Ghali of Egypt in his 1992 report *An Agenda for Peace*. (See Introduction in this volume.) Boutros-Ghali argued that regional organisations should play a more robust security role, not only as a means of alleviating mounting UN overstretch but also to contribute to a deeper sense of participation, consensus, and democratisation in international affairs.[1]

Indeed, it has become increasingly clear that Africa must build and operationalise its own effective security and governance architectures. The problems facing the continent today remain complex and massive, while its institutions are relatively weak and lack resources. This is supported by the fact that the first 18 situations before the International Criminal Court (ICC) have concerned

D. Kuwali (✉)
Centre for Human Rights, University of Pretoria, Tshwane (Pretoria), South Africa

T. Karbo, K. Virk (eds.), *The Palgrave Handbook of Peacebuilding in Africa*, https://doi.org/10.1007/978-3-319-62202-6_3

eight AU member states: the Central African Republic (CAR), the Democratic Republic of the Congo (DRC), Côte d'Ivoire, Kenya, Libya, Mali, Sudan, and Uganda. (See Nouwen in this volume.) In June 2017, nine of the UN's 16 peacekeeping operations were deployed in Africa, with nearly 80,000 blue helmets there, which is indicative of the continued prevalence of conflicts on the continent.[2] Consider further that about 60 per cent of the deliberations of the UN Security Council focus on Africa.[3] (See also Ugarte in this volume.) The fact that the six countries on the UN Peacebuilding Commission's agenda (as of June 2017)—Burundi, the CAR, Guinea, Guinea-Bissau, Liberia, and Sierra Leone—were all African also explains why Africa should take the lead in institution-building and reconstruction in post-conflict settings on the continent.[4] (See Omeje, Otobo, and Richmond in this volume.)

The APSA is built around structures, objectives, principles, and values, as well as decision-making processes relating to the prevention, management, and resolution of conflicts; post-conflict reconstruction; and socio-economic development on the continent. The 2002 Protocol Relating to the Establishment of the Peace and Security Council (PSC) of the AU outlines the various components of the APSA and their respective responsibilities, and African leaders have since taken further legal and policy steps to expedite the operationalisation of the APSA. The APSA comprises the PSC, which is a political decision-making body; the AU Commission, which is the oversight and coordinating organ; the Panel of the Wise, which is an auxiliary advisory and mediation body; the Continental Early Warning System (CEWS), which is an information-gathering and analysis centre; the African Standby Force (ASF), which contains military, police, and civilian components (see Nagar in this volume); and the Peace Fund, which is a special fund to cover APSA costs. The interaction between the PSC and other AU organs, such as the Pan-African Parliament and the African Commission on Human and Peoples' Rights (ACHPR), as well as with civil society organisations, is key to the promotion of peace, security, and stability in Africa. The APSA is further built on, or around, Africa's regional economic communities (RECs) and regional mechanisms for conflict prevention, management, and resolution.[5] (See Vogt in this volume.)

The deployment of the AU Mission in Sudan (AMIS), in 2004, demonstrated the Union's commitment to the protection of African citizens across borders. But, at the same time, it also revealed the limitations of the APSA.[6] The AU mission, comprising about 7,730 peacekeepers by 2005,[7] was able neither to effectively contain the violence on the ground in Sudan nor to carry out its civilian protection mandate. It, quite simply, lacked the necessary material and human resources to be effective. For example, it had no attack helicopters, which are necessary for rapid response activities. There were too few interpreters, and the mission also lacked experienced female staff to address issues of sexual and gender-based violence. AMIS further suffered from, among other things, a lack of information-sharing among its various elements (military observers, protection force, and police).[8] In 2007, it was merged into the

AU-UN Hybrid Operation in Darfur (UNAMID). (On Sudan, see Deng; and on UNAMID, see Gambari, both in this volume.)

The APSA also faces shortcomings related to the lack of sufficient political will of its member states to engage in military intervention, as evident in the AU's ambivalence to act against Libya's Muammar Qaddafi following the popular uprising against him in 2011. Given Africa's lack of capacity to respond to crises, such as that in northern Mali in 2012, the continent has continued to need to look to Europe and the United States (US)—sometimes bilaterally, sometimes under a UN umbrella—when intervening in complex conflicts, mediating the most difficult problems, and implementing peace agreements. (See Adebajo, Rashid, and Yates in this volume.) Additionally, no clear operational doctrine has been developed by the ASF for the protection of civilians and prevention of atrocities. Institutional weaknesses are another mounting problem, exacerbated by the apparent dominance of influential countries in deploying the ASF (see Nagar in this volume).

Therefore, the primary challenge for the APSA is to summon the political will needed to develop effective mechanisms for conflict prevention, early warning, and decisive rapid response, as well as post-conflict reconstruction and peacebuilding, all while maximising scarce resources. In this context, the establishment of preventive interventions should be the main preoccupation of the AU, as opposed to acting after conflict has begun.

The Peace and Security Council: Politics, Problems, and Patronage

The AU Peace and Security Council has effectively replaced the OAU's Central Organ of the Mechanism for Conflict Prevention, Management, and Resolution.[9] To move from the confinement of a purely reactive posture, the Peace and Security Council was established in July 2002, based on the recognition that the AU would require more effective policy channels through which it could confront conflicts proactively. The PSC is "a collective security and early-warning arrangement to facilitate timely and efficient response to conflict and crisis situations in Africa".[10] As such, the PSC is at the heart of the APSA and has considerable powers in its role as the standing decision-making vehicle for the prevention, management, and resolution of conflicts. Pursuant to, and buttressed by, the need to promote peace, security, and stability in Africa, the main objectives of the PSC are to anticipate conflicts and undertake preventive diplomacy; make peace through use of good offices, mediation, conciliation, and inquiry; undertake peace support operations and interventions; engage in peacebuilding and post-conflict reconstruction; and undertake humanitarian action and disaster management.[11]

The Peace and Security Council also forms a vital part of Africa's regional human and peoples' rights system, given that it is mandated to enforce the decisions of the AU and, under Article 19 of its founding protocol, to seek cooperation with the African Commission on Human and Peoples' Rights. As the central organ of the APSA, the Council legitimises and coordinates the actions of all its other elements. The PSC is supported by the chair of the AU Commission, who, importantly, also has official oversight of the APSA. It is further supported by a Military Staff Committee, which provides advice on military and security issues, and is composed of representatives from the countries that sit on the PSC. The Council comprises 15 members, with ten elected for a two-year term and five for a three-year term to ensure continuity (see also Gambari in this volume). The PSC meets regularly and recommends action to the AU Assembly of Heads of State and Government, which can delegate authority to the PSC to make decisions on its behalf. The AU Assembly, though, stands as the supreme organ of the Union. For example, in December 2015—ahead of the 26th AU Assembly summit in January 2016—the Peace and Security Council decided to authorise the deployment of a 5,000-strong African Prevention and Protection Mission in Burundi (MAPROBU), in an effort to quell the violence precipitated by Burundian president Pierre Nkurunziza's controversial winning bid for a third term in the country's July 2015 elections.[12] At the January 2016 summit, though, AU heads of state and government decided against the intervention.

There are several means by which an item may be placed on the agenda of the Peace and Security Council. These include submission by a member state, by the chair of the AU Commission, by the Panel of the Wise, by a REC or regional mechanism, or by the Pan-African Parliament.[13] Civil society organisations may also make representations to the PSC. This provision is designed to address the problems of political will and sovereignty of member states, and to ensure that the initiation of action is not left to member states alone.[14] Although civil society on the continent has been increasingly vocal, AU member states have, in general, turned a deaf ear to it in exercise of the principle of state sovereignty.

As American scholar Jeremy Levitt has observed, the PSC seems to be "more democratic than its UN counterpart as it does not provide for permanent membership or for any veto power", and because all decisions are taken by consensus, no member state can deadlock the activities of the PSC.[15] Yet, despite the broad powers accorded to the PSC, it lacks authority to make the final decision to implement an intervention under Article 4(h) of the 2000 AU Constitute Act, which grants the Union the right to intervene in a member state in grave circumstances in the form of genocide, war crimes, and crimes against humanity. Even if the Council becomes aware of actual grave human rights violations as enumerated under Article 4(h), the final decision for intervention lies with the AU Assembly. Such a requirement is necessary, on the one hand, to avoid possible abuse, especially by dominant states whose power is checked in the AU Assembly by the requirement of making decisions based on consensus or, failing that, a two-thirds majority. On the other hand, though, it convolutes the decision-making procedure. The AU Assembly also meets only twice a year. Moreover, in situations where urgent direct intervention is needed, the AU Assembly, because of its inherent political nature, may decide not to intervene at all. The process of responding to grave circumstances against the will of a target state can therefore be time-consuming and replete with challenges, as the crisis in Burundi in 2015 showed.[16]

The Continental Early Warning System: Early Warning or Early Action?

Established in 2004, the CEWS is intended to facilitate the anticipation and prevention of conflicts in Africa.[17] The heart of the CEWS is an observation headquarters called the "Situation Room", located in the Conflict Management Directorate under the AU's Peace and Security Department, which is charged with the task of collecting and analysing data on potential conflicts and threats to peace and security in Africa. More specifically, the CEWS has developed an early warning module to analyse developments on potential conflicts and threats to peace and security on the continent and to recommend the best course of action. Using open-source information, CEWS staff compile reports identifying potentially dangerous activity to determine the gravity and potential consequences of such action.

In theory, the Situation Room is connected to the observation and monitoring units of the sub-regional mechanisms in each of Africa's five sub-regions—Southern, Eastern, West, Central, and North Africa—to share information on impending conflicts with the Peace and Security Council. The information collected and analysed through the CEWS is meant to be used by the chair of the AU Commission to provide the PSC with timely advice on appropriate responses to potential or actual conflict. The CEWS is well positioned to give early warning of conflicts that could brew into crises if the international community does not act. But it still lacks the capacity to analyse raw conflict-related data, and continues to need more highly-trained and experienced analysts. Furthermore, the creation of an early warning network also requires establishing early action mechanisms and, more crucially, preventive mechanisms. While the CEWS is mandated to "advise the PSC, on potential conflicts and threats to peace and security in Africa", the PSC does not always act on warnings about imminent crises, due to poor communication between the two organs.[18]

The Panel of the Wise: Where Is the Right of Initiative?

In addition to its conflict mediation role, the Panel of the Wise has the responsibility to advise the PSC and the chair of the AU Commission on all issues pertaining to conflict prevention and the promotion and maintenance of peace, security, and stability in Africa.[19] The five-member panel consists of highly-respected African personalities, from various segments of society, who have made outstanding contributions to conflict prevention on the continent.[20] Acting on the instruction of the PSC or the chair of the AU Commission, or on its own initiative, the Panel meets regularly and undertakes action in support of the PSC's objectives and gives opinions on issues relating to peace, security, and stability in Africa.[21] In practice, this entails mediating between warring groups or in situations where conflict looks likely. Since its establishment in 2007, the panel has also been involved in behind-the-scenes roles, raising issues with the PSC that are too politically sensitive for serving politicians to address.[22] For example, following post-election violence in 2007–2008 in Kenya (see also Wamai in this volume), the panel assisted in mediating between the warring factions; and produced a thematic report on election-related disputes and violence in Africa, which was adopted in July 2009. The panel was also actively involved in mediation in the wake of the "Afro-Arab Spring" of 2011.[23]

This underscores the importance of the "right of initiative" of the Panel of the Wise to serve as an alternative avenue for conflict resolution and mobilise support for action when this is needed, with the aim of conflict prevention on the continent. As well, the importance of adopting a coherent and integrated approach to conflict prevention by strengthening the relationship between and among the key organs of the APSA, to ensure better coordinated and more effective action by the AU. To this end, with its multiple roles, the Panel of the Wise can coordinate the myriad activities of AU organs and human rights institutions and promote a culture of prevention among AU member states, in accordance with their respective mandates. The Panel of the Wise should be supported by a dedicated mediation mechanism, with a focus on the effective prevention and resolution of conflicts on the continent. (See also Wamai in this volume.)

The African Standby Force: Stillborn or Shifting Goals?

The role of the African Standby Force is to enable the AU Peace and Security Council to perform its responsibilities, with respect to the deployment of peace support missions and intervention under Article 4(h), and intervention by invitation for the restoration of peace and security under Article 4(j), of the 2000 AU Constitutive Act.[24] The ASF comprises standby, multi-disciplinary contingents, with civilian and military components in their countries of origin that are ready for rapid deployment at appropriate notice.[25] Inspired by the theme of building robust African regional capacities for peace operations, the ASF is intended for rapid deployment for a multiplicity of peace support operations, including preventive deployment; peacekeeping; peacebuilding; post-conflict disarmament, demobilisation, and reintegration (DDR); and humanitarian assistance.[26] (See Nagar in this volume.) The ASF is not a *standing* but a *standby* force, because it is an arrangement achieved on the basis of pledges from member states and preparations by the RECs and regional mechanisms. To this end, member states identify and earmark military, police, and civilian personnel and forward their names and details to the regional communities and mechanisms.[27]

Given that most of the staff, logistics, and equipment are to be drawn from regionally based resources, the term "African" in the name of the ASF may be misleading by virtue of presenting it as an AU-owned entity when, in fact, it is comprised of national contingents.[28] The original plan also envisaged that each REC and regional mechanism will have to prepare a force capability, consisting of military, police, and civilian elements, of about 5,000 personnel. In this sense, the term "force" is similarly misleading, as it seems to detract from the ASF's civilian components working on "good governance", human rights, and post-conflict reconstruction. In view of the complex and long-standing nature of African conflicts, the proposed force strength of the ASF will likely be adequate for just one peace support operation at a time, if it is also to be effective.[29] The question remains, therefore, as to whether the ASF will be able to deal with multiple operations, given the number and gravity of conflicts on the continent such as in the DRC, the Central African Republic, and South Sudan, among others.[30]

The deadline for the establishment of the ASF was shifted from 2010 to 2015, and at the time of writing in mid-2017, it continued to be a work in progress. With continued delays in the creation of the ASF, in April 2013, the AU decided to establish the African Capacity for Immediate Response to Crises (ACIRC), as a transitional arrangement aimed at facilitating speedy responses to urgent situations. Though the ACIRC is a commendable idea, the experience of the Force Intervention Brigade (FIB)—deployed since 2013 in the DRC—has shown that the more multinational a force, the more difficult it is to train and to operate. Multinational forces also take longer to deploy if not pre-assembled at a staging area.[31] Furthermore, one wonders whether the ACIRC is not a duplication in some respects of the ASF. Instead of establishing new mechanisms and shifting the goals of the ASF, African leaders should focus on operationalising the ASF, lest it be stillborn. It is urgent, now more than ever, to expedite the operationalisation of the regional standby forces[32] within the policy framework of the ASF. AU member states are expected to provide well-equipped contingents rapidly, and to provide "all forms of assistance and support" to their troops once deployed.[33] However, in the words of American scholar Douglas C. Peifer:

> Although African militaries are rich in peacekeeping experience and leadership talent ... few of them possess specialized units in addition to their basic needs, and many lack necessary skills and equipment. With the exception of South Africa, and to a lesser extent Ghana and Nigeria, none are capable of regional force projection or sustained, intense combat operations. In particular, militaries in sub-Saharan Africa are weak at maintenance of complex equipment, strategic mobility, advanced command, control, and intelligence, airpower, and naval power.[34]

Regarding a force being told to do more with less, the former force commander of the AU-UN Hybrid Operation in Darfur, Nigerian General

Martin Luther Agwai, once equated the consequences of lack of resources for his mission to being "sent to the boxing ring with our hands tied behind us".[35] (See Gambari in this volume.) The ASF also lacks the firepower, deployability, interoperability, and efficient force generation processes necessary to succeed. The conflicts in the eastern DRC, Darfur, Somalia, and Mali show that it takes combat forces, not ordinary peacekeepers, to stop large-scale killing. (See Adebajo, Hirsch, Gambari, and Mahiga in this volume.) The existence of well-equipped forces in their countries of origin will undoubtedly provide Africa with the capacity for rapid deployment in conflicts on the continent, as well as under the auspices of the UN. Considering the nature and number of conflicts in Africa, the AU should pay more attention to institution-building and reconstruction work than simply to ending the gunfire and achieving a political settlement between factional leaders.[36] Therefore, subject to the availability of resources, the ASF should also assume mandates to contribute to preventing the relapse of societies in transition into conflict, through peacebuilding and reconstruction, in order to establish sustainable peace.[37] (See also Nagar in this volume.)

The emerging scenario is that the AU will deploy first, opening up the possibility for a follow-on, multi-dimensional peace support operation by the UN. The ASF will therefore be deployed to a situation as part of the peacemaking process at an earlier stage than UN forces would be allowed to engage. The ASF could thereby help to create conditions on the ground that could lead to a comprehensive peace agreement before deployment of UN forces. In this scenario, under a mandate from the AU, the ASF would deploy a regional standby brigade using, for example, US strategic airlift.[38] In this context, it is vital for the ASF to reconcile the incoherence in the doctrines of the regional brigades that form the force and their respective peacekeeping duties on the continent. For the ASF to have the capability to protect, it also needs better training and equipment, as well as robust mandates, to protect civilians and prevent atrocities through deterrence and compellence.[39] Furthermore, given that the exit strategy for ASF missions is a transition to UN operations, the latter should include the reallocation of substantial ASF resources as blue-helmeted contingents.[40]

Regional Economic Communities and Regional Mechanisms: Lack of Harmonisation

The relationship between the AU and Africa's RECs and regional mechanisms is a key component of the APSA, as outlined in the 2008 Memorandum of Understanding on Cooperation in the Area of Peace and Security between the African Union, Regional Economic Communities and the Coordinating Mechanisms of the Regional Standby Brigades. Regional organisations' proximity to conflict provides them with a better understanding of dynamics, key players, and context-specific management and resolution options. At least in theory, this proximity also allows regional organisations to initiate more rapid and less expensive responses to conflict compared to those of the UN. Furthermore, regional leaders and organisations may be seen as more accountable and legitimate compared to more distant powers, and may have a greater stake in finding a peaceful solution to conflict.[41] Regional organisations also play an important role within the APSA, as they serve as the main interlocutors between each individual African state and the continental body.[42] The Economic Community of West African States (ECOWAS), for example, deployed major peacekeeping missions in Liberia, Sierra Leone, and Côte d'Ivoire between 1990 and 2003.[43]

However, regional organisations have manifold shortcomings. Apart from the usual resource and capacity constraints, regional organisations' proximity to conflict can also compromise the neutrality and impartiality of their response. Nigerian diplomat Sam Ibok succinctly notes that "proximity generates tension and undermines the spirit of impartiality between neighbours, sometimes to the extent that neighbours become part of the problems".[44] Another challenge is the existence of regional hegemonic actors that may influence the shape of regional peace and security agendas to suit their national interests. Reliance on regional powers also raises questions about how to fashion regional responses to conflicts in which the hegemonic state is party to the conflict, as in the case of Nigeria in the struggle against Boko Haram extremists.[45] In terms of organisation and management, regional organisations lack capacity to organise coherent entities, owing to the uneven political and economic development of member states, differing political and security agendas and visions, and competition between states. This undermines the consensus required to pursue a collective security mandate and execute effective responses to conflicts.

There are myriad challenges confronting the inter-operability and harmonisation of the AU and regional organisations, as well as between regional organisations themselves. For instance, the broad differences in the peace and security mandates of regional organisations, including the interventionist tradition of ECOWAS versus the strong non-intervention norms in Eastern Africa, will complicate a coherent pan-African approach to conflict.[46] Also, the construction of a continental security architecture built on regional capacities may be undermined by the fact that the AU, and the RECs and regional mechanisms have not been able to formalise a clear division of labour and a clear set of responsibilities for conflict prevention, management, and resolution on the continent. For example, the deployment of troops from Malawi, South Africa, and Tanzania in the eastern DRC started as a Southern African Development Community (SADC) initiative, but this Force Intervention Brigade ended up being taken over by the UN. There is, furthermore, a clear need for Africa's RECs and regional mechanisms to devise a uniform doctrine for training and coherent operations strategy to effectively complement the AU. If the AU is to construct a formidable APSA using regional arrangements as building blocks, then significant effort must be made towards harmonising the respective agendas of the RECs and regional mechanisms. Regional and sub-regional capacity-building in conflict prevention and management needs to be given the highest priority, for when action is needed, it is most likely to take the form of sub-regional action.

The Peace Fund: More Money, More Problems

The Peace Fund was created in July 2016 to finance AU peace support operations.[47] The fund itself is to be financed from the AU's regular budget and through voluntary contributions from member states and other fundraising activities. The latter includes innovative fundraising techniques such as a 0.2 per cent levy on eligible imports and services such as airlines, customs, and hospitality, to address the funding challenges the AU has faced since its inception.[48]

The Peace Fund is a commendable initiative considering that "nowadays Western donors appear to react less enthusiastically when confronted with another bill for another peace operation in yet another conflict in Africa. As a result, AU operations are generally underfunded, deployed late, difficult to expand, and often replaced by UN operations if possible".[49] One fundamental flaw in the APSA is its heavy dependence on external support for pursuing the implementation of its peace and security agenda. Close to 90 per cent of the funding for APSA activities comes from external partners (including, in particular, the European Union [EU] and its member states).[50] If Africa does not address this gap, the APSA will face serious challenges in achieving adequate control over the peace and security agenda of the continent and in credibly delivering on its mandate.[51]

The AU also faces problems with regard to the administration of funds for its operations. The Union does not have the necessary fiscal discipline or the management capacity, to shoulder the administrative burden that comes with donor funding. As UN Secretary-General Ban Ki-moon reported in March 2008, "even if funding existed, the AU does not have the capacity to turn dollar figures into resources", and the experience of AMIS has shown that the AU does not have an effective and transparent financial administration system.[52] This led, for example, to allegations that a substantial sum of money that was meant for financing AMIS cannot be accounted for.[53] Such allegations undermine the ability of the APSA to attract the necessary funding from external development partners who demand financial prudence. Therefore, the challenge for the AU is not just that of mobilising the required funding for APSA operations, but also that of developing the necessary financial administrative and regulatory framework to ensure the efficient and transparent management of funds.[54]

The Elusive Quest for African Solutions to African Problems

A capacity gap is the most significant challenge facing the APSA, along with the dearth of emphasis on, commitment to, and prioritisation of conflict prevention.[55] Driven by the experiences of the Rwandan genocide of 1994 and Western disengagement after the US disaster in Somalia in October 1993 (see Hirsch, Mahiga, and Mzali in this volume), Africa is experiencing a revival of the belief that peace enforcement can best be conducted by regional groupings of the willing, with traditional peacekeeping left to the UN. The AU is striving for "African solutions to African problems", a somewhat clichéd slogan coined by Ghanaian economist George Ayittey.[56] Whether the AU has the resources to act is the question, and experience seems to give a negative answer. This scepticism is deepened by the fact that the AU had to rely upon Western funding to conduct its first two peace operations, the African Union Mission in Burundi (AMIB, 2003–2004) and AMIS (2004–2007).

African-led interventions have been undertaken against the backdrop of limited human, financial, and logistical capacities, with little or no experience in dealing with complex humanitarian emergencies. The AU has established a robust peace and security architecture, but this needs to be structured in a manner such as to address effectively the challenges facing the continent. Nine of the 16 UN peacekeeping operations worldwide were deployed in Africa in June 2017, with five of the world body's 11 political and peacebuilding missions located on the continent (as of January 2017). Yet the AU does not have its own organ that can ensure compliance with the laws of armed conflict, similar to that of the International Committee of the Red Cross (ICRC) in the international arena. In all cases concerning Africa, the continent must aim to ensure that it has the capacity to provide political leadership as well as to take effective action on the ground. The African Union Mission in Somalia (AMISOM, since 2007) and ECOWAS operations in Liberia (1990–1998 and 2003) and Sierra Leone (1997–1999) are reminders that the right tool for conflict resolution can be found from within the continent, if African countries are prepared to pool their resources. (On Somalia, see also Hirsch, and Mahiga in this volume.)

The Two-Legged Tripod: The APSA's Lack of Preventive Mechanisms

The APSA is a "two-legged tripod" in that it contains early warning mechanisms and corresponding early response mechanisms, but lacks adequate preventive mechanisms in the context of the continuing challenges facing the Panel of the Wise and the Continental Early Warning System. It remains true that the conceptual development of preventive action has not been matched by corresponding willingness on the part of governments to back the prevention agenda. Ad hoc, short-term military interventions are effective only when underpinned by a coherent political framework that clarifies the operational mandates and goals of deployed forces. But conflict prevention is inherently political, and promoting "good governance" and preventing conflict are two sides of the same coin. Kenyan human rights advocate Binaifer Nowrojee characterises the response to conflicts in Africa like this:

> [H]and-wringing when hostilities break out, but little if anything in the way of serious preventive action. Yet there are often obvious signs that war may be coming—in particular official policies that violate human rights through systematic

discrimination and disregard for the rule of law, stolen elections (if any are held at all), and impunity for gross abuses.[57]

Too often, responses to conflicts in Africa have been reactive and have focused on mid- or post-crisis interventions involving the deployment of military forces. An over-reliance on military action increases the risk of a disproportionately large share of the AU's meagre resources being used for reactive rather than proactive strategies geared towards addressing the structural causes of conflict. The question is why crises are allowed to escalate to disastrous proportions before serious political attention is paid, and why military responses often seem to be preferred to non-military ones. These concerns have exposed a fundamental unwillingness to understand and confront the deeper structural causes of conflict. As such, more attention should be paid to conflict prevention through measures that address the kinds of political and socio-economic problems such as poverty and marginalisation that have tended to lead to violent conflict on the continent.[58]

The APSA is inclined towards the "fire-fighting" approach, which tends to employ conflict management and conflict resolution mechanisms as opposed to conflict prevention tools. Conflict prevention through early warning and a corresponding early reaction mechanism is much less expensive than reacting after the conflict occurs, as shown in the case of the 2007–2008 post-electoral violence in Kenya (see Wamai in this volume). Early warning on governance abuse is one of the many critical challenges facing the AU; others include resource conflicts and post-electoral violence.[59] Seemingly, the realisation of an effective early warning system in Africa is a political rather than technical, sociological, or financial question.[60] As South African analysts Jakkie Cilliers and Kathryn Sturman have observed, the fact that the AU's Peace and Security Department has four times the staff of its Department of Political Affairs reflects the inevitable focus of the AU on more expensive conflict management as opposed to much less expensive conflict prevention.[61] Rather, an appropriate focus on conflict prevention would have seen a much expanded role for the Department of Political Affairs, which is responsible for human rights; the development of democratic institutions, transparency, and accountability; refugees; humanitarian crises; and the monitoring of elections. In this way, an effective Department of Political Affairs could also capture early warning indicators of impending mass atrocity crimes, especially where there are widespread and systematic violations of human rights, breakdown of the rule of law, or a lack of democratic institutions.[62]

The reactive stance of the APSA implies that it lacks the capacity and required tools to deal with the underlying causes of conflict on the continent, particularly human rights and governance-related issues.[63] This means that the APSA should be structured in a way that persuades African leaders to respect human rights, the rule of law, and "good governance"—factors that are indispensable to the prevention of conflict. The APSA is currently based on the assumption that there are democratic systems and a desire to respect human rights and governance on the continent, even though several African states have been accused of poor governance and oppressing their populations.[64] Since respect for human rights is a viable and less costly method of conflict prevention compared to reaction after violence erupts, human rights monitoring constitutes an effective means for early warning and preventive action. For this reason, the AU human rights system should closely coordinate with the CEWS as a key institution, for better prevention strategies.

The 2000 Memorandum of Understanding on the Conference on Security, Stability, Development, and Cooperation in Africa (CSSDCA) requires that the infrastructure and capacity for an effective early warning system be based on a model of indicators that provides a "vulnerability index" of African countries, which would serve as an objective basis for early warning action. That mechanism should incorporate effective inter-linkages and coordination at regional, continental, and international levels. As part of this process, member states need further to facilitate early political action aimed at the prevention of conflicts. As well, the CEWS ought to be able to analyse trends and patterns of human rights violations in specific countries and regions; prevention of human rights violations should not be left to human rights institutions in Banjul alone. In addition to primary involvement, the CEWS—in conjunction with the PSC—should, whenever relevant and feasible, assist in follow-up activities to ensure implementation of recommendations of the African Commission for Human and Peoples' Rights. Communication and information-sharing between human rights institutions, governance institutions such as the New Partnership for Africa's Development (NEPAD) and the African Peer Review Mechanism (APRM), and AU organs should be enhanced. By systematically summarising reports and activities undertaken, better coordination would be achieved.[65]

Conclusion

Despite the construction of the APSA and the adoption of myriad instruments on governance, human rights, and humanitarian law by African states, numerous conflicts and violations of human rights and international humanitarian norms still take place on the continent. This points to the need to create a "climate of compliance".

First, although the AU has set up the APSA with an early warning system, still to be constructed is an effective early response mechanism for decisive and timely preventive action. This suggests the need to cultivate a culture of prevention on the continent. Timely and adequate response to early warning will enhance the chances of preventing conflict. The major defect in the APSA is the de-linking of governance and human rights institutions. Apart from the information gleaned from the CEWS, the PSC should utilise the human rights information and analysis emanating from various AU human rights and governance institutions as indicators for potential preventive action. Strategic partnerships and collaboration among regional and sub-regional early warning systems, and human rights, humanitarian law, and governance monitoring bodies need to be established with the CEWS. Also, the Pan-African Parliament is intended to be a common platform to involve African peoples and grassroots organisations in discussions and decision-making regarding issues facing the continent.[66] As such, this should be linked to the APSA, as it can examine, discuss, express opinions, and make recommendations on matters relating to human rights, democratic governance, and the rule of law.

Second, there should be a clear link between the African Governance Architecture (AGA)—established in 2011—given the gaping hole in the APSA's capacity to address effectively the challenge of helping countries with the transition from war to lasting peace. The APSA ought to focus beyond ceasefires and political settlements in ongoing conflicts, such as in South Sudan, and pay attention to eradicating the root causes of armed violence through institution-building and post-conflict reconstruction. This means that ASF deployments need to include mandates for institution-building and post-conflict reconstruction to prevent the relapse of societies in transition into conflict, and to build sustainable peace.[67]

Third, the AU should establish a committee within its machinery to oversee compliance with international humanitarian law, to complement the work of the International Committee of the Red Cross. The AU should also consider creating early warning and urgent action procedures akin to the Framework of Analysis for Atrocity Crimes, which has been developed by the UN Office for the Prevention of Genocide and the Responsibility to Protect to serve as a guide for international, regional, and local actors to assess the risks of atrocity crimes.[68] In armed conflicts, redress to the victims is central, and therefore the AU needs as well to develop appeal mechanisms within its framework to redress victims' grievances and ensure punishment of violators.

Fourth, the absence of effective controls on the transfer of small arms, light weapons, and anti-personnel landmines, along with their low cost and easy availability to untrained combatants, have facilitated the commission of atrocities on the continent. This exposes the need for a continent-wide moratorium on small arms and light weapons, to better protect Africa's civilians.[69]

Fifth, the integration of NEPAD into the APSA could encourage more AU states to subscribe to the African Peer Review Mechanism, thereby strengthening governance-related standards. However, because APRM membership is not mandatory, the mechanism has less impact than it could, since states requiring review can deliberately avoid peer evaluation.[70] Development, security, and human rights share a symbiotic relationship, encompassed in the concept of human security. The APSA should not be seen through the prism of military force alone. The focus should instead be on the entire spectrum of preventive strategies at the disposal of the AU for conflict prevention, vigilant early warning, and corresponding early response; and for timely and decisive action.

With regard to financial resources, Nigerian scholar-diplomat Ibrahim Gambari advised as early as 1994 that:

> Africans must realize that these days of "passing the buck" with regards to its [the continent's] development and other problems are over. Africans must mobilize its human, physical and other resources for the good of its entire people. Africans must truly become the masters of their own destiny rather than remain objects of international relations.[71]

If African states are unable or unwilling to mobilise resources for the continental peace and security agenda, and if the APSA continues to take the reactive "fire brigade" approach to responding to conflicts on the continent, in the words of Nigerian scholar Adekeye Adebajo, "the elusive quest for *Pax Africana*, a peace that is protected and maintained by African institutions themselves, will remain endless".[72] (See Mazrui in this volume.) For the APSA to be a formidable structure, African actors need to go beyond discussing African solutions to African problems, to finding effective solutions, mobilising resources, and garnering the political will to act decisively.

Notes

1. Boutros Boutros-Ghali, *Supplement to* An Agenda for Peace: *Position Paper of the Secretary-General on the Occasion of the Fiftieth Anniversary of the United Nations*, UN Doc. A/50/60-S/1995/1, 1995, para. 64.
2. Stale Ulriksen and Giovanna Bono, "Conclusion: Economic and Diplomatic Tools vs. Military Might", *International Peacekeeping* 11, no. 3 (2004), p. 561.
3. Centre for Conflict Resolution (CCR), "Towards a New Pax Africana: Making, Keeping, and Building Peace in Africa", concept paper for research seminar, 28–30 August 2013, Stellenbosch, South Africa, p. 6.
4. *See* United Nations Association in Canada, "UN Peacekeeping: From Peacekeeping to Peacebuilding", http://www.unac.org/peacekeeping/en/un-peacekeeping/fact-sheets/from-peacekeeping-to-peacebuilding (accessed 26 August 2013).
5. George B.N. Ayittey, "African Solutions to African Problems", speech at Calvin College, Grand Rapids, Michigan, United States (US), 22 January, 2010, https://freeafrica.org/wp-content/uploads/2014/03/012210-African-Solutions-For-African-Problems-Calvin-College.pdf (accessed 28 July 2016). The Peace and Security Council (PSC) protocol also provides for partnerships between the African Union (AU) on the one hand, and the UN and other relevant international stakeholders on the other. AU, *Protocol Relating to the Establishment of the Peace and Security Council of the African Union*, First Ordinary Session of the Assembly of Heads of State and Government, 9 July 2002, Durban, South Africa.
6. Arvid Ekengard, *The African Union Mission in Sudan (AMIS): Experiences and Lessons Learned* (Stockholm: Swedish Defence Research Agency, August 2008).
7. CCR, *Towards a New Pax Africana: Making, Keeping, and Building Peace in Post-Cold War Africa*, Seminar Report no. 46 (Stellenbosch, June 2014), p. 21.
8. Human Rights Watch, "Lessons Learned from Darfur's Peacekeepers", https://www.hrw.org/reports/2007/sudan0907/10.htm (accessed 18 July 2016).

9. The fourth recital of the preamble of the PSC Protocol states that pursuant to a decision of the 37th Ordinary Session of the Organisation of African Unity (OAU) Assembly of Heads of State and Government in Lusaka, Zambia, in July 2001, the Assembly "decided to incorporate the Central Organ of the OAU Mechanism for Conflict, Prevention, Management, and Resolution as one of the organs of the Union".
10. *See* Article 2 of the PSC Protocol.
11. *See* Article 7 of the PSC Protocol.
12. AU Peace and Security Council, "Communiqué", PSC/PR/COMM.(DLXV), Addis Ababa, Ethiopia, 17 December 2015, para 13.
13. According to Article 8(10)(c) of the PSC Protocol.
14. Greg Puley, "The Responsibility to Protect: East, West, and Southern African Perspectives on Preventing and Responding to Humanitarian Crises", Working Paper no. 05-5 (Waterloo, ON: Project Ploughshares, 2005).
15. Jeremy I. Levitt, "The Peace and Security Council of the African Union: The Known Unknowns", *Transnational Law & Contemporary Problems* 13, no. 1 (2003), p. 116.
16. The AU Constitutive Act of 2000, in general terms, provides that the AU Assembly will ensure compliance with the decisions of the AU pursuant to Article 23(2) of the act. Although this may apply to the decisions of the PSC as well, it is unclear as to what measures the AU Assembly may take, and the process is certain to be lengthy and ineffective.
17. *See* Article 12 of the PSC Protocol.
18. Institute for Security Studies (ISS), "An Early Warning on Africa's Early Warning System", *Peace and Security Council Report*, 11 August 2015, https://www.issafrica.org/pscreport/addis-insights/an-early-warning-on-africas-early-warning-system (accessed 28 July 2016).
19. *See* Article 11 of the PSC Protocol.
20. In 2016, the five-member panel comprised: former Angolan government minister Albina Faria de Assis Pereira Africano, from Central Africa; former Ugandan vice-president Speciosa Wandira Kazibwe, from Eastern Africa; former Algerian foreign minister Lakhdar Brahimi, from North Africa; former Mozambican prime minister Luisa Diogo, from Southern Africa; and former Togolese prime minister and former OAU secretary-general Edem Kodjo, from Western Africa. African Union, "Panel of the Wise (PoW)", Addis Ababa, 9 March 2016, http://www.peaceau.org/en/page/29-panel-of-the-wise-pow (accessed on 18 July 2016).
21. The Panel builds on a long-standing African tradition of mediation by African "elder statesmen" to help bring an end to armed conflicts, and is seemingly a derivative of the Council of Elders of the Economic Community of West African States' (ECOWAS) peace and security architecture.
22. Alex Vines, "A Decade of African Peace and Security Architecture", *International Affairs* 89, no. 1 (2013), p. 99.
23. ISS, "New Panel of the Wise Has a Lot on Its Plate", *Peace and Security Council Report*, 1 October 2014, https://www.issafrica.org/pscreport/addis-insights/new-panel-of-the-wise-has-a-lot-on-its-plate (accessed 20 July 2016).
24. Article 4(j) of the 2000 AU Constitutive Act provides for "the right of Member States to request intervention from the Union in order to restore peace and security". *See also* Article 13(1) of the PSC Protocol.

25. *See* Jakkie Cilliers, "The African Standby Force: An Update on Progress", Paper no. 160 (Pretoria: Institute for Security Studies, March 2008), p. 4.
26. *See* Article 13 of the PSC Protocol.
27. Solomon Dersso, "The Role and Place of the African Standby Force Within the African Peace and Security Architecture", Paper no. 209 (Pretoria: ISS, January 2010), p. 7.
28. Puley, "The Responsibility to Protect", pp. 3–4.
29. *See* AU, "Policy Framework for the Establishment of the African Standby Force and the Military Staff Committee", Exp/ASF-MSC/2 (I), document adopted by the Third Meeting of African Chiefs of Defense Staff, Addis Ababa, 15–16 May 2003, http://www.peaceau.org/uploads/asf-policy-framework-en.pdf (accessed 29 July 2016).
30. Dersso, "The Role and Place of the African Standby Force", p. 7.
31. Cilliers, "The African Standby Force", p. 4.
32. The regional standby forces were initially referred to as regional standby "brigades". However, the term "forces" is now used, given that they may have more personnel than the 1,500 to 3,500 personnel required for a standard "brigade" and that they will include military as well as civilian and police components.
33. Article 15 of the PSC Protocol.
34. Douglas C. Peifer, "Introduction to Genocide", in Douglas C. Peifer (ed.), *Stopping Mass Killings in Africa: Genocide, Airpower, and Intervention* (Montgomery, AL: Air University Press, 2008), pp. 1–20, 6.
35. General Martin Luther Agwai, Force Commander of AU–UN Hybrid Operation in Darfur (UNAMID), *quoted in* Kofi Annan, "Establishing a Culture of Prevention" (Lund: Raoul Wallenberg Institute, 2008), p. 7, http://www.rwi.lu.se/index.shtml (accessed 25 August 2013).
36. Dersso, "The Role and Place of the African Standby Force", p. 7.
37. Dersso, "The Role and Place of the African Standby Force", pp. 7, 18.
38. Dersso, "The Role and Place of the African Standby Force", p. 46.
39. United Nations, *Report of the Secretary-General on the Implementation of the Report of the Panel on United Nations Peace Operations* [Brahimi Report], UN Doc. A/55/305-S/2000/809, 21 August 2000, p. xi and paras. 48–64.
40. Cilliers, "The African Standby Force", p. 7.
41. Monica Juma and Aida Mengistu, "The Infrastructure of Peace in Africa: Assessing the Peace-Building Capacity of African Institutions" (New York: International Peace Academy, September 2002).
42. Human Rights Watch, *Liberia: Waging War to Keep the Peace: The ECOMOG Intervention and Human Rights*, Vol. 5, No. 6 (June 1993), https://www.hrw.org/reports/1993/liberia/ (accessed 8 August 2016).
43. CCR, *Towards a New Pax Africana*, p. 11.
44. Sam B. Ibok, "The OAU Mechanism for Conflict Prevention, Management, and Resolution" (Addis Ababa, 1999), pp. 7–9, http://www.dpmf.org/conflict-sam.html (accessed 26 August 2013).
45. Dan Kuwali, "How to Eradicate Extremism", *Mail & Guardian*, Thought Leader blog, 6 May 2015, http://www.thoughtleader.co.za/readerblog/2015/05/06/how-to-eradicate-extremism/ (accessed 7 August 2016).
46. Kristiana Powell, "The African Union's Emerging Peace and Security Regime: Opportunities and Challenges for Delivering the Responsibility to Protect", Monograph no. 119 (Pretoria: ISS, 2005), p. 69.

47. AU, "The African Union Adopts the AU Peace Fund", press release, Kigali, Rwanda, 18 July 2016, http://www.peaceau.org/uploads/auc-pr-peace-fund-18.07.2016.pdf (accessed 7 August 2016).
48. Vines, "A Decade of African Peace and Security Architecture", p. 99.
49. Jaïr van der Lijn, "Scenarios for Intervention in Darfur", *Utrecht Journal of International and European Law* 24, no. 65 (2007), p. 45.
50. The African Union-European Union Partnership, "Financing the Partnership", http://www.africa-eu-partnership.org/en/about-us/financing-partnership (accessed 7 August 2016).
51. Solomon Dersso, "Reflections on the 50th Anniversary of the OAU through the Prism of the Launch of the 'Annual Review of the PSC 2012/2013'", *Addis Standard*, 27 March 2013, http://addisstandard.com/peace-and-security-in-africa-a-compressive-review-looks-at-the-challenges-and-opportunities-ahead-2 (accessed 23 August 2013).
52. UN Security Council, *Report of the Secretary-General*, UN Doc. S/2008/178, 14 March 2008.
53. Ekengard, *The African Union Mission in Sudan (AMIS)*.
54. Dersso, "The Role and Place of the African Standby Force", p. 15.
55. Puley, "The Responsibility to Protect", pp. 3, 19–20.
56. Puley, "The Responsibility to Protect", pp. 19–20; African Union, "Final Communiqué: African Mini-Summit on Darfur", Tripoli, Libya, 17 October 2004, p. 2. *See also* Alex J. Bellamy, "Whither the Responsibility to Protect? Humanitarian Intervention and the 2005 World Summit", *Ethics & International Affairs* 20, no. 2 (2006), p. 160.
57. Binaifer Nowrojee, "Africa on Its Own: Regional Intervention and Human Rights", Human Rights Watch World Report, 2004, p. 1, http://www.hrw.org/legacy/wr2k4/download/4.pdf (accessed 24 August 2013).
58. Dan Kuwali, "Just Peace: Achieving Peace, Justice, and Development in Post Conflict African Countries", policy paper, Africa Peacebuilding Network, Social Science Research Council, New York, 2014, http://webarchive.ssrc.org/workingpapers/APN_WorkingPapers02_Kuwali.pdf.
59. Kuwali, "Just Peace".
60. Jakkie Cilliers and Kathryn Sturman, "The Right of Intervention: Enforcement Challenges for the African Union", *African Security Review* 11, no. 3 (2002), pp. 98–102.
61. Cilliers and Sturman, "The Right of Intervention".
62. Cilliers and Sturman, "The Right of Intervention", pp. 98–102.
63. Dersso, "Reflections on the 50th Anniversary of the OAU".
64. Mo Ibrahim Foundation, "Ibrahim Index of African Governance (IIAG)", http://mo.ibrahim.foundation/iiag/ (accessed 7 August 2016).
65. OAU, *Towards a Conference on Security, Stability, Development, and Cooperation in Africa* [Kampala Document], 19–22 May 1991, Kampala, Uganda, pp. 14–15.
66. Gerhard Hugo, "The Pan-African Parliament: Is the Glass Half-Full or Half-Empty?", Paper no. 168 (Pretoria: ISS, 2008), p. 1.
67. Dersso, "The Role and Place of the African Standby Force", p. 7.

68. United Nations, *Framework of Analysis for Atrocity Crimes: A Tool for Prevention*, 2014, http://www.un.org/en/preventgenocide/adviser/pdf/framework%20of%20analysis%20for%20atrocity%20crimes_en.pdf (accessed 30 April 2015).
69. *See* OAU, *Bamako Declaration on an African Common Position on the Illicit Proliferation, Circulation, and Trafficking of Small Arms and Light Weapons*, 1 December 2000, http://www.smallarmssurvey.org/files/portal/issueareas/measures/Measur_pdf/r_%20measur_pdf/Africa/20010309_sadc_declaration.pdf (accessed 15 March 2009).
70. United Nations, *Declaration on the New Partnership for Africa's Development*, UN Doc. GA/57/L.2/Rev.1, 16 September 2002.
71. Ibrahim A. Gambari, "The Role of Foreign Intervention in the Reconstruction of Africa's Collapsed and Collapsing States", address at the School of Advanced and International Studies, Johns Hopkins University, Washington, DC, 1994.
72. Adekeye Adebajo, "The Elusive Quest for Pax Africana Continues", *Business Day*, 27 January 2013. *See also* Ali A. Mazrui, *Towards a Pax Africana: A Study of Ideology and Ambition* (Chicago: Chicago University Press, 1967).

CHAPTER 4

Pillars of Africa's Peace and Security Architecture: The African Standby Force

Dawn Nagar

The main aim of this chapter is to assess the progress, problems, and prospects of achieving the objectives of the African Standby Force (ASF), which has been conceived as a continental rapid deployment force composed of troop contributions—regional standby brigades—from Southern, West, Eastern, Central, and North Africa. The African Union (AU), together with Africa's regional economic communities (RECs), has sought to develop and conceptualise the ASF as a key contributor to the achievement of peace and security on the continent.[1] The chapter poses two fundamental questions with reference to the standby force: What have the AU and the RECs achieved in their efforts towards greater security convergence? And what are the important actors and factors promoting or hindering regional security?

Historical Background

The idea of a continental security arrangement goes as far back as the late 1950s to the early 1960s. Steeped in pan-Africanism, Ghanaian leader Kwame Nkrumah, in particular, believed in the importance of seeking a political union for the continent. Other newly independent African states, though, sought functional regionalism through the creation of sub-regional organisations that they envisaged would become economically and politically independent through freer trade and interlinking customs unions. Nkrumah raised the idea of an African High Command for discussion at the 1958 All-African Peoples' Conference, but it dissipated, with African leaders divided on the issue. There were two major factions that developed on the issue of African integration—the Monrovia group and the Casablanca group. The Monrovia group—

D. Nagar (✉)
Former Senior Researcher, Centre for Conflict Resolution, Cape Town, South Africa

T. Karbo, K. Virk (eds.), *The Palgrave Handbook of Peacebuilding in Africa*, https://doi.org/10.1007/978-3-319-62202-6_4

comprising Benin, Burkina Faso, Cameroon, the Central African Republic (CAR), Congo-Brazzaville, Côte d'Ivoire, Gabon, Liberia, Madagascar, Mauritania, Niger, Nigeria, Senegal, and Togo—called for the gradual establishment of a joint defence command instead, so as to allow for time and space to strengthen the political and economic bases of African states; whereas the Casablanca group—Algeria, Egypt, Ghana, Guinea, Libya, Mali, and Morocco—had called for the establishment of a joint high command as expeditiously as possible.[2] With states jealously guarding their newly established sovereignty and steering away from any form of supra-national power, Nkrumah's idea did not take root. (See Introduction in this volume.)

In 1963, the idea of an African armed force resurfaced in the Organisation of African Unity's (OAU) charter under the rubric of a defence commission.[3] The reality, however, was that Africa's states were troubled with Cold War rivalries and proxy wars, the fight against colonialism, and the struggle against white supremacy. African leaders were not yet fully committed to a notion of pan-African solidarity that encompassed security, with several countries embroiled in regional conflicts. In Southern Africa, for example, Tanzania, Angola, and Mozambique were active members of the group of Frontline States (FLS) struggling against white supremacy and racism in the sub-region. The group also included Botswana, Zambia, and Zimbabwe. FLS states played a key role in supporting liberation struggles in Southern Africa. Angola and Mozambique, for instance, were under Portuguese colonial control until the mid-1970s, and Dar es Salaam—Tanzania having gained its independence in 1961—provided a safe haven for the Mozambique Liberation Front (FRELIMO) as well as the Popular Movement for the Liberation of Angola (MPLA). The independence of Angola and Mozambique, however, brought about regional violence and conflict. This provoked nervousness in the racist white-minority government in South Africa, which feared that a Marxist power could emerge to dominate the entire region, placing Pretoria's apartheid ideology in jeopardy.[4] Meanwhile, radical members of Angola's MPLA supported secessionist forces in Zaire—now the Democratic Republic of the Congo (DRC)—by invading the country twice, first in 1977 and then again in 1978, which effectively destroyed relations between the two countries. Zaire's Mobutu Sese Seko responded by seeking support from Western allies, in particular the United States (US), France, and Belgium; and within Africa, from Morocco.[5] (On France's role in Africa, see Adebajo, and Yates in this volume.)

The OAU's first military mission was mandated and deployed in Chad in December 1981, after years of efforts to address the country's civil war, and the organisation received no assistance from the United Nations (UN). In June 1982, the OAU peacekeeping force had to be withdrawn due to a host of problems mainly related to logistics and financial shortages, as well as instability in Chad. On the whole, the organisation's efforts to maintain peace and security in Africa during the Cold War period were largely weak and ineffectual.

Africa has long realised that it needs its own conflict response mechanism.[6] Its current conflicts call for robust and effective deployment of well-resourced, efficient, and effective peacekeeping missions. The African Standby Force was conceived at the AU's 2002 Durban summit and created as part of the Union's Protocol Relating to the Establishment of the Peace and Security Council (PSC), which came into force in December 2003. In addition to the PSC and the ASF, the protocol also provided for the creation of a Continental Early Warning System (CEWS), a Panel of the Wise, and a Special Fund (the Peace Fund). These all together form the main pillars of the African Peace and Security Architecture (APSA) (see Kuwali in this volume). The protocol also provides for the establishment of a Military Staff Committee. However, the ASF is arguably the most critical element of the APSA, and the standby force must be able to undertake interventions timeously and robustly. Crucially, such interventions will require the political will of its member states. But, as this chapter suggests, the parochial interests of major troop-contributing states (for example, South Africa, Rwanda, and Uganda) have been, and continue to be, a major obstacle, making the eventual operationalisation of an effective ASF a somewhat unlikely prospect.

The Role and Mandate of the African Standby Force

Established in 2002, the African Standby Force was intended to become operational in 2010, but this deadline was missed and moved to 2015 (and again missed). At the time of writing, in mid-2017, the ASF remained a work in progress. The main idea of the ASF is to strengthen the capacity of regional brigades for peace support operations through, among other things, enhancing the capacity of national defence forces and training civilian police for such peace missions. Five such brigades are envisaged: the Southern African Development Community (SADC) Brigade (SADCBRIG); the Eastern Africa Standby Brigade (EASBRIG); the Economic Community of West African States (ECOWAS) Brigade (ECOBRIG); the North African Standby Brigade (NASBRIG); and the Economic Community of Central African States (ECCAS) Brigade (ECCASBRIG). The nomenclature has changed over time as the development of the ASF has progressed.

The AU has developed a roadmap for the five brigades and a Planning Element (PLANELM)— a framework to guide their operationalisation based on six mission scenarios. Scenarios 1 to 4 are aimed at deployment within 30 days from a mandating AU resolution. More specifically, Scenario 1 describes AU/regional military advice to a political mission; Scenario 2, an AU/regional observer mission co-deployed with a UN mission; Scenario 3, a stand-alone AU/regional observer mission; and Scenario 4, an AU/regional peacekeeping force for peacemaking and preventive deployment missions. Scenario 5 involves the deployment, within 30–90 days, of an AU peacekeeping force for complex multidimensional peacekeeping missions. Scenario 6 calls for deployment in a situation of genocide, where the international community has failed to act promptly, with the AU envisaged to have the capability to deploy a robust military force within 14 days. Furthermore, the first phase of operationalisation (Scenarios 1 and 2) was expected to have been completed by June 2005, and the second phase by June 2010 (a missed deadline). By this time, it was conceived that the AU would have developed the capacity to manage complex peacekeeping operations, while the different regions continued to develop their capacities to deploy a mission headquarters for Scenario 4 involving AU/regional peacekeeping forces.[7]

Operationalising the African Standby Force

Since its creation, the African Union, which replaced its predecessor, the OAU, in 2002, has undertaken major missions including those in Burundi (2003–2004), Sudan's Darfur region (2004–2007), and Somalia (since 2007). (On Sudan, see Deng, and Gambari; and on Somalia, see Hirsch, and Mahiga, all in this volume.) The history of Africa's RECs in peacekeeping dates further back.[8] Since 1992, peace operations have been conducted by African regional economic communities such as ECOWAS, SADC, and ECCAS. There is thus considerable experience among these regional bodies, to feed into the operationalisation of the regional brigades in West, Southern, and Central Africa.

Furthermore, Nigeria and South Africa—the regional hegemons in West and Southern Africa respectively—have significant peacekeeping experience, and, as the continent's two largest economies, have an important role to play in efforts towards the operationalisation of an effective continental standby force. For example, the South African National Defence Force (SANDF) deployed about 5,000 personnel to UN-led regional peacekeeping missions between 2000 and 2015.[9] Nigeria (see Adebajo in this volume), meanwhile, has played a leadership role and deployed troops in several regional interventions, and was, in April 2017, among the top ten African troop-contributing countries to UN missions, with over 1,600 police and military personnel deployed, the vast majority of these in Africa.[10] The operationalisation of the ASF's building blocks, therefore, is reliant quite heavily on the two regional hegemons—South Africa in SADCBRIG and Nigeria in ECOBRIG—for logistics support and for compensating for weaker members in their cohorts—those with less developed infrastructure and fewer economic resources.

In Eastern Africa, the Intergovernmental Authority on Development (IGAD) oversaw the region's initial efforts to establish its standby brigade. In September 2004, the first meeting of EASBRIG—later renamed the Eastern Africa Standby Force (EASF)—adopted a draft policy framework establishing the standby brigade. In July 2005, the regional Planning Element was adopted. In September 2005, the chiefs of defence staff met to discuss the operationalisation of the AU Roadmap and PLANELM and the skeleton brigade headquarters, as well as the establishment of an independent coordination mechanism (EASBRICOM, later EASFCOM), with the operationalisation of the logistics base deferred until the AU had finalised the logistics concept for the ASF. By 2007, the EASBRIG structure had made fair progress, with the establishment of EASFCOM (previously EASBRICOM) in March of that year.[11] The status of EASFCOM was elevated to that of a full secretariat in 2014 by the Eastern Africa Council of Ministers of Defence and Security. This, along with the regional PLANELM, are located in Nairobi, while the logistics base and the command headquarters of the EASF are in Addis Ababa. As of 2017, the active membership of the Eastern Africa Standby Force comprised ten countries: Burundi, Comoros, Djibouti, Ethiopia, Kenya, Rwanda, Seychelles, Somalia, Sudan, and Uganda.[12] It is worth noting that the EASF was set up amid several regional conflicts, including the aftermath of the Ethiopia and Eritrea border conflict of 1998–2000; the electoral crisis in Kenya in 2007–2008 (see Wamai in this volume); the ongoing conflict in Somalia (see Hirsch, and Mahiga in this volume); the Ethiopia-Sudan Nile River water dispute;[13] as well as the water conflict between Tanzania (EAC and SADC member) and Malawi (SADC member) over Lake Malawi.[14]

Meanwhile, the SADC Brigade—later renamed the SADC Standby Force (SADC SF)—was formally launched in August 2007 at the SADC Summit in Lusaka, Zambia.[15] In launching the brigade, SADC was guided by its 2001 Protocol on the Organ on Politics, Defence, and Security Cooperation (OPDSC).[16] It is worth noting that the concept and design of regional security in Southern Africa is based on a broad understanding of human security, as reflected in key SADC documents. The OPDSC protocol, for instance, indicates that security should be based in peaceful cooperation, enhance mutual security, and include the management of humanitarian disasters, among other things.[17] Southern Africa's collective security arrangement also includes the 2004 Mutual Defence Pact, with the 2001 and 2010 Strategic Indicative Plans of the Organ (SIPO I and II respectively) providing further policy guidance for regional security cooperation.[18] It is envisaged that the SADC Standby Force—similar to the other four regional brigades of the ASF—will undertake observation and monitoring missions, peace support operations, and interventions to restore regional peace and security. The standby force is also expected to serve as a preventive deployment mechanism to keep conflicts from escalating; to conduct post-conflict reconstruction activities, such as disarmament and demobilisation; and to provide humanitarian assistance to civilians in war-ravaged areas.

South Africa, in keeping with its greater capacity, has sought to fill the gaps left by other SADC member states, through its contributions to the SADC Standby Force. The SANDF has pledged a parachute battalion, engineering capability, sanitation, patrol boats, signal capacity, divers, naval support vessel, air transport, as well as a field hospital.[19] In this context, it is important to note also the weaknesses and shortfalls in South Africa's own defence capacities, as made evident in 2013 by its lack of airlift capacity to rescue SANDF personnel under attack in the Central African Republic, with 13 soldiers losing their lives as a consequence.[20]

Overall, peacekeeping operations undertaken by the AU and the RECs have faced serious difficulties in Burundi, Comoros, Côte d'Ivoire, Guinea-Bissau, Liberia, Sierra Leone, Somalia, and Sudan. There are thus a set of general problems, related to resource and capability deficits, that the ASF faces and, once fully operational, is likely to face. Modern peacekeeping is complex, and requires adequate logistics capacity—often neglected—as well as specialised assets. In September 2007, for example, the AU-UN Hybrid Operation in Darfur (UNAMID) had no combat helicopters, which limited mobility and support, contributing to the loss of ten peacekeepers in an attack, as it took about eight hours for the injured to be moved.[21] (On UNAMID, see Gambari in this volume.) According to the AU's logistics concept paper,[22] South Africa has been tasked to develop a road and rail strategic lift concept for the SADC Standby Force, while Algeria has been similarly requested to develop air and sea lift capabilities for the North African Standby Brigade. But the question of resources remains. The AU and its RECs have yet to address issues related to the acquisition of resources and development of mechanisms for operationalising ASF-related initiatives.

Furthermore, civilian police have become an important part of peacekeeping operations. The ASF, in particular, envisages having a standby roster of at least 240 individual police officers, as well as two company-level formed units, able to deploy rapidly for peacekeeping missions.[23] Greater cooperation between police and military staff is thus important. South Africa's Tsepe Motumi, for example, has highlighted the importance of having a joint planning component that must be well synchronised.[24] This remains a challenge. Moreover, the operationalisation of the civilian dimension of the ASF has lagged behind, and this remains one of the least-developed components of the still evolving standby force.[25]

Key Challenges Facing the African Standby Force

It took Africa nearly five decades after independence to consider the establishment of a continental peacekeeping force. As the "military pillar" of the African Peace and Security Architecture developed by the AU, the African Standby Force is one of the most important mechanisms for addressing Africa's conflicts.[26] Yet progress to date has been slow, and this standby force, with over a decade and a half having passed since its 2002 conception, is still not brigade-ready. As mentioned, the ASF has missed two deadlines—2010 and 2015—for achieving full operational capacity.

Challenges of Region-Building and Regional Integration

The delays in the formation and operationalisation of a standby force owe to several factors, including those related to the broader challenges of region-building and regional integration on the continent. There exists, for example, a memorandum of understanding between the AU, Africa's eight main RECs,[27] and the coordinating mechanisms of EASBRIG and NASBRIG—agreed in June 2008—binding them to cooperation in the area of peace and security, including operationalisation of the APSA and the ASF.[28] But the multiple and overlapping memberships of regional economic communities have been a source of unwieldiness: 26 African countries are members of two different RECs, and 20 are members of three, while the DRC notably belongs to four RECs.[29] The lack of a binding legal framework further allows member states to criss-cross regional communities in the service of their economic or security interests, regardless of the impact this might have, for example, on the regional brigades—the first steps in the formation of the larger ASF.

Although Africa's RECs were mainly created for economic reasons, the divergence from their initial objective to security came in response to the major conflicts facing the continent. This varied by region. For example, between 1960 and 1990, West Africa experienced 37 military coups. Beginning in the 1990s, civil wars took place in Liberia, Sierra Leone, Côte d'Ivoire, and Guinea-Bissau. There was no provision made for political and defence areas in the ECOWAS Treaty of 1975; this was agreed to only much later by ECOWAS member states with the adoption of the Protocol on Non-Aggression in 1978 and the subsequent Protocol on Mutual Assistance on Defence in 1981.[30] ECOWAS's Ceasefire Monitoring Group (ECOMOG) in Liberia and Sierra Leone in the 1990s received widespread praise as a first real attempt by African countries to solve African conflicts.[31] With regard to Southern Africa, the Southern African Development Coordination Conference (SADCC) was transformed into the Southern African Development Community in 1992 to pursue a market-led regional economic integration plan, but it also has a peace and security role through its Organ on Politics, Defence, and Security Cooperation. Furthermore, there are differences in economic size, capacity, and resources between regions to consider. As well, within sub-regions, there are major political tensions between and among states. For example, the DRC, Rwanda, and Uganda are all members of the International Conference on the Great Lakes Region (ICGLR)—a regional security mechanism—but Rwandan and Ugandan involvement in the conflicts in the Congo has inhibited the DRC from sharing in regional missions alongside them. Meanwhile, in North Africa, the dispute over Western Sahara has contributed to tensions between Morocco and its regional peers, leading to the estrangement of Rabat from NASBRIG. Such tensions prevent and delay the processes of establishing the regional brigades. In this context, it was somewhat unrealistic to expect that all regional brigades would meet the 2015 missed deadline for full ASF operational capacity.

The AU must more firmly consider the concept of variable geometry, whereby brigades that have achieved the ASF's roadmap for operationalisation are integrated much sooner into the ASF than the slower-progressing brigades, instead of waiting for all five regional brigades to gain readiness before fully operationalising the ASF. Instead of applying the principle of variable geometry, the ASF is based on the principal of its weakest link (the brigades), at the pace of its slowest-progressing and weakest brigade. It is possible that these lagging brigades will never become deployment-ready. Meanwhile, the AU cannot allow hegemonic powers, such as South Africa, to "go it alone" and dominate continental security. The African Peace and Security Architecture is, after all, based on a multilateral approach incorporating regional peacekeeping efforts in a manner that is comprehensive, systematic, and practical from the regional up to the continental levels.[32]

Difficulties between the AU and the RECs are also apparent. The AU coordinates peacekeeping activities, but the links among member states of regional economic communities have progressed much faster than those with the AU in terms of their peace and security agenda. As Nigerian scholar Adekeye Adebajo has noted, African regional organisations such as ECOWAS and SADC have been far ahead of the AU in terms of establishing security mechanisms, and "often feel that the AU has more to learn from them than vice versa".[33] At the same time, tensions between the UN and Africa's RECs during missions have also increased. As the AU has strengthened its capacities, its engagement with the world body has also developed: the AU Peace and Security Council and the UN Security Council have held annual meetings since 2007, alternating between New York and Addis Ababa, to exchange ways for strengthening cooperation between them. However, the UN has failed to fully acknowledge the role of Africa's RECs during peacekeeping missions, and has maintained tight political control over these missions. As Adebajo writes, for example, tensions were apparent "during the ECOWAS peacekeeping missions in Liberia and Sierra Leone in the 1990s … when the UN deployed military observers alongside much larger ECOWAS forces, but refused to provide the financial and logistical muscle to strengthen the regional peacekeepers".[34] In 2013, South Africa, Tanzania, and Malawi contributed troops to a 3,000-strong Force Intervention Brigade (FIB) in support of the DRC's efforts against rebels, while the UN was "dragging its feet" in responding to the violence in the Congo.[35]

Political Will and National Interests

The national interests of states set the pace for the continental peace and security agenda, including the ASF, and not the African Union. Such interests have tended to be guided by a state's own domestic conditions, and have yielded a nationalist approach to dealing with external affairs. Africa's continental peacekeeping has also become squarely linked to the economic interests of the state, with security issues coming to be viewed by governments through the lens of realism and trumped by concerns of political economy over regional and human security. Furthermore, neorealists define a hegemonic state as a powerful, strong economy that sets the rules of the game, has a greater advantage over its partner states, and exerts power. The theory of "neorealist security convergence" goes further in proposing that a hegemon has the ability to converge the security apparatuses of other member states within a region or regional bloc, based on its own conception of interests. In other words, a regional hegemonic power—a state with immense political clout and authority within a regional bloc, but bound by the need to address its own domestic socio-economic concerns—will set the rules of the game for its own benefit. Moreover, such a state will have the political will to militarily intervene in support of other states in its region, or to address regional security issues, only when this is linked to its own national interests. This also means that national-level challenges, particularly in the case of regionally powerful states, will tend to filter into the continental-level aim of achieving convergence of regional security mechanisms.

Consider, for example, the violent conflicts in the Great Lakes region, directly and indirectly involving countries such as Burundi, the Central African Republic, and the DRC. Rather than involve the African Union, neighbouring countries like Rwanda, Uganda, and Tanzania—as well as South Africa, which has taken a lead role in conflict resolution efforts in the region—have preferred to rely on their own strategies and security mechanisms, using regional platforms such as the International Conference on the Great Lakes Region, where they are able to exert greater power; in the case of South Africa, this mechanism has been the SADC summits. However, the ICGLR lacks the impartiality to deal with the violence in the Great Lakes region, particularly in the DRC, given the vested state interests in the region. For example, three tonnes of minerals mined in the DRC have been smuggled across borders to Burundi (and Rwanda and Uganda), including gold, diamonds, cobalt, and copper, as reported in 2015.[36] Other smuggled resources include fish, ivory, timber, and charcoal.[37] Yet Uganda's President Yoweri Museveni was the chair of the ICGLR from December 2011 to December 2013. Questions have also been raised about South Africa's motivations for its involvement in the Great Lakes region,[38] where it deployed troops—alongside Tanzania and Malawi—as part of the Force Intervention Brigade that helped defeat March 23 Movement (M23) rebels in 2013 in the eastern Congo. South Africa, to meet its domestic demands for power, has secured 2,500 megawatts of hydro-electricity (of an expected output of 4,800 megawatts) from the Ingra III Dam—part of the Congo's Grand Inga Dam project—through an agreement with the DRC.[39]

Africa's continental peacekeeping has arguably become linked to the weak socio-economic conditions of key African countries (such as Angola, the DRC, Nigeria, South Africa, Tanzania, and Uganda), which are still engaged in decade-long efforts to deal with their own state-building and socio-economic challenges. These countries also have seemed to become selective and more strategic in their security interventions, bearing in mind as well the costly nature of such interventions. As for regional security, this has thus become dependent on, and vulnerable to, governments that have the capacity and willingness to use the region as an enabling mechanism to pursue their own national interests.

But whither the African Standby Force? The capacity of regionally powerful states to shape and converge regional security apparatuses around their interests has yielded a variety of initiatives such as the Force Intervention Brigade in the DRC and the African Capacity for Immediate Response to Crises (ACIRC).[40] These improvised and largely state-driven initiatives reflect, in part, delays in the operationalisation of the African Standby Force, but they also arguably divert from efforts to make the ASF brigades fully operational and available for deployment as envisaged.

Funding Challenges

The ASF was initially envisaged as a force of between 25,000 and 30,000 personnel; this number has since increased to about 40,000.[41] But peacekeeping is costly, and the AU has experienced enormous difficulties—financial and logistical—in conducting its peacekeeping missions, such as in Burundi, Rwanda, Comoros, and Darfur.[42] For example, the United Nations Organisation Stabilisation Mission in the Democratic Republic of the Congo (MONUSCO) had an approved budget of $1.2 billion in 2017, for an operation comprising over 18,000 uniformed personnel.[43] It is worth noting that the ASF concept is entirely based on ideas imported from the Nordic model (the Standby High-Readiness Brigade [SHIRBRIGG]) that are likely not applicable to the African context, given differences in conflict complexities, institutional structures, and political dynamics; not to forget that the Nordic countries have access to more advanced military equipment and are further ahead of Africa.

Africa's convergence of its regional security brigades has been heavily influenced by its dependence on financial contributions from external actors such as the United States and the European Union (EU). The AU has received $1 billion for its peace and security architecture from the EU since 2008. The artificial timeframe set by the AU to have all five brigades operational by 2010 appears to have been set based on the 2008–2010 deadlines provided by Brussels under the EU-Africa strategy, in order not to lose out on the €300 million that had already been secured.[44] This pressure was evident in February 2010, at a meeting of the European Commission and the African Union in Addis Ababa to ensure that the ASF was on track and funding criteria were being adhered to.[45] Similarly, at the regional level, the funding secured has tended to be linked to the interests of the EU, with frameworks and objectives in support of getting the ASF brigade off the ground lacking funding priority. For example, aside from its support to the AU, the EU is also providing funds to SADC and the Common Market for Eastern and Southern Africa (COMESA) for combating maritime piracy. In 2014, for example, COMESA received €37.5 million of EU funds to implement a comprehensive programme to fight piracy in the Indian Ocean.[46] The EU and the US are significant trade partners for the continent, with commitments including those linked to Africa's economic partnership agreements (EPAs) with Europe and agreements under the US African Growth and Opportunity Act (AGOA). With up to 90 per cent of Africa's trade volume conveyed by maritime transport, it is critical that trade cargo shipping is secured and that funding is provided to key African regional blocs for regional efforts to fight piracy on the shores of Kenya, Seychelles, Madagascar, and Mauritius.

Conclusion

In summary, the inability of most African countries to implement effective policies, along with the parochial national interests of militarily strong regional actors, are major obstacles to creating effective regional and continental security structures such as the African Standby Force. This is not to say that initiatives such as ACIRC and the Force Intervention Brigade in the DRC, or African troop contributions to peace operations, are not in some way assisting with gaps in regional security. Although full operationalisation of the ASF may be an overly ambitious goal, it remains vitally important for achieving continental stability and regional security. The AU cannot easily dispose of its role in building the ASF, nor abandon the idea, no matter how slow the pace of operationalisation. The continent cannot continue to rely too heavily on the United Nations.

A 2015 report of the UN High-Level Panel on Peace Operations notes: "UN peace operations have proven to be effective and cost-efficient tools when accompanied by a political commitment to peace."[47] In an echo of the report, this chapter has sought to suggest that a new *Pax Africana* can be achieved only when Africa's leaders and its regional economic communities, and the African Union, work together to create the ASF. (On the concept of *Pax Africana*, see Mazrui in this volume.) The standby force is, on paper, a sound pillar for the African Peace and Security Architecture that can help the continent deal with conflicts, such as those in the Great Lakes region and the troubled Horn of Africa, among others, but this requires greater political will, and requires key African actors to look beyond their narrow parochial interests. At the same time, it is also important for there to be an understanding of the role played by the economic interests of powerful states—African and non-African—in the construction and assessment of security frameworks. Resource-based conflicts further have major spill-overs that involve rebel groups, corruption, as well as the abuse of women and children. These must be taken into account when member states are involved in decision-making on regional security.

Though it is critical to operationalise the ASF—and it must be a priority—Africa also needs to address the root causes of conflict and avoid the relapse of societies into conflict. This, in turn, requires looking beyond peacekeeping, and finding ways and strategies to work with the UN, as well as key external donors and the rest of the international community, for more effective peacebuilding interventions and post-conflict reconstruction activities.

Notes

1. This chapter is based on my completed doctoral thesis in international relations, submitted to the University of the Witwatersrand (Wits), South Africa: Dawn Nagar, "The Politics and Economics of Regional Integration in Africa: A Comparative Study of COMESA and SADC, 1980–2015". *See also* Dawn Nagar, "Towards a New Pax Africana: Africa's Conflict Management Techniques and the Architects of Convergence", *Journal of Global Peace and Conflict* 5, no. 1 (June 2017), pp. 56–66.
2. Adebayo Adedeji, "Comparative Strategies of Economic Decolonization in Africa", in Ali A. Mazrui and C. Wondji (eds.), *General History of Africa*, vol. 8, *Africa Since 1935* (Oxford: Currey, 1999), pp. 407–417.
3. *See* "History of the Organisation of African Unity (OAU) and African Union (AU)", https://www.au.int/en/history/oau-and-au (accessed 1 September 2016).
4. Omari Abillah H. Omari and Paulino Macaringue, "Southern African Security in Historical Perspective", in Gavin Cawthra, Andre du Pisani, and Abillah Omari (eds.), *Security and Democracy in Southern Africa* (Johannesburg: Wits University Press, 2007), pp. 50–51.
5. Omari and Macaringue, "Southern African Security in Historical Perspective", pp. 50–51.
6. Solomon A. Dersso, "The Role and Place of the African Standby Force Within the African Peace and Security Architecture", Paper no. 209 (Tshwane [Pretoria]: Institute for Security Studies [ISS], January 2010).
7. Protocol Relating to the Establishment of the Peace and Security Council of the African Union, adopted at the First Ordinary Session of the African Union, Durban, 9 July 2002. *See also* Jakkie Cilliers, "The African Standby Force: An Update on Progress", Paper no. 160 (Tshwane: ISS, 2008).
8. Arthur Boutellis and Paul D. Williams, *Peace Operations, the African Union, and the United Nations: Toward More Effective Partnerships* (New York: International Peace Institute [IPI], April 2013).
9. Dawn Nagar, "Defence Review: Who Will Keep the Peace?", *Sunday Independent*, 12 April 2015.
10. Based on data from United Nations (UN) Peacekeeping, http://www.un.org/en/peacekeeping/resources/statistics/contributors.shtml, 30 June 2017 (accessed 27 July 2017).
11. Franke Benedikt, *Security Cooperation in Africa: A Reappraisal* (Boulder, CO, and London: Rienner, 2009), pp. 166–176; Eastern Africa Standby Force (EASF), "History and Background", http://www.easfcom.org/index.php/en/about-easf/history-and-background (accessed 27 July 2017).
12. EASF, "History and Background"; and EASF, "EASF Structures", http://www.easfcom.org/index.php/en/about-easf/easf-structures (accessed 27 July 2017).
13. "Egypt, Ethiopia, and Sudan to Start Negotiations on Nile Water Dispute", *Ahram Online*, 18 June 2013, http://english.ahram.org.eg/NewsContent/1/64/74322/Egypt/Politics-/Egypt,-Sudan-and-Ethiopia-to-start-negotiations-on.aspx (accessed 30 June 2013).
14. *See* Rex Chikoko, "Chissano, Mbeki to Visit Malawi over Lake Border Row", *Africa Review*, 11 July 2013, http://www.africareview.com/news/Chissano--

Mbeki-to-visit-Malawi-over-lake-border-row/979180-1911710-sqgxovz/index.html (accessed 31 July 2013).

15. Southern African Development Community (SADC), "SADC Brigade Launch", n.d., http://www.sadc.int/archives/read/news/1100; SADC, "Standby Force & SADC Brigade", http://www.sadc.int/themes/politics-defence-security/regional-peacekeeping/standby-force (accessed 31 July 2013). *See also* Jorge Cardoso, "Peace and Security Operations in the Southern African Development Community: Institutional and Operational Frameworks", in Jonathan Mayuyuka Kaunda and Farai Zizhou (eds.), *Furthering Southern African Integration: Proceedings of the 2008 FOPRISA Annual Conference* (Gaborone: Lightbooks, 2009), pp. 109–116.
16. SADC Organ on Politics, Defence, and Security Cooperation (OPDSC), http://www.sadc.int/index/browse/page/157 (accessed 31 March 2013).
17. SADC OPDSC.
18. Cardoso, "Peace and Security Operations in the Southern African Development Community".
19. Thomas Mandrup, "South Africa and the SADC Stand-By Force", *South African Journal of Military Studies* 37, no. 2 (2009), p. 19, http://scientiamilitaria.journals.ac.za/pub/article/viewFile/66/94 (accessed 30 July 2017).
20. Nagar, "Defence Review", p. 16.
21. Dersso, "The Role and Place of the African Standby Force", p. 14.
22. Dersso, "The Role and Place of the African Standby Force", p. 14.
23. African Union, "Policy Framework for the Establishment of the African Standby Force and the Military Staff Committee", Exp/ASF-MSC/2 (1), Third Meeting of African Chiefs of Defence Staff, Addis Ababa, 15–16 May 2003, p. 21, http://www.peaceau.org/uploads/asf-policy-framework-en.pdf (accessed 27 July 2017).
24. Tsepe Motumi, "Logistical and Capacity Considerations Surrounding a Standby Force", in Shannon Field (ed.), *Peace in Africa: Towards a Collaborative Security Regime* (Johannesburg: Institute for Global Dialogue [IGD], 2004), pp. 251–261.
25. ISS, "PSC Interview: 'The African Standby Force Needs Political Buy-In from Member States'", *Peace and Security Report*, 8 November 2016, https://issafrica.org/pscreport/addis-insights/psc-interview-the-african-standby-force-needs-political-buy-in-from-member-states (accessed 27 July 2017); Cedric de Coning, "The Civilian Dimension of African Peace Support Operations", in Cedric de Coning and Yvonne Kasumba (eds.), *The Civilian Dimension of the African Standby Force* (Addis Ababa: AU Commission; and Durban: African Centre for the Constructive Resolution of Disputes [ACCORD], 2010), pp.20–32,https://www.files.ethz.ch/isn/121430/2010_TheCivilianDimension.pdf (accessed 27 July 2017).
26. On the African Standby Force, *see* http://www.africa-union.org/root/au/AUC/Departments/PSC/Asf/asf.htm# (accessed 30 June 2014).
27. These are: the Southern African Development Community; the Economic Community of West African States (ECOWAS); the Intergovernmental Authority on Development (IGAD); the Arab Maghreb Union (AMU); the Community of Sahel-Saharan States (CEN-SAD); the Common Market for Eastern and Southern Africa (COMESA); the East African Community (EAC); and the Economic Community of Central African States (ECCAS).

28. AU Commission, "Memorandum of Understanding on Cooperation in the Area of Peace and Security Between the AU, the RECs, and the Coordinating Mechanisms of the Regional Standby Brigades" (Addis Ababa: Department of Peace and Security, Conflict Management Division, June 2008), https://unoau.unmissions.org/sites/default/files/african_peace_and_security_architecture.pdf (accessed 30 June 2014).
29. *See* Nagar, "The Politics and Economics of Regional Integration", especially chaps. 5 and 6.
30. Adebayo Adedeji, "ECOWAS: A Retrospective Journey", in Adekeye Adebajo and Ismail Rashid (eds.), *West Africa's Security Challenges: Building Peace in a Troubled Region* (Boulder, CO: Rienner, 2004), pp. 21–49; Abass Bundu, "ECOWAS and the Future of Regional Integration in West Africa", in Real Lavergne (ed.), *Regional Integration and Cooperation in West Africa* (Asmara: Africa World Press, 1997), pp. 22–47.
31. Adekeye Adebajo, "Prophets of Africa's Renaissance: Nigeria and South Africa as Regional Hegemons", Occasional Paper no. 3 (Lagos: Nigerian Institute of International Affairs, 2006).
32. AU Commission, "Memorandum of Understanding on Cooperation".
33. Adekeye Adebajo, *The Curse of Berlin: Africa After the Cold War* (New York: Columbia University Press, 2010), p. 34.
34. Adebajo, *The Curse of Berlin*, p. 35.
35. *See* ISS, "Peace and Security Council Report", 3 March 2015, https://issafrica.org/pscreport/situation-analysis/kinshasa-government-attacks-fdlr-rebels-without-the-un (accessed 30 June 2016).
36. United Nations Environment Programme (UNEP) and Mission des Nations Unies en République Démocratique du Congo (MONSUCO), "Experts' Background Report on Illegal Exploitation and Trade in Natural Resources Benefitting Organized Criminal Groups and Recommendations on MONUSCO's Role in Fostering Stability and Peace in Eastern DR Congo", 15 April 2015, http://postconflict.unep.ch/publications/UNEP_DRCongo_MONUSCO_OSESG_final_report.pdf (accessed 1 June 2015).
37. UNEP and MONUSCO, "Experts' Background Report".
38. *See also* Centre for Conflict Resolution (CCR), *Security and Governance in the Great Lakes Region*, Seminar Report no. 51 (Franschhoek, August 2015).
39. CCR, *Security and Governance in the Great Lakes Region*, p. 30. *See* World Bank, "Proposed Grant of $73.1 Million for the DRC", 5 March 2014, http://www-wds.worldbank.org/external/default/WDSContentServer/WDSP/IB/2014/03/05/000456286_20140305164405/Rendered/INDEX/774200REPLACEM0140Box382121B00OUO90.txt (accessed 21 August 2015). *See also* John Vidal, "Construction of World's Largest Dam in DR Congo Could Begin Within Months", *The Guardian*, 28 May 2016, https://www.theguardian.com/environment/2016/may/28/construction-of-worlds-largest-dam-in-dr-congo-could-begin-within-months (accessed 12 March 2017 and 26 July 2017).
40. *See* ISS, "New Super Combat Brigade: Creation of an African Elite?", 14 June 2013, https://issafrica.org/iss-today/new-super-combat-brigade-creation-of-an-african-elite (accessed 30 July 2013).
41. Dersso, "The Role and Place of the African Standby Force", p. 7 and n. 53 on p. 20. *See also* Johan Potgieter, "Peacekeeping Forces for Peace Support

Operations in Africa", 4 August 2009, http://www.apsta-africa.org/news/article040809.php (accessed 30 March 2010).
42. Adebajo, *The Curse of Berlin*, p. 37.
43. UN Department of Peacekeeping Operations, UN Organisation Stabilisation Mission in the Democratic Republic of the Congo (MONUSCO), http://www.un.org/en/peacekeeping/missions/monusco/facts.shtml (accessed 30 July 2017).
44. *See* Council of the European Union, "Communiqué: EU-SADC Double Troika Ministerial Meeting", EN 15597/08 (Presse 326), Brussels, 11 November 2008, http://europa.eu/rapid/press-release_PRES-08-326_en.pdf (accessed 31 March 2010), *cited in* Dawn Nagar, "Towards A *Pax Africana*: Southern African Development Community's Architecture and Evolving Peacekeeping Efforts, 1996–2009", master's thesis, University of Cape Town, South Africa, 2010, p. 39, https://open.uct.ac.za/bitstream/item/3575/thesis_hsf_2010_nagar_di.pdf?sequence=1 (accessed 7 August 2017).
45. AU and European Union (EU), "6th Meeting of the Joint Coordination Committee of the African Peace Facility", joint communiqué, Addis Ababa, 3 February 2010, http://www.europarl.europa.eu/meetdocs/2009_2014/documents/dpap/dv/6-joint_communique_6th_jcc_2010_/6-joint_communique_6th_jcc_2010_en.pdf (accessed 30 June 2013).
46. Common Market for Eastern and Southern Africa, "COMESDA-EU Launch a Programme to Fight Piracy", 12 September 2014.
47. UN, "Report of the High-Level Independent Panel on United Nations Peace Operations", 16 June 2015, p. 18, http://www.un.org/sg/pdf/HIPPO_Report_1_June_2015.pdf (accessed 21 August 2015).

PART II

Conflict Prevention and Peacemaking

CHAPTER 5

The International Criminal Court and Conflict Prevention in Africa

Sarah M.H. Nouwen

What does a chapter on the International Criminal Court (ICC) do in a book section on conflict prevention in Africa? This question raises at least three sub-questions. First, what does the ICC have to do with *prevention*? Second, what does the Court have to do with the prevention of *conflict* in particular? And finally, even more specifically, what does it have to do with the prevention of conflict *in Africa*? This chapter reflects upon these questions, and in so doing, highlights some of the most frequent assumptions underpinning claims about the ICC and conflict prevention on the African continent.

The ICC and Prevention

From a close-up perspective, the Hague-based International Criminal Court may seem to have little to do with prevention. The ICC is a court, not a preventive neighbourhood watch, police force, or social worker; it investigates, prosecutes, and tries crimes that have already been committed. Congolese rebel leader Thomas Lubanga was tried because he had already recruited children in the eastern part of the Democratic Republic of the Congo (DRC); Ansar Eddine member Ahmad Al Mahdi was prosecuted for having directed attacks against historic and religious buildings in Timbuktu, Mali, in 2012;

I finalised this chapter while on research leave funded by the Economic and Social Research Council (grant no. ES/L010976/1), the Leverhulme Trust (PLP-2014-067), and the Isaac Newton Trust (RG79578).

S.M.H. Nouwen (✉)
Lauterpacht Centre for International Law, University of Cambridge, Cambridge, UK

T. Karbo, K. Virk (eds.), *The Palgrave Handbook of Peacebuilding in Africa*, https://doi.org/10.1007/978-3-319-62202-6_5

while Sudanese militia leader Ali Kushayb is being sought for attacks in Darfur, Sudan, in 2003–2004. The Court's direct work is, thus, *ex post facto* rather than preventative. (On Mali, see Adebajo; and on Sudan, see Deng, in this volume.)

Yet, advocates of the International Criminal Court have promoted the ICC not only on deontological grounds, by arguing in favour of backward-looking retribution: the meting out of a punishment because this response is morally required and because the criminal deserves it. More and more, the justification for international criminal justice has been forward-looking and consequentialist.[1] One of the claimed consequences is that the Court prevents. Proponents find support for this objective in the preamble to the 1998 Rome Statute,[2] which created and governs the ICC,[3] and in which the states parties express their determination "to put an end to impunity for the perpetrators of [the] crimes [within the Court's jurisdiction] and thus to contribute to the *prevention* of such crimes".[4] In its first strategic plan, the Court confirmed that part of its mission is to "contribute to the long lasting respect for and the enforcement of international criminal justice, to the *prevention* of crime and to the fight against impunity".[5] Furthermore, according to the ICC's first Prosecutor, Argentinian Luis Moreno-Ocampo: "The goal of the Rome Statute is to end impunity for the most serious crimes of concern to the international community as a whole and to contribute to their prevention".[6] In 2006, he further noted: "I think that in seven or ten years the Court will have an impact. We can stop genocide, prevent crimes against humanity, and prevent massive crimes".[7] Seven years later, in 2013, the Court's second President, Sang-Hyan Song of South Korea, for his part observed: "[T]he long-term significance of the Rome Statute framework … does not lie in the punishment of past atrocities. What makes this new system fundamentally different from earlier efforts is its potential for the prevention of future crimes".[8]

Prevention as a Justification for Criminal Courts Generally

In claiming prevention as a key reason for its existence, the ICC fits in a long and rich history of theory arguing that criminal courts, in particular domestic criminal courts, can prevent, and setting forth how they can do so. Some of these theories focus on the effects of the enforcement of criminal law on potential future offenders; others stress the influence on specific individual perpetrators who have already offended; and yet others on society more generally. These theories are well known, so here follows but a brief overview, in which I organise the theories on the basis of their focus and worldview.

Some theories focus on the effect of international criminal law on society. Let us start with the ones based on an optimistic worldview. According to theories that rely on ideas of *norm infiltration*, the enforcement of criminal law exerts a moral and educative influence on the general public, who possibly even without realising it, internalise the norms of criminal law and adjust their conduct accordingly.[9] Based on a more pessimistic worldview, the theory of *general deterrence* justifies criminal law on the basis that the enforcement of criminal law serves to deter people, through fear of consequences, from violating the norm, thus discouraging them from committing offences.[10]

For these theories to hold, three kinds of factors are relevant: factors pertaining to the norm, to the system creating and administering the norm, and to the person of the offender. First, the norm must be well known, there must be a high likelihood of incurring negative consequences if one violates the norm, and those consequences must be sufficiently severe, especially when compared with the perceived benefits of offending. Second, for the norm internalisation function to work, the system meting out the punishment must be considered legitimate and authoritative, while there must be social agreement that the criminalised act deserves punishment. Finally, the character, mental capacity, and personal circumstances of the potential offender must allow her or him to act in a way that does not violate the norm.

Other theories focus on the effect of criminal law on the individual offender. To start again with the optimistic worldview, theories of *rehabilitation* justify punishment, often "alternative" punishment (alternative to incarceration), because it would help the perpetrator to review and reform her or his conduct.[11] More pessimistically, according to the theory of *specific* or *special deterrence*, the enforcement of criminal law will prevent future crime because the individual who is being punished will not wish to experience the punishment again.[12] On an even more pessimistic note, the theory of *incapacitation* argues that for criminal law to prevent crimes it must reduce the person's ability to commit crimes. Such incapacitation can take place to various degrees: the most extreme is the death penalty, which literally eliminates the person from society. Imprisonment disables the criminal's ability to commit crime to a lesser but still great extent. Even the mere subjugation to criminal investigations can "marginalise" a person by limiting her or his (political) influence and therefore ability to commit crimes.[13]

For both specific and general deterrence, procedural justice is key. As Lawrence Sherman has argued, if offenders experience sanctions as illegitimate, have weak bonds to the sanctioning agent and community, and deny their shame and become proud of their isolation from the sanctioning community—*defiance*, in other words—*more* crime is more likely than deterrence.[14]

Finally, some theories setting forth the preventative impact of criminal law focus on the rehabilitative impact on the society surrounding the criminal, rather than the potential (repeat) offender. To begin on the optimistic note again, what can be called *history lessons* theories hold that society can consciously learn from the truth that emerges during the trial, drawing lessons on how to prevent such crimes in the future.[15] When this truth is not merely known, but also acknowledged, this could foster consensus on moral values within society. Second, prosecution can cement the rule of law by showing society that the law is stronger than criminal individuals.[16] A more pessimistic version justifies punishment—a trial alone is insufficient for this purpose—on the basis that it is necessary to prevent victims from taking recourse to private justice, which could set in motion cycles of vengeance.[17]

Statements on the need for international criminal courts seem inspired by several of the aforementioned theories. For example, the ICC's Office of the Prosecutor (ICC-OTP) invoked general deterrence in its 2009–2012 Prosecutorial Strategy document:

> Crimes under the Statute are normally committed by large groups of individuals or organizations and require extensive planning; mere announcement of ICC activities can have a preventive impact on this process. The monitoring of a situation can deter future crimes. It increases the risk of punishment even before trials begin. This effect is not limited to the situation under investigation but extends to all States Parties and reverberates worldwide.[18]

A few years earlier, in a 2006 draft paper on criteria for the selection of situations and cases, the ICC-OTP heavily relied on the incapacitation theory when writing:

> As noted in the preamble to the Statute, a goal of the Court is to help put an end to impunity and thus to contribute to the prevention of crimes. For this reason, the Office may for example pay particular attention to groups or individuals responsible for ongoing serious crimes, *since arrest and prosecution of such persons can put an end to crimes.*[19]

The paper also referred to general deterrence, or perhaps even norm infiltration, with the ICC-OTP noting: "Consideration of impact may also lead to charges on matters such as the use of child soldiers, since this is a prevalent crime that is not widely prosecuted; international *prosecution and attention* may help bring an end to the use of child soldiers".[20]

Prosecutor Luis Moreno-Ocampo also referred to deterrence, and possibly incapacitation, when calling upon the United Nations (UN) Security Council, in December 2007, to put pressure on Sudan to execute the Court's arrest warrant for government official Ahmad Harun:

> The only realist solution today is to request the removal and arrest of Harun as a first step to any solution. It will send a signal to the perpetrators of crimes in Darfur that the international community is not only watching, but will hold them accountable for their actions. You can make a difference; you can break the criminal system. What is at stake is, simply, the life or death of 2.5 million people.[21]

It is not just ICC actors who rely on these theories as justification for the Court's work. So do states. For example, when referring the "situation concerning the Lord's Resistance Army" (LRA) to the ICC in December 2003, Uganda argued that the Court's investigations would be in the interests of justice on the following grounds: "[B]eyond the need for retribution, deterrence, and social rehabilitation … incapacitation of the LRA commanders and their benefactors through arrest and prosecution would most probably result in the organization's collapse and dispersal, and consequently, the prevention of future crimes".[22]

Generally speaking, the difficulty with theories of a preventative impact of criminal law is roughly two-fold. First, the theories are based on assumptions that do not always hold.[23] For example, the theory of general deterrence is based on the premise that people can be deterred by the prospect of punishment; in other words, the assumption is that people act rationally. But crimes are also committed out of paranoia or euphoria. Those that do act rationally may not consider the risk of being caught or the severity of the punishment high enough, compared to the expected benefit of committing the crime (for example, avoiding military defeat).[24] The theories of norm internalisation and avoidance of vengeance, for their parts, assume that both the norms and the courts are generally accepted as legitimate, which they are not necessarily, especially not at the international plane. The theory of incapacitation assumes that the enforcement system is either strong enough to arrest a criminal, or at least legitimate enough to reduce the criminal's influence. But particularly in conflict situations, law enforcement agencies may visibly lack the power to do their work or may be seen as partisan. A second type of difficulty with the theories of criminal law's preventative effects is that they are infamously hard to test, let alone prove, empirically: there are so many factors influencing crime rates that it is difficult to establish that people abstained from committing crimes because of criminal law.

Prevention as a Justification for International Criminal Courts Specifically

Many of the assumptions underpinning the preventative theories are problematic when applied to international crimes such as genocide, crimes against humanity, and war crimes—crimes that are often within the jurisdiction of international courts.[25] For example, international law is not always well known. The fact that international courts often lack enforcement powers reduces the risk of being caught and weakens the system's ability to incapacitate offenders. The perception that there is little risk of being caught could be self-fulfilling in times of mass violence: with crime becoming the rule, the likelihood of being prosecuted decreases.[26] Moreover, paradoxically, an international criminal tribunal's sentence for murder as a crime against humanity is often less severe than a national punishment for an "ordinary crime" of murder.[27] And the perceived interests of offending may be extremely high, for example, when it is believed that commission of war crimes or crimes against humanity is necessary for military or even physical survival.

Furthermore, with respect to the legitimacy and authority of the norm and the tribunal, the process of making international law differs from that in the domestic context, and so does that of the establishment of courts, thereby possibly further challenging (or in some instances advancing) their legitimacy and authority. For example, if an international criminal court is seen to mete out victor's justice or partial justice (focusing on one party to a conflict), this reduces the court's authority and legitimacy, leading to less moral consensus about the promoted norm in the affected society. Indeed, the circumstances that Sherman has identified for defiance (offenders experiencing sanctions as illegitimate, having weak bonds to the sanctioning agent and community, and denying their shame and becoming proud of their isolation from the sanctioning community) are common phenomena in international criminal justice.[28] Finally, it is questionable whether people who commit international crimes can be deterred like ordinary criminals. In situations of conflict, in which crime is often the rule rather than an instance of social deviation, perpetrators may feel they lack a choice, or may believe that they are acting justly.[29]

In sum, the assumptions underpinning general prevention theories are even more challengeable in the context of international criminal law than in that of domestic criminal law. Moreover, the theories are yet more difficult to test at the international plane because of the greater number of intervening variables and confounding factors.

At the same time, international criminal law in general, and the ICC in particular, may have features that enhance a potential preventative effect. For example, international criminal law's mode of liability called "command responsibility", pursuant to which a superior can be held responsible for failing to *prevent* the crimes committed by inferiors, could encourage preventive action.[30] The Rome Statute, more than the statutes of previous international criminal tribunals (such as those for the former Yugoslavia and Rwanda), also criminalises "attempts" to commit international crimes, defined as "action that commences its execution by means of a substantial step", theoretically allowing early intervention by the ICC.[31] However, the preventative effects of these modes of liability also depend on the validity of the general theories set out above.

That said, international criminal law has features based on which theories of prevention could be developed that would not hold for domestic courts. Thus, whereas the preventative impact of the ICC is in some ways weakened by the fact that it is not part of a domestic legal order, it could be strengthened by the fact that it is, in some way, part of an international order. For example, the ICC could have a different deterrent effect in different places. Even if the Court's actions do not have a preventative effect in the state in which it intervenes, they could have a preventative effect in other states. Second, with respect to the state in which it does intervene, ICC action could, theoretically, trigger other international action.[32] For example, it has been argued that charges of the particular international crime of genocide put states on notice that genocide is being committed; remind them of their obligation under the 1948 Genocide Convention to "prevent" that crime; and possibly encourage them to intervene militarily, if not to prevent the occurrence of the crime, then at least to halt it.[33] In light of the development of the concept of an international responsibility to protect (R2P)—which relates to preventing almost precisely those crimes over which the ICC has jurisdiction—the Court may play this alarm function not just with genocide, but also with war crimes and crimes against humanity. However, the outcome of such action, as Libyan leader Muammar Qaddafi's death in October 2011 illustrates, may well be incapacitation by means other than a criminal process. (In other contexts, recourse to international criminal justice may, in fact, operate as an *alternative* to other forms of intervention—under pressure to do something, but not willing to intervene militarily, the UN Security Council may be more inclined to get judges involved, than soldiers [such as in Bosnia in 1993]).

Some have argued that the ICC's preventative effect could be stronger than that of other international criminal tribunals because the Rome Statute has created, in the words of Luis Moreno-Ocampo, a "system" that consists of both the Court and all the states parties. The argument is that all these actors have signed up to investigating and prosecuting international crimes, thus exponentially enhancing the system's deterrent effect.[34] The principle of complementarity, according to which a case is admissible before the ICC only if it is not, or has not been, genuinely investigated or prosecuted by a state,[35] plays a particular role in this system theory.[36] The assumption is that this principle encourages more states to investigate and prosecute international crimes, which enhances the risk of being caught and increases the number of exemplary proceedings, which, in turn, amplify the deterrent and normative effects of the Court. The key weakness in this chain of assumptions is that neither the principle of complementarity nor any other provision in the Rome Statute *obliges* states to investigate and prosecute;[37] the Statute merely gives them the primary right. And some of the first situations before the ICC—for example, Uganda—have shown that states do not necessarily (want to) make use of that right.[38]

Prevention in the Rome Statute

More important than the grand claims in speeches and the literature is what role the Rome Statute expects the ICC to play with respect to prevention. According to its preamble, and as previously cited, the states parties are determined "to put an end to impunity for the perpetrators of [the] crimes [within the Court's jurisdiction] and thus to contribute to the prevention of such crimes". That little word "thus" is of the essence: it transforms crime prevention from a direct into an indirect objective. As David Bosco has argued: "The phrasing [of the preambular paragraph] suggests that prevention will be a consequence of the court's activities rather than a conscious goal; ending impunity will prevent future crimes, but the court's actual role is prosecution".[39] In contrast to the grander claims cited above, the ICC's Office of the Prosecutor has at times recognised this, for example, where it stated: "As the Preamble acknowledges, deterrence is a consequence of prosecution and accountability, not an independent objective".[40] The states parties' theory of change is thus that they contribute to the prevention of crimes by establishing a Court that works towards ending impunity

On the one hand, the aim of ending impunity to which the preambular recital refers is a much more ambitious goal than, for example, promoting norm internalisation or general deterrence. For the purposes of norm infiltration and general deterrence, not every crime requires punishment: a single prosecution could remind the public of the norm and instil fear of punishment. The aim of ending impunity, however, requires each and every crime to be prosecuted. On the other hand, the preamble's specific theory of change also narrows the ambitions of the full range of preventative theories. It is only by ending impunity that the ICC is expected to contribute to preventing the crimes within its jurisdiction.

Indeed, it seems that the ICC's Chambers, in contrast to the Office of the Prosecutor in some of its more sweeping policy statements,[41] have interpreted the Court's mandate to be addressing impunity only, irrespective of whether this prevents crime or not. According to the Appeals Chamber in 2009, the object and purpose of the Rome Statute, a factor relevant for its interpretation,[42] is "to put an end to impunity" and to ensure that "the most serious crimes of concern to the international community as a whole must not go unpunished".[43]

From the perspective of theories justifying criminal law, addressing impunity is a deontological justification: ending impunity requires accountability (in fact punishment, when impunity is taken literally)[44] for each and every crime within the Court's jurisdiction for the sake of accountability (or even for the sake of punishment). This deontological character of the ICC's mandate has implications for the relevance of empirical findings on the actual preventive impact of the Court's work for its own operations. Because its mandate is only to investigate, prosecute and try crimes, empirical evidence on whether the ICC actually, let alone effectively, prevents crimes is irrelevant for the Court. It may be the states parties' assumption that the Court, by investigating, prosecuting, and trying crimes, will also prevent crimes. However, for the Court itself, this consequentialist presumption is irrebuttable. It is allowed only to act in accordance with its Statute, even if following the proceedings in this Statute does not seem to prevent crimes, or if other types of actions, not provided for in the Statute, would seem more effective. Only the states parties could revise the presumption, the theory, and the mandate.[45]

The ICC and Prevention *of Conflict*

The ICC is a *criminal* court: it responds to crimes, rather than conflict or violence per se. Yet, many statements on the Court suggest a preventative effect on conflict or violence, or a positive impact on peace and security more broadly. For example, the ICC's 2009–2012 Prosecutorial Strategy suggested that its preliminary examinations can "prevent recurrence of violence".[46] And a former ICC investigator, American Christine Chung, justified the Court's first interventions thus: "The perceived benefit of each of the early ICC interventions ... was the possibility of maximizing the opportunity to have a preventive effect on the conflict, rather than letting the violence run its course before attempting to punish the perpetrators of past atrocities".[47]

Violent Conflict Equals Crime?

Just like conflict and violence are not the same, violent conflict need not be criminal. Most of the crimes in the Rome Statute concern certain *methods* of engaging in violence, rather than criminalising engaging in violence per se. That said, a significant step in the direction of giving the Court jurisdiction over some forms of engaging in armed conflict was made in Kampala, Uganda, in May–June 2010, when the Review Conference of the Rome Statute agreed on a definition of the crime of aggression. However, the criteria are strict. First, acts of aggression concern only international armed conflict, not those conflicts where there is no use of force by one state vis-à-vis another. International law, in contrast to most domestic legal systems, does not establish individual criminal responsibility for, indeed does not even prohibit, the act of taking up arms against a government. Second, an act of aggression is criminal only if, "by its character, gravity and scale, [it] constitutes a manifest violation of the Charter of the United Nations".[48] It has been argued that the requirement that the act is manifest in character excludes uses of force, the legality of which is in a "grey zone" of contestation (for example, humanitarian intervention) from the scope of the crime of aggression.[49] Third, as a result of the jurisdictional provisions applicable specifically to the crime of aggression, states will be able to exclude their nationals from falling within the Court's jurisdiction over aggression, either by refraining from becoming a state party, or by opting out from the Court's jurisdiction over the crime of aggression.[50]

Just as violent conflict is in itself not necessarily conflict, violent conflict is no prerequisite for the commission of international crimes. The crime of aggression and war crimes by definition require a link with armed conflict, but crimes against humanity and genocide can be committed without the legal threshold of "armed conflict" having to be met.[51]

Preventing Further Crimes Equals Preventing Escalation of the Conflict?

Rather than equating crime and conflict, the theory implicit in the statements cited above can also be that ICC intervention prevents further crimes and thus prevents escalation of the conflict. The problem with this theory is that, as Kenneth Rodman has argued, once criminal activity has begun, there is more of a role for compellence than for deterrence.[52] Compellence concerns halting or reversing actions already taken, either through brute force aiming at defeat or through forms of coercion trying to convince the target to change its behaviour through the threat of punishment.[53] And as Anthony Dworkin has argued: "If the threat of prosecution acts as a spur to seek an end to conflict, this is only true where a settlement is possible in which the threat of prosecution is lifted—an objective which the internal logic of international justice generally forbids".[54] So while ICC involvement in ongoing armed conflict might deter some who have not yet committed crimes, it may also lead to those who have already gone down that path to entrench in their positions and intensify the conflict.[55]

Institutional Links Between Violent Conflict and International Crimes: The Role of the UN Security Council

While not all engagement in violence amounts to an international crime and while not all crimes within the ICC's jurisdiction are by definition committed during violent conflict, institutional connections between the UN Security Council and the ICC and its ad hoc predecessors do suggest a positive correlation between violent conflict and international crimes. The Security Council established the International Criminal Tribunal for the Former Yugoslavia (ICTY) in May 1993 and the International Criminal Tribunal for Rwanda (ICTR) in November 1994, pursuant to the powers granted to it by the UN Charter of 1945 to serve international peace and security.[56] By creating these tribunals under its powers under Chapter VII of the Charter, the Council seemed to endorse theories according to which the enforcement of international criminal justice can support international peace and security. An ICTY Trial Chamber, referring to the Council's considerations in the resolution establishing the ICTY, thus concluded in the *Erdemovic* case: "The International Tribunal's objectives as seen by the Security Council—i.e. general prevention (or deterrence), reprobation, retribution (or 'just deserts') as well as collective reconciliation—fit into the Security Council's broader aim of maintaining peace and security in the former Yugoslavia."[57]

The International Criminal Court was created by states, rather than the UN Security Council, but the Rome Statute does grant the Security Council, acting under Chapter VII of the UN Charter, the power to trigger the ICC's jurisdiction by referring a situation to the Court.[58] This institutional link, thus, again implies that the Security Council can consider the Court's exercise of jurisdiction in the interests of peace and security. This is how the ICC's Office of the Prosecutor has interpreted Security Council referrals of situations to the Court, as illustrated in a 2006 report:

> On 31 March 2005, under Resolution 1593, the Security Council referred the situation in Darfur, the Sudan to the Prosecutor, affirming that justice and accountability are critical to achieving lasting peace and security in Darfur. The intrinsic link between peace and justice was reinforced in Resolution 1674 on the protection of civilians in armed conflict which concluded that the prevention of armed conflict requires a comprehensive approach and that ending impunity—through appropriate national and international mechanisms—is essential to ensuring the non-recurrence of abuses. This clear acknowledgement of the important links between justice, peace and security, just two years into the development of the Court, is a great achievement in the evolution of the role of international justice.[59]

Commenting on the same referral—the first of its kind—by the Security Council, Prosecutor Luis Moreno-Ocampo stated in a similar vein: "A new model to control violence is being tested. It is a test of our commitment to use the law to prevent atrocities."[60]

These statements do not render explicit how ICC intervention will serve peace and security or, more specifically, help prevent conflict. To fill that gap, we can develop at least three theories. Two of these can be categorised as "dependence" theories, because in both theories the ICC prevents conflict *because* it prevents something else first: crimes or impunity. By contrast, the third theory can be labelled as an "independent" theory because it suggests that the ICC prevents conflict *irrespective* of whether it prevents crime or impunity.

The Dependence Theories: The ICC Prevents Crime and/or Impunity and Thus Conflict

The first dependence theory relies on the aforementioned preventative theories to argue that ICC prosecutions prevent *crimes* and that prevention of crime, in turn, prevents (further) conflict. This is the theory that seems to be behind statements such as that of the first President of the Court, Canada's Philippe Kirsch: "The International Criminal Court was created to break this vicious cycle of crimes, impunity and conflict. It was set up to contribute to justice and the prevention of crimes, and thereby to peace and security."[61] The second dependence theory holds that the ICC prevents *impunity* for the crimes within its jurisdiction, rather than the crimes per se, and in doing so prevents conflict.

Yet, does the prevention of crime and/or impunity prevent conflict? It could, *if* crime and/or impunity are a *cause* of the conflict. In many instances, both crime and impunity will be a *consequence* of conflict. At times, they could also be conduits to conflict. Addressing impunity could then show that law is stronger than violence. However, two factors should not be overlooked. First, impunity is usually not caused by a lack of law, but by a lack of enforcement. This lack of enforcement may be due, for example, to the physical weakness of the police when confronted with militias. It can also be a political phenomenon, for example when someone is not prosecuted because of patronage. In the short term, the ICC could theoretically address a state's impunity vacuum, *if* it could rely on law enforcement powers. However, this is the ICC's own Achilles' heel: for enforcement, the Court usually depends on the powers of the state in which it intervenes. For example, if Sudanese government official Ahmad Harun does not travel abroad, it is only the state of Sudan that can arrest him (unless the UN Security Council were to authorise the intervention by a foreign arrest team).

Second, when the ICC addresses impunity, it addresses impunity only for a very few internationally selected crimes. Pervasive impunity for corruption or economic exploitation, for example, is not addressed. While the ICC may thus be able to address some instances of impunity, it is unlikely to be able to address the structural causes of the impunity in the particular state, such as the political economy of patronage (see Omeje in this volume).

In sum, the dependence theories work to the extent that crimes and/or impunity are the cause of the conflict, and to the extent that the ICC actually addresses these phenomena. It does, and can do so, only to a limited extent.

The Independent Theory: The ICC Prevents Conflict (and Possibly Also Crime/Impunity)

According to the independent theory, ICC action prevents conflict *by analogy* to crime prevention, but not *through* crime or impunity prevention. Recall the theories suggesting that the enforcement of international criminal law leads societies to learn lessons from the past, or prevent victims' vengeance: irrespective of whether these processes would prevent crime, they could also help prevent future conflict. Incapacitation, too, could serve both crime prevention and conflict prevention, if it is believed that the incapacitated persons are not just at risk of reoffending, but also a threat to peace.[62] Thus, reasons that explain why the enforcement of international criminal law prevents crime are also, independently, factors in theories that hold that the enforcement of international criminal law prevents conflict. Accordingly, the Court contributes to the prevention of conflict independently, that is, irrespective of whether it also contributes to the prevention of crime or of impunity. The ways in which it does so may also have a bearing on crime prevention, but it is not the crime or impunity prevention per se that prevents future or further conflict.

The Conflict Theory: The ICC May Prevent Crime or Impunity But Can Also Spur Conflict

If the aim of the International Criminal Court is the prevention of both crime and impunity, as well as conflict, there may be scenarios in which, rather than the ICC leading harmoniously to all three things at the same time, the pursuit of one objective becomes an obstacle to the pursuit of another. This may happen if, for example, trials do not lead to reconciliation, but to further division; the threat of prosecution prevents the conclusion of a peace agreement (the classic peace-versus-justice scenario);[63] or ICC involvement becomes a justification for military intervention to stop international crimes.

In case of conflicting objectives, the ICC is likely to prioritise the ending of impunity. As argued earlier, the Court has identified ending impunity as its direct mandate, with the other aims merely as potential beneficial outcomes of its work. The anti-impunity mandate lends itself to absolutism: peace, justice, and crime prevention may be objectives of degree, but *ending* impunity requires each and every international crime to go punished. Moreover, the ICC's operations in one country are aimed not merely to serve the community in which it intervenes, but also to have a global effect. In other words, even if ICC intervention creates an obstacle to, say, the conclusion of a peace agreement in a particular situation, the Court can argue on the basis of its mandate that it must still intervene to end impunity and aim to have a deterrent effect elsewhere in the world.[64] Conversely, this desire for a deterrent effect elsewhere in the world may also mean that the Court is against impunity in a particular situation, even if this were to serve peace in that situation. As Nick Grono of the International Crisis Group (ICG) has argued: "if peace deals regularly trump justice, then the deterrent impact of international justice will likely be negligible".[65]

The possibility of ICC involvement going against the interests of peace and security has been foreseen in the Rome Statute. Article 16 of the Statute provides that when the United Nations Security Council adopts a resolution under Chapter VII of the UN Charter (that is, in the interests of international peace and security) requesting the ICC to defer proceedings for a period of 12 months, the Court shall defer its proceedings. The article also provides for the Security Council renewing this request under the same conditions. Note that the Council can thus temporarily defer proceedings, and theoretically continue doing so on an annual basis (if there is agreement to that effect in the Council), but not stop them. In practice, the Security Council has been reluctant to use this prerogative. One explanation may be that even though formally the Council always acts in the interest of peace and security, the aim of promoting international justice has become an independent Council objective, irrespective of whether this criminal justice promotes peace and security. (See Ugarte in this volume.) As Frédéric Mégret has argued, "international criminal justice gradually emancipates itself from the confines of 'international peace and security' and becomes a logic unto itself".[66]

Another provision in the Rome Statute that, according to some, allows the ICC to take into account the interests of peace, including conflict prevention, is Article 53(1)(c), according to which the Prosecutor may decide to refrain from proceedings if he or she considers that these would not serve "the interests of justice". The Office of the Prosecutor, however, has issued a policy paper, arguing against a broad interpretation of the "interests of justice" that would encompass the interests of peace.[67] It emphasised that the UN Security Council, not the Court, is responsible for peace.

The key question then is, if the ICC does not consider conflict prevention its mandate, and the Security Council at times promotes justice irrespective of whether this actually promotes peace and security, who does prioritise conflict prevention? This leads us to the final part of our three-pronged question.

The ICC and Conflict Prevention *in Africa*

The International Criminal Court seems to have much to do with Africa: in 2016, all but one of the Court's ten situations under investigation were on the continent.[68] However, there are at least six reasons not to overemphasise its potential role in conflict prevention in Africa. First, there is little empirical evidence that international criminal law has a preventative impact on conflict.

Indeed, many of the assumptions underpinning the great claims regarding the relationship between the ICC, in particular, and prevention are challengeable.[69]

Second, and paradoxically, the ICC's work, while entirely focusing on Africa, is not Africa-specific. In other words, its key business—investigating, prosecuting, and trying—is not inspired by an analysis of the character of the current conflicts in Africa and what needs to be done to prevent these. Its analysis is crime-driven, not conflict-driven. The primary question for the Office of the Prosecutor when deciding whether or not to open an investigation is, and must be, whether there is evidence that crimes of sufficient gravity have been committed that have not been, or are not being, genuinely investigated or prosecuted domestically; the Rome Statute does not require the Court to do a conflict analysis with a view to assessing its potential impact on that conflict per se. A potentially good (or bad) effect may be a side-effect of its work, but is not its core business, or the focus of its attention.

Third, the ICC *could* contribute to conflict prevention if, and to the extent that, impunity is a cause of the problem; but the Court cannot address other causes of the problem. For example, in terms of grievances, the only injustice that the ICC can see through the lens of criminal law is injustice done as a result of impunity; distributive injustices or even most human rights violations are invisible to it.

Fourth, while there is much rhetoric on the Court's cooperation with other international organisations (such as the African Union [AU]), the ICC must institutionally remain independent and execute its mandate, irrespective of the views of other organisations. Accordingly, the Office of the Prosecutor states that it "will seek to work constructively with and respect the mandates of those engaged in other areas, but will pursue its own judicial mandate independently".[70] This leaves little room for negotiation, accommodation, and compromise with organisations having a conflict-prevention and conflict-resolution mandate, such as the AU.

Fifth, an institution whose mandate is to prosecute crimes will analyse every situation through the frame of criminal law. One of the implications of seeing a conflict through the lens of criminal law is that the cause is identified as the criminal intent of individuals, rather than a political structure within which such individuals can commit their crimes.[71] The Court may address the problem of individuals with criminal intent; it does not, and cannot, address the political context, even if one could validly hypothesise that changing that political situation is a more effective policy to prevent both crime and violence, as well as conflict, than conducting criminal trials.

A final reason not to overemphasise the Court's potential role in conflict prevention in Africa is that in all circumstances the ICC, like any other institution, is likely to prioritise its institutional mandate (to exist and function as a court) over the specific consequences of its intervention in a particular situation.

All in all, this means that the Court may theoretically help to prevent crime and perhaps conflict internationally and generally, but that in a specific (pre-)

conflict situation it cannot be used as a tool in a toolkit. Those who are trying to resolve or prevent a conflict must analyse the drivers of the conflict and how these can best be addressed, and then assess whether there is any role for the ICC in this.

Conclusion

Current debates in the African Union about proposals for a mass withdrawal of African states from the ICC have mostly focused on allegations of the Court "targeting" Africa, and seem to have been inspired by frustration with the Court prosecuting sitting African heads of state (Sudan and Kenya). A more significant factor for consideration may be the question as to how the ICC has influenced the AU's attempts to prevent and address conflicts on the continent. Meanwhile, states should be aware that signing up to the Rome Statute, let alone referring a situation to the Court, means a commitment to an instrument, irrespective of whether this proves to prevent conflict.

Notes

1. *See also* Leslie Vinjamuri, "Deterrence, Democracy, and the Pursuit of International Justice", *Ethics & International Affairs* 24, no. 2 (2010), pp. 191–211; Sarah Nouwen, "Justifying Justice", in James Crawford and Martti Koskenniemi (eds.), *The Cambridge Companion to International Law* (Cambridge: Cambridge University Press, 2012), pp. 327–351.
2. *See, for example*, Juan Mendéz and Jeremy Kelley, "Peacemaking, Justice, and the ICC", in Christian de Vos, Sara Kendall, and Carsten Stahn (eds.), *Contested Justice: The Politics and Practice of International Criminal Court Interventions* (Cambridge: Cambridge University Press, 2015), chap. 19, pp. 479–495, at p. 479.
3. *Rome Statute of the International Criminal Court*, 2187 UNTS 90, 17 July 1998, entry into force 1 July 2002. At the time of writing in July 2017, the Rome Statute had 124 states parties, 34 of which were African.
4. *Rome Statute*, fifth preambular paragraph, emphasis added.
5. Strategic Plan of the International Criminal Court, ICC-ASP/5/6, 4 August 2006, p. 2, emphasis added, http://www.icc-cpi.int/library/asp/ICC-ASP-5-6_English.pdf (accessed 26 August 2016).
6. Luis Moreno-Ocampo, "A Positive Approach to Complementarity", in Carsten Stahn and Mohamed El Zeidy (eds.), *The International Criminal Court and Complementarity: From Theory to Practice*, vol. 1 (Cambridge: Cambridge University Press, 2011), pp. 21–32, at p. 21. *See also* Luis Moreno-Ocampo, "Combating Genocide and Other Massive Crimes—The International Criminal Court's Contribution", speech given at "Commemoration of the 60 Years of the Genocide Convention", the Hague, the Netherlands, 7 December 2008, p. 2; Luis Moreno-Ocampo, "The Tenth Anniversary of the ICC and Challenges for the Future: Implementing the Law", London School of Economics and Political Science (LSE), Britain, 8 October 2008, p. 2.

7. Luis Moreno-Ocampo, "Keynote Address: Integrating the Work of the ICC into Local Justice Initiatives", *American University International Law Review* 21, no. 4 (2006), p. 503.
8. Sang-Hyun Song, "Preventive Potential of the International Criminal Court", *Asian Journal of International Law* 3, no. 2 (2013), pp. 203–213, at p. 206.
9. For strong support of this theory in the context of international criminal law, *see* Payam Akhavan, "Justice in the Hague, Peace in the Former Yugoslavia? A Commentary on the United Nations War Crimes Tribunal", *Human Rights Quarterly* 20, no. 4 (1998), pp. 737–816. *See also* Guido Acquaviva, "International Criminal Courts and Tribunals as Actors of General Deterrence? Perceptions and Misperceptions", *International Review of the Red Cross* 96, nos. 895–896 (2014), pp. 784–794, at pp. 789–790 (discussing this norm internalisation under the concept of general deterrence "in the broader sense").
10. On deterrence generally, *see* Johannes Andenæs, *Punishment and Deterrence with a Foreword by Norval Morris* (Ann Arbor: University of Michigan Press, 1974).
11. On which *see* Fergus McNeill, "Punishment as Rehabilitation", in Gerben Bruinsma and David Weisburd (eds.), *Encyclopedia of Criminology and Criminal Justice* (New York: Springer, 2014), pp. 4195–4206.
12. *See* Andenæs, *Punishment and Deterrence*, chap. 3.
13. For examples in the context of international criminal justice, *see* Payam Akhavan, "Beyond Impunity: Can International Criminal Justice Prevent Future Atrocities?", *American Journal of International Law* 95, no. 1 (2001), pp. 7–31.
14. Lawrence Sherman, "Defiance, Deterrence, and Irrelevance: A Theory of the Criminal Sanction", *Journal of Research in Crime and Delinquency* 30 (1993), pp. 445–473.
15. *See, for example*, Stephen Landsman, "Alternative Responses to Serious Human Rights Abuses: Of Prosecution and Truth Commissions", *Law & Contemporary Problems* 59, no. 4 (1996), pp. 81–92, at p. 83.
16. *See, for example*, Neil Kritz, "Coming to Terms with Atrocities: A Review of Accountability Mechanisms for Mass Violations of Human Rights", *Law & Contemporary Problems* 59, no. 4 (1996), pp. 127–152, at p. 128.
17. Kritz, "Coming to Terms with Atrocities", pp. 127–152, at p. 128.
18. International Criminal Court (ICC)-Office of the Prosecutor (OTP), *Prosecutorial Strategy 2009–2012*, 1 February 2010, p. 7, para. 23.
19. ICC-OTP, "Criteria for Selection of Situations and Cases", draft paper, June 2006, p. 13, emphasis added.
20. ICC-OTP, "Criteria for Selection of Situations and Cases", p. 13, emphasis added.
21. ICC-OTP, "Statement of the Prosecutor of the International Criminal Court to the United Nations Security Council Pursuant to UNSCR 1593 (2005)", 5 December 2007.
22. Government of Uganda, "Referral of the Situation Concerning the Lord's Resistance Army Submitted by the Republic of Uganda", 16 December 2003, para. 31, on file with author.
23. *See* James Alexander, "The International Criminal Court and the Prevention of Atrocities: Predicting the Court's Impact", *Villanova Law Review* 54, no. 1 (2009), pp. 1–56.

24. *See more elaborately* Kate Cronin-Furman, "Managing Expectations: International Criminal Trials and the Prospects for Deterrence of Mass Atrocity", *International Journal of Transitional Justice* 7, no. 3 (2013), pp. 434–454.
25. Miriam J. Aukerman, "Extraordinary Evil, Ordinary Crime: A Framework for Understanding Transitional Justice", *Harvard Human Rights Journal* 15 (2002), pp. 39–98; Tom Buitelaar, "The ICC and the Prevention of Atrocities: Criminological Perspectives", *Human Rights Review* 17 (2016), pp. 285–302; Mark Drumbl, *Atrocity, Punishment, and International Law* (Cambridge and New York: Cambridge University Press, 2007); Immi Tallgren, "The Sensibility and Sense of International Criminal Law", *European Journal of International Law* 13, no. 3 (2002), pp. 561–595; David Wippman, "Atrocities, Deterrence, and the Limits of International Justice", *Fordham International Law Journal* 23, no. 2 (1999), pp. 473–488.
26. Anonymous, "The Promises of International Prosecution", *Harvard Law Review* 114, no. 7 (2001), pp. 1957–1982, at p. 1964, n. 44.
27. *See, for example,* Jens Ohlin, "Towards a Unique Theory of International Criminal Sentencing", in Göran Sluiter and Sergey Vasiliev (eds.), *International Criminal Procedure: Towards a Coherent Body of Law* (London: Cameron May, 2009) pp. 373–403, at p. 373.
28. *See more elaborately* Kjell Anderson, "Punishment as Prevention? The International Criminal Court and the Prevention of International Crimes", in Evelyn Ankumah (ed.), *The International Criminal Court and Africa: One Decade On* (Cambridge and Antwerp: Intersentia, 2016), pp. 461–487, at pp. 469–472.
29. *See* Drumbl, *Atrocity, Punishment, and International Law*; Tallgren, "The Sensibility and Sense of International Criminal Law"; Aukerman, "Extraordinary Evil, Ordinary Crime".
30. *Rome Statute*, art. 28.
31. *Rome Statute*, art. 25(f). *See also* Héctor Olásolo, "The Role of the International Criminal Court in Preventing Atrocity Crimes through Timely Intervention: From the Humanitarian Intervention Doctrine and Ex Post Facto Judicial Institutions to the Notion of Responsibility to Protect and the Preventative Role of the International Criminal Court", inaugural lecture as Chair in International Criminal Law and International Criminal Procedure, Utrecht University, the Netherlands, 18 October 2010.
32. For this theory of prevention, *see* Song, "Preventive Potential of the International Criminal Court", p. 208.
33. Christine Chung, "The Punishment and Prevention of Genocide: The International Criminal Court as a Benchmark of Progress and Need", *Case Western Reserve Journal of International Law* 40, nos. 1–2 (2007–2008), pp. 227–242.
34. *See, for example,* Moreno-Ocampo, "Keynote Address".
35. *Rome Statute*, art. 17.
36. James Alexander even goes as far as identifying, and coining, "complementary deterrence" as an independent theory of prevention, *see* Alexander, "The International Criminal Court and the Prevention of Atrocities". However, complementarity is better considered as a factor that can amplify or diminish the normal deterrent effect, rather than an independent theory of prevention, because the theory of complementarity deterrence still rests on ordinary deterrence theory.

37. The sixth preambular recital, "recalling that it is the duty of every State to exercise its criminal jurisdiction over those responsible for international crimes", does not create such an obligation, but refers to other, more specific obligations under international law.
38. Sarah Nouwen, *Complementarity in the Line of Fire* (Cambridge: Cambridge University Press, 2013), chap. 3.
39. David Bosco, "The International Criminal Court and Crime Prevention: Byproduct or Conscious Goal?", *Michigan State Journal of International Law* 19, no. 2 (2011), pp. 163–200, at p. 174.
40. ICC, Situation in Darfur, Prosecutor's Response to Arbour's Observations of the United Nations High Commissioner for Human Rights Invited in Application of Rule 103 of the Rules of Procedure and Evidence, ICC-02/05-21, OTP, 19 October 2006, p. 6.
41. *See, for example*, Luis Moreno-Ocampo, "Statement to the Fourth Session of the Assembly of States Parties", the Hague, 28 November 2005, p. 5, in which the Prosecutor explicitly states that work of the Court will go beyond ending the culture of impunity: "The Rome Statute establishes an overarching goal: to contribute to the prevention of future crimes. The work of the Court will help to end the culture of impunity, but this is just a piece of the goal. … [L]et me focus on our common task to prevent future crimes."
42. *Vienna Convention on the Law of Treaties*, 1155 UNTS 331, 23 May 1969, entry into force 27 January 1980, art. 31.
43. ICC, Appeals Chamber, Situation in the Democratic Republic of the Congo, *Prosecutor v. Germain Katanga and Mathieu Ngudjolo Chui*, Judgment on the Appeal of Mr Germain Katanga against the Oral Decision of Trial Chamber II of 12 June 2009 on the Admissibility of the Case, ICC-01/04-01/07-1497, Appeals Chamber, 25 September 2009, p. 30, para. 79, footnotes omitted. In fact, it can be argued that the object and purpose of the Rome Statute is even more narrow, namely to create a permanent international criminal court that is complementary to national jurisdictions and acts in accordance with the Statute (*see Rome Statute*, preamble read in conjunction with art. 1).
44. The term "impunity" derives from the Latin "impunis": "unpunished".
45. *See also* Sarah Nouwen, "International Criminal Law: Theory All over the Place", in Anne Orford, Florian Hoffman, and Martin Clark (eds.), *The Oxford Handbook of the Theory of International Law* (Oxford: Oxford University Press, 2016), pp. 738–761, at p. 754.
46. *See* ICC-OTP, *Prosecutorial Strategy 2009–2012*, para. 40.
47. Chung, "The Punishment and Prevention of Genocide", p. 232.
48. *Rome Statute*, as amended by resolution RC/Res.6, 11 June 2010, art. 8 bis.
49. Claus Kress and Leonie von Holtzendorff, "The Kampala Compromise on the Crime of Aggression", *Journal of International Criminal Justice* 8, no. 5 (2010), pp. 1179–1217, at pp. 1192–1193.
50. *See Rome Statute*, as amended by resolution RC/Res.6, art. 15bis (4) and (5).
51. For crimes against humanity, *see* International Criminal Tribunal for the Former Yugoslavia (ICTY), *Prosecutor v. Duško Tadić*, Decision on the Defence Motion for Interlocutory Appeal, IT-94-1-Ar72, Appeals Chamber, 2 October 1995, para. 141.
52. Kenneth Rodman, "Darfur and the Limits of Legal Deterrence", *Human Rights Quarterly* 30, no. 3 (2008), pp. 529–560.

53. Rodman, "Darfur and the Limits of Legal Deterrence".
54. Anthony Dworkin, "International Justice and the Prevention of Atrocity", report, European Council on Foreign Relations, p. 34, http://www.ecfr.eu/page/-/ECFR115_International_Justice_Report.pdf (accessed 24 August 2016).
55. *See also* Sarah Nouwen and Wouter Werner, "Doing Justice to the Political: The International Criminal Court in Uganda and Sudan", *European Journal of International Law* 21, no. 4 (2010), pp. 941–965.
56. UN Security Council Resolution 827, UN Doc. S/RES/827, 25 May 1993; UN Security Council Resolution 955, UN Doc. S/RES/955, 8 November 1994.
57. ICTY, *The Prosecutor v. Drazen Erdemovic*, Sentencing Judgement, IT-96-22-T, Trial Chamber, 29 November 1996, para. 58.
58. *Rome Statute*, art. 13(b).
59. ICC-OTP, *Office of the Prosecutor Report on the Activities Performed During the First Three Years (June 2003–June 2006)*, para. 38.
60. Luis Moreno-Ocampo, "The International Criminal Court: Seeking Global Justice", *Case Western Reserve Journal of International Law* 40, nos. 1–2 (2007–2008), pp. 215–225, at p. 223.
61. Philippe Kirsch, President of the International Criminal Court, "Address to the United Nations General Assembly", 1 November 2007, p. 3.
62. However, the assumption that incapacitation leads to peace is based on the often wrong assumption that there is a peace-loving leader (a "Mandela") waiting in the corridors to succeed the incapacitated leader. Alex de Waal has argued, in the context of targeted killings, that the opposite is usually the case: the successors will be more radical. *See* Alex de Waal, "Assassinating Terrorists Does Not Work", *Boston Review*, 24 November 2015, http://bostonreview.net/blog/alex-de-waal-assassinating-terrorists-does-not-work (accessed 24 August 2016). *See also* Vinjamuri, "Deterrence, Democracy, and the Pursuit of International Justice", p. 195.
63. *See* Sarah Nouwen, "The International Criminal Court: A Peacebuilder in Africa?", in Devon Curtis and Gwinyayi A. Dzinesa (eds.), *Peacebuilding, Power, and Politics in Africa* (Athens: Ohio University Press, 2012), pp. 171–192; Anthony Dworkin, "International Justice and the Prevention of Atrocity", and the accompanying case studies at http://www.ecfr.eu/ijp (accessed 24 August 2016); Payam Akhavan, "Are International Criminal Tribunals a Disincentive Peace? Reconciling Judicial Romanticism with Political Realism", *Human Rights Quarterly* 31 (2009), pp. 624–654.
64. *See* Nouwen, "Justifying Justice".
65. Nick Grono, "Peace Versus Justice? Understanding Transitional Justice in Fragile States", speech to the Overseas Development Institute (ODI), 9 October 2009, http://www.worldpulse.com/en/community/users/marietta64/posts/8271 (accessed 24 August 2016). *See also* Akhavan, "Are International Criminal Tribunals a Disincentive Peace?", p. 646.
66. Frédéric Mégret, "A Special Tribunal for Lebanon: The UN Security Council and the Emancipation of International Criminal Justice", *Leiden Journal of International Law* 21, no. 2 (2008), pp. 485–512.
67. ICC-OTP, "Policy Paper on the Interests of Justice", 17 September 2007, p. 8, https://www.icc-cpi.int/NR/rdonlyres/772C95C9-F54D-4321-BF09-73422BB23528/143640/ICCOTPInterestsOfJustice.pdf (accessed 24 August 2016).

68. The Central African Republic (two situations); Darfur, Sudan; the Democratic Republic of the Congo (DRC); Georgia; Côte d'Ivoire; Kenya; Libya; Mali; and Uganda.
69. For some empirical evidence, *see* Anthony Dworkin, "International Justice and the Prevention of Atrocity" and the symposium "Can the International Criminal Court Deter Atrocity", http://jamesgstewart.com/new-symposium-can-the-international-criminal-court-deter-atrocity (accessed 24 August 2016).
70. ICC-OTP, "Policy Paper on the Interests of Justice", p. 8.
71. *See, for example*, ICC-OTP, *Thirteenth Report of the Prosecutor of the International Criminal Court to the UN Security Council pursuant to UNSCR 1593 (2005)*, 2011, para. 81, on the Court's investigation in Darfur, suggesting that the causes of crimes and other problems are the crimes themselves: "UNSC Resolution 1593 (2005) triggered an effort to address '*crimes problems and their causes*'. Those were described in the arrest warrants issued by the Court, which unveiled and documented war crimes, crimes against humanity and a genocidal policy of extermination of three ethnic groups, implemented since 2003 ... The crimes in Darfur are the consequence of a strategic decision taken by the highest authorities of the Government of the Sudan and not the by-product of a conflict" (emphasis in original).

CHAPTER 6

Preventing Mass Atrocities in Africa: The Case of the Two Sudans

Francis M. Deng

The notion of mass atrocities implies a devastating level of violence often reflected in genocide, war crimes, ethnic cleansing, and crimes against humanity. In addition to the 1948 Convention on the Prevention and Punishment of the Crime of Genocide and a wide array of other human rights instruments, international commitment to preventing such atrocities is embodied in the outcome document of the 2005 World Summit of Heads of State and Government, which enshrined the emerging concept of the responsibility to protect (R2P).[1] The evolution of this concept has been widely documented.[2] It is rooted in the normative principle of "sovereignty as responsibility"—developed through the Washington-based Brookings Institution's Africa Program, which I founded and directed for 12 years (1989–2001)—as a conceptual framework for approaching post–Cold War conflicts in Africa.[3] The Brookings Africa Program conducted regional and country-specific studies, which resulted in the publication of a series of books, with *Sovereignty as Responsibility*—published in 1996—among the concluding volumes in which we synthesised our major findings.[4]

We framed the program around two conceptual questions. First, what were the policy priority areas of concern in Africa that the program should address? Second, to what extent had the end of the Cold War by 1990 affected the way we should approach and address these issues on the continent? The answer to the first question was almost self-evident. The Africa policy agenda had to address violent conflicts, democratic governance, human rights, sustainable development, and gender equality. Although we carried out, or commissioned, studies in all these areas, our focus was mainly on conflict prevention, management, and resolution.[5]

F.M. Deng (✉)
Former Permanent Representative of South Sudan to the United Nations, New York, United States

T. Karbo, K. Virk (eds.), *The Palgrave Handbook of Peacebuilding in Africa*, https://doi.org/10.1007/978-3-319-62202-6_6

Our approach to post–Cold War conflicts in Africa entailed a key shift from viewing these conflicts as part of the proxy confrontation between the United States (US) and the Soviet Union—prevented, managed, resolved, or aggravated through the bipolar control mechanisms of the two superpowers—to seeing them in their proper national and regional contexts, with responsibilities for addressing them re-appropriated accordingly. Apart from our research agenda at the Brookings Institution, I also acquired considerable insights through my experiences as the Representative of the United Nations (UN) Secretary-General on Internally Displaced Persons (IDPs) from 1992 to 2004 and as Special Advisor of the UN Secretary-General on the Prevention of Genocide from 2007 to 2012.

In order to prevent mass violence and related atrocities in Africa, the root causes of conflicts must be identified and addressed. Drawing on my extensive engagement with issues related to the prevention of mass atrocities, in this chapter I focus on the experience of the Sudan, a country that before the independence of South Sudan in July 2011 was, in many ways, a microcosm of Africa. Located at the heart of the continent, Sudan and South Sudan are surrounded by nine neighbours—Egypt and Libya to the north; Chad, the Central African Republic (CAR), and the Democratic Republic of the Congo (DRC) to the West; Kenya and Uganda to the south; and Ethiopia and Eritrea to the east—with Saudi Arabia across the Red Sea, all of whom have contributed to their pluralistic population composition. Despite the partitioning with the independence of South Sudan, the two countries remain intrinsically interconnected by shared history, ongoing tensions, and conflicts over several unresolved issues.

Context: Conflict and Peacemaking in the Sudan—A Struggle Ongoing

Making peace is always a lengthy process that involves countless people. In the Sudan, the peace process that ended in the Comprehensive Peace Agreement (CPA) of 2005 between the government of Sudan and the Sudan People's Liberation Movement/Army (SPLM/A) began in earnest in 1993–1994, with the Intergovernmental Authority on Development (IGAD) proposing a Declaration of Principles, in 1994, for resolving the country's North-South conflict.[6] The declaration stipulated that, as the South Sudanese had never participated in the self-determination exercise that gained the Sudan its independence in January 1956, they were entitled now to exercise that right. Furthermore, the exercise of the right should include secession, but give priority to the unity of the Sudan. Preserving that unity had to, however, be based on guaranteeing full equality to all citizens without any discrimination on the basis of race, ethnicity, religion, or culture. That meant secularism, decentralisation, and respect for democracy and fundamental rights.

However, the IGAD process stalled. The Friends of IGAD group—including the US, Britain,[7] and Norway—provided crucial support, including in the form of financial assistance and third-party mediation, to the process, with due regard for the principle of seeking "African solutions for African problems". Several African leaders—in particular, Nigeria's then president, Ibrahim Babangida, in his capacity as the head of the Organisation of African Unity (OAU)—became actively engaged in the process. But third-party mediation remained marginal, and progress continued to be slow. The Friends of IGAD eventually transformed into the IGAD Partners Forum, who became more actively engaged in the peacemaking effort and cumulatively mounted pressure on the warring Sudanese parties. The Troika—comprising the US, Britain, and Norway—became particularly active in the peace process. The role of the United States under President George W. Bush, who appointed John Danforth as the US Special Envoy to the Sudan, was especially important. The high-level international involvement in the peacemaking process led eventually to the signing of the CPA in January 2005 and eventually to South Sudan's landmark independence referendum in January 2011.

South Sudan's independence was the fulfilment of an aspiration to which its people had struggled for half a century. I was privileged to accompany the then UN Secretary-General, Ban Ki-moon, to attend that spectacular moment in the history of South Sudan, and observed how nearly the whole of Juba turned up to witness the event—the new country's inaugural independence ceremony on 9 July 2011—in the blazing African heat. The swift universal recognition of South Sudan's independence, the warm and speedy acceptance of the new state by the UN and the wider international community, and the strong pledges of support from a wide range of sources, were nothing short of extraordinary.[8] This was in striking contrast to the earlier prophecies of doom, as many had feared that the independence of the South would be a bad example for Africa, that South Sudan would become a failed state, that its failure would be a disaster not only for the two Sudans but also for the region, and that the crisis would threaten international peace and security.

Those of us who were in a position to counter these negative predictions argued that the Sudan had suffered from "too many agreements dishonoured", in the famous words of South Sudanese statesman Abel Alier;[9] that the 2005 Comprehensive Peace Agreement had to be honoured; that the referendum envisaged by the CPA had to be held on time; that the will of the people of then Southern Sudan had to be respected; and that, if this meant independence, their decision ought to be accepted and recognised. The sources of the predicted failure, whether internally or externally generated, needed to be identified, though, and it was clear the new state would need assistance from the international community to succeed as a positive example of self-determination in Africa.[10]

Almost miraculously, by the time UN Secretary-General Ban Ki-moon convened a high-level meeting on then Southern Sudan in September 2010, global opinion had shifted in favour of the referendum being held on time and the results being honoured. Since then, the world has stood steadfastly with South Sudan, a clear indication that the justness of the cause for which the South Sudanese struggled for so long and sacrificed so much has been recognised.

However, since the internal conflict that erupted in December 2013 and, after a brief halt, resumed in July 2016, a serious rift has developed between South Sudan and the international community. Atrocities and mass human rights violations, including allegations of genocide, have resulted in a series of condemnations by the UN Security Council and other international actors, including many who had been instrumental to the achievement of South Sudan's independence.[11] This has confronted the country with major challenges that it still has to address to recover the goodwill it previously enjoyed in the international community, but it also calls for intensifying internal peace efforts as they relate to ethnic conflicts that call for the constructive management of diversity aimed at promoting inclusivity, equality, and non-discrimination.

On the Concept of Identity and Conflict in Divided Nations

A crisis of identity lies at the heart of the conflicts in the two Sudans.[12] Identity constitutes the core of our humanity. It begins with our self-awareness as individuals, extends to the family, the lineage or clan, the tribe or ethnic group, national affiliation, and multiple other configurations, such as those based on region, religion, language, culture, and gender.

While malleable and constantly changing, identity is a deeply felt phenomenon that often transcends material considerations, even though there is a mutually reinforcing interplay between identity and material considerations. It is generally argued that conflicts over material resources or assets are more amenable to resolution, while conflicts over identity are more elusive and difficult to resolve.[13] The two are, however, interconnected. What often generates conflict is an inequitable distribution of material resources based on identity differentiation. The argument often advanced by scholars and policy analysts that identity is a fiction exploited by political entrepreneurs to advance their own interests or to disguise their material objectives is only partially true. Indeed, it underestimates both the power of self-perception that determines identity considerations and the fact that identity is often a source of access to power, wealth, and other assets. One cannot exploit something that does not exist, even if it is a constructed phenomenon or a myth that has become a reality.[14]

Identity has subjective and objective dimensions. The widely held view among social scientists is that it is what you perceive yourself to be, and not what you objectively are, that determines your identity, even where there is a gap between subjective and objective factors.[15] This would be innocuous if one's self-perception were purely personal, with no negative impact on others. However, where the impact of distorted self-perception becomes a basis for discrimination—as in the case of the Sudan—it must be corrected by exploding the myth of such self-perception.

A vitally important ingredient of group identity is the correlative complex of cultural values, institutional structures, and patterns of behaviour associated with the group. These are the elements that give the identity "skeleton" its "flesh and blood". Unfortunately, most African countries inherited constitutions at independence that did not build on indigenous African values and institutional structures. They were based on European models that the colonialists did not apply to moderate even their own authoritarian rule. For example, democratic values, and fundamental rights and civil liberties were antithetical to colonial authoritarianism, and yet they were central to the Eurocentric constitutions that African countries inherited. These constitutions were, therefore, not rooted in African realities, which is why they tended to be generally discarded without resistance or the shedding of tears.[16] The continent cannot go back to outdated traditions, of course, but it can at least try to build on what is best and adaptable from its indigenous cultural values.[17] This requires studying Africa's own indigenous social organisations and systems of governance, and engaging African communities from the grassroots level up to determine the system that best reflects their aspirations and value systems.

Identity can also be defined in a uniting way that "includes" or in a divisive way that "excludes". The notion of "us" can be narrowly defined to marginalise the "them" group, or broadened to include the latter, depending on the normative dictates of the context. A nation can be united or divided, depending on how its national identity framework is conceptualised and the factors that define that framework.

Although a system of global governance is emerging, the United Nations, itself not yet fully united, is an organisation of divided nations.[18] My experience as Representative of the UN Secretary-General on Internally Displaced Persons introduced me to countries in conflict that are so acutely divided that I wondered how they would ever become united as nations.[19] To illustrate with examples from around the world, on my missions to affected countries I would first meet with the leadership and then visit the IDPs. As I left the IDPs, I would ask them what message they wanted me to convey to their national leaders. Their responses were almost identical, wherever I went. They did not see those in government as their leaders, because they did not feel themselves identified with the nation. "To those rulers, we are not citizens, but criminals, and our only crime is our poverty", one community leader in a Latin American country responded to my question. "None of our people is in that government", a spokesman in a Central Asian country responded in terms of ethnicity. In an African country, the prime minister said to the senior UN official, "The food you give to those people [his country's IDPs] is killing my soldiers". What these reactions indicate is that in such divided nations, there is an "in-group" who enjoy the rights of citizenship, and an "out-group" who are excluded and denied these rights—categorisations that can generate genocidal conflicts and mass atrocities.

The Emergence of Diversity and Disparity in Africa

In most African countries, the sources and causes of conflict are generally recognised to have been inherent in the traumatic experiences of state formation and nation-building. The starting point is the colonial state, which brought together diverse groups that were paradoxically kept separate and offered unequal opportunities for education, development, and employment. Ethnic groups were broken up and affiliated with others within the artificial borders of the new state. Potential conflicts were suppressed because colonial authorities imposed a superstructure of law and order to maintain relative peace and tranquillity.[20]

The independence movement was a collective struggle for self-determination that reinforced the notion of unity within the artificial framework of the newly established state. Initially, independence came as a collective gain that did not delineate who was to get what and how from the legacy of centralised power and wealth. Because colonial institutions had divested the local communities and ethnic groups of much of their indigenous autonomy and sustainable livelihood, replacing this with a degree of centralised authority and dependency on the welfare-state system, the struggle for control became unavoidable, once power passed on at independence to those nationals privileged by colonial empowerment. The outcome was often conflict over power, wealth, services, and development opportunities, often based on identity configuration. This led to gross violations of human rights, denial of civil liberties, disruption of economic and social life, and the consequential frustration of efforts for socioeconomic development.

As the Cold War raged, however, these conflicts were seen not as domestic struggles for power and resources, but as proxy wars in the bipolar superpower confrontation. Rather than help resolve these conflicts peacefully, the United States and the Soviet Union often aggravated them by providing military and economic assistance to their respective allies. Although the end of the Cold War by 1990 removed this external factor, it also diminished the moderating role of the superpowers, both as third parties and as mutually neutralising allies. In acutely divided countries, the result became unmitigated brutalities and devastating identity conflicts.

The larger the gap in the participation and distribution patterns based on racial, ethnic, or religious identity, the more likely the breakdown of civil order and the escalation of political confrontation into violent conflict. When the conflict turns violent, the issues at stake become transformed into a fundamental contest for state power. The objectives may vary in degree from a modest demand for autonomy to a more radical call for a major re-structuring of the national framework, either to be captured by the demand-making group or to be more equitably shaped. When the conflict escalates into a contest for the "soul" of the nation, it runs into an intractable zero-sum confrontation. The critical issue is then whether the underlying sense of injustice, real or perceived, can be remedied in a timely manner, to avert the zero-sum level of genocidal violence.

The colonial state and even the post-colonial state in Africa failed in two fundamental respects that are interconnected: they did not recognise and manage diversity constructively; and they did not build on indigenous cultural values, institutions, and operational patterns. Both failures accentuated identity-related conflicts. Since identity conflicts tend to be zero-sum, they also tend to be genocidal.

De-mystifying Genocide and Mass Atrocities

The term *genocide* is often used loosely to describe mass atrocities that may not meet the legal criteria of the 1948 Convention on the Prevention and Punishment of the Crime of Genocide. Article 2 of the convention takes genocide to mean

> any of the following acts committed with intent to destroy, in whole or in part, a national, ethnical, racial or religious group, as such: killing members of the group; causing serious bodily or mental harm to members of the group; deliberately inflicting on the group conditions of life calculated to bring about its physical destruction in whole or in part; imposing measures intended to prevent births within the group; [and] forcibly transferring children of the group to another group.[21]

However defined, genocide is one of the most heinous crimes that humanity should be expected to unite in preventing, halting, and punishing. By the same token, it is a highly emotional issue that is often seen as too sensitive for comfortable discussion. Therefore, the general response is denial. Both the perpetrators and those called upon to prevent or stop it usually fall into such denial. This is why we mostly recognise genocide after the fact, in historical hindsight. Prevention before the situation escalates to the point of denial is, therefore, the best course of action.[22] It is also critically important to de-mystify genocide from being seen as something untouchable—too difficult to deal with—to something more manageably conceptualised as an extreme form of identity-related conflict, whether the groups involved are identified by the factors specified in the 1948 convention, which include national origin, race, ethnicity, and religion, or by some other criteria, including political affiliation.

It must be emphasised that it is not the mere fact of being different that causes genocidal conflicts; just as important is how differences are managed, especially the extent to which people are differentiated and politically, economically, and socially stratified. As earlier noted, in acutely divided nations, some groups are marginalised, discriminated against, excluded, de humanised, and denied the dignity and the rights that should normally accrue from citizenship. It is the reaction of these extremely disadvantaged groups that generates a conflict of resistance to the indignity; a conflict emanating from despair as a result of not having constructive, peaceful alternatives for pursuing equitable belonging to the nation. Resistance then generates a counter-reaction that can result in genocide or mass atrocities, depending on the balance of power.[23]

It is paradoxical that the powerful feel an existential threat from the weaker antagonists, which then motivates the powerful to react with a genocidal onslaught. Unless the perpetrators are defeated militarily, it usually takes the involvement of a third party to mediate, to ensure both equity and face-saving. The irony of all this, of course, is that the subjectivity with which people define themselves, as opposed to the objective realities of their identities, often means that what divides the parties in conflict has more to do with myth than reality.

The people at war are often not as different from one another as they think they are. In a mid- to long-term public policy strategy, this distorted perception needs to be exposed and corrected.

I have been to Bosnia at the peak of the conflict there, to Central Asia amid civil wars, and to a number of African countries undergoing internal conflicts. Usually, when looking at the people in conflict, it is not easy to tell who belongs to which side of the divide. I remember addressing crowds in Burundi in the aftermath of the 1994 Rwandan genocide, some of whom looked typically Tutsi, in a way we are told Tutsis look, and some of whom looked Hutu, but many of whom I could not tell whether they were Tutsis or Hutus. I asked the foreign minister after those meetings: "Can you always tell a Tutsi from a Hutu?" His response was: "Yes, but with a margin of error of 35 percent." And that margin of error is common in many parts of the world torn apart by internal conflicts. A Sudanese scholar, Suleiman Ali Beldo, who subsequently heard me tell of this experience, commented that in the Sudan, especially in regions such as Darfur, Southern Kordofan, and Blue Nile, the margin of error would be even larger.

If we take the challenge posed by identity conflicts as being one of how to manage diversity constructively—to promote inclusivity, a sense of equality, a sense of belonging to the nation on an equal footing, a sense of pride in being a citizen who enjoys the dignity and rights associated with citizenship—then this is an objective that no self-respecting government can question, far less oppose. This is a challenge that provided a positive basis of engagement with governments in my UN mandates on IDPs and genocide prevention. Diversity is a global phenomenon; hardly any country can claim to be fully homogeneous. Even Somalia, once considered one of the most homogeneous countries in the world, is torn apart by clan differences and conflicting views on Islam (see also Hirsch, and Mahiga in this volume). Yet, despite the pervasiveness of diversity, not all countries characterised by diversity experience genocidal identity conflicts. Some manage well, others not so well, and yet others perform dismally. Sadly, the Sudan is one of those cases that have failed dismally in managing diversity constructively.

Sudan's Crisis of National Identity

I have always maintained that the conflicts that have ravaged the Sudan since independence emanate from an acute crisis of national identity.[24] There are two dimensions to this crisis. The first is the distorted self-perception of a hybrid Arab-African minority who see themselves as homogenously Arab in race, language, and culture, with Islam as a reinforcing ingredient. The second is the imposition of this distorted self-perception as the framework for defining a nation that is racially, ethnically, religiously, and culturally pluralistic.[25]

While this inevitably created a basis for discriminating against non-Arabs and non-Muslims in both the North and the South of Sudan, the situation was simplistically viewed in terms of a North-South dualism, perceived as an Arab-African dichotomy. The normative historical context in which this dualism developed was that if one became a Muslim, was Arabic-speaking, was culturally Arabised, and could trace or concoct descent from an Arab ancestry, one was elevated to a status of dignity and respectability, with little or no regard to the colour of their skin. If one were black, African, and a "heathen", one fell into the category of those considered legitimate targets for slavery. Over time, the North assumed an identity of assimilation in which even the non-Arab groups were subsumed into the Arab-Islamic mould. Since the South remained African, with indigenous belief systems and increasing conversion to Christianity, Southerners developed an identity of resistance to Arabism and Islam, not for what they were or are, but as tools of domination, discrimination, and oppression.

The British, the dominant partner in the Anglo-Egyptian condominium (1899–1955), governed the Sudan as a set of two regions: the central Arab riverine regions were relatively more developed, while the peripheral regions in the North and the South were marginalised, with the South the most neglected and subordinated. Initially, the British left open the option of the South becoming independent or being annexed to East Africa. Toward the end of colonial rule, though, the decision was taken to unify the country under a centralised system of government.

Two Contrasting Wars of Liberation

With independence imminently approaching, the South, apprehensive that the gross mistreatment of the past would once again be inflicted upon it by the Arab-Muslim successors of the British colonialists, started a secessionist rebellion in August 1955, barely four months before independence in January 1956. Seventeen years later, this first war was ended with a compromise under the 1972 Addis Ababa Agreement, which granted the South regional autonomy within a united Sudan.[26] The war had devastated the South, leaving at least half a million dead, hundreds of thousands displaced externally as refugees in neighbouring countries, villages burnt to the ground, crops decimated, and livestock looted or killed.[27] In this context, the peace agreement, although a major compromise, was welcomed by the South.

The unilateral abrogation of the Addis Ababa accord ten years later by the Sudan's President, Jaafar Nimeiri—the very man who had made it possible in the first place—led to the outbreak of the second war in 1983, under the leadership of the Sudan People's Liberation Movement/Army, which ended with the 2005 Comprehensive Peace Agreement.[28] Unlike the first war, the objective of the second war, as stated by the SPLM/A, was not Southern secession, but the liberation of the whole country from the distortions of Sudan's identity and the creation of a "new Sudan" that would be free from any discrimination based on race, ethnicity, religion, culture, or gender.[29]

This vision of a "new Sudan"—the brainchild of John Garang, the intellectual, military, and political leader of the SPLM/A—was initially not taken seriously by either the North or the South, except as a ploy for achieving limited

Southern objectives, which the fighting men in the South expressed in the coded words, "We know what we are fighting for"—implying independence. For Garang, the vision was both an ideal and a pragmatic way of protecting the more limited goal of South Sudanese independence. Be as it may, with time, the vision of a "new Sudan" began to inspire many, in particular, those from the marginalised areas of the North.[30] In the 1980s, the Nuba of Southern Kordofan and the Ingassana (or Funj) of Blue Nile joined the SPLM/A in the liberation struggle for the "new Sudan". Later, the Beja of eastern Sudan rebelled, in cooperation with the SPLM/A. The Darfurians first rebelled in 1992, but were crushed, and then resumed their struggle in 2003. Indeed, the struggle in Darfur rages to this day, inflicting atrocities that some have called genocidal and others have defined as crimes not less heinous than genocide.[31] With fighting continuing between government forces and rebel groups, there were an estimated 2.1 million IDPs in need in Darfur in 2017.[32] (See also Gambari in this volume.)

South Sudan's Independence and Its Implications for the North

The Washington-based Centre for Strategic and International Studies (CSIS) launched a Task Force on US Sudan Policy in July 2000, which I was honoured to co-chair with J. Stephen Morrison, director of the CSIS Africa Program. In February 2001, the task force recommended that the United States should play a leading role in the Sudan peace process initiated by IGAD in 1993–1994.[33] The task force further proposed a formula of "one country, two systems" to reconcile the two visions for the Sudan: aspirations for unity in the North, supported by the international community, and the understandable quest of the Southerners for independence, in reaction to their gross and persistent mistreatment by the North. However, the formula unwittingly became a mechanism for entrenching the division of the country during the six-year interim period, from 2005 to 2011, stipulated by the 2005 Comprehensive Peace Agreement, after which the South was to decide whether to remain within a united Sudan or secede as an independent state. In January 2011, the South voted overwhelmingly in favour of independence, which was subsequently declared in July of the same year.

The 2005 CPA also stipulated popular consultations for the marginalised regions of Southern Kordofan and Blue Nile, although what this meant and what the outcome would be remained uncertain. What I foresaw when I visited these states before South Sudan's landmark referendum leading to independence in July 2011, which was by then predictable, is that the marginalised regions of the North would remain committed to the struggle for a "new Sudan", and, understandably, hope for support from the independent South. However, Southern support for the marginalised regions of Sudan would almost certainly provoke inter-ethnic conflicts in South Sudan and de-stabilise the nascent country.[34] This is, indeed, what is now happening in the border areas of Southern Kordofan and Blue Nile, not to mention Darfur, whose struggle predates the signing of the CPA. And, of course, Sudan's alleged support of David Yau Yau's rebel group in South Sudan's Jonglei region, following his loss in the 2010 elections in the South, was the expected retaliation to any support Khartoum believed Juba was offering its previous northern allies in Kordofan and Blue Nile.

The Crisis in Abyei

As recent developments have demonstrated, the situation in Abyei on the North-South border poses an even more imminent threat in Sudan–South Sudan relations. The Abyei Protocol of the 2005 CPA gave the members of the nine chiefdoms of the Ngok Dinka and other regular residents of the area the right to choose whether to join the South or remain under the administration of the North, to which they were annexed by the British in 1905. It also established the Abyei Boundaries Commission (ABC) in January 2005, whose demarcation of the borders of the area—presented in its report in July 2005[35]—was to be final and binding. Sudan's ruling National Congress Party government's rejection of the commission's findings, followed by a military confrontation in the area, led to submission of the case to the Permanent Court of Arbitration in July 2008, which in July 2009 revised the ABC borders by ceding more land to the North than the commission had demarcated.[36]

The National Congress Party government has so far (at the time of writing in January 2017) also resisted implementation of the ruling of the Permanent Court of Arbitration. Instead, it decided to occupy Abyei militarily, just at the time of the referendum in the South in January 2011, perhaps with the intent of provoking the South Sudanese to retaliate and trigger an all-out war that would have subverted the independence of the South. The government of South Sudan, under President Salva Kiir Mayardit, wisely resisted that provocation. Rather, Kiir repeatedly said that South Sudan would not go back to war with Sudan over Abyei, but would press for the implementation of the Abyei Protocol of the 2005 CPA. He has also stated, though, that he would not be able to control developments on the ground, which might lead to the resumption of hostilities over Abyei. The earlier failure of the Sudan's government to implement a similar provision of the 1972 Addis Ababa Agreement on Abyei had led to a local rebellion that contributed to the resumption of North-South conflict in 1983. History could repeat itself, with the current situation in Abyei a potential trigger for a return to war.[37]

Conclusion: The Challenge in Perspective

A crisis of national identity and their persistent failure to manage diversity constructively since independence confront both Sudan and South Sudan with several contextual challenges. First, independent South Sudan must correct the mistakes of the past by adopting a South Sudanese national identity framework that promotes inclusivity, equality, and dignity for all ethnic groups, without discrimination—a "new Sudan" in the South Sudan context.

Second, Sudan must address the genuine grievances of its marginalised regions (in particular, Abyei, Southern Kordofan, and Blue Nile), in order also to promote the same principles and similarly embodied in the concept of a "new Sudan" in the Northern context. This should ensure regional autonomy similar to what South Sudan enjoyed during the CPA interim period from 2005 to 2011, without the option of separation, but with equitable participation at the centre.

Third, the cause of the people of Abyei that drove them to join the South in the two wars between the North and South, and that has been recognised in several agreements, must be effectively addressed by implementing the Abyei Protocol of the 2005 CPA and the subsequent findings of the Permanent Court of Arbitration, or it will continue to threaten peaceful and cooperative relations between Sudan and South Sudan.

Fourth, both Sudan and South Sudan cannot be indifferent to the genuine grievances of disadvantaged and marginalised groups in their respective contexts. As South Sudan's president, Salva Kiir, said in his Independence Day speech in July 2011,[38] both countries should help each other cooperatively to address these grievances in order to promote peace, security, stability, and equality for all.

Fifth, South Sudan, being among the African countries least affected by modernity and the blanket importation of outside models of governance, must endeavour to make effective use of its indigenous cultural values, institutional structures, and patterns of behaviour, as the essence of genuine self-determination. These indigenous principles can be used effectively in developing norms and operational measures for conflict prevention, management, and resolution; reinforcing international human rights standards; promoting equitable socio-economic development; and reforming gender relations such as to ensure mutual respect and equality between the sexes.

Since independence, the Sudan has been intermittently at war with itself. If the 2005 CPA is credibly implemented and holds, it would offer the people of Sudan and South Sudan the first opportunity to resolve their chronic crisis of national identity. What is needed is a shift in mindset, away from hostility and acrimony and towards peaceful co-existence and cooperation. Degrees of unity and separation vary in ongoing relationships that can be strengthened or weakened, depending on the will of the people and particularly of their leaders. The international community, in its entire configuration—governmental and non-governmental, regional, continental, and global—will continue to be needed to support both Sudan and South Sudan in consolidating and sustaining the new dispensation based on peaceful co-existence, good neighbourliness, and productive cooperation.

South Sudan, for its part, struggled for a long time on the basis of ideals that it is now called upon to respect, and pursue the building of a system that constructively manages diversity, adheres to the principles of democracy and "good governance", respects fundamental rights and civil liberties, ensures equitable socio-economic development, and promotes gender equality—all essential elements of the vision of a "new Sudan" that the SPLM/A championed from its inception. The leaders of South Sudan struck the right note in all their statements upon independence. The challenge was to live up to the commitments made in those statements. However, the ongoing conflict in Sudan, particularly in Blue Nile and South Darfur; the unresolved situation in Abyei; and the outbreak of the civil war in South Sudan in 2013 that briefly halted and then resumed in 2016, spill over the borders of the two Sudans, rendering them "bound by conflict".[39]

Although the case of the now divided Sudan is an extreme example of mismanaged diversity, the lessons from this experience are relevant to most African countries and indeed many states worldwide, wherever identity differences threaten peace, unity, and stability. The challenge in all these situations is how to develop a working framework that fosters inclusivity, equality, and human dignity for all, irrespective of identity differences based on race, ethnicity, religion, or culture. Divisive self-perceptions, especially those that distort realities, should be corrected to foster the commonalities of shared elements and the unifying framework of inclusive national identity.

The twin concepts of sovereignty as responsibility and the responsibility to protect link two principle objectives: first, determining what needs to be done to prevent mass atrocities, respond to them where they occur, and reconstruct societies and consolidate peace after conflict; and second, determining who is to do what needs to be done, which calls for partnership involving the state, international support for the state, and a more robust intervention to provide protection and assistance where the state manifestly fails to fulfil its national obligations. In essence, this is a strategy for bridging idealism and realism, a means of negotiating sovereignty in divided nations.[40]

Notes

1. United Nations (UN) General Assembly, *2005 World Summit Outcome*, UN Doc. A/RES/60/1, 24 October 2005, paras. 138–139.
2. *See* International Commission on Intervention and State Sovereignty (ICISS), *The Responsibility to Protect: Research, Bibliography, Background—Supplementary Volume to the Report of the International Commission on Intervention and State Sovereignty* (Ottawa: International Development Research Centre [IDRC], 2001); Gareth Evans, *The Responsibility to Protect: Ending Mass Atrocity Crimes Once and For All* (Washington, DC: Brookings Institution Press, 2008); Julia Hoffman and André Nolkaemper (eds.), *Responsibility to Protect: From Principle to Practice* (Amsterdam: Pallas Publications—Amsterdam University Press, 2012). *See also* Alex J. Bellamy, *Responsibility to Protect: The Global Effort to End Mass Atrocities* (Cambridge: Polity, 2009); Francis M. Deng, "From 'Sovereignty as Responsibility' to the 'Responsibility to Protect'", *Global Responsibility to Protect* 2, no. 4 (2010), pp. 353–370; Luke Glanville, *Sovereignty and the Responsibility to Protect: A New History* (Chicago: University of Chicago Press,

2014); Alex J. Bellamy and Tim Dunne (eds.), *The Oxford Handbook of the Responsibility to Protect* (Oxford: Oxford University Press, 2016).

3. The program began with a research conference in 1989, resulting in the first edited volume: Francis M. Deng and I. William Zartman (eds.), *Conflict Resolution in Africa* (Washington, DC: The Brookings Institution, 1991). This was to be followed by a series of regional and country-specific studies.
4. Francis M. Deng, Sididiel Kimaro, Terrence Lyons, Donald Rothchild, and I. William Zartman, *Sovereignty as Responsibility: Conflict Management in Africa* (Washington, DC: Brookings Institution, 1996).
5. Program publications included: Abdullahi Ahmed An-Na'im and Francis M. Deng, *Human Rights in Africa: A Cross-Cultural Perspective* (1990); I. William Zartman (ed.), *Governance as Conflict Management: Politics and Violence in West Africa* (1991); Francis M. Deng and Larry Mineer, *The Challenges of Famine Relief: Emergency Operations in Sudan* (1992); Thomas Ohlsen and Stephen John Stedman, with Robert Davis, *The New Is Not Yet Born: Conflict Resolution in Southern Africa* (1994); Claude Ake, *Democracy and Development in Africa* (1996); Francis M. Deng and Terrence Lyons, *African Reckoning: A Quest for Good Governance* (1998); Francis M. Deng and I. William Zartman, *A Strategic Vision for Africa* (2002). All published by the Brookings Institution in Washington, DC.
6. *The IGAD Declaration of Principles*, Nairobi, Kenya, 20 May 1994, http://peacemaker.un.org/sites/peacemaker.un.org/files/SD_940520_The%20IGAD%20Declaration%20of%20principles.pdf (accessed 25 June 2017).
7. Britain is used synonymously with the United Kingdom (UK) in this volume.
8. *See* Francis M. Deng, *Bound by Conflict: Dilemmas of the Two Sudans* (New York: Fordham University Press, 2016); Hilde F. Johnson, *South Sudan: The Untold Story* (London and New York: I.B. Tauris, 2016).
9. Abel Alier, *Southern Sudan: Too Many Agreements Dishonoured*, second edition (Ithaca: Exeter, 1999).
10. *See* Francis Mading Deng, *Sudan at the Brink: Self Determination and National Unity* (New York: Fordham University and Institute for International Humanitarian Affairs, 2010).
11. *See, for example*, Security Council Press Statement on Fighting in South Sudan, UN Doc. SC/12713, 10 February 2017, https://www.un.org/press/en/2017/sc12713.doc.htm (accessed 25 June 2017). *See also* Security Council Report, "UN Documents for South Sudan", http://www.securitycouncilreport.org/un-documents/south-sudan (accessed 25 June 2017).
12. Deng, *Bound by Conflict*, pp. 1–9.
13. *See, for example*, Donald Rothchild, "An Interactive Model for State-Ethnic Relations", in Deng and Zartman, *Conflict Resolution in Africa*, pp. 190–215.
14. Deng, *Sudan at the Brink*. *See* Francis M. Deng, *Identity, Diversity, and Constitutionalism in Africa* (Washington, DC: United States Institute of Peace Press, 2008). *See also* Muna Ndulo, "Ethnic Diversity: A Challenge to African Democratic Governance", in Francis M. Deng (ed.), *Self-Determination and National Unity: A Challenge for Africa* (Trenton, NJ: Africa World Press, 2010), pp. 11–56.
15. *See* Crawford Young, *The Politics of Cultural Pluralism* (Madison and London: University of Wisconsin Press, 1976); Joseph V. Montville (ed.), *Conflict and Peacemaking in Multiethnic Societies* (Washington, DC: Heath and Company,

1991); Peter Woodward, *Sudan 1898–1989: The Unstable State* (Boulder, CO: Lynne Rienner, 1990).

16. *See* Deng, *Identity, Diversity, and Constitutionalism in Africa.*
17. *See* Francis M. Deng, *Tradition and Modernization: A Challenge for Law Among the Dinka of the Sudan* (New Haven, CT: Yale University Press, 1971).
18. Francis M. Deng, "Divided Nations: The Paradox of National Protection", *Annals of the American Academy of Political and Social Science* 603, no. 1 (2006), pp. 217–225.
19. Thomas G. Weiss and David A. Korn, *Internal Displacement: Conceptualization and Its Consequences* (London and New York: Routledge, 2006).
20. *See* Ricardo Rene Laremont (ed.), *Borders, Nationalism, and the African State* (Boulder, CO: Lynne Rienner, 2005). *See also* Mark R. Beissinger and Crawford Young, *Beyond State Crisis? Postcolonial Africa and Post-Soviet Eurasia in Comparative Perspectives* (Washington, DC: Woodrow Wilson Center Press, 2002).
21. Convention on the Prevention and Punishment of the Crime of Genocide, 9 December 1948, art. 2, https://treaties.un.org/doc/publication/unts/volume%2078/volume-78-i-1021-english.pdf (accessed 21 December 2016).
22. David Hamburg, *Preventing Genocide: Practical Steps Toward Early Detection and Effective Action* (Boulder, CO: Paradigm, 2008); David Hamburg *Give Peace a Chance: Preventing Mass Violence* (Boulder, CO: Paradigm, 2013).
23. I. William Zartman, *Preventing Identity Conflicts Leading to Genocide and Mass Killings* (Baltimore, MD: Johns Hopkins University Press, 2010).
24. My writings on the crisis of identity in Sudan include the books *Dynamics of Identification: A Basis for National Integration in the Sudan* (Khartoum: Khartoum University Press, 1974) and *War of Visions: Conflict of Identities in the Sudan* (Washington, DC: Brookings Institution, 1995), as well as numerous journal articles and book chapters, among them: "Sudan: A Nation in Turbulent Search for Itself", *Annals of the American Academy of Political and Science* 603, no. 1 (2006), pp. 155–162; and "Sudan's Turbulent Road to Nationhood", in Laremont, *Borders, Nationalism, and the African State*, pp. 33–85.
25. *See* Deng, *Bound by Conflict.*
26. Francis M. Deng, *Peace and Unity in the Sudan: An African Achievement* (Khartoum. Khartoum University Press, 1973).
27. Matthew LeRiche and Matthew Arnold, *South Sudan: From Revolution to Independence* (London: Hurst, 2012), p. 1.
28. Alier, *Southern Sudan.*
29. Deng, *Sudan at the Brink*, p. 7. *See* Francis M. Deng, *New Sudan in the Making? Essays on a Nation in Painful Search of Itself* (Trenton, NJ: Red Sea Press, 2010).
30. Deng, *New Sudan in the Making?*
31. The United States (US) held the position that it was genocide, while the UN maintained the opposite position, though admitting that crimes had been and were being committed there that were "not less heinous than genocide".
32. UN Office for the Coordination of Humanitarian Affairs (OCHA), "Sudan: Darfur Humanitarian Overview", 1 April 2017, http://reliefweb.int/sites/reliefweb.int/files/resources/Darfur_Humanitarian_Overview_A3_01_Apr_2017.pdf (accessed 25 June 2017).
33. Centre for Strategic and International Studies (CSIS), Task Force on US Sudan Policy, *US Policy to End Sudan's War* (Washington, DC, February 2001). On

the Intergovernmental Authority on Development (IGAD) initiative, *see* Francis M. Deng (ed.), *Their Brothers' Keepers: Regional Initiative for Peace in Sudan* (Addis Ababa: InterAfrica Group, 1997).

34. Deng, *Sudan at the Brink*.
35. For the text of the Abyei Boundaries Commission report, *see* http://www.sudantribune.com/TEXT-Abyei-Boundary-Commission,11633 (accessed 25 June 2017).
36. *See* Permanent Court of Arbitration, *In the Matter of an Arbitration Before a Tribunal Constituted in Accordance with Article 5 of the Arbitration Agreement Between the Government of Sudan and the Sudan People's Liberation Movement/Army on Delimiting Abyei Area—Final Award*, the Hague, the Netherlands, 22 July 2009, http://www.haguejusticeportal.net/Docs/Court%20Documents/PCA/Abyei_Final_Award_EN.pdf (accessed 25 June 2017). *See also* John R. Crook, "Abyei Arbitration—Final Award", *ASIL Insights* 13, no. 15 (September 2009), https://www.asil.org/insights/volume/13/issue/15/abyei-arbitration-%E2%80%93-final-award (accessed 25 June 2017).
37. Francis M. Deng, *Frontiers of Unity: An Experiment in Afro-Arab Cooperation* (Abingdon, Oxon: Routledge, 2010).
38. For the text of President Salva Kiir Mayardit's speech, *see* http://www.gurtong.net/ECM/Editorial/tabid/124/ctl/ArticleView/mid/519/articleId/5440/President-Kiirs-Independence-Speech-In-Full.aspx (accessed 25 June 2017).
39. Deng, *Bound by Conflict*.
40. Francis Deng, "Idealism and Realism: Negotiating Sovereignty in Divided Nations", 2010 Dag Hammarskjöld Lecture, Uppsala University, Sweden, 10 September 2010.

CHAPTER 7

The 2008 Kenyan Mediation Process: Lessons and Dilemmas for Conflict Prevention in Africa

Njoki Wamai

The Kenya National Dialogue and Reconciliation (KNDR) process was facilitated by the African Union's (AU) Panel of Eminent African Personalities—led by former United Nations (UN) Secretary-General, Kofi Annan of Ghana—in the wake of violence after the country's December 2007 general elections. The incumbent president, Mwai Kibaki of the Party of National Unity (PNU), was controversially declared the winner of a second term, after what was considered to have been a flawed electoral process, with local as well as international observers reporting that the presidential election was characterised by rigging and falsification of tallied results.[1] The then Chairperson of the Electoral Commission of Kenya, Samuel Kivuitu, admitted that widespread electoral malpractices had occurred, before swearing in Kibaki as the president in a hurried ceremony.[2] This triggered widespread violence after Kibaki's main opponent, Raila Odinga of the Orange Democratic Movement (ODM), refused to concede defeat, citing electoral malpractices condoned by the national electoral commission and judiciary. Between December 2007 and February 2008, over 1,130 people lost their lives and more than 350,000 people were displaced in the violence.[3]

After 41 days of negotiations, the Annan-led Panel of Eminent African Personalities brokered a power-sharing agreement, the National Accord and Reconciliation Act, in February 2008, which ended the political crisis and resulting humanitarian emergency. Based on the speed at which the crisis was resolved, the mediation process was lauded as a triumph of the norm of responsibility to protect (R2P) by Annan as well as several Western actors.[4] However, Kenyan observers and scholars were critical of Annan and the UN, as well as

N. Wamai (✉)
Centre of Governance and Human Rights, Department of Politics and International Studies, University of Cambridge, Cambridge, UK

T. Karbo, K. Virk (eds.), *The Palgrave Handbook of Peacebuilding in Africa*, https://doi.org/10.1007/978-3-319-62202-6_7

others, for failing to acknowledge the process as an example of a successful African-led mediation.[5]

In this chapter, I argue that the Kenyan mediation process presents three sets of lessons and dilemmas for conflict prevention in Africa. First, it demonstrates how a single, well-resourced African-led mediation team, with status and leverage, can be effective in conflict resolution. Second, it confirms the importance of a domestic movement as a source of support for the mediation team. Local civil society groups, including Kenyan politicians, business and women leaders, and ordinary citizens, supported the Annan–led Panel of Eminent African Personalities to pressure the protagonists for a peaceful resolution to the crisis. Third, Annan and his mediation team's perceived impartiality were critical in ensuring confidence in the mediation process. This process also exposed the limits of a liberal peacemaking process, though, in generating a meaningful, political transformation that goes beyond accommodating national elites, as indicated by recent developments at the International Criminal Court (ICC). The ICC case against Kenyan president, Uhuru Kenyatta, for his role in the 2007–2008 violence, was dropped in December 2014; and that against his deputy, William Ruto, who faced similar charges, in April 2016. (See Nouwen in this volume.)

The chapter begins with a discussion on mediation as a form of conflict prevention in Africa. I then trace the background of the post-electoral violence that erupted in Kenya in December 2007, before discussing local and international efforts towards initiating a mediation process to resolve the crisis. Next, I discuss the strategies employed by the Annan–led Panel of Eminent African Personalities, and draw out the general lessons and dilemmas that the Kenyan mediation process presents for conflict prevention in Africa, before offering some concluding reflections.

Mediation as a Form of Conflict Prevention in Africa

Definitions of mediation vary depending on several factors such as the focus and essence of mediation, the level of impartiality, and mediator behaviour.[6] New Zealand scholar Jacob Bercovitch defines mediation as:

> a process of conflict management related to but distinct from the parties' own negotiations where those in conflict seek the assistance of, or accept an offer of help from an outsider (who may be an individual, an organization, a group or a state) to change their perceptions or behavior, and to do so without resorting to physical force or invoking the authority of law.[7]

Documenting lessons learnt in the practice of mediation is complex and difficult, because every context presents different dynamics. However, liberal peace scholars like Jacob Bercovitch, Saadia Touval, and William Zartman have identified a number of generic conditions across situations that can guarantee varying levels of success when applied in other contexts.[8] Bercovitch, for example, identifies three factors that contribute to effective mediation: the parties to the conflict, the ripeness of the conflict, and the appropriate mediator.[9] Indeed, there is general agreement among scholars, as well as practitioners, that effective mediation is possible when the parties to the conflict are motivated to end the conflict, and when a mutually hurting stalemate exists to orchestrate a ripe moment, coupled with a mediator who possesses tact, intelligence, and knowledge and is high ranking. Furthermore, the effectiveness of international mediation can be evaluated using subjective criteria such as party satisfaction, perceptions of fairness, and changes in relationships; as well as objective criteria, which focus on reductions in violent behaviour, the agreements reached, and the endurance of settlements.[10] Despite the development of scholarship on the subject, though, successful mediation is often difficult to replicate in different situations, as Kofi Annan learned in Syria, in 2012, despite his previous success in leading the Kenyan mediation.[11] Nevertheless, this limitation does not prevent the identification of some critical lessons from the Kenyan experience for policymakers in Africa.

As Chester Crocker, Fen Osler Hampson, and Pamela Aall argue, the end of the Cold War and the resulting intractability of conflicts led to an increased interest in mediation as a form of conflict prevention after 1990.[12] They identify four factors that influenced the nature of international mediation in the post-Cold War period.[13] First, there was increased interest in mediation on the part of intergovernmental organisations such as the United Nations, following UN Secretary-General Boutros Boutros-Ghali of Egypt's 1992 report, *An Agenda for Peace*, which called for greater involvement of regional organisations in preventive diplomacy, peacemaking, peacekeeping, and post-conflict reconstruction.[14] (See Introduction in this volume.) Second, there was increased involvement by humanitarian, religious, and development non-governmental organisations (NGOs) in pre-negotiations and track one-and-a-half mediation processes. Susan Nan defines track one-and-a-half as "an unusually direct way for unofficial activities to contribute to peace making".[15] Third, there was realisation that mediation is a low-cost alternative to large-scale military intervention. The fourth factor was the emergence of the norm of R2P, which legitimises intervention by the international community and regional organisations as a moral responsibility.[16] (See also Deng in this volume.) That said, there are others—for example, Ugandan scholar Mahmood Mamdani and American academic Adam Branch—who have been sceptical about international mediation efforts, considering the impact that Western interventionist peace projects have had in terms of imparting liberal and market economies to Africa, without corresponding political transformation that addresses the structural causes of conflicts.[17]

The 2000 AU Constitutive Act allows for intervention by the Union in the internal affairs of its member states; this is unlike the charter of its predecessor, the Organisation of African Unity (OAU), which did not.[18] In 2002, the African Peace and Security Architecture (APSA) was established to address post-Cold War security challenges and conflicts on the continent (see Kuwali in this volume). This architecture is composed of five pillars: the Peace and

Security Council (PSC); the Panel of the Wise; the Continental Early Warning System (CEWS); the African Standby Force (ASF) (see Nagar in this volume); and the Peace Fund. However, these structures have continued to face significant political, financial, and logistical challenges. Both the Peace Fund and the ASF, for example, have struggled with notable capacity constraints due, in large part, to the reluctance of African countries to pay their annual contributions to cover operating costs, making peace operations such as the AU Mission in Somalia (AMISOM) very dependent on external actors such as the European Union (EU) and the UN.[19] (On Somalia, see Hirsch, and Mahiga in this volume.)

African-led mediation efforts over the years have produced mixed results, with varying levels of success and failure. Various actors have been involved in, and contributed towards, mediation efforts on the continent. They include: appointed special envoys, as in the Kenyan case and in the Darfur conflict; Africa's regional economic communities (RECs), such as the Southern African Development Community (SADC) in Zimbabwe and the Intergovernmental Authority on Development (IGAD) in South Sudan (see Deng in this volume); and high-level panels, as in Côte d'Ivoire. The AU Panel of the Wise also supports the conflict prevention efforts of the PSC by brokering peace agreements between warring parties; and provides help to the AU Commission in mapping out threats to peace and security on the continent. The relative success of mediation efforts in ending post-electoral violence in Kenya and Zimbabwe, for example, has generated increased support for mediation as a form of conflict resolution, while failures, such as in Libya and Côte d'Ivoire, point to some of the challenges that these efforts continue to face.

Background to the 2008 Kenyan Mediation Process

Before the unprecedented outbreak of post-electoral violence in December 2007, Kenya was considered an island of peace in a troubled sea relative to its neighbours in turmoil in Eastern Africa, such as Burundi, Rwanda, Somalia, Sudan, and Uganda in the 1980s and 1990s.[20] This erroneous image of an island of peace served the regimes of Jomo Kenyatta (1963–1978), the country's first post-independence president, and his successor, Daniel arap Moi (1978–2002), who cultivated an international image of a stable Kenya, notwithstanding the despotism that characterised their leadership. Britain and the United States (US) bolstered this image during the Cold War, as Kenya served as a strategic foothold in the Horn of Africa then, and as it now does again after the terrorist attacks of September 2001 in the US.[21]

The formation of the Kenyan nation was tumultuous, owing to the country's colonial legacy and post-independence leadership. According to Kenyan scholar John Oucho, the British colonial legacy affected Kenya's governance in four ways: it provided the basis for (1) ethnic-administrative provincial boundaries and for (2) the drafting of an imperialist constitution, while giving rise to (3) a land crisis and (4) the emergence of squatters.[22] Kenya's first president,

Jomo Kenyatta, instead of reforming this inherited and flawed system of boundaries, land ownership, and constitution, skewed it further, using his imperialist presidency to disproportionately reward his ethnic group, the Kikuyu, but more so the Kikuyu elite, with *matunda ya uhuru* (fruits of independence), as Tanzanian scholar Issa Shivji has argued.[23] These "fruits" included land for development and political appointments, further exacerbating inequalities between the Kikuyu and other ethnic groups.[24]

Upon Kenyatta's death in August 1978, his vice-president, Daniel arap Moi from the Kalenjin ethnic group (which is dominant in the Rift Valley province), succeeded him. Moi, during his tenure, diverted socio-economic entitlements such as education, infrastructure development, and healthcare provision to the Rift Valley region, prompting outrage from courageous politicians, civil society, and university students and staff.[25] Moi responded by institutionalising repression in his 24-year-rule using the country's security forces, who detained, tortured, and assassinated all critics, under the guise of "national security". Domestic and international pressure to reform the government led to the re-introduction of multi-party politics in December 1991, with multi-party elections following in 1992 and 1997 amidst state-sponsored violence, resulting in the displacement of more than 75,000 people perceived as opposition supporters.[26]

In 2002, opposition parties united under one presidential candidate, Mwai Kibaki, in an attempt to re-capture the Kenyan state after 24 years of predation on state resources. With Moi constitutionally barred from running again, Kibaki was elected, in December 2002, by an overwhelming margin on a platform that sought to correct ethnic inequalities, address historical injustices, punish grand corruption, reduce presidential powers, and improve the economy. During his first term (2002–2007), Kibaki succeeded in turning around the economy—growth increased from 2 per cent in 2002 to 7 per cent in 2007—but failed to deliver everything else that Kenyans wanted: a new constitutional order, limiting of presidential powers, punishment of grand corruption, and reduction of ethnic and regional inequalities.[27] By the time of the 2007 presidential election, most Kenyans were frustrated with Kibaki's politics. As French scholar Gerard Prunier has asserted, Raila Odinga, of the opposition Orange Democratic Movement, was able easily to capitalise on these failures in his presidential campaign.[28]

The declaration of Kibaki as the winner of the 2007 presidential election by a biased national electoral commission; Odinga's refusal to concede defeat; and the immediate, and secret, swearing-in of Kibaki as the president, provided the trigger for Kenya's descent into anarchy.[29] Protests, riots, and violence broke out nationwide. The leadership and supporters of the ODM were outraged by what they considered to have been electoral fraud. The leadership and supporters of the Party of National Unity, meanwhile, obstinately insisted that they had won the election fairly and asserted that Kibaki was the president.[30]

Explaining the origin and role of political ethnicity in Kenyan politics is important in understanding why elections have been violently contested since the advent of multi-party politics in 1992. According to Kenyan scholar Karuti Kanyinga, the origins of ethnicised politics in Kenya lie in the colonial state's attempt to undermine local pan-territorial mobilisation and political pluralism.[31] The post-colonial Kenyatta and Moi governments intensified these ethnic divisions through the manipulation of ethnic ideology to increase support from ethnic voters. The repeal of Section 2A of Kenya's Constitution introduced multi-party politics in 1991, further deepening political competition. Since Moi's defeat by a coalition of opposition parties in 2002, such alliances have become central to politics in Kenya as the means to achieving and sustaining political power. Although Kenya has over 70 distinct ethnic groups, the five largest groups—the Kikuyu, the Luhya, the Luo, the Kalenjin, and the Kamba—dominate winning coalitions, resulting in the exclusion of minorities. As British analyst Gabrielle Lynch has further observed, these coalitions are fluid and constantly changing to reflect new elite partnerships.[32] (On the role of ethnicity in conflict in Africa, see also Deng in this volume.)

The Post-Electoral Violence of 2007–2008 and Pre-Annan Mediation Efforts

By January 2008, the post-electoral violence had escalated significantly, with 35 Kikuyu women and children burned in a church at Kiambaa in Uasin Gishu district in one attack. This incident increased tensions and retaliatory attacks against perceived supporters of the Orange Democratic Movement, including Luos and Kalenjins living in strongholds of the Party of National Unity, such as Naivasha and Nakuru. Three categories of the violence that occurred have since been identified: (1) organised violence by the Kalenjin against the Kikuyu in Kalenjin-dominated regions in the northern Rift Valley; (2) retaliatory violence by the Kikuyu against other ethnic groups in Kikuyu-dominated regions in Nakuru and Naivasha; and (3) spontaneous violence in urban centres such as Nairobi, Kisumu, and Mombasa by youth.[33]

There are four sets of factors that can explain this post-electoral violence: first, structural causes resulting from the absence of strong institutions of governance (including the rule of law); second, political causes arising from an imperialist constitution that favoured a powerful president without accountability; third, historical causes arising from the legacy of colonial borders and demarcations, as well as the culture of violence and coercion used by British colonial authorities; and fourth, socio-economic causes, in particular, sustained inequalities resulting from the exclusion and marginalisation of different ethnic groups and regions by different post-independence regimes.

Immediately after the outbreak of violence in December 2007 in Kenya, various local and international actors gathered in the capital of Nairobi in an attempt to broker peace. Bethuel Kiplagat and Lazaro Sumbeiywo, who had experience mediating in Somalia and Sudan respectively, made the first attempt to end the crisis, but in vain. South African Nobel Peace laureate, Archbishop

Desmond Tutu, under the auspices of the All Africa Council of Churches, soon joined them as the first international mediator between Kibaki and Odinga. According to Kenyan scholar Gilbert Khadiagala, accepting international mediation was a challenge for Kibaki, in particular, who saw this as an affront to Kenya's "sovereignty"; one compounded by a legacy of national pride after years of mediating among Kenya's turbulent neighbours.[34]

AU and Western diplomats also joined in the attempts to end the crisis. British foreign secretary, David Miliband, and US secretary of state, Condoleezza Rice, called for a compromise that put Kenya's interests first in January 2008.[35] British prime minister, Gordon Brown, and Rice also pledged their support for the AU's efforts—led by former Ghanaian president, John Kufuor—to find an international mediator as part of what was called "African solutions to African problems".[36] Soon thereafter, US assistant secretary of state, Jendayi Frazer, joined the diplomatic efforts in Nairobi, threatening the principals that "it would not be business as usual with Kenya if the stalemate continued."[37] The EU development commissioner, Frenchman Louis Michel, also threatened to reduce European aid in the face of the Kenyan government's reluctance to accept mediation.[38]

Regional leaders—in particular, Ugandan president, Yoweri Museveni, then chair of the East African Community (EAC); Collin Bruce, then World Bank country director in Kenya; and four other former African heads of state (Tanzania's Benjamin Mkapa, Mozambique's Joachim Chissano, Botswana's Ketumile Masire, and Zambia's Kenneth Kaunda)—also joined the frantic shuttle diplomacy in Nairobi, but similarly in vain. Disruption of transport networks by ethnic militias was threatening to choke other East African economies by mid-January 2008, prompting Rwanda's president, Paul Kagame, to suggest a military intervention if the crisis continued, in order to prevent Kenya from sliding into genocide like his own country had in 1994.[39] Finally, on 15 January 2008, the two adversarial Kenyan sides—the PNU and the ODM—agreed on John Kufuor's proposal for former UN Secretary-General Kofi Annan to mediate between them.

The Annan-Led Mediation Process

On 23 January 2008, a three-member mediation team—the Panel of Eminent African Personalities—began the task of resolving the conflict through what the parties called the Kenya National Dialogue and Reconciliation process. Kofi Annan led the team, with the other two members being Benjamin Mkapa, the former president of Tanzania, who had the advantage of familiarity with Kenya as a regional actor; and Graça Machel, former education minister of Mozambique, with a particular interest in women's and children's issues. Indeed, Machel played a critical role in the mediation process by conveying the concerns of women who were not at the mediation table.[40] She also understood the structural causes of the Kenyan conflict, having previously led the Kenya review process under the African Peer Review Mechanism (APRM).

Annan and his team persuaded the protagonists, Kibaki and Odinga, to shake hands publicly as a sign of good will and as a confidence-building measure.[41] This famous handshake, on 26 January 2008, was critical in de-escalating the violence and reducing tensions, for mediation to proceed.[42] At the onset of the mediation, the Annan–led team established three critical elements to manage the process. The first was Annan's insistence that there would be only one mediation process, led by the Panel of Eminent African Personalities. In his words:

> ... when we got there, three of the four leaders in the Africa Leaders' Forum were in town, so I wanted to know what their plans were. And I also wanted to let them know that we were not attempting any power grab at all ... They thought they could stay on—they were establishing an office—and deal with the social aspects by encouraging social cohesion ... And I said, "No, I think that will lead to confusion, when you have the panel of eminent persons negotiating and three or four former heads of states [*sic*] leading a process that is trying to get the Kenyans to talk to each other." I said that we should leave it to the Kenyans, and that we should encourage them to do so ... And they understood, so they left town.[43]

The UN Security Council supported Annan and his team's strategy and warned that it could intervene if the parties failed to resolve the crisis.[44] The UN Secretary-General, Ban Ki-moon, and the incoming AU Commission chairperson, Gabonese Jean Ping (who replaced Kufuor in Nairobi in February 2008), also met Annan in the Kenyan capital and issued a statement in support of the mediation process. The second strategy that underpinned the mediation process involved deliberate consultation with parties not at the mediation table such as the business community, civil society, youth, women, and religious leaders, through regular meetings; and the use of the media to inform the wider public of progress.[45]

The third strategy that Annan's team deployed, was the use of a two-prong mediation strategy, which involved mediating between the two principals (Raila Odinga and Mwai Kibaki) as well as between the eight PNU and ODM negotiators appointed by the principals as the main mediation team.[46] The former were only engaged intermittently, while Annan's team worked full-time with the eight-strong main mediation team. This strategy proved very useful in salvaging the talks, when the main mediation team became deadlocked on the proposed power-sharing arrangement between Kibaki (the incumbent president) and Odinga (his closest challenger). Domestic and international pressure to end the stalemate mounted, after the negotiation teams failed to reach an agreement. Local civil society organisations, including church leaders; transport associations; the Kenyan Association of Manufacturers; the Kenyans for Peace, Truth, and Justice (KPTJ) group; the Kenya Civil Society Congress; and the Women Caucus, all pressured the party principals to end the stalemate. The Secretary–General of the Central Organisation of Trade Unions, Francis Atwoli, warned Kibaki that workers would strike if the crisis remained unresolved.[47] International pressure also mounted on the Kenyan principals to end the stalemate, with the US secretary of state, Condoleezza Rice, warning the

Kenyan politicians that "it would no longer be business as usual with the US if they continued with their hard line positions."[48] Kofi Annan noted in an interview, later in 2008, with Martin Griffiths, the Director of the Geneva-based Centre for Humanitarian Dialogue, that he relied on powerful external actors such as Washington to provide the "carrots and sticks" when the Kenyan parties were recalcitrant.[49]

With the main Kenyan mediation team at a stalemate, the Annan–led team involved Kibaki and Odinga, who agreed to a power-sharing agreement after discussions. This showed the critical importance of higher-level communications during a negotiation, with the principals able to reach agreement faster than the negotiators. Once the political crisis was resolved, the mediation team could then start deliberating on its root causes and take the mediation process forward. Thus, Annan and his team successfully guided the main negotiating team in discussing four key issues through the mediation process. These were, in order of priority: (1) the cessation of violence; (2) addressing the humanitarian crisis; (3) resolving the political crisis; and (4) addressing the root causes of the conflict. The first two agenda items were quickly resolved, and the third was addressed through the afore-mentioned power-sharing agreement. The root causes of the conflict—as identified in the discussion earlier—were to be addressed through a number of measures including: constitutional reform to devolve governance and reduce the imperial powers of the presidency; the introduction of land reform policies; security sector reform (SSR); judicial reform; and affirmative action policies.

Dilemmas and Lessons Learned from the Kenyan Mediation Process

In this section, I focus on three sets of dilemmas and lessons learned from the Kenyan mediation process. I include dilemmas because some of the issues that arise from the Kenyan case are not necessary lessons, but challenges that scholars and practitioners will continue to have to grapple with in different contexts. The three sets of lessons and dilemmas from Kenya are as follows: the first set relates to the effectiveness of a single, well-resourced African-led mediation team with status and leverage, though the extent to which the Kenyan process was "African-led" was questionable; the second to the role of the domestic movement that supported the mediation team; and the third to the perceived impartiality of individual mediators, such as Kofi Annan, who are not institutional mediators as such from the AU or the UN.

Unity of Purpose of a Single, Well-Resourced African-Led Mediation Team

The use of a single, well-resourced African-led mediation team, with support from all key external and internal actors, was critical in ensuring its success in ending the violence in the Kenyan case. The Panel of Eminent African

Personalities achieved positive outcomes (cessation of violence and political agreement) in the short term, by ensuring that national efforts were focused on a single peace process—the Kenya National Dialogue and Reconciliation Process. As noted earlier, Kofi Annan, as the leader of the team, made certain that there would be only one mediation process on the ground. According to Annan, this helped in ensuring that the negotiators from both the Party of National Unity and the Orange Democratic Movement remained focused on the process, and did not lose time and energy in "shopping" for alternatives.[50] Other regional and international actors interested in supporting the peace process were encouraged to channel their support through the Panel of Eminent African Personalities as the only framework for intervention.[51]

This was an important lesson that was subsequently reinforced by the experience in Libya, specifically the failure of the AU and other actors to mediate between former president Muammar Qaddafi and the National Transitional Council in 2011. Several uncoordinated mediators attempted to facilitate the process in Libya, including individual leaders, for example, Venezuelan president Hugo Chávez and Turkish president Recep Tayyip Erdogan; the UN-appointed special envoy for Libya, Abdel-Elah Al-Khatib; the Arab League; and the AU's High-Level Ad Hoc Committee on Libya, comprising presidents Jacob Zuma of South Africa, Amadou Toumani Touré of Mali, Denis Sassou Nguesso of Congo-Brazzaville, Mohamed Ould Abdel Aziz of Mauritania, and Yoweri Museveni of Uganda. These numerous mediators failed to achieve much, and in this respect, the use of a single mediation channel in Kenya serves as a key lesson.

Furthermore, unlike the others who tried brokering peace before them in the Kenyan case, the Annan-led team had significant financial and human resources at its disposal. Drawing on his experience at the UN, Kofi Annan marshalled experts from the world organisation on thematic issues particular to the Kenyan mediation process including: Hans Corell, Annan's former legal counsel at the UN, who helped Annan turn the politically divisive issue of governance into a technical one; and Craig Jenness, director of the Electoral Assistance Division, and Margaret Vogt, director of the Africa Division, both at the UN Department of Political Affairs (DPA). In addition, Martin Griffiths, from the Geneva-based Centre for Humanitarian Dialogue, was invited to advise Annan's team on mediation, and Gernot Erler, Minister of State in the German Federal Foreign Office, to share his experience of coalition governments. The United Nations Development programme (UNDP) and the UN Office in Nairobi (UNON) coordinated financing and other logistics to ensure the smooth running of the process.

Annan and his team also had the requisite and complementary knowledge, skills, and experience regarding both mediation and the specific situation in Kenya. Annan's prior experiences in his role as UN Secretary-General were particularly useful, especially his mediation of the conflicts in Iraq and East Timor, as well as the Israeli-Palestinian conflict.[52] His skills as a mediator enabled him to capture ripe moments for mediation, created by the top-down pressure from regional and international actors and that from the bottom-up from Kenyan citizens. The other mediators in Annan's team, Graça Machel and Benjamin Mkapa, had considerable knowledge of Kenya, though they lacked international mediating experience. Machel had led the APRM mission in Kenya in 2004–2006 to assess the level of economic, social, and political governance in the country, and Mkapa, heralding from Eastern Africa, was familiar with Kenya's politics and politicians. With their combined experience, the team was able to facilitate and formulate strategies that orchestrated ripe moments for mediation, which eventually contributed to ending the violence and finding a political solution.

In this context, some scholars have argued that the Annan-led team succeeded because they were an African-led mediation team with status and leverage.[53] Kenyan scholar Kathina Juma, for example, has praised the Kenyan process as a triumph of "African solutions to African problems". But I argue that, although the Kenyan process was African in appearance because it was African-led, Annan's overreliance on Western powers to finance and to influence the protagonists—as discussed earlier—demonstrates that it was not wholly African. The process was largely a case of neoliberal interventionism, as Kofi Annan's interviews reveal.[54] As he noted: "I would call Condi [Rice] to say, 'Look, things are not going well and I have just suspended the talks and a statement would be in order.' ... Particularly when we had all said, 'whoever is responsible for failure must pay a price'. And I got Condi, the EU and even the Swiss to fly in to back it up."[55] Hence the Kenyan mediation process cannot be termed purely as an "African solution" since other international actors were involved within a liberal peace framework, but was more so a case of hybrid interventionism, perhaps.

A Strong Domestic Movement to Support the Mediation Process

While the formal mediation process, led by the Panel of Eminent African Personalities, was ongoing, a strong domestic movement emerged to support their efforts. The domestic movement was important in holding to account the political elites who were negotiating on behalf of their political parties. This organic movement cut across sectors and included various organised groups such as the East African Business Council and the Kenya Association of Manufacturers; as well as religious and civil society organisations like the Kenyans for Peace, Truth, and Justice and the Concerned Citizens for Peace groups. The Kenya Women's Consultative Group—an ad hoc group of women activists and politicians from across ethnic divides and political parties—was instrumental in lobbying the mediation team to ensure that women's concerns were mainstreamed in the peace agreements, drawing inspiration in this regard from UN Security Council Resolution 1325 of 2000 on women, peace, and security. (On the role of women in peacebuilding, see Porter in this volume.) At the local level, community-based organisations initiated local dialogues, while encouraging Kofi Annan and his team through the media and through murals drawn on Kenyan *matatus* (the most popular form of public transport in the country).

The Kenyan media also played a critical role in creating this movement to support the mediation team. The country's leading dailies, including *The Daily Nation*, *The Standard*, *The Star*, and *The People*, partnered in an unprecedented way by publishing joint headlines urging politicians to support the Annan-led team, for the sake of the country. These rare acts of unity among the media helped in galvanising Kenyans behind the Annan-led initiative. Other public spaces such as transport murals also depicted the mood of the country at the time, urging the two principals, Mwai Kibaki and Raila Odinga, to put Kenya first by securing a peace agreement. The Kenyan parliament was also part of this domestic movement, and amended the Kenyan constitution in record time, in March 2008, to allow for an executive prime minister after the power-sharing agreement was agreed as a way out of the political crisis.

The Importance of the Perceived Impartiality of the Mediation Team

Annan and his team's perceived impartiality were critical in garnering the support of Mwai Kibaki's Party of National Unity and Raila Odinga's Orange Democratic Party, and persuading them to accept the mediation process at the start. South African politician and businessman, Cyril Ramaphosa, for example, was dismissed as a potential chief mediator by the Kibaki-led government, due to his perceived partiality based on his business links with Odinga. Annan, though, was perceived as a powerful, impartial mediator. He was a Ghanaian, without any prior personal relationships with the Kenyan protagonists, and thus, was considered to be an impartial outsider who would be fair, because he was not known to be sympathetic to any of the parties before the crisis. Annan's impartiality earned him credibility and legitimacy among local and international actors, all of whom supported the single process. Graça Machel could have been considered impartial because of the fairness she had demonstrated in her previous role in leading the Kenya review process under the APRM in 2004–2006. As a former neighbouring president, Benjamin Mkapa, was at risk of being considered partial to president Kibaki who was his counterpart between 2005 and 2007, but there were no recorded concerns raised by the opposition, probably because he was not the lead mediator.

The relative success of the Annan-led team in deescalating the violence and resolving the political crisis in the short term raises the issue of the effectiveness of individual mediators compared to that of official, or institutional, mediators.[56] Individual mediators are usually high-ranking individuals who do not have an official role or who do not represent their country in any capacity.[57] The three members of the Panel of Eminent African Personalities were not official representatives of organisations, nor were they representing their respective counties, when they mediated the Kenyan crisis. Individual mediators are, in general, thought to have greater flexibility than official state mediators, and this notion was reinforced by the Kenyan case. Although they may not themselves possess significant resources for mediation, individual mediators can command resources based on their goodwill, as the Annan-led team did in Kenya.

There are lessons here for the AU, given the limits that institutional mediators such as its highly publicised high-level ad hoc panels of presidents in Libya and Côte d'Ivoire have faced. High-level panels face bureaucratic challenges from their institutions that stifle their effectiveness; and can be further limited by the political and geo-strategic calculations that states make in the international arena, which may not always be supportive of a mediation process. In Libya, for example, the AU committee failed to mediate between the parties because the AU was perceived as partial by the National Transitional Council; and because of a lack of support for a single process from other actors such as the UN, the North Atlantic Treaty Organisation (NATO), and the Arab League.

At the same time, although the Kenyan case demonstrates the advantages of individual mediators like Kofi Annan and his team, it also points to their limitations in the context of Annan's exclusion and isolation by the PNU after the International Criminal Court intervened, in 2010, in the case. The ICC indicted six high-ranking officials suspected of orchestrating the post-election violence. Annan, in his capacity as a former chief mediator, tried to dissuade Kenyans from electing Uhuru Kenyatta and William Ruto who were among those indicted by the ICC for crimes against humanity. Their followers, however, went ahead and elected them as president and deputy president respectively in the March 2013 general election, with Annan's popularity as the "impartial voice of reason" waning as he came to be seen as a biased liberal intervener in Kenya's deeply ethnicised politics. It is difficult to say, though, as to what might have happened if Annan had been an official mediator from the AU in terms of the developments in the Kenyan cases at the ICC. (On the ICC and conflict prevention in Africa, see Nouwen in this volume.)

Conclusion

Mediation as a conflict prevention mechanism offers opportunities for conflict resolution and for transformation of the long-term causes of conflict. The Kenya National Dialogue and Reconciliation Process provides key lessons and dilemmas for peacemaking. The first lesson is that all actors interested in brokering peace should consider supporting a single mediation process instead of initiating various peace processes. The Kofi Annan-led mediation team succeeded in deescalating the violence and in securing a power-sharing agreement to end the political crisis in Kenya, because it ensured that a single well-resourced mediation team with status and leverage, both in Africa and internationally, was the only engagement channel with the two Kenyan rivals. This also meant that all other internal and external actors focused their efforts towards supporting the efforts of the Panel of Eminent African Personalities. The second lesson is the importance of a strong domestic movement to support the mediation process. The Kenyan process was successful in the short term due to the pressure from below from Kenyan business, religious, and political leaders, as well as ordinary citizens who supported the process. The third lesson, rather dilemma, relates to the extent that the perceived impartiality of the mediation team was important in the mediation process. Although the Kenyan case demonstrates the advantages of an individual mediator like Annan and his team in resolving a crisis, it also illustrates their lack of influence on political developments beyond the mediation process.

The Kenyan mediation process further exposes the limits of neoliberal peacemaking in creating any meaningful political transformation beyond the accommodation of national elites. Though supporters of "African solutions to African problems" and of the R2P norm have variously claimed success from the Kenyan case, it is neither an African success story nor a successful case of R2P in its entirety. Rather, it was a hybrid process involving an African-led initiative supported by a neoliberal interventionist logic. Political transformation in Kenya needs to address the root causes of the conflict and to involve challenging power relations that provide elites with the power to form ethnic coalitions, while reducing the agency of their voters to mere numbers in their quest for political survival. The recent collapse of the Kenyan cases at the International Criminal Court provides further evidence of the limits of liberal intervention. I would argue that, although national ethnic elites initially supported the mediation process and the resulting ICC process as a show of commitment to addressing the root causes of conflict and impunity in Kenya, their participation in the peace and resulting accountability processes was, to borrow from Carl von Clausewitz, just a continuation of politics by any other means. Eight years on from the 2008 Kenyan mediation process, in 2016, a number of radical changes had been effected, such as a new constitutional order that guarantees equality through development and resource distribution, but power relations between national ethnic elites and their voters remained untransformed.

The Kenyan case thus illustrates several dilemmas that need to be navigated in mediation for conflict prevention in Africa, so as to ensure that not only short-term resolutions are achieved, but also that there is long-term transformation of society and the root causes of conflicts are addressed. The AU should strive to document the major lessons and dilemmas arising from mediation processes on the continent—such as the Kenyan case—to strengthen its peacemaking efforts under the umbrella of the African Peace and Security Architecture.

Notes

1. "Kenya's Dubious Election", *BBC News*, 8 January 2008, http://news.bbc.co.uk/1/hi/world/africa/7175694.stm (accessed 7 April 2016).
2. "Kenya's Dubious Election".
3. Government of Kenya, *Commission of Inquiry into Post-Election Violence Report* (Nairobi: Government Printers, 2008).

4. Kofi Annan, cited in Roger Cohen, "How Kofi Annan Rescued Kenya", *New York Review of Books* 55, no. 13 (2008), p. 51.
5. Kathina Juma, "African Mediation of the Kenyan Post-2007 Election Crisis", *Journal of Contemporary African Studies* 27, no. 3 (2009), pp. 407–430; Gilbert Khadiagala, "Regionalism and Conflict Resolution: Lessons from the Kenya Crisis", *Journal of Contemporary African Studies* 27, no. 3 (2009), pp. 431–444; Makumi Mwagiru, *The Water's Edge: Mediating Violent Electoral Conflict in Kenya* (Nairobi: University of Nairobi Press, 2008).
6. Jacob Bercovitch and Allison Houston, "The Study of International Mediation: Theoretical issues and Empirical Evidence", in Jacob Bercovitch (ed.), *Resolving International Conflicts: The Theory and Practice of Mediation* (Boulder: Lynne Rienner, 1996), p. 27.
7. Jacob Bercovitch, "International Mediation and Intractable Conflict", in Guy Burgess and Heidi Burgess (eds.), *Beyond Intractability*, Conflict Information Consortium, University of Colorado, Boulder, 2004, http://www.beyondintractability.org/essay/med-intractable-conflict (accessed 25 March 2016).
8. Bercovitch, "International Mediation and Intractable Conflict"; William Zartman and Saadia Touval, "International Mediation in the Post-Cold War Era", in Chester A. Crocker, Fen Osler Hamson, and Pamela Aall (eds.), *Managing Global Chaos: Sources of and Responses to International Conflict* (Washington, DC: United States Institute of Peace Press, 1996), pp. 445–461.
9. Bercovitch and Houston, "The Study of International Mediation", p. 21.
10. Bercovitch and Houston, "The Study of International Mediation", p. 22.
11. Scott Baldauf, "After Two Months of Discord, Finally a Handshake", *The Christian Science Monitor*, 8 August 2008, http://www.csmonitor.com/World/Africa/2008/0808/p25s04-woaf.html (accessed 25 March 2016).
12. Chester A. Crocker, Fen Osler Hamson, and Pamela Aall, "Introduction", in *Herding Cats: Multiparty Mediation in a Complex World* (Washington, DC: United States Institute of Peace, 1999), pp. 6–7.
13. Crocker, Hamson, and Aall, "Introduction", p. 7.
14. Boutros Boutros-Ghali, *An Agenda for Peace: Preventive diplomacy, Peacemaking, and Peacekeeping* (New York: United Nations [UN], 1992).
15. Susan Nan, "Track One and a Half Diplomacy", in Ronald J. Fisher (ed.), *Paving the Way: Contributions of Interactive Conflict Resolution to Peacemaking* (Oxford: Lexington Books, 2005), p. 161.
16. Crocker, Hamson, and Aall, "Introduction", p. 7.
17. Mahmood Mamdani, *Saviors and Survivors: Darfur, Politics, and the War on Terror* (New York: Pantheon, 2009); Adam Branch, *Displacing Human Rights: War and Intervention in Northern Uganda* (New York: Oxford University Press, 2011).
18. Elisabeth Lindenmayer and Josie Kaye, *A Choice for Peace? The Story of Forty-One Days of Mediation in Kenya* (New York: International Peace Institute [IPI], 2009), p. 6.
19. Yohannes Tekalign Beza, "The 'African Solutions for African Problems': Challenges for the African Standby Force (ASF)", *Journal of Social Sciences and Humanities* 1, no. 4 (2015), pp. 450–457.
20. Gilbert Khadiagala, "Forty Days and Nights of Peacemaking in Kenya", *Journal of African Elections* 7, no. 2 (2008), p. 5.

21. Musambayi Katumanga, *Militarized Spaces and the Post 2007 Electoral Violence* (Nairobi: Society for International Development, 2010), p. 538. Britain is used synonymously with the United Kingdom (UK) in this volume.
22. John Oucho, *Undercurrents of Post-Election Violence in Kenya: Issues in the Long-Term Agenda* (Nairobi: Society for International Development, 2010), p. 498.
23. Issa Shivji, quoted in Susanne Mueller, "The Political Economy of Kenya's Crisis", *Journal of Eastern African Studies* 2, no. 2 (2008), p. 189.
24. Francis Stewart, "Horizontal Inequalities in Kenya and the Political Disturbances of 2008: Some Implications for Aid Policy", *Conflict, Security, and Development* 10, no. 1 (2010), p. 140.
25. Stewart, "Horizontal Inequalities in Kenya and the Political Disturbances of 2008", p. 140.
26. "Clashes, Elections and Land—Church Keeps Watch in Molo", *IRIN*, 19 July 2007, http://www.irinnews.org/report/73319/kenya-clashes-elections-and-land-church-keeps-watch-molo (accessed 7 April 2016).
27. Gérard Prunier, "Kenya: Roots of Crisis", *openDemocracy*, 7 January 2008, http://www.opendemocracy.net/article/kenya_roots_of_crisis (accessed 8 August 2011).
28. Prunier, "Kenya".
29. International Crisis Group (ICG), "Kenya in Crisis", *Africa Report* no. 137 (Brussels, 2008), p. 2.
30. ICG, "Kenya in Crisis".
31. Karuti Kanyinga, "The Legacy of the White Highlands: Land Rights, Ethnicity and the Post-2007 Election Violence in Kenya", *Journal of Contemporary African Studies* 27, no. 3 (2009), p. 328.
32. Gabrielle Lynch, "Negotiating Ethnicity: Identity Politics in Contemporary Kenya", *Review of African Political Economy* 33, no. 107 (2007), pp. 49–65.
33. Duncan Okello and Ben Sihanya, "The Constitutional Politics of Kenya's Post Elections Mediation Process", in Karuti Kanyinga and Duncan Okello (eds.), *Tensions and Reversals in Democratic Transitions: The Kenyan 2007 General Elections* (Nairobi: Society for International Development, 2010), p. 652.
34. Khadiagala, "Forty Days and Nights of Peacemaking in Kenya", p. 5.
35. Baldauf, "After Two Months of Discord, Finally a Handshake".
36. Baldauf, "After Two Months of Discord, Finally a Handshake".
37. Okello and Sihanya, "The Constitutional Politics of Kenya's Post Elections Mediation Process", p. 676.
38. Okello and Sihanya, "The Constitutional Politics of Kenya's Post Elections Mediation Process", p. 676.
39. Lindenmayer and Kaye, *A Choice for Peace?*, p. 5.
40. Meredith Preston McGhie and E. Njoki Wamai, *Beyond the Numbers: Women's Participation in the Kenya National Dialogue and Reconciliation*, Centre for Humanitarian Dialogue, Geneva, 2011.
41. Baldauf, "After Two Months of Discord, Finally a Handshake".
42. Martin Griffiths, "The Prisoner of Peace: An Interview with Kofi A. Annan", Centre for Humanitarian Dialogue, Geneva, 9 May 2008, p. 8.
43. Griffiths, "The Prisoner of Peace", p. 8.
44. Lindenmayer and Kaye, *A Choice for Peace?*, p. 5.
45. Baldauf, "After Two months of Discord, Finally a Handshake".

46. Njoki Wamai, "Mediating Kenya's Post-Election Violence: From a Peacemaking to a Constitutional Moment", in Godwin Murunga, Duncan Okello, and Anders Sjögren (eds.), *Kenya: The Struggle for a New Constitutional Order* (London: Zed Books, 2014).
47. Wamai, "Mediating Kenya's Post-Election Violence".
48. Griffiths, "The Prisoner of Peace", p. 11.
49. Griffiths, "The Prisoner of Peace", p. 11.
50. Griffiths, "The Prisoner of Peace", p. 8.
51. Griffiths, "The Prisoner of Peace", p. 8.
52. Kofi Annan and Nader Mousavizadeh, *Interventions: A Life in War and Peace* (New York: Penguin Press, 2012).
53. Juma, "African Mediation of the Kenyan Post-2007 Election Crisis", pp. 407–430; and Mwagiru, *The Water's Edge*.
54. Griffiths, "The Prisoner of Peace", p. 11.
55. Griffiths, "The Prisoner of Peace", p. 11.
56. Bercovitch, "International Mediation and Intractable Conflict".
57. Bercovitch, "International Mediation and Intractable Conflict".

CHAPTER 8

Peacemaking in Somalia: AU and UN Peace Operations

John L. Hirsch

This chapter discusses the prospects of peace in Somalia from the vantage point of 2017, over a quarter century after the fall of Siad Barre's military regime in 1991 and the concomitant efforts of the African Union Mission in Somalia (AMISOM) and the United Nations Assistance Mission in Somalia (UNSOM) as they seek to assist the Somali people and government to restore viable governance and move towards social and economic recovery (see Mahiga in this volume). It also includes an assessment of the key factors that have shaped United Nations (UN) engagement in Somalia, from peacekeeping missions in the 1990s to support for the African Union (AU) peace operation since 2007. In this respect, the Somali experience, spanning more than two decades, provides an opportunity to consider the evolving roles of both the AU and the UN in responding to civil wars and crises in Africa. The chapter's main argument is that a mix of opportunities and dual constraints—both internal and international—have slowed, but not prevented, efforts aimed at the establishment of democratic governance and the restoration of peace and security in Somalia.

The Political-Security Context

New leadership in Somalia after the 2016–2017 "electoral process", as well as at the UN and the AU since January 2017, presage re-energised efforts aimed at resolving existing problems, to bring about a secure and viable Somali state. The London Somalia Conference, held in May 2017, has led to a wide range of political, security, and humanitarian commitments by 42 international partners to assist the government in achieving this key goal. In June 2017, the UN Security Council adopted Resolution 2358, welcoming the Somali government's

J.L. Hirsch (✉)
International Peace Institute, New York, United States

T. Karbo, K. Virk (eds.), *The Palgrave Handbook of Peacebuilding in Africa*, https://doi.org/10.1007/978-3-319-62202-6_8

commitment to holding a "one person, one vote" election by 2021 and its adoption of a new National Security Architecture intended to integrate Somali security forces incrementally with UN and AU peacekeepers.[1] There are thus new opportunities for peacemaking in Somalia, with the "election" of Abdullahi Mohamed Farmajo as the country's new president and the appointments of António Guterres as the ninth UN Secretary-General and Moussa Faki Mahamat as the third AU Commission chairperson. At the same time, however, there are also concerns about commitments from the United States (US) to the UN and the AU, in light of statements by the Donald Trump administration regarding a possible reduction in American support to UN development and peacekeeping missions. Were these cuts to happen, it would have a significant adverse impact on UN and AU operations in Somalia, as well as elsewhere in Africa.

From 1991 to 1995, the international community supported three successive United Nations peace operations in Somalia, including the UN-authorised, but US-led, Unified Task Force (UNITAF) in 1992–1993. Two decades later, neither the UN nor the African Union (since 2007) have been able to overcome clan rivalries and restore a viable Somali state. Following the withdrawal of the second United Nations Operation in Somalia (UNOSOM II) in April 1995, UN-brokered conferences in Djibouti, Kenya, and Ethiopia proved unable to establish the basis for a new government. Major efforts by successive Special Representatives of the UN Secretary-General eventually led to an agreement among the major Somali faction leaders in 2007 to form a transitional federal government, which convened first in Jowhar and then in Baidoa. The transitional government later transformed into the Federal Government of Somalia (FGS), which was established in Mogadishu by September 2012 after AMISOM forces drove fighters belonging to the militant group al-Shabaab from the city.

In 2017, the Federal Government of Somalia was in partial control of the country. The Somali National Army (SNA) remained unable fully to defeat al-Shabaab militants, leaving the government unable to exert its authority and deliver services to many parts of south-central Somalia. Progress on a new political compact since 2012 has been slower than hoped for by the UN, and at the time of writing, negotiations were continuing on the terms of a new constitution. The 2016–2017 "electoral process" involved a limited electorate of parliamentarians and senior clan leaders; a fully democratic election with the participation of all Somali citizens has been deferred until 2021.[2]

Meanwhile, the African Union and the UN have encountered great difficulty in coordinating, deploying, and financing the AU Mission in Somalia (see Mahiga in this volume)—a 22,126-strong operation comprising police and troops from Uganda, Burundi, Ethiopia, Kenya, and Djibouti, among other countries.[3] Established by the AU Peace and Security Council in January 2007, AMISOM was authorised by the UN Security Council a month later to, among other things, "provide, as appropriate, protection to the Transitional Federal Institutions ... [and] [t]o contribute, as may be requested and within capabilities, to the creation of the necessary security conditions for the provision of humanitarian assistance".[4] Recent studies have underscored strategic operational shortcomings in coordinating deployments, obtaining requisite equipment, and providing sustainable financing for AMISOM peace operations.[5] Furthermore, in 2016, the African Union reviewed AMISOM's Concept of Operations and recommended, among other things, a two-year exit strategy for the mission, though there were expectations in June 2017 that the strategy would be revised.[6] The pervasive financial shortage, non-permissive operational environment, absence of "enablers" (for example, helicopters), command and control challenges, as well as the threat of possible precipitous withdrawal of Ugandan or Kenyan forces in the interim, have necessitated the need for an exit strategy. These difficulties continue to constrain progress toward the establishment of a fully viable Somali state. Both the UN and the AU retain the goal of having a new federal constitution and popular democratic elections by 2021. Towards that end, the deployment of AMISOM continues to need sustained political commitment as well as mobilisation of personnel and resources. (On the African Peace and Security Architecture [APSA], see Kuwali, and Nagar in this volume.)

The UN Security Council has played a major role, in coordination with the European Union (EU) and continental actors, in helping the AU mission to meet its wide-ranging objectives, by providing essential financial and logistical as well as political support. Ultimately, however, the measure of success or failure in Somalia is not just the outcome of the international community's military peace enforcement role, but also its commitment to sustained post-conflict peacebuilding, recovery, and reconstruction. And after more than two decades of near total state collapse and the failure of the UN interventions of the 1990s, the establishment of the Federal Government of Somalia in Mogadishu has provided a new opportunity for sustainable peace and reconstruction. This turnaround has been due, in large measure, to the evolving relationship between the UN and the AU (see Vogt in this volume), the initial success of the AMISOM deployment since 2007, and the greater commitment of the new Somali federal government elected in 2016–2017 (see Mahiga in this volume). Considerable risks and uncertainties persist, however, ranging from clan rivalries that continue to limit the writ of the federal government, to the rise of al-Shabaab, corruption, and transnational organised crime. Whether the new Somali government, with the support of the large AU and UN presence, will ultimately be able to restore a viable state remained to be seen at the time of writing in 2017.

The Peacekeeping Role of the United States

In the immediate aftermath of the Cold War, United Nations peacekeeping in Africa evolved significantly from the optimism and euphoria following UN successes in facilitating negotiated transitions in Mozambique and Namibia in 1992–1993 and South Africa's first free and fair democratic elections in 1994, to the mid-decade failures to avert genocide in Rwanda in 1994 and UNOSOM II's precipitous withdrawal from Somalia in 1995 (see also Jonah in this volume). The role of the United States in Somalia, as in the case of France in Mali and the Central African Republic (CAR) (see Adebajo, and Yates in this volume), has been pivotal. These two permanent members of the UN Security Council have been the driving force for the Council's decisions to establish, or end, peacekeeping operations in Africa. In addition, Britain remained the "penholder" for the Council's resolutions on Somalia in 2017 (the US has the responsibility on piracy).[7] The perceived interests, other international obligations, domestic politics, and financial considerations of the US and France, in particular, have determined the extent and duration of their staying power, and hence of Council engagement in Africa (see Ugarte in this volume). In the specific case of Somalia, continued US financial support will remain key to the future of AMISOM and UNSOM roles in that country.

American engagement in Somalia was initially a humanitarian response at the end of President George H.W. Bush's tenure in office. This took the form of the US-led Unified Task Force, authorised by the UN Security Council in December 1992 to create a secure environment for the delivery of humanitarian assistance in the war-torn country.[8] The "Black Hawk Down" incident of October 1993 (see Mzali in this volume), in which 18 US soldiers were killed while trying to capture Somali warlord Mohamed Farah Aideed, led to American disengagement after 1995, reflecting Washington's limited interest in Africa at a time of major engagement in the Balkans and the Middle East. In the aftermath of US withdrawal from Somalia by March 1994 (UNOSOM II withdrew one year later) and of the international failure to prevent genocide in Rwanda in April 1994, the United States backed away from UN peacekeeping altogether. Without US support, there were no new UN peacekeeping operations for four years, until the Security Council established peace operations and transitional administrations in Sierra Leone, the Democratic Republic of the Congo (DRC), Ethiopia-Eritrea, East Timor, and Kosovo in 1999.

The emergence of al-Shabaab in southern Somalia and its role in international terrorism, as well as the rise of maritime piracy in the Gulf of Aden and the threat that it poses to Western shipping interests, were key factors in giving shape to renewed engagement in Somalia by the United States, the UN, and the AU in 2007. For the US, the restoration of stability in Somalia and the defeat of al-Shabaab are linked to its broader interest in stability in the Gulf of Aden, Yemen, and the Middle East and to its wider efforts in the "war on terrorism". It remains to be seen, though, whether and how the Trump administration will continue to support these objectives.

The Peacekeeping Role of the African Union

A major new development of the past two decades has been the transformation of the Organisation of African Unity (OAU) into the African Union in 2002 and the corresponding shift in African policy from non-intervention to non-indifference in responding to African regional conflicts (see Introduction in this volume). In the words of former AU Commission chair Alpha Oumar Konaré: "We have to assume our principle of non-indifference, [defined as] the courteous and united interference [in member countries]".[9] Article 4(h), in particular, of the AU's landmark Constitutive Act of 2000 provides for the right of the Union to intervene in cases of war crimes, genocide, and crimes against humanity.[10] The shift towards non-difference, meanwhile, has been evident on the ground in AU military interventions in Burundi (2003–2004), Sudan's Darfur region (2004–2007), Somalia (since 2007), Mali (2013), and the Central African Republic (2013–2014).

At the 2005 World Summit, the UN General Assembly committed itself to a ten-year capacity-building plan for the African Union. There has since been increased engagement between the UN and the AU on peace and security issues (see Vogt in this volume), and their operational relationship has been steadily improving. Since 2007, the AU Peace and Security Council (PSC) and the UN Security Council have held annual meetings, which alternate between Addis Ababa and New York. The two secretariats have also established closer coordination. Established in 2010, the UN Office to the African Union (UNOAU) in Addis Ababa—led, since July 2013, by Under-Secretary-General Haile Menkerios, formerly Special Envoy for Sudan and South Sudan—has further been strengthened. The UN has, since 2011, significantly expanded the staffing of the office, and as of 2016 the UNOAU comprised 52 staff, 26 professional staff, and 26 support staff.

The AU Mission in Somalia comprised over 22,126 African troops and police personnel on the ground in 2016 and, since deployment, has suffered significant casualties.[11] The UN Security Council has, meanwhile, provided the essential logistical support for AMISOM troop contingents from assessed contributions at an estimated annual cost of $485 million.[12] In 2016, however, the European Union reduced its contributions for AMISOM salaries by 20 per cent, leaving AMISOM troops with lower salaries than heretofore. This was presumably attributable to broader EU engagement in peacekeeping operations in Africa, including Mali and the CAR. France reportedly pushed for the reduction, in order to utilise the available funds for the UN peacekeeping operations in the two Francophone countries (see Adebajo in this volume). Such developments, while complex and at times controversial, underscore the continued evolution of the UN–AU peace and security partnership. From the perspective of 2017, what happens in Somalia over the next four years will depend in significant measure not only on the political will of the Somali leadership to transcend clan differences, but also on how the UN–AU–EU partnership continues to evolve.

Three Phases of the UN Role in Somalia

The UN's role in Somalia falls broadly into three phases: (1) active engagement (1992–1995); (2) disengagement and abandonment (1995–2007); and (3) political-security re-engagement through the establishment of AMISOM in

2007 and the transfer of UNSOM and the UN Support Office in Somalia (UNSOS) from Nairobi to Mogadishu starting in 2012. In 2016, there were 1,512 UN staff in Somalia—including 411 international and 1,101 national personnel—and 22,126 AMISOM military and police deployed in the capital, Mogadishu, and the south.[13] Albeit operating under security restrictions, senior UN staff and agency personnel were able to travel frequently throughout the country under AMISOM protection; though the staff of diplomatic missions, including Britain and China, were largely limited to the area adjacent to the international airport (with the US Mission to Somalia constructing a new building in the same compound).

UN Peacekeeping Engagement, 1992–1995

Somalia came onto the agenda of the United Nations in January 1992, a year after Somali military dictator Siad Barre's hasty flight from Mogadishu and the onset of the civil war (see Mahiga in this volume). Three peacekeeping operations (two UN-led operations and one US-led mission) lasted barely three years. The first UN Operation in Somalia (UNOSOM I) was established in April 1992, but its 500 Pakistani peacekeepers proved unable to deploy beyond the international airport (see also Virk in this volume). The outgoing Bush administration's offer of American assistance to the UN, which took the form of the US-led Unified Task Force (deployed in December 1992), was made with the clear proviso that UNITAF would be a short-term operation until a new UN operation—UNOSOM II—could be established. Following the failed American effort to capture Somali warlord Mohamed Farah Aideed and the death of 18 US soldiers in October 1993 (in an incident popularly known as "Black Hawk Down"—see Mzali in this volume), President Bill Clinton—in response to US congressional concerns—decided to withdraw all American forces from Somalia. UNOSOM II formally closed operations in April 1995.[14]

Security Council Abandonment, 1995–2007

As then Special Representative of the UN Secretary-General for Somalia, Tanzania's Augustine Mahiga, put it in September 2011, the international community had effectively abandoned Somalia to its fate.[15] (See Mahiga in this volume.) From 1995 to 2007, the UN Security Council assumed three roles: (1) encouraging, through the adoption of hortatory resolutions and presidential statements, regional efforts by the Intergovernmental Authority on Development (IGAD), the League of Arab States, and the Organisation of Islamic Cooperation (OIC, formerly the Organisation of the Islamic Conference) to re-start the Somali peace process; (2) monitoring implementation of the arms embargo established in January 1992, including the appointment in July 2002 of a panel of experts to make recommendations on strengthening enforcement of the embargo; and (3) authorising humanitarian and other aid from the UN's specialised agencies (such as the United Nations Development Programme [UNDP], the Office for the Coordination of Humanitarian Affairs [OCHA], and the Food and Agriculture Organisation [FAO]).

Meanwhile, the UN Secretary-General and his successive special representatives at the helm of the UN Political Office for Somalia (UNPOS), then based in Nairobi, Kenya, sought unsuccessfully to develop a viable peace process with regional and Somali leaders to restore the Somali state.[16] The Security Council periodically considered authorising a new UN peace operation, but the circumstances were never deemed appropriate.

AMISOM and Security Council Re-engagement, 2007–2016

As early as March 2005, IGAD was authorised by the AU Peace and Security Council to establish a peace support mission in Somalia—the IGAD Peace Support Mission in Somalia (IGASOM)—but it never deployed given the uncertain security situation in the country at the time. By January 2007, Somalia's security situation had become precarious. Ethiopian forces—deployed in July 2006—had left the country after installing the transitional federal government in Mogadishu. Al-Shabaab was in control in most of the south. The transitional government, initially in exile, held control over only a few streets in Mogadishu and was clearly incapable of providing security for the Somali population. In January 2007, the AU Peace and Security Council authorised the deployment of AMISOM to provide protection for the recently re-instated transitional federal institutions. In so doing, the AU outlined an ambitious set of peace enforcement objectives and projected deployment of nine infantry battalions, as well as maritime and air components, for an initial six-month period.[17]

This set the stage for the active re-entry of the UN Security Council into Somalia. In January 2007 itself, only a day after the AU decision, the Security Council endorsed the deployment of AMISOM and mandated the force to, among other matters, protect the Somali transitional federal institutions and provide security for key infrastructure as well as for humanitarian assistance and repatriation of refugees.[18] The AU Peace and Security Council, cognisant of the African Union's material and financial limitations, had also "urge[d] the United Nations Security Council to consider authorizing a United Nations operation in Somalia that would take over from AMISOM at the expiration of its initial six months mandate".[19] The AU was reportedly led to believe that a UN operation was under active consideration in the Security Council.[20] This, as it turned out, was not the case.

Since 2007, the African Union has focused primarily on improving the internal security situation in Somalia. Meanwhile, the UN Security Council—especially the United States and Britain—have been concerned mainly with containing the international repercussions of the Somali crisis; preventing al-Shabaab terrorism from going beyond Somalia's borders; responding to the new challenge of maritime piracy (a clear threat to international shipping and a source of funding fuelling the conflict on land); and preventing al-Shabaab forces linking with the Islamic State of Iraq and al-Sham (ISIS) and other radical elements in Yemen. This has had the advantage of keeping the UN Security Council engaged on Somalia. At the same time, the establishment of the Federal Government of Somalia in 2012 provided a new framework within which the Somali leadership and clans could begin to shape their own destiny. Five years later, in early 2017, given the continuing limitations of the Somali National Army, AMISOM—with the support of the UN Security Council—remained primarily responsible for ensuring and expanding security for the government and the population.

AMISOM and the UN Security Council: Against All Odds

Somalia has been a major test case of the UN Security Council's evolving relationship with the African Union. The first test case came in Sudan, with the establishment of the AU–UN Hybrid Operation in Darfur (UNAMID) in July 2007, which has had mixed results. The dual-hat setup, with an AU military commander and a UN political representative, has proven difficult to implement (see Gambari in this volume). The AU Constitutive Act of 2000, committing the African Union to act in cases of war crimes, crimes against humanity, and genocide, created a new situation for the Security Council. Whereas UN peacekeeping had traditionally been predicated on the idea that there is already a peace to keep, the AU was clearly prepared to deploy in order to create the conditions necessary for peacekeeping, even where a peace agreement was not yet at hand. The Security Council has consequently been compelled to consider and authorise new strategies for UN peacekeeping in Africa (see Ugarte in this volume).

AMISOM was established in difficult political and economic circumstances, immediately on the heels—as mentioned earlier—of Ethiopia's defeat of Union of Islamic Courts (UIC) forces and the establishment of the transitional federal government in Mogadishu. At the time, most outside observers believed that AMISOM had little prospect of achieving its mandate, and some even questioned its moral and political legitimacy.[21] Even though approved by the AU Peace and Security Council and endorsed by the UN Security Council,[22] AMISOM was seen by many Somalis as "a tool of Western interests",[23] given the immediately prior US-supported Ethiopian campaign against the UIC. The US continued to view al-Shabaab as a regional rather than a Somalia-specific threat. Moreover, AMISOM was perceived as supporting "a weak, divided and (in the view of many Somalis) illegitimate transitional government" that could barely control a few streets around Villa Somalia (the official presidential residence).[24] For many Somalis, the transitional federal government was a dysfunctional, warlord-dominated government beholden to Ethiopia rather than committed to the best interests of the Somali people.[25]

At the operational level, the AU took a big risk in establishing AMISOM. It lacked sufficient troop commitments as well as the financial resources and logistics to deploy the initial 8,000-strong authorised force. Despite deep scepticism by various analysts, there was no alternative—as AU member states soon found out. Over the next two years, the UN Security Council periodically considered various options to replace AMISOM. In December 2008, the US under President George W. Bush wanted the Security Council to approve a new UN peacekeeping mission. Only the US and the Netherlands, however, were prepared to commit funds, and no country was prepared to send troops. This perhaps reflected the scepticism of Council members regarding the prospects of an international force to stabilise Somalia. When the Barack Obama administration came into office in January 2009, the idea of a UN peacekeeping force was quietly dropped.

Following its initial deployment, to the surprise of many observers, AMISOM, comprising forces mainly from Uganda and Burundi, significantly improved security in parts of southern Somalia. Additional forces have come subsequently from Ethiopia and Kenya. After two years of intense fighting, al-Shabaab was "forced out" of Mogadishu and subsequently the southern port city of Kismayo by September 2012. However, AMISOM forces have been unable to completely liberate the south from al-Shabaab and have been unable to consolidate their control. The Somali National Army has lacked the capacity to take over from AMISOM troops, preventing normalisation and post-conflict development from taking place. Restructuring the Somali army is to be a major component of the transformation envisaged under the National Security Architecture as agreed at the May 2017 London Somalia Conference.

AMISOM has continued to provide key security functions for the Somali government, with the re-training of the Somali army and police proceeding slowly. This has come at a great price in manpower. AMISOM forces have taken heavy troop losses; though AMISOM does not provide official casualty counts, estimates range from 2,000 to 3,000 troops—numbers that would be unacceptable for a UN peacekeeping operation.[26]

Maintaining AMISOM has involved multiple challenges for the African Union and the UN Security Council, requiring a new degree of consultation and cooperation. A key issue has been financing for logistics, equipment, salaries, and other operational requirements. The AU and the UN recognised early on that the international community would need to provide the financial resources and support to sustain AMISOM operations. Since AMISOM's inception, the UN Security Council has—as mentioned earlier—provided logistical support, through assessed contributions, at an estimated annual cost of $485 million.[27] In April 2008, on the recommendation of then UN Secretary-General, Ban Ki-moon, the Security Council established a joint AU–UN high-level panel, named after its chair, former Italian prime minister Romano Prodi, to consider options for supporting AU peace operations. The Council, however, has been reluctant to accept the panel's main recommendation—an open-ended commitment to provide a reliable and consistent funding stream from assessed contributions for AU peace operations.[28] The five permanent members (P-5) of the Security Council—the US, Britain, France, China, and Russia—insist on approving the concept of operations and maintaining effective oversight on an annual basis. (See Ugarte in this volume.)

Ten years on from their inception, in 2017, AMISOM operations face considerable difficulties. An in-depth examination of AMISOM, contained in a May 2016 report by the New York-based International Peace Institute (IPI), highlighted a number of major challenges: the absence of a shared stabilisation strategy between the Somali federal government and AMISOM; the separation of political and security dimensions in force planning; the fragmented system of AMISOM command and control; the inability to degrade al-Shabaab's fighting capabilities, resulting in no perceptible increase in security and no significant peace dividends for the civilian population in the south; the lack of sufficient logistical support including helicopters and other equipment; and the inability of the Somali army to play either a leading or supporting security role.[29] For the first six months of 2016, AMISOM had no force commander. While formally operating as a unified command, in reality the Kenyan, Ethiopian, Ugandan, Djiboutian, and Burundian contingents operated separately in their areas of operations with little coordination. The AU, at its Military Operational Coordination Committee (MOCC) meeting in May 2016, finally appointed General Osman Soubagleh, former chief of staff at AMISOM force headquarters, as the new force commander.

Challenges for the AU and UN in Somalia

As of mid-2017, Somalia continued to face three major challenges: (1) reaching a new domestic consensus on whether the structure of the Somali state would be federal or centralised; (2) determining whether the future international security role would comprise an AU or UN peacekeeping operation; and (3) developing a new foundation for sustainable peace, "good governance", and development within the realities of the Somali clan system (see Richmond in this volume).

A Centralised or Federal State?

The new Somali federal government, selected through the 2016–2017 limited "electoral process", is headed by Abdullahi Mohamed Farmajo, who returned to Somalia in mid-2016 after having worked for many years as a US state government official in Buffalo, New York.[30] At the time of writing, in mid-2017, work had begun on a new federal constitution, but much remained to be done both at the political and administrative levels. The regions in the south and north had yet to be formally delineated; nor had regional representatives to a constitutional conference been chosen. Long-standing tensions between the Marehan clans, who have controlled Somali politics for decades, and other clan groups in the north and the south, continued to persist. This is even as

Somaliland stayed apart as an independent state, and the status of Puntland in the north and Hiram and Middle "Shabelle" in the south remain undecided.

The key to Somalia's future is whether it will remain a weak centralised state or become a federal state based on a reasonable sharing of power and resources within the clan system. The AU, IGAD, and the UN have sought to promote the idea of a federal state through extensive consultations with local leaders. Though the UN and the AU cannot make these decisions, they need to continue to encourage thoughtful and responsible consultations among the major actors in the country.

Security: A Possible Transition

After ten years of AMISOM operations, the issue of a new UN peacekeeping force to replace AMISOM has resurfaced. Uganda and Kenya have made clear their intention to withdraw from the AU mission, rather than face the prospect of an indefinite deployment in Somalia in order to provide security—at considerable expense—without any noticeable improvement in the Somali army's capacity to take over the responsibility. There is considerable reluctance, however, in the UN Security Council to establish a new "blue-helmet" peacekeeping operation to replace AMISOM, given the previous failures of UN peacekeeping in Somalia, the world organisation's many other peacekeeping commitments, uncertainty about US funding, and doubts about overcoming the internal structural constraints of the Somali political system. To avert a precipitate withdrawal of Ugandan and Kenyan forces, in June 2016 the AU conducted a review of its Concept of Operations, in consultation with its troop-contributing countries and international partners, and recommended a two-year exit strategy. In April 2017, the United Nations and the African Union entered into a Joint UN-AU Framework for Enhanced Partnership in Peace and Security.[31] While acknowledging the achievement of the AU-UN benchmarks on the steps needed for an effective transition to a UN peacekeeping force and the commitment to work more closely together, the UN Security Council had, at the time of writing, requested the Secretary-General to keep the future of AMISOM under continuous review, in consultation with the AU. Whether AMISOM continues, or is replaced by a UN peacekeeping or hybrid AU-UN force, it is widely recognised that an international peacekeeping presence in Somalia will be needed for many years to come.

A New Development Strategy for Somalia

International assistance to Somalia has been largely humanitarian in the form of support for refugees and displaced persons. There is a resilient economy in Mogadishu and parts of the south. However, there also are large areas in the south where al-Shabaab's presence has prevented or disrupted development efforts. A major challenge for the Somali federal government is to establish the security conditions that would allow development projects in areas from which

AMISOM has dislodged al-Shabaab. Somalis will need to see new investments in infrastructure and economic opportunities if confidence in the federal government is to be established. The United States and the EU will need to sustain their engagement and to continue to provide financial support for strengthening the Somali security sector and enabling the government to direct resources to smaller cities and rural communities beyond Mogadishu.

Conclusion: The African Union at a Crossroads

The AMISOM role in Somalia, as well as ongoing AU and UN consultations on the situation, underscore the importance of sustained international commitment to improving the prospects of peace in the country. At the political level, the roles of the US, Britain (the "penholder" on Somalia), and France in the UN Security Council remain key, as does the support, where possible, of the other permanent members—Russia and China—with American and French interests, in particular, having tended to determine the level and duration of Security Council commitment. Tensions over the respective roles of the UN and the AU in political and military decision-making may well persist. There remains a need for a more flexible partnership, a reliable logistical and funding stream for AMISOM, a reduction of bureaucratic delays in military decision-making, and guaranteed delivery of essential equipment to the peacekeepers on a timely basis.

The major interest of the US in Somalia pertains to its broader concern of preventing terrorist attacks against its own territory and nationals. The same applies to British and French interests on the continent. In this respect, it is noteworthy that the UN Security Council only re-engaged in Somalia with the rise of al-Shabaab and the emergence of maritime piracy. The AU Peace and Security Council, as well as African representatives on the UN Security Council, have an important role to play in the decisions affecting both Somalia and its neighbours. A key issue before the next federal election in 2021 will be ensuring that the dialogue on Somalia also meets African regional and national interests. Furthermore, greater attention to the protection of civilians in the peacekeeping mandate of AMISOM underscores growing awareness of the need to reduce civilian casualties when dealing with difficult insurgencies.

Peacekeeping and the Security of UN and AU Missions

Another important issue is the security of international staff. Al-Shabaab attacks on UN staff in Mogadishu in June 2013, and periodic attacks since then on civilians in hotels or restaurants frequented by international staff (most recently in June 2017) have repeatedly highlighted the vulnerability of the entire UN presence in Somalia. Most international staff remained confined, at the time of writing in mid-2017, to a large compound adjacent to the international airport. Both AMISOM and the UN face the challenge of maintaining security for their staff, as well as for the local population in Mogadishu, while asserting control in southern Somalia where al-Shabaab elements remain active. Al-Shabaab successfully launched mortar attacks in May and June 2016 on Mogadishu's international airport, as well as on other AMISOM bases, causing slight injury and damage to property. The accuracy and success of these attacks suggest that it is only a matter of time until a major attack happens. A further unaddressed and politically sensitive issue is the question of a possible dialogue with the al-Shabaab leadership. It is hard to imagine a strictly military outcome in Somalia; as with other global insurgencies, such as against the Taliban in Afghanistan, it may be necessary to open up a direct or indirect dialogue to explore al-Shabaab's goals and objectives.

A Final Word

It is neither realistic nor feasible to predict future outcomes. Somalia remains fragile and vulnerable, and government institutions are weak, while AMISOM forces continue to face a resilient al-Shabaab insurgency in the south of the country. While there is a new level of international engagement, much more needs to be done to strengthen the partnership between the AU and the UN to improve the prospects of a sustainable peace in Somalia. (See Vogt in this volume.) Political tensions over the appropriate balance of responsibility between the AU and the UN need to be openly addressed. As a new generation of Somalis look ahead to their future, they will need encouragement that a better more peaceful future is possible. Ultimately, however, only the Somalis can determine their own future.

Notes

1. United Nations (UN) Security Council Resolution 2358, UN Doc. S/RES/2358, 21 June 2017.
2. For further background information, *see* John L Hirsch and Robert Oakley, *Somalia and Operation Restore Hope: Reflections on Peacekeeping and Peacemaking* (Washington, DC: United States Institute of Peace, 1995); John L Hirsch, "Somalia", in Sebastian von Einsiedel, David M. Malone, and Bruno Stagno Ugarte (eds.), *The UN Security Council in the 21st Century* (Boulder, CO: Lynne Rienner, 2016), pp. 595–614.
3. *See* African Union Mission in Somalia (AMISOM), http://amisom-au.org (accessed 24 June 2017).
4. UN Security Council Resolution 1744, UN Doc. S/RES/1744, 20 February 2007, para. 4.
5. *See, for example*, Walter Lotze and Paul Williams, *The Surge to Stabilize: Lessons for the UN from the AU's Experience in Somalia* (New York: International Peace Institute [IPI], May 2016).
6. As of June 2017, those working on Somalia at the UN expected that AMISOM's Concept of Operations would be revised again that year. At the time of writing, a joint African Union (AU)–UN review of the mission was expected to report to the UN Security Council by July 2017 and include a focus on a conditions-based

exit strategy for AMISOM, with a gradual handover of responsibility of security to Somali forces. The timelines of withdrawal were as well expected to shift somewhat, and it looked likely that AMISOM would stay deployed beyond 2018, with projections of a drawdown of the main body of the force by 2022, but with small reaction capability still in place.

7. Security Council Report, "2017 Chairs of Subsidiary Bodies and Penholders", 2 February 2017, http://www.securitycouncilreport.org/un-security-council-working-methods/pen-holders-and-chairs.php (accessed 24 June 2017). Britain is used synonymously with the United Kingdom (UK) in this volume.
8. UN Security Council Resolution 794, UN Doc. S/RES/794, 3 December 1992.
9. Baffour Ankomah, "African Union: From Non-Interference to Non-Indifference", *New African* no. 460 (March 2007), https://www.questia.com/magazine/1G1-160922404/african-union-from-non-interference-to-non-indifference (accessed 22 June 2016).
10. AU, *Constitutive Act of the African Union*, adopted by the 36th Ordinary Session of the Assembly of Heads of State and Government, 11 July 2000, Lomé, Togo.
11. No official statistics are available. In 2013, UN Under-Secretary-General Jan Eliasson indicated that up to 3,000 AMISOM troops had been killed in combat, far higher than would be acceptable to any UN Peacekeeping operation. *See* "Press Conference by Deputy Secretary-General Jan Eliasson at United Nations Headquarters", UN Doc. DSG/SM/668, 9 May 2013.
12. Matt Freear and Cedric de Coning, "Lessons from the African Union Mission for Somalia (AMISOM) for Peace Operations in Mali", *Stability: International Journal of Security and Development* 2, no. 2 (2013), pp. 1–11.
13. Pursuant to UN Security Council Resolution 2245, adopted 9 November 2015, the United Nations Support Office for the African Union Mission in Somalia (UNSOA) was renamed the United Nations Support Office in Somalia (UNSOS).
14. For a detailed account of the events in Somalia from 1992 to 1995, *see* Hirsch and Oakley, *Somalia and Operation Restore Hope*, pp. 3–16.
15. "Stabilizing Somalia: Featuring Augustine Mahiga", video, IPI Special Representatives of the Secretary-General Series Policy Forum, New York, 20 September 2011, https://vimeo.com/29850921 (accessed 12 June 2016).
16. Special Representatives of the UN Secretary-General for Somalia since 1995: David Stephen (Britain), 1997–2002; Winston Tubman (Liberia), 2002–2005; Francis Lonsey Fall (Senegal), 2005–2007; Ahmedou Ould Abdullah (Mauritania), 2007–2010; Augustine Mahiga (Tanzania), 2010–2013; Nicholas Kay (Britain), 2013–2015; and Michael Keating (Britain), appointed November 2015.
17. AU Peace and Security Council, *Communiqué of the 69th Meeting of the Peace and Security Council*, AU Doc. PSC/PR/COMM (LXIX), 19 January 2007.
18. UN Security Council Resolution 1744.
19. AU Peace and Security Council, *Communiqué of the 69th Meeting of the Peace and Security Council.*
20. Confidential discussion.

21. For a detailed account of the AMISOM situation in 2007, *see* Paul Williams, "Into the Mogadishu Maelstrom: The African Union Mission in Somalia", *International Peacekeeping* 16, no. 14 (October 2009), pp. 514–530.
22. UN Security Council Resolution 1744.
23. Paul D. Williams, "AMISOM's Five Challenges", commentary (Washington, DC: Center for Strategic and International Studies, 15 November 2009), https://www.csis.org/analysis/amisom's-five-challenges (accessed 10 June 2016).
24. Williams, "AMISOM's Five Challenges".
25. Ken Menkhaus, "Somalia: A Country in Peril, a Policy Nightmare", strategy paper (Washington, DC: Enough Project, September 2008), pp. 7, 10.
26. UN, "Press Conference by Deputy Secretary-General Jan Eliasson at United Nations Headquarters".
27. The United States (US) is the leading provider of financing, airlift, and pre-deployment training for AMISOM. Assessed contributions are delivered to the mission through the UN Support Office in Somalia. In addition, the European Union (EU), through its Peace Support Fund, voluntarily contributes an estimated $200 million a year for salaries and other requirements. *See* Adam C. Smith, "United States of America", in Alex J. Bellamy and Paul Williams (eds.), *Providing Peacekeepers: The Politics, Challenges, and Future of United Nations Peacekeeping Contributions* (Oxford: Oxford University Press, 2013), http://www.oxfordscholarship.com/view/10.1093/acprof:oso/9780199672820.001.0001/acprof-9780199672820-chapter-4 (accessed 13 June 2016).
28. UN General Assembly and Security Council, *Report of the African Union–United Nations Panel on Modalities for Support to African Union Peacekeeping Operations*, UN Doc. A/63/666-S/2008/813, 31 December 2008.
29. *See* Lotze and Williams, *The Surge to Stabilize*.
30. Abdullahi Mohamed Farmajo was State Commissioner of Education in Buffalo, New York, from 2002 to 2010, before his return to Somalia.
31. Joint United Nations-African Union Framework for Enhanced Partnership in Peace and Security, 19 April 2017, https://unoau.unmissions.org/sites/default/files/signed_joint_framework.pdf (accessed 24 June 2017).

PART III

The Practice of Peacekeeping

CHAPTER 9

A Life in Peacekeeping

James O.C. Jonah

In present-day diplomatic, political, and media usage, the term *peacekeeping* has come to mean many different things.[1] To some, it represents a splendid tool in the diplomatic and security toolbox of the international community to tackle a whole array of political difficulties. Others view it as a modern cottage industry to keep military personnel busy, or the means by which powerful states and entities employ Machiavellian astuteness to control unstable situations.

There was a time, however, when the term *peacekeeping* was used with greater precision. It emerged in the United Nations (UN) with the aim of resolving a deficiency in the security architecture mapped out in the UN Charter of 1945. This envisaged that all military actions by the world organisation would be authorised by its Security Council; and that peacekeeping operations would be conducted with the assistance of a Military Staff Committee, as provided for in Chapter VII of the Charter.[2] Furthermore, this instrument of force was to be used only when the UN Security Council had determined that there was a threat to the peace, breach of the peace, or act of aggression.

But the Cold War (1945–1990), which emerged at the end of the Second World War, made it extremely difficult for the UN Security Council to operate as envisaged by its founders.[3] It had been assumed, during the planning for the world organisation at Dumbarton Oaks between August and October 1944, that the five permanent members of the Security Council (P-5) would work together harmoniously in maintaining international peace and security.[4] This

This chapter draws partly on my memoirs: James O.C. Jonah, *What Price the Survival of the United Nations? Memoirs of a Veteran International Civil Servant* (Ibadan: Evans Brothers [Nigeria Publishers] Limited, 2006).

J.O.C. Jonah (✉)
Ralph Bunche Institute for International Studies, City University of New York Graduate Centre, New York, United States

T. Karbo, K. Virk (eds.), *The Palgrave Handbook of Peacebuilding in Africa*, https://doi.org/10.1007/978-3-319-62202-6_9

assumption was based on the successful cooperation among the five Allied Powers—the United States (US), the Soviet Union, Britain,[5] France, and China—during the Second World War. As it turned out, not only were there frequent deadlocks in the Council, but also the P-5 could not even agree on the proper modalities for the functioning of the Military Staff Committee. (See Ugarte in this volume.)

Emergence of the Notion of Peacekeeping

In July 1956, Egyptian President Gamal Abdel Nasser nationalised the Anglo-French Suez Canal Company, precipitating a serious crisis in the Middle East. Three months on, in October 1956, Israel launched an armed attack against Egypt. This was shortly followed by a joint British and French intervention and occupation of the Egyptian Canal Zone, ostensibly to separate the Egyptian and Israeli armed forces.[6] The UN Security Council was unable to take any action, with Britain and France vetoing separate proposals by the United States and the Soviet Union calling for a ceasefire and withdrawal of all armed forces from the Canal Zone. The US also rejected a proposal by Moscow for a joint American and Soviet peace force. With the Security Council thus paralysed, imaginative measures were taken to tackle the situation. Under the so-called Uniting for Peace Resolution of 1950,[7] the UN General Assembly convened, and in November 1956, authorised the establishment of the United Nations Emergency Force (UNEF).[8] This contravened the UN Charter, which assigns the conduct of military operations to the Military Staff Committee. However, with the committee unable to meet due to the politics of the Cold War, the General Assembly skilfully interpreted Article 98 of the UN Charter on the roles and responsibilities of the Secretariat and requested the Secretary-General—then Sweden's Dag Hammarskjöld—to manage the day-to-day operations of the force.[9]

Fortunately, prior to that date, the UN had carried out an experiment when the Security Council established two observer missions of unarmed military officers in the Middle East and India/Pakistan in May 1948 and January 1949 respectively.[10] These observer missions—the UN Truce Supervision Organisation (UNTSO) and the UN Military Observer Group in India and Pakistan (UNMOGIP)—became models for the establishment of the first emergency force in 1956—UNEF I. When the Congo crisis later broke out in 1960, some elements of UNTSO also helped in establishing the force on the ground that became known as the UN Operation in the Congo (ONUC).[11]

Under the ground rules for these two types of peacekeeping machinery—unarmed observer forces, and military operations with lightly armed contingents—it was clearly understood that both types were and would be consent-type operations, meaning that they could only operate fully with the consent of the host country or parties involved. It was necessary to differentiate these operations from the enforcement measures outlined under Chapter VII of the UN Charter, which allows the Security Council to authorise the use of force without seeking the consent of the parties. In any event, peacekeeping could only be productive if the parties involved cooperated.

The prospects of having the UN Security Council authorise the use of force in those bleak years of acute Cold War confrontations between East and West were not bright. Of course, the police action in Korea, which was authorised in June/July 1950 by the Security Council under the command of the United States,[12] was made possible only because the Soviet Union was boycotting the Council at the time on the grounds that Peking (now Beijing) was not properly represented in the body following the communist victory in China in 1949.

My own interest in making the study of peacekeeping a preoccupation arose before I joined the UN Secretariat in October 1963. While I was a research assistant at the Center for International Studies at the Massachusetts Institute of Technology (MIT) in the United States, in 1961, I was a member of the Harvard-MIT consultations on arms control and disarmament. Those were exciting and interesting times, with much discussion of the possibility of peaceful change in a disarmed world. Under the Dwight Eisenhower administration (1953–1961), strengthening of peacekeeping capabilities was contemplated. Peacekeeping machinery and progress on disarmament were first enunciated by US Secretary of State Christian Herter in an address delivered to the National Press Club in February 1960, in which he stressed that peacekeeping could provide a stable military environment in a disarmed world.[13] The John Kennedy administration (1961–1963) later proposed general and complete disarmament in the context of a viable peacekeeping structure. In a speech to the UN General Assembly in September 1961, President Kennedy said, among other things: "To destroy arms … is not enough. We must create even as we destroy—creating world-wide law and law enforcement as we outlaw world-wide war and weapons".[14]

Scholars were hopeful of a new world order. A symbol of the active academic contribution to a disarmed and peaceful world was a book published in 1958 and co-authored by Louis B. Sohn and Granville Clark, both of Harvard Law School. The book, *World Peace Through World Law*,[15] proposed changes in the UN Charter to provide for a peacekeeping machinery. In those days, there were doubts as to whether peacekeeping could be justified under the plain language of the Charter. In my view, a controversial part of the book was the recommendation to introduce weighted voting in the UN General Assembly. This idea—shared by others in the US—was inimical to the principle of sovereign equality as enshrined in Article 2(1) of the UN Charter, and to my mind, unacceptable when considering the fact that extraordinary power, in the form of permanent membership and the right to veto, was already vested in five members of the Security Council. The book further called for a standing army for the world organisation. It was in this atmosphere that I set my mind to focusing on improving the peacekeeping capability of the United Nations.

The Cuban missile crisis of October 1962 only deepened the world's awareness of the enormous danger of a nuclear war. It was a sobering experience for the two superpowers. The deadlock in the Congo over how to end the secession of Katanga between July 1960 and February 1963, meanwhile, focused our minds regarding the operational difficulties of UN peacekeeping. The UN Emergency Force in the Sinai was operating smoothly, without major problems, because it was an interpositional force deployed between two organised armies under effective national command and control. But ONUC was a much more complex operation, with the UN essentially in control of a huge African country in the midst of varied civil conflicts and the secession of Katanga—the richest province in the Congo.[16]

Negative Impact of the Congo Crisis on Peacekeeping

Amidst the gathering momentum of rapid decolonisation in Africa in the 1950s, Belgium was reluctant to grant independence to the Congo. When it finally conceded to the demands for Congolese independence, contrary to Belgian expectations, Patrice Lumumba emerged as the first elected prime minister of Congo-Léopoldville—today's Democratic Republic of the Congo (DRC)—in June 1960. At the independence ceremony, attended by Belgium's King Baudouin, Lumumba lashed out at decades of Belgian economic exploitation and maladministration. Fearful of the direction that the newly independent country might take, the Belgians colluded with Congolese leader, Moise Tshombe, to have the mineral-rich province of Katanga secede and declare its independence. The UN became involved when Belgian troops intervened purportedly to quell widespread internal disorder in the country, but really to support the secession and gain control of the resources of Katanga.[17]

I arrived at the UN when the functioning of peacekeeping had damaged the reputation of the world organisation and its Secretary-General, Dag Hammarskjöld, who eventually lost his life during a peace mission to the Congo in September 1961. The Congo crisis called into question the efficacy of the entire enterprise of peacekeeping. It provoked a virulent attack against the UN Secretary-General by Soviet Premier Nikita Khrushchev, who accused Hammarskjöld of being complicit in the assassination of Congolese leader Patrice Lumumba. The sentiment was shared by the Afro-Asian members of the world organisation. Lumumba's assassination further disillusioned several African states about the usefulness of peacekeeping and the UN's ability to protect their hard-won sovereignty through the colonial struggle, as these countries came to believe that the superpowers were using it as a ploy to extend their hegemony, particularly in Africa. The UN Operation in the Congo also raised fundamental questions about the authorisation, financing, and day-to-day conduct of the peacekeeping mission.

But fortunately, the Congo crisis also stimulated pan-Africanists, such as Ghana's Kwame Nkrumah, Guinea's Sékou Touré, Tanzania's Julius Nyerere, and Ethiopian Emperor Haile Selassie, to redouble their efforts to create Africa's own continental organisation in May 1963—the Organisation of African Unity (OAU),[18] which was replaced by the African Union (AU) in July 2002. While African states had in mind to solve African problems by African means, they were not ready to abandon the global organisation, because the UN's principle of the sovereign equality of states safeguarded their independence. (See also Mazrui in this volume.) That is why they did not endorse Premier Khrushchev's proposal in 1960 that a troika of representatives—capitalist, socialist, and neutral—should jointly run the United Nations, since this could have weakened the office of the UN Secretary-General and thereby made the world organisation less effective.[19]

However, by October 1963, when I joined the UN Secretariat, there was considerable evidence that a fascinating chapter in the imaginative experiment of international peacekeeping was coming to a close. The Soviet Union, having failed in its efforts to radically restructure the UN through the replacement of the office of the Secretary-General with a troika and frustrated over his role in the Congo, became determined to end all peacekeeping operations by the UN, including ONUC. This, of course, did not preclude the Soviets' own policy of providing support and assistance to countries, including the Congo, to end colonialism or Western neo-colonialism in Africa. In this regard, it should also be kept in mind that the strategic policy of the US and other Western powers in the Congo crisis was to prevent the Soviet Union from gaining what they perceived as a foothold in the heart of Africa.[20]

Troublesome Questions Raised About Peacekeeping

ONUC raised some fundamental questions that darkened the prospects for a new peacekeeping role for the UN. First, who should authorise peacekeeping operations? Second, which organ of the organisation should finance such operations? And third, who should manage the day-to-day operational activities?

East and West were bitterly divided on these issues. The Western powers argued that although the UN Security Council had the primary responsibility for security matters of the organisation, this was not an exclusive responsibility. The UN General Assembly, as it did with respect to establishment of the first peacekeeping operation in the Sinai, could take action if the Security Council failed to act. The Soviet Union held the firm position that only the Council, where it had the right of veto, should authorise peacekeeping operations.

The Western and Eastern powers also diverged on which organ should apportion the expenses for peacekeeping. The West, along with the majority of the General Assembly, insisted that the costs of the UN Operation in Congo, for example, were organisational expenses under Article 17(2) of the world body's 1945 Charter, and as such, should be covered through assessed contributions made by the members of the General Assembly. For their part, the Soviet Union and its Eastern European allies argued that the financing of peacekeeping operations such as UNEF and ONUC should be based on Articles 43 and 48 of the Charter. In other words, decisions on expenditures for the maintenance of international peace and security—in essence, peacekeeping—were, in their view, the exclusive responsibility of the UN Security Council.

With respect to the day-to-day management of peacekeeping, the Soviet Union rejected any role for the UN Secretary-General and insisted on an exclusive role for the Military Staff Committee—an organ of the Security Council. The Western powers pointed to the obvious fact that the Military Staff Committee, although it met from time to time, was not a functioning mechanism. Furthermore, they argued that a committee could not conceivably undertake the day-to-day management of peacekeeping. They observed that under Article 98 of the Charter, the Council could delegate such function to the Secretary-General.

With no agreement in sight, the UN was faced with a serious financial crisis, with arrears in contributions to both UNEF and ONUC posing a threat to the continuation of these operations. Both the Soviet Union and its allies, as well as France, refused to pay for the operations. The Soviet Union maintained that if the operations were not authorised by the Security Council, or if the Secretary-General did not act according to the Charter, it would not pay. The position of the French was different. Relying on consent-type peacekeeping, they asserted that because contribution was voluntary, they could decide which operations to pay for.[21]

Fate of the 19th Session of the General Assembly and Its Promise

As the financial crisis deepened, because of the refusal by some member states to pay, the matter was referred in December 1961 by the UN General Assembly to the International Court of Justice (ICJ) for its advisory opinion. In July 1962, the Court advised that member states were obliged to pay for all expenses of the UN.[22] But because this was an advisory opinion, it was not binding on member states. That did not prevent the US from deciding to seek the penalty, under Article 19 of the UN Charter, according to which a member state that is in financial arrears for more than two years can lose its vote in the General Assembly. The African states were in a dilemma; they supported the principle that was being espoused by the US, but feared the consequence of the loss of the Soviet vote in the General Assembly. At that time, the Soviet Union and its allies were stout supporters of the agenda of the African Group, which was to end colonialism, end apartheid, and promote economic development.

Under these circumstances, at the start of its 19th session in 1964, the General Assembly, under the presidency of an African representative, Ghana's Alex Quaison-Sackey, decided by consensus to suspend voting on substantive matters during the session, to avoid a debacle, more specifically the application of a penalty against any member state under Article 19 of the Charter. The Assembly proceeded to conduct its work on that basis until Albania, which as a matter of policy consistently opposed both East and West, called for a vote in a dramatic fashion at a meeting. However, in a timely intervention, Saudi Arabia challenged the Albanian attempt to overturn the Assembly's consensus. In February 1965, the 19th session of the General Assembly established the Special Committee on

Peacekeeping Operations to examine all aspects of peacekeeping,[23] and called on all members to make voluntary contributions to ease the financial burden of the world organisation. Although the committee worked tirelessly, few governments made any meaningful voluntary financial contributions.

It was my good fortune to be assigned to work with the committee and participate fully in all the discussions. The first report of the committee was most useful.[24] It not only dealt with peacekeeping operations but also proposed that peacekeeping must be accompanied by *peacemaking*—the first time the latter concept had ever been mentioned. Hitherto, the deployment of a peacekeeping operation was expected to provide the space for active negotiations to resolve the dispute that had given rise to the establishment of the operation. But reality turned out to be quite different, as the case of UNMOGIP illustrates.[25]

One practical advance of the Peacekeeping Committee, after many fruitless sessions, was its decision to establish a working group, under a mandate received from the General Assembly in December 1967,[26] to prepare a model for peacekeeping operations. I became the secretary of that working group, and in May 1968, we produced a first draft model on UN military observer missions established or authorised by the Security Council and the principles that should guide such missions. In reality, the working group became a cover for serious and significant bilateral negotiations between US Ambassador Maxwell Finger and Soviet Deputy Ambassador Lev Mendelovich. I was kept fully informed about their discussions and kept record of their progress. These records became critical, and useful in future planning. There was no expectation of a new UN peacekeeping role due to the continuing divergence of positions.

Until the establishment of the United Nations Peacekeeping Force in Cyprus (UNFICYP) in March 1964,[27] it appeared that UN peacekeeping was dying. The Soviet Union had agreed to the Cyprus operation only because it was opposed to a possible North Atlantic Treaty Organisation (NATO) force to keep peace in Cyprus. In agreeing to the operation, it introduced the now common practice of placing limits on the duration of the mandate period, with the possibility of extension. That approach became necessary for the Soviet Union because it was helpless to stop open-ended mandates such as in the Congo when it became disillusioned by the conduct of the operation. With the limited mandate, it could use its veto to stop any peacekeeping operation it was unhappy with.[28] The Soviet Union also made this a condition for its approval of the Cyprus mission when insisting that the mission should be financed by voluntary contributions—an unstable way to finance peacekeeping operations.

Re-Birth of Peacekeeping with Guidelines

In July 1973, the United States vetoed a draft resolution, tabled by nonaligned states, in the UN Security Council, which would have expressed the Council's regret at the lack of progress in peace initiatives concerning the Middle East under the auspices of the UN Secretary-General. It would have also had the Council deplore Israel's continued occupation of Arab territories since the 1967 Arab-Israeli conflict. Subsequently, in October 1973, Egypt launched an attack on Israeli military positions in an effort to re-take Egyptian territories under Israeli occupation. In the wake of this October 1973 War, no one considered the dispatch of another peacekeeping operation to the troubled region. The untimely withdrawal of UNEF I in May–June 1967—when the government of Egypt, under President Gamal Abdel Nasser, withdrew its consent for the continued deployment of the force on Egyptian territory—had caused major problems and was seen as a direct cause of the Six Day War of June 1967, when Israel occupied the West Bank of the Jordan, Golan Heights, and Sinai.

However, then in the midst of the Watergate scandal, US President Richard Nixon issued a nuclear alert (Def Con 3)[29] to prevent Soviet intervention to rescue Egypt's Third Army, which was being surrounded by Israeli forces. The Soviet Union had also indicated that it might consider intervening in the conflict. These signs of potential superpower confrontation notwithstanding, the US and the Soviet Union took the unprecedented step of co-sponsoring draft resolutions in the Security Council in October 1973 calling for cessation of the Israeli-Egyptian hostilities. The non-aligned members of the UN Security Council decided to act independently of the permanent members and drafted a resolution on establishing a peacekeeping force. Since I was deeply involved in these meetings, I knew that some of the permanent members were caught off-guard by this action of the non-aligned. The US, in agreeing to go along with the request to ask the UN Secretary-General—then Austria's Kurt Waldheim—to prepare a report for a peacekeeping operation, insisted that the authorisation must state that no permanent member should participate in the operation.

Since I was the officer closely linked with the negotiations on the Peacekeeping Committee, I was requested to prepare draft guidelines for the force. After almost a decade of no UN peacekeeping operations, it was not an easy task. Nevertheless, I made use of the negotiations between Ambassadors Finger and Mendelovich to find a compromise between the divergent positions of the Americans and the Soviets—in fact they had mostly closed the gap, though with some issues outstanding. The new guidelines for peacekeeping were part of the Secretary-General's report that went before the Security Council in October 1973,[30] and which the Council used as the basis of its decision to authorise the second United Nations Emergency Force (UNEF II) for an initial period of six months.[31] The Council was to maintain overall control of the operation and determine its approximate cost, with the caveat that only the General Assembly could appropriate the funding. The day-to-day management was assigned to the Secretary-General. It was also proposed that the composition of the force should be on a broad geographic basis. That enabled the Secretary-General to propose countries from Africa, Asia, Western Europe, Latin America, and Eastern Europe—this for the first time. Canada and Poland jointly provided the logistical support for the force.[32] Interestingly, it was only later during the liberal policies of Mikhail Gorbachev in the mid-1980s that the Soviet Union accepted that the Secretary-General could have political functions beside that of chief administrative officer of the world organisation.

Establishing UNEF II on the Ground

With the approval of the Secretary-General's report, including the new guidelines—still being used today—a new era of peacekeeping began under the UN flag. As soon as the Security Council took the decision to create UNEF II in October 1973, I was immediately requested to proceed to Cairo to supervise the establishment of the force on the ground. With fighting still continuing in some parts of the Egyptian Canal Zone, the designated commander of the force, Lieutenant-General Ensio Siilasvuo of Finland, and I had to make contacts with the parties to ensure full respect for the ceasefire by both Egypt and Israel.

The new peacekeeping force in Egypt was an innovation. It became an active participant in negotiations between Egypt and Israel, established an appropriate modality to stabilise the ceasefire, and made arrangement for the supply of food and water for Egypt's Third Army, which was still partially surrounded by Israeli forces. This provided the impetus for the now famous "Kilometer 101" talks, held immediately after the October 1973 war, on the Egyptian Cairo-Suez desert road. I participated fully in these talks, the first between Egyptian and Israeli military officers.[33]

The talks at Kilometer 101 transformed the UN peacekeeping force from one of interposition to a buffer force, as it was requested to supervise a buffer zone between the parties as well as zones of limited forces and armaments. That model was later followed in the Geneva conference, held under UN auspices and co-chaired by the United States and the Soviet Union, which ended with the signing of a disengagement agreement between Israel and Syria in May 1974. Under this agreement, and through a UN Security Council resolution co-sponsored by Washington and Moscow, the Council established the United Nations Disengagement Observer Force (UNDOF) in May 1974 to supervise the implementation of the ceasefire between Israel and Syria and the disengagement of their forces in the Golan Heights.[34] The UN team, of which I was a part, conducted the negotiations for the establishment of the force between Israel and Egypt—acting for Syria, but with the presence of a Syrian representative. UNDOF was able to keep the peace in the Golan Heights, to the appreciation of both Israel and Syria, while the buffer force in the Sinai—UNEF II—became the model force to supervise the peace treaty between Egypt and Israel that was signed in March 1979. Although provisions were made for the United Nations to supervise the peace treaty, the UN Security Council could not authorise the operation because of Soviet and Arab opposition to the visit of President Anwar Sadat to Israel and Jerusalem in November 1977.

Despite the fate of the UN role in the Sinai between Israel and Egypt, I continued my supervisory role of the UN peacekeeping operations in Lebanon and Golan Heights. As with UNEF II, I was sent to supervise the establishment of UNDOF on the ground. UNDOF represented a combination of the two types of peacekeeping operations—an observer force with military contingents. I was also in place to give directions on how best to establish on the ground the UN Interim Force in Lebanon (UNIFIL), authorised by the Security Council in March 1978.[35] Its original mandate was to maintain international peace and security, confirm the withdrawal of Israeli forces from southern Lebanon, and assist the Lebanese government in ensuring its effective authority in the area. Although it was supposed to be an interim peacekeeping operation, the Security Council, in response to the situation on the ground, subsequently revised the mandate, and following the July–August 2006 Israeli-Hizbullah war, assigned UNIFIL significant additional responsibilities.[36]

Interregnum and Return to the Peacekeeping Stage

When, in the late 1970s, it became clear that the UN was assuming a less active role in peacekeeping, the UN Secretary-General—then Austria's Kurt Waldheim—requested me to turn my attention to administrative and personnel responsibilities at the UN Secretariat, where there were difficulties with UN staff. It was not a wholly popular decision in some quarters. There was a strong feeling among some governments that I should continue my engagement in political and peacekeeping activities.

But the election of Peru's Javier Pérez de Cuéllar as UN Secretary-General in December 1981 (with effect from January 1982) brought me back to the management of peacekeeping. The new Secretary-General had served in the same 38th floor office at UN headquarters in New York, where I was a staff member. This office—the Office of the Under-Secretaries-General for Special Political Affairs—had been established by Dag Hammarskjöld in 1954, originally with an American under-secretary and a Soviet under-secretary as co-heads. It became the premier office to provide daily advice and analyses to the Secretary-General, and was also responsible for management of all UN peacekeeping operations.

The new Secretary-General was well aware of my responsibilities for peacekeeping prior to my appointment as head of Personnel Service in 1979. He was among those who believed it had been a mistake to transfer me away from my political and peacekeeping activities. For that reason, he requested me to return to my previous involvement with peacekeeping. His initial idea was for me to return to the Office of Special Political Affairs, but there he ran into some difficulties. The British wrongly claimed that the post belonged to them. This was incorrect, because the post had been held by an American, a Soviet, a Latin American national (Argentine), and also a British national—Brian Urquhart—who was a respected and trusted international civil servant. However, the

Secretary-General was not prepared to lock horns with Britain and proposed an alternative position for me.

The new post he established was to deal with the troublesome problem of peacekeeping logistics. Having served as the UN Secretary-General's Special Representative in Cyprus from 1975 to 1977, Pérez de Cuéllar was familiar with the problems of logistical support for peacekeeping, and therefore wanted me to focus on improving this support. The office I headed, between 1982 and 1985, was called the Office for Field Operations and External Support Activities (OFOESA). I was also asked to prepare regular political analyses to determine global trouble spots in my role. To my surprise, there were some who opposed a separate office on logistical support. In the past, the logistics support function was part of the Office of General Services; the responsible head of the relevant Field Service Unit, was a highly qualified staff member who had considerable experience in planning for the technical aspect of peacekeeping, American George Lansky (who retired two years prior to my appointment as head of this office). In 1982, as part of the reforms undertaken by Secretary-General Pérez de Cuéllar, the peacekeeping support function was moved to become part of OFOESA. In subsequent reforms in 1985, when OFOESA was abolished, this support function was returned to the Office of General Services. The relevant unit has since been made a part of the Department of Peacekeeping Operations (DPKO) under Secretary-General Ban Ki-moon (2007–2016), succeeded in 2017 by António Guterres.

In an attempt to modernise logistical support, I included in my staff a trained logistician, who had previously headed the logistics department of the Australian army. I further requested a US army logistician to prepare a plan for UN logistics. However, many of the staff in the office did not welcome these appointments. It was only later during the oil-for-food scandal, which was uncovered in the mid-2000s, that I realised the reason for the opposition. The Field Service Unit had been responsible for all procurement of the UN (which runs into the billions of dollars annually) in the Office of General Services, which was headed and thus controlled by a US national. The wishes of the staff opposed to my appointments were fulfilled during the administrative reform of 1985, subsequent to which I was moved to head a new office—the Office for Research and the Collection of Information (ORCI). This was the first attempt by the UN to have an early warning unit. I was given a free hand by the Secretary-General, Javier Pérez de Cuéllar, to select my own staff, because of the special skills required for the assignment.

The new office, which I was proud to lead, was given the unusual permission to maintain contacts with rebel movements, or freedom fighters, to assess what their plans were and to determine whether the UN could be of help. In carrying out these duties, I was able to suggest to the Secretary-General where a peacekeeping option might be necessary to end a conflict. My staff and I held constant contacts with many rebel leaders, which proved beneficial—as in Ethiopia, when the rebel leaders there as well as in Eritrea sought the help of my office to manage affairs following the defeat of the Dergue in May 1991.

Growth of Peacekeeping in Africa

When I was promoted to the rank of UN Under-Secretary-General in 1990 as head of the Department of Political Questions, Regional Cooperation, Decolonisation, and Trusteeship, I essentially became the most senior African in the UN Secretariat and the principal African advisor to the Secretary-General. The most urgent task before me was the decision of Sudanese leader Omar al-Bashir, following a coup in July 1989, to halt the useful Operation Lifeline Sudan, which had been facilitating timely delivery of humanitarian assistance to Southern Sudan since April that year. (On Sudan and South Sudan, see Deng in this volume.) I immediately travelled to Sudan and was able to secure the agreement of President Omar al-Bashir to resume the delivery. Thus, instead of political analyses, I was preoccupied with the coordination and delivery of humanitarian assistance in Africa.

Fortunately in 1971, I had been tutored by an energetic and experienced expert on technical assistance—Sir Robert Jackson, an Australian who was instrumental on the allied side during the Second World War. At the end of the war between India and Pakistan over the creation of Bangladesh in December 1971, I was assigned to work with him with the aim of learning how best to conduct such disaster operations. That lesson served me well as I confronted the humanitarian crises in the Horn of Africa and Angola.

Boutros-Ghali Orders a Political Role in Somalia

But it was the focus on humanitarian relief rather than finding a political solution to underlying problems that drew international criticism. That was particularly relevant in the case of Somalia (see Hirsch, and Mahiga in this volume). Although the UN and its agencies were doing their utmost to deliver humanitarian assistance, the world organisation had no presence in the country as the security situation profoundly deteriorated in late 1991 and early 1992. In November 1991, the UN Security Council recommended Egypt's Boutros Boutros-Ghali to be the organisation's new Secretary-General, with effect from January 1992. I was the first UN official he requested to meet at his hotel upon his arrival in New York from Cairo soon after the Council's recommendation. When we met he wanted to know why, with my long experience in the Middle East, I had done nothing to tackle the Somali crisis.

I was taken aback by the question and explained that my efforts to get outgoing Secretary-General Pérez de Cuéllar to approach the Security Council on the matter had been fruitless. With the OAU taking no overt action, Pérez de Cuéllar had not wished to intervene. I then informed Boutros-Ghali that I had already prepared a letter for the Secretary-General to send to the Security Council. To my surprise, Boutros-Ghali told me that he wanted me to undertake an urgent mission to Somalia; he wanted me to leave immediately. I gently reminded him that he would not officially be Secretary-General until he was elected by the General Assembly the following week in December 1991.

I added that I was prepared to proceed, but that he should prevail on Pérez de Cuéllar to send a letter to the Security Council about my mission. He picked up the phone and called the outgoing Secretary-General, who graciously agreed to immediately send such a letter. And so, early in 1992, I commenced the first UN intervention in Somalia, which was in a state of full-scale civil war following the fall of Mogadishu and the overthrow of President Siad Barre in January 1991. The humanitarian situation was so precarious that on several occasions UN agencies were forced temporarily to suspend their humanitarian assistance operations.

Somalia was in utter turmoil at the time and a very dangerous place. Nevertheless, I undertook the mission. My initial goal was to obtain a ceasefire between the forces of General Mohamed Farah Aideed and Interim President Ali Mahdi Mohammed. The ceasefire was achieved in March 1992. My team, which included representatives from the OAU, the League of Arab States, and the Organisation of the Islamic Conference, then turned its attention to safeguarding the delivery of humanitarian assistance. Despite General Aideed's initial strong opposition to the intervention of UN forces to resolve the problem, an agreement was reached to deploy UN military observers to accompany humanitarian teams. In April 1992, the UN Security Council established the first United Nations Operation in Somalia (UNOSOM I),[37] authorising the immediate dispatch of UN observers to monitor the ceasefire and subsequently the deployment of UN security forces to protect humanitarian relief. However, over the next several months, the situation on the ground continued to deteriorate. There was lawlessness and banditry through Somalia amidst an alarming level of human suffering.[38] The strength of UNOSOM had to be increased, together with a substantial increase in the airlift operation, as a matter of priority.

At that point, in November 1992, US President George H.W. Bush, who had previously served as the American ambassador to the UN, wrote to the Secretary-General and offered US assistance to stop the warlords. I immediately agreed to that offer and indicated to the Secretary-General my full support. However, my colleague, Britain's Marrack Goulding, who headed the UN Department of Peacekeeping Operations, was resolutely opposed. He believed the involvement of the US would end in disaster. The Secretary-General accepted my recommendation and agreed to accept the US offer of assistance. The multinational Unified Task Force (UNITAF) was established in December 1992,[39] under the authority of the UN Security Council and led by the US (in an operation known as Restore Hope), and which worked with UNOSOM to create and ensure a secure environment for the delivery of humanitarian assistance. Operation Restore Hope was successful. (See also Mzali in this volume.)

Nevertheless, the overall security situation in Somalia did not improve much. When Bill Clinton took over the American presidency from Bush in January 1993, the US adopted a different approach. There was a change of leadership at the DPKO, with Goulding replaced by his deputy, Ghana's Kofi

Annan. Goulding was transferred and joined me in the Department of Political Affairs. For reasons unknown to me, or Secretary-General Boutros-Ghali, the UN force on the ground then decided to seek the arrest of General Aideed. I learned from Kofi Annan that he had been informed of the proposed move, and he showed me the prepared statement that was to be issued once Aideed was arrested. Both Boutros-Ghali and I had no objection to the removal of Aideed from the scene, but the point was that we did not know what was happening.

The security situation on the ground in Somalia continued to deteriorate and UN troops were being killed. Twenty-four Pakistani soldiers, for example, were killed in an attack in June 1993 (see Virk in this volume), and in September in the same year, seven Nigerian peacekeepers lost their lives in a street ambush. When American soldiers were killed and dragged through the streets in October 1993, though, in an incident known as Black Hawk Down (see Mzali in this volume), there was uproar in the US Congress and soon, by March 1994, US troops were withdrawn from Somalia (see Hirsch in this volume). Other withdrawals followed soon afterwards. It was then that the US announced its new policy on UN peacekeeping.

At a luncheon meeting at the UN Secretary-General's residence in early 1994 in New York, US Secretary of State Warren Christopher elaborated on the new US policy. In essence, in the future, the US would be extremely cautious in authorising peacekeeping operations. I did not hesitate to let Christopher know that the new policy was wrongheaded. I expressed doubts that any government could make such a declarative policy without evaluating each situation as it arises. The immediate response of Christopher was that the United States could not conduct policy based on ground reports on CNN.[40] I left the luncheon worried that there were dangers ahead for UN peacekeeping.[41]

Prior to its adventure in Somalia, the UN played a useful role in tackling the security situation in Liberia as a result of the civil war that began in 1989. In 1990 I received a call from my countryman Abbas Bundu, Executive Secretary of the Economic Community of West African States (ECOWAS).[42] He sought my assistance in crafting a plan for the deployment of a peacekeeping force in Liberia. I did obtain the green light from UN Secretary-General Pérez de Cuéllar and was pleased to work with Bundu. In a meeting held in Freetown in August 1990, ECOWAS's Standing Mediation Committee decided to establish the ECOWAS Ceasefire Monitoring Group (ECOMOG).[43] At the request of the Chair of ECOWAS Heads of State and Government, I participated at all ECOWAS summit meetings until an agreement was reached in August 1996 in Abuja to conduct elections in Liberia in May 1997, which Charles Taylor won when they were finally held in July 1997.

However, before that event, it was at one of the group's summit meetings—between 1990 and 1993—that I managed to obtain the agreement of the ECOWAS Heads of State and Government to allow deployment of a UN peacekeeping force in Liberia. The agreement came about when Charles

Taylor—leader of the rebel National Patriotic Front of Liberia (NPFL)—refused to accept demobilisation of his force because he had no trust in ECOMOG. I held several consultations with him during this period, and proposed that the UN could send an unarmed observer force to monitor ECOMOG as the latter conducted the demobilisation process. Once Taylor agreed, I had to convince the ECOWAS Heads of State and Government to agree, as there were some strong objections to any UN military involvement in an operation under the sub-regional organisation.

At an informal meeting of the ECOWAS Summit, held in Cotonou, Benin, in July 1993, the Chair—Benin's Nicéphore Soglo—asked me to address the meeting and make the case for a UN observer force in Liberia. Following my statement, General Ibrahim Babangida of Nigeria and President Félix Houphouët-Boigny of Côte d'Ivoire endorsed the recommendation. The summit then decided to formally ask the UN to send an observer force. When I returned to UN headquarters, there was opposition to the plan. Marrack Goulding, still head of the DPKO at that time, asserted that a UN peacekeeping force should not co-exist or operate alongside a regional operation like ECOMOG. But the Secretary-General endorsed my position and the request went to the Security Council. By that time, the ECOWAS summit in Bamako had taken place in November 1990, and there had been a convergence of positions between the francophone and the anglophone members of ECOWAS. All three African members of the Security Council—Côte d'Ivoire, Ethiopia, and Zaire—spoke in support of the ECOWAS request and eventually the Council approved the establishment of the UN Observer Mission in Liberia (UNOMIL) in September 1993.[44]

Mozambique and Rwanda

Between 1991 and 1994, I became very much involved with the establishment of peacekeeping operations in both Mozambique and Rwanda. The prolonged civil war between the government of newly independent Mozambique and the Mozambique National Resistance (RENAMO), backed by South Africa, which ended in October 1992 with the signing of a General Peace Agreement in Rome, provided the backdrop of the UN peacekeeping operations in that country. In the process leading to the signing of the agreement, I was able to convince the initially hesitant Mozambican government to agree to UN involvement in resolving the conflict. Once the Mozambican government had relented, the UN was invited to participate as an observer in the Rome talks. I sent an experienced officer, Tayeb Merchoug, to Rome to follow the discussions. The negotiators requested a plan for peacekeeping from the UN, and I sent the request to the DPKO for a draft. The UN presented a peacekeeping plan along with another relating to the conducting of elections, and both documents were approved. In the final stages of the Rome talks, I represented the UN Secretary-General. I also represented the UN at the signing ceremony. There was a sense of urgency, and immediately after the signing ceremony I rushed to fly directly to New York to start the process of seeking the approval of the Security Council for the establishment of a peacekeeping force in Mozambique. In December 1992, the Council approved the force, which was named the UN Operation in Mozambique (ONUMUZ).[45] Since it would take time to set up the force on the ground, I recommended that a small number of UN unarmed observers be sent immediately to Maputo, to show the UN flag, and by so doing, reassure the population, which had endured 14 years of a bitter civil war, that the world organisation was there to help consolidate peace.

Under the terms of the Rome Agreement and its mandate from the UN Security Council, ONUMUZ played a significant role in Mozambique. It monitored and verified implementation of the ceasefire, as well as disarmament, demobilisation, and reintegration of combatants, monitored elections, and assisted in the implementation of humanitarian relief programmes until its mandate ended in December 1994. On the whole, the UN peacekeeping operation in Mozambique was a success.

Much has been written about the genocide in Rwanda in 1994, and also about what the UN did, or failed to do in preventing the catastrophe which claimed the lives of some 800,000 people.[46] From my own vantage point, I believe that the full story about the events in Rwanda has not yet been revealed. Unfortunately, many Western scholars, publicists, governments, and journalists have been too ready and willing to accept the narrative of events as written and proclaimed by General Roméo Dallaire of Canada—the commander of the UN Assistance Mission for Rwanda (UNAMIR)—while ignoring or rejecting the version of the head of UNAMIR, Special Representative of the Secretary-General Jacques-Roger Booh–Booh of Cameroon.[47]

I started to reflect on what the UN could do in Rwanda when I began, in late 1992, to receive frequent visits from the Rwandan ambassador to the UN, Jean-Pierre Bizimana, after the signing of a ceasefire agreement, in July 1992, between the mainly Hutu Rwandan government and the Tutsi-led Rwandan Patriotic Front (RPF). Bizimana was keen to convince me that the UN should be more involved in the question of Rwanda and send a peacekeeping force to the country. I was hesitant because the OAU had deployed an observer mission to Rwanda as part of the July 1992 ceasefire agreement. When I contacted Tanzania's Salim Ahmed Salim, the Secretary-General of the OAU, he confirmed that the organisation's observer mission was functioning, but that it would request logistical and financial support from the UN. I also received a French envoy, who warned me that unless the UN dispatched a force to Rwanda, there would be grave consequences. He went on to tell me that the government of Rwanda had no confidence in the OAU mission. I continued to keep the matter under review.

A step forward was taken when the OAU presented an invitation to the UN to attend the joint politico-military meetings that led eventually to the signing of the Arusha Accords, in August 1993, aimed at ending the Rwandan civil war. Once I was convinced that the OAU would support UN involvement, I engaged a retired UN Secretariat officer, Macaire Pedanou, with whom I had worked closely in the past, to represent my office at the talks in Arusha. He kept me informed of the discussions and suggestions that the UN might be requested to field a peacekeeping force. Once I was informed that a request would be made for a UN force, I alerted Secretary-General Boutros-Ghali.

Meanwhile, some Western governments began to intimate that they would not support a peacekeeping force for Rwanda. In our planning, we were convinced that the UN should act. I later sent a formal request to the Secretary-General that based on the agreements at the Arusha talks, he should request the establishment of a peacekeeping force, and copied the memo to my colleagues in the departments of peacekeeping and humanitarian affairs. To my surprise, the head of the DPKO at the time sent a counter-memo to the Secretary-General that no such requests should be made, as they would be opposed by some of the permanent members of the Security Council. Fortunately, the Secretary-General supported my recommendation and signed a letter to the Council requesting the establishment of a peacekeeping force for Rwanda.

Anticipating some opposition in the Security Council, I held consultations with non-permanent members, underscoring the importance of the Council agreeing to the request of the Secretary-General. There is no doubt in my mind that the consensus of the non-permanent members made it difficult for the permanent members to veto the request. In any case, the Council, in October 1993, decided to establish UNAMIR.[48] (See Ugarte in this volume.) Significantly, it was not long before we heard voices calling for reduction of the force. I left the UN Secretariat at the end of March 1994 and the rest is history.

Conclusion

Subsequent developments have demonstrated that UN peacekeeping has become a major feature of the African continent. Interestingly, the hesitation of some permanent members to deploy peacekeeping in Africa in the past has now disappeared. It may well be that in the eyes of some of the major powers peacekeeping as a form of monitoring and control has become a useful tool in their toolbox. Whereas the management of peacekeeping in Africa during the time of Boutros-Ghali was mainly in the hands of African nationals, non-Africans today are the major players in peacekeeping operations in Africa. Even when countries like the DRC are calling for the withdrawal of UN peacekeeping forces there is strong opposition in the Council to do so. The question that should be raised perhaps by Africans is whether UN peacekeeping in Africa has an exit strategy.

At the same time, the Security Council is experimenting by linking to peacekeeping some form of enforcement action, now often called "prevention forces", as has been proposed for the DRC and South Sudan. Nevertheless, the international community has a greater responsibility to protect civilians in armed conflict, and maybe, these new developments are appropriate for this task. However, it would be far more useful for the Security Council to re-evaluate its hesitation to provide appropriate financing and logistics support for regional peacekeeping such as that by the AU and Africa's regional economic communities (RECs) (see Vogt in this volume).[49] It is possible to work out some arrangements by which the Security Council can have overall responsibility for these regional peacekeeping forces, since it would be in conformity with the provisions of Chapter VIII of the UN Charter. African states have demonstrated their capacity to conduct peacekeeping operations. Their deficiency is in the areas of financing and logistic support. Whatever the outcome of this exercise, it is amazing that the African states, who became so disenchanted with the first United Nations peacekeeping operation in Africa, ONUC, have finally embraced the concept of United Nations peacekeeping as a useful exercise in the maintenance of international peace and security.

Notes

1. On peacekeeping, *see generally* Alex J. Bellamy and Paul D. Williams, *Understanding Peacekeeping* (Cambridge: Polity Press, 2010); Mats Berdal, "The Security Council and Peacekeeping", in Vaughan Lowe, Adam Roberts, Jennifer Welsh, and Dominik Zaum (eds.), *The United Nations Security Council and War: The Evolution of Thought and Practice Since 1945* (Oxford: Oxford University Press, 2008), pp. 175–204; Paul F. Diehl and Alexandru Balas, *Peace Operations*, second edition (Cambridge: Polity Press, 2014); Michael W. Doyle and Nicholas Sambanis, "Peacekeeping Operations", in Thomas G. Weiss and Sam Daws (eds.), *The Oxford Handbook on the United Nations* (Oxford: Oxford University Press, 2007), pp. 323–348; Marrack Goulding, "The Evolution of United Nations Peacekeeping", *International Affairs* 69, no. 3 (1993), pp. 451–464; Joachim A. Koops, Norrie MacQueen, Thierry Tardy, and Paul D. Williams (eds.), *The Oxford Handbook of United Nations Peacekeeping Operations* (Oxford: Oxford University Press, 2015).
2. *Charter of the United Nations*, San Francisco, United States (US), 26 June 1945, entry into force 24 October 1945, chap. VII; *see especially* arts. 45–47 on the role and composition of the Military Staff Committee.
3. For case studies of United Nations (UN) peacekeeping operations during the Cold War, *see* William J. Durch (ed.), *The Evolution of UN Peacekeeping: Case Studies and Comparative Analysis* (New York: St. Martin's Press, 1993). *See generally* Thomas G. Weiss, David P. Forsythe, and Roger A. Coate, *The United Nations and Changing World Politics* (Boulder, CO: Westview Press, 2001), pp. 47–64.
4. In reality, the Dumbarton Oaks proposals envisaged three permanent members of the UN Security Council: the US, the Soviet Union, and Britain. However, at the Yalta Conference in February 1945, the question arose as to whether France, at the request of General Charles de Gaulle, should also be made a permanent member of the Security Council. While US President Franklin D. Roosevelt and Russian President Joseph Stalin were initially reluctant, they finally agreed to it. However, Roosevelt insisted that China should also be made a permanent member of the Council. In compensation to the Soviet Union, two of the 15 republics

of the Soviet Union—Belorussia and Ukraine—were made separate members of the UN, thus giving the Soviets three seats in the world body.

5. Britain is used synonymously with the United Kingdom (UK) in this volume.
6. *See* Adekeye Adebajo, *UN Peacekeeping in Africa: From the Suez Crisis to the Sudan Conflicts* (Johannesburg: Fanele; and Boulder, CO, and London: Lynne Rienner, 2011), pp. 26–31.
7. The Uniting for Peace Resolution, adopted by the UN General Assembly in November 1950, states: "if the Security Council, because of lack of unanimity of the permanent members, fails to exercise its primary responsibility for the maintenance of international peace and security in any case where there appears to be a threat to the peace, a breach of the peace, or an act of aggression, the General Assembly shall consider the matter immediately with a view to making appropriate recommendations to Members for collective measures, including in the case of a breach of the peace or act of aggression the use of armed force when necessary, to maintain or restore international peace and security". UN General Assembly Resolution 377 (V), Uniting for Peace, UN Doc. A/RES/377 (V), 3 November 1950, pt. A, para. 1.
8. UN General Assembly Resolution 1000 (ES–I), UN Doc. A/RES/1000 (ES–I), 5 November 1956.
9. Brian Urquhart, *Ralph Bunche—An American Life* (New York and London: W.W. Norton and Company, 1993), pp. 264–290.
10. The UN Truce Supervision Organisation (UNTSO) was established by UN Security Council Resolution 50, UN Doc. S/RES/1950, 29 May 1948. With regard to the UN Military Observer Group in India and Pakistan (UNMOGIP), key documents include: UN Security Council Resolution 39, UN Doc. S/RES/39, 20 January 1948; UN Security Council Resolution 47, UN Doc. S/RES/47, 21 April 1948; and UN Security Council Resolution 91, UN Doc. S/RES/91, 30 March 1951. The first cohort of unarmed military observers who came to compose the basis of UNMOGIP deployed to India/Pakistan in January 1949. UN Peacekeeping, "UNMOGIP Background", http://www.un.org/en/peacekeeping/missions/unmogip/background.shtml (accessed 10 June 2017).
11. Urquhart, *Ralph Bunche*, pp. 299–360. For one of the best accounts of the Congo crisis, *see* Madeleine G. Kalb, *The Congo Cables: The Cold War in Africa—From Eisenhower to Kennedy* (New York: Macmillan Publishing Co., Inc., 1982).
12. UN Security Council Resolution 83, UN Doc. S/RES/83, 27 June 1950; and UN Security Council Resolution 84, UN Doc. S/RES/84, 7 July 1950.
13. Christian Herter, National Press Club luncheon speech, Washington, D.C., 18 February 1960.
14. Address to the UN General Assembly, New York, 25 September 1961, UN Doc. A/PV/1013, para. 66.
15. Louis B. Sohn and Granville Clark, *World Peace Through World Law* (Cambridge: Harvard University Press, 1958).
16. *See* Kalb, *The Congo Cables*; Conor Cruise O'Brien, *To Katanga and Back: A UN Case History* (New York: Grosset & Dunlap, 1966). For one of the best critiques of Dag Hammarskjöld's role in the Congo, *see* Stanley Hoffmann, "In Search of a Thread: The UN in the Congo Labyrinth", *International Organisation* 16, no. 2 (1962), pp. 331–361.

17. In a letter to the UN Secretary-General, dated 12 July 1960, Congolese Prime Minister Patrice Lumumba and President Joseph Kasabuvu noted that the real cause of the internal disturbances was the colonialist machinations of the Belgians, and they accused the Belgian government of orchestrating the secession of Katanga. They further requested the urgent deployment of UN military assistance to protect their country and put an end to the secession. *See* UN Doc. S/4382, 13 July 1960. In his statement to the UN Security Council on 25 July 1960, Secretary-General Dag Hammarskjöld clarified the legal basis of the Council's decision to establish the UN Operation in the Congo (ONUC). *See* UN Doc. S/PV.913, para. 25. Hammarskjöld, in recommending action by the Security Council, acted under Article 99 of the UN Charter. This was the first time that this article was invoked. On this point, *see also* Brian Urquhart, *Hammarskjöld* (New York: Alfred A. Knopf, 1972).
18. *See* James O.C. Jonah, "The Security Council, the General Assembly, the Economic and Social Council, and the Secretariat", in Adekeye Adebajo (ed.), *From Global Apartheid to Global Village: Africa and the United Nations* (Scottsville, South Africa: University of KwaZulu-Natal [UKZN] Press, 2009), pp. 67–69.
19. African leaders coordinated their position on the Troika proposal with Indian Prime Minister Jawaharlal Nehru. Khrushchev had assumed that the bitterness of Afro-Asian states would lead them to support the Soviet position, and was disappointed when they did not.
20. In August 1960, at a pan-African conference held in the Congolese capital, Prime Minister Patrice Lumumba noted that the Congo did not want either the US or the Soviet Union to be directly involved in his country, and that non-alignment was the only viable policy for newly independent countries. *See* Kwame Nkrumah, *Challenge of the Congo: A Case Study of Foreign Pressures in an Independent State* (New York: International Publishers, 1967).
21. Based on the principles of constitutionality and collective responsibility, the UN General Assembly, in December 1960, recognised that the expenses involved in UN operations in the Congo for that year constituted expenses of the organisation within the meaning of Article 17(2) of the Charter, and that the assessment against member states creates binding legal obligations on them to pay their assessed shares. *See* UN Doc. A/RES/1583 (XV), 20 December 1960. Subsequently, the General Assembly urged the permanent members (P-5) of the Security Council to make sizeable additional contribution and also Belgium, as a state directly concerned with the situation in the Congo, to make a substantial contribution.
22. *Certain Expenses of the United Nations* (Advisory Opinion), ICJ Reports 1962, p. 151, in D.J. Harris, *Cases and Materials on International Law*, fifth edition (London: Sweet & Maxwell, 1998), pp. 975–984.
23. UN General Assembly Resolution 2006 (XIX), Comprehensive Review of the Whole Question of Peace-Keeping Operations in All Their Aspects, UN Doc. A/RES/2006 (XIX), 18 February 1965.
24. A five-part report on the work of the committee between March and May 1965 was submitted by the Secretary-General and the President of the General Assembly, in their capacity as its chairs. *See* UN Doc. A/AC.121/4. A report by the committee as a whole was presented on 15 June 1965. *See* UN Doc. A/5915 and A/5915/ADD.1. Another was issued on 31 August 1965. *See* UN Doc.

A/5916 and A/5916/ADD.1. *See also* UN General Assembly Resolution 2053 A and B, Comprehensive Review of the Whole Question of Peace-Keeping Operations in All Their Aspects, UN Doc. A/RES/22053 (XX), 15 December 1965.

25. On UNMOGIP, *see generally* Rahul Roy-Chaudhury, "The Security Council and the India-Pakistan Wars", in Lowe et al., *The United Nations Security Council and War*, pp. 324–345; Christy Shucksmith and Nigel D. White, "United Nations Military Observer Group in India and Pakistan", in Koops et al., *The Oxford Handbook of United Nations Peacekeeping Operations*, pp. 133–143.
26. UN General Assembly Resolution 2308 (XXII), UN Doc. A/RES/2308, 13 December 1967.
27. UN Security Council Resolution 186, UN Doc. S/RES/186, 4 March 1964.
28. In this context, it is worth noting, for example, UN General Assembly Resolution 33/114, adopted in December 1978, which reiterated the General Assembly's conviction that "peace-keeping operations of the United Nations, conducted with the consent of the host country and respect for its sovereignty and territorial integrity, consistent with the Charter, are an essential function of the United Nations, though not a substitute for the peaceful settlement of disputes and therefore of a temporary nature". UN Doc. A/RES/33/114, 18 December 1978, preamble.
29. US intelligence had determined that the Soviet Union was shipping nuclear weapons to Egypt.
30. UN Doc. S/11052/Rev.1, 27 October 1973.
31. UN Security Council Resolution 340, UN Doc. S/RES/340, 25 October 1973; and UN Security Council Resolution 341, UN Doc. S/RES/341, 27 October 1973.
32. Jonah, *What Price the Survival of the United Nations?*, pp. 115–120.
33. *See* James O.C. Jonah, "The Military Talks at Kilometer 101: The UN's Effectiveness as a Third Party", *Negotiation Journal* 6, no. 1 (1990), pp. 53–70.
34. UN Security Council Resolution 350, UN Doc. S/RES/350, 31 May 1974.
35. UN Security Council Resolution 425, UN Doc. S/RES/425, 19 March 1978; and UN Security Council Resolution 426, UN Doc. S/RES/426, 19 March 1978.
36. UN Security Council Resolution 1701, UN Doc. S/RES/1701, 11 August 2006.
37. UN Security Council Resolution 751, UN Doc. S/RES/751, 24 April 1992.
38. Report of the Secretary-General to the Security Council, UN Doc. S/24480, 24 August 1992; and UN Security Council Resolution 775, UN Doc. S/RES/775, 28 August 1992.
39. UN Security Council Resolution 794, UN Doc. S/RES/794, 3 December 1992.
40. The so-called "CNN effect"—a term used in the context of the US intervention in Somalia—refers to the effect of 24-hour media coverage on the making of foreign policy.
41. Jonah, *What Price the Survival of the United Nations?*, p. 460.
42. Jonah, *What Price the Survival of the United Nations?*, pp. 324–333.
43. On the ECOWAS Ceasefire Monitoring Group (ECOMOG) in Liberia, *see, for example*, Adekeye Adebajo, *Liberia's Civil War: Nigeria, ECOMOG, and*

Regional Security in West Africa (Boulder, CO, and London: Lynne Rienner, 2002).

44. UN Security Council Resolution 866, UN Doc. S/RES/866, 22 September 1993. On UN peacekeeping in West Africa (including Liberia), *see generally* Adebajo, *UN Peacekeeping in Africa*, pp. 139–170; Comfort Ero, "UN Peacekeeping in West Africa", in Adebajo, *From Global Apartheid to Global Village*, pp. 283–304.
45. UN Security Council Resolution 797, UN Doc. S/RES/797, 16 December 1992.
46. In the large body of literature on the Rwandan genocide, there are two accounts, in particular, written by competent UN functionaries who were in Rwanda in 1994: Canadian General Roméo Dallaire, who was commander of the UN Assistance Mission for Rwanda (UNAMIR); and Cameroon's Jacques-Roger Booh-Booh, who was Special Representative of the UN Secretary-General in Rwanda. Roméo Dallaire, *Shake Hands with the Devil: The Failure of Humanity in Rwanda* (Toronto: Random House Canada, 2003); Jacques-Roger Booh-Booh, *Le patron de Dallaire parle: Révélations sur les dérives d'un général de l'ONU au Rwanda* (Paris: Duboiris, 2005).
47. *See* previous note.
48. UN Security Council Resolution 872, UN Doc. S/RES/872, 5 October 1993.
49. *See also* Margaret Vogt, "The UN and Africa's Regional Organisations", in Adebajo, *From Global Apartheid to Global Village*, pp. 251–268.

CHAPTER 10

The UN Security Council and Africa: Playing New Games and Applying New Rules and Moves

Bruno Stagno Ugarte

Here begins the Great Game.
—Rudyard Kipling, *Kim* (1900)

This chapter is about the games played by the United Nations (UN) Security Council in Africa.[1] It addresses how the Council has dared to innovate, introducing entirely new games and drastically changing the rules and moves of existing games in its efforts to maintain peace and security on the continent. It is mainly in Africa that the Council has overcome its conservative instincts as the pre-eminent expression of the world order established in 1945, and in so doing, made progressive strides that challenge the inviolability of sovereignty. The chapter also addresses, in passing, how Africa itself has gradually moved from being on the receiving end of the games to becoming a player of its own destiny. Finally, the chapter posits the question of whether the innovations introduced by the Security Council in Africa should be applied elsewhere, or confined to the continent.

Historically, the term *games* alludes to the "Great Game" in Afghanistan as coined by British Lieutenant Arthur Conolly and later immortalised by the poet Rudyard Kipling.[2] In advocating for the outbreak of the Boer War (1899–1902), Sir Alfred Milner, then High Commissioner for South Africa and Governor of the Cape Colony, was one of the first to make reference to a "great game for mastery" in an African context.[3] While there may be such an undertone to the games played by the UN Security Council in Africa covered in this chapter, the term is borrowed from, and meant to be understood

B. Stagno Ugarte (✉)
Human Rights Watch, New York, United States

T. Karbo, K. Virk (eds.), *The Palgrave Handbook of Peacebuilding in Africa*, https://doi.org/10.1007/978-3-319-62202-6_10

as it is in, game theory.[4] In this sense, games leading to interdependent decision-making—in this case, the members of the Security Council—are structured by the choices they face, the outcomes arising from the choices, and, eventually, the evaluations they make of the outcomes and accompanying consequences.[5] The term is therefore not used pejoratively, as it can encompass engagement and disengagement, cooperation and competition, and lead to positive and negative outcomes. In fact, these are multi-faceted games, in which Council members are, at times, playing with one another while playing with the parties on the ground. At times, the games also involve other players, such as neighbouring states, regional or sub-regional organisations, and other parties with interests at stake. The games usually involve values and principles, interests and counter-interests, and are generally played within the Council in line with its mandate to maintain international peace and security.

The Security Council and Africa During the Cold War, 1946–1989

When the UN Charter was adopted at the San Francisco Conference in June 1945, only four of the 51 founding member states were from Africa (Egypt, Ethiopia, Liberia, and South Africa). As the most under-represented continent at the UN at the time, it probably comes as no surprise that Africa was also the last to come to the attention of the Security Council. Whereas the Council addressed situations in Western Europe, Eastern Europe, and Asia as early as 1946,[6] it did not begin addressing situations in Latin America and the Caribbean, and Africa until 1954 and 1956 respectively,[7] and sub-Saharan Africa as late as 1960. In the case of Africa, the low prevalence of situations or questions on the agenda of the Council would come to an end as of 1960, as more African states were admitted to the UN.[8] In fact, throughout the 1946–1989 period, agenda items regarding Africa would total no less than 54 of the 156 (35 per cent) agenda items that came to the formal attention of the Council. Interestingly, the first two African situations addressed by the Council, Egypt and the Congo (present-day Democratic Republic of the Congo [DRC]), would introduce game-changing precedents in terms of Council action (see Jonah in this volume).

In regard to the situation in Egypt, brought to the attention of the Security Council in September 1956 by a joint complaint by France and Britain[9] due to what they characterised as the "unilateral action of the Egyptian government in bringing to an end the system of international cooperation of the Suez Canal",[10] a number of interesting precedents were established. First, although two permanent members (France and Britain) brought the situation to the attention of the Council, both suffered a humiliating reverse within the Council, having to resort twice to the veto in order to contain the damage and prevent the adoption of damning draft resolutions. This rare affront by the Council was in part possible due to an equally rare instance of Cold War cooperation between the

United States (US) and the Soviet Union, as both worked in tandem in order to restrain the aggression committed against Egypt. Second, the failure of the Council to act, due to the joint vetoes by France and Britain,[11] led the UN General Assembly to become seized of the situation under its Uniting for Peace Resolution of 1950.[12] As a result, the General Assembly held its first emergency special session in November 1956 to address the situation in Egypt. Third, the General Assembly established the UN Emergency Force (UNEF I), the first ever armed deployment by the UN, as an intercession force between the warring parties, which set the basic rules for subsequent UN peacekeeping: consent of the host state, impartiality of the UN and non-use of force except in self-defence. Due to the inexistence of the special arrangements whereby UN member states would provide forces to the world organisation as intended in Article 43 of the Charter, peacekeeping thereby emerged as an ad hoc solution to address the situation in Egypt (see Jonah in this volume).

In regard to the situation in the Congo, the Security Council similarly set a number of game-changing precedents, including its first expression, contained in Resolution 161 of 1961, of "deep regret and concern for the systematic violations of human rights and fundamental freedoms and the general absence of the rule of law".[13] No previous Council decision had so comprehensively addressed human rights, which had previously been trumped by the principle of domestic jurisdiction enshrined in Article 2(7) of the UN Charter.[14] Resolution 161 was also ground-breaking in authorising an investigation into a specific assassination—that of Congolese Prime Minister Patrice Lumumba and two associates in January 1961—in order to ascertain that the perpetrators be punished. Adopted under Chapter VII, Resolution 161 furthermore introduced what has of late been termed "robust peacekeeping", as it allowed the UN Operation in the Congo (ONUC) to take "all appropriate measures" to prevent the occurrence of civil war, including "the use of force, if necessary, in the last resort". Finally, according to some scholars, Resolution 161 "contained elements which arguably fell under Article 42", making it the first Council decision to venture into the enforcement powers enshrined in the UN Charter.[15]

Despite the game-changing nature of ONUC, keeping the centripetal forces at bay in the Congo proved to be an impossible challenge. The UN operation not only came under intense criticism, most notably and violently from Soviet premier Nikita Khrushchev, but also produced disillusionment in a number of African states. The latter had the fortunate effect of inducing the establishment in May 1963 of the Organisation of African Unity (OAU), in what amounted to an effort to find "African solutions to African problems". The OAU was not the sole regional organisation indirectly spawned by the UN. Chapter VIII of the UN Charter on regional arrangements unintentionally inspired a number of such arrangements.[16] However, the OAU is probably the first to have done so not in the abstract, but in part as a result of the perceived failings of a UN peacekeeping operation. As a result of what some have termed the "Congo allergy",[17] no subsequent peacekeeping mission was deployed to sub-Saharan African during the remainder of the Cold War, nor to anywhere else in Africa with the sole exception of the second UN Emergency Force (UNEF II) from 1973 to 1979.

Another situation in Africa that would likewise introduce unprecedented expressions of concern for human rights from the Security Council was South Africa. In Resolution 182 of 1963, the Council acknowledged "the need to eliminate discrimination in regard to basic human rights and fundamental freedoms for all individuals" and first referenced the Universal Declaration of Human Rights, some 15 years after its adoption by the General Assembly in December 1948.[18] Moreover, it requested the UN Secretary-General to constitute what would subsequently become the Group of Experts on South Africa, the first of its kind, "to examine methods of resolving the present situation in South Africa through full, peaceful and orderly application of human rights and fundamental freedoms to all inhabitants". The inviolability of domestic jurisdiction enshrined in Article 2(7) of the UN Charter was further called into question in the case of South Africa, with the Council urging South Africa, in Resolutions 190 and 191 (both in 1964),[19] to "renounce the execution of any persons sentenced to death" and to "grant immediate amnesty to all persons detained or on trial, as well as clemency to all persons sentenced" for their opposition to apartheid. The Council furthermore asked South Africa to "abolish the practice of imprisonment without charges, without access to counsel or without the right of prompt trial". In 1988, in adopting its last decisions on the situation in South Africa, mainly Resolutions 610, 615, and 623 (all in 1988), the Council urged the country's white minority government to "stay the execution" and "commute the death sentences" of the Sharpeville Six among other anti-apartheid activists.[20]

The Security Council would likewise break new ground on a different front with the adoption of Resolution 181 of 1963 on the situation in South Africa. In Resolution 181, it for the first time ever hinted at the possibility of mandatory sanctions in calling on member states to "cease forthwith the sale and transfer of arms and ammunition of all types" to South Africa.[21] Though the Council would fail to impose mandatory sanctions on South Africa until 1977, when it became concerned that South Africa was "at the threshold of producing nuclear weapons". In adopting Resolution 418 in 1977, after uncharacteristically recognising that its previous sanctions against South Africa were "voluntary", the Council imposed a mandatory arms embargo while also deciding that "all states shall refrain from any cooperation with South Africa in the manufacture and development of nuclear weapons".[22] In so doing, the Council for the first time tackled the issue of non-proliferation, which would later become a regular part of its agenda, most notably regarding Iraq, Iran, and North Korea. Following the adoption of Resolution 421 in 1977,[23] the Council furthermore established its longest-serving sanctions committee to date, the 421 South Africa Sanctions Committee, which was only terminated in 1994 with the adoption of Resolution 919.[24]

South Africa has also been the only UN member state to date threatened with expulsion by the General Assembly. In November 1962, the General

Assembly adopted Resolution 1761 requesting the Security Council to consider action under Article 6 of the UN Charter, which enables the Council to recommend expulsion of a member state if it has "persistently violated" the principles contained in the Charter.[25] The Council later adopted Resolution 269 in 1969, condemning South Africa for its "persistent defiance of the authority of the United Nations" and reminding the country of "its responsibilities under Article 6", yet falling short of threatening expulsion.[26] In 1974, however, the Council did actually discuss a draft resolution,[27] which was eventually vetoed by three permanent members (the US, Britain, and France), "recommending to the General Assembly the immediate expulsion of South Africa from the United Nations in compliance with Article 6".[28]

The situation in Southern Rhodesia (present-day Zimbabwe) would also provide fertile ground for the Security Council to innovate. Southern Rhodesia was the first state in 1965 to be condemned by the Council for what it termed a "unilateral declaration of independence" by "a racist minority". In Resolution 216 of 1965, the Council also issued its first call on all states not to recognise, and to deny any assistance to, the regime in Southern Rhodesia, in this case one it furthermore characterised as an "illegal racist minority regime".[29] In addition, in Resolution 217 of 1965, the Council determined that the proclamation of independence by Southern Rhodesia in November 1965 had "no legal validity",[30] the first such legal determination by the Council. Resolution 221 of 1966 upped the ante, with the Council stating unequivocally that the situation in Southern Rhodesia "constituted a threat to the peace",[31] in what would be its only explicit determination of a threat to the peace under Article 39 of the UN Charter—a necessary pre-requisite for any mandatory measures including the use of force—made during the entire Cold War.[32] The Council also hinted at its first ever naval blockade in calling on all states "to ensure the diversion of any of their vessels reasonably believed to be carrying oil destined for Southern Rhodesia", and additionally called on Britain "to prevent, by the use of force if necessary", the arrival of any such vessels. Although Resolution 221 failed to explicitly invoke Article 42, which enables the Council to authorise the use of force, the legal basis for the mandate given to Britain nonetheless rested in the article. This was therefore only the second Article 42–based resolution, after Resolution 161 on the Congo, adopted during the Cold War.[33] With the adoption of Resolution 232 of 1966, the Council moreover adopted its first measures, not involving the use of force, against a non-UN member state, acting under Article 41 of the UN Charter, and imposed mandatory commodity import and export sanctions and an arms embargo on Southern Rhodesia.[34] Additionally, in adopting Resolution 253 in 1968, the Council established its first ever sanctions committee, the 253 Southern Rhodesia Sanctions Committee, thereby setting an important precedent for subsequent sanctions regimes.[35] With Resolution 253, the Council also issued its first blanket condemnation of "all measures of political repression, including arrests, detentions, trials and executions which violate fundamental freedoms and rights". Finally, the case of Southern Rhodesia further set an interesting precedent, as the

Council actually declared the country's 1979 elections, held under the auspices of the "illegal racist regime", to be "null and void", in its Resolution 448 of 1979.[36]

The adverse economic impact of the sanctions imposed on Southern Rhodesia would also induce its neighbouring states to file, as provided for in Article 50 of the UN Charter, the first and only requests for special assistance from the Security Council during the Cold War. With the obvious exception of South Africa, all the neighbouring countries (Botswana, Mozambique, and Zambia) appealed to the Council at some point. The Council responded by adopting Resolutions 253 in 1968, 277 in 1970, 327 in 1973, and 329 in 1973, in the case of Zambia; Resolution 386 in 1976, in the case of Mozambique; and Resolutions 403 and 406, both in 1977, in the case of Botswana. Although the measures adopted by the Council largely fell short of the needs and expectations of the appealing states, these cases at least demonstrated the limitations that bedevilled the implementation of the envisaged special assistance.

Another situation in Africa that similarly set game-changing precedents for the Security Council was South West Africa (present-day Namibia), then occupied and administered by apartheid South Africa. In Resolution 246 of 1968, the Council called on South Africa to discontinue the "illegal trial" of 37 defendants from South West Africa, and to release and repatriate them forthwith. In so doing, the Council expressed unprecedented concern for "arbitrary laws whose application has been illegally extended" from apartheid South Africa to another territory.[37] More significantly, with Resolution 284 of 1970 the Council for the first time invoked Article 96 of the UN Charter in seeking an advisory opinion from the International Court of Justice (ICJ) on the situation in Namibia.[38]

This, in turn, played a decisive role in clarifying the at times binding nature of Security Council decisions taken outside Chapter VII, thanks to the advisory opinion rendered in 1971 by the ICJ in the case of Namibia. The ICJ determined that "in deciding the binding force of a decision, the provisions of the Charter on which it is based, as well as the intent of the Security Council as documented by the wording of the decisions, have to be taken into account; and the context in which the decision is taken also has to be recognized".[39] The situation in South West Africa also set an interesting precedent, in that the General Assembly and the Security Council characterised the situation differently in awarding the South West Africa People's Organisation (SWAPO) different status. Four General Assembly resolutions adopted between 1973 and 1985 recognised SWAPO as "the sole and authentic representative of the Namibian people and granted observer status to it".[40] However, the Council remained mute on the status conferred on SWAPO, merely commending it in Resolution 566, adopted in 1985, for "its preparedness to cooperate [and] its expressed readiness to sign and observe a cease-fire agreement with South Africa".[41] Interestingly, however, the Council never challenged the General Assembly, despite some Council members not agreeing with the characterisation of SWAPO as an armed struggle for national liberation.[42]

In 1971, in adopting Resolution 294,[43] the Security Council first acknowledged the existence of the UN Commission of Human Rights in taking note of a report by its ad hoc group of experts concerning acts of violence by Portugal in Senegal. More generally, the Council also cautiously addressed condemnation of Portugal for its practices in its overseas dominions in Africa (Angola, Guinea-Bissau, and Mozambique), walking a fine line between what some permanent members of the Council considered to be legitimate acts of self-defence by Portugal against internal disturbances, and what most UN member states considered to be legitimate acts of self-determination. The voting record of Resolution 312, adopted in 1972, is quite eloquent as to this fine line, with three permanent members—the US, Britain, and France—abstaining on the matter.[44] Angola also set an interesting precedent after independence, when the Council unusually asserted the right to self-defence of Angola against South Africa—a right protected under Article 51 of the UN Charter—in Resolutions 546 of 1984 and 574 of 1985.[45]

In terms of taking the game abroad or to the field, Africa was furthermore the prime destination of Security Council visiting missions during the Cold War. Of the ten missions undertaken by Council members during this period, all save the first, to Cambodia and Vietnam (1964), were to Africa: Guinea (1970, 1971), Senegal (1971), Zambia (1973), Lesotho (1976), Botswana (1977, 1985), Benin (1977), and Angola (1985). The Council moreover also held its first meetings away from its New York headquarters for substantive reasons in Africa. It agreed to meet in Addis Ababa, Ethiopia, in January–February 1972 in response to a request from the OAU and a follow-up request from the General Assembly, both received in 1971.[46] To prepare the meetings, the Council established a still extant subsidiary body charged with the preparation of meeting away from headquarters. It moreover decided, in Resolution 308 of 1972, that the meetings would be exclusively devoted to the "consideration of questions relating to Africa with which the Security Council is currently seized and the implementation of the Council's relevant resolutions".[47] The Council held 13 meetings in Addis Ababa and adopted four resolutions, all concerning Africa.[48]

The Security Council also first acknowledged resort to regional agencies, as envisaged in Chapter VIII of the UN Charter, in addressing the situation in the Congo in Resolution 199 of 1964. This resolution not only encouraged the OAU "to pursue its efforts" in the Congo while keeping the Council "fully informed of any action it may take", but also requested all states to assist the OAU in the matter. In addition, it expressed more generally that the OAU "should be able, in the context of Article 52 of the Charter of the United Nations, to help find a peaceful solution to all the problems and disputes affecting peace and security in the continent of Africa".[49]

All in all, during the Cold War, the Security Council established no less than five of its 18 (28 per cent) peacekeeping operations in Africa, although the last two were authorised at the tail end of the Cold War: the first UN Angola Verification Mission (UNAVEM I) by Resolution 626 of 1988, and the UN

Transition Assistance Group (UNTAG) by Resolution 632 of 1989.[50] Although Africa was not the main playing ground for UN peacekeeping at the time, the first two operations—UNEF in Egypt and ONUC in the Congo—invented UN peacekeeping and so-called robust peacekeeping respectively. Situations in Africa also led to the first convocation of a General Assembly special emergency session, the first Council request for an advisory opinion by the ICJ, the first resort to a regional organisation, and the first near threat of expulsion from the United Nations. As mentioned, the Council moreover established its first two and only sanctions regimes and committees during the entire Cold War period in Africa, including adopting its first decisions and sanctions on non-proliferation and mandating its first authorisation for the use of force, as well as the first applications for special assistance due to the adverse effects of the sanctions on neighbouring countries. The Council also started to play with the inviolability of Article 2(7) in Africa, adopting its first comprehensive and intrusive language on human rights and making its first legal determinations as to the illegality of sovereign acts of colonial administration, declarations of independence, and elections. During the Cold War, situations in Africa thus allowed the Council to introduce new games, rules, and moves to its practice, setting the stage for the arguably more intrusive stance adopted by the Council towards Africa in the post–Cold War period.

The Security Council and Africa Since the End of the Cold War, 1990–2015

Although comparatively few situations in Africa came to the attention of the Security Council during the Cold War, the end of the East-West confrontation by 1990 brought a host of situations to the fore. Between 1990 and 2015, 57 agenda items relating to Africa came to the attention of the Council, slightly more than the previous period in almost half the time (54 in 44 years compared to 57 in 25 years). No longer distorted by the prism of Cold War bipolarity, the true nature of most of these conflicts came to light, with the Council addressing them as either internal conflicts, mostly civil wars, or trans-national conflicts among African states with, at times, African proxies (see also Deng in this volume). According to one recent study highlighting a trend that has since continued, between 1989 and 2006, 50 per cent of all Council decisions addressing civil wars globally were on conflicts in Africa.[51]

Shortly after the end of the Cold War, the Security Council started to authorise an unprecedented number of UN peacekeeping missions—17 from 1990 to 1993 alone, compared to 18 between 1946 and 1989—deploying nearly 70,000 uniformed personnel by December 1993 compared to about 10,000 just three years earlier. The Council was soon overwhelmed, however, as there was simply too much peace to keep, leading it to mandate its first ever UN peacekeeping mission to a theatre already occupied by a sub-regional organisation. In Resolution 866 of 1993, the Council mandated deployment of the UN Observer Mission in Liberia (UNOMIL) to operate simultaneously with the Military Observer Group already deployed by the Economic Community of West African States (ECOWAS). As UNOMIL was "the first peace-keeping mission undertaken by the UN in cooperation with a peace-keeping mission already set up by another organization", the Council requested the UN Secretary-General and ECOWAS to conclude "an agreement defining, before deployment of UNOMIL, the roles and responsibilities" of each operation.[52] This first experiment in parallel deployments would be followed in 2007 with the first ever hybrid deployment, the African Union–United Nations Hybrid Operation in Darfur (UNAMID), authorised by Resolution 1769 (see Gambari in this volume).[53] In 2013, the Council would authorise a second hybrid deployment in the form of the UN Multidimensional Integrated Stabilisation Mission in Mali (MINUSMA), as mandated by Resolution 2100.[54] Despite the previous precedents set by UNOMIL and UNAMID, the establishment of MINUSMA would prove quite contentious, with both the African Union (AU) and ECOWAS faulting the Council for not taking into consideration their requests for a peace enforcement mandate for MINUSMA and denying them a logistical and financial support package for the pre-existing African-Led International Support Mission in Mali (AFISMA).[55] (See Adebajo in this volume.) Notwithstanding the contentions, to date Africa has provided the sole contexts in which the Council has deployed hybrid peacekeeping missions.

The threat of terrorism was first concretely addressed by the Security Council in an African context after Libya refused to cooperate fully in establishing responsibility for the bombing of PanAm flight 103 and Union de Transports Aériens flight 772 in December 1988 and September 1989 respectively, and in extraditing the alleged terrorists as requested by Britain and the United States. After adopting Resolution 731 in 1992, urging Libya "immediately to provide a full and effective response",[56] the Council determined in Resolution 748—also adopted in 1992—that "the failure by the Libyan Government to demonstrate by concrete actions its renunciation of terrorism and in particular its continued failure to respond fully and effectively to the requests in Resolution 731 (1992) constitute a threat to international peace and security".[57] In Resolution 748 the Council moreover imposed its first ever sanctions for aiding, abetting, or assisting terrorism.

The measures taken against Libya were likewise game-changing, due to two novel challenges faced by the Security Council. First, in 1992, Libya countermanded the Council in appealing before the ICJ, alleging that the Montreal Convention for the Suppression of Unlawful Acts Against the Safety of Civil Aviation of 1971 was the sole legal basis for addressing the situation and asking the Court to order Britain and the United States to "immediately cease and desist from … the use of any and all force or threats against Libya".[58] The ICJ disagreed with Libya and upheld the decisions of the Council. Second, in 1998, the OAU challenged the authority of the Council with its adoption of a resolution on Libya deciding "not to comply any longer with Security Council Resolutions 748 (1992) and 883 (1993) … owing to the fact that the said resolutions violate … the United Nations Charter, and the considerable human and economic losses suffered by Libya and a number of other African peoples as a result of the sanctions".[59] To date, along with an ICJ application filed by Bosnia and Herzegovina against the Council in 1993, these have been the most serious legal challenges to the authority and legitimacy of Council decisions.

In regard to mass crimes, although the Security Council first established an ad hoc international criminal tribunal to address a non-African situation—the International Criminal Tribunal for the Former Yugoslavia (ICTY)—its replication in an African context was almost immediate. Whereas the ICTY was established in Resolution 827 of 1993,[60] the International Criminal Tribunal for Rwanda (ICTR) was mandated in Resolution 955 of 1994.[61] However, the Council expanded its subsidiary bodies, established under its Article 29 prerogatives, in mandating its first "treaty-based sui generis court of mixed jurisdiction and composition" to address an African situation:[62] the Special Court for Sierra Leone (SCSL). In Resolution 1315 of 2000, the Council requested the UN Secretary-General to negotiate an agreement with Sierra Leone "to create an independent special court".[63]

On the accountability front, Africa further provided the first and, at the time of writing, only situations referred by the Security Council to the International Criminal Court (ICC): the situation in Darfur in Resolution 1593 of 2005,[64] and the situation in Libya in Resolution 1970 of 2011.[65] Although other situations have been considered, most recently and openly Syria, none have garnered sufficient support within the Council. Africa has also provided the only case yet of a potential challenge to the judicial authority of the ICC in the form of a Council deferral under Article 16 of the Court's 1998 Rome Statute. Nonetheless, despite the efforts by Kenya to convince the Council to agree to a one-year deferral of the ICC cases against Kenyan President Uhuru Kenyatta and Deputy Vice-President William Samoei Ruto, such a decision had not garnered the required majority in the Council when the ICC dropped the two cases. The charges against Kenyatta were withdrawn due to insufficient evidence in December 2014, while those against Ruto were vacated in April 2016. (On the ICC, see Nouwen; and on Kenya, see Wamai, in this volume.)

On a related matter, Africa also spawned the emerging concept of the responsibility to protect (R2P), which was acknowledged by the Security Council in Resolution 1674 in 2006.[66] Although the concept was first conceived as "sovereignty as responsibility" by the Africa Program of the Brookings Institution (see Deng in this volume), and later coined the "responsibility to protect" and expanded globally by the Canadian-sponsored International Commission on Intervention and State Sovereignty (ICISS) in 2002, by 2015 nine of the ten country-specific Council references employing R2P language concerned Africa. These occurred in Resolution 1653 of 2006 on Burundi and the DRC; Resolutions 1970, 1973, and 2016 of 2011, and 2040 of 2012 on Libya; Resolution 1975 of 2011 on Côte d'Ivoire; Resolution 1996 of 2011 on South Sudan; and Resolutions 2085 and 2100 of 2012 on Mali.[67] In fact, the situation in Burundi and the DRC warranted a first reference three months before the adoption of Resolution 1674 acknowledging R2P.

With the adoption of the outcome document of the 2005 World Summit, an additional tool was added to the Security Council toolbox: the Peacebuilding Commission (PBC). Although the PBC is the only joint subsidiary body of the General Assembly and the Security Council, through Resolution 1646 of 2005 the Council surreptitiously altered its composition by enshrining its five permanent members (the P-5)—the United States, Britain, France, Russia, and China—as permanent members of the PBC.[68] The PBC was not established to address situations in Africa only, though most of the thinking behind its establishment was informed by the alleged recurrence of recent conflict in Africa and the need to secure the gains brought on by peacekeeping with follow-up peacebuilding activities. Yet Africa had, at the time of writing, provided all the situations on the agenda of the PBC—Burundi, the Central African Republic (CAR), Guinea, Guinea-Bissau, Liberia, and Sierra Leone—all of which were referred by the Council with the exception of Guinea.[69] (See Otobo in this volume.) Before the PBC, the Council had in 2002 already created an Africa-specific subsidiary body, the Ad Hoc Working Group on Conflict Prevention and Resolution in Africa, the only working group of its kind with a specific geographic focus.[70] Although it has largely under-performed, it is nonetheless striking that the mandate of the working group is not open-ended geographically but explicitly confined to Africa.

As Africa has through time developed more sub-regional organisations, it has given the Security Council options to go "forum-shopping" for the regional or sub-regional organisation that best fits its interests.[71] Although the AU, through its Peace and Security Council (PSC), is by design, composition, and jurisdiction the best counterpart in principle, the Council has at times shunned the AU and turned to a sub-regional organisation deemed more in tune with its interests.[72] (See Kuwali, Nagar, and Adebajo in this volume.) This attitude has at times exacerbated the already tense relations between the AU and Africa's sub-regional organisations, as they contend with issues of primacy and subsidiarity akin to those that likewise bedevil the relationship between the Council and regional and sub-regional organisations more generally (see Vogt in this volume).

The AU PSC, however, has established the most routine meetings with the members of the Security Council. Starting in 2007, the members of both councils have met on an annual basis, alternating between Addis Ababa and New York, to discuss situations in Africa. No other regional organisation enjoys something akin, although both the European Union (EU) and its equivalent to the AU PSC, the Political and Security Committee, have had informal meetings with members of the Council since 2010 (with the exception of 2012) and 2013 respectively, and the Council endorsed UN-EU cooperation on international peace and security in 2014.[73] However, situations in Africa have dominated most of the agenda of the EU dialogues with the members of the Council, in light of EU peacekeeping, training, or funding efforts in the CAR, Mali, and Somalia. In addition, since the end of the Cold War, Africa has continued to be the prime destination of Security Council visiting missions. In fact, since 2000,

Council members have undertaken at least one annual trip to Africa, a routine that is unique to the continent.

This overview of the new games, rules, and moves introduced by the Security Council following the Cold War clearly demonstrates that Africa continues to be a prime testing ground for innovation. Despite some important challenges from affected or interested states, during the post–Cold War period the Council has had more opportunities to work in tandem with African institutions, setting them quite apart from most other regional organisations. Yet the games, rules, and moves introduced by the Council in strictly African contexts, whether through mandating parallel or hybrid peacekeeping deployments, establishing hybrid courts or referring specific situations to the ICC, addressing terrorism and mass crimes, or establishing new subsidiary bodies or consultative routines, have all created precedents and instruments for the Council to address the maintenance of peace and security more globally. The question remains, however, whether these and other games, rules, and moves first played in Africa will likewise be played elsewhere. There is abundant evidence that some of the precedents have been applied elsewhere, including in the form of parallel peacekeeping deployments with the EU or the North Atlantic Treaty Organisation (NATO) in the former Yugoslavia and of addressing several terrorism or mass crimes situations beyond Africa. However, many of the tools that have become available, such as ICC referrals and hybrid courts or peacekeeping missions, have yet to be applied in other latitudes and longitudes.

Conclusion

Africa will likely continue to be the prime playing ground of the Security Council in the near future, for several reasons. First, the power of precedent: the Council has repeatedly introduced new games, rules, and moves in addressing situations in Africa for many decades. Although the trend is not necessarily ingrained, it has arguably become more customary to play new games and apply new rules or moves to situations in Africa compared to other continents. Whether due to the pliability of the states concerned, the asymmetry of power compared to the P-5, the guilty conscience or agenda of the former colonial powers (Britain and France), or other factors, such as history—"an element that the West looks upon as irrelevant and tries to evacuate through the abstract bureaucratic language of 'peace and security'"[74]—Africa has undoubtedly been the place where the Security Council has dared, and been able, to innovate.

Second is the power of the present, which practically ensures that Africa will continue to be the prime playing ground for the Security Council at least in the immediate future. Between 2013 and 2015 Africa represented about one-third of the situations on the agenda of the Council,[75] and it was the subject of 90 of a total of 167 (53.9 per cent) Council meetings scheduled in 2015 as well as 60 of the 90 (66.7 per cent) Council decisions adopted.[76] In June 2017, the continent hosted nine of the 16 (56.2 per cent) peacekeeping missions deployed. Even if all situations in Africa were to evolve positively, the lifting of

Security Council–mandated measures currently in place would take some time. Agenda items become inactive after three years of inactivity, and can be subsequently reactivated on the request of any member state within the subsequent three years. Peacekeeping missions generally undergo gradual downsizing before full withdrawal and, taking into account the inordinate size of some of the current deployments in Africa, any downsizing is likely to be extended. Moreover, with France, Britain, and the United States each leading about a third of the agenda items pertaining to the continent under the so-called penholder arrangements that have come to the fore of late, the timing and framing of Council decisions on Africa are mostly in the hands of external actors.

Third, in terms of agenda-setting, Africa is the only continent to have continental or regional agenda items enabling the Security Council to become seized of an issue without necessarily undergoing extended procedural debates. Agenda items such as "Peace Consolidation in West Africa", "Central African Region", or the "Situation in the Great Lakes Region", not to mention "Peace and Security in Africa", provide pre-established agenda items with which to initiate discussion, if not consideration, of practically any situation in Africa. The closest approximations elsewhere are the agenda items "Situation in the Middle East", which despite its geographic ambiguity is nonetheless more confined compared to continental Africa, and the now defunct "Situation in Central America" and "Situation in Southeast Asia". Situations as diverse as Zimbabwe in 2008, Libya in 2011, and Mali in 2012 all came to the attention of the Council through the item "Peace and Security in Africa". What is interesting about these agenda items is that they were added when significant stakeholders from Africa were members of the Security Council: Egypt, along with Botswana and Guinea-Bissau, for the "Situation in the Great Lakes Region" in 1996; Angola, along with Cameroon and Guinea, for the "Central African Region" in 2003; Ghana and Tanzania, along with the Congo, for "Peace Consolidation in West Africa" in 2006; and Ghana and South Africa, along with the Congo, for "Peace and Security in Africa" in 2007.

Last, and probably most important, despite the emergence of the OAU-AU and a host of sub-regional organisations in Africa, the Security Council will most likely continue to exert its right to primacy as enshrined in Chapter VIII of the UN Charter whenever it sees fit. The Council reminds the AU PSC of its primacy every time they meet for their annual consultative meetings in opposing any reference that would suggest a meeting of equals.[77] Some may argue that so long as Africa is deprived of permanent membership in the Council—a prospect that seems improbable so long as the 2005 Ezulwini Consensus continues to hold Africa to an impossible maximalist position among other factors, including the byzantine rules of Article 108 of the UN Charter, which give the current permanent members a "veto" over any such reform—the Council will not be deterred from playing the games it can in Africa.

However, it would be false to portray the introduction of new games, rules, and moves as having been directed against Africa, in that all the innovations mentioned in this chapter, save five, were adopted with the acquiescence of the

African members of the Council at the time. Resolutions 221 and 232 on Southern Rhodesia were adopted in 1966 with the support of Nigeria and Uganda; only Mali abstained. Resolution 1593 on Sudan was likewise supported in 2005 by Benin and Tanzania; only Algeria abstained. Only Rwanda voted against Resolution 955 establishing the ICTY in 1994, not Djibouti or Nigeria. In fact, there was only one Security Council decision—the imposition of sanctions on Libya via Resolution 748 of 1992—that was rejected by the African states in the Council at the time, with Cape Verde, Morocco, and Zimbabwe abstaining but not voting against the measures. At the same time, one or more Western members of the Security Council either abstained or voted against 18 of the resolutions referenced here.

Africa has allowed the Security Council to explore new boundaries, serving as the prime testing ground for new games, rules, and moves, mostly pertaining to Chapters VII and VIII of the UN Charter. In maintaining peace and security in Africa, first or significant precedents were introduced to Articles 39, 41, 42, 43, 50, and 51 of Chapter VII. This is no small feat, as most of the remaining articles of Chapter VII (44–47) have been largely superseded in light of the development of peacekeeping, or deal with provisional measures (Article 40). If one takes into account that Chapter VII is where the most intrusive powers of the Security Council reside, the most robust tools available to the Council have found a prime testing ground in Africa. Regarding Chapter VIII (Articles 52–54), the Security Council first tested the waters of cooperation with regional organisations with the OAU in 1964 and then with ECOWAS in 1993.

Kipling immortalised the term "Great Game" in 1900, and declared that the Boer War would give "no end of a lesson". In many ways, Africa has given the UN Security Council "no end of a lesson" in providing the Council with a prime playing ground to innovate, for good and bad, and to set game-changing precedents. Let us hope that in the future the lessons learned in and from Africa enable the Security Council to play a better game—for the sake of the innocent populations most directly affected by the threats or breaches to the peace in Africa and beyond—and, whenever possible, to do so cooperatively in tandem with African partners.

Notes

1. *See* Adekeye Adebajo, *UN Peacekeeping in Africa: From the Suez Crisis to the Sudan Conflicts* (Boulder, CO: Lynne Rienner, 2011), p. 1. Adebajo uses the phrase "the games that great powers play".
2. Arthur Conolly, *Journey to the North of India, Overland from England, Through Russia, Persia, and Afghanistan* (London: R. Bentley, 1834); Rudyard Kipling, *Kim* (London: Macmillan, 1901).
3. Thomas Packenham, *The Boer War* (London: Abacus, 2012), p. 64.
4. *See* John von Neumann and Oskar Morgenstern, *Theory of Games and Economic Behavior* (Princeton: Princeton University Press, 1944).
5. James D. Morrow, *Game Theory for Political Scientists* (Princeton: Princeton University Press, 1994), p. 1.

6. The first situations or questions addressed by the United Nations (UN) Security Council were Iran (2nd meeting, 25 January 1946), Spain (39th meeting, 29 April 1946), and Greece (82nd meeting, 10 December 1946, which also involved Albania and Bulgaria).
7. The first situations or questions addressed by the UN Security Council were Guatemala (675th meeting, 20 June 1956) and Egypt (735th meeting, 5 October 1956). Egypt had previously been addressed not as a situation in itself but as one of the Arab parties to the Armistice Agreements for Palestine (1949).
8. Just in 1960, Benin, Burkina Faso, Cameroon, the Central African Republic (CAR), Chad, Congo, Côte d'Ivoire, the Democratic Republic of the Congo (DRC), Gabon, Madagascar, Mali, Niger, Nigeria, Senegal, Somalia, and Togo were admitted. Current official names are used here, for consistency. Morocco and Tunisia had been admitted in 1956, Ghana in 1957, and Guinea in 1958.
9. Britain is used synonymously with the United Kingdom (UK) in this volume.
10. Letter from the Representatives of France and the United Kingdom addressed to the President of the Security Council, UN Doc. S/3645, 12 September 1956.
11. As acknowledged in UN Security Council Resolution 119, S/RES/119, 31 October 31 1956; adopted 7-2-2, with France and Britain voting against and Australia and Belgium abstaining.
12. This resolution, adopted to address the Korean War, allows the General Assembly to seize itself of a situation already under consideration by the Security Council, when the Council is deadlocked due to the use, or threat of use, of the veto by its permanent members. UN General Assembly Resolution 377 A (V), 3 November 1950.
13. UN Security Council Resolution 161, S/RES/161, 21 February 1961; adopted 9-0-2, with France and the Soviet Union abstaining.
14. *See* Bruno Stagno Ugarte and Jared Genser, "Evolution of the Security Council's Engagement on Human Rights", in Jared Genser and Bruno Stagno Ugarte (eds.), *The United Nations Security Council in the Age of Human Rights* (Cambridge: Cambridge University Press), pp. 3–31.
15. Bruno Simma, Hermann Mosler, Albrecht Randelzhofer, Christian Tomuschat, and Rüdiger Wolfrum (eds.), *The Charter of the United Nations: A Commentary* (Oxford: Oxford University Press, 2002), p. 751.
16. *See* Bruno Stagno Ugarte, "Collaborating with Regional Organizations", in Sebastian von Einsiedel, David M. Malone, and Bruno Stagno Ugarte, (eds.) *The UN Security Council in the 21st Century* (Boulder, CO: Lynne Rienner, 2015), pp. 475–490; Stephen A. Schlesinger, *Act of Creation: The Founding of the United Nations—A Story of Superpowers, Secret Agents, Wartime Allies and Enemies, and Their Quest for a Peaceful World* (Boulder, CO: Westview, 2003).
17. Adebajo, *UN Peacekeeping in Africa*, p. xvi.
18. UN Security Council Resolution 182, S/RES/182, 4 December 1963; adopted unanimously.
19. UN Security Council Resolution 190, S/RES/190, 9 June 1964; adopted 7-0-4, with Brazil, France, Britain, and the United States (US) abstaining. UN Security Council Resolution 191, S/RES/191, 18 June 1964; adopted 8-0-3, with Czechoslovakia, France, and the Soviet Union abstaining.
20. UN Security Council Resolutions 610 and 615, S/RES/610 and S/RES/615, 13 March and 17 June 1988; adopted unanimously. UN Security Council

Resolution 623, S/RES/623, 23 November 1988; adopted 13-0-2, with Britain and the US abstaining.

21. UN Security Council Resolution 181, S/RES/181, 7 August 1963; adopted 9-0-2, with France and Britain abstaining.
22. UN Security Council Resolution 418, S/RES/418, 4 November 1977; adopted unanimously.
23. UN Security Council Resolution 421, S/RES/421, 9 December 1977; adopted unanimously.
24. UN Security Council Resolution 919, S/RES/919, 25 May 1994; adopted unanimously.
25. UN Charter, Article 6.
26. UN Security Council Resolution 269, S/RES/269, 12 August 1969; adopted 11-0-4, with Finland, France, Britain, and the US abstaining.
27. UN Security Council Draft Resolution, S/11543, 6 June 1974; adoption failed due to vetoes cast by France, Britain, and the US.
28. Simma et al., *The Charter of the United Nations*, p. 213.
29. UN Security Council Resolution 216, S/RES/216, 12 November 1965; adopted 10-0-1, with France abstaining.
30. UN Security Council Resolution 217, S/RES/217, 20 November 1965; adopted 10-0-1, with France abstaining.
31. UN Security Council Resolution 221, S/RES/221, 9 August 1966; adopted 10-0-5, with Bulgaria, France, Mali, the Soviet Union, and Uruguay abstaining.
32. Simma et al., *The Charter of the United Nations*, pp. 126–127. The situation in the Korean peninsula was considered to be a breach of the peace.
33. Simma et al., *The Charter of the United Nations*, p. 751.
34. UN Security Council Resolution 232, S/RES/232, 16 December 1966; adopted 11-0-4, with Bulgaria, France, Mali, and the Soviet Union abstaining.
35. UN Security Council Resolution 253, S/RES/253, 29 May 1968; adopted unanimously.
36. UN Security Council Resolution 448, S/RES/448, 30 April 1979; adopted 12-0-3, with France, the United Kingdom, and the United States abstaining.
37. UN Security Council Resolution 246, S/RES/246, 14 March 1968; adopted unanimously.
38. UN Security Council Resolution 284, S/RES/284, 29 July 1970; adopted 12-0-3, with Poland, the Soviet Union, and Britain abstaining.
39. Simma et al., *The Charter of the United Nations*, p. 461.
40. UN General Assembly Resolutions 3111 (XXVIII), 12 December 1973; 31/146 and 31/152, 20 December 1976; and 40/97, 13 December 1985.
41. UN Security Council Resolution 566, S/RES/566, 15 June 1985; adopted 13-0-2, with Britain and the US abstaining.
42. Simma et al., *The Charter of the United Nations*, p. 293.
43. UN Security Council Resolution 294, S/RES/294, 15 July 1971; adopted 13-0-2, with Britain and the US abstaining.
44. UN Security Council Resolution 312, S/RES/312, 4 February 1972; adopted 9-0-6, with Argentina, Belgium, France, Italy, Britain, and the US abstaining.
45. UN Security Council Resolution 546, S/RES/546, 6 January 1984; adopted 13-0-2, with Britain and the US abstaining. UN Security Council Resolution 574, S/RES/574, 7 October 1985; adopted unanimously.

46. UN General Assembly Resolution 2863 (XXVI), 20 December 1971.
47. UN Security Council Resolution 308, S/RES/308, 19 January 1972; adopted unanimously.
48. UN Security Council Resolution 309, S/RES/309, 4 February 1972; adopted 14-0-0, as China registered no vote. UN Security Council Resolution 310, S/RES/310, 4 February 1972; adopted 13-0-2, with France and Britain abstaining. UN Security Council Resolution 311, S/RES/311, 4 February 1972; adopted 14-0-1, with France abstaining. And the previously cited UN Security Council Resolution 312, S/RES/312, 4 February 1972; adopted 9-0-6, with Argentina, Belgium, France, Italy, Britain, and the US abstaining.
49. UN Security Council Resolution 199, S/RES/199, 30 December 1964; adopted 10-0-1, with France abstaining.
50. UN Security Council Resolution 626, S/RES/626, 20 December 1988; adopted unanimously. UN Security Council Resolution 632, S/RES/632, 16 February 1989; adopted unanimously.
51. James Cockayne, Christoph Mikulaschek, and Chris Perry, "The United Nations Security Council and Civil War: First Insights from a New Dataset", International Peace Institute, September 2010, p. 19.
52. UN Security Council Resolution 866, S/RES/866, 22 September 1993; adopted unanimously.
53. UN Security Council Resolution 1769, S/RES/1769, 31 July 2007; adopted unanimously.
54. UN Security Council Resolution 2100, S/RES/2100, 25 April 2013; adopted unanimously.
55. Security Council Report, "July 2013 Monthly Forecast" (New York, 28 June 2013), p. 12.
56. UN Security Council Resolution 731, S/RES/731, 21 January 1992; adopted unanimously.
57. UN Security Council Resolution 748, S/RES/748, 31 March 1992; adopted 10-0-5, with Cape Verde, China, India, Morocco, and Zimbabwe abstaining.
58. Letter from the Secretary of the People's Bureau of the Great Socialist People's Libyan Arab Jamahiriya to the Kingdom of the Netherlands to the Registrar of the International Court of Justice, 3 March 1992, http://www.icj-cij.org/docket/files/88/7207.pdf, p. 5
59. Organisation of African Unity (OAU) Resolution AHG/Dec.1–27 (XXXIV), 10 June 1998.
60. UN Security Council Resolution 827, S/RES/827, 25 May 1993; adopted unanimously.
61. UN Security Council Resolution 955, S/RES/955, 8 November 1994; adopted 13-1-1, with Rwanda voting against and China abstaining.
62. Report of the Secretary-General on the Establishment of a Special Court for Sierra Leone, UN Doc. S/2000/915, 4 October 2000.
63. UN Security Council Resolution 1315, S/RES/1315, 14 August 2000; adopted unanimously.
64. UN Security Council Resolution 1593, S/RES/1593, 31 March 2005; adopted 11-0-4, with Algeria, Brazil, China, and the US abstaining.
65. UN Security Council Resolution 1970, S/RES/1970, 26 February 2011; adopted unanimously.

66. UN Security Council Resolution 1674, S/RES/1674, 28 April 2006; adopted unanimously.
67. *See* Global Center for Responsibility to Protect, http://www.globalr2p.org/resources/335 (accessed 25 March 2016).
68. Security Council Report, "The Security Council and the UN Peacebuilding Commission" (New York, 18 April 2013), p. 3.
69. Letters from the President of the Security Council Addressed to the Chairman of the Peacebuilding Commission, UN Doc. PBC/1/OC/2, 21 June 2006, in the case of Burundi and Sierra Leone; UN Doc. S/2008/419, 12 June 2008, in the case of the Central African Republic; UN Doc. S/2007/744, 11 December 2007, in the case of Guinea-Bissau; UN Doc. S/2010/389, 9 July 2010, in the case of Liberia.
70. Note by the President of the Security Council, UN Doc. S/2002/207, 1 March 2002.
71. Adebajo, *UN Peacekeeping in Africa*, p. 237.
72. *See* Stagno Ugarte, "Collaborating with Regional Organizations", pp. 486–487.
73. UN Security Council Presidential Statement, S/PRST/2014/4, 14 February 2014.
74. Gerard Prunier, *Africa's World War: Congo, the Rwandan Genocide, and the Making of a Continental Catastrophe* (New York: Oxford University Press, 2011), p. 336.
75. *See* Summary Statement by the Secretary-General, UN Doc. S/2016/10, 4 January 2016.
76. UN Security Council Affairs Division, "Highlights of Security Council Practice 2015", http://www.un.org/en/sc/inc/pages/pdf/highlights/2015.pdf (accessed 25 March 2016).
77. *See* Joint communiqué of the Ninth Annual Joint Consultative Meeting Between the Peace and Security Council of the African Union and Members of the United Nations Security Council, UN Doc. S/2015/212, 27 March 2015.

CHAPTER 11

The Politics of Peacekeeping

Ibrahim A. Gambari

With all its imperfections, the United Nations (UN) can work more effectively to strengthen African peace and security, if it treats initiatives undertaken by the African Union (AU) and Africa's regional economic communities (RECs) seriously rather than perfunctorily. At the same time, African states must do more to promote and adhere to unified, common positions and perspectives on continental and global issues. Against that background, this chapter discusses the responsibility and practice of the 15-member UN Security Council as a partner with African countries and the AU in the maintenance of peace and security on the continent. This partnership is currently an unequal and uneasy one. The challenge is to make it a more balanced one based on mutual respect, and to make it more beneficial to Africa. By examining the failure of the international community to respond to the genocide in Rwanda in 1994, in which 800,000 people were killed, and the deployment of the AU-UN Hybrid Operation in Darfur (UNAMID) by the UN Security Council in 2007, this chapter provides an anatomy of the politics of peacekeeping in Africa.

The chapter is based on my almost two-and-a-half decades of experience with the UN, where I served in several roles, including as Permanent Representative of Nigeria and chair of the UN Special Committee on Peacekeeping Operations between 1990 and 1999, Special Representative of the UN Secretary-General in Angola between 2002 and 2003, and Under-Secretary-General for Political Affairs between 2005 and 2007. The chapter also draws from my recent experience as the AU-UN joint special representative and head of UNAMID from 2010 to 2012.[1] Furthermore, from 1994 to

I thank Dan Kuwali for research assistance in preparing this chapter.

I.A. Gambari (✉)
Savannah Centre, Abuja, Nigeria

T. Karbo, K. Virk (eds.), *The Palgrave Handbook of Peacebuilding in Africa*, https://doi.org/10.1007/978-3-319-62202-6_11

1995, I represented Nigeria as one of Africa's three non-permanent members of the Security Council. This period coincided with momentous changes in the international political environment, including the events leading up to the Rwandan crisis of 1994 and the genocide that followed.

The UN Security Council and the End of the Cold War

The euphoria that followed the fall of the Berlin Wall in November 1989, culminating in the end of the Cold War by 1990 and the defeat of Iraq in the first Persian Gulf War in February 1991 by a United States (US)-led coalition of forces authorised by the UN Security Council, may have encouraged the grandiose declaration about the advent of a "New World Order". In this euphoric atmosphere, American scholar Francis Fukuyama boldly claimed that the world had come to the "end of history",[2] precipitated by the apparent victory of the free market and liberal democracy over command economies and totalitarian political systems.[3] Nonetheless, the end of the Cold War presented Africa and the international community with the opportunity to resolve some of the long-standing and internecine conflicts on the continent—in Namibia, South Africa, Angola, and Mozambique—through UN peacekeeping missions. I was fortunate to have served as the last chair of the UN Special Committee Against Apartheid from 1990 to 1994.

However, the disappearance of the ideological rivalry between East and West, and its induced competition for friends and influence within Africa by the erstwhile superpower adversaries—the US and the Soviet Union—unleashed some of the negative forces of sub-nationalism and ethnic rivalry (see also Deng in this volume). African leaders, with the help of powerful external patrons, had previously suppressed many of these conflicts. Consequently, some of the client states that were artificially held together by Cold War patrons unravelled, resulting in a new wave of conflicts in Africa, from Liberia to Somalia to Rwanda and Burundi, among others. The post–Cold War era, therefore, presented the continent with positive opportunities for conflict resolution as well as an array of new pitfalls. The combination of old and new types of conflict in Africa invariably meant that the majority of issues that were before the UN Security Council were African cases, and today about 60 per cent of the Council's agenda involves African issues.[4] (See Ugarte in this volume.) The potentially positive aspect of this is that the Council is engaged with Africa in addressing its peace and security challenges, but the downside is that the continent is portrayed as one of endemic conflicts and wars, especially at a period when it is registering impressive and consistent growth and receiving a higher share of foreign direct investments. In 2016 Africa remained one of the world's fastest-growing regions—second behind only South Asia—with average economic growth of 2.2 per cent and expected to improve in 2017 and 2018.[5]

In this regard, and in an effort to promote the cause of peace in Africa, the Nigerian delegation that I headed while on the UN Security Council between 1994 and 1995 made it a cardinal and guiding principle in all our activities to work as hard as we could, in cooperation and collaboration with other Council members, to try to de-congest the Council's agenda of African issues. This approach was informed by the feeling that the multiplicity of crises raging in Africa had sapped the continent's meagre resources and hampered longer-term investment. Nigeria began by consulting the other two African members of the Council—Djibouti and Rwanda in 1994, and Botswana and Rwanda in 1995—before moving to encompass all non-aligned members of the Council and subsequently all other interested Council members.[6]

The crises in the Balkans, Burundi, and Rwanda in the 1990s, for which the UN appeared to be ill-prepared, soon led to the sober realisation that the world remained a dangerous place. Indeed, the root causes of conflicts and instability, especially those with economic origins, or with deep historical and ethnic antagonisms, did not disappear with the end of the Cold War. Rather, the case of Rwanda became emblematic of post–Cold War intra-state conflicts and exemplified the inability of the Security Council to address them effectively.

The UN's Failure to Respond to the 1994 Rwandan Genocide

While the work of the International Criminal Tribunal for Rwanda (ICTR) between 1995 and 2011 was key in achieving many victories for justice, these successes on the part of the international community cannot detract from the fact that the case of Rwanda exemplified the UN Security Council's inability to address post–Cold War conflicts effectively. The Rwandan genocide of 1994 exposed serious structural and policy failures in the UN system. The case revealed that the UN Security Council, which had received plenty of warnings about the impending tragedy in Rwanda, failed to fulfil its primary responsibility under the UN Charter to maintain international peace and security.[7] Without a doubt, it was the Security Council, especially its most powerful members that failed the people of Rwanda in their gravest hour of need. This conclusion is clear from the testimony of General Roméo Dallaire, the Canadian former force commander of the UN Assistance Mission for Rwanda (UNAMIR), at the ICTR in February 1998. Dallaire opined that "with a well-armed group of 5,000 men [and a proper mandate] the United Nations could have stopped the slaughter of hundreds of thousands of Rwandans".[8] There are several vital lessons to be learned from the UN Security Council's paralysis and the international community's failure to respond effectively to the genocide in Rwanda in 1994.

Peacekeeping Should Not Be Used to Advance Parochial National Interests

It will be recalled that, as the Rwandan genocide began in April 1994, 10 Belgian soldiers were killed while serving in the 2,500-strong UNAMIR. As a result, Belgium not only decided to withdraw its battalion from the country, but also embarked on diplomatic efforts to bring down the entire mission.

Bangladesh (see also Virk in this volume) followed the Belgian lead and withdrew its own contingent and, within two weeks, the first batch of UNAMIR soldiers had already been evacuated to Kenya. In a real sense, therefore, the Belgians triggered the collapse of UNAMIR. The withdrawal of the UN contingents was a clear signal to the *génocidaires* that the world was not interested in halting their slaughter of Rwandans. In hindsight, one of the most serious flaws in the mandated mission in Rwanda was that Belgium—an ex-colonial power, which could not be perceived as a neutral and impartial actor in the politics of Rwanda—was allowed to contribute troops to UNAMIR. Peacekeeping should never be used or abused to advance parochial national interests. Furthermore, actors with a direct stake in the conflict should not be permitted to take part in a peacekeeping mission in which they have a clear conflict of interest.

States Not Willing to Implement the Mandate Should Not Contribute Troops

Equally disturbing during the Rwandan crisis were the political positions adopted by many member states at the UN in New York. These states seemed concerned only about their own troops and the potential political repercussions, in their respective capitals, of peacekeepers returning home in body bags. Even as the massacre continued after the death of Rwandan president Juvenal Habyarimana in April 1994, the US, for example, did not publicly use the word "genocide" until much later in May–June of the same year—even then describing the killings merely as "acts of genocide"—due, in large part, to avoid intervening militarily and risking the lives of American soldiers.[9] While such concerns may be legitimate, they ignored the moral and overriding duty to help save defenceless civilians who were being massacred under the noses of UN peacekeepers. If a member state is not ready and willing to walk the talk, it should not contribute troops to peacekeeping operations. Contributing to peacekeeping is a serious exercise, and unless the member state is willing to implement the UN mandate fully, the international community is better served if that state does not contribute troops to the mission.

The UN Secretary-General Should Be Clear, Persuasive, and Consistent When Engaging the Security Council

In response to the pressure on the UN to act, the UN Secretary-General at the time, Egypt's Boutros Boutros-Ghali, presented a report to the Security Council in April 1994 that offered three possible options. The first was the deployment of an immediate and massive reinforcement of several thousand additional troops to UNAMIR and a change in its mandate from Chapter VI (peacekeeping) to Chapter VII (peace enforcement) in order to coerce the opposing forces into a ceasefire. Following the fiasco in Somalia, in which the deaths of 18 American soldiers in Mogadishu in October 1993 had led to the withdrawal of UN peacekeepers (see Mzali in this volume on its portrayal in film), this was not a politically feasible option for some members of the Security Council such as the US, which is often the most powerful voice on the Council. The second option envisaged a reduction in UNAMIR's size to a small group to be headed by the mission's force commander, Roméo Dallaire. This deployment would remain in Kigali and act as an intermediary between the two parties in an attempt to bring about a ceasefire, and would assist with the resumption of humanitarian relief operations. For this reduced mandate, the UN Secretary-General estimated that a force of about 270 observers would be sufficient. The third option foresaw a complete withdrawal, which Boutros-Ghali did not favour. This would have amounted to a complete abandonment of the people of Rwanda and a total betrayal of the ideals of the United Nations to promote human rights and collective security.[10]

Faced with these three options, the Security Council chose the second, ordering a sharp reduction in the size of UNAMIR's force. Not only did this reinforce the message of a passive international community, but it also exacerbated the genocide on the ground, which eventually resulted in 800,000 deaths within one month. In retrospect, the UN Secretary-General should have endorsed the first option for strong action more clearly, despite the almost certain opposition to such action by the most powerful members of the Council. It was Boutros-Ghali's duty to persuade the Council to do the right thing. Under similar circumstances, the Secretary-General should be clear and forceful in his engagement with the Council. He should ensure that the fate of a defenceless population does not become the victim of the politics of the most powerful nations. At the least, the Secretary-General should assume the high moral ground in defence of the powerless.

The Security Council Must Be Reformed to Ensure Less Selective and More Effective Engagement in Violent Conflicts

The Rwandan tragedy also illustrated an enormous contrast between the international community's will to prevent, or halt, genocide, on the one hand, and the Security Council's support for interventions authorised by its most powerful members, on the other. While the Council refused to deploy a robust, large-scale force to stop the genocide, it stood behind the French when they asked for a mission that served a specific, limited purpose. While the entire world watched the ongoing tragedy unfold, the Council authorised France to carry out *Operation Turquoise* under Chapter VII (peace enforcement) of the UN Charter.[11] UNAMIR, by contrast, was only authorised under Chapter VI (peacekeeping), which remained the platform for its mandate. (On French interventionism in Africa, see Adebajo, and Yates in this volume.)

Thus, the Council proved itself to be what it is—a political institution that functions in concentric circles of interests and relative influence. The outer ring of that circle consists of the non-permanent members that do not belong to the Non-Aligned Movement (NAM), unless they have other connections with members of the North Atlantic Treaty Organisation (NATO). The next inward circle comprises the Non-Aligned Movement, whose members meet regularly and try, with occasional success, to harmonise their positions on issues before the Council. Then there are the five permanent members, in their various configurations (the P-5, the P-4 plus China, the circle of the P-3 [France, Britain,[12] and the United States], and the P-2 [Russia and China]), and finally the most powerful inner circle, the P-1, which is, of course, the United States.[13] Unless the membership of the UN Security Council is reformed and democratised, and comes to reflect today's economic, demographic, and political realities, and unless Africa is fully represented and taken into consideration, the body will continue to be an institution that selectively safeguards narrow interests and is of limited value to the people who need it the most.

The AU-UN Hybrid Operation in Darfur

In striking contrast to the UN Security Council's response to the Rwandan crisis has been its response to the events in Sudan's Darfur region, where a long-running dispute erupted in February 2003, resulting in an estimated 200,000 deaths by 2004.[14] In a real sense, the Security Council's more engaged and proactive response to the violence being directed against the civilian population in Darfur owed significantly to the Council's earlier failure to respond to the tragedy in Rwanda. The cry of "Never again!" seemed to have been heard. While some argue that the UN response in Darfur was not as prompt as, or in the form that, they would have preferred,[15] no one can dispute that the Security Council moved forward in Darfur, rather than retreating. Subsequently, however, the Council slowed down when it came to the need to apply effective sanctions against the armed movements who clearly became "spoilers" in the peace process.

The genocide in Rwanda a decade earlier had the additional and perhaps unintended consequence of reawakening governments in Africa to an appreciation of their own responsibility to protect civilian populations beyond their territorial borders and narrow political interests. Rwanda taught Africans not to rely purely on the goodwill of the larger international community to police and resolve conflicts on their continent. The need for *Pax Africana*, for Africa to develop its own resources and mechanisms to initiate effective and robust engagements to resolve the problems of the continent,[16] was becoming increasingly apparent (see Introduction, Mazrui, Kuwali, and Nagar in this volume). The Constitutive Act of the African Union, which replaced the Organisation of African Unity (OAU) in 2002, accorded the AU a collective right to intervene to prevent mass atrocities, and a new African Peace and Security Architecture (APSA) was created (see Kuwali in this volume).[17] Although members of the Economic Community of West African States (ECOWAS) had, through the deployment of the ECOWAS Ceasefire Monitoring Group (ECOMOG) in Liberia between 1990 and 1998 and later in Sierra Leone between 1997 and 1999, shown their resolve in this regard (see Adebajo in this volume on

ECOWAS peacekeeping in Mali), it was in Darfur that the continent demonstrated forcefully and concretely its determination to provide security and protection for its own people, to which the international community was more inclined to respond in kind.

From the beginning of the international conversation on Darfur, Africa and the UN Security Council were jointly engaged in the protection of the civilian population there and seeking peaceful, political solutions to the conflict. A critical lesson had been learned that if an issue is of vital importance to Africa, it must be championed by Africans themselves. The deployment of the African Union Mission in Sudan (AMIS), consisting of troops from Nigeria, Rwanda, Senegal, Gambia, Kenya, and South Africa, in June 2004, was a testament to such engagement.[18] AMIS showed that Africa was willing to put its boots where its politics lay. The 5,000 AMIS troops worked nobly under harsh conditions, with 60 of them paying the ultimate sacrifice after the inception of the mission in April 2004.[19] They embodied another important lesson learned from Rwanda: the troop-contributing countries in AMIS put their troops in harm's way to stem a potential humanitarian and human rights disaster. When the final history of Darfur is written, the work of those troops, from 2004 to the deployment of UNAMID beginning in December 2007, will be viewed as a flawed, but nonetheless essential, contribution to averting what could have been another Rwanda.

Today, through UNAMID, the UN and the AU have found an innovative form of engagement in the area of peace and security—the first hybrid AU–UN mission. Having begun operations in 2008, UNAMID had by August 2012 become the world's largest peacekeeping mission at the time, with 26,000 personnel, and the protection of civilians as its core mandate.[20] In 2016–2017 it remained one of the largest UN missions—second only after the UN Organisation Stabilisation Mission in the DRC (MONUSCO)—with more than 19,000 uniformed and civilian personnel, and a budget of over $1 billion.[21] As the joint special representative for UNAMID for two years, between 2010 and 2012, I represented both the UN and the AU in leading the mission. Despite some complexities that were inherent to implementing such a mission, the AU's engagement in the daily workings of UNAMID provided a much-needed balance to the political interests of key members of the UN Security Council. This engagement enabled strong and clear communication of the views of the region and the continent on how the peacekeeping mandate should be implemented in Darfur. Through the AU, the voices of the continent could be heard over those emanating from the capitals of the permanent members of the UN Security Council.

Furthermore, UNAMID has served as a real testing ground for the AU's 15-member Peace and Security Council (PSC), established in 2004. The demonstrated reluctance of many nations to put their troops in harm's way on the continent indicates that the type of hybrid operation seen in Darfur may represent the future. If this approach is to succeed, the AU's Peace and Security Council must play a vital role in mobilising African leaders to adopt unified perspectives on intra- and inter-state conflicts on their own continent. Through UNAMID, the AU has dealt with the practical realities of peacekeeping and, hopefully, learned lessons that will encourage it to seek a more active engagement with UN peacekeeping in future collaborative cases such as Somalia (on Somalia, see Hirsch, and Mahiga in this volume).

For African countries on the UN Security Council, the AU's engagement with UNAMID provides a unified African approach that these states can use to bolster their positions on the Council. In a real sense, the three African members of the Security Council should become the institutional voice of the AU and thus represent all the countries of the continent on the Council. Although such an approach may not in every important case overcome the UN Security Council's reluctance to act, or free it of its dominance by its most powerful members, it could temper the language employed in the chamber, and shift debates to take better account of African views. Furthermore, the more effective that African nations are in articulating their perspectives and positions, the more difficult it becomes to ignore their calls for reform of the Council.

UNAMID could potentially represent a new kind of engagement between Africa and the Security Council. However, Africans must be thoughtful and visionary, as well as vigorous enough to seize the opportunity that this mission presents. Rwanda was a case of the Security Council at its least effective in responding—or more accurately, not responding—to security challenges in Africa. If Africans continue to engage the Council, speak with one voice on behalf of the AU Peace and Security Council and as members of the UN and its Security Council, and are vigilant in monitoring and balancing the rhetoric and policies of the powerful members of the Council as they address the mission in Darfur, UNAMID has the potential to be one of the continent's finest moments.

UNAMID has clearly demonstrated that the hybrid model can work, and that it has several comparative advantages politically, operationally, and financially. The approach of hybrid operations as a viable way to develop and maintain regional and international engagement in resolving conflict situations should be encouraged and strengthened. Persistence to maintain the traditional business-as-usual decision-making frame of mind will likely strengthen the voices of dissatisfaction about the effectiveness of the UN's responses to conflicts in Africa, and lead African nations, and the regional organisations of which they are members, to limit their engagement with the UN on issues of common concern.

An internal challenge noted in the UNAMID deployment is to make sure that all the troop-contributing countries take three important actions. (On South Asian troop-contributing countries, see Virk in this volume.) First, ensure that the quality and quantity of contingents' equipment are up to UN standards; second, ensure that the pre-deployment training provided to national troops is adequate, thorough, and rigorous; and third, ensure that the soldiers who are sent to UN missions are of the highest calibre, and that these troops operate cohesively in the field. We had some contingents in UNAMID, including sadly from Nigeria, who did not perform adequately according to expectations. Fortunately, the Nigerian government sought to address this issue by repatriating one battalion, sending new troops, and re-equipping them. The UN and the AU should jointly examine the state of preparedness, the training, and the equipment of all peacekeeping contingents before deployment.[22]

UN-AU Coordination and Cooperation

There are three major points of contact and coordination between the UN and the AU that are relevant to the partnership between the two organisations in the area of peace and security: between the UN Security Council and the AU Peace and Security Council; between the UN Secretariat (Departments of Political Affairs and Peacekeeping) and the African Union Commission; and between the UN Secretary-General and the chair of the AU Commission. In all three cases, the contacts, cooperation, and coordination tend to be ad hoc and often perfunctory. (See Vogt in this volume.) To be fair, efforts have been made to improve the situation through the creation of the UN Office to the African Union in Addis Ababa and, on the part of the AU, through its permanent observer mission at the UN Secretariat in New York. (See also Hirsch in this volume.) Furthermore, both the UN and the AU, with the participation of Sudan, jointly created the Tripartite Mechanism in 2008 to coordinate their efforts in support of implementing UNAMID's mandate, although the mechanism has tended to address more logistical than substantive political issues. But these efforts are inadequate to ensure that the UN and the AU are two sides of the same coin when it comes to strengthening Africa's peace and security architecture.

Part of the difficulty in developing the required synergy is that whereas there is a P-5 that drives the agenda of the UN Security Council, there is no core group of the "able and willing" to do the same in the AU Peace and Security Council. Furthermore, the resources for maintaining full-scale peacekeeping operations by the AU or regional organisations on the continent are not always internally generated, with the AU relying on external donors for over 90 per cent of its funding in the security area.[23] Finally, the AU Commission chair, Chad's Moussa Faki Mahamat (since 2017), does not have the same authority over his nine commissioners that the UN Secretary-General, Portugal's António Guterres (since 2017), has over his Under-Secretaries-General and department heads in the UN Secretariat. As is well known, the AU commissioners and the AU Commission chair are elected, while the UN Under-Secretaries-General are appointed by the Secretary-General, whom they directly report to. Indeed, the chair of the AU Commission is more like a "super" commissioner with no specific portfolio, whereas the elected commissioners and deputy chairs have specific portfolios.

In addressing the deficiencies of the AU, it is essential and urgent that a review and re-organisation of the AU Commission be undertaken. Furthermore, with regard to the financing of AU-led but UN-authorised peacekeeping operations, the recommendations of the Prodi Report of December 2008 should be adopted with the proviso that financing by the UN should also extend beyond six months and to hybrid arrangements.[24] The African Group at the UN should be more proactive than it has been in recent times, and devise ways to ensure that the actions of the three African members of the Security Council reflect the AU's positions on issues before the Council. After all, the elections of these three African states to the UN Security Council have been hugely facilitated by the endorsement they receive from the AU, and with endorsement should come responsibility. In essence, what Africa needs is not a new dependency syndrome in peace and security areas, but increased assistance from the international community in capacity-building to undertake preventive diplomacy through enhanced early warning mechanisms, as well as logistical and financial support to both regional and sub-regional initiatives.[25]

Towards Strengthening Peacekeeping in Africa

As Africa continues its elusive quest for *Pax Africana* (see Mazrui in this volume), the continent has become a major contributor to the maintenance of international peace and security. The deployment of the AU Mission in Sudan in 2004 (replaced by UNAMID in 2007) and then the AU Mission in Somalia (AMISOM) three years later illustrates the need for a change in paradigm from analysis of the African continent as a mere consumer of international peace and security to a producer of security. AMISOM has made significant contributions to improving the security situation in Somalia that have facilitated positive political developments, especially the transfer of power from the transitional federal government to the federal government of Somalia in September 2012 (see Hirsch, and Mahiga in this volume).[26] As my specific two-year experience in Darfur (2010–2012) and my engagement towards the resolution of many other conflicts throughout the African continent over two decades has shown, successful intervention, whether through political engagement or with the help of a peacekeeping force, requires a sound understanding of the local, regional, and external dimensions of conflicts, including of the stakeholders involved and their interests.

Indeed, it can be argued that "pure" UN peacekeeping missions in Africa are losing their credibility and value, as evidenced by the experiences of the UN Mission in Ethiopia and Eritrea (UNMEE) between 2000 and 2008, the UN Mission in the Central African Republic and Chad (MINURCAT) between 2007 and 2010, and more recently, the UN Organisation Stabilisation Mission in the Democratic Republic of the Congo (previously the UN Organisation Mission in the DRC [MONUC]). And conversely, robust and preferably hybrid operations now appear to be the wave of the future in international peacekeeping on the African continent. In January 2013, AMISOM's review team, which I headed, recommended that a new joint AU-UN mission should be established in Somalia. We noted that such a mission should comprise an AU peace support operation, a UN peacebuilding office, and a joint mission support office, with the mission led by an AU-UN joint special representative appointed by both the AU and the UN.[27] Emboldened by their relative peacekeeping successes in theatres like Liberia, Sierra Leone, and Darfur, and confident in their keen understanding of the realities on the ground, Africa's regional organisations will increasingly resist any attempt to impose a unilateral decision-making process on peace and security matters on the continent (see Vogt in this volume). Such hybrid missions should have a structural arrangement that ensures joint AU-UN political direction and leadership and that AU troops have the necessary resources from the UN to pursue their mandates in the field effectively.[28]

Now over a decade and a half into its establishment, the AU has had to intervene in several conflicts, with mixed results, in the quest to maintain peace and security on the continent. In some instances, the AU has been commended for its efforts towards the prevention, management, and peaceful resolution of conflicts in cases such as Burundi (2003–2004) and Darfur (2004–2007); in others, it has faced considerable criticism concerning the way it responded to an evolving crisis, such as the case of Libya in 2011.

As the crisis in Libya demonstrated, African states continue to have limited influence on strategic decisions made by the UN Security Council and other multilateral bodies, including international financial institutions, all of which continue to be dominated by the great powers. Western countries have often resisted the push by African states for greater inclusion in key decisions affecting the African continent, including through a more proactive and flexible application of Chapter VIII of the UN Charter, relating to the role of regional organisations in peace and security issues.

The exclusion or weakening of African voices in the international arena can be reversed, however, through increased coordination among African countries and the joint development of new foreign policy approaches. This will require, among other things, a strengthening of the African diplomatic missions in Addis Ababa so as to ensure that they have the requisite human resources and expertise required to participate effectively in the deliberations of important AU bodies such as the Peace and Security Council. African representatives in multilateral fora in New York, Geneva, and Vienna should also be called upon to fulfil their duties towards the African continent and better coordinate their positions to reflect the collective views of African states, in order to increase the continent's leverage in world politics. African representation on the UN Security Council also needs urgent review. In this connection, I strongly endorse the idea that the three African non-permanent seats on the UN Security Council should be agreed as follows: rotation of one seat between Africa's major powers; the second between the continent's middle powers; and the third between the smaller countries. This would ensure that, at any given time, Africa is represented on the Council, and that the Council reflects the power configuration on the continent.

Conclusion

The international community has the power to end conflicts in theatres like Africa, but does not always choose to do so. The real key to this puzzle is the political will to act promptly and decisively. In the case of Rwanda in 1994, there was a glaring and tragic lack of political will to intervene to stop the genocide, particularly on the part of the most powerful members of the UN Security Council. In Darfur, the Council has shown greater will. As a result, while the conflict is estimated to have led to over 200,000 deaths since 2003,[29] the AU and the UN have together acted as a buffer and a facilitator for peace. When member states collectively make disastrous decisions, such as in Rwanda, there is a tendency to blame the UN as an institution, especially its Secretary-General. The Brahimi Report of August 2000 recommended that the UN Secretariat should always tell the Security Council, especially the Council's key members, what it needs to know and not what it wants to hear about situations of potential or actual conflict, in order for the body to reach informed and effective decisions.[30] Unfortunately, the tendency in recent times is the reverse, in my view. However, as Lord Caradon, the late British statesman and Permanent Representative to the UN from 1964 to 1970, famously noted: "There is nothing wrong with the UN that is not attributable to its members."[31] The UN is nothing more than an aggregation of its members, a tool that can be no more effective and responsive to world crises than its 193 member states—especially the most powerful ones—allow it to be.

I have two further observations. First, special responsibilities must be assumed by those with special privileges, especially on the Security Council, which, according to the UN Charter of 1945, has primary responsibility for the maintenance of international peace and security. Second, the Security Council must be reformed, as a matter of urgency, in terms of both its membership and its methods. It is a fact of international life that the AU is a regional organisation while the UN is a global one. It is also the case that under the UN Charter, the Security Council has primary responsibility for the maintenance of international peace and security. However, *primary* does not mean *exclusive* responsibility, and Chapters VI, VII, and VIII of the UN Charter are meant to be complementary, not stand-alone, provisions. Therefore, in order to address the challenges of peace and security in Africa, responsibility should be shared by the UN and the AU in a spirit of genuine partnership based on a creative and robust application of Chapter VIII of the UN Charter. The future of UN-Africa relations in the area of peace and security depends on a cohesive approach with a global perspective involving collective responsibility.

UNAMID represents a new kind of engagement between Africa and the UN Security Council. To be successful, the AU needs the support of its member states, every African citizen, and the larger international community. Happily, efforts have recently been moving in the right direction. Prospects for peace, stability, and prosperity in Africa are contingent on our ability and willingness to pursue opportunities with persistence, unwavering commitment, and relentless vigour. Populations affected by the scourge of violent conflicts; the refugees and internally displaced persons; the women, youth, the elderly, and everybody else—all require our attention and active engagement to be able to leave behind suffering and sorrow and attain the peace, security, justice, and dignity they truly deserve. Given the track record of the past decade, the AU is gradually measuring up to the challenges and can do much better in the next decade. However, achievement of these goals requires continued engagement and focus, as well as the understanding and support—both political and financial—of Africa's international partners.

Notes

1. Ibrahim Gambari, "The Politics of the United Nations Security Council: Lessons Learned from Rwanda and Darfur", keynote address delivered at the Centre for Conflict Resolution (CCR) seminar "South Africa, Africa, and the United Nations' (UN) Security Architecture", Cape Town, South Africa, 13–14 December 2011.
2. *See* Francis Fukuyama, "The End of History?", *The National Interest*, no. 16 (Summer 1989), pp. 3–18.
3. Ibrahim A. Gambari, "Rwanda: An African Perspective", in David M. Malone (ed.), *The UN Security Council: From the Cold War to the 21st Century* (Boulder, CO: Lynne Rienner, 2004), pp. 512–520.
4. CCR, *Towards a New* Pax Africana: *Making, Keeping, and Building Peace in Post-Cold War Africa*, Seminar Report no. 46 (Stellenbosch, May 2014), p. 12.
5. African Development Bank (AfDB), "Africa Remains World's Second-Fasted Growing Region", 24 May 2017, https://www.afdb.org/en/news-and-events/africa-remains-worlds-second-fastest-growing-region-17036 (accessed 8 August 2017).
6. Gambari, "Rwanda", p. 512.
7. *See* Article 24(1) of the UN Charter. *See also* Gambari, "Rwanda", pp. 512–513.
8. Lara Santoro, "Rwanda Massacres Were Avoidable, General Says", *Christian Science Monitor*, 27 February 1998, p. 7. *See also* Gambari, "Rwanda", p. 514.
9. Douglas Jehl, "Officials Told to Avoid Calling Rwanda Killings 'Genocide'", *New York Times*, 10 June 1994, http://www.nytimes.com/1994/06/10/world/officials-told-to-avoid-calling-rwanda-killings-genocide.html (accessed 25 November 2016); Rory Carroll, "US Chose to Ignore Rwandan Genocide", *The Guardian*, 31 March 2004, https://www.theguardian.com/world/2004/mar/31/usa.rwanda (accessed 25 November 2016).
10. *See* United Nations, *Special Report of the Secretary-General on the United Nations Assistance Mission for Rwanda*, S/1994/470, 20 April 1994, pp. 3–5.
11. UN Security Council Resolution 929, S/RES/929, 22 June 1994.
12. Britain is used synonymously with the United Kingdom (UK) in this volume.
13. Gambari, "Rwanda", p. 519.
14. United Nations, "Security Council Refers Situation in Darfur, Sudan, to Prosecutor of International Criminal Court", press release, 31 March 2005. *See also* United Nations, *Report of the International Commission of Inquiry on Darfur to the United Nations Secretary-General, Pursuant to Security Council Resolution 1564 of 18 September 2004*, Geneva, 25 January 2005, http://www.un.org/News/dh/sudan/com_inq_darfur.pdf#search=%22un%20report%20darfur%20genocide%22 (accessed 15 August 2013).
15. *See, for example*, Louis Charbonneau, "World Response to Darfur Is 'Anemic': US Envoy", *Reuters*, 3 April 2008, http://www.reuters.com/article/us-sudan-darfur-usa-idUSN03306185200804O3 (accessed 25 November 2016).

16. *See* Ali A. Mazrui, *Towards a Pax Africana: A Study of Ideology and Ambition* (Chicago: Chicago University Press, 1967).
17. *See* Adekeye Adebajo, Mark Paterson, and Jeremy Sarkin (eds.), "Africa's Responsibility to Protect", special issue, *Global Responsibility to Protect* 2, no. 4 (2010), especially Musifiky Mwanasali, "The African Union, the United Nations, and the Responsibility to Protect: Towards an African Intervention Doctrine", pp. 388–413.
18. African Union (AU), "Current Status of the Military Deployment for the Enhanced AMIS", Darfur Integrated Task Force, Information Update no. 3, 7 August 2005, http://www.africa-union.org/darfur/ditf%20info%20update%20No%203.pdf (accessed 15 August 2013).
19. Martin Binder, *The United Nations and the Politics of Selective Humanitarian Intervention* (Cham: Palgrave Macmillan, 2017), p. 108.
20. UN News Centre, "Interview with Ibrahim Gambari, African Union–United Nations Joint Special Representative for Darfur", 13 August 2012, http://www.un.org/apps/news/newsmakers.asp?NewsID=65 (accessed 10 August 2013). As of June 2017, the over 22,000-strong UN Organisation Stabilisation Mission in the Democratic Republic of the Congo (MONUSCO) was the world's largest peacekeeping operation.
21. UN Peacekeeping, "Peacekeeping Fact Sheet", 30 June 2017, http://www.un.org/en/peacekeeping/resources/statistics/factsheet (accessed 8 August 2017).
22. UN News Centre, "Interview with Ibrahim Gambari".
23. CCR, *The African Union at Ten: Problems, Progress, and Prospects*, international colloquium report, Berlin, Germany, 30–31 August 2012, p. 29.
24. United Nations, *Report of the African Union–United Nations Panel on Modalities for Support to African Union Peacekeeping Operations* [Prodi Report], UN Doc. A/63/666-S/2008/813, 31 December 2008.
25. Ibrahim A. Gambari, "Nigeria at Home and Abroad: The Dynamics of Nation Building", in Thomas Okpaku (ed.), *Selected Speeches* (Atlanta, GA: Chaneta International, 2007), p. 310.
26. AU, *Report of the African Union Commission on the Strategic Review of the African Union Mission in Somalia (AMISOM)*, 16 January 2013, p. i.
27. AU, *Report of the African Union Commission on the Strategic Review of AMISOM*, p. iii.
28. AU, *Report of the African Union Commission on the Strategic Review of AMISOM*, p. iii.
29. UN Department of Public Information, Peace and Security Section, "The United Nations and Darfur", August 2007, http://www.un.org/News/dh/infocus/sudan/fact_sheet.pdf (accessed 8 August 2017); "Genocide Fast Facts", *CNN*, 14 March 2017 (accessed 8 August 2017).
30. United Nations, *Report of the Panel on United Nations Peace Operations* [Brahimi Report], A/55/305-S/2000/809, 21 August 2000, pp. x, 12, 54.
31. Quoted in Ibrahim A. Gambari, "The Role of Africa in the United Nations", *American Foreign Policy Interests* 34, no. 4 (2012), p. 178.

CHAPTER 12

Pax Nigeriana Versus *Pax Gallica*: ECOWAS and UN Peacekeeping in Mali

Adekeye Adebajo

Late Kenyan scholar, Ali Mazrui, noted in 1993: "In the twenty-first century ... France's West African sphere of influence will be filled by Nigeria—a more natural hegemonic power in West Africa. It will be under those circumstances that Nigeria's own boundaries are likely to expand to incorporate the Republic of Niger, the Republic of Benin, and conceivably Cameroon."[1] Mazrui's bold prophesy of an expansionist *Pax Nigeriana* displacing the French *gendarme* in West Africa, remains unfulfilled over two decades after it was first uttered. This is despite praiseworthy Nigerian-led peacekeeping missions in Liberia, Sierra Leone, and Guinea-Bissau since 1990. Not only is Nigeria yet to swallow up Niger, Benin, and Cameroon, but it has faced its own potentially existential threats from Islamic militants Boko Haram (the group was driven out of major cities by 2016); communal violence that has killed over 20,000 people since 1999; secessionist groups in some of its eastern states[2]; and an increase in attacks by Niger Delta militants by 2016 that had cut a third of the country's oil supplies. In stark contrast, *Pax Gallica* appears to persist in francophone West African states such as Côte d'Ivoire and Mali in which France has deployed military troops to pursue parochial interests subsidised by United Nations (UN) peacekeeping missions. (See Yates in this volume.)

France has historically had more political clout than Nigeria in francophone West Africa. What makes the Mali case different, however, is that Boko Haram was fighting alongside militants in northern Mali, meaning that Abuja had a direct national security interest in resolving this crisis in its own sub-region. Even though Nigeria's immediate interests in defeating the terrorists coincided with those of France, Abuja also had a real interest in ensuring a reduced

A. Adebajo (✉)
Institute for Pan-African Thought and Conversation, University of Johannesburg, Johannesburg, South Africa

T. Karbo, K. Virk (eds.), *The Palgrave Handbook of Peacebuilding in Africa*, https://doi.org/10.1007/978-3-319-62202-6_12

French role in Mali. This is the background that explains why *Pax Nigeriana* was pitted against *Pax Gallica* in Mali. I argue in this chapter that Nigeria's response to this challenge was weak, and that France has effectively used the UN as an instrument to protect its parochial interests in Mali and neighbouring Niger.

Nigeria and France are countries with an inflated sense of their own importance. Both engage in a *politique de grandeur* that sometimes exaggerates style over substance. Both suffer from a nostalgic longing for past glory that often exposes their pretensions to be great powers. Both have citizens with a sense of fashion, good food, and *joie de vivre*. Both are competing on their respective continents with regional hegemons which sometimes appear to have more influence than them. South Africa and Germany, not Nigeria and France, have the most industrialised economies on their respective continents. But Nigeria's geo-strategic position is weaker than France's in several ways. While South Africa remains the only African country in the Brazil, Russia, India, China, and South Africa (BRICS) economic grouping and the Group of 20 (G-20) major economies, and is the only African country out of 11 global strategic partners of the European Union (EU), France is one of five veto-wielding permanent members of the UN Security Council: a club to which Germany does not belong. While Nigeria is one of the most important members of the Economic Community of West African States (ECOWAS) and the African Union (AU), France wields greater influence within the EU and the UN, giving it not just *regional* but—sometimes in African cases—*global* clout. (See Ugarte in this volume.) However, France is not a great power globally, but an African power. It is only in Africa that Paris can wield such influence. In this case study of Mali, France used the UN and the EU much more effectively to pursue its interests than Nigeria used ECOWAS and the AU. France even arguably used ECOWAS—through its francophone leaders—more effectively than did Nigeria.

Though political relations between Nigeria and France have historically been characterised by "deep distrust, hostility and conflict",[3] economic relations have paradoxically been profitable, developing almost independently of political tensions.[4] Since 1960, the Gallic nation has been the major obstacle to the realisation of Nigeria's hegemonic ambitions in West Africa. France provided diplomatic support to Cameroon in its long-running dispute with Nigeria over the Bakassi peninsula (largely ceded to Cameroon in 2002). The end of the Cold War made some Western countries wary of military interventions in Africa, particularly after United States (US)–led and Belgian-led UN peacekeeping debacles in Somalia (1993) and Rwanda (1994) respectively. (On Somalia, see Hirsch, and Mahiga; and on Rwanda, see Gambari, in this volume.) The Nigerian-led ECOWAS Ceasefire Monitoring Group (ECOMOG) interventions in Liberia and Sierra Leone between 1990 and 1999 seemed to mark Nigeria's opportunity to dominate its sub-region free of the constraints of the interventionist French *gendarme*. France, however, has proved an exception to the non-interventionist allergy among major Western states. It has continued, since 2003, to launch military interventions into countries such as Côte d'Ivoire, Chad, the Central African Republic (CAR), Libya, and more recently Mali.

Franco-Nigerian diplomatic relations had an inauspicious start. French president Charles de Gaulle was particularly irked by Nigerian prime minister, Tafawa Balewa's severing of diplomatic ties with France in January 1961 to protest French atomic tests in the Sahara. Full diplomatic relations were only resumed in May 1966. Between 1963 and 1966, Paris frustrated Nigeria's negotiation of a trade deal with the European Economic Community (EEC).[5] During the Nigerian civil war of 1967–1970, France—along with francophone Côte d'Ivoire and Gabon—provided Biafran secessionists with arms in an effort to reduce the potential threat to its "sphere of influence" from a dismembered Nigerian federation.[6] Paris also frustrated the economic integration efforts of the Nigerian-led ECOWAS by encouraging its former colonies to form rival trade blocs. By 1990, however, some signs pointed to a possible end to the Franco-Nigerian rivalry in West Africa. With Nigeria having become France's largest market for its investments in sub-Saharan Africa, with $23 billion worth of trade, French political and business interests argued that Nigeria should play a greater role in regional integration and seemed more prepared to accommodate Nigerian economic interests in its francophone neighbours, Benin and Niger.

Following a deep crisis of *Françafrique*—a corrupt and cosy system that had guided relations between Paris and its former colonies for three decades—after the end of the Cold War, a new generation of French policymakers emerged pushing for a change in its Africa policy; encouraging greater democracy; reaching out to anglophone countries like Nigeria, South Africa, and Ghana; and pushing for reducing the francophone African burden on the French treasury. Both Nigerian leader Olusegun Obasanjo and French president Jacques Chirac paid each other reciprocal state visits between 1999 and 2007. The election of the conservative, right-wing politician Nicolas Sarkozy as French president in May 2007, however, led to a resumption of Paris's former interventionist policies, most notoriously in Libya in 2011. The socialist regime of François Hollande, which came into office in May 2012 vowing to adopt a non-interventionist approach to Africa, undertook instead an old-style neo-colonial intervention into Mali barely nine months later. (See Yates in this volume.)

This essay assesses the leadership ambitions and roles of Nigeria and France in historical context under the rubric of *Pax Nigeriana* and *Pax Gallica*. I then use the specific case of the Mali peacekeeping mission in 2013 to examine the outcome of the paradoxical confluence and clash of both countries' foreign policies in the West African state, arguing that Paris outmanoeuvred Abuja by using the UN, the EU, and ECOWAS more effectively to promote its goals. I analyse the failure of the Nigerian-dominated African-led International Support Mission in Mali (AFISMA) to gain external logistical and financial support, as well as the speed with which this mission was provided with some of these resources and converted into a UN mission after the French military intervention in Mali in January 2013. The chapter concludes with some reflections on the lessons of the Mali case for the regional roles of Nigeria and France, as well as for future peacekeeping missions in Africa.

Pax Nigeriana: Gulliver's Troubles

Since its independence in 1960, over 150,000 Nigerian soldiers have been deployed to international peacekeeping missions, and the country has contributed troops to about 40 major United Nations and regional peacekeeping missions in Africa, Asia, Europe, and the Middle East. In July 2013, Nigeria had 5450 UN peacekeepers deployed around the world: the fifth largest contribution after Bangladesh, Pakistan, India, and Ethiopia (see Virk in this volume). Nigerian military and police were serving on UN missions in Mali, Sudan's Darfur and Abyei regions, Liberia, Côte d'Ivoire, the Democratic Republic of the Congo (DRC), South Sudan, Western Sahara, Haiti, and Lebanon. Between 2000 and 2011, Nigeria was the fourth largest contributor of peacekeepers to UN peacekeeping.[7] In June 2017, the country had 1667 peacekeepers deployed in ten missions.

This peacekeeping activism has been part of a *Pax Nigeriana*: Nigeria's historical quest to pursue a hegemonic leadership role and to secure a permanent seat on a reformed UN Security Council. The idea of "concentric circles" has historically guided Nigeria's foreign policy. The innermost circle represents Nigeria's own security, independence, and prosperity and is centred on its immediate neighbours—Benin, Niger, Chad, and Cameroon; the second circle revolves around Nigeria's relations with its ECOWAS neighbours; the third circle focuses on continental African issues of peace, development, and democratisation; while the fourth circle involves Nigeria's relations with organisations, institutions, and states outside Africa.[8] In this conceptual framework, the importance of ensuring that West Africa remains a "zone of peace" has often been stressed in Nigeria's diplomacy.[9] Aside from its peacekeeping efforts in its sub-region, Abuja has thus also provided support to democratic processes in Liberia, Sierra Leone, Ghana, Senegal, Niger, Mali, and Guinea-Bissau.

Under Nigerian president Goodluck Jonathan's administration between 2010 and 2015, the country's foreign policy suffered terminal decline, and Nigeria's international voice became muted. The country became a giant with clay feet, a regional Gulliver tied down by the petty ambitions and often inhumane greed of Lilliputian politicians who have consistently prevented a country of enormous potential from fulfilling its leadership aspirations in Africa. Abuja's feeble efforts to prevent South Africa's Nkosazana Dlamini-Zuma from assuming the chair of the AU Commission in 2012 failed despite Abuja's principled position that no representative of a large African power should occupy the post. Although Nigeria had the largest troop contingent in the AU-UN Hybrid Operation in Darfur (UNAMID), the UN brushed aside Abuja's objections and removed its special representative, Ibrahim Gambari, from leadership of the mission in 2012. The quality of Nigeria's soldiers had been questioned; its military and police contingents had often not been equipped to UN standards; and many of the country's armoured personnel carriers (APCs) had broken down in the mission area. (See Gambari in this volume.) These incidents have damaged the country's impressive peacekeeping record painstakingly built up over five decades.

Nigerian governments have also been criticised for not incorporating UN peacekeeping into broader foreign and security policy goals in a coherent manner.[10] Critics have pointed to the lack of a strategic approach to peacekeeping and poor coordination between key policymakers in Nigeria's ministries of foreign affairs, defence, and police affairs that has led to a lack of a clearly articulated rationale of the national interest involved in UN peacekeeping.[11] Parliamentary oversight of the country's UN contributions is also weak due to a lack of expertise and research capacity within the national legislature, and the dominant role of the executive, particularly under the presidency of Olusegun Obasanjo (1999–2007). Others have criticised the lack of battle-readiness of the Nigerian military, with its obsolete weapons and an air force cannibalised and grounded by the regime of General Ibrahim Babangida following its central role in an alleged coup plot in December 1985. Nigeria has been slow to modernise its weaponry and lacks the capacity to repair and service that weaponry, which led President Obasanjo to seek US support in professionalising his army from 1999.[12]

By the time of the return to civilian rule in 1999, the 94,500-strong Nigerian army was also not short of domestic and international trouble spots to police: nearly one-third of the military was being used during Obasanjo's first presidential term, between 1999 and 2003, for missions in Sierra Leone and on the Nigeria-Cameroon border, as well as in the Niger Delta and various parts of the country where conflicts with religious and ethnic undertones resulted in an estimated 12,000 deaths between 1999 and 2007. In March 2012, the Nigerian military and police contingents in UNAMID could not meet 20 per cent of the needs of the contingent-owned equipment (COE) required by the UN, while less than seven out of 45 of its armoured personnel carriers in the mission were functional.[13] Less than 30 per cent of these APCs were serviceable.[14] The country also experienced similar problems with its APCs deployed in Liberia.[15] Abuja was never able to meet the equipment needs in pre-deployment agreements signed with the UN Secretariat, causing much frustration within the UN Department of Peacekeeping Operations (DPKO) in New York.

Nigeria faced more serious threats. Particularly from 2009, terrorist attacks by a radical Muslim sect, Boko Haram, were killing scores of Nigerians in increasingly sophisticated attacks, including a suicide bombing of the UN's headquarters in Abuja in August 2011. By July 2013, an estimated 18,000 Nigerians had been killed by the terrorist group,[16] provoking the government to declare a state of emergency in three northeastern states (Adamawa, Borno, and Yobe), and to launch a military campaign against Boko Haram operations in these areas. This is the difficult domestic environment in which *Pax Nigeriana* has had to operate.

Pax Gallica: The Stubborn Persistence of Françafrique

Since 1960, France has pursued a neo-colonial six-decade relationship with Africa known as *Françafrique*.[17] (See Yates in this volume.) Africa has historically represented a stage on which France has sought to maintain the illusion of being a global power. As former French president François Mitterrand remarked in 1957: "Without Africa, France will no longer have a history in the twenty-first century."[18] An intricate network of political, military, economic, and cultural ties have been used since 1960 to promote French interests on the continent. Though all francophone African countries were eventually granted nominal independence by 1963, most signed military and economic pacts that gave France continued influence over their sovereign affairs. Paris maintained military bases across Africa, acting like a "pyromaniac fireman" in intervening over 50 times to prop up or depose assorted tyrants in countries such as Zaire (now the DRC), Gabon, Togo, and the Central African Republic. Thirteen francophone African states tied their currencies to the French franc. An important aspect of French policy was to keep trespassers out of its *pré carré* (backyard) or *chasse gardée* (private hunting-ground), often frustrating efforts at regional integration across Africa.

By 1990, pro-democracy demonstrations across Africa forced many francophone African governments to adopt various forms of multi-party democracy. But Paris continued to condone sham elections in countries like Burkina Faso, Cameroon, and Togo. Autocratic African governments also funded French electoral campaigns. Events in Africa's Great Lakes region eventually exposed the bankruptcy of Paris's Africa policy: France trained and armed the genocidal Hutu-led militias before the Rwandan genocide of 1994, in which about 800,000 people were killed, while its post-genocide Operation Turquoise helped *génocidaires* to escape into eastern Congo.[19] In neighbouring Zaire three years later, Paris supported a sinking Mobutu Sese Seko long after he had passed his sell-by date. Despite closing three military bases and renegotiating neo-colonial defence treaties, France still had about 7000 troops in Africa in 2013, and continued to act as an African *gendarme*.

In 2013, France had 450 troops in Côte d'Ivoire working alongside UN peacekeepers; and maintained a military presence in Senegal, Chad, Djibouti, Gabon, and the CAR. Paris has used its presence on the UN Security Council as one of five veto-wielding permanent members to pursue its parochial interests in Africa. (See Ugarte in this volume.) It pushed the Security Council to approve a 1350-strong UN Mission in the Central African Republic (MINURCA)—consisting largely of francophone troops from Gabon, Burkina Faso, Chad, Mali, Togo, and Senegal who had been part of a French-funded 800-strong force deployed in 1997—that sought to provide stability to an important French neo-colony between April 1998 and February 2000. This allowed 1400 French troops to depart a country in which Paris had maintained a military base until 1998.[20]

France also deployed 4600 troops to monitor a ceasefire in Côte d'Ivoire in 2003, and simultaneously financed the deployment of 1288 largely francophone African troops from Senegal, Niger, Togo, Benin, and Ghana to the country under the auspices of ECOWAS. Paris then influenced the deployment in 2004 of what became an 8000-strong United Nations peacekeeping mission in Côte d'Ivoire. After President Laurent Gbagbo refused to concede defeat to the French-backed Alassane Ouattara following UN-monitored elections in November 2010, French and UN forces helped pro-Ouattara Republican forces militarily to secure his presidential mandate. Genuine suspicions persisted about the stance of France, whose previous self-interested interventions in Africa, and continuing support for local autocrats, cast the Gallic power in the role of a fox guarding a hen-house. In the still volatile CAR in August 2013, French troops still controlled this supposedly sovereign country's airport, even as instability continued from a rebel invasion in March 2013 that toppled the autocratic rule of François Bozizé.

In more economically austere times following a eurozone crisis after 2008, France is now seeking to "Europeanise" its military interventions to reduce the political and financial costs of past unilateral interventions by convincing its EU partners to share the burden of neo-colonial interventions in pursuit of parochial national interests. The French military project Reinforcement of African Capacities to Maintain Peace (RECAMP) has been transformed into EURORECAMP in a bid to foster collaboration between regional training and operational centres in Africa, and purportedly to assist the AU to deploy peacekeepers to trouble-spots on the continent. EURORECAMP is based in Paris and involves personnel from France, Britain, Belgium, Finland, and Italy.[21]

The Roots of Mali's Conflict

The roots of Mali's conflict lay in two decades of poor governance after a 1968 military coup, followed by a fragile democratic transition from 1992. The country has been characterised by weak state institutions and a nepotistic, corrupt, and sometimes insensitive ruling elite. The 500,000-strong Tuaregs in the north felt that they had been marginalised since independence from France in 1960 with allegations of neglect of the development needs of the region and a lack of representation in the central government in Bamako. They therefore initiated a rebellion that raged particularly in the early 1990s. They felt that neither the National Pact for the Re-establishment of Peace, Brotherhood, and National Unity in Northern Mali in 1992 nor the Algiers Accord of 2006 had addressed their grievances.[22] These plans had integrated some Tuareg elements into the Malian army and police. (Many would later defect to join armed militants in 2013.) In Mali as a whole, nearly 80 per cent of the population of 14 million lived under the poverty line in 2013,[23] suggesting that the central government was also neglecting other regions and groups in the country.

The more proximate cause of the Mali conflict lay in the perception of junior officers that their senior officers were diverting resources for the counterinsurgency in northern Mali into their own pockets. This led to low morale and inoperable equipment among government troops. President Amadou Toumani

Touré—himself a former general and military head of state between 1991 and 1992—was seen as having mismanaged both this situation and the militant threat in the north. This coup was reminiscent of the military putsch staged by military officers in Sierra Leone in April 1992, when junior officers toppled the regime of former general Joseph Momoh, who was felt to have neglected their military needs in fighting Revolutionary United Front (RUF) rebels (see Rashid in this volume).

On 10 January 2012, the National Movement for the Liberation of Azawad (MNLA), a Tuareg group; Ansar Dine, an Islamic splinter group from the MNLA (whose political leadership was based in Mauritania); as well as Islamic extremists, al-Qaeda in the Islamic Maghreb (AQIM), and the Movement for Unity and Jihad in West Africa (MUJAO) launched attacks against government forces that led to them taking over the northern two-thirds of the country, including the key towns of Gao, Timbuktu, and Kidal. Several thousand heavily armed Tuareg fighters had returned to Mali in October 2011 having fought with Libya's deposed Muammar Qaddafi: this was a blow-back from the French-led military intervention in that country. Ansar Dine worked with AQIM towards its goal of imposing Sharia law across the Sahel, and was fighting against the MNLA.[24] The MNLA declared what it called the "independent state of Azawad", which no country recognised. These groups numbered around 3000 core fighters and also involved criminal networks. MUJAO and Ansar Dine were reported to be fighting alongside Nigerian militants Boko Haram, giving Abuja a direct stake in defeating this rebellion.

The Malian government's response to the mujahidin threat was weakened by the coup staged by the United States–trained Captain Amadou Sanogo in March 2012. In the same month, ECOWAS appointed Bukinabè head of state Blaise Compaoré as its mediator (he was himself ironically toppled in a "people's revolt" in October 2014 which revealed that he had lost the support of his military). The sub-regional body also announced plans to deploy a 3000-strong standby force if the rebels refused to settle the situation peacefully. The following month, an ECOWAS deal forced the resignation of the Malian president Amadou Touré and the appointment of Dioncounda Traoré as interim president. Compaoré urged the MNLA and Ansar Dine to negotiate collectively with Bamako. Led by Sanogo, however, the putschists continued to wield tremendous influence over the interim government.

Following the March 2012 coup, a support and follow-up group on the situation in Mali consisting of representatives from ECOWAS, the "core countries" (Algeria, Mauritania, and Niger), the AU, the EU, and key bilateral donors started to meet regularly. The AU pushed for greater coordination of domestic and international efforts, and stressed the need to restore state authority, security sector reform (SSR), and elections. Even as 412,000 Malians were displaced by the conflict (including 208,000 refugees in Algeria, Burkina Faso, Guinea, Mauritania, Niger, and Togo) by November 2012, tensions erupted between the rebels in the north, with Ansar Dine and MUJAO repelling the MNLA out of the main towns it had occupied. AQIM notoriously destroyed many historic and cultural sites in Timbuktu. These attacks also closed down the country's gold-mining industry.

AFISMA: Dead on Arrival

It is important to provide some brief background on *Pax Nigeriana*'s anaemic response to the Mali crisis. While Nigeria clearly has both economic and political interests in stabilising West Africa, its domestic political and economic problems continued to take up much of its attention and resources.[25] Nigeria's decision not to contribute troops to the ECOMOG mission in Guinea-Bissau (1999), and its decisions to reduce significantly its troops in Sierra Leone (1999–2000) and to subsume missions in Liberia, Sierra Leone, and Sudan's Darfur region under a UN umbrella between 1999 and 2007, were signs of a growing wariness at the costs and frustrations with regional peacekeeping. It is unlikely that civilian administrations will be able to sustain these casualties and costs without some loss of political support. The government of Goodluck Jonathan also decided not to deploy troops to the AU mission in Somalia in 2011 following an assessment by Nigeria's defence ministry.[26] This was another sign of growing caution about over-committing troops abroad amid Nigeria's own domestic security challenges. Nevertheless, in May 2012, Nigeria deployed peacekeepers to Guinea-Bissau as part of a 600-strong ECOWAS mission. Its domestic battles with Boko Haram, deployment of troops to Guinea-Bissau, and substantial commitments to UN missions in Liberia and Darfur, however, made it difficult to make another heavy commitment to Mali.

ECOWAS's leadership was, at the time that the Mali crisis erupted, francophone-dominated, allowing France to wield great influence among its major players. The organisation's key mediator was Burkinabè leader Blaise Compaoré, who had hosted French Gazelle helicopters in his country before they were deployed for military combat in Mali in January 2013[27]; its chair after February 2012 was Alassane Ouattara, leader of Côte d'Ivoire, whose presidential mandate had been largely restored by French arms; while the ECOWAS president, between 2012 and 2016, Kadré Ouédraogo, was former Burkinabè prime minister and a member of Compaoré's Congress for Democracy and Progress (CDP) party. All three were, in a sense, French Trojan horses within ECOWAS. Nigeria seemed diplomatically encircled and linguistically deficient.

In June 2012, the ECOWAS Commission in Abuja started to discuss the possibility of deploying a stabilisation force to re-establish state authority in northern Mali. The UN and external donors provided support to ECOWAS's planning. The Malian army, ECOWAS, and the AU all requested the UN Security Council to authorise deployment of an ECOWAS stabilisation force with a peace-enforcement mandate (under Chap. 7 of the UN Charter) to restore the country's territorial integrity and also to secure its border areas, while the Malian army re-established state authority. The concept of operations of the ECOWAS force was refined at two meetings involving senior Malian military officers, ECOWAS, the "core countries" (Algeria, Mauritania, and Niger), the AU, the UN, and other partners such as France, the US, and the EU in Bamako in August and October/November 2012.

A harmonised joint concept of operations—the "strategic operational framework"—emerged that sought to align the Malian army's plans with those of a sub-regional force, AFISMA. The mission would back a poorly equipped 5000-strong Malian army in three phases: to build its capacity; to recover occupied parts of the north and reduce the terrorist threat; and to transition to stabilisation activities in order to consolidate state authority in northern Mali. The plan also stressed the importance of longer-term security sector reform of the Malian army.[28] A joint coordination mechanism was established involving the ministers of defence of Mali, ECOWAS troop-contributing states, and the neighbouring "core countries", as well as the AU, the UN, and other international donors.[29]

Both ECOWAS and AU leaders endorsed the plan in November 2012, and asked the UN Security Council to authorise a 3300-strong African-led International Support Mission in Mali—with infantry units, air assets, and formed police units—for an initial one-year period. The force was authorised in December 2012 in a resolution drafted by France,[30] with the UN Security Council urging AFISMA to take all necessary steps to rebuild Mali's army; help the government to extend its authority to the north; protect civilians; and help stabilise the country after military operations.[31] The force was to be deployed by September 2013, crucially signalling to armed militants that they had nine months in which to defeat the Malian army. In order to ensure efficient deployment of AFISMA to Mali, the AU asked for a logistical support package to be provided to the mission through assessed UN contributions, as had occurred with the AU-UN Hybrid Operation in Darfur in 2007 (see Gambari in this volume).

This plan was great on paper, but would be difficult to implement in practice given the logistical and financial challenges of sub-regional armies, and Nigeria's peacekeeping over-commitments. AFISMA was mandated to train, equip, and provide logistical support to the Malian army, but could hardly equip or provide logistics to sustain itself in the field without substantial external assistance. The UN Secretariat and Department of Peacekeeping Operations—headed by Frenchman Bernard Miyet—had been particularly hostile to the Nigerian peacekeeping presence in Sierra Leone,[32] and was later (under another Frenchman, Jean-Marie Guéhenno) critical of the AU-UN hybrid model in Darfur. (The French have headed the UN Department of Peacekeeping Operations since Ghana's Kofi Annan promised it to them in 1996 in order to win their support to secure the post of UN Secretary-General that year.)

The UN Secretariat was therefore lukewarm towards AFISMA as reflected in the reports of its Secretary-General, Ban Ki-moon, to the UN Security Council. Ban regarded AFISMA as an instrument of "last resort" despite the fact that only military force would clearly dislodge hardened militants in northern Mali. He continually warned that an ill-conceived intervention by AFISMA could worsen the situation on the ground, and noted that the deployment of such a force could result in human rights abuses. He condescendingly and persistently cautioned that these troops would have to be "held accountable" for their actions, and called for UN human rights monitors to be deployed who would effectively "police" AFISMA peacekeepers. Ban also kept asking for more details of how AFISMA would be led, financed, equipped, and coordinated.

Most cynically, the South Korean UN Secretary-General refused to consider the logistical support package that AFISMA was requesting to fulfil a task that was clearly in the interests of not just the West Africans, but also the entire international community, and particularly powerful Western states like France and the US.[33] Ban absurdly called for funding of the military operations to be done by bilateral or voluntary contributions: a clearly unsustainable basis to approach such a dangerous mission. France's fingerprints appeared to be all over several of the UN Secretary-General's reports. Ban, for example, left open the possibility of member states directly supporting military action to combat armed groups in Mali.[34] Instead of the logistics and funding needed by AFISMA, the UN offered patronising platitudes about human rights observance. By March 2013, the Consolidated Appeals Process for Mali had received only $73.7 million, representing only 20 per cent of its $368 million target.[35]

The Strange Reappearance of the *Gendarme*

As militants from Ansar Dine, MUJAO, and AQIM came to within 680 kilometres of Bamako on 10 January 2013, routing weak and demoralised Malian government forces, President Dioncounda Traoré requested French assistance to prevent a march on the capital. The fact that a supposedly sovereign African country was turning to a former colonial power to protect its sovereignty was itself the greatest indictment of *Pax Africana*: Ali Mazrui's call in 1967 for Africans to keep peace on the continent through their own exertions (see Introduction and Mazrui in this volume). The same day as this attack, Paris pushed the UN Security Council to declare Mali's crisis a "threat to international peace and security", thus legitimising its impending military actions.

Even before this militant drive to Bamako, French special forces had already reportedly been fighting in Mali alongside the Malian army.[36] In a well-coordinated move, France launched Operation Serval a day after the French-drafted UN Security Council resolution, with its troops eventually reaching 4000. (Appropriately, "serval" is an African cat of prey that urinates 30 times an hour to mark out its territory!) In a *Blitzkrieg* conducted closely with 2000 troops from autocratic Chad rather than AFISMA, France retook major northern towns like Gao, Konna, and Timbuktu by the end of January 2013, as the militants withdrew north into the desert and the Adrar des Ifoghas mountains. Some of the jihadists staged suicide bombings and hit-and-run strikes against French and Malian units, as well as the MNLA.[37] By March 2013, the militants retained a presence in Kidal, Gao, and along the Niger

River and Ouagadou Forest, with some also retreating to neighbouring countries. Northern Mali had been rendered a "Wild West" featuring drug cartels, cross-border banditry, ransom kidnapping, human trafficking, and money-laundering.[38] The US, Britain, Germany, Canada, and Denmark rushed to provide France with the logistical support that AFISMA had earlier been denied.[39]

French president François Hollande—suffering from low domestic poll ratings—pledged that France would stay in Mali as long as it took to defeat the terrorists.[40] He argued in January 2013 that "Mali would have been entirely conquered and the terrorists would be in a position of force not just to submit the Malian population to a regime it did not want but to put pressure on all the countries of West Africa".[41] France was thus astonishingly—and humiliatingly for Nigeria—presenting itself as a guarantor of peace not just in Mali, but in West Africa as a whole. French foreign minister Laurent Fabius announced that Paris would maintain a 1000-strong garrison in Mali,[42] a country that obtained 14 per cent of its imports from France in 2012.[43]

The long-delayed AFISMA deployment also started to move into Mali by February 2013 following assurances of logistical and financial support that had previously been withheld. By March 2013, a 6288-strong AFISMA (out of a revised authorised strength of 9500) was expanding its presence into parts of north and central Mali under the leadership of Nigeria's General Shehu Abdulkadir. Other ECOWAS troop-contributing countries included Benin, Burkina Faso, Ghana, Guinea, Niger, Senegal, and Togo. Predictably, the troops faced logistical challenges including food, fuel, and water; and required bilateral donor support to overcome these deficiencies.[44] A hastily created UN Trust Fund had provided AFISMA with $26.7 million by March 2013.[45] Five logistics bases were established in Mali and Niger to supply the force by June 2013.[46] Serious questions were raised in Africa as to why these arrangements had not been put in place to support the regional troops before the French military intervention. Confirming the cynicism of powerful Western countries in watching AFISMA struggle to mobilise troops, Ban Ki-moon confirmed, in June 2013, what everyone had known all along: that AFISMA lacked the enabling units to act as an effective peacekeeping force. The troops were given four months to reach UN standards.[47]

A surprising voice of support for French efforts in Mali came from Nigeria's late foreign minister, Olugbenga Ashiru, who noted in April 2013: "If the French had not intervened at the time they did, the situation in Mali would have been different today. Nigeria and indeed all members of the AU are grateful for the French intervention."[48] At their summit in the Ivorian town of Yamoussoukro in February 2013, ECOWAS leaders had also expressed "profound gratitude" to Paris for its "decisive action".[49] Led by Nigeria, these West African governments were acting like supplicants to a French patron, not recognising the embarrassment of a former colonial power intervening in the core responsibilities of a supposedly sovereign state five decades after its independence. A poll conducted by the Washington, D.C.–based Pew Research Center in March and April 2013 suggested that these leaders did not always accurately reflect the views of their populations. While 42 per cent of Nigerians approved of the French intervention, 25 per cent disapproved; 39 per cent of Ghanaians approved, while 41 per cent disapproved; in francophone Senegal, 91 per cent approved, while only 5 per cent disapproved.[50]

The Politics of MINUSMA

France's clout within the UN Security Council and its Department of Peacekeeping Operations, led by Frenchman Hervé Ladsous, was evidenced by the deployment of a UN Office in Mali (UNOM) in January 2013 weeks after the French military intervention. Paris was the "pen-holder" for the Mali dossier on the UN Security Council, meaning that it drafted all the resolutions relating to this country. Aside from its influence in the UN, Paris also used its clout to ensure that the EU approved a training mission for the Malian army by March 2013. A coordinating mechanism was put in place involving the UN, ECOWAS, the AU, and the EU.

Aside from France, another veto-wielding permanent member of the UN Security Council that played an important role in Mali was the US. Throughout 2012, Washington had consistently warned against a premature deployment of AFISMA to Mali, doubting its capacity to rout the militias. It proposed instead a two-step process for AFISMA to train the Malian army first before engaging in peace-enforcement activities.[51] Washington had spent $41 million between 2009 and 2012 training the coup leaders in Mali, including its meddling chieftain, Captain Amadou Sanogo.[52] Before the Malian coup in 2012, the US had shifted resources from Mali to Mauritania and Niger because it felt that the Malians were not focused enough on America's own counter-terrorism and anti-narcotics priorities. Washington thus remained wary of supporting the Malian army and AFISMA, even after the French intervention.[53]

The obsessive American and French push for elections in this fragile West African country, however, seemed misguided, with the north of the country still full of rebels in mountain and desert territory, and with a weak government in Bamako with no effective army under firm civilian control. Washington provided logistical support to France's deployment in Mali. By 2013, it had deployed drones to Niger to target militants in Mali, and also had a small numbers of soldiers operating on the ground in Mali, a key country for Washington's Trans-Sahara Counter-Terrorism Partnership.[54] The US further pressured Algeria (which has historically been wary of French influence in the region) to back an African-led military intervention in Mali following a visit by then–secretary of state Hillary Clinton to Algiers in October 2012.[55] One of the greatest disappointments of Barack Obama's presidency for Africa was that he continued to support neo-colonial French actions—instead of UN-supported regional efforts—in countries like Mali, Côte d'Ivoire, the CAR, Chad, and Libya.

The UN Secretary-General, Ban Ki-moon, noted in March 2013 that the UN could not absorb the numbers of casualties likely to be incurred in Mali, condescendingly implying that African organisations like the AU and ECOWAS could. He then proposed two options for peacekeeping in Mali. The first was a UN presence operating alongside AFISMA, which could now potentially be provided with the logistics package and funding that Ban had rendered impossible just four months earlier.[56] This cynical idea would involve troops clearly lacking sufficient logistical capacity being asked to act as cannon fodder in softening up rebels until a UN peacekeeping force could be deployed. Ban arrogantly suggested that the UN Security Council would decide when the time was right to re-hat AFISMA into a UN peacekeeping operation. This was an idea similar to the one Nigeria's then president, Olusegun Obasanjo, had rejected in Sierra Leone in 1999, insisting that Nigerian troops must be subsumed under a new UN force and not be used for dangerous peace-enforcement actions. Obasanjo thus refused to allow UN peacekeepers to stand aside, while Nigerian troops suffered casualties and were blamed if things went wrong with the mission.[57]

Ban Ki-moon's second option would be the deployment of a full-fledged UN mission with peace-enforcement powers with robust rules of engagement to address threats and protect populations at risk. Under this option, most of AFISMA would be incorporated into the UN mission with an authorised strength of 11,200 troops and 1440 civilian police. In a proposal that again appeared to have been heavily influenced by France, Ban suggested that a parallel force operate outside the UN chain of command to conduct combat and counter-terrorism operations.[58]

Both the UN Security Council and UN Secretariat rejected the idea of a hybrid mission implicit in the first option (as attempted in Darfur by the UN and the AU), preferring the single command of a full-fledged UN mission suggested by the second option, but without robust peace-enforcement powers.[59] In April 2013, the UN Security Council established the UN Multidimensional Integrated Stabilisation Mission in Mali (MINUSMA). The mission—which at the time became the third largest UN operation in the world after missions in Darfur and the DRC—was tasked with helping the Malian government to extend state authority throughout the country; to be present in main population centres; and to promote civilian security. The UN Security Council called on France to report to it on the Gallic power's role in supporting MINUSMA to undertake peace-enforcement and counter-terrorism activities at the request of the UN Secretary-General. This clause was inserted in the mandate following concerns expressed by other Security Council members about the relationship between the French and UN forces.[60] Russia (along with others) was particularly sceptical about what it saw as the undue haste in establishing MINUSMA without sufficient understanding of the situation on the ground.[61]

Reinforcing Gallic influence in creating the mission, a back office for MINUSMA[62] was to be established in Abidjan, where France had 450 troops and had earlier ensured the deployment of a UN peacekeeping mission. AFISMA was transformed into MINUSMA by July 2013. Exposing the folly of deploying an ill-equipped regional force unable to sustain itself in the field,

MINUSMA called for logistics, engineering and transport units, as well as contractors to construct camps for the peacekeepers. Underlining the triumph of *Pax Gallica* over *Pax Nigeriana*, ECOWAS and the AU had asked the UN Security Council for a peace-enforcement mandate for MINUSMA, as well as for a logistical and financial package for AFISMA's transition. Both requests were declined, leading to the two organisations sending a letter of protest to the UN. They also felt that their mediation process, which had achieved some results, was not being properly acknowledged.[63]

The appointment of a Dutch special representative, Albert Koenders, to head MINUSMA was a further slap in the face of the AU, which had pushed (without much support from ECOWAS) for former Burundian military leader Pierre Buyoya, special representative of AFISMA, to be appointed to this position. Adding further insult to injury, the Nigerians and ECOWAS were snubbed in their request to transfer the AFISMA force commander, General Shehu Abdulkadir, into the military head of MINUSMA. Instead, General Jean Bosco Kazura of Rwanda—a country the UN had publicly accused of fuelling instability in the DRC—was appointed MINUSMA force commander. Much to the chagrin of ECOWAS and the AU, the UN was also to take over the coordination functions of the Follow-Up Group on the Situation in Mali, which had been initiated by both African regional bodies. Italian politician Romano Prodi was appointed special envoy for the Sahel, continuing Ban Ki-moon's penchant for appointing non-African diplomats to these roles on the continent. Having lost the political leadership of MINUSMA, ECOWAS and the AU scrambled to establish political offices in Bamako, as well as to deploy military and human rights observers: a wasteful duplication of activities that would have been better left to the UN.

Both ECOWAS and the AU—instinctively anti-secessionist African intergovernmental institutions—pushed strongly for the MNLA to disarm without preconditions and to ensure that it renounced the declaration of the "independent state of Azawad", which had broken a traditional African diplomatic taboo against secession. This was a central issue for both organisations.[64] The inability of ECOWAS and the AU to exert more influence on the situation in Mali, however, also involved tensions between both bodies. Based on the principle of subsidiarity, ECOWAS saw itself as being in the lead in peace efforts on Mali, and felt that the AU should have been coordinating rather than implementing peacemaking efforts. The issue of which organisation had the mandating authority over AFISMA thus remained ambiguous, creating much confusion for the UN.[65] Both African organisations had their own special envoys in Mali (Pierre Buyoya, AU, and Cheaka Touré, ECOWAS), and both announced the creation of separate offices in the country. (See Vogt in this volume.)

Burkina Faso—and not Nigeria—continued to drive mediation efforts with Mali's armed groups and government through its head of state, Blaise Compaoré, and foreign minister, Djibril Bassolé. Nigeria's president at the time, Goodluck Jonathan, was given the honorific of "Associate Mediator", which sounded more like an empty chieftaincy title. It was Compaoré, not

Jonathan, who briefed ECOWAS leaders on the situation on Mali at their summits, even after Jonathan asked to be included as a co-mediator at an extraordinary ECOWAS summit in Abidjan in April 2012.[66] The lack of guile of Nigerian diplomacy was astonishing.

By June 2013, the MNLA appeared to be softening its stance and was engaging in meaningful dialogue on the future status of the north. Most combat operations had ceased by this time, and the French and AFISMA had gained control of most of the north, though clashes continued between the MNLA (which still controlled Kidal), MUJAO, and Tuareg and Arab militias.[67] The Support and Follow-Up Group on the Situation in Mali also continued to meet in Bamako, and even in Brussels: again demonstrating France's influence in drawing the EU into supporting peacebuilding efforts in Mali. An international donor conference for Mali in Brussels in May 2013 was co-chaired by France, the EU, and the government of Mali, and pledged €3.25 billion for the reconstruction of the country.[68] (An AU pledging conference in Addis Ababa four months earlier had pledged $455 million, of which African governments were to provide a paltry $50 million.) A 540-strong EU Training Mission in Mali—under French general François Lecointre—had also been deployed by May 2013, meaning that Paris would continue to wield significant influence over Mali's future armed forces.

By July 2013, Nigeria appeared to be fed up with the machinations of *Pax Gallica* in dominating decision-making in MINUSMA's operations and ignoring ECOWAS and AU requests for more political and military influence over the mission. Abuja therefore announced that it would withdraw 800 of its 1200 troops from Mali. (It had only 83 soldiers—and 141 police—in Mali by June 2017). This was ostensibly because the troops were needed in the fight against Boko Haram back home. But Nigerian military sources later reported that the action was being taken in protest against the UN's "shabby treatment" of Nigeria's peacekeepers; the world body's failure to recognise the country's past and current peacekeeping contributions to the UN; and the appointing of a non-Nigerian to head MINUSMA.[69] Presidential elections were held in Mali in July and August 2013 in which Ibrahim Boubacar Keita, a former prime minister between 1994 and 2000, became president. The turn-out was predictably low in much of the country's volatile north.

Despite these polls and the efforts of Algerian foreign minister Ramtane Lamamra to promote political reconciliation among the country's disputing parties, the situation in Mali remained unstable, particularly in the country's volatile north. By 2017, government administration was still absent from large parts of the five northern regions. Groups such as AQIM, Ansar Dine, MUJAO, the MNLA, and the Macina Liberation Front, killed civilians—including brutal beheadings, particularly in Kidal and Timbuktu—and attacked UN and French peacekeepers, as well as Malian soldiers, inflicting serious fatalities. These attacks involved the use of roadside explosive devices, rockets, mortars, and suicide vehicle-borne explosives. Fighting between the Coordination of Movements of the Azawad (CMA) and the Platform—a loose collection of armed movements broadly seen as pro-government—in places in and around Kidal, also resulted in scores of fatalities.

The Malian armed forces remained largely unable to control demonstrations, and continued to be accused of human rights abuses. Serious security sector reform was still proceeding slowly by June 2017. The Malian army was redeploying to the north, while the 10,756-strong $1 billion a year UN force struggled to stabilise the country, even despite sporadic "pacification" missions undertaken with French soldiers that echoed the colonial era actions of *Pax Gallica*. MINUSMA continued to lack the two helicopter units and 88 armoured personnel carriers it needed by June 2017. An astonishing 78 UN peacekeepers, about 20 French soldiers, and over 180 members of the Malian security forces had also been killed in hostile attacks in Mali.[70]

Conclusion

The Mali case has exposed the cynical politics behind peacekeeping missions in Africa. France has now used UN-sanctioned missions in Mali, Rwanda, the CAR, Côte d'Ivoire, and Chad to subsidise its parochial interests in Africa under the cover of a UN flag. It has effectively sought to multilateralise its past discredited unilateral interventions on the continent. While stability may have occurred in some of these cases, it was incidental to primary Gallic interests of maintaining its own political, strategic, and economic interests in its African *chasse gardée*.

AFISMA had clearly been set up to fail. It was a phantom force that was still-born and dead on arrival in Mali, and clearly had to be resurrected as MINUSMA. In the international community's grisly "aristocracy of death", the lives of African peacekeepers are still considered to be worth less than those of Western peacekeepers. The fact that, after the French military intervention in 2013, the UN authorised a force that was four times as large as the proposed African force, exposed the duplicity of its Western-dominated Security Council. AFISMA was the cheap way of sending African troops as sacrificial rams to be slaughtered by Islamic militants in the full knowledge that the force lacked the size, logistics, and financing to sustain itself in the field. Its initial strength of 3300 was tripled to 9500 as soon as the French intervention occurred, and some of the support that had previously been denied it suddenly appeared. As with previous African-led missions in Liberia, Sierra Leone, Burundi, and Darfur, the Africans felt that the UN was coming to steal the glory after tortuous regional peacemaking and peacekeeping that the world body failed properly to acknowledge.

This approach of first deploying ill-equipped African peacekeepers and then converting them into a larger, better-resourced UN force (strongly condemned by the Prodi Report on UN peacekeeping in 2008)[71] had previously been practised with the conversion of a 13,000-strong ECOWAS force in Sierra Leone into a 20,000-strong UN force by 2000; a 2645-strong AU force in Burundi into a UN force of 5650 by 2004; and an 8000-strong AU force in Darfur into a 26,000-strong AU-UN hybrid force by 2008 (see Vogt in this volume). In all of these cases, powerful Western members of the UN Security Council only belatedly supported the deployment of sufficient forces after ill-equipped and poorly funded regional peacekeepers had sacrificed much blood and treasure. This was the duplicitous model that was to have been followed by AFISMA in Mali. One therefore wonders why African countries like Nigeria continue to set themselves up for failure in the full knowledge that they lack the logistics and finance to sustain peacekeeping interventions in places like Mali without substantial external support. The plans to set up an African Standby Force (ASF) by 2010 were postponed until 2015 (another missed deadline; see Nagar, and Kuwali in this volume), even as talk continues of establishing an African Capacity for Immediate Response to Crises (ACIRC) force. Yet *Pax Africana* will not be achieved through an alphabet soup-bowl of acronyms, but by greater political commitment and resources being provided, led by Africa's regional powers like Nigeria, South Africa, and Ethiopia.

Perhaps the most damaging sign of the loss of influence in Nigeria's recent foreign policy was the French-led military intervention into Mali. While the elimination of the militant threat in northern Mali was in the interest of both Africa and the West, France still effectively launched an old-style neo-colonial intervention into a country in Nigeria's backyard. Paris's simultaneous sending of troops to guard uranium mines in neighbouring Niger exposed some of the other interests at the heart of its regional role. Rather than seeking to ensure that parochial Gallic interests were not entrenched in its sub-region, and that a genuine international security force was established in Mali under a unified UN military command, Nigeria instead acted as a cheerleader, deploying troops that effectively became auxiliaries of French foreign policy in the country. Only when Abuja failed to secure the position of force commander of MINUSMA did the scales finally fall from its eyes. Nigeria largely reacted to events in Mali rather than shaped them.

Though Nigeria's contribution of peacekeepers to the new UN mission in Mali was consistent with its foreign policy objectives, the country's actions abroad lacked strategic vision. Abuja should perhaps work more closely in future cases like Mali with regional powers like Algeria and South Africa, which both share a profound antipathy to French military interventions in Africa. Algeria is a neighbouring state that has led mediation efforts in Mali, with the sub-region's largest army and the widest intelligence network in the Sahel, while South Africa is Africa's most industrialised state, and a key bilateral partner of Nigeria that has played an important role in restoring Mali's ancient scripts in Timbuktu. Even as Nigeria returned to the UN Security Council in January 2014, there were continuing reports of delays in paying its UN dues. Within AU circles, there were reports in 2013 of Abuja dragging its feet on delivering on promises of financial support to the AU Mission in Somalia (AMISOM). Even within ECOWAS on Mali, Nigeria appeared to be leading from behind, with Burkina Faso largely overseeing mediation efforts. Nigeria's response to the Mali crisis was subservient, weak, and incoherent, reversing five decades of Nigerian foreign policy. It has proved too difficult for Abuja to pursue "hegemony on a shoestring" in this peacekeeping mission. Nigeria's foreign policy under the Goodluck Jonathan administration resembled a battered jalopy with a rookie driver asleep at the wheel on a road to nowhere. Many wondered whether this accident could be avoided.

Despite its supposedly "humanitarian intervention" in Mali, France has historically had economic interests in both Mali's and Niger's uranium sectors. About a quarter of French electricity production relies on uranium. An April 2013 French government white paper on defence and national security—with its advisory group chaired by Jean-Marie Guéhenno, the French former UN Under-Secretary-General for Peacekeeping—specifically singled out Africa (the Sahel, the Gulf of Guinea, and the Maghreb) as a priority area for Gallic defence and security policy. While the white paper noted that France would help strengthen African peacekeeping capacity, Paris envisaged undertaking future interventions like the one in Mali, and planned to maintain at least four military bases on the continent. The white paper also recognised Africa's economic potential, while urging the EU to acknowledge that African security was a key interest for the whole organisation.[72]

As France's economy has declined and its military spending reduced, Paris has sought to multilateralise its past neo-colonial interventions through UN and EU missions. In addition to cuts of 54,000 military personnel in 2008, an additional cut of 24,000 was announced in France's April 2013 defence review (leaving a total operational force of 66,000 instead of 88,000), and the defence budget was frozen at €31.4 billion: 1.5 per cent of gross domestic product (GDP). The number of French ships, transport aircraft, tanks, and helicopters were also reduced. Despite its continued *folie de grandeur*, Paris can no longer afford to pay for its imperial role in Africa on its own. Like Nigeria, this *gendarme* is also an invalid. The French military presence in Africa costs €400–450 million annually, and the long-term bill for French taxpayers of the Mali intervention is estimated to reach €300–400 million.[73] It is the Ivorian model, in which France—with about 10,000 soldiers in Africa in 2016—kept troops outside the UN chain of command while the world body subsidised stability in a country in which Paris has political, strategic, and economic interests, that was applied to Mali. *Pax Gallica* had decisively trumped *Pax Nigeriana* in this small West African country.

Notes

1. Ali A. Mazrui, "The Bondage of Boundaries", *The Economist*, 11 September 1993, http://www.economist.com.
2. *See* Peter M. Lewis, *Nigeria: Assessing Risks to Stability* (Washington, DC: Center for Strategic and International Studies, June 2011); Karl Maier, *This House Has Fallen: Midnight in Nigeria* (New York: PublicAffairs, 2000); Ali Mazrui, "Shari'ahcracy and Federal Models in the Era of Globalization: Nigeria in Comparative Perspective", in Alamin Mazrui and Willy Mutunga Mazrui

(eds.), *Governance and Leadership: Debating the African Condition—Mazrui and His Critics*, vol. 2 (Asmara: Africa World, 2003), pp. 261–276; John N. Paden, *Muslim Civic Cultures and Conflict Resolution: The Challenges of Democratic Federalism in Nigeria* (Washington, DC: Brookings Institution, 2005), pp. 13–36.

3. *See* Jean-François Médard, "Crisis, Change, and Continuity: Nigeria/France Relations", in Adekeye Adebajo and Raufu Mustapha (eds.), *Gulliver's Troubles: Nigeria's Foreign Policy After the Cold War* (Scottsville: University of KwaZulu-Natal Press, 2008), pp. 314–333.
4. *See* Bola Akinterinwa, *Nigeria and France, 1960–1995: The Dilemma of Thirty-five Years of Relationship* (Ibadan: Vintage, 1999); Bassey E. Ate and Bola Akinterinwa (eds.), *Nigeria and Its Immediate Neighbours: Constraints and Prospects of Sub-Regional Security in the 1990s* (Lagos: Nigerian Institute of International Affairs, 1992); Emeka Nwokedi, "Nigeria and France", in G.O. Olusanya and R.A. Akindele (eds.), *Nigeria's External Relations* (Ibadan: Ibadan University Press, 1986), pp. 284–293.
5. *See* Wenike Briggs, "Negotiations Between the Enlarged European Economic Community and the African, Caribbean, and Pacific Countries", *Nigerian Journal of International Affairs* 1, no. 1 (July 1975); and Pius Okigbo, *Africa and the Common Market* (Evanston, IL: Northwestern University Press, 1967).
6. For accounts of the Nigerian civil war, *see* Anthony Kirk-Greene, *Crisis and Conflict in Nigeria*, 2 vols. (London: Oxford University Press, 1971); John Stremlau, *The International Politics of the Nigerian Civil War* (Princeton: Princeton University Press, 1977).
7. *See* Adekeye Adebajo, "Nigeria", in Alex J. Bellamy and Paul D. Williams (eds.), *Providing Peacekeepers: The Politics, Challenges, and Future of United Nations Peacekeeping Contributions* (Oxford: Oxford University Press, 2013), pp. 245–268.
8. *See, for example*, Ibrahim Gambari, "From Balewa to Obasanjo: The Theory and Practice of Nigeria's Foreign Policy", in Adebajo and Mustapha, *Gulliver's Troubles*, pp. 58–80. *See also* Gabriel Olusanya and Raufu Akindele, "The Fundamentals of Nigeria's Foreign Policy and External Economic Relations", in Olusanya and Akindele, *Nigeria's External Relations.*
9. Telephone interview with Segun Apata, Deputy Permanent Representative of Nigeria to the United Nations (UN), 1999–2003, 13 May 2012.
10. Telephone interview with Joy Ogwu, Permanent Representative of Nigeria to the United Nations, 17 May 2012.
11. I have relied for these points on Julie Sanda, "Nigeria's Global Role", in Attahiru M. Jega and Jacqeline W. Farris (eds.), *Nigeria at Fifty* (Abuja: Shehu Musa Yar'Adua Foundation, 2010), pp. 92–95.
12. W. Alade Fawole, "Militaries, Militias, and Mullahs: National Security in Nigerian Foreign Policy", in Adebajo and Mustapha, *Gulliver's Troubles*, pp. 108–111. *See also* Joy Ogwu, "We Need a Doctrine on National Security", *The Punch* (Lagos), 17 June 2005, p. 32.
13. Nasir el-Rufai, "Failing State, Fading Peacekeepers", *This Day* (Lagos), 16 March 2012.
14. Telephone interview with Ibrahim Gambari, Special Representative of the African Union (AU)–United Nations Hybrid Operation in Darfur (UNAMID) and Nigeria's Permanent Representative to the UN between 1990 and 1999, 18 May 2012.

15. Telephone interview with General Chikadibia Isaac Obiakor, former Force Commander of the United Nations Mission in Liberia (UNMIL), 12 May 2012.
16. "Nigeria 'to Withdraw Some Troops from Mali'", *BBC News Africa*, 19 July 2013, http://www.bbc.com/news/world-africa-23369865 (accessed 25 December 2016).
17. *See* Adekeye Adebajo, "Folie de Grandeur", *World Today* 53, no. 6 (1997), pp. 147–150; John Chipman, *French Power in Africa* (Oxford: Blackwell, 1989); Paul Gifford and W.R. Lewis (eds.), *The Transfer of Power in Africa: Decolonization 1940–1960* (New Haven: Yale University Press, 1982); Victor T. Le Vine, *Politics in Francophone Africa* (Boulder, CO: Lynne Rienner, 2007); Guy Martin, *Africa in World Politics: A Pan-African Perspective* (Asmara: Africa World, 2002); Douglas A. Yates, *The French Oil Industry and the Corps des Mines in Africa* (Asmara: Africa World, 2009).
18. *Quoted in* Christopher M. Andrew, "France: Adjustment to Change", in Hedley Bull (ed.), *The Expansion of International Society* (Oxford: Clarendon, 1984), p. 337.
19. For two detailed studies on French complicity in Rwanda's genocide, *see* Daniela Kroslak, *The Role of France in the Rwandan Genocide* (London: Hurst, 2007); Andrew Wallis, *Silent Accomplice: The Untold Story of France's Role in the Rwandan Genocide* (London: Tauris, 2006).
20. *See* Norrie MacQueen, *United Nations Peacekeeping in Africa Since 1960* (London: Pearson Education, 2002), pp. 96–104.
21. *See* the rich essay by Douglas A. Yates, "France, the EU, and Africa", in Adekeye Adebajo and Kaye Whiteman (eds.), *The EU and Africa: From Eurafrique to Afro-Europa* (New York: Columbia University Press; London: Hurst; and Johannesburg: Wits University Press, 2012), pp. 317–342.
22. The information in this section relies on United Nations, *Report of the United Nations Secretary-General on the Situation in Mali*, UN Doc. S/2012/894, 29 November 2012, pp. 1–10.
23. United Nations, *Report of the United Nations Secretary-General on the Situation in Mali*, UN Doc. S/2013/189, 26 March 2013, p. 5.
24. Economist Intelligence Unit, Country Report, "Mali", May 2012, pp. 18–19.
25. *See* Stephen Wright and Julius Emeka Okolo, "Nigeria: Aspirations of Regional Power", in Stephen Wright (ed.), *African Foreign Policies* (Boulder, CO: Westview, 1999), pp. 125–130.
26. Telephone interview with General Chikadibia Obiakor, 12 May 2012.
27. "Sand on Their Boots", *The Economist*, 26 January 2013, https://www.economist.com/news/briefing/21570718-french-action-mali-seems-be-workingso-far-sand-their-boots (accessed 25 December 2016).
28. *See* "Final Communiqué of the Extraordinary Session of the Authority of ECOWAS Heads of State and Government", Abuja, 11 November 2012.
29. This paragraph and the next are based largely on United Nations, *Report of the United Nations Secretary-General on the Situation in Mali*, UN Doc. S/2012/894, 29 November 2012, pp. 11–17.
30. "Sand on Their Boots".
31. Security Council Report, Monthly Forecast, "Mali", January 2013, p. 4.
32. James Jonah, "The United Nations", in Adekeye Adebajo and Ismail Rashid (eds.), *West Africa's Security Challenges: Building Peace in a Troubled Region* (Boulder, CO, and London: Lynne Rienner, 2004), p. 331.

33. Security Council Report, Monthly Forecast, "Mali", January 2013, p. 5; United Nations, *Report of the United Nations Secretary-General on the Situation in Mali*, UN Doc. S/2012/894, 29 November 2012, pp. 18–21.
34. United Nations, *Report of the United Nations Secretary-General on the Situation in Mali*, UN Doc. S/2012/894, 29 November 2012, p. 22.
35. United Nations, *Report of the United Nations Secretary-General on the Situation in Mali*, UN Doc. S/2013/189, 26 March 2013, pp. 2–3.
36. Xan Rice, "French Troops Bolster Flagging Ground Campaign", *Financial Times*, 17 January 2013, p. 5.
37. United Nations, *Report of the United Nations Secretary-General on the Situation in Mali*, UN Doc. S/2013/189, 26 March 2013, pp. 1–2.
38. United Nations, *Report of the United Nations Secretary-General on the Situation in Mali*, UN Doc. S/2013/189, 26 March 2013, p. 11.
39. Economist Intelligence Unit, Country Report, "Mali", Second Quarter 2013, p. 9.
40. *See, for example*, Seamus Milne, "The Fastest Blowback Yet in This Disastrous War on Terror", *The Guardian* (London), 23 January 2013, p. 27.
41. Rice, "French Troops Bolster Flagging Ground Campaign", p. 5.
42. Paul Melly and Vincent Darracq, "A New Way to Engage? French Policy in Africa from Sarkozy to Hollande" (London: Chatham House, May 2013), p. 13.
43. Economist Intelligence Unit, Country Report, "Mali", Third Quarter 2013, p. 6.
44. United Nations, *Report of the United Nations Secretary-General on the Situation in Mali*, UN Doc. S/2013/189, 26 March 2013, p. 8.
45. United Nations, *Report of the United Nations Secretary-General on the Situation in Mali*, UN Doc. S/2013/189, 26 March 2013, p. 16.
46. United Nations, *Report of the United Nations Secretary-General on the Situation in Mali*, UN Doc. S/2013/338, 10 June 2013, p. 14.
47. United Nations, *Report of the United Nations Secretary-General on the Situation in Mali*, UN Doc. S/2013/338, 10 June 2013, p. 15.
48. Olugbenga Ashiru, "Nigeria's Foreign Policy in a Changing World", speech delivered on 16 April 2013.
49. Economic Community of West African States (ECOWAS), "Final Communiqué of the Forty-second Ordinary Session of the ECOWAS Authority of Heads of State and Government", Yamoussoukro, 27–28 February 2013, p. 5.
50. Pew Research Center, "As Mali Votes, Mixed Reception to French Intervention from Publics in Africa and Middle East", 25 July 2013, p. 1, http://www.pewglobal.org/2013/07/25/as-mali-votes-mixed-reception-to-french-intervention-from-publics-in-africa-and-middle-east/ (accessed 25 December 2016).
51. Security Council Report, Monthly Forecast, "Mali", January 2013, pp. 5–6.
52. *See* Simon Tisdall, "Mali: Fragile Democracy and Clumsy US Policy", *The Guardian* (London), 18 January 2013, https://www.theguardian.com/commentisfree/2013/jan/18/mali-fragile-democracy-clumsy-us-policy (accessed 25 December 2016).
53. Security Council Report, Monthly Forecast, "Mali", March 2013, p. 20.
54. Economist Intelligence Unit, Country Report, "Mali", Third Quarter 2013, p. 10.

55. Economist Intelligence Unit, Country Report, "Mali", First Quarter 2013, p. 14.
56. United Nations, *Report of the United Nations Secretary-General on the Situation in Mali*, UN Doc. S/2013/189, 26 March 2013, pp. 13–14.
57. Adekeye Adebajo, *UN Peacekeeping in Africa: From the Suez Crisis to the Sudan Conflicts* (Boulder, CO, and London: Lynne Rienner, 2011), p. 150.
58. United Nations, *Report of the United Nations Secretary-General on the Situation in Mali*, UN Doc. S/2013/189, 26 March 2013, pp. 14–15.
59. Security Council Report, Monthly Forecast, "Mali", March 2013, p. 20.
60. Security Council Report, Monthly Forecast, "Mali", May 2013, p. 7.
61. Security Council Report, Monthly Forecast, "Mali", May 2013, p. 7.
62. United Nations, *Report of the United Nations Secretary-General on the Situation in Mali*, UN Doc. S/2013/338, 10 June 2013, p. 12.
63. Security Council Report, Monthly Forecast, "Mali", July 2013, p. 3.
64. Confidential correspondence.
65. Confidential correspondence.
66. ECOWAS, "Final Communiqué: Extraordinary Summit of ECOWAS Heads of State", Abidjan, 26 April 2012, p. 6.
67. United Nations, *Report of the United Nations Secretary-General on the Situation in Mali*, UN Doc. S/2013/338, 10 June 2013, p. 5.
68. United Nations, *Report of the United Nations Secretary-General on the Situation in Mali*, UN Doc. S/2013/338, 10 June 2013, p. 11.
69. *See* Senator Iroegbu, "Real Reason Why Nigeria Is Withdrawing Troops from Mali", *This Day* (Lagos), 21 July 2013, http://www.thisdaylive.com; Chidi Okoye, "Nigeria in Strategic Withdrawal from Mali", *Nigerian Telegraph*, 22 July 2013, p. 3; "Nigeria 'to Withdraw Some Troops from Mali'".
70. Information in the three preceding paragraphs gleaned from United Nations, *Reports of the Secretary-General on the Situation in Mali*, UN Doc. S/2016/281, 28 March 2016; UN Doc. S/2016/498, 31 May 2016; UN Doc. S/2016/819, 29 September 2016; UN Doc. S/2017/478, 6 June 2017.
71. United Nations General Assembly and Security Council, "Comprehensive Review of the Whole Question of Peacekeeping Operations", UN Doc. A/63/666-S/2008/813, 31 December 2008.
72. Cited in Melly and Darracq, "A New Way to Engage?", pp. 12–13.
73. Melly and Darracq, "A New Way to Engage?", p. 13.

PART IV

Themes in Peacekeeping

CHAPTER 13

Accountability of Peacekeepers in Peacekeeping Missions

Kwame Akonor

United Nations (UN) peacekeepers generally comprise civilian, police, and military personnel who contribute voluntarily to help assist war-torn countries create conditions for lasting peace.[1] Overall, the work of the UN peacekeepers has been portrayed positively, with a large body of literature (scholarly, journalistic, as well as documentary accounts) on how "blue helmets" and peacekeeping personnel function. According to the UN, peacekeepers are "called upon not only to maintain peace and security, but also to facilitate the political process, protect civilians, assist in the disarmament, demobilization and reintegration of former combatants; support the organization of elections, protect and promote human rights and assist in restoring the rule of law."[2] By and large then, peacekeepers are perceived to be selfless troops who volunteer their time, and even risk their lives, to bring normalcy to civilians in conflict-torn countries. As Italian scholar Alice Gadler notes, UN peacekeepers are sometimes also the victims of violent crimes, who themselves need protection.[3]

But what about cases when UN peacekeepers do not function at their best? What happens when peacekeepers become perpetrators of crimes against the very people they are supposed to protect? Indeed, there have been some instances, both confirmed and alleged, though not widespread, of UN peacekeepers committing crimes, including sexual exploitation and abuse (SEA), trafficking in children and arms, and corruption.[4] Cases of alleged criminal misconduct were documented, for example, in the case of peacekeepers deployed to the UN Organisation Mission in the Democratic Republic of the Congo (MONUC), since renamed the UN Organisation Stabilisation Mission in the Democratic Republic of the Congo (MONUSCO) in 2004. A report by

K. Akonor (✉)
Department of Political Science and Public Affairs, Seton Hall University, South Orange, New Jersey, United States

T. Karbo, K. Virk (eds.), *The Palgrave Handbook of Peacebuilding in Africa*, https://doi.org/10.1007/978-3-319-62202-6_13

the UN Office of Internal Oversight Services (OIOS) found that in 2005, some Congolese women and girls had been sexually abused or exploited by peacekeepers. The payment for sexual services in some instances ranged from two eggs to five dollars, and the victims included abandoned orphans and illiterates.[5] Similar abuses by UN peacekeepers occurred in 2012 in the Congo. Though such criminal activity in the host country by blue-helmet peacekeepers—the "dark side" of UN peacekeeping—is not extensive, it remains a fundamental problem,[6] because there are no existing mechanisms in the international arena for prosecution of offending peacekeepers. It is only the troop-contributing country, and not the UN, that ultimately has the right to exercise criminal jurisdiction.

This chapter is informed by my belief that if impunity remains the norm rather than the exception for UN peacekeepers who commit crimes, then their mission of protecting the most vulnerable groups of people risks becoming meaningless and counter-productive. Forms of criminal misconduct involving peacekeepers include women trafficking and involvement with prostitution rings,[7] rape and murder,[8] as well as gold smuggling.[9] In this chapter, though, I focus mainly on sexual exploitation and abuse by UN peacekeepers due, in part, to space constraints, but also because this is one of the most widely-documented areas in which the lack of accountability for the transgressions of peacekeepers is most evident.

I begin with a brief overview of alleged criminal conduct, particularly sexual exploitation and abuse, by African peacekeepers and their African victims. Of course, peacekeeping abuses, when they do occur, are generally not restricted to race or geography, but in the spirit of the pursuit of a new *Pax Africana*—the theme of this volume (see Introduction and Mazrui)—the abuses of African peacekeepers, in particular, are worth placing in focus here. Two points are worth noting in this regard. First, Africa remains in the top ten troop-contributing countries globally. In 2015, five African countries—Ethiopia, Rwanda, Senegal, Ghana, and Nigeria—were among the ten largest providers of troops for UN peacekeeping, with 24,000 blue helmets deployed (as of December that year), comprising more than one-fifth of the world body's total.[10] Second, notwithstanding this substantial African contribution to peacekeeping, much of it on the continent, abuses in Africa are not always perpetrated by African personnel. Non-African countries are major contributors of UN peacekeeping contingents deployed in Africa (see Virk in this volume). In the Congo, for example, the three largest contingents deployed to MONUSCO, as of June 2017, were from India (3,697), Pakistan (3,486), and Bangladesh (1,907), which altogether comprised nearly half of the mission's strength.[11] Next, I review the literature on UN peacekeeping, as it relates to the challenges of accountability for peace operations, and also why criminal activity, specifically sexual exploitation and abuse, is high among blue helmets.[12] I conclude with suggestions and scenarios for transforming the culture of impunity for peacekeepers into a culture of accountability and justice.

Sexual Exploitation and Abuse in UN Peacekeeping

In 1996, a landmark study by the United Nations Children's Fund (UNICEF), *The Impact of Armed Conflict on Children*, reported that "in 6 out of 12 country studies, the arrival of peacekeeping troops has been associated with a rapid rise in child prostitution"; this being one of the first of several UN-commissioned high-level reports on the problem of sexual exploitation and abuse.[13] SEA is defined by the UN as "any actual or attempted abuse of a position of vulnerability, differential power, or trust, for sexual purposes, including, but not limited to, profiting monetarily, socially or politically from the sexual exploitation of another."[14]

The United Nations only began keeping records and tracking data on allegations of SEA and other criminal misconduct in 2006—a year after the publication of the Zeid Report in 2005. Former UN Secretary–General, Kofi Annan of Ghana, described the report as "the first comprehensive analysis of the problem of sexual exploitation and abuse by United Nations peacekeeping personnel."[15] Much of the data on SEA can now be obtained from the Investigations Division of the UN Office of Internal Oversight Services. This data appears to show a downward trend in the total number of SEA allegations reported. In 2015, for example, there were 69 allegations reported in UN field missions, which is significantly lower than the peak of 127 in 2007.[16]

But, as I noted at the outset, the United Nations does not have the authority, or mechanisms, to prosecute sexual offenders in its ranks of peacekeeping troops. All it can do is follow up with the relevant troop-contributing country, to ascertain if the perpetrators have been held to account. This makes achieving accountability difficult. Even when a troop-contributing country acts in good faith in carrying out an investigation and prosecution, there are several obstacles to bringing offenders to justice. Often, the relevant troop-contributing country is likely to be in a different part of the world from the scene of the crime, making it difficult to find witnesses and gather evidence. Also, complaints are often delayed, and offending soldiers may have already been rotated out of a region by the time reports are received.[17] The very wording of the rules is sometimes the problem; what, for example, can be done legally with the idea of consensual sexual relations between peacekeepers and local adults being "strongly discouraged" (rather than, say, it being prohibited).[18]

Over the years, there have been numerous accounts of sexual exploitation and abuse, coupled with a lack of accountability, by African peacekeepers specifically and UN peacekeepers more generally. While my focus in this chapter is on UN peacekeepers (including African blue helmets), it is worth noting briefly that the problem of sexual exploitation and abuse is not limited to them. About two decades ago, abuses by African peacekeepers in Sierra Leone, deployed under the umbrella of the Economic Community of West African States (ECOWAS) gained wide notoriety. Similarly, the blatant sexual violence and banditry committed against the local population by personnel deployed to the

ECOWAS Ceasefire Monitoring Group in Liberia (ECOMOG), in the early 1990s, has been well-documented. Some accounts contend that there were approximately 6,000 births as a result of rape committed by ECOMOG soldiers (a phenomenon given the distasteful name "ECOMOG babies").[19] So much criminal behaviour, particularly theft, became associated with ECOMOG soldiers that they earned a new meaning for their namesake acronym: "Every Car or Moving Object Gone".[20]

More recently, in July 2013, a confidential report by UN monitors accused Kenyan soldiers, deployed to the African Union Mission in Somalia (AMISOM), of "facilitating illegal charcoal exports from the port city of Kismayu"; a trade that is estimated to generate millions of dollars each year for Islamic militants with political and ideological goals in the region.[21]As well, in August 2013, a Somali woman reported that she had been drugged and repeatedly raped by AMISOM peacekeepers. The African Union (AU) and the Somali government set up a joint team to investigate this allegation, with the outcome of the probe yet to be announced at the time of writing.[22]

That said, a common thread that runs through the various reported cases of sexual exploitation and abuse by UN peacekeepers—both African and non-African—relates to the lack of accountability. Some examples from the world body's missions in Africa illustrate the problem. The cases presented here are based mainly on anecdotal, public news sources. But I include them here for emphasis, as the problem they illustrate is real. For example:

- In June 2002, a Bangladeshi peacekeeper allegedly raped a 14-year-old boy near the Jui transit camp for Sierra Leonean returnees, outside of the capital of Freetown. The boy had been fishing with friends before the incident, and the peacekeeper reportedly gave the boy the equivalent of US$ 0.25 to silence him. The alleged incident came to light after a six-month UN investigation into sexual exploitation of refugees by aid workers and UN personnel in West Africa. The UN, however, was unable to confirm the extensive SEA allegations.[23]
- In 2005, two 14-year-old girls were allegedly raped by two Uruguayan peacekeepers in Uvira in the eastern Congo, leaving them pregnant. However, the two men returned to Uruguay. This incident, among many other cases of local abuse allegedly perpetrated by Uruguayan soldiers, led to the entire Uruguayan contingent being withdrawn from the Congo.[24]
- In March 2010, 14 Moroccan peacekeepers in Côte d'Ivoire were implicated in sexual exploitation and abuse, by a confidential probe conducted by UN and Moroccan investigators. There was reportedly DNA evidence to indicate that some of the troops had fathered children with their victims. But the UN never officially released the results of the investigation, and the Moroccan government stated that there was no conclusive evidence, leading to all charges being dropped.[25]

Challenges to Accountability for Peacekeeping Operations

In July 2004, after evidence emerged of blue helmets having sex with—and even raping—women and girls in the DRC in exchange for food and money, then UN Secretary-General Kofi Annan appointed Prince Zeid Ra'ad Zeid al-Hussein, then Permanent Representative of Jordan to the United Nations, to act as his special adviser on sexual exploitation and abuse committed by peacekeeping personnel. In March 2005, the Zeid Report, touted as "a comprehensive strategy to eliminate future sexual exploitation and abuse in United Nations Peacekeeping operations", was published.[26] Commenting on the report, Annan stated that "such abhorrent acts are a violation of the fundamental duty of care that all United Nations peacekeeping personnel owe to the local populations they serve".[27] The role of a UN adviser on sexual exploitation and abuse, however, ended with the conclusion of Prince Zeid's term as Jordan's ambassador to the UN in 2007.

Writing in 2008, American scholar Elizabeth Defeis concurred with the Zeid Report on several issues, such as the need for community outreach, and educating UN peacekeepers on sexual exploitation and abuse. But, at the same time, she does not view sexual exploitation and abuse by UN peacekeepers as habitual; rather she maintains that what is habitual is the willingness of blue helmets, who are predominantly male, to cover up such exploitation and abuse when it does occur.[28] According to Defeis, a "culture of dismissiveness", one that is "hyper-masculine", exists within the UN peacekeeping structure that allows impunity. Cambodian UN envoy Yasushi Akashi's famous explanation that "boys will be boys", when civil society organisations tried to bring cases of sexual abuse against Cambodian peacekeepers to his attention in 1993, comes to mind.[29] The logic here is that the military culture surrounding the male-dominated blue helmets makes them more physically aggressive than they would otherwise be, and that the UN lacks structures for accountability. Defeis goes on to argue that reforms need to be implemented on the ground to require and facilitate reporting of abuse, in order to break through this "wall of silence"; the UN needs not only to propose draft conventions on sexual exploitation and abuse by peacekeeping personnel, but also to impose sanctions and blacklist troop-contributing countries whose governments do not take sexual misconduct of personnel seriously. There is also a need for more women in the ranks of peacekeepers, including in positions of authority, with women constituting only about 9 per cent of UN police and 4 per cent of UN military personnel, as of June 2017.[30] (See Porter in this volume.)

Melanie O'Brien, meanwhile, has argued that the UN's codes of conduct—in particular, its *Ten Rules: Code of Personal Conduct for Blue Helmets*[31]—if enforced could help prevent SEA and other gender-based crimes.[32] This includes "rules" such as "Treat the inhabitants of the host country with respect, courtesy and consideration"; and "Do not indulge in immoral acts of sexual, physical or psychological abuse or exploitation of the local population or United Nations staff, especially women and children". O'Brien also cites the "zero tolerance policy" bulletin issued by the UN Secretary-General, Kofi Annan, in October 2003 that requires suspicions of abuse to be reported. She further points out the steps that have already been taken towards ensuring action by troop-contributing countries to prosecute offenders. For instance, a model Memorandum of Understanding (MOU)—a document short of a treaty—agreed to by sending countries for every deployment, starting in 2007, contains guidelines for preventing sexual exploitation and abuse, and for prosecuting offenders.

The problem with this line of reasoning, though, is that the status-of-forces agreement (SOFA), signed between the UN and a host country, is unenforceable in the latter, since in reality it is the troop-sending country that has exclusive extra-territorial jurisdiction over its military personnel, with civilian personnel more likely to come under host-country jurisdiction. Indeed, the SOFA, among other provisions, assures UN peacekeepers immunity from prosecution in the courts of the host country (though it also calls upon troops to respect the host country's laws). At the same time, the MOU between the UN and a troop-sending country provides that the latter will have sole responsibility for the conduct of the troops that it is deploying. Thus, UN authorities, when they learn that blue-helmeted soldiers have committed offenses, can do nothing beyond ordering their removal from the field, back to their sending countries. Meanwhile, under the status-of-forces agreements, host countries typically defer the conduct of any disciplinary or criminal prosecution to the troop-sending country.

Apart from sovereignty claims, accountability for sexual exploitation and abuse is further complicated within the peacekeeping systems of the UN, as well as the AU and Africa's regional economic communities, due to lack of uniformity in certain norms. For example, does soliciting a prostitute during a peacekeeping mission fall under SEA? This is a contested point, because not all governments will agree that sexual solicitation among consenting adults constitutes misconduct. Indeed, prostitution, though prohibited by UN guidelines, may be legal in both the troop-contributing country and the host country. The same issue can arise with regard to the age of consent, where the definition of a minor is concerned. Even scholars do not all agree on the definition of misconduct. Olivera Simic, for example, has argued that treating all prostitution as exploitative, and all sexual relations between peacekeepers and locals as something to be discouraged, denies the agency of women at the community level, while over-generalising about the power inequality and the circumstances behind prostitution and other sex acts. (On women, gender, and peacebuilding, see Porter in this volume.)

O'Brien, meanwhile, further argues that the Draft Convention on Criminal Accountability of UN Officials and Experts on Mission,[33] which she finds ambiguous, should be broadened to apply more generally to personnel on mission, and signed and put into effect. Such a move, according to O'Brien, would quash relativist claims and force countries where prostitution is legal domestically to criminalise solicitation of prostitutes by their peacekeepers in a host country.

In this regard, O'Brien is aware of the UN's limited juridical authority in such matters, and indeed points out the fact that the world body has only administrative sanctions at its disposal, not criminal jurisdiction. As a solution, she thus emphasises that all troop-sending countries be signatories to a UN convention that obligates them, first, to accept extra-territorial jurisdiction over all their nationals when serving on UN peacekeeping missions in any capacity, and second, to criminalise the full range of offences destructive to the peacekeeping mission, including some actions that may not be criminal under other circumstances and on their own soil. She also acknowledges the value of training and the importance of recreational outlets and other amenities for peacekeeping personnel, citing a case study showing that access to recreational facilities for UN peacekeeping personnel reduces sexual exploitation and abuse. In the model Memorandum of Understanding, everything involving the welfare of peacekeeping personnel is the responsibility of the sending country; a model that O'Brien suggests should be re-thought, in order to standardise access to recreational facilities across nationalities and different types of personnel.

New Zealand scholar Andrew Ladley notes that troop-contributing countries have vast disparities in their own domestic criminal codes, and that conviction of a crime can be difficult when the trial takes place on the other side of the globe and in a cultural milieu different from that of the crime scene. He also suggests the creation of a standardised judicial structure under UN auspices, through an international treaty, for peacekeepers, in cooperation with the International Criminal Court (ICC) (see Nouwen in this volume) and not precluding home-country prosecutions.[34] Ladley puts more emphasis on prosecution of civilian offenders, seeing less of an impunity problem where military personnel are concerned. Alongside issues of variation between criminal codes of troop-contributing countries and jurisdictional discrepancies between civilian and military personnel, he adds the difficulty of bringing effective evidence into a court in the sending country of a crime committed across the globe in the host country. Ladley goes on to suggest that a UN court could be created to prosecute violations of a uniform UN code for peacekeeping missions. He proposes that such a court might also, in some instances, waive the diplomatic immunity that shields civilian personnel from host-country jurisdiction. The agreement of troop-contributing countries to the court's jurisdiction could be established in mission-specific treaties or in a standard convention (regardless, this would require the power of a treaty).

The UN also has the option of disciplining troops by sending them home or blacklisting countries whose troops have a record and pattern of misconduct. This it did in February 2016, for example, when it sent 120 peacekeepers from the Republic of Congo and the Democratic Republic of the Congo (DRC), serving under the UN mission in the Central African Republic (CAR), home following allegations of sexual exploitation and abuse. Unfortunately, this is a double edged sword, as it risks alienating the UN's troop-contributing member states, on which the world body relies for its operations since it has no standing army of its own.

Finally, another factor to consider, in addressing the problem of sexual exploitation and abuse by peacekeepers, is the vulnerability of local populations to sexual exploitation—that is, a situation in which the necessity is felt of providing sexual favours for money. This depends on, and relates to, the conditions of acute poverty prevailing in the countries affected by conflict, and to which peacekeeping missions are deployed. The fact that a country needs peacekeeping troops is, of course, a function of being war-torn, which in itself breeds poverty.[35]

Conclusion: "Policing the Police"—Some Reflections

Based on the preceding discussion, there are four sets of explanations as to why peacekeeping abuses take place, but criminal prosecution for them rarely happens. The first is that the institutional structure of UN peacekeeping operations is male-centric, with peacekeepers having inculcated aspects of military culture that tend to make them physically aggressive and encourage them to form close bonds to protect one another when a fellow "brother" gets into trouble with civilians. The second is that economic deprivation may create an environment that views abuse as permissible. In most cases of conflict in which peacekeeping is required, poverty is a common characteristic of the most vulnerable populations. The reasoning goes that it may be, therefore, tempting for peacekeepers to take advantage of the dire conditions of the local population, and engage in sexual exploitation and abuse. The third explanation relates to the reality of variations in cultural and legal systems across troop-contributing countries. The challenge here is to standardise norms in a way that could satisfy relativist claims. Making matters more complicated is the fact that some countries have sub-standard legal systems. Moreover, even if prosecutors were willing to try peacekeepers in their domestic courts, they may not be able to do so due to logistical constraints, such as gathering evidence and interrogating victims from distant lands. Fourth, and finally, there is the school of thought which holds that the psychological impact of conflict on victims makes them vulnerable to sexual exploitation and abuse. (This explanation is not stressed as much in the scholarly literature compared to the other three explanations, though the Zeid Report does allude to it.) The rationale here is that victims of conflict tend to internalise norms of sexual violence because they themselves have already been victimised by violence, and hence, are more likely to tolerate sexual exploitation and abuse in exchange for their personal and community protection.

Since the options for holding peacekeepers accountable for such abuses are less than perfect, one could argue that the most effective way to prevent misconduct by UN peacekeepers from happening in the first place would be to create a culture of change and accountability, despite the absence of universal legal codes of prosecution. Based on prevailing trends and norms, three inter-related questions (and possible preventative scenarios) would then need to be addressed. First, should there be a convention or binding treaty, to which all sending countries become signatories, thereby standardising relevant laws and criminalising all behaviour destructive to the understood intent of UN missions, for both civilian and military personnel? For example, should seemingly voluntary sexual encounters with prostitutes, and other sexually exploitative behaviour by UN peacekeepers, be prosecuted, even if the laws of a peacekeeper's own country do not categorically prohibit acts of prostitution? Related to this is the question of whether troop-contributing countries can provide the most effective venues of prosecution. Second, should there be an international tribunal, whether a special UN/regional court or the ICC, with expanded powers and operating under a standardised code of law, through which civilian and military personnel on UN missions can be prosecuted? And third, under what circumstances is it legally possible to have troop-contributing countries waive immunity for offenders to allow them to face prosecution in the host country's own justice system for crimes committed on that country's soil while on mission for the UN?

There are a few possible ways out of this conundrum. At the international level, the UN could begin to hold member states accountable by raising the public profile of sexual exploitation and abuse. The UN might consider restoring the position of a special adviser on sexual exploitation and abuse committed by UN peacekeeping personnel, and perhaps eventually elevate this position to that of a permanent under-secretary. This office could, among other duties, be responsible for naming and shaming offenders in the UN's peacekeeping forces (especially among the top brass), and provide a record of peacekeeping forces that enforce discipline and are willing to subject accused peacekeepers to trial. Similarly, this office could lobby to condition foreign aid on the presence of norms and laws against sexual exploitation and abuse. Such an office could also be charged with implementing the much-needed global curriculum and instruction that would universalise rules of behaviour.

From the standpoint of moving "towards a new *Pax Africana*" (see Introduction in this volume), one strategy would be to properly constitute and empower the African Court on Human and Peoples' Rights (AfCHPR). Due to deficits in logistics, resources, and political commitment, the AfCHPR cannot, at present, take on the task of handling cases of sexual exploitation and abuse. To make matters worse, African leaders have granted themselves immunity from prosecution in the new African Court of Justice and Human Rights (ACJHR).[36] This new court, in accordance with a 2008 Protocol on the Statute of the African Court of Justice, merges the AfCHPR (established in 1998) and the African court of justice envisaged by the 2000 AU Constitutive Act, into one institution.[37] Still, the AU could demonstrate leadership, and a serious commitment to halting sexual exploitation and abuse, by altering the ACJHR's mandate to allow African peacekeepers to face prosecution outside their home countries, when they commit offences while on missions.

Notes

1. This chapter focuses, for the most part, on military and police personnel deployed as peacekeepers.
2. *See* United Nations (UN), "What is Peacekeeping?", http://www.un.org/en/peacekeeping/operations/peacekeeping.shtml (accessed 4 July 2016). *See also* Michael Doyle and Nicholas Sambanis, *Making War and Building Peace: United Nations Peace Operations* (Princeton, Princeton University Press, 2006).
3. Alice Gadler, "The Protection of Peacekeepers and International Criminal Law: Legal Challenges and Broader Protection", *German Law Journal* 11, no. 6 (2010), pp. 585–608.
4. The point here is that allegations do not always indicate criminal activity. Indeed, there have been cases where allegations of UN peacekeeping abuses were pressed for other motivations.
5. UN News Centre, "Peacekeepers' Sexual Abuse of Local Girls Continuing in DR of Congo, UN Finds", http://www.un.org/apps/news/story.asp?NewsID=12990#.V4-XGnmV9aQ (accessed July 18, 2016).
6. In an interview with the author (November 2013), Barbara Crossette, a former writer for the *New York Times*, illustrated the mixed picture that UN peacekeepers present, when she noted that in Cambodia, for instance, Bangladeshis had a good record of enforcing discipline, even if there were slippages; whereas Bulgarian troops in that country were known locally as the "Vulgarians" due to their bad conduct.
7. Daniel McGrory, "Woman Sacked for Revealing UN Links with Sex Trade: How a Tribunal Vindicated an Investigator Who Blew Whistle on Workers in Bosnia", *Times of London*, 7 August 2002. Her story became a bestseller as well and the basis of a film titled, *The Whistleblower*.
8. David Smith and Paul Lewis, "UN Peacekeepers Accused of Killing and Rape in Central African Republic", *The Guardian*, 12 August 2015, http://www.theguardian.com/world/2015/aug/11/un-peacekeepers-accused-killing-rape-central-african-republic (accessed 7 January 2016).
9. Colum Lynch, "Pakistani Forces in Congo Aided Gold Smugglers, the U.N. Finds", *Washington Post*, 23 July 2007, http://www.washingtonpost.com/wp-dyn/content/article/2007/07/22/AR2007072201242.html (accessed 8 July 2016).
10. UN Peacekeeping, "Contributors to UN Peacekeeping Operations", December 2015, http://www.un.org/en/peacekeeping/resources/statistics/contributors.shtml (accessed 10 July 2016).
11. UN Peacekeeping, "Summary of Contributions to Peacekeeping by Mission, Country and Post", 30 June 2017, http://www.un.org/en/peacekeeping/contributors/2017/jun17_5.pdf (accessed 9 August 2017).
12. When it comes to sexual exploitation and abuse (SEA), Celhia de Lavarene, a reporter and author of the book *Un Visa Pour l'Enfer [A Visa to Hell]* (Paris: Fayard, 2006) who has been on seven missions with the UN—not as a journalist, but as a UN staff member—says bluntly that, most of the time, "peacekeepers are part of the problem, not even to say, *the* problem"; interview with author, November 2013.
13. Graça Machel, *Promotion and Protection of the Rights of Children: Impact of Armed Conflict on Children*, Report of the Expert of the Secretary-General, UN

Doc. A/51/306, 26 August 1996, http://www.unicef.org/graca/a51-306_en.pdf (accessed 1 March 2014).
14. *See* UN, "The Conduct and Discipline Unit", https://cdu.unlb.org/Policy/SexualExploitationandAbusePolicy.aspx (accessed 19 July 2016).
15. UN General Assembly, "Letter Dated 24 March 2005 from the Secretary-General to the President of the General Assembly", UN Doc. A/59/710, 24 March 2005, p. 2, https://cdu.unlb.org/Portals/0/Documents/KeyDoc5.pdf (accessed 6 December 2016). This document contains the full text of the Zeid Report, "A Comprehensive Strategy to Eliminate Future Sexual Exploitation and Abuse in United Nations Peacekeeping Operations".
16. Based on data from the reports of the UN Office of Internal Oversight Services (OIOS) up until 31 December 2015, https://cdu.unlb.org/Statistics/AllegationsbyCategoryofPersonnelSexualExploitationandAbuse/AllegationsforAllCategoriesofPersonnelPerYearSexualExploitationandAbuse.aspx (accessed 21 February 2016).
17. Róisín Burke, *Troop-Discipline and Sexual Offences by UN Military Peacekeepers: The UN's Response – Moving Beyond the Current Status Quo?*, Working Paper no. 1.5, Centre for International Governance and Justice, Canberra, Australia, http://regnet.anu.edu.au/research/publications/2945/working-paper-no-15-troop-discipline-and-sexual-offences-un-military (accessed 4 July 2016).
18. Kathleen Jennings, *Protecting Whom? Approaches to Sexual Exploitation and Abuse in UN Peacekeeping Operations* (Oslo: Fafo, 2008), http://www.fafo.no/media/com_netsukii/20078.pdf (accessed 19 July 2016).
19. Kwesi Aning and Funmi Olonisakin, "Humanitarian Intervention and Human Rights: The Contradictions in ECOMOG", *International Journal of Human Rights* 3, no. 1 (1999), pp. 16–39.
20. Christopher Tuck, "'Every Car or Moving Object Gone': The ECOMOG Intervention in Liberia", *African Studies Quarterly* 4, no. 1 (2000), http://asq.africa.ufl.edu/files/ASQ-Vol-4-Issue-1-Tuck.pdf (accessed 15 July 2016).
21. Louis Charbonneau, "Kenyan Peacekeepers Aided Illegal Somalia Charcoal Export", *Reuters*, 14 July 2013, http://uk.reuters.com/article/uk-somalia-charcoal-un-idUKBRE96D01C20130714 (accessed 15 July 2013).
22. Nicholas Kulish, "African Union and Somalia to Investigate Rape Accusation", *New York Times*, 15 August 2013.
23. UN News, "Investigation into Sexual exploitation of Refugees by Aid Workers in West Africa", http://www.un.org/news/dh/infocus/a-57-465.pdf (accessed 12 July 2016).
24. Gerald Caplan, "Peacekeepers Gone Wild: How Much More Abuse Will the UN Ignore in Congo?", *The Globe and Mail*, 3 August 2012, http://www.theglobeandmail.com/news/politics/second-reading/peacekeepers-gone-wild-how-much-more-abuse-will-the-un-ignore-in-congo/article4462151 (accessed 19 July 2016).
25. Steve Stecklow and Joe Lauria, "U.N. Mum on Probes of Sex-Abuse Allegations," *Wall Street Journal*, 22 March 2010, pp. A1, A18, http://www.wsj.com/articles/SB10001424052748704188104575083334130312808 (accessed 6 May 2015).
26. The full text of the Zeid Report can be found in UN Doc. A/59/710), https://cdu.unlb.org/Portals/0/Documents/KeyDoc5.pdf (accessed 10 July 2016).

27. Warren Hoge, "Report Calls for Punishing Peacekeepers in Sex Abuse", *New York Times*, 25 March 2005, http://www.nytimes.com/2005/03/25/politics/report-calls-for-punishing-peacekeepers-in-sex-abuse.html (accessed 7 October 2013).
28. Elizabeth F. Defeis, "U.N. Peacekeepers and Sexual Abuse and Exploitation: An End to Impunity", *Washington University Global Law Studies Review* 7, no. 2 (2008), pp. 185–214.
29. Barbara Crossette, "When Peacekeepers Turn Into Troublemakers", *New York Times*, 7 January 1996, p. 6. *See also* "Profile: Bureaucrat at Large in the Balkans: Yasushi Akashi, Almost Painfully Diplomatic UN Envoy", *The Independent*, 29 April 1994, http://www.independent.co.uk/voices/profile-bureaucrat-at-large-in-the-balkans-yasushi-akashi-almost-painfully-diplomatic-un-envoy-1373287.html (accessed 18 December 2014).
30. Sahana Dharmapuri, "Not Just a Numbers Game: Increasing Women's Participation in UN Peacekeeping", Providing for Peacekeeping no. 4 (New York: International Peace Institute, July 2013); UN Peacekeeping, "Summary of Troop Contributions to UN Peacekeeping Operations by Mission, Post and Gender", 30 June 2017, http://www.un.org/en/peacekeeping/contributors/gender/2017gender/jun17.pdf (accessed 9 August 2017).
31. UN Peacekeeping, "Ten Rules: Code of Personal Conduct for Blue Helmets", http://www.un.org/en/peacekeeping/documents/ten_in.pdf (accessed 6 December 2016).
32. Melanie O'Brien, "National and International Criminal Jurisdiction over United Nations Peacekeeping Personnel for Gender-Based Crimes Against Women", PhD thesis, University of Nottingham, 2010.
33. *See* http://www.un.org/en/ga/sixth/67/CrimAcc.shtml (accessed 7 July 2016).
34. Andrew Ladley, "Peacekeeper Abuse, Immunity, and Impunity: The Need for Effective Criminal and Civil Accountability on International Peace Operations", *Politics and Ethics Review* 1, no. 1 (2005), pp. 81–90.
35. "Liberia Sex-for-Aid 'Widespread'", *BBC News*, 8 May 2006, http://news.bbc.co.uk/2/hi/africa/4983440.stm (accessed 9 November 2014).
36. "Proposed Court," *New York Times*, 2 July 2014, p. A10. *See also*, "Justice for Dictators: History Rules", *The Economist*, 21 April 2012.
37. *See* African Union (AU), "Judicial and Human Rights Institutions", http://www.au.int/en/organs/cj (accessed 6 December 2016).

CHAPTER 14

Managing HIV/AIDS in Peace Support Operations in Africa

Paul Mulindwa and Oscar Siwali

In June 2017, nine of the 16 United Nations (UN) peacekeeping missions worldwide were in Africa.[1] The continent also accounted for about 69 per cent of people living with HIV globally.[2] Because the HIV/AIDS pandemic can jeopardise effective implementation of these missions, as well as exacerbate existing insecurity in their areas of operation, the disease represents a significant threat to peace and security on the continent.

In July 2000, the UN Security Council adopted Resolution 1308,[3] acknowledging the severity of the HIV/AIDS pandemic globally and its potential impact on international peace and security. The resolution highlighted how HIV/AIDS was contributing to social instability, as well as the potential damaging impact of the spread of the disease on the health of international peacekeepers. It acknowledged countries that had made efforts to address the problem through national programmes; and encouraged those that had not yet done so to consider putting in place measures including HIV/AIDS education, voluntary and confidential testing and counselling, and treatment of their personnel, in cooperation with the international community, to address the spread of the disease. It further called on the Joint UN Programme on HIV/AIDS (UNAIDS) and the UN Department of Peacekeeping Operations (DPKO), as well as member states, to take steps to address "the effects of HIV on the health of peacekeeping and support personnel and develop long-term strategies for HIV prevention as an important part of Member States' prepara-

P. Mulindwa (✉)
Centre for Conflict Resolution, Cape Town, South Africa

O. Siwali
Southern African Development and Reconstruction Agency,
Cape Town, South Africa

T. Karbo, K. Virk (eds.), *The Palgrave Handbook of Peacebuilding in Africa*, https://doi.org/10.1007/978-3-319-62202-6_14

tion for participation in peacekeeping operations".[4] This chapter focuses on efforts to manage the pandemic in peace support operations, while offering recommendations to enhance relevant programmes and policies, in Africa.

HIV/AIDS and Peacekeeping in Africa

Data on HIV prevalence in African militaries are scarce, patchy, and difficult to obtain, with infection rates tending to be treated as sensitive or classified information by military officials for fear that the knowledge, if made publicly available, may compromise national security. Be that as it may, military personnel are widely considered to be at high risk for contracting HIV, as well as other sexually transmitted infections (STIs), due to various factors including long periods of separation from their families and concomitant susceptibility to high-risk sexual behaviour. In 2006, South Africa's Department of Defence reported that 30 per cent of the 34,810 members of the South African National Defence Force (SANDF) who were tested for HIV/AIDS that year had contracted the virus.[5] However, the prevalence rate in the SANDF was estimated to have decreased to 8.5 per cent by 2013,[6] and the country's defence department has, as indicated in its 2015–2016 annual report, continued to strengthen strategy, policies, and plans to manage the disease in the defence force.[7] More recent data on HIV/AIDS prevalence in the SANDF, though, have been difficult to obtain, with the information increasingly treated as classified. In several sub-Saharan African countries, as many as 50–60 per cent of soldiers were estimated in the mid-2000s to have contracted HIV.[8] In Nigeria, random testing for HIV infection among a selected group of soldiers revealed an HIV prevalence rate of 14.7 per cent in 2012.[9] Meanwhile, HIV prevalence among personnel of Rwanda's national defence force has been estimated at 4.5 per cent.[10] In 2004, HIV prevalence rates among urban and rural recruits to Ethiopia's military stood at 7.2 and 3.8 per cent respectively.[11] The troops from these African militaries are deployed in several African Union (AU) and UN-sanctioned peacekeeping missions on the continent including those in the Central African Republic (CAR), Côte d'Ivoire, the Democratic Republic of the Congo (DRC), Liberia, Mali, Somalia, South Sudan, Sudan, and Western Sahara. In 2016, about 42,000 of the over 98,500 peacekeeping and support personnel in peace support missions on the continent came from 14 African countries.[12]

The troops from national militaries on the continent also constitute the five African regional brigades that form the AU's African Standby Force (ASF), which was to have been established by 2015 (with the previous deadline of 2010 having been missed). In October–November 2015, the Amani Africa II field training exercise was held at the South African Army Combat Training Centre with the aim of assessing the rapid deployment capacity of the force. Though declared to have attained "full operational capability" after the exercise, the ASF was yet to be actually deployed at the time of writing.[13] The ASF has been devised as a peacekeeping force comprising both civilian and military components able to intervene in cases of conflict and instability across the continent. Consisting of five rapidly deployable regional brigades—in Southern, Central, West, Eastern, and North Africa—the ASF is supposed to prevent the emergence or escalation of African conflicts and thus foster the peace and stability necessary for foreign investment and strong economic growth on the continent.[14] (See Nagar, and Kuwali in this volume.)

Over the past decade and a half, African leaders have sought to devise various policy mechanisms and commitments to coordinate their efforts—at both the continental and regional levels—to address the spread of HIV as a shared challenge. They include: the 2001 Abuja Declaration on HIV/AIDS, Tuberculosis, and Other Related Infectious Diseases; the 2003 Maputo Declaration on Malaria, HIV/AIDS, Tuberculosis, and Other Related Infectious Diseases; the AU Commission's HIV/AIDS Strategic Plan 2005–2007; the 2012 Roadmap on Shared Responsibility and Global Solidarity for AIDS, Tuberculosis, and Malaria Response in Africa; and the Africa Health Strategy 2016–2030. However, despite these pledges and commitments towards a continental effort to combat the HIV/AIDS pandemic in Africa, a coherent and coordinated set of policies to prevent the spread of the disease among regional peacekeeping forces has yet to be promoted. Notably, HIV/AIDS is not even mentioned in the policy frameworks, and peace and security memorandum agreed for the African Standby Force.[15] The omission is glaring considering the increasing military readiness of the regional brigades that will make up the standby force and the high rates of HIV/AIDS prevalence among the national armies contributing to the brigades.

HIV/AIDS Among Peacekeepers in Africa and Globally

According to a 2011 UNAIDS review of HIV programmes among international peacekeepers and uniformed service personnel: "The prevalence of HIV infection among peacekeeping personnel tends to reflect the prevalence among young men of similar age groups in their countries of origin. The HIV prevalence in national uniformed services (including national police services) is similar to that of the general population, with some exceptions in countries in sub-Saharan Africa—but not, as was postulated in 2000, 2–5 times higher than in comparable civilian populations." However, the report also noted: "The incidence of HIV infection tends to rise with increasing duration of deployment in a duty area."[16] This is likely the case because HIV/AIDS prevalence is still high in the sub-Saharan African countries where troops tend to be deployed, which creates a risk to already vulnerable soldiers.[17]

Generally speaking, peacekeeping missions can create specific vectors and conditions for the spread of HIV. Peace support operations often feature a high turnover of troops, and they include soldiers from a range of contributing countries that may have widely varying rates of HIV prevalence and degrees of access to medical care on duty and at home. These soldiers often conduct their tours of duty in unfamiliar and insecure environments, and can spend long periods away from their home countries, far from their accustomed communities and families, and removed from contact with their spouses or regular sexual partners. This often encourages the growth of the sex industry in the areas where they are deployed, while increasing the probability of sexually risky behaviour, as well as involvement in extra-marital relations, which can, in turn, lead to contracting STIs. In addition, peacekeepers in Africa and elsewhere have at times been associated with inappropriate behaviour and sexual exploitation known to facilitate HIV infection. Cases of rape, sexual violence, and engagement with sex workers have been reported in almost every UN peacekeeping mission worldwide, including in Burundi, Côte d'Ivoire, the DRC, Liberia, Sierra Leone, Haiti, and Kosovo.[18] (See Akonor in this volume.) Peacekeepers can, thus, be a source of HIV infection to local populations, as well as a vector for infection by host populations, taking the virus home with them on their return from duty.

But military personnel are also potentially strong agents of change in preventing the spread of the virus "within the army and beyond. If equipped with the right information, knowledge and tools, the military can achieve lower HIV prevalence rates than the national average, as can be seen from the experiences among the armed forces of Ethiopia and Uganda".[19] Similarly, the HIV/AIDS Unit of the AU-UN Hybrid Operation in Darfur (UNAMID) reported a decrease in the HIV infection rate among peacekeepers in 2012, due to behaviour-change programmes carried out by trained peer educators within the mission.[20] (On UNAMID, see Gambari in this volume.) As agents of change in stemming the spread of HIV, peacekeepers have the potential to make a significant impact both within the uniformed services as a whole and among the communities with which they interact.

It is also important to note that HIV/AIDS-related concerns have not been limited to African peacekeepers and armed forces. For example, in Russia, the new HIV infection rate in the country's military forces increased precipitously "from about 0.1 cases per 100,000 soldiers in 1995 to nearly 40 per 100,000 in 2003".[21] An intelligence assessment, published in 2002 by the United States (US) National Intelligence Council, noted that China and India were likely to "increasingly … monitor AIDS in the military to ensure that the disease does not complicate staffing among smaller, more highly trained units operating sophisticated weapons systems".[22] Pre- and post-deployment testing of Indonesian peacekeepers to the UN Transitional Authority in Cambodia (UNTAC) (1992–1993) indicated that 11 of the 12 personnel found to be HIV-positive had contracted the infection in the "mission area".[23] Blue helmets from other countries, in particular India, Uruguay, and the United States, were similarly found to have returned from serving in UNTAC with HIV infection thought to be contracted while they were on deployment.[24]

Impacts of HIV on Peacekeeping

High HIV prevalence rates among militaries can have significant budgetary implications for countries contributing troops to peacekeeping missions. Costs include those related to making anti-retroviral (ARV) treatment available to

HIV-positive soldiers; providing medical attention for those suffering from AIDS-related illnesses; and replacing troops who are too ill to do their jobs. Such costs can have a disproportionate effect on the national budgets of developing countries. For example, HIV prevalence in the South African National Defence Force has, as mentioned earlier, been estimated at 8.5 per cent.[25] The impact of this can be seen in relation to the force's budget and absenteeism.[26] The defence budget to address HIV/AIDS increased from R32 million in the 2009–2010 financial year to R48 million in the 2011–2012 financial year,[27] and the force was losing at least 400,000 days and as many as 560,000 days a year to absenteeism.[28] Moreover, the economic and social costs to troop-contributing countries can be compounded when peacekeepers return home with HIV infection—or when their partners have contracted the virus in their absence. The risk of infection in these cases can be substantial because condoms are often not used due to lack of education on prevention of STIs among peacekeepers and their families.[29] South Africa had about 1,500 peacekeepers deployed in various parts of Africa—including the DRC, South Sudan, and Sudan's Darfur region—in June 2017.[30]

Those who argue against the deployment of HIV-positive military personnel to peacekeeping missions also rely on concern for the welfare and well-being of those affected, citing, among other things, the poor availability of adequate medical treatment to meet the special requirements of HIV-infected personnel in the field; pre-deployment vaccinations and on-deployment exposure to diseases that could further compromise their health; and the additional risk of forward transmission to medical personnel, other soldiers, as well as local civilians.[31] However, it is important to weigh these factors against considerations of fairness and equality, as well as the importance of taking a human rights-based approach to HIV-positive personnel.

That having been said, transmission of the virus by HIV-positive peacekeepers to local populations can exacerbate the significant, existing health and socio-economic challenges in the conflict-prone countries to which they are deployed. As well, the issue has created diplomatic tensions, with peacekeepers from militaries that do not conduct HIV testing and screening of recruits being refused entry by host countries. For example, Sudan in the mid-2000s, when it opposed the idea of increasing the number of AU peacekeepers in Darfur, raised fears that troops from sub-Saharan African countries who do not undergo testing before deployment might bring HIV/AIDS into its territory, and in this context suggested screening the incoming peacekeepers for HIV.[32]

High HIV prevalence rates can also have a serious impact on the capacity of peacekeepers to complete their missions. Military personnel who are HIV-positive potentially jeopardise the health of their fellow soldiers. Other troops as well may feel reluctant to work closely with HIV-positive peers in a team or unit, fearing they might become infected by the blood of HIV-positive soldiers. The virus may be transmitted through sex, intravenous drug use, or open wounds (such as the kind often caused by accidents or in armed fighting). Fear of infection may lower morale. In addition to such real psychological impacts, the virus can detract from readiness for deployment, as sick soldiers cannot be readily deployed, which can, in turn, delay the timely arrival of peacekeepers to prevent conflicts.[33]

Responding to HIV/AIDS in Peace Support Operations

Military organisations, including peace support operations, provide a highly structured and disciplined workplace in which personnel can be readily mobilised to participate in HIV/AIDS education, prevention, and testing campaigns, as well as being closely monitored for treatment. Information and material resources (such as condoms and therapeutic drugs) to address the spread of HIV/AIDS, voluntary counselling and testing, and preventive safer-sex training can be efficiently provided through military structures both for soldiers and for the general population. If such structures are streamlined, they can enhance the effective management of the HIV/AIDS pandemic in Africa and elsewhere.

In 2001, the UN Department of Peacekeeping Operations established new positions within every peacekeeping mission for an HIV/AIDS focal point and HIV/AIDS policy advisor, mandated to provide technical input and support to the HIV/AIDS units within the missions. When adopting Resolution 1528, in February 2004, establishing the United Nations Operation in Côte d'Ivoire (UNOCI), the UN Security Council welcomed and encouraged "efforts by the United Nations to sensitise peacekeeping personnel in the prevention and control of HIV/AIDS and other communicable diseases in all its peacekeeping missions".[34] Similar language was used by the Security Council later in the same year when establishing the UN Stabilisation Mission in Haiti (MINUSTAH) and the UN Operation in Burundi (ONUB).[35] In December 2007, the DPKO's Department of Field Support on HIV issued a policy directive on the role of the HIV/AIDS units in UN missions. The units are mandated to provide HIV/AIDS awareness and prevention programmes to mission personnel. Missions that have featured such HIV/AIDS units have included the UN operations in the DRC, Ethiopia and Eritrea, Liberia, Côte d'Ivoire, South Sudan, Timor-Leste, and Haiti. In addition, between January 2011 and December 2014 the UN Integrated Office in Burundi (BINUB) provided counselling services, while the UN Interim Administration Mission in Kosovo (UNMIK) focal point provided voluntary HIV/AIDS counselling and testing services within the medical facilities. However, many of these units lack sufficient resources and capacity to properly identify the relevant HIV/AIDS issues for their missions. The effective integration of HIV/AIDS concerns into the programmes of peace support operations is thus reduced, and important opportunities for cooperation with other actors in the sphere of a mission's operations—such as the pooling of resources, the sharing of training materials, and the development of joint outreach projects—are missed.

Meanwhile in Africa, the AU, since its creation in 2002, has sought to build and develop the African Peace and Security Architecture (APSA), with the ASF, in particular, envisaged—as mentioned earlier—as an integrated pan-African force with robust, rapid deployment capability to conduct a wide range of missions. Side by side with the evolution of the APSA, African armed forces have been increasingly deployed under various umbrellas to help keep the peace, manage humanitarian crises, and serve a policing function in several newly democratic and post-conflict states on the continent. In this context, it is vital that security challenges such as HIV/AIDS are managed effectively. As also mentioned earlier, the AU and Africa's regional economic communities (RECs) have developed various initiatives to mitigate and manage HIV/AIDS on the continent. Many of these call for robust and intensive approaches towards the pandemic. The 2001 Abuja Declaration, for example, includes a pledge by African governments to set a target allocation of at least 15 per cent of their annual budgets to achieving improvements in the health sector, including, in particular, the fight against HIV/AIDS, tuberculosis, and other related infectious diseases.[36] It is worth noting, though, that this and other pledges have not been directly or specifically aimed at security institutions. Yet, militaries are among the most vulnerable to, and high-risk groups for, HIV infection, and the security sector across Africa could benefit enormously from greater budget allocations at the national level for HIV/AIDS programmes. Several individual African countries have sought to implement various measures, such as mandatory testing, to combat the spread of HIV/AIDS in their armed forces. In Uganda and South Africa, for example, HIV testing is mandatory at the time of recruitment into the military and recommended on a regular basis thereafter.

Among Africa's RECs, the Southern African Development Community (SADC) has made progress towards putting in place policies, frameworks, and protocols aimed at managing the effects of HIV/AIDS, including in security institutions. For example, the SADC HIV and AIDS Strategic Framework 2010–2015[37] includes an action plan to facilitate mainstreaming of HIV/AIDS activities across its core sectors, including defence and security (such as through capacity building for the SADC Brigade), and to ensure access to treatment, care, and support for security personnel. The Economic Community of West African States (ECOWAS),[38] the Intergovernmental Authority on Development (IGAD), and the East African Community (EAC) have similarly sought to design mechanisms to manage the problem of HIV/AIDS in their member states. The 2016–2020 Strategic Plan of the West African Health Organisation (WAHO)—the specialised ECOWAS institution for health issues—identifies interventions to, among other things, manage the prevalence of HIV/AIDS in the sub-region.[39] Similarly, the IGAD Regional HIV and AIDS Partnership Program (IRAPP) articulates detailed strategies to address the disease.[40] The EAC has a similar plan and implementation framework.[41] However, neither the IGAD plan nor that of ECOWAS mentions or considers specific measures to deal with HIV/AIDS within the militaries of their member states or even their regional standby brigades.

The development of appropriate structures and channels to disseminate information and promote awareness about the impact of HIV/AIDS, and how to prevent its spread, is critical in peace support operations. For its part, the UN Department of Peacekeeping Operations has developed standardised pre-deployment training courses to equip peacekeepers with such knowledge. HIV/AIDS policy advisors are increasingly facilitating pre-deployment awareness sessions in African missions. For instance, Namibian and Ethiopian troops deployed to Liberia in 2003 and 2004 received such training, as did Rwandan troops deployed, more recently, to Darfur in 2011; Burundian and Rwandan troops deployed to the CAR in 2015 and 2016; and Ugandan troops deployed to Liberia, Somalia, and South Sudan in 2015 and 2016. The DPKO has also produced an HIV/AIDS awareness card,[42] which it distributes to all peacekeeping personnel. This supports in-mission training programmes, and consolidates the information already disseminated. It provides basic information on HIV/AIDS and how personnel can protect themselves against sexual and occupational risk of exposure, and includes a pocket for a condom.

UNAIDS and the DPKO have jointly adopted several policies to implement the UN Security Council's 2011 declaration[43] that prevention should be regarded as the major strategy to combat HIV/AIDS. In 2004, the DPKO established an HIV Voluntary Confidential Counselling and Testing (VCCT) policy for uniformed peacekeepers that conforms to international human rights norms, making such testing voluntary for peacekeepers while respecting the right of troop-contributing countries to implement mandatory testing. The provision of voluntary counselling and testing services enables individuals to make informed and independent decisions in relation to learning their HIV status and acquiring information about safer sex practices. The availability of such services can influence behaviour and help to prevent further transmission of the virus. However, many missions lack basic VCCT amenities such as test kits and a dedicated facility from which the service can operate.

HIV/AIDS prevention can also be fostered through the promotion of safe-sex practices such as using condoms. The DPKO has agreed with the United Nations Population Fund (UNFPA) to ensure a consistent and economical supply of male and female condoms. Five condoms a week are supposed to be given to every peacekeeper. However, the distribution of condoms at the battalion level relies heavily on successful negotiation of often delicate cultural and religious issues, and on the cooperation of contingent commanders. In one case, such a commander reportedly burned a consignment of condoms.[44] The distribution of condoms also needs to be supported by the promotion of their benefits, and practical instructions on usage. In addition, the effectiveness of these distribution programmes would be significantly enhanced if they were extended to engage with local communities in the areas of operation through appropriate outreach and prevention campaigns.

Another option to manage HIV/AIDS within peace support missions is to build the capacity of the national militaries of troop-contributing countries to provide HIV/AIDS awareness training. Such training contributes, among other things, to making personnel realise that it is important for others to know their HIV status; to empowering and increasing the alertness of personnel with regard to HIV/AIDS and its impact; and to ensuring the effective management and availability of support systems. This, in turn, further encourages early testing and lifestyle changes that can reduce and prevent further infection. Cohorts of peer educators should be created to implement such training, creating sustainable awareness programmes with a multiplier effect that could reach beyond those in uniform to the population at large. Such networks of peer educators have yet to be created—and would probably require the joint support of national militaries as well as agencies and institutions working with these militaries, such as the DPKO, UNAIDS, and the AU, as well as Africa's sub-regional bodies through the brigades of the African Standby Force.

Although the UN Department of Peacekeeping Operations is responsible for providing training, executive direction, management, and logistical support for its missions, the engagement of troop-contributing countries is crucial to the success of initiatives to manage the HIV/AIDS pandemic among peacekeepers. As part of its train-the-trainer programme, the DPKO provides senior officers from contributing countries with intensive two- to three-week peacekeeper training. The focus of this training includes encouraging troop-contributing countries to develop national strategies to address the spread of HIV among national uniformed services and to ensure the inclusion of HIV/AIDS awareness in pre-deployment training for peacekeepers. However, it remains unclear how many countries have developed HIV/AIDS strategies specifically for their uniformed services, and how actively such strategies are being implemented.

Management of the HIV/AIDS pandemic among peace support operations needs to be addressed through a comprehensive, multi-sectoral approach. This should extend HIV/AIDS management efforts beyond the medical sphere to include areas such as social practices and behaviour, and seek to provide holistic support to soldiers infected with HIV. It is essential that senior military officers and political figures take the lead in campaigning, creating awareness, mobilising resources, and ensuring that programmes are implemented. For example, in the Ugandan military, senior commanders were involved in a national HIV/AIDS prevention strategy, launched in 1987, to reduce HIV/AIDS prevalence among uniformed personnel as well as civilians around the army barracks. The success of such campaigns also depends on HIV/AIDS issues being addressed in a full and frank manner.

Challenges of Managing HIV/AIDS in Peace Support Operations

In January 2000, HIV/AIDS was formally recognised by the United Nations as a potential impediment to the effectiveness of militaries—especially those engaged in UN peacekeeping missions—because of the prevalence of the disease among armed forces personnel. Subsequently, Peter Piot, then Executive Director of UNAIDS, further declared that HIV/AIDS was not only a health matter, but also a security issue that militaries needed to address because of the destabilising effects of the pandemic among militaries themselves as well as society at large, and on socio-economic development and stability more widely.[45] Altogether this led to a debate on HIV/AIDS prevalence that emphasised the rate of infection among African militaries, as well as in many African countries; although critics noted that the terms of this debate in the 2000s did not appear to be supported by the available evidence and that more research was needed.[46] For example, as noted earlier, reliable and accurate data about the prevalence of HIV/AIDS in armed forces are often unavailable, partly because militaries work, in general, in secrecy and are unwilling to publish information deemed sensitive.[47] It remains unclear as to how many soldiers are actually infected with the HIV virus in many national militaries, and correspondingly, as to how many of those are participating in peacekeeping missions—although some countries, such as South Africa, are increasingly seeking to make information available on the prevalence of HIV in their armed forces. Furthermore, the link between high HIV prevalence and the presence of militaries, where it does exist, is often found to be of a different nature than previously assumed. For instance, research conducted since 2000—when the existence of the link was confidently announced by the UN—has indicated that HIV/AIDS spreads more widely after conflicts end.[48] This confounded expectations and challenged existing assumptions that had been made about the role of African militaries as vectors for the virus.

In addition to this debate, in recent years a series of media and research reports have appeared noting that international peacekeepers are often identified as perpetrators of sexual abuse by local populations in the areas of their deployment.[49] Peacekeepers have been variously described as "rapists, patrons of prostitutes, child pornographers, molesters, absentee fathers, tormentors, [and] spreaders of contagion and disease".[50] Such voices have also been critical of the UN for failing to sanction a sexually predatory culture among peacekeepers and for even encouraging it through the distribution of condoms.[51] The allegations and the reported evidence of sexual abuse by peacekeepers—for example, in Côte d'Ivoire, the DRC, Liberia, Sudan, and Haiti[52]—raise important questions about the ethical nature of sexual relations between peacekeepers and members of host populations.

It is also important to note that negative perceptions of the role of peacekeepers as vectors for HIV transmission are further exacerbated by the inconsistent availability of data on the prevalence of HIV/AIDS in host countries during and after conflicts. During war, little HIV testing is conducted; often it is only afterwards, as the peacekeepers arrive, that proper tracking of prevalence of the virus begins again, and that fuller reporting of the sexual abuse that often accompanies war—for example, in recent conflicts in the DRC and Haiti—starts to emerge. As the peacekeepers become the focus of attention, and in the context of reports of sexual abuse inflicted by them, they—rather than the greater accuracy of reporting—are often perceived as the cause of higher reported rates of HIV infection.

That having been said, the problem of sexual exploitation and abuse during peace support operations is real. The UN's Executive Committee on Humanitarian Affairs (ECHA) and the Executive Committee on Peace and Security (ECPS), and the non-governmental Task Force on Protection from Sexual Exploitation and Abuse have been running a campaign, since 2006, dubbed "Serving with Pride" that has sought to dissuade and prevent soldiers from having sex with the people they are meant to protect. The initiative has created an important space for dialogue on the issue of sexual abuse. In addition, UN Security Council Resolution 1325 of 2000 recognises that women require special protection from gender-based violence during armed conflict. The resolution creates a clear duty for peacekeepers to protect vulnerable women.[53] (See Porter in this volume.)

Nonetheless, challenges remain. A key issue relates to the enforcement of HIV/AIDS policies among African militaries in the absence of UN involvement in promoting such policies in the armies of troop-contributing countries *before* peacekeepers are deployed. The matter is complicated, since the policies of the world body and those of troop-contributing militaries can contradict each other. For example, the UN requests that HIV testing and screening should be done before deployment, but it remains optional. Though such testing is mandatory in some national militaries, others conduct no testing or screening at all.

Another key challenge in the management of HIV/AIDS in peace support operations relates to issues of gender and masculinity. While both men and women have significant contributions to make to the security sector, the experiences and voices of women on security issues are often discounted, with debates and on-the-ground realities tending, by and large, to favour men. Gender remains one of the most overlooked issues in militaries, despite efforts by the UN and others to devise mechanisms to ensure the inclusion and prioritisation of gender perspectives in security matters (see Porter in this volume). UN Security Council Resolution 1325 of 2000 on women, peace, and security is of particular note in this regard. This resolution calls, among other things, for the increased representation of women at all decision-making levels in conflict resolution and peace processes; the adoption of a gendered perspective in the negotiation and implementation of peace agreements; the protection of women and girls from sexual and gender-based violence; and an end to impunity for genocide, crimes against humanity, and war crimes, including those related to violence against women and girls.[54] Yet in most African societies, sexual and gender-based violence—one of the vectors of HIV transmission—remains pervasive both during and after conflict. Meanwhile, within military and police ranks, female uniformed personnel, as well, are especially vulnerable. Not only are women biologically more vulnerable than men, but they are also often at a disadvantage in sexual negotiations, including negotiations for condom use. In this context, it is critical for HIV/AIDS programmes in national militaries, as well as those that are part of peacekeeping training, to include gender components such as having female peer leaders talk to female military personnel, having peer facilitation groups organised according to gender, promoting and distributing female condoms, and introducing a gender-based approach for HIV prevention to men.

Just as important in the struggle against HIV/AIDS are the needs to mainstream gender equality, and to increase women's representation and meaningful participation in African uniformed services and peace support operations. Service women's access to meaningful assignments in their national armed forces continues too often to be influenced by traditional attitudes towards "women's work", and the deployment of women to conflict situations is rare, with a notable imbalance between the numbers of men and women in top military echelons. As Yolande Bouka and Romi Sigsworth note, for example, in a recent study: "[In Uganda] less than 2% of colonels and lieutenant colonels are female; 3% of majors and 8.5% of captains are women. In Rwanda [often cited as a case of best practice for women's empowerment and participation in governance], an estimated 0.8% of the defence force is female. A mere 0.46% of the National Defence Force in Burundi is female, with no women represented in decision-making positions. ... The low level of women's participation in domestic security institutions is reflected at the regional level where the presence of women in peacekeeping is also not prioritised. ...[T]he total number of female personnel in the UN Organisation Stabilisation Mission in the Democratic Republic of the Congo (MONUSCO), for example, stands at only 2%."[55] However, experience has shown that female security and peacekeeping personnel deployed in volatile countries are able to play a positive role in engaging with communities and, in particular, with women and children, who are among the worst affected by conflict. In Darfur, for instance, female peacekeepers (police) have played critical roles, including in information gathering and dealing with sexual and gender-based violence, in a local context where women and girls find it easier to relate to these female peacekeepers than to male authority figures.[56] (See also Porter in this volume.)

Conclusion

It is vital for the African Union, through its 2004 Common Defence and Security Policy (CDSP), and for the UN Department of Peacekeeping Operations, through its various policies and directives, to try to develop a common approach to managing HIV/AIDS in peace support operations. Towards that end, the DPKO, together with the AU and other stakeholders including member states, needs, in particular, to formulate a strategy for uniformed officers on managing HIV/AIDS in national militaries as well as in peace support operations. Military commanders, for their part, need as well to be encouraged to contribute towards the formulation of effective policies and programmes on managing HIV/AIDS through performance-related incentives and deterrents. It is important, furthermore, for such policies to take into consideration country-specific cultures and experiences, and also to be harmonised with regional and continental policies on the issue. As well, they should define mechanisms that will enable policymakers to allocate adequate resources for implementation and effectively monitor their impact.

Based on the preceding discussion, we conclude with several concrete recommendations for stakeholders at different levels, to guide more effective management of HIV/AIDS in peace support operations in Africa.

First, the AU and Africa's RECs, as well as the UN through its Department of Peacekeeping Operations, need to integrate HIV/AIDS prevention into the design and command structures of their peace support operations on the continent. There is a further need for HIV/AIDS to be addressed in the policy frameworks, and peace and security memorandum for the ASF, in view of the robust and interventionist role envisaged for the standby force.

Second, cohorts of peer educators should be created to implement HIV/AIDS training, creating sustainable awareness programmes with a multiplier effect that could reach beyond those in uniform to the population at large. The creation of such networks in Africa, however, needs the support of national militaries as well as key external institutions such as the AU and Africa's RECs (through the ASF brigades) and UN actors including the DPKO and UNAIDS.

Third, in a related vein, the role of African peacekeepers as agents of change in stemming the spread of HIV within their institutions and beyond to their local/host communities should be promoted. Towards that end, organisational structures need to be further streamlined to facilitate the provision of information, resources, and facilities such as voluntary counselling and testing, and preventive safer-sex training for soldiers and the populations with whom they interact. Troop-receiving countries, for their part, could be more proactive in engaging positively with peacekeepers, for example, though joint and competitive sporting events that incorporate the dissemination of HIV/AIDS prevention messaging.

Fourth, there is a need for lessons to be learned from effective country- and mission-specific approaches to preventing the spread of HIV among militaries and for these to be shared. As Alex de Waal writes: "In Ethiopia, for example … HIV prevention integrated incentives and disincentives for HIV outcomes into the mainstream functioning of the army as an institution. Units that remain free from HIV will be rewarded with promotions, more desirable missions, and bonuses."[57] This collective approach has been shown to encourage greater concern among soldiers about their HIV status.

Fifth, sufficient resources and capacity need to be allocated to HIV/AIDS units within UN peacekeeping missions for them to implement their mandates effectively and enhance cooperation with other actors in their sphere of operations.

Finally, managing HIV/AIDS in peace support operations effectively requires a comprehensive, multi-sectoral approach that extends beyond the medical sphere to include areas such as social practices and behaviour, and seeks to provide holistic support to HIV-infected peacekeeping and support personnel.

Notes

1. United Nations (UN) Peacekeeping, "United Nations Peacekeeping Operations", fact sheet, 30 June 2017, http://www.un.org/en/peacekeeping/documents/bnotelatest.pdf (accessed 8 August 2017).
2. AVERT, "Global HIV and AIDS Statistics: 2015 Global HIV Statistics", http://www.avert.org/global-hiv-and-aids-statistics (accessed 19 December 2016).
3. UN Security Council Resolution 1308, UN Doc. S/RES/1308, 17 July 2000.
4. Joint UN Programme on HIV/AIDS (UNAIDS) and UN Department of Peacekeeping Operations (DPKO), *On the Front Line: A Review of Programmes That Address HIV Among International Peacekeepers and Uniformed Services 2005–2010* (Geneva and New York, 2011), p. 3.
5. South African Department of Defence, *Annual Report FY 2005–2006* (Pretoria, 2006), p. 163.
6. Kim Helfrich, "HIV Prevalence in the SANDF Less Than Half the National Average", 18 March 2013, http://www.defenceweb.co.za/index.php?option=com_content&view=article&id=29896:hiv-prevalence-in-the-sandf-less-than-half-the-national-average&catid=111:sa-defence (accessed 11 April 2017).
7. South African Department of Defence, *Annual Report FY 2015–2016*, p. 143.
8. Martin R. Rupiya (ed.), *The Enemy Within: Southern African Militaries' Quarter-Century Battle with HIV and AIDS* (Pretoria: Institute for Security Studies [ISS], 2006), p. 40.
9. Obioma Azuonwu, Osaro Erhabor, and Omokaro Obire, "HIV Among Military Personnel in the Niger Delta of Nigeria", *Journal of Community Health* 37, no. 1 (2012), pp. 25–31.
10. Government of Rwanda, *Rwanda Demographic and Health Survey 2005.*
11. United States (US) Department of State, *The President's Emergency Plan for AIDS Relief (PEPFAR/Emergency Plan): Ethiopia Operational Plan 2012.*
12. UN Peacekeeping, "Monthly Summary of Military and Police Contribution to United Nations Operations", 31 August 2016, http://www.un.org/en/peacekeeping/resources/statistics (accessed 19 December 2016).
13. "What Is Holding the African Standby Force Back", 10 May 2017, https://issafrica.org/pscreport/on-the-agenda/what-is-holding-the-african-standby-force-back (accessed 8 June 2017); African Union (AU), Declaration, Ninth Ordinary Meeting of the Specialised Technical Committee on Defence, Safety, and Security, Addis Ababa, Ethiopia, 4 June 2016, http://www.peaceau.org/uploads/9th-stcdss-final-declaration-english-.pdf (accessed 8 June 2017).
14. Bailey Jackson, "Standing By for the African Standby Force", Center for Global Prosperity, 5 March 2013, http://globalprosperity.wordpress.com/2013/03/05/standing-by-for-the-african-standby-force (accessed 20 December 2016).
15. AU, "Policy Framework for the Establishment of the African Standby Force and the Military Staff Committee (MSC)", 15–16 May 2003; AU, "Roadmap for the Operationalisation of the African Standby Force", 22–23 March 2005; AU, "Experts' Meeting on the Relationship Between the AU and the Regional Mechanisms for Conflict Prevention, Management, and Resolution", EXP/AU-RECs/ASF/4(I), March 2005; AU, "Draft Framework for a Common

African Defence and Security Policy", January 2004, MIN/Def and sec 3.(I) 20–21.

16. UNAIDS and UN DPKO, *On the Front Line*, p. 59. *See* Alan Whiteside, Alex de Waal, and Tsadkan Gebre-Tensae, "AIDS, Security, and the Military in Africa: A Sober Appraisal", *African Affairs* 105, no. 419 (2006), pp. 201–218.
17. South African Department of Defence, *Annual Report FY 2015–2016*, p. 143.
18. Kwame Akonor, *UN Peacekeeping in Africa: A Critical Examination and Recommendations for Improvement* (Cham, Switzerland: Springer, 2017), p. 35.
19. UNAIDS, *Fighting AIDS: HIV/AIDS Prevention and Care Among Armed Forces and UN Peacekeepers: The Case of Eritrea* (Geneva, 2003), p. 6.
20. AU, "Efforts to Address HIV/AIDS in Darfur: Case Study Series on Implementation of UNSCR 1983" (Addis Ababa, 2011).
21. Laurie Garrett, "The Lessons of HIV/AIDS", *Foreign Affairs* 84, no. 4 (2005), p. 54.
22. US National Intelligence Council, *The Next Wave of HIV/AIDS: Nigeria, Ethiopia, Russia, India, and China* (Washington, DC, 2002), p. 26.
23. Roxanne Bazergan, *HIV/AIDS: Policies and Programmes for Blue Helmets*, Paper no. 96 (Pretoria: ISS, 2004), p. 5.
24. Bazergan, *HIV/AIDS*, p. 5. *See* Chris Beyrer, *War in the Blood: Sex, Politics, and AIDS in Southeast Asia* (London and New York: Zed, 1998), pp. 64–65.
25. Helfrich, "HIV Prevalence in the SANDF".
26. Lindy Heinecken, "The Potential Impact of HIV/AIDS on the South African Armed Forces: Some Evidence from Outside and Within", *African Security Review* 18, no. 2 (2009), pp. 57–77.
27. Leon Engelbrecht, "SANDF to Spend R48m on Combating HIV/AIDS in 2011", 6 January 2011, http://www.defenceweb.co.za/index.php?option=com_content&view=article&id (accessed 12 April 2017).
28. Jani Meyer, "SANDF Unveils Shock AIDS Data", *IOL News*, 1 August 2004, http://www.hst.org.za/news/sandf-unveils-shock-aids-data (accessed 20 December 2016).
29. UNAIDS, *Report of the UNAIDS Expert Panel on HIV Testing in United Nations Peacekeeping Operations*, Bangkok, Thailand, 28–30 November 2001, p. 14.
30. UN Peacekeeping, "Summary of Contributions to UN Peacekeeping by Country, Mission and Post", 30 June 2017, http://www.un.org/en/peacekeeping/contributors/2017/jun17_3.pdf (accessed 8 August 2017).
31. Heinecken, "The Potential Impact of HIV/AIDS", p. 70.
32. Alex de Waal, "AIDS and Peacekeepers: Reason for Good Policy, Not Fear", *African Arguments*, 9 August 2009, http://africanarguments.org/2009/08/09/aids-and-peacekeepers-reason-for-good-policy-not-fear (accessed 20 December 2016).
33. Alex de Waal, Jennifer F. Klot, and Manjari Mahajan, with Dana Huber, Georg Frerks, and Souleymane M'Boup, "HIV/AIDS, Security, and Conflict: New Realities, New Responses" (New York: AIDS, Security, and Conflict Initiative, 2010), p. 12.
34. UN Security Council Resolution 1528, UN Doc. S/RES/1528, 27 February 2004, preamble.
35. UN Security Council Resolution 1542, UN Doc. S/RES/1542, 30 April 2004; UN Security Council Resolution 1545, UN Doc. S/RES/1545, 21 May 2004.

The language in Resolution 1545 differs slightly: "Welcoming with satisfaction and encouraging the efforts of the United Nations Organization to enhance the awareness of peacekeeping personnel on the need to prevent and combat HIV/AIDS and other communicable diseases."

36. *Abuja Declaration on HIV/AIDS, Tuberculosis, and Other Related Infectious Diseases*, Abuja, Nigeria, 27 April 2001, para. 26.
37. *SADC HIV and AIDS Strategic Framework 2010–2015*, October 2009.
38. Ayodele Akenroye, "The ECOWAS Regional Framework on HIV/AIDS and the Military in West Africa", in Obijiofor Aginam and Martin R. Rupiya (eds.), *HIV/AIDS and the Security Sector in Africa* (Tokyo and New York: United Nations University Press, 2012), p. 46.
39. West African Health Organisation (WAHO), *Strategic Plan 2016–2020*, http://www.wahooas.org/IMG/pdf/VERSION_ANGLAISE_CORRIGEE.pdf (accessed 8 June 2017).
40. Intergovernmental Authority on Development (IGAD), Declaration by IGAD Ministerial Committee on Health, HIV, and AIDS, Nairobi, Kenya, 18 March 2010, https://www.igad.int/communique/184-declaration-by-igad-ministerial-committee-on-health-hiv-and-aids (accessed 13 June 2017).
41. East African Community (EAC), *HIV and AIDS/STI and TB Multi-Sectoral Strategic Plan and Implementation Framework 2015–2020* (Arusha, Tanzania, 2015), https://static1.squarespace.com/static/5519047ce4b0d9aaa8c82e69/t/5551b87fe4b0872f41a62138/1431419007743/EAC+HIV+and+AIDS++Strategic+Plan.pdf (accessed 13 June 2017).
42. The card is in different languages—Arabic, Bahasa, Bengali, Chinese, English, French, Hindi, Kiswahili, Nepalese, Portuguese, Russian, Spanish, and Urdu.
43. UN, "Security Council Unanimously Adopting 1983 (2011): Security Council Encourages Inclusion of HIV Prevention, Treatment, Care, Support in Implementing Peacekeeping Mandates", press release, UN Doc. SC/10272, 7 June 2011.
44. Roxanne Bazergan, "HIV/AIDS: Policies and Programmes for Blue Helmets", Paper no. 96 (Pretoria: ISS, 2000).
45. UNAIDS, "Fighting Aids: HIV/AIDS Prevention and Care Among Armed Forces and UN Peacekeepers" (Geneva, 2003); Voice of America (VOA), "UN Security Council Notes Peacekeepers Role in Combating HIV/AIDS", *VOA News*, 6 June 2011, http://www.voanews.com/content/un-security-council-notes-peacekeepers-role-in-combating-hivaids-123390593/158259.html (accessed 20 December 2016).
46. Joseph U. Becker, Christian Theodosis, and Rick Kulkarni, "HIV/AIDS, Conflict, and Security in Africa: Rethinking Relationships", *Journal of the International AIDS Society* 11 (2008), pp. 1–7.
47. Harley Feldbaum, Kelley Lee, and Preeti Patel, "The National Security Implications of HIV/AIDS", *PLOS Medicine* 3, no. 6 (June 2006), p. 775. *See also* Aginam and Rupiya, *HIV/AIDS and the Security Sector in Africa*.
48. Nancy B. Mock et al., "Conflict and HIV: A Framework for Risk Assessment to Prevent HIV in Conflict-Affected Settings in Africa", *Emerging Themes in Epidemiology* 1, no. 6 (2004), https://ete-online.biomedcentral.com/articles/10.1186/1742-7622-1-6 (accessed 18 June 2017).
49. "Peacekeepers or Sexual Abusers?", *Carte Blanche* documentary, broadcast 11 August 2013.

50. Alexandra R. Harrington, "Victims of Peace: Current Abuse Allegations Against U.N. Peacekeepers and the Role of Law in Preventing Them in the Future", *ILSA Journal of International & Comparative Law* 12 (2005), p. 126.
51. Harrington, "Victims of Peace".
52. Gwinyayi Albert Dzinesa, "Culture and HIV/AIDS in African Peacekeeping Operations", in Aginam and Rupiya, *HIV/AIDS and the Security Sector in Africa*, p. 101.
53. UN Security Council Resolution 1325, UN Doc. S/RES/1325, 31 October 2000. The resolution calls for more involvement of women in conflict resolution and greater consideration of gender issues in peace processes.
54. UN Security Council Resolution 1325.
55. Yolande Bouka and Romi Sigsworth, "Women in the Military in Africa: Kenya Case Study", ISS *East Africa Report* no. 7 (September 2016), p. 5.
56. Sharon Lukunka, "Women Advocate for Peace in Darfur", AU-UN Hybrid Operation in Darfur (UNAMID), 10 February 2015, https://unamid.unmissions.org/women-advocate-peace-darfur (accessed 9 June 2017).
57. Alex de Waal, "HIV/AIDS and the Challenges of Security and Conflict", *The Lancet* 375, no. 9708 (2 January 2010), pp. 22–23.

CHAPTER 15

Staging the Peacekeeping Narrative: Hollywood's Portrayal of Peacekeeping Efforts in Africa

Ines Mzali

Hollywood's interest in Africa has always expressed itself through the deployment of codes of polarised notions of "self" and "other". Although films on Africa have evolved over the years, this polarisation, now recoded and revamped, continues to underlie cinematic productions and to encourage a particular perception and interpretation of African realities. Some of the most recent films on Africa correspond to the rise of the so-called human rights/humanitarian film or documentary genre, itself reflecting the development of "military humanitarianism".[1] Often in dialogue with certain political, media, and other cultural representations, these films still project familiar stereotypical tropes and largely de-contextualised renditions of African conflicts and international responses to them. By looking at the films *Black Hawk Down* (2001), *Hotel Rwanda* (2004), and to a lesser extent *Blood Diamond* (2006), I propose to examine the ways in which African conflicts and Africans are portrayed, on the one hand, and how international interventions are constructed, through their mandates and changing objectives on the ground, on the screen. Not all of these three films focus on peacekeeping missions per se, but they all reflect and contribute to a "peacekeeping narrative" that comes to bear on how we perceive the notions of intervention, responsibility, and agency. Because Hollywood holds ideological sway and has power to influence and mobilise public opinion in the highly politicised world of peacekeeping, such stereotypes and truncated narratives cannot simply be dismissed as harmless misrepresentations. I propose that the polarisation between African victims or African ruthless fighters on the one hand, and Western saviours on the other, that often permeates filmic representations of

I. Mzali (✉)
Woosong University, Daejeon, South Korea

T. Karbo, K. Virk (eds.), *The Palgrave Handbook of Peacebuilding in Africa*, https://doi.org/10.1007/978-3-319-62202-6_15

conflict and intervention in Africa, hinders imagining alternatives and rethinking international peacekeeping in other terms, namely through cooperation and collaboration.

By gleaning the continuities among the three films, I am not suggesting that they use the same strategies of representation. Rather, their different approaches to conflict reflect the common and hardly challenged perception of Africa, underlying other political, media, and literary constructions of the "peacemaking narrative". The films studied here tend to draw from, or build on, media representations of conflicts and peacekeeping produced at the time of the events. On the other hand, they tap and recode an old and persistent "archive"[2] of images associated with Africa and African wars, in particular. As Irish scholar Susan L. Carruthers aptly puts it when she writes about the representation of Western humanitarian missions in Africa, "sub-Saharan Africa continues to feed the West's subconscious ... enabling identities to be fashioned around the polarity of Western civilization and African 'barbarism'".[3]

Unlike reportage, cinema functions through and with a delay that allows it to tap and reinterpret earlier representations of war and international intervention. This hindsight, however, does not necessarily imply a departure from the discourses generated hastily in the media and in the official presentation of peacekeeping operations. The films thus hark back to the discourse generated at the time of the particular war they depict, but given the narration in retrospect, they are often harnessed to different and new spaces of intervention. More specifically, the release of *Black Hawk Down* coincided with the mounting rhetoric of war that followed the terrorist attacks on the World Trade Centre in New York in September 2001, while *Hotel Rwanda*—released in 2004—became a powerful reference for the US-based Save Darfur Coalition in its campaign to generate a response to the atrocities committed against civilians by the Sudanese government in the region of Darfur. The ways in which films interact with other representations of war and peacekeeping and contribute to the public perception, support, or rejection of certain policies warrant careful attention to the codes they deploy in constructing their narratives.

Black Hawk Down attempts to uncritically produce a peacekeeping narrative consistent with the one evoked at the beginning of the American peacekeeping operation in Somalia—Operation Restore Hope (1992–1993)—during which the action is set (see also Hirsch, and Mahiga in this volume). The construction of the narrative of intervention in the film is itself reminiscent of the narrative produced by the United States (US) government and the media prior to and during the operation. With *Hotel Rwanda*, the peacemaking narrative is severely challenged and questioned after the international failure to act and prevent the 1994 Rwandan genocide, in which an estimated 800,000 people were killed. This narrative is also largely articulated through notions of guilt and trauma expressed by the Western characters in this film. Finally, *Blood Diamond*, though not focusing on a peacekeeping mission, deploys the trope of white saviours and their voiceless victims in the context of the Sierra Leone civil war (1991–2002), extrapolating the notion of peacekeeping to include acts understood as contributing to war or peace, such as trading in blood diamonds.

Black Hawk Down: Maintaining the Peacekeeping Myth

The film *Black Hawk Down*, directed by British filmmaker Ridley Scott, portrays the 1993 Battle of Mogadishu, which pitted US Rangers and Delta Force soldiers against Somali forces and resulted in the death of about a thousand Somalis and 18 US soldiers. The US forces had been deployed in Somalia since December 1992 in a joint (but US-led) peacekeeping mission with the United Nations (UN) (see Hirsch, and Mahiga in this volume). The unexpected US debacle in Somalia in October 1993 led to the early (and hasty) withdrawal of most US forces from the country by May 1993 and had a significant impact on US responses, or lack thereof, to subsequent crises, particularly in Rwanda. The film was released in 2001, several years after the US operation. Yet despite the vantage point of hindsight, *Black Hawk Down* maintains the narrative produced by both the US government and media in the wake of the battle in 1993. The ways in which the battle, the operation, and the different parties are portrayed imply a problematic conception and perception of peacekeeping and, more particularly, of US involvement in peacekeeping, which was based on polarised identities, lack of knowledge of local culture and terrain, and lack of attempts to cooperate with Somalis. The latter point also characterises the making of the film itself. Here I examine the peacekeeping narrative in the film through the construction of the conflict in Somalia, the US/UN intervention, and finally the Mogadishu battle itself.

It seems that the US operation in Somalia was a "Hollywood production"[4] before it was even brought to the big screen. While my analysis here focuses on filmic rather than journalistic representations of the peacekeeping mission, it is important to briefly examine the media construction of the US operation in Somalia before and after the Battle of Mogadishu. In fact, the film builds on the collective memory of the events as reported at the time of their occurrence and taps what Nigerian scholar Harry Garuba and Puerto Rican researcher Natasha Himmelman call the "system of citation" related to the history of representations of Africa in general and the operation in Somalia in particular.[5] Much has been said and written about the alleged role of media reports in convincing the George H.W. Bush administration in December 1992 to authorise an operation in Somalia.[6] Reports on the dire humanitarian crisis and the failure of the first United Nations Operation in Somalia (UNOSOM I) to ensure the safety of humanitarian workers, while UN Secretary-General Boutros Boutros-Ghali pressed the US to join the United Nations in Somalia, functioned as a "builder of support".[7] As a result, when the US government finally announced its decision, there was already public support for an operation that had been packaged as both humanitarian and, simplistically enough, easy.[8] Both Somalis and Americans were soon to confront another reality.

The Unified Task Force (UNITAF), known in the US as Operation Restore Hope, was supposed to inaugurate a new post–Cold War role for the country: that of the peacekeeper (see also Hirsch, and Mahiga in this volume). In 1990–1991, the US had been involved in the Persian Gulf War precipitated by Iraq's invasion of Kuwait in August 1990. Image was paramount in these early post–Cold War operations, and the war propaganda machine was in full swing. The operation in Somalia was to complement the image of the US in war with images of American forces involved in a peacekeeping operation. In this operation, as US scholar Thomas Keenan aptly puts it, "the agenda—the tactics and strategy—was the imagery: the creation of images".[9] Generating and controlling these images was not simply part of the propaganda. Rather, it was at the core of the mission.[10] Ironically, then, before US Marines set foot on Somali soil in December 1992, reporters advised by the Pentagon had already taken position on the Somali beaches to film the Marines landing, so that, in the words of the late Kenyan public intellectual Ali Mazrui, "[t]he whole thing resembled a Hollywood production, rather than a military operation".[11]

Of course, before long, the US mission would become a full-fledged military operation. Even as the US government and media insisted on the peacekeeping vocation of Operation Restore Hope (alongside the UN), the images circulated reveal all the trappings of a military force involved in a war and in a manhunt for Somali warlord Mohamed Farah Aideed,[12] rather than dedicated to negotiating and facilitating peace between warring factions. Nevertheless, some of the most striking images of the first phase of the operation were those of Somali crowds cheering and welcoming the US soldiers upon their arrival, and those of US soldiers doing humanitarian work. *Black Hawk Down* focuses only on the battle, but the first phase is evoked when towards the end of the film one of the soldiers imagines, or probably remembers, crowds of Somalis cheering and celebrating the arrival of US forces.

The peacemaking narrative in the media continued to operate even through the mission's shift. The American public had been conditioned to expect gratitude rather than hostility, and was thus not prepared to see fallen soldiers. The Battle of Mogadishu resulted from a gradual escalation of the confrontation between Aideed's militia and US and UN troops through a series of events and a priority shift for the US command in Somalia. While the Battle of Mogadishu has been rightly perceived as a turning point both in Operation Restore Hope itself and in the media and public perception of the operation in the US, the discourse around Somalia did not shift radically. In fact, the peacekeeping narrative was maintained and reinforced. Aside from the loss of 18 Rangers, other images emerged from the battle. Footage showing the bodies of two Rangers stripped and dragged through the streets of Mogadishu amid a cheering and jeering crowd (among whom many appear to be civilians) unleashed an emotional response that reinforced rather than disrupted the identity paradigm opposing "the West" to "Africa". The real motivation behind the mission was not questioned by the mainstream media; rather, it was now presented as a series of faux pas. However, the basic and underlying identity paradigm at work, deployed in the early media representations of the mission, never shifted; rather, what was questioned was the wisdom of US involvement in uncharted territory.

It is at this level of the Somalia narrative, as deployed by the US mainstream media, that *Black Hawk Down* situates itself after "summarising" the events in the opening text. The film builds on the confusion generated by the circulation of images of a full-fledged war. The Battle of Mogadishu did not lead to any serious attempt at tracing the hostilities back to a series of incidents and the gradual but increasingly deadly escalation. Instead, the turn of events is presented on the screen as a sudden outburst of violent Somalis. Before the battle, Somalis were presented as either brutal militiamen who needed to be contained, or victims who needed to be saved from warlords or from themselves. The lack of self-assessment after the battle, however, seems only to confirm the perception of Africa as a land of chaotic and incomprehensible outbursts of violence. As American public opinion had been conditioned to expect gratitude for US involvement while ignoring the inconsistency of a peacekeeping mission involved in increasingly belligerent actions (with a rising civilian death toll), so is the film's audience expected to unquestioningly accept the narrative of well-intentioned heroism on the American side, opposed to irrational and ungrateful hostility on the Somali side.

Black Hawk Down builds on the collective memory of the stark defeat, death, and humiliation of the US contingent on 3 October 1993. The film summons what the audience knows and remembers from the coverage of the war, and reproduces the truncated and selective representation of the events. The opening text, somewhat typical of fictionalised true stories, purports to contextualise the narrative. In fact, it reflects the official narrative circulated in the US media at the outset of the mission. The opening text establishes the "factuality" of the film by announcing that it is "based on an actual event": "Years of warfare among rival clans cause a famine on a biblical scale. 300,000 civilians died of starvation ... The world responds. Behind a force of 20,000 US Marines, food is delivered and order is restored."

The text immediately conjures the apocalyptic and ahistorical visions now associated with Somalia, through its references to clan warfare and a famine on a biblical scale that led the world to respond. This summary text deploys the familiar codes of anarchy, violence, or helplessness on the one hand, and civilisation, order, and humanitarian conscience and duty on the other. As it reinforces such a polarisation, this introduction also functions as a way to reassert the moral imperative of the mission (despite its failure), and thus paves the way for the narrative of heroic, brave, and loyal Marines involved in a foreign quagmire. Thus the film seeks to salvage one of the most embarrassing instances of US international intervention of recent years and turn it into a tale of heroism. In so doing, the film draws upon and reconstructs the old identity paradigms at work in war as in peacemaking. This old, albeit modernised and revamped, paradigm permeates the confused and unstable representation of humanitarian intervention and peacekeeping, on the one hand, and the attempt to regain symbolic and discursive control of the narrative after the unexpected fiasco, on the other.

While often cited as a war film, *Black Hawk Down* is ironically about a peacemaking mission. This, in fact, reflects the confusion ensuing the shift of the mission on the ground from a peacemaking one to a manhunt and a war against Mohamed Farah Aideed. The confusion was also compounded by a lack of knowledge about Somalia and its political context. The slide from a peacekeeping mission focused on securing supply routes for humanitarians, to the rhetoric of war, is cursorily summarised in the text at the opening of the film, as we are informed that Aideed waited for the withdrawal of US forces to declare war on the UN. In fact, quite early in the mission, Aideed is identified as the main enemy and the mission starts to revolve around the manhunt. Except for Sergeant Eversmann (played by Josh Hartnett), who evokes the humanitarian motif he associates with the presence of US forces in Somalia, the soldiers' indiscriminate and prejudiced references to Somalis, to Somalia, to the upcoming battle, and to their presence there are all framed in a military and belligerent mindset. Problematically enough, this ubiquitous war mentality and rhetoric is left unquestioned. By the time the soldiers are preparing for the operation that was to become the Battle of Mogadishu, there are very few reminders of the peacekeeping nature of the mission. *Black Hawk Down* eventually unfolds then as a war film that creates a narrative of bravery and principled fighting in the face of an anomic context of war.

I would argue that the slide from the peacekeeping narrative to the rhetoric of war is facilitated by the fact that both discourses rely on a similar premise opposing "the West" to "the other". For humanitarianism, as German scholar Heike Härting argues, "is also a cultural practice … that makes and manages codes of otherness in the service of particular identity politics".[13] In the peacekeeping narrative, "the other" is epitomised by helpless victims who can be saved from themselves only by a rescue mission organised by the West. In the more belligerent intervention steeped in war rhetoric and strategy, "the other" is represented by a ubiquitous tendency for inexplicable violence and cruelty. In *Black Hawk Down*, in a rare scene where the soldiers are shown discussing their mission, Sergeant Eversmann surprises his fellow soldiers by voicing what US academic Maryellen Higgins terms "his humanitarian credentials".[14] When pressed to explain why he "likes" Somalis, as another soldier puts it, Eversmann explains: "I respect them. Look, these people, they have no jobs, no food, no education, no future. I just figure that we have two things we can do. We can either help, or we can sit back and watch a country destroy itself on CNN [Cable News Network]." Yet his attempt to humanise Somalis is not supported by any scene or Somali character in the film. Rather, one of the soldiers discards Eversmann's position as "idealistic", while another asserts his own lack of interest in any causes, as he has "been trained to fight". In fact, even Eversmann's discourse reproduces the "classical Hollywood trope of Africans being children in need of help of benevolent western saviours".[15] A problematic vagueness about the implications of the intervention marks the slide from peacekeeping, with the objective of securing the delivery of food aid, to a full-fledged battle, occasionally through the "just war" motif[16] as in Eversmann's perspective. Although the US was attempting to create and buttress its image as a peacekeeping force (and not just as a war-maker), the peacekeeping narrative is constructed around a conflict between good and evil in the movie.

The opening text of the film and the soldiers' perception of Somalis pave the way for the representation of the Battle of Mogadishu, which is the main concern of the film. If at the beginning of the mission Somalis seem to be classified as either helpless starving victims or ruthless warlords and their acolytes, the film's reconstruction of the battle, based as it is on the "good guys versus bad guys" motif, cements a radical opposition between Americans and Somalis. Civilians mingle with the gun-toting militia as they are seen thronging the fallen helicopter to extract the bodies of dead Rangers. We also see children working for the militia by keeping watch and relaying messages. One particular scene illustrates the "disappearance", so to speak, of Somali civilians, as all Somalis become potential enemies. While the US soldiers are engaged in urban warfare, one of them stops shooting to spare an escaping woman and her baby. Yet the woman turns around and, now holding a baby in one arm and a gun in the other hand, aims at him. As the soldiers stare incredulously at this improbable fighter, they shoot her. In the absence of references to the thousand Somali civilians killed during the battle,[17] this scene, along with the one portraying a crowd around the helicopter, reifies the complete "otherness" of Somalis and precludes any reaction other than empathy for the brave soldiers and certainly not for Somalis, who seem to have chosen embattlement against the peacekeepers.

The film does not seek to contextualise such war scenes nor to explain the reasons behind the civil war, let alone mention the previous involvement of the US (from 1978) in supporting the long and devastating dictatorship of Somali president Siad Barre (1969–1991). Why would this woman pick up a gun and aim it at a US soldier? Why would crowds of people cheer at the desecrated body of a US soldier? Neither the film nor its characters seem to be interested in exploring these questions, for the suggested answer is that violence and irrationality are inherently engrained in the land and its inhabitants, just as the "famine" that prompted the intervention is often understood to be solely the result of an apolitical state of "anarchy".[18] Not delving into the gradual escalation of the conflict, or the root causes of a civil war, has the certain advantage of imagining a disinterested and genuinely humanitarian intervention in a land where the US supposedly had no interests and no previous history. Somalis, in turn, remain mysterious, indistinguishable from each other and from other Africans. A blurred perception also facilitates a recoding of the relation of American forces with the local population when hostility becomes predominant. Not only are Somali voices and perspectives erased from the narrative, but also men, women, and children have all become indiscriminate enemies. In the face of this incomprehensibility, which itself harks back to the motif of a dark, cryptic Africa, US soldiers are seen acting with bravery and loyalty towards each other, thus maintaining against all odds the marks of civilisation.

The US/UN joint mission in Somalia was supposed to inaugurate a new era of interventionism as the US engaged directly and uncharacteristically in a humanitarian mission alongside the UN. In the US, the ensuing debacle led some politicians to blame the UN rather than examine the mistakes of US command that led to the ill-advised shift in the mission towards a full-fledged war.[19] The perspective of the film continued to fuel the confusion between war and peacekeeping. Even though *Black Hawk Down* had been made before the terrorist attacks of September 2001, it was released after these events in a context fraught, as it was, with war rhetoric, and therefore propitious for a polarised depiction of military interventions. Especially in this context, the stereotypical depiction of Somalis does not simply deny them agency but also locks them into an "enemy" position, easily interpreted as a warning for future "foreign" encounters.

Hotel Rwanda: Distributing Trauma

The unexpected and disastrous outcome of the Somali mission had a direct impact not only on the withdrawal of the US and UN from Somalia but also on the response, or rather lack thereof, of the international community in the face of a proven genocide in Rwanda in 1994 that claimed the lives of nearly 800,000 mostly Tutsi Rwandans. The crisis generated by the intervention in Somalia, and prefigured to a certain extent in *Black Hawk Down*, translated into refusal to act as the impotence of the UN was coupled with the decision of European countries to send forces to Rwanda only to evacuate their nationals. If Somalia raised many questions as to the problematic mandate of peacekeeping forces engaging in acts of war, Rwanda revealed an international community crippled by the so-called Somalia syndrome[20] and entangled in a linguistic and definitional exercise to justify inaction. One of the most damning episodes during the Rwandan genocide was the successful attempt of the US government to pre-empt any UN intervention by instructing US officials not to use the word "genocide" and only concede that "acts of genocide may have occurred".[21] This inaction came to define the contours of the discourse on the genocide in Rwanda in the West. Numerous documentaries and works of fiction have since reproduced the dual representation of the scope of the massacres and the non-intervention.[22]

Hotel Rwanda, directed by Irish filmmaker Terry George and released in 2004, portrays the genocide through the story of Paul Rusesabagina (played by Don Cheadle), a hotel manager who sheltered more than a thousand endangered Rwandans in his hotel during the tragedy. The film reproduces some of the most common leitmotifs now characteristic of fictional and documentary representations of the tragedy in Rwanda. For example, it unfolds along a narrative of abandonment and indictment of those who committed atrocities and, more pointedly, of those who refused to act, including the UN. I examine here the ways in which international intervention, or lack thereof, are represented in the film. I also address the representation of the genocide, especially through the motif of "Western/white guilt".[23] *Hotel Rwanda* has been commended for departing from some modalities of representation characteristic of Hollywood films on Africa. Notably, the main character and "hero", in Hollywood parlance, is African, rather than Western as is usually the case, and we follow him as the genocide unfolds and he slowly realises that the expected help will never come despite the presence of UN forces on the ground. Yet to what extent does this perspective, and the denunciatory tone associated with it, break the mould of a typically de-historicised and de-politicised approach to the portrayal of violence in Africa?

The peacekeeping narrative at work in *Hotel Rwanda* both results and differs from the one developed in *Black Hawk Down*. In the latter, political and propagandist calculations behind Operation Restore Hope are constantly denied, while the narrative of a rather moral, albeit naive and misguided, rationale for the mission is maintained throughout the film, notwithstanding the deeply prejudiced frame through which the US Marines see Somalis, whom the plot itself reduces to an irrationally angry and dangerous throng of people. *Hotel Rwanda*, in contrast, claims that issues of racism and the little importance attributed to African matters in the world accounted for the refusal to act. These ideas are voiced by Western characters, which demarcates their statements from the anti-colonial discourse harnessed by Hutu extremists to the cause of "Hutu power". In one scene, a hopeful Paul expresses his belief in an imminent intervention prompted by an American journalist's footage proving that mass killings are under way. The journalist, Jack Daglish (played by Joaquin Phoenix), in turn, can already anticipate the general reaction to such images: "If people see this footage, they'll say 'Oh, my God, it's horrible', then they'll go on eating their dinner." It is not until later that Paul realises the validity of this statement. The expected international intervention forces finally arrive, only to comply with their strict mandate to evacuate their respective nationals. Again it is a military man, Colonel Oliver (played by Nick Nolte, and based on real-life Canadian general Roméo Dallaire, who was in charge of the United Nations Assistance Mission for Rwanda [UNAMIR]), who voices it crudely: "You're dirt. We think you're dirt ... The West, all the superpowers, everything you believe in ... They think you're worthless." This scene dramatises the extent to which humanitarian and peacekeeping operations are politicised.[24]

While the inaction of the international community had direct and dire consequences for the Rwandans facing torture and death, this failure has often been explored "as an event that traumatised the United Nations ... peacekeepers and white civilians left in the country".[25] Unlike *Black Hawk Down*, in which the plight of Somalis is completely erased, *Hotel Rwanda* is told from the perspective of a Rwandan whose family faces death in more than one instance. Yet a ubiquitous sense of guilt is expressed through Jack, who feels ashamed and unworthy when being evacuated. When Paul tries to congratulate him on the arrival of foreign troops, Colonel Oliver expresses a similar sense of guilt, saying that Paul "should spit in [Oliver's] face". Aware of the sentiment, Paul advises the refugees at the hotel to call their influential acquaintances abroad and "shame them into sending help".

The denunciation of the shameful international consensus to avoid intervention has often functioned as the core axis for narrating the Rwandan genocide, and in the context of the release of *Hotel Rwanda* was also harnessed to the campaign by Save Darfur to push for intervention in Darfur. The Save Darfur Coalition was formed in New York in 2014 in order to, as it states on its website, raise awareness and pressure political leaders to "put an end to the first genocide of the twenty-first century".[26] The coincidence of the birth of this coalition with the tenth anniversary of the Rwandan genocide made the latter a reference and a warning of what could happen again. (On Sudan, see Deng in this volume.) While non-intervention was indisputably a determining factor in the scale of the massacres in Rwanda, which also revealed the highly politicised world of humanitarianism, the systematic deployment of this guilt often precludes an in-depth analysis of the roots of the atrocities and the complex national and international factors at play. In other words, on the one hand *Hotel Rwanda* frames the genocide in the vague, generic, and mysterious notion of "hatred, insanity", as Paul puts it to explain mass killings. On the other hand the film unfolds through the theme of what is often dubbed "white guilt". From this perspective, then, and as Härting puts it, "the West [becomes the] primary critical reference rather than the genocide's political dimension".[27] A largely de-politicised narrative facilitates the conflation between different African conflicts and contexts.

Thus the film straddles the past context of the genocide in 1994 and the new setting of war and debate on intervention in Darfur. While each context of war and intervention naturally informs the international response to subsequent crises, what is problematic about the deployment of a certain representation of situations of conflict and peacekeeping is that it relies on analogies between different contexts, as Higgins puts it, borrowing Ugandan academic Mahmood Mamdani's term, rather than on "historical or political knowledge".[28] It is crucial to decrypt the ways in which fiction encodes and deploys particular tropes of "self" and "other".

By focusing on an African as its main character, *Hotel Rwanda* departs from Hollywood's trend of focusing on Western characters either exclusively as in *Black Hawk Down* or as main characters as in *Blood Diamond*. Nevertheless, the film still evinces an underlying de-historicising and de-politicising tendency that re-circulates, though not necessarily purposely, the familiar "Manichean binary of good and evil".[29]

Blood Diamond: This Is Africa

US director Edward Zwick's *Blood Diamond* (2006) testifies to Hollywood's continued interest in exploring (or exploiting) human rights issues as long as they can be packed with fighting action. Although the film does not address the question of peacekeeping interventions, its portrayal of the violent war and fierce fights over gems, driven by international demand for them, seems to suggest that the battle for peace, so to speak, must be waged outside of Sierra Leone (here read "Africa"). The Western audience is further encouraged to think that they have a choice to "consume" responsibly and boycott blood diamonds (diamonds mined and sold to fund armed conflict). In the film, Danny Archer (played by Leonardo DiCaprio), former mercenary turned arms dealer and diamond smuggler, pairs up with an improbable partner, Solomon Vandy (played by Djimon Hounsou), a fisherman seized by the rebels after their attack on his village. Archer promises Vandy to help him find his family in exchange for a sizable diamond the whereabouts of which only Vandy knows. As Sierra Leonean scholar Iyunolu Osagie points out, the "buddy" motif in this film is in fact replete with racial stereotypes expressed through "hegemonic relations within the narrative".[30] And yet, as South Africa–based academics Martha Evans and Ian Glenn say about "racist" Archer, "the film redeems him constantly and he ends up as a sacrificial westerner".[31]

Why is this relevant to the peacekeeping narrative? Analysis of the representation of local conflicts in *Black Hawk Down* and *Hotel Rwanda* reveals how non existing or dismissive references to the roots of violence, to the context, and to the perspectives of either Somalis or Rwandans reduce them to victims at best. This representation through lack of history, so to speak, denies them agency and rules out Africans as potential actors and partners in making and rethinking peacekeeping narratives. *Blood Diamond* ends with the meeting in Kimberley, South Africa, held in May 2000, that led to the adoption of the Kimberley Process Certification Scheme, in order to prevent the trade of conflict diamonds. While *Blood Diamond* seeks to expose the devastating effect of the diamond trade in war zones and encourages uncritical support for a boycott of conflict diamonds, it also seems to suggest that any change would have to be staged outside of Africa. Vandy's salvation is actualised when, thanks to Western assistance, he escapes to England and becomes involved in the campaign against conflict diamonds. We never see Vandy transcend his secondary role, and even if he is set to speak at the Kimberley convention, we never hear him. And we are left to wonder, in Higgins's words: "[Are there] no grassroots African authorities, no African humanitarians who can take the microphone and offer a new perspective?"[32]

Conclusion

Black Hawk Down, *Hotel Rwanda*, and *Blood Diamond* reflect a particular interest in representing African realities through conflict, as this is one of the most common themes through which Africa makes headlines in the West. More specifically, all three movies reflect debates on the question of intervention in the context of post–Cold War US engagement in Africa. *Hotel Rwanda* and *Blood Diamond* also register a shift in this debate towards an international consensus—at least in theory—redefining intervention as a humanitarian responsibility. However, by framing the question of intervention in a de-contextualised rendition based on recycled binaries of "the West" and "the other", the films reveal the limitations of intervention, as action and discourse, if envisioned and conceived from a Western perspective only.

Hollywood's interest remains related to topical issues relevant to US audiences. However, alternative sources of film are also making headway as more and more, albeit not enough, African movies gain visibility and acclaim in film festivals, such as *Ezra* (2007) by Nigerian-born filmmaker Newton Aduaka, in which the narrative is told from the perspective of a child soldier. Interestingly, while Hollywood(-like) productions have little room for African voices or agency, the child soldier narrative seems to be generating interest in Western cinema. Two examples of such films, *Johnny Mad Dog* (2008) by French director Jean-Stéphane Sauvaire and, more recently, *Beasts of No Nation* (2015) directed by US filmmaker Cary Joji Fukunaga, are adaptations of novels by Africans—Congolese writer Emmanuel Dongala and Nigerian Uzodinma Iweala respectively. While these films do not break the trend of portraying Africa through its conflicts and tales of victimisation, they do offer a more complex and multilayered glimpse into the conflicts in Africa, as the narratives bring the novelists' voices, as well as more African actors, to the screen and to a larger audience. Such perspectives will remain limited, however, until the representation and distribution of African movies, and of movies about Africa, becomes more balanced.

Notes

1. *See* David Chandler, "The Road to Military Humanitarianism: How the Human Rights NGOs Shaped a New Humanitarian Agenda", *Human Rights Quarterly* 23 (2001), pp. 678–700.
2. Harry Garuba and Natasha Himmelman, "The Cited and the Uncited", in Maryellen Higgins (ed.), *Hollywood's Africa After 1994* (Athens: Ohio University Press, 2012), p. 16.
3. Susan L. Carruthers, "Tribalism and Tribulation: Media Constructions of 'African Savagery' and 'Western Humanitarianism' in the 1990s", in Allan Stuart and Barbie Zelizer (eds.), *Reporting War: Journalism in War Time* (London: Routledge, 2004), p. 157.
4. Ali Al'Amin Mazrui, *The African Predicament and the American Experience: A Tale of Two Edens* (Westport: Greenwood, 2004), p. 29.
5. Garuba and Himmelman, "The Cited and the Uncited", p. 16.
6. *See* Piers Robinson, *The CNN Effect: The Myth of News, Foreign Policy, and Intervention* (London: Routledge, 2005).
7. Robinson, *The CNN Effect*, p. 62.
8. When former American president George H.W. Bush was asked why the United States (US) government had opted for an intervention in Somalia when Yugoslavia was also mired in a civil war, Bush's rather revealing answer was that Somalia was "doable" in comparison to Yugoslavia; quoted in Bruce Nelan, "Taking on the Thugs", *Time*, 14 December 1992, pp. 41–43. In his televised

address of 4 December 1992 on Somalia, Bush insisted that "[o]ur mission has a limited objective, to open the supply routes, to get the food moving, and to prepare the way for a UN peacekeeping force [UNOSOM II] to keep it moving". Addressing the Somali population directly, he added: "we come to your country for one reason only, to enable the starving to be fed". "Mission to Somalia: Transcript of President's Address on Somalia", *New York Times*, 5 December 1992, http://www.nytimes.com/1992/12/05/world/mission-to-somalia-transcript-of-president-s-address-on-somalia.html (accessed 22 February 2016).

9. For more on the media representation of the intervention in Somalia, *see* Ines Mzali, "Wars of Representation: Metonymy and Nuruddin Farah's *Links*", *College Literature* 37, no. 3 (2010), pp. 84–105.
10. Thomas Keenan, "Mobilizing Shame", *South Atlantic Quarterly* 103, nos. 2–3 (2004), p. 442.
11. Mazrui, *The African Predicament*, p. 29.
12. *See* William Shawcross, *Deliver Us from Evil: Peacekeepers, Warlords, and a World of Endless Conflict* (New York: Simon and Schuster, 2000), p. 221.
13. Heike Härting, "Foreign Encounters: The Political and Visual Aesthetics of Humanitarianism in Contemporary Canadian Film Vulture", *University of Toronto Quarterly* 82, no. 2 (2013), p. 332.
14. Maryellen Higgins, "Hollywood's Cowboy Humanitarianism", in Higgins, *Hollywood's Africa*, p. 70.
15. Adekeye Adebajo, "Africa's Image Suffers in the Hands of Hollywood", *Business Day* (South Africa), 11 March 2013.
16. South African–born US scholar Ashley Dawson argues that the scene in which Eversmann argues that "the U.S. has a burden to help those suffering human rights violations ... recirculates World War II themes of just war". Ashley Dawson, "The New World Disorder: Black Hawk Down and the Eclipse of US Military Humanitarianism", *African Studies Review* 54, no. 2 (2011), p. 184.
17. When the film ends, and after the names of the 18 US soldiers killed in the battle are listed, a single line informs the audience about the staggering number of Somali victims.
18. Alex de Waal, *Crimes, Politics, and the Disaster Relief Industry in Africa* (Bloomington: Indiana University Press, 1997), p. 159.
19. For example, Paul Wolfowitz, US Undersecretary of Defense for Policy at the time Operation Restore Hope was launched, blames the UN for the tragic turn of the mission; "Clinton's First Year", *Foreign Affairs*, January/February 1994, p. 32. Also, US scholar Ryan Hendrickson notes a general "anti-UN stance" in Congress in the aftermath of the battle; *The Clinton Wars, the Constitution, Congress, and War Powers* (Nashville: Vanderbilt University Press, 2002), p. 36.
20. By "Somalia syndrome", US scholar Thomas Weiss refers to the fact that, in the wake of the debacle in Somalia, "multilateral interventions to thwart starvation, genocide, the forced movement of people and massive violations of human rights are no longer politically or operationally feasible". Thomas Weiss, "Overcoming the Somalia Syndrome: 'Operation Rekindle Hope'", *Global Governance* 1 (1995), p. 171.
21. Adekeye Adebajo, "Africa, African Americans, and the Avuncular Sam", *Africa Today* 50, no. 3 (2004), p. 102.

22. Examples include the documentary film *When Good Men Do Nothing*, directed by British BBC correspondent Steve Bradshaw. The tenth anniversary of the genocide also marked a renewed interest in the events with the release of several long feature films, such as *Shooting Dogs* (2005), by Scottish director Michael Caton-Jones; *A Sunday in Kigali* (2006), directed by Canadian Robert Favreau; and *Shake Hands with the Devil* (2007), by British-Canadian director Roger Spottswoode. The latter two films are based respectively on the novel *A Sunday at the Pool in Kigali* by Gil Courtemanche (translated by Patricia Claxton) (Toronto: Vintage Canada, 2004) and the autobiography *Shake Hands with the Devil: The Failure of Humanity in Rwanda* by Roméo Dallaire (Toronto: Random House Canada, 2003)—two examples of a large corpus of books on the Rwandan tragedy.
23. For a more thorough analysis of the representation of the genocide in literature and film, *see* Alexandre Dauge-Roth, *Writing and Filming the Genocide of the Tutsis: Dismembering and Remembering Traumatic History* (Lanham, MD: Lexington Books, 2010).
24. Heike Härting, "Global Humanitarianism, Race, and the Spectacle of the African Corpse in Current Western Representations of the Rwandan Genocide", *Comparative Studies of South Asia, Africa, and the Middle East* 28, no. 1 (2008), p. 62.
25. Härting, "Global Humanitarianism", p. 62.
26. *See* savedarfur.org (accessed 26 February 2016).
27. Härting, "Global Humanitarianism", p. 64.
28. Quoted in Higgins, *Hollywood's Africa*, p. 4.
29. Kenneth W. Harlow, "Again the Darkness: Shake Hands with the Devil", in Higgins, *Hollywood's Africa*, p. 83.
30. Iyunolu Osagie, "Situating Agency in *Blood Diamond* and *Ezra*", in Higgins, *Hollywood's Africa*, p. 227.
31. Martha Evans and Ian Glenn, "'TIA—This Is Africa': Afropessimism in Twenty-First-Century Narrative Film", *Black Camera* 2, no. 1 (2010), p. 24.
32. Maryellen Higgins, "Introduction: African Blood, Hollywood's Diamonds?", in Higgins, *Hollywood's Africa*, p. 1.

PART V

Peacebuilding

CHAPTER 16

The Political Economy of Peacebuilding in Africa

Kenneth Omeje

Peacebuilding is essentially a post-conflict activity, and the practical approach adopted by most regional and international organisations—including the African Union (AU), Africa's regional economic communities (RECs), and the United Nations (UN) Peacebuilding Commission—to the process of (re-) building societies emerging from conflict. As such, peacebuilding involves a range of targeted measures to reduce the risk of relapse into conflict and solidify peace by strengthening national capacities at all levels for conflict management, and to lay the foundation for sustainable peace and development.[1] This can be described as a minimalist approach. However, there are a number of proponents that advocate for a more generic or maximalist approach to peacebuilding—one that should encompass the entire conflict spectrum, beginning with the pre-conflict phase and continuing through the armed violence phase and ultimately the post-conflict phase.[2]

There are both conceptual and practical difficulties associated with this maximalist paradigm, particularly its tendency to subsume within the peacebuilding framework other more established methods and processes of conflict intervention, such as, on the one hand, conflict prevention in the pre-conflict phase and, on the other, conflict management, conflict settlement, and conflict resolution in the armed violence phase. Although the maximalist framework has, or rather claims to have, the advantage of being an inclusive approach to addressing conflict, it also renders the concept and practice of peacebuilding into an omnibus process. A halfway point between the two contending approaches might be to remove pre-conflict intervention from the maximalist framework and to limit peacebuilding to the turbulent conflict and post-conflict phases.

K. Omeje (✉)
John and Elnora Ferguson Centre for African Studies, University of Bradford, Bradford, UK

T. Karbo, K. Virk (eds.), *The Palgrave Handbook of Peacebuilding in Africa*, https://doi.org/10.1007/978-3-319-62202-6_16

This could be analytically helpful, because the progression from the turbulent armed conflict phase to the post-conflict dispensation is, in practice, hardly a linear transition, but often a convoluted process of continuities and discontinuities, political factionalism, elite horse-trading, cooperation and co-optation, as well as organised resistance and occasional relapse into insurgency and armed conflict.

African Conflicts from a Political Economy Perspective

In the context of armed conflict and peacebuilding, political economy analysis is broadly concerned with issues of (neo-)patrimonial governance, rent-seeking, competition for power and resources, and prebendal corruption.[3] Prebendal corruption, or prebendalism, refers to a political culture in which the governing elite and other public office holders have a sense of entitlement to public funds and resources, which they misappropriate for themselves, their kin, and/or their ethnic or identity group.[4] A cursory insight into the political economy of armed conflicts in Africa is important for understanding peacebuilding because of the nexus between the economic agendas of conflict and peacebuilding. The violent and predatory economies that feature prominently in many armed conflicts in Africa and elsewhere around the world do not suddenly disappear in the post-conflict phase, but remain available sources of revenue for disaffected criminal entrepreneurs, peace spoilers, and other actors at the margins of the war-to-peace transition process. Canadian analyst Karen Ballentine and German scholar Heiko Nitzschke have argued that where shadow economies have become implicated in the political economy of conflict, economic criminality and related opportunities tend to be systemic and well-integrated into regional and global criminal networks in such a way that they can seriously undermine peacebuilding and post-conflict recovery.[5]

A plethora of studies already exist on the economic agendas of wars and armed conflicts in Africa and other developing regions in the global South.[6] "Resource curse" perspectives, notably the theories of greed-grievance and predation, have featured prominently in the debates on these agendas. Armed rebellion in many natural resource–rich states, as some leading proponents have argued, are largely instigated or aggravated and prolonged by factional greed for lootable natural resources and criminal obstructibility of the largely non-lootable resources.[7] Broadly speaking, lucrative natural resources (such as diamonds, oil and gas, timber, and cobalt) have been associated with fuelling rebel insurgencies, civil wars, and war economies on the continent, for example, in Angola, the Democratic Republic of the Congo (DRC), Liberia, Sierra Leone, and Sudan. The long-standing militia insurgency in Nigeria's Niger Delta, which has de-escalated since the introduction of the government's Amnesty, Disarmament, Demobilisation, and Rehabilitation (ADDR) programme in 2009, has also been partly associated with the opportunities for economic criminality presented by the local oil economy (such as the kidnapping of oil workers for ransom, the running of protection rackets, and the stealing of crude oil from perforated pipelines, with the latter colloquially known as oil bunkering).

In 1995 alone, for instance, Liberian warlords managed to export an estimated \$300–500 million worth of diamonds and gold, \$53 million worth of timber, and \$27 million worth of rubber.[8] During the civil war in neighbouring Sierra Leone (1991–2002), the rebel Revolutionary United Front (RUF), led by Foday Sankoh, fought long and hard to control the diamond-mining fields in Kono and Makeni districts for the purposes of illicit accumulation and financing the war project. The illegal logging and export of timber was also a key feature of Sierra Leone's war economy. Sankoh's RUF received significant support from Liberian warlord Charles Taylor, both as rebel leader and later in his capacity as president of Liberia. Among other things, Taylor was linked to a diamond-for-arms deal with the RUF, one of the multiple war crime charges for which he was later indicted and jailed in April 2012 by the UN-backed Special Court for Sierra Leone.[9] (On security sector reform [SSR] in Sierra Leone, see Rashid in this volume.)

Similarly, favourable variations in the price of coltan in 2000–2001 impacted the war in eastern Congo in fundamental ways. When the price of coltan, previously sold at \$80 per kilogramme on the export market in January 2000, sky rocketed to \$800 per kilogramme by December of the same year, the appreciated commodity price meant a windfall for the RCD-Goma (a faction of the ferocious Rally for Congolese Democracy [RCD]), the rebel movement that controlled significant parts of the mining basin; as such, the rebel group first decreed a monopoly on the export of coltan, imposing a tax of \$10 per kilogramme, and then refused to trade with syndicates that could not produce at least five tonnes per month.[10] Other commodities, like diamonds and timber, have also fuelled the conflict in eastern Congo, with rebel factions and their external allies at different times vying for control of mining territories and revenues.

None of these civil wars was caused by the rebels' quest for economic opportunities, but there is little doubt that, once the internal conflicts had started, natural resources progressively became a major aggravating factor driving the war economies and fuelling insecurity. More systemic issues lie at the root of most civil wars in African natural resource–rich states. These include: misgovernance, prebendal corruption by a privileged oligarchy, impoverishment of the vast majority of the population, decay of public institutions and infrastructures, development failure, authoritarian rule, and high levels of youth unemployment, as well as a general atmosphere of cynicism and hopelessness.[11]

Linkage between the political economy of armed violence in Africa and the continent's "worrying youth bulge"—the prevalence of a large percentage of hopelessly unemployed and underemployed young people in the population—is, in particular, a major concern.[12] Africa has the fastest-growing and most youthful population in the world: over 20 per cent of the continent's population is aged between 15 and 24 years.[13] In fact, in most sub-Saharan African countries, at least 50 per cent of the population is below the age of 25 years, and a further 43 per cent are below the age of 15.[14] Extreme poverty (less than $1.25 per day) and working poverty (underemployed working people living on less than $3.10 per day) are key characteristics of this youth population, and sub-Saharan Africa continues to suffer the highest youth working poverty rates globally, at almost 70 per cent.[15] The situation is especially worrying in volatile conflict-prone and conflict-affected countries on the continent. In several such fragile contexts, such as Sudan's Darfur region, South Sudan, the DRC, the Central African Republic (CAR), Chad, Nigeria, and, to a lesser extent, Sierra Leone and Liberia, wily politicians and ethnic warlords can find it fairly easy to mobilise, arm, and use the marginalised youth, to perpetuate self-serving political violence and to do so with relative impunity.[16]

Furthermore, it is worth noting that a vital impetus for the political economy of rebellions and armed conflicts in Africa comes from the fact that the costs of prosecuting wars are excessively high for the relatively poor parties to the conflicts (both rebels and governments). The situation is compounded for the protagonists by the post–Cold War disinclination of the wealthier great powers—such as the United States (US)—to fund warring parties in Africa, as they had during the Cold War era (1945–1990). The result is that wars and armed conflicts on the continent have become mostly self-financed, a reality that predisposes belligerents to desperate predatory devices that have far-reaching implications for post-conflict reconstruction and peacebuilding.[17]

Third-Party Intervention, Conflict Settlement, and Peacebuilding

Whereas economic agendas have featured prominently in most armed conflicts in Africa, most conflict settlements through third-party intervention have tended to focus more on political issues, notably elite power-sharing and appeasement of consequential rebel leaders and their constituencies, with the result that the economic agendas and drivers of the hostilities are either neglected or perfunctorily handled. Third-party intervention often takes the form of diplomatic action, peacekeeping by a regional or international body, bilateral military deployment (usually to bolster the strength and survival chances of the government), and efforts at mediation. Viewed from a political economy perspective, another major practical feature of the war-to-peace transition in Africa is the sharing of the peacebuilding resource largesse to ensure both the survival and the continuity of a fragile government. These inordinate externalities of post-conflict reconstruction and peacebuilding are flawed and defective, not least because they predispose excluded, disadvantaged, and disaffected parties to reject peace deals in practice and resort possibly to armed violence to challenge them.

Most wars, furthermore, end in mediated conflict settlement, which usually culminates in power-sharing over a transitional period that could lead to a neoliberal democratic dispensation characterised by constitutional reforms, liberalisation of the political space, multi-party elections, and market reforms—

essentially, a restructuring of the state following the liberal peace paradigm.[18] There has been a wide range of liberal peacebuilding projects in modern African history. Post-war Namibia and Mozambique are often cited as examples of countries where liberal peacebuilding has been most successfully implemented. However, Canadian scholar Devon Curtis has challenged the "qualified successes" of the liberal peacebuilding projects in Namibia and Mozambique on account of the "high rate of inequality and persistent insecurity among some communities" within the two countries.[19] (On the impact of inequality on peacebuilding, see Richmond in this volume.) It is further debatable whether the multiplicity of democratic transitions and elections in post-conflict societies in Africa have yielded the desired levels of peace and security on the continent in line with core assumptions of liberal peace theory; these being that democracy is a necessary condition for peace, especially in the aftermath of war, and that peacebuilding is all about liberal democratic governance.[20] In this regard, conflict-affected countries such as South Sudan and Burundi attest to the tenuous link between democracy and peace. (On Sudan and South Sudan, see Deng in this volume.)

By its very nature, the politics of power-sharing, especially as a conflict settlement measure, is always extremely interest-driven, and the underlying interests are hardly what anyone could label "national interests", but rather the parochial self-serving interests of the elite. The analysis below of a few key peace agreements highlights the different ways that these agreements have related to the economic agendas and drivers of war.

West Africa: Liberia, Sierra Leone, and Côte d'Ivoire

In a highly revealing study, carried out in 2010 to assess the extent to which civil war–centred peace agreements in West Africa have addressed the economic agendas and drivers of the underlying conflicts, Ghanaian scholars Kwesi Aning and Samuel Atuobi have shown that out of a total of 13 peace agreements signed by warring parties between 1990 and 2005 to end the civil wars in Liberia, Sierra Leone, and Côte d'Ivoire, nine made no reference to the economic dimensions of the civil wars.[21] With regard to the Liberian civil war (1989–1996 and 1999–2003), all the key peace agreements signed between 1990 and 1995, in Banjul, Gambia; Yamoussoukro, Côte d'Ivoire; Lomé, Togo; Cotonou, Benin; Accra, Ghana; and Abuja, Nigeria, had no economic components. This is ironic given that the Liberian civil war had profound economic drivers that verged on illegal exploitation and export of the country's natural resources. It was only the 2003 Comprehensive Peace Agreement—signed in Accra, ending the 14–year civil war—that made reference to an economic agenda, by creating the Contracts and Monopolies Commission to help regulate macro-economic policy formulation and implementation under the national transitional government of Liberia.[22]

In Sierra Leone, unlike in Liberia, two major peace agreements took into account the economic dimensions of the war, albeit in a rather perfunctory manner. Both agreements were negotiated by the Economic Community of West

African States (ECOWAS) and signed by the warring parties, in Abidjan, Côte d'Ivoire, in 1996 and Lomé in 1999. While Article 26 of the Abidjan peace accord "recognised that there is a socio-economic dimension to the conflict which must be addressed in order to consolidate the foundation of peace", Article 27 proposed that a "broad-based Socio-Economic forum, in which the RUF/SL [RUF of Sierra Leone] shall participate, shall be established with a view to enriching policy formulation and execution in the socio-economic sector".[23] The Lomé Comprehensive Peace Agreement, on the other hand, outlawed all illegal mining of natural resources and proposed a new strategy for natural resource governance under its Article 7, which, among other things, demanded the government's creation of a new commission to oversee management of strategic resources, national reconstruction, and development.[24] Article 26 of the agreement awarded the chairmanship of this commission's governing board to RUF leader Foday Sankoh, an appeasement that elevated him to the equivalent of the country's second-in-command, but that ironically was not able to guarantee the peace in practice, because of Sankoh's inordinate ambition for the topmost political office in the land. Some analysts have lampooned the failed appeasement of Sankoh as a neo-patrimonial extravaganza and a blunder akin in proportion to the European powers' 1938 failed territorial appeasement of the Nazi leader Adolf Hitler in a bid to achieve peace in Europe.[25] Sankoh was arrested less than a year later, in May 2000, for recklessly violating the ceasefire provision of the peace agreement. He was subsequently indicted, in March 2003, on 17 counts of various war crimes by the Special Court for Sierra Leone, under whose custody he later died, in July 2003, of ill health.

In the case of Côte d'Ivoire, three of the four major peace agreements signed by the warring parties to end the civil war—Lomé in 2002; Pretoria (Tshwane), South Africa, in 2005; and Ouagadougou, Burkina Faso, in 2007—did not address the economic dimensions of the civil war. It was only the January 2003 Linas-Marcoussis peace agreement, signed in France, that made some marginal reference to economic drivers of the conflict in a proposal requiring the Government of National Reconciliation to submit a bill to the National Assembly for an amendment of the land tenure system; specifically by repealing the conflict-ridden, retroactive landholding restrictions enshrined in a December 1998 law on rural land tenure, adopted unanimously by the National Assembly.[26] Article 8 of the Linas-Marcoussis agreement made a vague reference to economic recovery: "The Government of National Reconciliation will restore free circulation of persons and goods throughout the national territory and facilitate the resumption of educational, administrative, economic and social activity."[27]

Eastern and Central Africa: Sudan and the Democratic Republic of the Congo

In Sudan and the DRC, the more recent peace agreements of the 2000s have made stronger references to the economic dimensions of the underlying wars, but implementation of these agreements has proved problematic. Among other things, the 2005 Comprehensive Peace Agreement (CPA) between the government of Sudan and the Sudan People's Liberation Movement/Army (SPLM/A)—signed in Machakos, Kenya—provided for incorporation of the SPLM/A into a Government of National Unity, with 50/50 sharing of oil revenue between the North and the South; restriction of Sharia law to the North; review of the boundary demarcation between the North and the South; and holding of a national election and a self-determination referendum for the South, after a six-year period, in which Southerners could vote to either remain in Sudan or secede as an independent state.[20] (See Deng in this volume.)

The sharing of oil revenue between the North and the South was a particularly sensitive issue before the independence referendum—held in January 2011—and also a complex one that is yet to be completely resolved, notably with regard to pipeline oil transportation fees payable by Juba to Khartoum.[28] Other highly sensitive conflict issues between Sudan and South Sudan include the postponed referendum to determine the status of the oil-rich Abyei region and border demarcation in the restive oil-rich frontier territories, including the ultimate status of the socio-demographically mixed states of Blue Nile and South Kordofan (see Deng in this volume). Regarding the sharing of oil revenue under the 2005 CPA, Global Witness—a London-based independent, not-for-profit organisation—published a report, in September 2009, in which it claimed that the Sudanese central government had widely under-reported its oil revenue receipts. Moreover, discrepancies between what Khartoum reported as oil receipts and what the major oil companies reported as remittances to it indicated at least a 12 per cent revenue disadvantage against the government in then Southern Sudan.[29] This discrepancy, the report further claimed, amounted to a shortfall of over $700 million in Juba's total revenue receipts between 2005 and 2009.[30]

After at least six major failed peace agreements on the war in eastern Congo, a regional approach was adopted by the AU's conflict mediators, leading to the unprecedented "Peace, Security, and Cooperation Framework Agreement for the DRC and the Region", signed in Addis Ababa, Ethiopia, in February 2013. The agreement was designed to solicit the support of regional states and the international community in helping the Congolese government to, among other things, consolidate state authority, especially in eastern Congo; foster decentralisation and economic development; and undertake further structural reform of state institutions, with particular reference to financial reform. The agreement recognised in its preamble that "the DRC government has begun some reforms, with partners' support, that are intended to lay the ground for economic recovery and for democratization of the country".[31] All nine of the DRC's neighbours (Angola, Burundi, the CAR, Congo-Brazzaville, Rwanda, South Sudan, Tanzania, Uganda, and Zambia) and the regional hegemon, South Africa, were signatories to the agreement. Four international organisations also signed the framework agreement—the UN, the AU, the International Conference on the Great Lakes Region (ICGLR), and the Southern African Development Community (SADC). A regional oversight mechanism involving signatories to the agreement was created to monitor implementation and review progress.

Regarding mitigating the economic agendas of the civil war in the DRC, the 2013 framework agreement and other national and international arrangements (including the 2003 Extractive Industries Transparency Initiative and the 2003 Kimberley Process Certification Scheme to prevent export and sale of conflict diamonds) have not been effective in reining in the following subversive players, agencies, and structures:

1. Corruptible senior figures in the Congolese government, especially regarding opacity in the award of mining contracts, privatisation of assets, and accountability of mining revenues;
2. Unscrupulous local and foreign mining companies that evade scrutiny and sometimes export, sell, or buy minerals linked to illegal extractions;
3. Armed groups, rebels, and the Congolese army, who by their various clandestine operations tend to perpetuate the illicit trade in various minerals;
4. External investors and corrupt officials alike, who are able to use loopholes in the international (economic) legal system to transfer revenues out of the resource-rich state and into the international financial system, with limited reporting requirements; and
5. Neighbouring countries (especially Rwanda and Uganda), which are backing armed groups by providing them with weapons, and in turn secure and export Congolese minerals.[32]

Beyond the superficiality and perfunctory nature of many peace agreements, other factors that conspire to hamper the practicality of diverse war-to-peace transitions and post-conflict peacebuilding initiatives in Africa include: the proliferation and erratic mutation of armed factions; the subversive devices of spoilers; subterfuge and opposition by demoralised soldiers; hostility by interest-driven neighbouring states towards peace agreements; and inadequate assistance from the international community, including incapacity or inability to sanction violations of peace agreements by any of the warring parties.[33] These observations, which are incidental to the so-called post–Cold War "new wars",[34] are clearly discernible whether one is considering the failed peace processes in civil wars in Burundi, Darfur, and pre-genocide Rwanda, or the ongoing turbulent peace processes in South Sudan, Mali, and the Central African Republic. (See also Richmond in this volume.)

The Politics of External Support and Sharing the Peacebuilding Largesse

Most post-conflict peace processes and governments in Africa are outcomes of peace settlements largely negotiated and bankrolled by external bodies and actors, including regional and international stakeholders. External support usually precedes the peace process, and may start from either the conflict formation and escalation phases or the wartime violence phase. Preventive diplomacy is one of the most prevalent features of external intervention in the pre-conflict phase, while targeted military strikes, humanitarian operations, and peacekeeping (including robust enforcement action) are among the most often used external support measures during the wartime violence phase. In the post-conflict phase, when a ceasefire regime is already in place, external support to peace operations includes funding for third-party-mediated peace talks, ceasefire monitoring and stabilisation activities, transitional justice, humanitarian relief operations, as well as political and economic governance reforms.[35] These peace (support) operations require enormous financial investment, multi-sectoral technical skills, and a carefully planned, comprehensive, time-lined operation.

In 2008, British economist Paul Collier estimated the cost of a typical civil war to be around $64 billion and the cost of conflict intervention and post-conflict reconstruction to be significantly higher.[36] The huge financial cost of peace operations entails a proliferation of institutions, actors, and funds, creating its own challenges, particularly with regard to coordination of roles and competition for space, resources, power, and influence. Too often, these peace operations are also interest-driven. Examples abound. The pro-government mercenary support services in the civil war in Sierra Leone provided by the South Africa–based private military and security company, Executive Outcomes, and its British collaborator, Sandline International, involved contracts tied to over $200 million worth of diamond mining using proxy multinational companies (mainly Diamond Works and Branch Energy) in the war-torn country.[37]

The first and second military invasions of the DRC by Rwanda and Uganda in 1996 and 1998 respectively, as well as the ultimate deployment of countervailing troops against them by Angola and Zimbabwe in 1998, were all calculations involving the use of national armies, by ruling elites, as tools for the short- and long-term exploitation of the Congo's mineral and forestry resources. In the case of Angola, pressure from business interests in the United States on the Bill Clinton administration (1993–2001) was key in Luanda's decision to replace Executive Outcomes with the US private military and security company Military Professional Resources Inc. in 1995, after the former had done most of the fighting to pacify resource enclaves that were threatened by the National Union for the Total Independence of Angola (UNITA) rebels.[38]

Similarly, French bilateral military interventions in the civil wars in Côte d'Ivoire (since 2002) and Mali (since 2013), though rationalised on humanitarian grounds, have ulterior political economy dimensions (on Mali, see Adebajo in this volume). France is the leading investor in, and destination for, Côte d'Ivoire's primary commodity exports (cocoa, cotton, and coffee)—a sector with a large ripple economy that prior to the civil war employed most of the estimated 14,000 French citizens living in that country. Mali, on the other hand, is of strategic importance to Paris because of the prospect of the Tuareg-led rebellion spreading into neighbouring Niger, as happened in the past (1990 and 2007). The uranium mines in Niger and the uranium deposits in Mali are of significant interest to France, which generates 78 per cent of its electricity from nuclear energy.[39]

Meanwhile, in Kenya, the British and American governments reportedly adopted an anti–President Mwai Kibaki posture in the run-up to, and aftermath of, the violent December 2007 election because their multinational companies lost out to Chinese firms in all the major construction, infrastructure development, and pharmaceutical contract bids, contracts that had hitherto been their exclusive monopoly.[40] (See also Wamai in this volume).

Peacebuilding is significantly interest-driven, and different perspectives and practices of peacebuilding tend to project different vested interests. Approached from a liberal governance perspective, post-conflict peacebuilding in Africa tends to markedly promote the shared interests of African political elites and external free market entrepreneurs. This is in line with the uncritical perception of liberalism as a universal good that accommodates the interests of all. All in all, peacebuilding initiatives in the aftermath of deadly conflicts in Africa have often created some form of transitional government that usually involves negotiated power-sharing between the beleaguered government camp and the opposition. In practice, the power-sharing settlements have often been about distributing the most lucrative positions in government among various factions of the political elite in such a way that the largesse of government can be more inclusively shared. The experiments of such transitional national governments in Burundi, Côte d'Ivoire, Guinea Bissau, Kenya, Liberia, Madagascar, Somalia, Sudan, and Zimbabwe have more or less culminated in enlarging and diversifying the frontiers of patronage politics, elite aggrandisement, and prebendal corruption.[41] Consequently, while most power-sharing arrangements have helped in de-escalating conflict and creating (fragile) peace, they have done little to stamp out the acrimonious "winner-takes-all" slant of electoral politics and to guarantee free and fair elections in the short run. Democratic elections and political transitions in the aftermath of the interim power-sharing coalition governments have often been marred by violence, with the result that political order is maintained primarily by the people's collective memory of the gravity of returning to armed hostilities, as opposed to any perceived sense of fairness, justice, and legitimacy in the prevailing dispensations.

An often-overlooked example of the politics of largesse-sharing in post-conflict peacebuilding is the case of Liberia. The country's president, Ellen Johnson-Sirleaf, since assuming office in January 2006 as Africa's first female head of state, has attracted significant international development assistance from the World Bank and various UN agencies; bilateral donors, most notably the US; and various Western charities. Different stakeholders took up implementation of key aspects of the country's 2003 peace settlement agreement. Security sector reform was undertaken, from scratch, by the US government. Disarmament, demobilisation, and reintegration (DDR) and the rehabilitation of child soldiers and ex-combatants were largely taken up by the United Nations Mission in Liberia (UNMIL) and various international as well as local charity organisations. The Liberian government was charged with institutional reform involving, among other things, the civil service, judiciary, legislative and electoral sectors, government ministries and departments, and public service delivery—a process supported with huge donor funding and technical assistance.

With this multi–billion dollar integrated approach to post-conflict reconstruction and peacebuilding, Liberia was rapidly reconstituted from a failed state into a functioning fragile state within a few years, a multi-stakeholder achievement that has incidentally earned President Johnson-Sirleaf international accolades as a reformer. However, beyond the façade of her "reformer" reputation, Johnson-Sirleaf's post-war Liberia reeks with neo-patrimonial corruption, nepotism, and impunity. Despite her loud anti-corruption rhetoric and legislation, the president has refused to prosecute any of the numerous cases of high-level corruption brought against her top appointees by the government's General Auditing Commission, while officers indicted of corruption are retained and recycled into top government positions.[42] In a dramatic twist of irony, Johnson-Sirleaf, who in the pre-war years was a vocal critic of former presidents William R. Tolbert and Samuel Doe for fostering nepotism by appointing their close relatives and kinsmen to top government positions, took nepotism to a bewildering crescendo in blatant violation of Article 5 of the Liberian constitution and Executive Order 38, the Code of Conduct, belatedly signed into law in January 2012.[43] The president has reportedly appointed several cronies and close relatives to top government positions, including three of her sons: Robert Sirleaf, who served as the advisor to the president and chair of the state-owned National Oil Company of Liberia (NOCAL), until his resignation in September 2013 following relentless public criticism regarding allegations of impropriety and corruption; Charles Sirleaf, who is deputy governor of the Central Bank of Liberia; and Fumba Sirleaf, who heads the National Security Agency.[44] In February 2016, Charles Sirleaf was appointed the interim governor of the Liberian Central Bank to replace John Mills Jones, who was allegedly forced out of office after he expressed interest in running for president in Liberia's 2017 election.[45]

Post-war Liberia is governed by a neo-patrimonial oligarchy that thrives on impunity, while a considerable number of honest public officers have been either sacked or compelled to resign their positions in government.[46] Among the prominent Liberians who have, in recent years, spoken out against President Johnson-Sirleaf's reign of nepotism and corruption are her co–Nobel Prize laureate, Leymah Gbowee, who resigned her post as head of the government's Peace and Reconciliation Commission in October 2012; Nagbalee Warner, who resigned as chairman of the Board of Directors of the Liberia Petroleum Refinery Corporation (LPRC) in February 2012; and renowned human rights lawyer, Tiawon Gongloe, who was relieved of his post as labour minister in November 2010 when the president made the controversial decision to send her entire cabinet on compulsory "administrative leave," with the exception of minister of state Edward McLain.[47]

Implementation of Liberia's development policies has been ridden with opacity and corruption. Johnson-Sirleaf's government reportedly "granted more than a third of Liberia's land to private investors for logging, mining and agro-industrial enterprises" between 2006 and 2011, while nearly three million hectares "have become forestry and agricultural concessions". As well, land deals with the Malaysian corporation Sime Darby for production of palm oil "have been particularly divisive, with about 150,000 people directly affected in the first five years of plantation development".[48] In November 2012, President Johnson-Sirleaf was forced to acknowledge that corruption had become "systemic and endemic" in post-war Liberia under her watch.[49]

The Liberian government has also treated issues of transitional justice with levity. The executive and legislative arms of government harbour several ex-warlords and individuals who allegedly bear the greatest criminal responsibility for the country's 14–year civil war. In July 2009, the president was indicted by her own Truth and Reconciliation Commission (TRC) for, among other things, providing financial support to rebel leader Charles Taylor during the civil war.[50] The TRC recommended a 30-year ban from holding public office for the president and 50 other alleged culprits. Little wonder that the TRC's report has not been released.

Beyond the example of neo-patrimonial peacebuilding in post-war Liberia, there is a sense in which peacebuilding is an agency for re-creating international order and maintaining both the regional and the global security status quo through a nexus of stabilisation activities. The emphasis of this approach is on building a militarily secure state that enjoys internal order and a monopoly on the legitimate use of force within its territorial jurisdiction. It is this view of peacebuilding as stabilisation that the US-led post–11 September 2001 "war on terror" has particularly tried to promote in Africa, the Middle East, and Southeast Asia. It is a paradigm that privileges military security cooperation with the West (notably the US) and high defence budgets, often at the expense of social services and development sectors like health, education, public infrastructure, and agriculture. Paradoxically, increased militarisation, as is the case in countries like Eritrea, Egypt, and different parts of the Sahara and the Sahel, becomes perceived as peacebuilding.[51] The UN has played a dual-mandate role in championing peacebuilding as stabilisation through its various multidimensional peacekeeping interventions in Africa (for example, in Sierra Leone [1999–2006]; Burundi [2004–2007]; and Liberia [2003–2015]), and also through promoting peacebuilding as liberal governance, especially (but not exclusively) since the establishment of the UN Peacebuilding Commission in December 2005 (see Otobo in this volume).

International peacekeeping and peace support operations are big business for the leading state funders of UN missions (the US, European Union [EU] member states, Japan, Canada, and Australia), which ironically, all together, contribute less than 6 per cent of the troops.[52] In his classic empirical study "The Economic Impact of Peacekeeping", American scholar William Durch[53] found the following startling details, which have been corroborated by other, similar studies:[54]

1. Only about 10 per cent of the budget of a UN peacekeeping operation lands in the mission area, on average.
2. The rest of the UN budget pays global vendors and international staff, and reimburses states for the cost of troops and police.

3. Of the 10 per cent spent locally, on average about half goes to spending of international staff per diems on housing, food, and incidentals; one-quarter to the mission's direct procurement of local goods and services; and one-quarter to salaries of local staff hired directly by the mission.
4. Military supplies; security sector reform; disarmament, demobilisation, and reintegration; and security contract services are among the biggest businesses in peacekeeping that impact both local and international economies in many ways, even influencing the extension of peacekeeping and peacebuilding missions.

Peacebuilding is further used as a vehicle for justice. Normatively, peacebuilding has been associated with social justice—the empowerment of underprivileged individuals and groups within national and international systems by working towards the elimination of structural violence and the advancement of positive peace. At the political economy level, this normative conception implies that peacebuilding should be used to address issues of historical marginalisation, exclusion, deprivation, and disempowerment of specific social classes, groups, and communities. More significantly, peacebuilding has been empirically associated with transitional justice, defined as a set of judicial and non-judicial measures implemented to redress the legacies of massive human rights abuses and to achieve accountability and reconciliation; measures that include truth commissions, judicial reforms, accountability for atrocities and prosecution for war crimes, compensation for losses, and inter-community confidence-building.[55] Used as a vehicle for transitional justice, peacebuilding is often instrumentalised to champion and maximise the "victor's peace"—the peace of the victorious party in an armed conflict. This is among the criticisms of transitional justice programmes in Sierra Leone, Rwanda, and Liberia, where it is widely believed that most of the indicted and/or prosecuted and convicted figures in the countries' transitional justice programmes were members of the vanquished parties.[56]

Conclusion

One of the greatest challenges of post-war recovery in Africa is the use of peacebuilding to revive neo-patrimonial accumulation, foster nepotism, and promote the sharing of the perquisites of public office. It is a phenomenon that has featured significantly in several African post-conflict countries, including Liberia; Sierra Leone; Côte d'Ivoire; Mali; Zimbabwe; Kenya; and, most recently, South Sudan, where a struggle for power and resources among the country's ethno-national elites triggered a relapse into armed conflict in December 2013. Nigeria's oil-rich Niger Delta has been the site of one of the few home-grown and internally funded and executed peacebuilding projects in contemporary Africa—the Amnesty, Disarmament, Demobilisation, and Rehabilitation programme, introduced in 2009, to help restore peace to the beleaguered region. Notwithstanding the programme's acclaimed success, it is telling, though, that under former president Goodluck Jonathan this success hinged on a large-scale patronage system. This system featured regular payment of millions of dollars to prominent ethnic militia leaders for so-called "security contract" services. The militia leaders, in turn, used part of the huge funds received from the government for appeasement of their group members and other local stakeholders, to encourage them to protect rather than vandalise oil infrastructures in their communities and environs. Other important components of the Niger Delta ADDR programme include a weapons-for-cash exchange and the relatively well-funded (but perfunctorily delivered) rehabilitation for ex-militants involving counselling, vocational skills training, and formal education or entrepreneurship skills acquisition tenable either in Nigeria or abroad.[57] Whether the Niger Delta's fragile peacebuilding process can be sustained is highly doubtful, especially if the new government of President Mohammadu Buhari (since May 2015) decides to discontinue the costly security contract service arrangement between the federal government and the ex-militants. Moving forward, it is important that post-conflict peacebuilding policies, programmes, and activities in Africa be divested, as much as possible, of self-serving hegemonic interests (both local and foreign) and other prebendal motives, to enable more effective delivery of public goods.

Notes

1. Boutros Boutros-Ghali, *An Agenda for Peace* (New York: United Nations [UN], 1992). *See also* Organisation for Economic Cooperation and Development (OECD), *The International Dialogue on Peace-Building and State-Building: Contribution by the Government of South Sudan* (Juba, March 2010), http://www.oecd.org/countries/sudan/44924610.pdf (accessed 8 February 2016).
2. *See* Funmi Olonisakin, *Peacekeeping in Sierra Leone: The Story of UNAMSIL* (Boulder, CO: Lynne Rienner, 2008).
3. Achim Wennmann, *The Political Economy of Peacemaking* (London: Routledge, 2011), p. 8.
4. Richard A. Joseph, *Democracy and Prebendal Politics in Nigeria: The Fall of the Second Republic* (Cambridge: Cambridge University Press, 1987).
5. Karen Ballentine and Heiko Nitzschke, "The Political Economy of Civil War and Conflict Transformation", (Germany: Berghof Research Centre for Constructive Conflict Management, 2005), p. 15, http://www.berghoffoundation.org/fileadmin/redaktion/Publications/Handbook/Dialogue_Chapters/dialogue3_ballentine_nitzschke.pdf (accessed 8 February 2016).
6. Mats Berdal and David M. Malone (eds.), *Greed and Grievance: Economic Agendas in Civil Wars* (Boulder, CO: Lynne Rienner, 2000); Michael L. Ross, *The Oil Curse: How Petroleum Wealth Shapes the Development of Nations* (Princeton: Princeton University Press, 2012).
7. Paul Collier and Anke Hoeffler, *Greed and Grievance in Civil War* (Washington, DC: World Bank, 2000), http://www.worldbank.org/research/conflict/papers/greedgrievance_23oct.pdf (accessed 10 June 2015); Ross, *The Oil Curse*.

8. Kwesi Aning and Samuel Atuobi, "The Neglected Economic Dimension of ECOWAS Negotiated Peace Accords in West Africa", *Africa Spectrum* 46, no. 3 (2011), p. 30.
9. "Charles Taylor Guilty of Aiding Sierra Leone's War Crimes", *BBC News*, 26 April 2012, http://www.bbc.co.uk/news/world-africa-17852488 (accessed 23 August 2014). *See also* John M. Kabia, "Postcoloniality, Conflict Intervention and Peacebuilding in West Africa: Opportunities and Challenges", in Kenneth Omeje (ed.), *The Crises of Postcoloniality in Africa* (Dakar: Council for the Development of Social Science Research in Africa [CODESRIA], 2015), pp. 103–122.
10. J.R. Mailey, *The Anatomy of the Resource Curse: Predatory Investment in Africa's Extractive Industries* (Washington, DC: Africa Centre for Security Studies, 2015), p. 2.
11. Mailey, *The Anatomy of the Resource Curse*, p. 6.
12. Kenneth Omeje, "Strengthening Peace Research and Peace Education in African Universities", *African Sociological Review* 19, no. 1 (2015), p. 24.
13. African Economic Research Consortium (AERC), *Youth and Unemployment in Sub-Saharan Africa*, seminar report, Senior Policy Seminar XV, Kigali, 21–22 March 2013, p. 1.
14. Omeje, "Strengthening Peace Research and Peace Education in African Universities", p. 24; AERC, *Youth and Unemployment in Sub-Saharan Africa*, p. 7.
15. International Labour Organisation (ILO), "World Employment and Social Outlook 2016: Trends for Youth", press release, 24 August 2016, http://www.ilo.org/global/abouttheilo/newsroom/news/WCMS_513728/langen/index.htm (accessed 5 July 2017); and "Youth Unemployment Challenge Worsening in Africa", 24 August 2016, p. 1, http://www.ilo.org/addisababa/mediacentre/pr/WCMS_514566/langen/index.htm (accessed 9 March 2017).
16. Omeje, "Strengthening Peace Research and Peace Education in African Universities", pp. 24–27.
17. Ballentine and Nitzschke, "The Political Economy of Civil War", p. 2.
18. Oliver Richmond, "Reclaiming Peace in International Relations", *Millennium: Journal of International Studies* 36, no. 3 (2008), pp. 439–470.
19. Devon Curtis, "The Contending Politics of Peacebuilding in Africa", in Devon Curtis and Gwinyayi A. Dzinesa (eds.), *Peacebuilding, Power, and Politics in Africa* (Athens: Ohio University Press, 2012), p. 10.
20. Michael W. Doyle, "Three Pillars of the Liberal Peace", *American Political Science Review* 99, no. 3 (2005), pp. 463–466.
21. Aning and Atuobi, "The Neglected Economic Dimension", p. 33.
22. *Comprehensive Peace Agreement between the Government of Liberia and the Liberians United for Reconciliation and Democracy (LURD) and the Movement for Democracy in Liberia (MODEL) and Political Parties*, Accra, 18 August 2003, part 8, art. 27, sec. 2(a), http://www.usip.org/sites/default/files/file/resources/collections/peace_agreements/liberia_08182003.pdf (accessed 10 June 2015).
23. *Peace Agreement between the Government of the Republic of Sierra Leone and the Revolutionary United Front of Sierra Leone (RUF/SL)*, 1996, http://www.ucdp.uu.se/gpdatabase/peace/SiL%2019961130.pdf (accessed 11 June 2015).

24. *The Lomé Agreement: Peace Agreement Between the Government of Sierra Leone and the Revolutionary United Front of Sierra Leone*, 7 July 1999.
25. *See* Ablam Benjamin Akoutou, Rike Sohn, Matthias Vogl, and Daniel Yeboah (eds.), "Understanding Regional Integration in West Africa: A Multi-Thematic and Comparative Analysis", Paper no. 17 (Praia: West Africa Institute; and Bonn: Centre for European Integration Studies, 2014).
26. *Linas-Marcoussis Agreement—Programme of the Government of National Reconciliation in Cote d'Ivoire*, 2003, art. IV, paras. 1–2, http://www.usip.org/sites/default/files/file/resources/collections/peace_agreements/cote_divoire_01242003en.pdf (accessed 16 June 2015).
27. *Linas-Marcoussis Agreement*, art. VIII, para. 1.
28. Being land-locked, South Sudan transports its crude oil through two pipelines that link the oil-producing fields in its south to Sudan's Red Sea export terminal in Port Sudan. This arrangement dates back to 1999, before South Sudan gained its independence from Sudan in July 2011. *See* Kenneth Omeje, "Dangers of Splitting a Fragile Rentier State: Getting It Right in Southern Sudan", Occasional Paper Series (Durban: African Centre for the Constructive Resolution of Disputes [ACCORD], Fall 2010), p. 18.
29. Global Witness, "Global Witness Highlights Oil Revenue Discrepancy Between North and South", September 2009, http://www.sudanradio.org/global-witness-highlights-oil-revenue-discrepancy-betweennorth-and-south (accessed 20 June 2014).
30. Global Witness, "Global Witness Highlights Oil Revenue Discrepancy".
31. *AU Peace, Security, and Cooperation Framework Agreement for the Democratic Republic of the Congo (DRC) and the Region*, 2013, http://www.peaceau.org/uploads/scanned-on-24022013-125543.pdf (accessed 18 June 2015).
32. Southern Africa Resource Watch (SARW), "Consultative Conference on Peace Agreements and Conflict Minerals in the DRC", Kinshasa, 2–3 May 2013, pp. 6–10, http://www.sarwatch.org/sites/sarwatch.org/files/Publications_docs/drc_conference_english_for_web.pdf (accessed 18 June 2015). *See also* Mailey, *The Anatomy of the Resource Curse*, p. 7.
33. Julius Mutwal, *Peace Agreements and Civil Wars in Africa: Insurgent Motivations, States Responses, and Third Party Peacemaking in Liberia, Rwanda, and Sierra Leone* (New York: Cambria, 2009).
34. Mary Kaldor, *New and Old Wars*, 2nd ed. (Cambridge: Polity, 2006).
35. Konrad Huber, "Conflict Analysis in Peace Processes: Pitfalls and Potential Remedies", in African Union (AU), *Managing Peace Processes: A Handbook for AU Practitioners*, vol. 1 (Addis Ababa, 2013), pp. 11–34.
36. Paul Collier, *The Bottom Billion: Why the Poor Countries Are Failing and What Can Be Done About It* (Oxford: Oxford University Press, 2008), pp. 105–107.
37. Abdel-Fatau Musah, "Privatization of Security, Arms Proliferation, and the Process of State Collapse in Africa", *Development and Change* 33, no. 5 (2002), p. 912.
38. Musah, "Privatization of Security", p. 923.
39. Roger Annis, "France Launches War in Mali in Bid to Secure Resources, Stamp Out National Rights Struggles", *Global Research*, 19 January 2013.
40. Macharia Munene, "Historical Perspectives on Security in Africa: The Refugee Problem", in Jamila Abubakar, Kenneth Omeje, and Habu Galadima (eds.),

Conflict of Securities: State and Human Security in Africa (London: Adonis and Abbey, 2010), pp. 101–107.

41. Carl A. LeVan, "Power-Sharing and Inclusive Politics in Africa's Uncertain Democracies", *Governance: An International Journal of Policy, Administration, and Institutions* 24, no. 1 (2011), http://carllevan.com/wp-content/uploads/2010/01/Governance-LeVan-power-sharing-2011.pdf (accessed 17 June 2015); John Perry and T. Debey Sayndee, *African Truth Commissions and Transitional Justice* (Lanham, MD: Lexington Books, 2015).
42. Government of the United States, "U.S. Human Rights Report Decries Corruption, Lack of Transparency in Liberia", in *2012 Human Rights Report on Liberia*, 2013, http://allafrica.com/stories/201304221656.html?viewall=1 (accessed 20 June 2015).
43. The New Dispensation, "Liberian Ruling Party Secretary General Admits to Nepotism and Corruption in Government", 19 October 2012, http://thenew-dispensation.com/2012/10/19/liberia-ruling-party-secretary-general-admits-to-nepotism-and-corruption-in-government (accessed 25 February 2016).
44. Liberian Listner, "Nepotism in Africa: Ellen Accused to Habored About17 Family Members in Govt.", 19 February 2016, http://www.liberianlistener.com/2016/02/19/nepotism-in-africa-ellen-accused-to-habored-about17-family-members-in-govt (accessed 26 February 2016).
45. John Morlue, "John Morlue Discusses President Sirleaf, Trajectory of Liberian Politics", *New Liberia*, 18 October 2012, http://newliberian.com/?p=1760#sthash.9a8diLjl.dpuf (accessed 20 June 2015).
46. Christopher Neyor, "Open Letter to President Ellen Johnson Sirleaf", *The Perspective*, 13 June 2014, http://www.theperspective.org/2014/0616201402.php (accessed 19 June 2015). *See also* The Analyst, "I am Angry—Says Minister Tiawon Gongloe", *AllAfrica*, 17 November 2010, http://allafrica.com/stories/201011190299.html (accessed 26 February 2016).
47. "Liberia's Johnson Sirleaf Defiant over Nepotism and Corruption Claims", *The Guardian* (London), 1 November 2012, http://www.theguardian.com/global-development/2012/nov/01/liberia-johnson-sirleaf-nepotism-corruption (accessed 20 June 2015).
48. "Liberia's Johnson Sirleaf Defiant".
49. "Liberia's Johnson Sirleaf Defiant". For a list of some of those indicted by the Truth and Reconciliation Commission (TRC) who hold or have previously held positions in the Liberian government, *see* Heritage, "Who Are Those Behind Liberia Purported War Crime List?", *AllAfrica*, 14 March 2015, http://allafrica.com/stories/201503150107.html (accessed 26 February 2016).
50. Perry and Sayndee, *African Truth Commissions and Transitional Justice.*
51. Curtis, "The Contending Politics of Peacebuilding in Africa", p. 12.
52. Thierry Tardy, "Funding Peace Operations: Better Value for EU Money", Briefing Issue (Brussels: European Union Institute of Security Studies, November 2013), p. 2, http://www.iss.europa.eu/uploads/media/Brief_38_Funding_peace_operations.pdf (accessed 18 June 2015).
53. William Durch, "The Economic Impact of Peacekeeping: An Update", 2009, http://www.xn--bundesheer-sterreich-ebc.net/pdf_pool/publikationen/eco_impacts_04_eco_impact_an_update_durch.pdf (accessed 15 June 2015).
54. Eric Mvukiyehe and Cyrus Samiiy, "Quantitative Impact Evaluation of the United Nations Mission in Liberia: Final Report", 9 February 2010, http://

www.columbia.edu/~enm2105/docs/unmil/unmil_final100209.pdf (accessed 16 June 2015); Ernst Brandon, Rajeev Sooreea, Gigi Gokcek, and Diara Spain, "The Economic Impacts of United Nations Peacekeeping Operations: Growth Versus Level Effects", *International Journal of Public Policy* 10, nos. 1–3 (2014), pp. 100–117.

55. Office of the United Nations Secretary-General, "Guidance Note to Secretary-General: UN Approach to Transitional Justice", March 2010, http://www.unrol.org/files/TJ_Guidance_Note_March_2010FINAL.pdf (accessed 15 June 2015); Anna Macdonald, "Local Understanding and Experiences of Transitional Justice: A Review of the Evidence" (London: Justice and Security Research Programme, London School of Economics, 2013), http://www.lse.ac.uk/internationalDevelopment/research/JSRP/downloads/JSRP6-Macdonald.pdf (accessed 15 June 2015).
56. Perry and Sayndee, *African Truth Commissions and Transitional Justice.*
57. Oluwatoyin O. Oluwaniyi, "Post-Amnesty Programme in the Niger Delta: Challenges and Prospects", *Conflict Trends* no. 4 (2011), pp. 46–54; Hinshaw Drew, "Nigeria's Former Oil Bandits Now Collect Government Cash", *Wall Street Journal*, 22 August 2012, http://www.wsj.com/articles/SB10001424052702304019404577420160886588518 (accessed 18 June 2015).

CHAPTER 17

The Impact of Inequality on Peacebuilding and State-Building in Africa

Oliver P. Richmond

The post-Cold War order has been marked by a combination of liberal internationalism, Northern-centrism, and a global system of neo-liberalism, interspersed with some relatively authoritarian states. The neo-liberal system is an outcome of the role of the World Bank and International Monetary Fund (IMF) in structural adjustment, state reform, and market promotion from the 1980s onwards. This system has made some sense in terms of addressing conflicts located in the industrialised North and implicated in the Cold War. In a functioning capitalist economy, if social and legal inequality are addressed, a relatively level playing field can enable material needs to be self-secured. There is an assumption that if legal equality can be secured through human rights, democracy, and the rule of law, material inequality will be less significant for peacebuilding efforts. However, peacebuilding in Africa needs to be designed bearing in mind the continent's historical experience of colonialism and of subsequent North-South relations in the context of the Cold War; all of which have created a complex and unique set of conditions for, and claims upon, the modern African state as well as the donor and international system. Yet post-conflict reconstruction in the global South has generally been amalgamated into the global, but Northern-driven peacebuilding and state building paradigm, which aims to build neo-liberal states within a global capitalist and international liberal peace framework for securing human rights.

This chapter draws on a previous article of mine, "The Impact of Socio-Economic Inequality on Peacebuilding and Statebuilding", *Civil Wars* 16, no. 4 (2014), pp. 449–467.

O.P. Richmond (✉)
Department of Politics, and Humanitarian and Conflict Response Institute, University of Manchester, Manchester, UK

T. Karbo, K. Virk (eds.), *The Palgrave Handbook of Peacebuilding in Africa*, https://doi.org/10.1007/978-3-319-62202-6_17

If legal and material inequality are at the root of some dimensions of conflict—especially as related to power, resources, and identity—then the state being built according to the neo-liberal approach is already a failure by design. Legal rights, though important, do not inevitably secure material needs in practice. Yet the framework of human rights, free markets, and political institutions in the global South tends to reflect Northern historical development, rather than be rooted in local contexts. Neo-liberalism represents the ideological belief that material inequality is not a political or moral issue, and does not lead to conflict, but instead promotes competition, innovation, and entrepreneurship, even in post-conflict and development environments.[1] It can even be justified for moral reasons, where it contributes to the public good.[2] Yet before neo-liberalism's influence on the agendas of peacebuilding and state-building prior to the end of the Cold War, the European Enlightenment project (the basis for the loose global consensus on the liberal peace/neo-liberal state), over its historical time span, tended to focus on political, economic, racial, class, and gender dynamics of inequality, in different combinations at different times.[3] Social forms of statehood were the result of many twentieth-century forms of conflict before the end of the Cold War by 1990.[4] Yet they have been excluded from post–Cold War peace models, often on the grounds of cost and ideology initially, or simply as a naturalised pathway of dependency on previously determined blueprints.

Inequality has historically caused conflict and therefore been mitigated by the state and the international community to avoid further conflict. Superficially, one might think that the post-colonial state system and international institutions were established for exactly this reason. Decolonised states were accepted into the existing hierarchy with the colonial and industrial powers at the top, but they were given legal equality without material support. The available historical data tend to show that inequality between African countries and the so-called advanced economies (former colonial powers and Northern states) remains relatively unchanged, and internal inequality is actually increasing worldwide.[5]

This chapter begins by surveying the general theoretical insights into inequality and its relationship with peace and development specifically in the post-colonial African context, and then turns to the implications of these insights for "neo-trusteeship" forms of peacebuilding, state-building, and development in the African context, which involves historical and structural inequality. Trusteeship has, in a sense, substituted, through subtle forms of external programming and adjustment, for more decisive economic policies related to peacebuilding in Africa and elsewhere.

A Puzzle for Peacebuilding, State-Building, and Development

The international focus on inequality, via contemporary indices such as the Human Development Index (HDI) used by the United Nations Development Programme (UNDP),[6] and various other indicators used by international financial institutions like the World Bank and IMF, points to inequality as a factor in inducing conflict. These indices also indicate that inequality is, to a certain degree, a natural part of the international order. So a starting point for contemporary conflict management, peacebuilding, state-building, and development thinking is that historical order is, to a large extent, natural and cannot be rectified, and that distributive justice is not necessary for peace, at least in its negative form and in the short to medium term. In fact, contemporary policy practices represent a form of neo-trusteeship through which international actors seek to guide the emergence of resilient and peaceful states, without the need for a global architectural (re-)design to redistribute wealth. At the same time, there is recognition that socio-economic inequality may well be a causal factor in conflict, which global governance and the state should hedge against if war is to be prevented. Thus, international efforts to support peacebuilding and state-reconstruction are based upon some contradictions between ethics, structural factors, geo-politics, and the claims made, often on humanitarian grounds, to establish more peaceful political systems after war.

For example, the much lauded developmentalism associated with the United Nations' (UN) Millennium Development Goals (MDGs)—launched in 2000 and since replaced by the 2030 Agenda for Sustainable Development comprising 17 Sustainable Development Goals (SDGs)—suggested lifting one-and-a-half billion people above a poverty line set at just over a $1 per day, ignoring the fact that the top 30 per cent of the world's population (over two billion people) live on many times more than the amount set by this most basic of developmental goals.[7] Even if this MDG had been achieved, a further one to two billion people would still be living in relative poverty, and this would be the case even under the framework of the new SDGs.[8] These indices represent the biases, interests, and ideologies of the key donors behind them (for example, the United States [US] and other Western governments, and the principles associated with sovereignty and neo-liberalism).[9] They define, to a significant degree, what is thought to represent development, peace, and order, at the elite level of the international system, and what the level of intolerance to poverty is before conflict (or even terrorism) ensues. Evidence of the relationship between inequality and peace since the end of the Cold War, is somewhat contradictory. For instance, many conflict-affected countries (for example, Côte d'Ivoire) have stabilised and improved their HDI ranking, but alternative readings of the data show socio-economic stagnation, and in some cases, even regression towards structural and direct forms of violence.[10]

It is notable that many development indices tend to show a small, but significant, overall improvement in post-conflict environments, though this improvement, when placed in the context of indices measuring specific elements (such as the indices provided by Freedom House, or the Gini index for inequality), becomes less significant.[11] Since the end of the Cold War, inequality and authoritarian features of regimes in countries hosting peacebuilding operations have been increasing. An inequality-adjusted version of the HDI has been published since 2011.[12] As well, a recent research project at the

University of Texas in the United States has outlined how the retreat from neo-liberal orthodoxy has reduced inequality in South America in particular.[13] In this context, a reduction in socio-economic inequality has also been connected to a decline in crime and violence, even though, in many cases, underlying issues such as land use and ownership have not been resolved. Political stability has tended to increase, as can be observed throughout history, in states where redistribution occurs, as a result of the fact that equality (domestic as well as international) tends to reduce emigration and produce more environmentally responsible societies.[14] This sort of evidence, placed in the context of the stabilisation of post-war Europe and Japan, also seems to indicate that the post-conflict integration into global and regional governance of a stable and liberal state, and the redressal of structural and social inequality within and between societies need to occur quickly if peace is to be sustainable.

Thus, a major puzzle exists as to why Northern-framed and Northern-dominated peacebuilding and state-building since the end of the Cold War have only selectively followed the patterns suggested by this evidence. Why risk changing the model offered by the European Union (EU) when it seems to have been so successful in ending violent conflict? But, although Europe has prospered, large parts of Africa have languished during and after decolonisation and since the end of the Cold War, relatively speaking. At best, development has been uneven and unequal. In the twentieth century, the successful model followed a pattern of increasing the equality of rights and needs (as well as representation, law, and institutional capacity), in order to mitigate the factors that led to conflict and to establish a long-term viable order. This can also be seen in the progression of certain concepts: from traditional state-centric to human security, from first- to third-generation human rights, and from procedural to participatory forms of democracy. Historically, governance has been either deployed to mitigate the effects of inequality through redistribution of resources and generation of public services as a form of pacification, or used to create space via markets wherein individuals can be "resilient" or engage in "self-help" within a liberal legal and institutional framework attractive to foreign direct investment (FDI). Government has been constructed around these two competing approaches, though more recent development, and post-conflict state-building and peacebuilding policies of the UN, the EU, and others in the international donor community have focused on rights and markets over needs and relative material equality. Mitigating inequality through state design is thought to undermine initiative and redistribution by generating dependency, and so the state's legal and security apparatus are designed to prevent this.

This is a complicated problem, of course. In post-colonial, post-socialist, custom-based, and socially networked countries (which make up most conflict-affected environments), such reform—related to building both social and neo-liberal states—may be disruptive of the very systems that moderate material rights and inequalities and produce a sustainable social order. Using neo-liberal governance to promote self-help even under the rubric of "peace" appears to lead to widening inequality, mirrored in a circumvention of the institutions of peacebuilding and the liberal state by a range of elites, and a distancing (or rejection) of the state by society in general. This also has the side-effect of allowing the state to be hijacked by predatory elites. It is indicative of an experimental, positivist (and methodologically unethical), insensitive, and internationally owned exercise of power rather than democratic accountability with the objective of a broadly just settlement. These dynamics are exaggerated in post-conflict settings where inequality is statistically at its highest, and self-help is least plausible. Variations of such dynamics may be seen around the world, from Liberia to Cambodia, from Bosnia to Timor-Leste.

The peace agreements in both Liberia and Sierra Leone, for example, followed the liberal rights framework and the neo-liberal developmental state model. Consequently, the post-conflict states that have been built have been very narrow in their remit and capacity. This has been a feature of modern state-building, which has sought to allow capital to do its work, while building only a very limited state apparatus sufficient to provide "good governance" through the rule of law and to offer security. However, these now appear to have been contradictory aims. A small state open to capital cannot provide security and development, and in particular, it cannot provide public services necessary to support human rights. During the 2013–2016 Ebola outbreak in West Africa, it became clear that states such as Liberia and Sierra Leone, both subjects of neo-liberal state-building, had not been designed to deal with medical crises common to the region. They simply did not have the public service capacity to respond to the crisis, because of the nature of the state design. Neo-liberal forms of state are not able to anticipate such security risks, and expect citizens to be sufficiently resilient to do so themselves. This assumption is problematic in an advanced economy; in a conflict-affected economy it has much more serious consequences. International support was required on a large scale to deal with West Africa's Ebola crisis, raising the question of what is the purpose of this type of state? Neo-liberal state-building disconnects the state from its historical and spatial context, and ultimately comes to depend on the charity of other states when crises arise; a fact which also has had the unfortunate effect of undermining the local capacity, and so social legitimacy, of these states. Indeed, these neo-liberal states have been designed bearing in mind the Northern priorities of efficiency and anti-corruption in the context of "good governance". Ironically, this model of state-building which focuses on security, deregulation, and capacity-building means, somewhat perversely, that these states can neither provide basic public services nor deal with crises without external assistance.[15] This has been seen in a range of recent crises that have affected conflict-affected sub-Saharan African states, which have had regional and global consequences. (On the political economy of peacebuilding in Liberia and Sierra Leone, see Omeje in this volume. On Sierra Leone, see also Rashid in this volume).

This is clear in the way that donor members of the Organisation for Economic Cooperation and Development (OECD), through its Development Assistance Committee (DAC), follow the mainstream neo-liberal, post–Washington Consensus on the probability that markets do not produce unintended consequences in post-conflict zones, and so widening inequality does not matter as long as growth is present within a rights-oriented legal system.[16] Yet the evidence from most sub-Saharan African states shows that for several reasons—including established power structures, differing systems of norms and governance, among other—liberal rights cannot be established under the conditions of neo-liberal capital. There has been a widespread realisation in the critical academic community that neo-liberal forms of capitalism undermine political rights even in stable states, because wealth concentrates in the hands of the few, allowing them to bypass law and its stipulation of legal equality and therefore, in effect, continue conflicts by other means.[17] Inequality exacerbates political competition over the distribution of scarce resources in any society, and is of course particularly problematic in post-conflict societies (such as in Liberia with its stratified society), where inequalities are already acute and weapons are widely available. (See Omeje in this volume.)

This perspective indicates that peacebuilding and state-building do not merely require strong legal and security capacities, or integration of material and identity forces, as represented by the state, into a bureaucratic set of political institutions to maintain order. This may produce state governance, but it may also depend upon a subjugated population, favouring powerful elites and high material inequality. In effect, it produces mixed continuities, with both colonial-era binaries of domination/subjugation, and North-South politics. Strong evidence exists that points to the need for social forms of legitimacy for democratic states, especially when they are built by external actors, if conflict is to be avoided.[18] Otherwise, contra Friedrich von Hayek's claim,[19] the state does not remain small and the market does not correct deficiencies; rather, the state/market formula becomes an instrument through which elites maintain a historical exploitation of society. As society resists the state, local agency mobilises, causing the state to revert to authoritarianism to maintain elite power (enabling the state, as camouflage, to claim it is following through on structural adjustment–style reform). This connects to the Weberian idea that the state is necessary to control the means of violence, but material inequality means that this control is open to co-optation by elites, as currently appears to be the case in many countries across Africa, from the Democratic Republic of the Congo (DRC) to Rwanda, and farther afield as in Cambodia and Bosnia-Herzegovina. For example, very high levels of inequality in the political economy of many conflict-affected African countries, such as the DRC, not only undermine the human rights of the population, but also enable political elites who have failed to bring about peace to maintain their rule by virtue of their material power and neo-patrimonial bypassing of democratic institutions.[20]

Implications for Peacebuilding in Africa

As a response to colonial conflicts and post-colonial transitions, as well as to authoritarian, nationalist, and ideological rule, the liberal peace framework appears to be plausible, especially in parallel to an economic development programme. Certainly, some kind of strategy has been required in response to the significant number of conflicts in Africa since 1990. One can understand why external actors would see local politics as the problem, one requiring external solutions (rather than the more post-colonial and anti-colonial theoretical view, which would reverse this understanding, with responsibility lying in historical external intervention and integrity in local models). In its early involvement in Africa in the post–Cold War environment, the UN facilitated the development of peacekeeping, as in Namibia (1989–1990) and Mozambique (1992–1994), away from a quasi-military and diplomatic system, towards one where the peace agreement and the UN's implementation of it were instrumental in the shaping of the constitutional framework of the new state, if not its very nature. Some form of military intervention was sometimes necessary, as in Sierra Leone (1999–2005), where there was experimentation by the UN with prevention, peace enforcement, and peacebuilding. (On security sector reform in Sierra Leone, see Rashid in this volume.) These doctrinal developments emerged in Africa and elsewhere in the world (the Balkans, for example), after the catastrophic genocide that ensued in Rwanda, in 1994, upon disengagement by a more traditional peacekeeping mission. (On the role of the UN Security Council in Africa, see Ugarte, and Gambari in this volume.)

All of these iterations in the evolution of the UN's peace paradigm have been tried out in the DRC, for example, in the shift from first-generation to multi-dimensional peacekeeping (from a basic peacekeeping mission aimed mainly at enforcing a ceasefire, to a peace operation with a more comprehensive mandate guided by the protection of human rights and democracy), and by the early 2000s, to peace enforcement (at least on paper), with the UN trying to use force to protect human rights and democracy; although the latter has proved to be a very difficult role. Promoting rights, democracy, and institutionalisation, alongside the rule of law, seems to have been used as a way of not engaging with very significant issues of development and control of the means of violence more directly. Indirectly, it came to be hoped by Western policy planners that building a "viable state" would eventually place the means of violence, corruption, rights, and matters of inequality within the control of the state. Despite the concerted engagement of the UN, EU, and many other donors with it, the case of the DRC indicates that state-building is not a viable approach, at least in the short to medium term, under the current liberal peace/neo-liberal state blueprint. Power, territory, land, borders, and resources are inextricably linked, meaning that any approach to peace that is predicated upon material inequality will tend to make sovereignty and related territorial disputes more visceral: neoliberal state-building would become the grounds for continuing violence, as seen most clearly in post-invasion Iraq since 2003.

What mattered more to external actors in the missions of the 1990s, after the failed intervention in Somalia (1992–1995), was that the core liberal states of the era—the US, Britain,[21] and France (see Rashid, Yates, and Adebajo in this volume)—stabilised the periphery as they saw it and maintained the veracity and legitimacy of their preferred approaches, using normative, legal, and constitutional frameworks projected through collective security mechanisms and international institutions. This meant that the international liberal architecture and the maintenance of the concept of the liberal state became more important than the "virtual" forms of peace on the ground in places like Somalia or Rwanda. Though this had elements of Northern dominance, reflecting the vanguardist leanings of these core liberal states, it also reflected a genuine belief in liberal democracy with its economic and social attributes and concurrent expectations for civil society and citizenship. It seemed possible that an international society was indeed coming into existence, tying citizens and states together in a common project, if only self-interest and predatory power could be tamed. Legal equality could compensate for material inequality under this system.

By the dawn of the twenty-first century, this picture had changed somewhat. There had been an anti-colonial-style backlash; security and economic development had not been as widely shared as many populations had hoped for; and the now mostly authoritarian and highly unequal states that had been brought into being were not competent enough to provide for the needs and rights of citizens in conflict-affected societies. Liberal peacebuilding had morphed into neo-liberal state-building as external actors backed away from the normative and rights elements of peacebuilding, and returned to security issues and the hope that global capital might succeed where more direct intervention had failed. The core international community was becoming seemingly less interested in welfare, services, and rights, and more focused on its own security and economic problems, leading to states with very limited rights and service-oriented cohesive capacity.

At the same time, social movements for rights and needs, as well as for some version of contextual identity, were becoming more organised, vocal, and mobile. There were a series of social movements, resistance processes, and even "revolutions" during and since the 2000s, many of them in favour of the liberal peace model, such as the "colour revolutions" of Eastern Europe in the 2000s, or the more recent popular uprisings across North Africa in 2010–2011. Individuals anywhere on the planet were suddenly able to use their access to the internet, for example, to work out the justice of their positionality vis-à-vis others, and this only accentuated the North-South divide and the internal class systems and their injustice for many. This also accentuated the divisions between predatory governments or elites and their populations. In Africa, this has played out in different ways across the continent. In some locations, liberal peacebuilding and neo-liberal state-building have been practiced, as in Sierra Leone, Liberia, and the DRC. Attempts have been made in countries such as South Sudan (see Deng in this volume), Burundi, and Mozambique focusing on diplomacy, elite agreements, some state reform, and piecemeal development efforts, with limited success. In other countries, such as Rwanda, a far less liberal version of the polity has emerged, mainly through the efforts of the local political elites, with international support. In Somalia and Somaliland, a very different permutation has arisen. None of the elite or externally driven contributions to peace or state-building have directly engaged with the underlying structural issues of inequality, instead focussing on security, development, or rights in ways that sidestep the materiality of peace and politics. Furthermore, these states, whether of international, elite, or social design, have been focused essentially on copying the neo-liberal model of statehood that emerged via the World Bank and IMF's legacy of the 1980s and 1990s, and that had broadly been taken up by all donors and the UN system by the 2000s.[22]

This was an answer to the politics—and age-old problem—of how material resources, starting with land and primary resources, and moving to taxation and private capital, may produce peace and development. In none of these cases has the peace become self-sustaining on the grounds of a just distribution of resources, but rather more because of power-sharing deals, authoritarianism, patrimonialism, and the like. In other words, politics has not been able to deal with the problem of peace within the system of global capital, but has maintained the latter by substituting power for justice, especially of the social kind. Hence the "big-man syndrome" of African politics mirrors the oligarchies of the West, which direct resources away from societies and towards favoured and often predatory elite enterprises that bring together patrimonialism with capitalism (or oligopoly) and sometimes the military-industrial sphere of the state.

Neo-liberal state-building, the most recent iteration of interventional practice, appears to pander to this authoritarian tendency that the modern neo-liberal state inadvertently makes possible, rendering authoritarian Singapore, for example, more of an acceptable model than say the more democratic United States or Britain. This might be normatively acceptable if it pointed to material redistribution, but this is not normally the case. Nor is such an approach capable of addressing regional conflicts or questions of distributive justice, not to mention historical restitution. Neo-liberal state-building has not been, in practice, suited to the complex local and regional conflicts on the African continent, and in fact can be seen as continuing to work in the interests of the former colonial powers and industrialised Northern states, by absolving them of any historical responsibility for material restitution. So the focus of peacebuilding, state-building, and development has been on knowledge transfer, in a disciplinary epistemological sense, in order to help build a bureaucratic and legal basis for rights, security, and development.[23] However, this approach has not been able to overcome historical or contemporary power relations and inequalities on the local and global scales, thus providing a weak basis for peace. Nor has it been able to generate states that are capable of dealing with contextual issues (witness the Ebola epidemic in West Africa, and the difficulty of, say, Sierra Leonean institutions in responding to it).

Somewhat problematically, Rwanda is often taken to be a good example of a desirable state-building outcome by Western planners and policymakers. Though its human rights record and military adventures across its western border with the Democratic Republic of the Congo are often criticised; Rwanda is also seen as a stable state that is reasonably democratic and focused on providing a peace dividend, developing a vibrant economy, and offering public services, education, and health in an accountable manner.[24] However, Rwanda also illustrates that state-building's normative dimension is secondary to its security, political, and economic architecture.

These areas are in a difficult system of balance, between the political claims made by conflict-affected populations (that is, the rights claimed by conflict-affected subjects) and the material resources made available by the state or international donors. But the exigencies of security and politics have meant that social and material dynamics are secondary to institutional design, even when the empirical evidence indicates that they are primary concerns for the population at large. In practice, the formal state often remains weak and incapable, is hijacked by previous state-formation elites who drove the war, or becomes endogenously donor-driven. As external actors have been unwilling to take complete control of post-conflict states without consent (for example, as in the case of Britain in Sierra Leone) (see also Rashid in this volume), they tend to be propped up by a mixture of external support allied with dominant and often problematic elites. In other words, their reality is a negative form of hybrid peace. Since the interventionary quagmires of the 2000s in Afghanistan and Iraq, an even more jaundiced version of state-building—a diluted, "good enough" version—has emerged.[25] Again, Rwanda, with its mix of an authoritarian and liberal state, is often presented as an example, on the basis that it offers hope that a stable present might lead to future reforms. This represents an uneasy compromise between mainstream state-formation approaches and state-building in order to stabilise existing inequalities.[26] At best, the root causes of conflict are not addressed, and the institutional framework of the state stabilises and benefits elites or existing power structures, enabling power-sharing but not an emancipatory peace, at least in the short to medium term.

Peacebuilding from Below

Indeed, much of the post-colonial raft of interventionary practices to build states and peace in Africa has been driven by Western preferences and ideology—indeed a neo-liberal imaginary of state-centric international order embedded in global capitalism—rather than an understanding of, or respect for, the organising principles of order in various African societies, and the often vertical cleavages of populist politics, ethnicity, and religion.[27] The politics of positionality in the global economy, and the experience of colonialism, are avoided at all costs. However, context is scalar and temporally complex (that is, physical geography no longer determines politics, and time cannot be guaranteed to nullify historical injustice), and so, it cannot be neatly delineated into horizontal levels of institutional organisation with the West at the apex. Furthermore, African conceptions of justice tend not to be rights-based nor guaranteed under law, as in the West, but rather more conservative and focused on mutual advantage or reciprocity and relationality.[28] However external actors may judge such a framework, it carries local legitimacy and cannot be ignored. The establishment of liberal versions of polity and law requires deep reform and long transitions, and may not in fact be the goal of African societies in general.

Related dynamics can be observed in Somalia, one of the longest-running failed states in modern times. (See Hirsch, and Mahiga in this volume.) After UN peacekeeping and US intervention failed in the country in the early 1990s in their attempt to create a showcase liberal state and set up a stable government, despite the clan and warlord alliance system, some security and marginal stability eventually emerged, in negative form. The conflict further led to the withdrawal of Somaliland (after a war between 1992 and 1996) and Puntland (in 1998 after a series of internal conferences convened partly because of frustration with the Somali state at the unstable situation in the rest of the country), and the emergence of their own state formation processes. Both Somaliland and Puntland have had a fair amount of success, completely based upon local resources and agency, without international support or recognition. Somaliland now has many of the attributes of a relatively peaceful state (fixed territory, borders, centralised governance, and some material means, and if not international recognition then respect).[29] Puntland, meanwhile, has become a self-governing territory awaiting the creation of a Somali federation. But the latter's peace is rather more negative, as Puntland is dominated by one particular clan and has some support from the international community. Even in rump Somalia, now long considered in Western circles as the most anarchic of places, local clan governance has emerged through local networks and organisations where the modern state and international actors are absent.[30] This is not to argue that the region has in any way moved away from direct or structural forms of conflict, or dealt with inequality at the social or material level, but there are interesting ways in which the social and political order is re-emerging, to the degree that it can through localised forms of governance with limited resources and international support. Indeed, it is telling that much of the policy and academic argumentation since the UN Operation in Somalia (UNOSOM) first started its mission, in 1992, has focused on the dysfunctional nature of security and political institutions in the state, as if the state was relevant to the positionality of the wider region in local and global political history and contemporary affairs. Likewise, the focus on political institutions and security matters has relegated the material and social questions faced by Somalis to a set of secondary concerns, as if these were not part of the conflict.

That said, some important institutions have been designed from below, according to existing power structures, identities, and networks, many of which are antithetical to Western liberalism. Indeed, Somali society is based on segregation, discrimination, and hierarchy, which means that in various ways inequality is part of its politics and history. Kenneth Menkhaus has described this as a "radical localisation" of politics via "informal, overlapping polities loosely held by clan leaders and others" also including elders, the business community, and clergy forming tense coalitions over power, resources, as well as judicial and law enforcement matters.[31] The centralised state has failed to stabilise or to provide order, security, development, or peace, but local peace-formation actors have been more successful in finding political arrangements, even if such arrangements are weak and temporary. Detailed formal agreements have been made and mediated between customary elders and district or state officials, however.[32] This has provided some level of social and material security, a rule of law, and a customary order, supported by elders, society, the business community, and even militias (as in Puntland and most obviously in Somaliland), through the Xeer framework of customary rules for cooperative responsibility.[33]

Indeed, respect for human dignity, equality, and non-discrimination have long been among the features of customary law in Somalia, even if society is organised along more segregated lines, as have norms of dialogue and a range of traditional conflict resolution methods required to negotiate differences in society.[34] This indicates that local peace actors could potentially form a state which is able to balance and mediate differences, as well as to mitigate against legal and economic inequality. It might well be argued that peace-formation would then work against external practices of liberal peacebuilding and neo-liberal state-building in Somalia.

The Challenge of Liberal Peacebuilding

A range of authors have long pointed to the pre-liberal dynamics that shape and nurture order, especially underlying cultural systems based upon reciprocity, justice, and participation, with institutions emerging from social experience rather than rational design.[35] Many point to the fragility of such processes, which did not evolve in the context of the modern military-industrial state or global capitalism (though they were affected by imperialism), but also to the need to base political institutions on society's common values and legitimacy (in a post-liberal sense).[36] Ultimately, this represents a fundamental challenge to Western conceptions of justice, institutions, and bureaucracy upon which the liberal order is assumed to rest. The imperialism, the global wars, and the unequal resource and knowledge distribution under globalisation of the past century are obvious concerns, not least because, from colonialism to globalisation, many of the West's preferred processes of development and progress have been disruptive in Africa, and have rarely been consented to by local populations. Relations over conflict management have generally been between external actors and "big men" or eminent elders, and social relations have not figured strongly in peace efforts governed in this way. The UN and the African Union (AU) have tended to follow this pattern, which in effect brings together elites who work to advance an order that often reflects their own interests and preferences. For this reason, social justice, historical justice, and distributive justice are not directly on the peace agenda, unless such forms of justice contribute to their own state or leadership projects.[37] Furthermore, global capitalism and neo-liberalism tend to encourage predatory elites rather than social movements for peace and development, as in many conflict-affected states (for example, Zimbabwe). Civil society has been disempowered by such a global framework for peace and development.

Thus, the state and the international architecture, in their liberal and neo-liberal forms, seem unable to produce state or regional settlements in Africa that support social forms of emancipation, connected to contextual dynamics; indeed, these settlements have led to a range of contradictory results, from ineffective and unsuitable international interventions to authoritarian and predatory states. Furthermore, it is probably fair to say that from the perspective of the IMF, World Bank, and donor community, such results have not been the aim, and authoritarian and unequal states have only been accepted in the short to medium term if they lead to security and to longer-term political and economic stability. But there is not much evidence that authoritarian and unequal states lay the ground for more emancipatory forms of governance.

Goran Hyden argues, contra liberal peacebuilding or neo-liberal state-building praxis, that restorative justice following, say, the example of South Africa's Truth and Reconciliation Commission is a more appropriate approach, because it is deliberative, creative, and empathetic, and connects communities to a broader associational life that the state should offer and that is part of African societies' history (which is also connected to Western critical thought).[38] From Kenya to Nigeria, the building of associational life is playing an increasing role in countering ethnic loyalties and neo-patrimonialism, and in preventing power-seekers from exploiting particularistic polarisation. Community peace councils have also played a role, as in Kenya and Ghana. Such approaches, however, run across the grain, intellectually and ideologically, as well as structurally, of liberal peace and global governance.

Indeed, some of the more critical literature has pointed to the alternative of localised peace movements, as in South Africa during the collapse of the apartheid system. However, it was ambiguous as to whether peace infrastructures formed from the top down following the liberal preferences of some elite groups interested in reconciliation within a liberal state model, or from localised peace-formation movements more focused on issues of inequality and poverty. In South Africa, racial segregation from 1948 to 1994 had meant that rights, associations, and movements were limited for the majority of society, with material consequences.[39]

In Kenya, ethnic and identity conflicts, as well as political unrest since the introduction of multi-party politics to replace one-party rule (see Wamai in this volume), have also resulted in the emergence of peace infrastructures since the early 1990s, when ad hoc local peace committees formed from women's groups, which also incorporated elders into a clan-based mediation process.[40] This model, first tried in Wajir district, soon proliferated across the country, after which donors began to support the process in the hope that they may begin to influence elite politics and, in particular, its inability to deal with longer-standing identity issues. A number of different models emerged for the local peace committees, some democratically run and led, with others run by a district commissioner.[41] However, a problem with such approaches is that they remain in the discursive realm, and have little impact on hard security or material problems. Globalisation, the introduction of Chinese and other sources of capital from the BRICS countries (Brazil, Russia, India, China, and South Africa), as well as the presence of patrimonial elites means that such approaches to peace have not been able to engage with power and material inequality, perhaps other than mitigating their localised effects to a degree. Indeed, the closer the peace committees move into the state, the more they experience power struggles that are configured by, rather than combating, conflict.[42] This is also mirrored by the tension between local legitimacy and inclusiveness, which is often not a significant feature of the interactions of highly localised systems, relating in particular to gender relations, identity, or the position of youth in society. (On women, gender, and peacebuilding, see Porter in this volume.) Of course, this is also to be expected: the process is also shaped by structural imperatives.

These peace-formation processes offer some direction for peacebuilding itself, but they cannot deal with basic and structural inequality. They cannot confront directly and quickly the sources of conflict, whether those sources lie in predatory elites, states, dysfunctional social processes, or global arms and capital flows. This surely would be the role of international actors, who since the end of the Cold War have made some progress, but with obvious shortcomings: security is patchy, states are weak, development is slow, and the provision of rights is thus also limited.

Conclusion

The evidence so far suggests that neo-liberal states are ill-equipped to deal with conflict and make peace, even under international tutelage, because their institutions are too weak to prevent competition spilling over into violence, or to redress historical inequality. Indeed, such states may provoke more inequality, which weakens the links between civil society, solidarity, social justice, human rights, and democracy. Even when social and peace-formation processes are mobilised, they can do no more than mitigate power relations until there is structural change, such as the construction of an enabling state and of concerted support among external actors for localised networks focused on peace, human rights, development, and material improvement. The lack of a range of peace dividends under the framework of neo-liberal state-building discourages integration and consensus-building. Such a critique contradicts much of the received wisdom about democratic peace and its relationship with capitalism. Current approaches mask a great deal of inequality and poverty correlated in many cases to low economic growth, crime, political unrest, as well as embedded structural violence—all key factors in provoking conflict. Thus, the World Economic Forum of 2012 stated that inequality was a major "global risk".[43] New rationalities (individualism, property rights, consumerism) displace established patterns of legitimate authority with perhaps insufficient regard for the disruption this may cause. Approaches to peacebuilding and state-building, to be worth their names in ethical terms, must deal with inequalities arising from colonialism and imperialism, from the demise of the welfare state, and from the inequalities arising from unfettered global capitalism.

Notes

1. David Harvey, *A Brief History of Neoliberalism* (Oxford: Oxford University Press, 2005).
2. John Rawls, "The Law of Peoples", *Critical Inquiry* 20, no. 1 (Autumn 1993), pp. 36–68.
3. *See, for example*, Jean-Jacques Rousseau, *Discourse on the Origin of Inequality* (Indianapolis, IN: Hackett, 1992 [1755]); Thomas Piketty, *Capital in the Twenty-First Century* (Cambridge: Harvard University Press, 2014).
4. Piketty, *Capital in the Twenty-First Century.*
5. Nancy Birdsall, "Rising Inequality in the New Global Economy", World Institute for Development Economics Research (WIDER), United National University, *WIDER Angle* no. 2 (2005), pp. 1–3.
6. *See* United Nations Development Programme (UNDP) Human Development Indices (HDI) spanning 1997 to the present. Note that for many developing countries, the data are incomplete. Since 2011, an inequality-adjusted HDI has also been calculated.
7. UNDP HDI spanning 1997 to the present.
8. Andy Sumner and Meera Tiwari, "Global Poverty Reduction to 2015 and Beyond: What Has Been the Impact of the MDGs and What Are the Options for a Post-2015 Global Framework?", Working Paper no. 348 (Sussex: Institute for Development Studies, 2010); Jan Vandemoortele, "The MDG Conundrum: Meeting the Targets Without Missing the Point", *Development Policy Review* 27, no. 4 (June 2009), pp. 355–371.
9. *See* Charles Mutasa and Mark Peterson (eds.), *Africa and the Millennium Development Goals* (Lanham, MD: Rowman and Littlefield, 2015).
10. *See* Oliver P. Richmond, *Failed Statebuilding: Intervention, the State, and the Dynamics of Peace Formation* (New Haven, CT: Yale University Press, 2014), Appendix 1.
11. *See, for example*, http://www.fundforpeace.org/global/?q=fsi (1 June 2015); and http://www.freedomhouse.org/report/freedom-world/freedom-world-2013 (1 June 2015).
12. *See, for example*, http://hdr.undp.org/en/statistics/ihdi (1 June 2015).
13. James K. Galbraith, "Inequality, Unemployment, and Growth: New Measures for Old Controversies", *Journal of Economic Inequality* 7, no. 2 (June 2009), pp. 189–206, especially p. 206.
14. Robert Skidelsky, *Keynes: The Return of the Master* (London: Penguin, 2009), p. 123.
15. Sue Ingram, *Statebuilding: Key Concepts and Operational Implications in Fragile States: The Case of Sierra Leone and Liberia* (Washington, DC: World Bank; and New York: UNDP, 2011).
16. Organisation for Economic Cooperation and Development–Development Assistance Committee (OECD-DAC), *Supporting Statebuilding in Situations of Conflict and Fragility: Policy Guidance* (Paris, 2011).

17. *See, for example,* Martin Gilens and Benjamin I. Page, "Testing Theories of American Politics: Elites, Interest Groups, and Average Citizens", *Perspectives on Politics* 12, no. 3 (2014), pp. 564–581.
18. Adam Przeworski, Michael Alvarez, Jose Antonio Cheibub, and Fernando Limongi, *Democracy and Development* (Cambridge: Cambridge University Press, 2000); Richard Sandbrook, Marc Edelman, Patrick Heller, and Judith Teichman, *Social Democracy in the Global Periphery: Origins, Challenges, Prospects* (Cambridge: Cambridge University Press 2007), pp. 67–89.
19. Friedrich von Hayek, "The Meaning of the Welfare State", in Christopher Pierson and Francis G. Castles (eds.), *The Welfare State Reader* (Cambridge: Polity, 2000), pp. 90–95.
20. Chukwuma Obidegwu, "Post-Conflict Peace Building in Africa: The Challenges of Socio-Economic Recovery and Development", Africa Region Working Paper Series no. 73, World Bank, Washington, DC, October 2004.
21. Britain is used synonymously with the United Kingdom (UK) in this volume.
22. For an excellent analysis of North-South relations, *see* Vijay Prashad, *The Poorer Nations: A Possible History of the Global South* (London: Verso, 2012).
23. Bertrand Badie, *The Imported State: The Westernisation of the Political Order* (Stanford, CA: Stanford University Press, 2000), p. 2.
24. Confidential interview with author, United Nations Peacebuilding Support Office (PBSO), New York, 10 February 2012.
25. World Bank, *World Bank Development Report 2011* (Washington, DC, 2011).
26. Robin Luckham and Tom Kirk, "The Two Faces of Security in Hybrid Political Orders", *Stability: International Journal of Stability and Development* 2, no. 2 (2013), pp. 1–30.
27. Goran Hyden, "Rethinking Justice and Institutions in African Peacebuilding", *Third World Quarterly* 36, no. 5 (2015), p. 1008.
28. Hyden, "Rethinking Justice and Institutions", p. 1013.
29. Mark Bradbury and Sally Healy, "Whose Peace Is It Anyway? Connecting Somali and International Peacemaking", *Accord: An International Review of Peace Initiatives* no. 21, Conciliation Resources, London, 2010, p. 11.
30. Christopher Clapham, "Peacebuilding Without a State: The Somali Experience", in Devon Curtis and Gwinyayi A. Dzinesa (eds.), *Peacebuilding, Power, and Politics in Africa* (Athens: Ohio University Press, 2012); Jutta Bakonyi, "Authority and Administration Beyond the State: Local Governance in Southern Somalia, 1995–2006", *Journal of Eastern African Studies* 7, no. 2 (2013), pp. 272–290.
31. Roland Marchal and Ken Menkhaus, *Somalia Human Development Report 1998* (Nairobi: UNDP, October 1998), p. 18.
32. Tobias Hagmann, "Bringing the Sultan Back In: Elders as Peacemakers in Ethiopia's Somali Region", in Lars Buur and Helene Maria Kyed, *State Recognition and the Democratisation of Sub-Saharan Africa* (London: Palgrave, 2007), pp. 6, 18.
33. Haroon Yusuf and Robin Le Mare, "Clan Elders as Conflict Mediators", in Catherine Barnes, "Weaving the Web: Civil Society Roles in Working with Conflict and Building Peace", in Paul van Tongeren, Malin Brenk, Marte Hellema, and Juliette Verhoeven (eds.), *People Building Peace II: Successful Stories of Civil Society* (Boulder, CO: Lynne Rienner, 2005), p. 460.

34. Mohamed Abdi Mohamed, "The Role of Somali Women in Search of Peace", in United Nations Educational, Scientific, and Cultural Organisation (UNESCO), *Women and Peace in Africa* (Paris, 2003), pp. 87–94.
35. On institutions emerging from social experience, *see* Hyden, "Rethinking Justice and Institutions", p. 1018.
36. Hyden, "Rethinking Justice and Institutions", p. 1007. *See also* Oliver P. Richmond, *A Post-Liberal Peace* (London: Routledge, 2011).
37. Hyden, "Rethinking Justice and Institutions", p. 1012.
38. Hyden, "Rethinking Justice and Institutions", p. 1019.
39. Nicole Ball, "Managing Conflict: Lessons from the South African Peace Committees", (Washington, DC: United States Agency for International Development [USAID], Centre for Development and Evaluation, 1988); Oliver P. Richmond, *Peace Formation and Political Order* (Oxford: Oxford University Press), 2016.
40. Tanja Chopra, "When Peacebuilding Contradicts Statebuilding: Notes from the Arid Lands of Kenya", *International Peacekeeping* 16, no. 4 (2009), p. 532.
41. Cited in Andries Odendaal, *A Crucial Link: Local Peace Committees and National Peacebuilding* (Washington, DC: United States Institute of Peace, 2013), p. 40.
42. Odendaal, *A Crucial Link*, p. 42.
43. World Economic Forum (WEF), *Global Risks 2012*, seventh edition (Geneva: WEF, 2012), p. 18, www3.weforum.org/docs/WEF_GlobalRisks_Report_2012.pdf (accessed 22 July 2016).

CHAPTER 18

Women, Gender, and Peacebuilding

Antonia Porter

As the issue of gender receives increasing attention globally and within Africa from mainstream domains that previously dismissed it as a "soft" issue, a distraction, or an inconvenient "box to tick", the complexities and contestations involved in making sense of gender, and achieving equality in this area, have emerged concomitantly. Perhaps attention and complexity are always bedfellows. Certainly, growing societal attention to, and awareness of, gender equality as a priority have not yet meant that seemingly straightforward policies around stopping discrimination and increasing women's participation are any more easily achieved. What is needed to respond to slow progress, misinterpretation, and backlash is a far more radical and personal approach than the mainstream discourses around gender equality in Africa and worldwide have so far included. The connection between the personal and the political, particularly in relation to—but not limited to—gender, needs to be acknowledged and explored to a far greater extent by all of us, and particularly by those with social, political, or economic power. The relationship between structural violence such as that resulting from patriarchy, and the physical violence of war, must be recognised, and this awareness should be reflected in the ways in which we seek to build peace. African feminist perspectives on militarism need to be taken seriously within the traditional peace and security domains, as does the need to value the feminine. We must turn power upside down for the benefit of all: for example, to develop the nascent focus on men and masculinities in gender equality and broader peacebuilding work, and to pay attention to, support financially, and be guided by the perspectives of grassroots women's groups that are showing success at building peace and equality.

These are some of the topics that are touched upon in this chapter. I begin with a description of the gender, peace, and security architecture in Africa, as

A. Porter (✉)
Independent Consultant, Cape Town, South Africa

T. Karbo, K. Virk (eds.), *The Palgrave Handbook of Peacebuilding in Africa*, https://doi.org/10.1007/978-3-319-62202-6_18

reflected in the policy frameworks of the African Union (AU) and Africa's sub-regional bodies, as well as major international policy frameworks, such as United Nations (UN) Security Council Resolution 1325 of 2000, as they pertain to the continent. I look, in particular, at the Southern African Development Community (SADC), the East African Community (EAC), the Intergovernmental Authority on Development (IGAD), the Economic Community of West African States (ECOWAS), and the International Conference on the Great Lakes Region (ICGLR). After a brief interrogation of perspectives on the numerical representation of women in peace and security structures, since this is the means through which equality is so often perceived as secured, I look at research on women in African peacekeeping missions, focusing on the South African National Defence Force (SANDF), before briefly exploring feminist perspectives on militarism. Building on the discussion, I next turn to describing four main ideas for advancing progress towards gender equality in the making, keeping and building of sustainable peace in Africa. Finally, I conclude by outlining seven recommendations on how to translate these ideas into practice on the continent, aimed at contributing productively to building peace and harmony for all in Africa and in our complex world.

Gender, Peace, and Security Architecture in Africa: Regional and Global Frameworks

Gender—at least as it pertains to women and as shown by policy instruments—is an area that seems to have been taken seriously by African institutions at the continental and regional levels, as well as at the national level in several countries (such as South Africa and Rwanda).[1] Even though their monitoring, implementation, and impact have been weak (as discussed later), the frameworks that exist are nonetheless important to consider, as they delineate a country or region's intentions for equality.

The Continental Level

At the continental level, the African Union's concern for gender equality mostly emerges through various policy instruments on gender equality and women's rights on the one hand, and through elements of its peace and security policies on the other.[2] The AU established the Women, Gender, and Development Directorate in 2000, to oversee implementation of its gender architecture, as well as to implement practical work on gender equality and the empowerment of African women.[3] The continental-level gender architecture consists of several instruments including, first and foremost, the AU's Constitutive Act of 2000, which enshrines the promotion of gender equality as a fundamental principle.[4] The New Partnership for Africa's Development (NEPAD), created in 2001, also places some emphasis on women in its provisions.[5] Unsurprisingly, a central element of Africa's gender architecture is the 2003 Protocol on the Rights of Women in Africa, part of the African Charter on Human and Peoples' Rights.

This protocol is the first comprehensive legally binding instrument on the promotion and protection of women's human rights in Africa.[6] It also supports the use of affirmative action to ensure the equal participation of women in politics.[7] The protocol had been ratified by 37 of the AU's 55 member states as of January 2017.[8] Another critical element is the Solemn Declaration on Gender Equality in Africa (SDGEA) of 2004, which strives to keep gender issues alive at the highest political level on the continent.[9]

Furthermore, the AU established a Gender Policy and Action Plan in 2009 with eight target areas.[10] The action plan sets its member states a target of 50/50 representation of women and men in politics and decision-making by 2020, which provides a numerical target for the intentions set out in Article 9 of the 2003 Protocol on the Rights of Women, Commitment 5 of the 2004 SDGEA, and UN Security Council Resolution 1325 of 2000.[11] The gender policy contains a commitment to the building of an enabling environment to ensure that all political declarations and decisions made by the AU foster the elimination of barriers that provide obstacles to achieving gender equality and women's empowerment.[12] The policy also includes specific references to peace and security issues. It commits to involving women in mediation processes, and to working in collaboration with the UN and certain AU organs to build truth and reconciliation structures that will reveal human rights violations against women and girls that occur during conflict.[13] Moreover, five of the ten commissioners of the AU Commission are women,[14] and efforts are being made towards achieving gender parity in other AU organs and institutions, such as the African Commission on Human and Peoples' Rights (ACHPR), and the African Court on Human and Peoples' Rights (AfCHPR). Regardless of one's confidence in the degree to which placing women in leadership positions, or achieving gender parity, may contribute towards achieving gender *equality*, the efforts made by the AU in these regards are notable, even if not sufficient, as I explore later in this chapter.

The AU also set up the Fund for African Women in 2010, which has been implemented at the national level through the creation of National Gender Equality Funds.[15] Several campaigns have also been organised by the AU over the past years, such as the Africa UNiTE Campaign to End Violence Against Women—the regional component of the UN Secretary-General's global campaign—which was launched during the AU heads-of-state summit in January 2010. Notably, the AU has declared 2010 to 2020 to be the African Women's Decade (AWD). The implementation of the AWD is taking place in two phases, with the first covering the period 2011–2015 and the second 2016–2020. In June 2014, the AU launched a Gender, Peace, and Security Programme (2015–2020) to oversee implementation of UN Security Council Resolution 1325, as well as later Council resolutions, on women, peace and security, across the African Peace and Security Architecture (APSA) (see Kuwali in this volume).[16] The AU also declared 2015 as the Year of Women's Empowerment and Development Towards Africa's *Agenda 2063*.[17] The AU's gender directorate has since undertaken a mid-point evaluation to assess AU member states' progress in implementing the first phase of the AWD,[18] and to present portraits of progress made towards gender equality in each African country. A status update on this evaluation was submitted at the July 2017 AU summit.[19] During 2017, the gender directorate is reviewing the current AU gender policy and developing a new gender strategy to inform implementation of its future activities,[20] to ensure that both are aligned with *Agenda 2063*.[21] The July 2017 AU summit also agreed upon the operationalisation of a Pan-African Network of Women Mediators, as a subsidiary body of the Panel of the Wise.

The Regional Level

The AU has assisted Africa's regional economic communities (RECs) and mechanisms in harmonising global and regional frameworks for gender equality, by translating various resolutions and commitments into relevant policies and actions. Each REC has a dedicated gender unit, with declarations and means for gender mainstreaming.[22] However, progress in both policy frameworks and implementation varies considerably across African sub-regions. For example, the AU notes that the International Conference on the Great Lakes Region has focused on the prevention of sexual and gender-based violence (SGBV). This may owe, in part, to the combination of high levels of fragility and SGBV in the Great Lakes region;[23] and in part, to the strong presence of women's groups and networks, such as Uganda's Isis-WICCE (Isis-Women's International Cross Cultural Exchange), who urged for this emphasis. In contrast, the Intergovernmental Authority on Development and the Southern African Development Community have placed emphasis on women's participation in decision-making.[24]

SADC, in particular, has made significant efforts to address gender equality as a regional economic community. It established a Gender Unit in 1998 that is responsible for working with national gender machineries that have been set up in all the member states, and to ensure that gender is mainstreamed into the overall SADC Programme of Action and the SADC Programme of Action and Community Building Initiative, which spanned 2008 to 2015.[25] In 2008, SADC adopted a Protocol on Gender and Development,[26] a unique instrument that brought together both African and international goals on gender equality, and applied targets and timeframes to them: additions that the other 22 SADC protocols did not have. Although Botswana and Mauritius had not yet signed the Gender Protocol at the time, it entered into force in September 2012 after nine countries had ratified it.[27] Lobbied by the Southern Africa Gender Protocol Alliance[28] to align the Gender Protocol with the Sustainable Development Goals (SDGs), the Beijing Plus Twenty Review, and the AU's *Agenda 2063*, SADC gender ministers agreed to review the protocol at their 2014 annual meeting in Malawi. A year later the gender ministers agreed that the Gender Protocol should be accordingly aligned,[29] and in August 2016 SADC heads of state signed the Post-2015 SADC Gender Protocol.[30]

The updated protocol uses stronger language in terms of rights relating to sexual reproductive health and child marriage, and refers to "eliminating", rather than merely "halving", gender-based violence.[31] The outside deadline for reaching all the protocol's objectives is 2030, in alignment with the deadline for achieving the SDGs.[32] Article 28 of the 2008 SADC Gender Protocol focused on peacebuilding and conflict resolution. Interestingly, the updated protocol includes a specific reference also to peacekeeping, as opposed to just conflict resolution and peacebuilding processes.[33] The protocol also urges state parties "to take the necessary steps during armed and other forms of conflict to prevent and eliminate incidences of human rights abuses, especially of women and children, and ensure that the perpetrators of such abuses are brought to justice before a court of competent jurisdiction".[34]

Although other RECs and regional mechanisms in Africa may not have achieved as much as SADC in terms of their translation of international and continental commitments to gender equality into policies and strategies, or commitment of resources to carry out gender work,[35] several have made significant progress in recent years. In March 2017, the EAC finally enacted a Gender Equality, Equity, and Development Bill, which had been sitting on the East African Legislative Assembly's (EALA) table since 2008. The EAC also launched a Gender Barometer in May 2017, which is a participatory, people-centred report from its member states with information and statistical data on gender equality conditions in areas such as the media, education, and health.[36] Furthermore, the EAC's Peace and Security Unit, and Gender Unit, are jointly working on a Regional Implementation Plan on UN Security Council Resolution 1325 for 2015–2019.[37]

IGAD would also at first glance seem to hold gender equality as a priority area: it established a gender desk at its secretariat as early as 1999.[38] An IGAD Gender Policy and Strategy was formulated and launched in 2004, and a new one has since been developed for 2016–2020, which outlines interventions to be undertaken by all staff, not merely the Gender Affairs Programme. Various additional efforts towards equality have been made since then, and in 2014 IGAD formally adopted a Regional Action Plan (RAP) for the implementation of UN Security Council Resolution 1325, although it continues to struggle with resources for implementation, such as helping member states develop National Action Plans (NAPs).[39] In 2015, IGAD established the Women and Peace Forum,[40] with the central goal of enhancing women's stewardship of the gender agenda in peacebuilding and conflict resolution in Eastern Africa and the Horn of Africa. Feminists have pointed out, though, that gender is not highlighted in IGAD's overall mission, vision, or objectives of the organisation.[41] Other than IGAD, the Economic Community of West African States is the only other REC to adopt a 1325 Regional Action Plan. There have been determined efforts by ECOWAS to bring about the mainstreaming of women's concerns in the West African regional peace architecture. An important accomplishment is that West Africa has the largest concentration of 1325 National Action Plans: 12 of the 15 ECOWAS member states (excluding Cape Verde, Benin, and Niger) have such action plans in various stages of implementation.

Other regional bodies related to the AU have also made efforts to address gender, peace, and security, some of which have been particularly lauded by some African feminists. One such body is the International Conference on the Great Lakes Region: this is an inter-governmental organisation of 11 countries[42] established in 2003 to address the regional dimension of conflicts impacting the Great Lakes region. The ICGLR initiated the Protocol on the Prevention and Suppression of Sexual Violence Against Women and Children in 2007, with the aim of addressing gaps in the respective laws of its member states around the prevention of rape of women and children.[43] The ICGLR also adopted model legislation on prevention and suppression of sexual violence against women and children, which identifies connections between sexual violence, trafficking, slavery, genocide, and war crimes. This was the first legislation in the area of protection against sexual violence in conflict and post-conflict environments in Africa.[44]

The Global Level

Beyond continental and regional efforts, there are various international policy frameworks that have been created to stop violence against women, achieve gender equality, and recognise the role of women in peacebuilding. These include the 1979 Convention on the Elimination of All Forms of Discrimination Against Women (CEDAW), which demands quotas and other measures to increase the number of women in political decision-making positions; the 1994 Dakar Platform for Action; and the 1995 Beijing Platform for Action, which is generally considered to be a turning point in the advancement of the rights of women.[45] Nine UN Security Council Resolutions with specific provisions on women, peace, and security have also been passed since 2000, which are applicable to Africa. Of these, the most renowned is still Resolution 1325 of 2000, which emphasises the importance of women's "equal participation and full involvement in all efforts for the maintenance and promotion of peace and security".[46] The resolution also recognises the need for mainstreaming a gender perspective in peacekeeping operations.[47] This landmark resolution has been followed by eight additional resolutions on women, peace, and security.[48] In addition to the gender and security–focused resolutions adopted by the UN Security Council, SDG 5 (following Millennium Development Goal [MDG] 3), aims to achieve gender equality and empower all women and girls worldwide.

"Quota Fever" and the Problem of Overemphasis on Mere Numerical Representation

While the various international, continental, and regional efforts broadly aimed at achieving gender equality are important—even apparently progressive and explicit—recognition of gender injustices reflected in legislation is not sufficient to transform and eliminate gender inequalities at a fundamental level.

Interestingly, the overall approach to gender taken by the AU, UN, and other inter-governmental bodies has been criticised by African feminists at the Nairobi-based African Leadership Centre for evolving "separately and as an additive to governance debates".[49] The Centre implies that the general separation between security and gender equality suggests that supposedly innovative security paradigms are not as transformative and relevant as they are touted to be.[50]

Perhaps most significant, as noted by Ugandan analyst Joyce Laker,[51] among other African feminists, too often the notion of women's involvement has merely been translated into an emphasis on filling quotas for women, or an expectation that gender parity will somehow achieve gender equality. While UN Security Council Resolution 1325 has enabled greater representation of women in decision-making structures in Africa, particularly in post-conflict countries such as Burundi, Liberia, Mozambique, Rwanda, and South Africa, as well as an increase in the proportion of women in national parliaments, this has not translated into greater overall equality between the sexes: this requires far more than merely a greater numerical representation of women. Many feminists, such as British scholar Donna Pankhurst and Indian theorist Aruna Rao,[52] have argued that large institutions and policymaking bodies worldwide, including those that are responsible for governance, and building, making, or keeping peace, are masculine in culture and practice, rather than gender-neutral. Consequently, as I have noted in earlier work (with South African researcher Elizabeth Otitodun),[53] despite increasing numbers of women staff and even leaders, state bureaucracies and international bodies operate according to masculine norms, with hierarchical structures.

An interesting case that feminists have paid attention to in recent years is the practice of injecting greater numbers of women into peace support operations. Although the representation of women among uniformed UN peacekeeping personnel (as opposed to civilian personnel) globally is still very small, at only about 4.4 per cent, there has been an increase of 243 per cent between August 2006 (when there were 1,235 women) and June 2017 (when there were 4,240 women).[54] Similarly, the number of women in African national militaries and peacekeeping forces is slowly but gradually increasing. For example, by 2015, the South African National Defence Force had met its gender equity target of the force constituting 30 per cent women, while female representation in the defence forces of Namibia and Zimbabwe stood at 23 per cent and 20 per cent respectively.[55] Zambian feminist scholar Yaliwe Clarke suggests that the global peace and security agenda has compelled African military structures to *purport* an interest in the needs of women.[56] However, this concern seems largely to manifest only as an intention for increasing the numbers of female peacekeepers, and the focus, furthermore, has mainly been on South African peacekeepers, as observed by South African scholar-activist Cheryl Hendricks.[57] The conventional arguments put forward for involving greater numbers of women in peacekeeping forces include the ideas that women are better than men at interacting with local communities (especially with other women, and children); that the incidence of gender-based and sexual violence will decrease due to the presence of women peacekeepers, while local women's access to services will increase; that the overall capacity of local women will be strengthened, including in the domain of politics; that community relations will improve; that traditional views that marginalise women will be dismantled;[58] and that misconduct by male soldiers will lessen.[59]

Most of these assumptions rest on essentialist ideas of women,[60] and have been proven incorrect. Research among male and female South African peacekeepers returning from missions in the Democratic Republic of the Congo (DRC) and South Sudan, for example, has shown that women peacekeepers felt that locals actually placed more trust in *male* peacekeepers.[61] Women peacekeepers also reported that they were not able to gather much information on the specific security concerns of women in local communities or to assist sexual violence survivors, because their pre-mission training included very little emphasis on gender.[62] Misconduct by men still seems to take place, even with women peacekeepers present. Moreover, women peacekeepers reported being mocked for their lesser physical strength and endurance, and even faced many forms of sexual harassment within these armed forces and in local communities. As South African scholar Lindy Heinecken maintains, even when national armed forces promote gender equality, women are under pressure to take on masculine values so as to be identified as "good" soldiers.[63] Yaliwe Clarke observes that this adoption of masculine roles by women in militaries results in an entrenchment, rather than a transformation, of traditional sexist ideologies.[64] Another South African scholar exploring the role of women peacekeepers in the SANDF, Angela Nicole Alchin, suggests that the main problem is that the hegemonic masculine culture of militaries promotes the building of a soldier identity in which only masculine qualities are allowed.[65] Alchin maintains that what is required is to give femininity equal priority to masculinity—a topic this chapter will return to later. (See also Mulindwa and Siwali in this volume.)

These findings and research speak to feminist work on militarism, which as it relates to Africa has been pioneered by Nigerian feminist Amina Mama. The concept of militarism is grounded in the recognition that war and conflict are simply an explicit expression of ongoing structural violence along fault-lines of gender, ethnicity, and class, and that violent conflict is the crudest form of militarism.[66] Implicit is the idea that in a patriarchal world there is no such thing as "peacetime", for patriarchy itself is violent, and ultimately produces behaviour that is termed "armed conflict" or "war". Indeed, there is the view that the recent discourse and specific focus on sexual violence and rape as a "weapon of war", apparent in the later UN resolutions on women, peace, and security, and other such policy frameworks,[67] is problematic because it implies that such types of violence are features only of "wartime", when in fact, as Kenyan feminist scholar Awino Okech states, for women "the distinction between 'war' and 'peace' is false. Their experience of violence is not restricted to situations of conflict".[68] The everyday forms of violence against women at home and in the streets, workplace, and community, are still not visible enough. Amina Mama maintains that militarism "reifies polarised gender relations and gender identities, and particular notions of masculinity and masculine prowess seem to be bound up with gender-based violence, which threatens women's security".[69] She claims that militarisation, and all the pervasive political, social, cultural, and economic effects of military institutions, discourses, and practices are fundamental impediments to Africa's progress. Accordingly, the idea that progress towards gender equality can be made through adding women peacekeepers to peacekeeping missions in Africa is antithetical to feminist perspectives on militarism. As Clarke asks: "[I]s there any critique of the militarised masculinities that are key to militarism, or indeed ... exploration of the possibility that these may in fact be a root source of violence and conflict, obstructing any hope for the attainment of security?"[70] While such explorations have undoubtedly expanded since 2008 when this question was framed, they have not yet led to serious efforts to transform militarised masculinities within militaries or peacekeeping forces.

Addressing Gender Inequalities and Building Peace in Africa: A Radical, Personal, and Trans-Disciplinary Approach Required

In July 2016 the AU produced a list of recommendations of what needs to be done at national, regional, continental, and international levels to advance the women, peace, and security agenda on the continent. Many of these are highly technical recommendations. The list includes recommendations such as developing predictable, accessible, and flexible funding mechanisms and instruments for local women's organisations and networks; building a critical mass of centres of excellence and research/academic institutions engaging in research and capacity-building on women, peace, and security; and enhancing the demand and utilisation of women mediators rosters.[71] This chapter endorses the recommendations made by the AU, and suggests some additional theoretical, and arguably unorthodox, recommendations, with associated practical implications.

Greater Focus on Transforming Militarised Masculinities

Greater emphasis needs to be placed on transforming militarised masculinities for gender equality to be achieved on the continent, a point I have emphasised in earlier work on masculinities in post-conflict societies in Africa.[72] Gender is still too often perceived as referring only to women's issues. Some international commitments, such as the 1994 International Conference on Population and Development and the 1995 Beijing Platform for Action,[73] for example, stress the importance of working with men for gender equality, and of involving men in eradicating gender stereotypes, although most gender policies in Africa to date, excluding the 2008 SADC Gender Protocol, do not make specific mention of the importance of engaging men. As noted earlier in this chapter, neither do they deal radically enough with militarism and the ramifications of military institutions. As Clarke has noted, security sector reform processes could provide an excellent opportunity to work towards transforming masculinities and cultures of militarism.[74]

Since 2012, on behalf of the MenEngage Africa Alliance, the South Africa-based non-governmental organisation (NGO) Sonke Gender Justice has been conducting a Regional Bodies Policy Advocacy project. This includes various activities to engage the AU and Africa's RECs, with a particular focus on SADC and the EAC, on the basis that regional policies are key to the goal of building the impact of work with men and boys to address gender inequalities.[75] Importantly, during the past few decades, a rapidly growing field of practical initiatives that strive to engage men and boys to address gender equality, and even, purportedly, to transform masculinities, has emerged worldwide, including in Africa.[76] However, much more is needed at theoretical, policy, and programmatic levels.

Recognise the Value of Grassroots Women's and Local Gender-Focused Groups in Africa to a Far Greater Extent, and Provide Associated Financial Support

Linked to various themes identified later in this section, such as the need to value the feminine and associated qualities such as flexibility and collaboration, and the importance of making the personal political and vice versa, is the need for greater recognition of, and financial support for, grassroots and local women's and gender-focused groups on the continent that work on peacebuilding. It must be acknowledged that the AU and even the RECs have increased their recognition of, meaningful engagement with, and support for local women's groups in recent years. For example, the AU Commission and its Women, Gender, and Development Directorate partner with the Gender Is My Agenda Campaign (GIMAC), a network of more than 55 civil society organisations that promote gender equality and accountability for women's rights.[77] The 30th GIMAC consultative meeting was held on 27–28 June 2017, ahead of the AU summit in June–July 2017 focusing on youth. Other important work supported by the AU with women's groups includes the Women's Situation Rooms (WSRs): a process initiated and led by women's groups that mobilises women and youth to address the gendered nature of electoral violence for women as candidates and voters.[78] In the WSRs, women are involved in peace advocacy, intervention, coordination, political analysis, observation, and documentation.[79]

The July 2016 AU list of recommendations includes the recommendation that "flexible funding mechanisms for local women's organisations and networks should be developed".[80] This chapter strongly endorses this recommendation, and calls for even greater recognition and support for grassroots women's groups not only by the AU but also by international donors, national governments, and inter-governmental organisations such as the UN. Local women's and gender-focused groups in Africa have the capacity to act as critical agents of change in transforming gender relations and building sustainable peace, and need more visibility and support as such. For example, 40 women's rights organisations in the Great Lakes region have formed the Women's Platform, launched by ground-breaking feminist donor the Global Fund for Women (GFW). These organisations have made remarkable gains in involving women at the grassroots level in conflict prevention and resolution through connecting them to local security committees, security forces, and peacekeeping missions.[81] The GFW recounts a noteworthy example from eastern DRC of how women's groups can safeguard peace: following various activities conducted by women's organisations supported by the Congolese Women's Fund, a woman informed a neighbouring community that some members of her community were gathering weapons and getting ready to launch an attack. Consequently, people could evacuate in time to avoid violence.[82] With local women's involvement, additional community efforts furthermore led to intercommunity reconciliation in the area. Greater funding is needed for multi-year grants for such local women's groups.[83]

Other such powerful local efforts to transform gender relations include the activities undertaken by the South Africa–based NGO GenderWorks, which implements Gender Equity and Reconciliation (GER) workshops and training programmes. As I have observed in earlier work,[84] the GER process is a highly effective approach that uniquely brings together women and men in carefully facilitated group forums. The invitation is to share in a safe space personal experiences related to lived experiences as women and men. The cross-gender storytelling and other such modalities undertaken in such a setting unlock a profound platonic intimacy between the genders. It provides insight and healing for both genders, and produces a cross-gender respect that overturns patriarchy at its roots. Despite achieving sustained changes in attitudes and behaviour among participants, GenderWorks faces immense funding challenges. This is perhaps because it conducts a process that transgresses social norms by shining a light on the personal impacts of societal gender conditioning among groups of women and men: something that does not happen in ordinary life and is consequently somewhat taboo. And yet it is the pioneering approaches such as Gender Equity and Reconciliation—that so directly link the personal to the political—that need to be financially and institutionally supported. Opportunities for increasing implementation of such methodologies at all levels is necessary: from grassroots communities, to staff in peace and security institutions and NGOs, to political decision-makers, and more.[85]

Making the Personal Political, and the Political Personal

I have argued in earlier work (which sought to establish why gender injustices continue to persist in Southern African post-conflict environments and in so-called peacetime)[86] that, despite the proliferation of policy frameworks and legal architecture for the continent described earlier in this chapter—and indeed the difficulties of bringing these frameworks to life—"gender fatigue" is a key problem.[87] This argument maintains that gender equality policies are usually not framed in ways that allow the larger issues behind women's disenfranchisement in peacebuilding to become clear; and that purely cognitive, cerebral explanations of gender norms often do not generate a full understanding of the devastation of patriarchy on different genders and the need to transform it. It advises that what is needed to stimulate action are experiential approaches that facilitate people's reflection on, and awareness of, the ways in which they themselves, whatever their gender, have been subject to gender conditioning, and facilitate their personal "gender journey". Here I argue along the same lines, but for an even more radical shift in the way in which political, governance, security, and peacebuilding institutions in Africa and globally need to conceptualise and address both gender inequality and violent conflict. As has been observed earlier in this chapter, the two are intimately connected, and so is their elimination. I draw on the long-standing feminist slogan of the 1960s, "the personal is political", and I dare us to actualise this idea fully, in conjunction with its converse that the "political is personal", in efforts to make, keep, and build peace in Africa.

What does this mean? In essence, I advocate for significantly greater recognition in the political and peacebuilding realms that violence and conflict, including structural violence such as gender inequality, cannot be dealt with effectively without all stakeholders, including political leaders and decision-makers in the arenas of peacemaking, peacekeeping, and peacebuilding, undertaking sustained internal reflective and self-awareness work as a critical accompaniment, and ideally fore-runner, to their professional activities. Nobel Peace Prize nominee and peacebuilding activist Scilla Elworthy frames this idea simply but insightfully:

> [W]hen we have strong emotions like fear or anger, if we're not awake to what's going on inside us we tend to project those emotions onto others. This projection, on a larger scale, is what causes wars. Leaders become … incensed with the aggress[ion] of the other side when they have not examined and dealt with their own internal anger. This demonisation of the other permits all kinds of horror. If we are to work effectively in conflict, whether in government or at the grassroots, we need to understand this kind of projection on a personal level. To do this can be deeply uncomfortable and can require real courage, because we are confronting our own deeply embedded convictions and emotions. But … we become ten times more effective.[88]

Globally, including within Africa, many political leaders, military leaders, peacebuilders, and peace or gender academics or activists, whether at policy-making or local levels, perceive their work endeavours as disconnected from their internal realities, emotions, and psychological functioning. There is a scepticism and a reluctance or caution to connect the professional and political to the psychological or personal. It is controversial and even somewhat taboo to raise such issues, or to turn the focus to the "self" in the political or peacebuilding spheres, especially when involving people with power. Too often in these arenas, psychological support or the notion of therapeutic healing is only deemed acceptable to mention or promote—if at all—for the likes of survivors of gender-based violence. Even here, it tends to be framed using a patronising rhetoric of "counselling" for "abused women". It is largely dismissed as an issue that is not really critical to serious matters of peace and security. It is certainly not acceptable to speak of the need to address and support the well-being of political or military leaders, UN special representatives, or the leaders of peacebuilding organisations. But as Elworthy, and psychologists such as South African trauma specialist Pumla Gobodo-Madikizela, imply,[89] this disconnect and lack of deep personal reflection is, arguably, what produces violent conflict and gender and racial injustices, among others.

Regardless of our professional, academic, or leadership status, our work or professional motivations, impetus, and decisions are intrinsically linked to our experiences in early life, family dynamics, management of conflict, and so on. Often, healing and therapeutic work needs to be done. This is important for all human beings to undertake, and it is particularly crucial for those with decision-making power over groups of people; for those engaged in peace or justice work, including mediators; and for those who inhabit post-conflict environments where there tends to be particularly high levels of trauma. This self-awareness may be fostered through different avenues, such as depth psycho-therapeutic approaches that work with unconscious mental processes, for example, as created by analytical psychologist Carl Jung; and through psycho-social approaches that encourage sustained self-awareness, such as the GER process described earlier or the Tree of Life process developed by Zimbabwean psychologist Ncazelo Ncube,[90] among others. What is required is a fundamental paradigm shift in awareness about the importance of individual inner development for effective political or peace-related work at all levels. The practical implications of this shift will emerge as it unfolds, with the understanding that avenues for fostering self-awareness are diverse and may vary considerably between cultures and faiths.

Integration of Feminine and Masculine Qualities on an Individual Level, and the Need for Greater Valuing of the Feminine in Societies Across Africa and Worldwide

Linked to the idea that individual self-awareness on the part of all stakeholders is important for effective peace-related work and gender justice in Africa and globally, is the notion that full equality between women and men requires a fundamental balancing and integration of the feminine and the masculine energies within everyone (whether female, male, or whatever the gender identity of an individual). This perspective, which sees the primary split in human consciousness as between masculine and feminine, is usually not spoken of in relation to the domains of politics, conflict, peacemaking and peacebuilding, but is important to reflect upon. Gradually gaining credence is the perspective that values associated with masculinity are generally given more worth in the world, including in Africa, than those associated with femininity, and that this prioritisation of masculine values (such as assertiveness, competition, success, and hierarchy) is a cause of violent conflict.[91] Exemplifying this is Heinecken's observation—also alluded to earlier in this chapter—that peacekeeping is "steeped in the warrior ethos and … the 'feminine' is not valued, is suppressed, seen as a threat, or a liability".[92] Grounded in the perspective that both masculine and feminine principles or ways of being exist in all women, men, and indeed any gender identity, this chapter supports the growing view that often-marginalised values associated with the feminine, such as flexibility, responsiveness, collaboration, nurturance, and compassion, need to be embraced and embodied by all gender identities worldwide to a far greater extent. This is because of the current over-prioritisation of the masculine. I enter slightly controversial territory by suggesting not only that a greater appreciation of the feminine is needed within society and all individuals, but also that a careful and deliberate internal integration of masculine and feminine qualities needs to be undertaken on an individual basis.

Conclusion

I conclude this chapter with the following seven recommendations. First, disarmament, demobilisation, and reintegration (DDR) and security sector reform (SSR) processes in Africa and globally should include specific interventions to transform hegemonic masculinities, using psycho-social and therapeutic approaches such as Gender Equity and Reconciliation, and other processes that promote self-awareness. Second, governments and other donors should divert considerable funding from national defence budgets to DDR and SSR processes that are structured accordingly. Third, institutional and government donors should adopt best practices from feminist donors such as GFW, and fund more flexibly and responsively with less demanding reporting requirements; and linked to this, they should increase funding to locally led grassroots women's and gender-focused groups in Africa. Fourth, peacebuilding, politically focused, and gender justice institutions and NGOs should incorporate an emphasis on personal development and self-awareness among all staff as a matter of course, including among leadership. Fifth, the AU and African governments should consider routine provision of psycho-therapeutic or other such support to political leaders, decision-makers, and mediators, and support the training, support, and credibility of more Jungian or other depth psychologists and equivalent traditional experts, in Africa. Sixth, more African-designed entertainment media should be created that links the personal to the political and promotes self-reflection, such as the MTV-Africa show *Shuga*, which showcases gendered experiences of young women and men (with the goal of HIV prevention) in Kenya, Nigeria, and South Africa. Seven, heteronormativity—which normalises behaviours tied to the presumption of heterosexuality and a strict gender binary—should be disrupted by promoting awareness of the experiences of gender and sexual minorities as a gender issue within all contexts of gender-related work on the continent. Implementation of these recommendations will help build a significantly more equal and peaceful continent.

Notes

1. By July 2017, 19 African countries had National Action Plans (NAPs) for the implementation of United Nations (UN) Security Council Resolution 1325. These countries were: Burkina Faso, Burundi, the Central African Republic (CAR), Côte D'Ivoire, the Democratic Republic of the Congo (DRC), Gambia, Ghana, Guinea, Guinea-Bissau, Kenya, Liberia, Mali, Nigeria, Rwanda, Senegal, Sierra Leone, South Sudan, Togo, and Uganda.
2. Awino Okech, *Gender and Security in Africa: Primer 2* (Accra: African Women's Development Fund [AWDF], 2016), p. 9.
3. "Mrs. Mahawa Kaba Wheeler Addressed the Press on Activities and Theme on Women's Rights", press release, 31 January 2016, https://www.au.int/web/en/pressreleases/19688/mrs-mahawa-kaba-wheeler-addressed-press-activities-and-theme-women%E2%80%99s-rights (accessed 30 June 2017).
4. Article 4(l) of the 2000 Constitutive Act of the African Union (AU) identifies the promotion of gender equality as a founding principle. Centre for Conflict Resolution (CCR), *Women in Post-Conflict Societies in Africa*, Seminar Report no. 20 (Johannesburg, 6–7 November 2006).
5. Thapo Rapoo, *Gender and the New Africa Agenda: Examining Progress Towards Gender Equality in SADC*, Policy Brief no. 49 (Johannesburg: Centre for Policy Studies, 2007), *cited in* Elizabeth Otitodun and Antonia Porter, "Gender and Peacebuilding", in Chris Saunders, Gwinyayi A. Dzinesa, and Dawn Nagar (eds.), *Region-Building in Southern Africa: Progress, Problems and Prospects* (London: Zed, 2012), pp. 107–127.
6. Known also as the Maputo Protocol, it provides a continental legal framework for addressing gender inequality matters, and aspects of the norms that perpetuate women's subordination.
7. Zanele Khumalo and Antonia Porter, "Promoting Gender Equality and Empowering Women (MDG Three)", in Charles Mutasa and Mark Paterson (eds.), *Africa and the Millennium Development Goals: Progress, Problems, and Prospects* (Lanham, MD: Rowman and Littlefield, 2015), pp. 69–90.
8. African Union, "Briefing Note: Mitigating Vulnerabilities of Women and Children in Armed Conflict", PSC/PR/3 (CCXXIII), 3 March 2010. The 2003 protocol has been ratified by 37 AU member states. A further 12 member states have signed the protocol but have not yet ratified it, and six member states have not yet signed the protocol.
9. The 2004 Solemn Declaration on Gender Equality in Africa (SDGEA) incorporates key issues raised during preparatory processes involving a range of women's networks in South Africa, Senegal, and Mozambique.
10. The eight targets are: (1) creating an enabling and stable political environment; (2) legislation and legal protection actions against discrimination for ensuring gender equality; (3) mobilising stakeholders for implementing the AU Gender Policy; (4) rationalisation and harmonisation of the gender policies and programmes of the regional economic communities (RECs); (5) mobilising resources for implementing the AU Gender Policy; (6) capacity-building for

gender mainstreaming; (7) implement gender mainstreaming in all sectors; and (8) maintaining peace and security, and promoting settlement of conflicts, reconstruction, and the effective participation of women in peacekeeping and security including efforts aimed at reconciliation in post-conflict reconstruction and development.

11. Khumalo and Porter, "Promoting Gender Equality and Empowering Women (MDG Three)".
12. "Mrs. Mahawa Kaba Wheeler".
13. Okech, *Gender and Security in Africa*, p. 9.
14. The five female AU Commission commissioners are: Cessouma Minata Samate of Burkina Faso; Amani Abou-Zeid of Egypt; Amira El Fadil of Sudan; Sacko Josefa Leonel Correa of Angola; and Sarah Mbi Enow Anyang Agbor of Cameroon.
15. Member states were requested to contribute 1 per cent of their annual national budgets to the fund. For more information, *see* Redi, "'Women's Decade': Greater Attention to Implementation", press release, 22 February 2010, http://www.ipsnews.net/2010/02/africa-womens-decade-greater-attention-to-implementation (accessed 2 August 2017).
16. AU Commission, *Implementation of the Women, Peace, and Security Agenda in Africa* (Addis Ababa, July 2016), http://www.un.org/en/africa/osaa/pdf/pubs/2016womenpeacesecurity-auc.pdf (accessed 3 July 2017).
17. The AU reports that *Agenda 2063* presents the impetus for enhanced political will to end conflict in Africa, while complemented by efforts to strengthen preventative capacity through enhanced early warning and structural vulnerability assessment tools and engagement in resolving conflict before it escalates, through a range of measures.
18. "Mrs. Mahawa Kaba Wheeler".
19. Author telephone call with Victoria Maloka, AU Gender Directorate, 1 August 2017.
20. One of the goals of the gender directorate for 2017 is to encourage the 17 member states that have not yet ratified the Women's Protocol of 2003 to do so.
21. Author telephone call with Maloka.
22. Khumalo and Porter, "Promoting Gender Equality and Empowering Women (MDG Three)".
23. "Closing the Gap in Sexual Violence Response in the Great Lakes Region", n.d., http://isis.or.ug/closing-the-gap-in-sexual-violence-response/# (accessed 29 July 2017).
24. AU Commission, *Implementation of the Women, Peace, and Security Agenda in Africa*.
25. Southern African Development Community (SADC), http://www.sadc.int/issues/gender (accessed 28 July 2017.)
26. The protocol draws together existing instruments that address gender equality and conditions for women in Southern Africa, including constitutional and legal rights, governance, education, productive resources, gender-based violence, health (especially HIV/AIDS), peacebuilding and conflict resolution, and the media.
27. This is because nine ratifications amounts to more than two-thirds of the 13 signatories.

28. The Global Alliance is a strong network of women's rights non-governmental organisations (NGOs) across SADC's 15 member states.
29. GenderLinks, "Region: Alliance Urges Resolute Action Post-2015", press release, 6 July 2016, http://genderlinks.org.za/pressreleases/southern-africa-alliance-urges-resolute-action-on-post-2015-gender-protocol (accessed 2 July 2017).
30. Southern Africa's gender ministers also decided that the protocol should be accompanied by a strong monitoring, evaluation, and results framework. For more information, *see* GenderLinks, "Region: Alliance Urges Resolute Action Post-2015".
31. It also upgrades the requirement for women's "equal" participation in decision-making to "equal and effective" participation, in alignment with the language of the Sustainable Development Goals (SDGs). However, the protocol no longer incorporates the timeframes that previously distinguished it from other protocols, a fact that disappoints the Global Alliance.
32. GenderLinks, "Region: Alliance Urges Resolute Action Post-2015".
33. This article now states that "state parties shall put in place measures to ensure equal representation and participation in key decision-making positions in conflict resolution, peacebuilding processes, and peacekeeping in accordance with United Nations Security Council Resolution 1325 on Women, Peace, and Security and other related resolutions". *Quoted in* Colleen Lowe Morna, Lucia Makamure, and Sifiso Dube (eds.), *SADC Gender Protocol Barometer 2016* (Johannesburg: GenderLinks, August 2016), p. 16.
34. Otitodun and Porter, "Gender and Peacebuilding", pp. 111–112.
35. Jan Vanheukelom and Talitha Bertelsmann-Scott, *The Political Economy of Regional Integration in Africa: The Southern African Development Community (SADC)* (Maastricht: European Centre for Development Policy Management [ECDPM], January 2016).
36. Eastern African Sub-Regional Support Initiative for the Advancement of Women (EASSI), "Policy Brief on Gender Equality in the East African Community," n.d., http://eacsof.net/EACSOF/wp-content/uploads/2017/05/EA-Policy-brief-copy.pdf (accessed 2 August 2017).
37. East African Community (EAC), "Regional Implementation Plan on United Nations Security Council Resolution 1325 on Women, Peace, and Security: 2015–2019", n.d., http://www.eassi.org/eassi/files/mydocs/final-report on the-eac-regional-implementation-fr.pdf (accessed 3 July 2017).
38. United Nations Economic Commission for Africa (UNECA), "Assessing Regional Integration in Africa, Volume 1", p. 216.
39. AU Commission, *Implementation of the Women, Peace, and Security Agenda in Africa*http://www.un.org/en/africa/osaa/pdf/pubs/2016womenpeacesecurity-auc.pdf.
40. Bernardo Monzani, "Women, Peace, and Security in the Horn of Africa: Between Rhetoric and Reality", 5 May 2016, http://www.peaceagency.org/en/2016/05/05/women-peace-and-security-in-the-horn-of-africa-between-rhetoric-and-reality (accessed 2 July 2017).
41. Make Every Woman Count, "Intergovernmental Authority for Development (IGAD)", 19 April 2012, http://www.makeeverywomancount.org/index.php/community/monitoring-african-regional-organisations/3374-intergovernmental-authority-for-development-igad (accessed 3 July 2017).

42. The membership of the International Conference on the Great Lakes Region (ICLGR) includes: Angola, Burundi, the Central African Republic, Congo-Brazzaville, the Democratic Republic of Congo, Kenya, Rwanda, South Sudan, Sudan, Tanzania, Uganda, and Zambia.
43. Okech, *Gender and Security in Africa*, p. 10.
44. Okech, *Gender and Security in Africa*, p. 10.
45. The Beijing Platform even included a chapter on "Women in Armed Conflicts", and called for greater participation of women in peace processes, reduction in military spending, and the promotion of peaceful means to resolve conflicts. For more information, *see* Otitodun and Porter, "Gender and Peacebuilding".
46. This resolution calls for all actors in peace agreements to protect and respect the human rights of women and girls, especially as they relate to the police, judiciary, and disarmament, demobilisation, and reintegration.
47. Okech, *Gender and Security in Africa*, p. 7.
48. The additional eight resolutions on women, peace, and security are: UN Security Council Resolutions 1820 (2008), 1888 (2009), 1889 (2009), 1960 (2010), 2106 (2013), 2122 (2013), 2242 (2015), and 2272 (2016).
49. African Leadership Centre, "Gender, Peace, and Security", n.d., http://www.africanleadershipcentre.org/index.php/research/research-projects/gender-peace-and-security (accessed 30 June 2017).
50. African Leadership Centre, "Gender, Peace, and Security".
51. Joyce Laker, "Gender and Democracy in Africa", paper presented at the biannual conference of the South African Association of Political Studies (SAAPS), Stellenbosch, 1–4 September 2010, *cited in* Otitodun and Porter, "Gender and Peacebuilding".
52. Donna Pankhurst, "Women, Gender, and Peacebuilding", Working Paper no. 5 (Bradford: Centre for Conflict Resolution, University of Bradford, 2000), p. 10, *cited in* Otitodun and Porter, "Gender and Peacebuilding"; Aruna Rao, cited in Jane S. Jaquette and Aruna Rao, "Setting the Context: Approaches to Promoting Gender Equity", in Elizabeth Bryan and Jessica Varat (eds.), *Strategies for Promoting Gender Equity in Developing Countries: Lessons, Challenges, and Opportunities* (Washington, DC: Woodrow Wilson International Center for Scholars, 2008), pp. 5–10.
53. Otitodun and Porter, "Gender and Peacebuilding".
54. *See* "Strategic Summary 2016: UN Peace Operations by the Numbers", n.d., http://peaceoperationsreview.org/strategic-summary-2016-un-peace-operations-by-the-numbers (accessed 2 August 2017); and UN Peacekeeping, "Summary of Troop Contributions to UN Peacekeeping Operations by Mission, Post, and Gender", 30 June 2017, http://www.un.org/en/peacekeeping/contributors/gender/2017gender/jun17.pdf (accessed 2 August 2017).
55. Yolande Bouka and Romi Sigsworth, "Women in the Military in Africa: Kenya Case Study", September 2016, https://issafrica.s3.amazonaws.com/site/uploads/ear7.pdf (accessed 2 August 2017).
56. Yaliwe Clarke, "Security Sector Reform in Africa: A Lost Opportunity to Deconstruct Militarised Masculinities", in "Militarism, Conflict, and Women's Activism", *Feminist Africa* no. 10 (August 2008), p. 52.
57. Cheryl Hendricks, "Gender and Security in Africa: An Overview", Discussion Paper no. 63 (Uppsala: Nordiska Afrikainstitutet, 2011).

58. Lindy Heinecken, "Challenges Facing Women in Peacekeeping", 5 May 2016, https://sustainablesecurity.org/2016/05/05/challenges-facing-women-in-peacekeeping (accessed 2 August 2017).
59. Angela Nicole Alchin, "Are Women Making a Difference in Peacekeeping Operations? Considering the Voices of South African Women Peacekeepers", MA thesis, Stellenbosch University, March 2015, http://scholar.sun.ac.za/handle/10019.1/96843 (accessed 2 August 2017).
60. Some such essentialist ideas are that women are non-competitive, more emotional, and more nurturing than men.
61. Lindy Heinecken, "Are Women 'Really' Making a Unique Contribution to Peacekeeping? The Rhetoric and the Reality", *Journal of International Peacekeeping* 19, nos. 3–4, (2015), pp. 227–248.
62. Heinecken, "Challenges Facing Women in Peacekeeping".
63. Heinecken notes that the findings show that the ability of women peacekeepers to make a difference is limited by their training, in which they are expected to perform "just like men". For more information, *see* Heinecken, "Are Women 'Really' Making a Unique Contribution to Peacekeeping?".
64. Clarke, "Security Sector Reform in Africa", p. 60.
65. Sandra Whitworth, *Men, Militarism and UN Peacekeeping: A Gendered Analysis* (Boulder, CO: Rienner, 2004), *cited in* Alchin, "Are Women Making a Difference in Peacekeeping Operations?".
66. "Militarism, Conflict, and Women's Activism", *Feminist Africa* no. 10 (August 2008).
67. *See, for example*, UN Security Council Resolution 1820 of 2008, which explicitly links sexual violence as a tactic of war, with women, peace, and security issues. Resolution 1820 also requires parties to armed conflict to take immediate action to protect civilians from sexual violence, such as by training troops appropriately. *See also* Resolution 1888 of 2009, as a follow up to Resolution 1820, which mandates that peacekeeping missions protect women and children from sexual violence during armed conflict, and requested the UN Secretary-General to appoint a special representative on sexual violence during armed conflict. Resolutions 1960 of 2010 and 2106 of 2013 place even greater operational detail on responding to conflict-related sexual violence.
68. Okech, *Gender and Security in Africa*, p. 5.
69. Amina Mama and Margo Okazawa-Rey, "Editorial: Militarism, Conflict, and Women's Activism", in "Militarism, Conflict, and Women's Activism", *Feminist Africa* no. 10 (August 2008), p. 3.
70. Yaliwe Clarke, *A Lost Opportunity to Deconstruct Militarised Masculinities?*, in "Militarism, Conflict, and Women's Activism", *Feminist Africa* no. 10 (August 2008), p. 50.
71. For the list of recommendations, *see* AU Commission, "Implementation of the Women, Peace, and Security Agenda in Africa", July 2016, pp. 42–44, http://www.un.org/en/africa/osaa/pdf/pubs/2016womenpeacesecurity-auc.pdf (accessed 3 July 2017).
72. Antonia Porter, "'What is Constructed Can be Transformed': Masculinities in Post-Conflict Societies in Africa", *International Peacekeeping* 20, no. 4 (2013), pp. 486–506.

73. According to Sonke Gender Justice, others include the 1994 International Conference on Population and Development; the 1995 Programme of Action of the World Summit on Social Development and its review in 2000; the 26th special session of the UN General Assembly on HIV/AIDS (2001); and the 48th and 53rd sessions of the UN Commission on the Status of Women (CSW) (2004 and 2009).
74. Clarke, "Security Sector Reform in Africa".
75. Sonke Gender Justice, http://www.genderjustice.org.za/regional-programmes/menengage-africa/african-union-regional-economic-communities (accessed 2 July 2017).
76. Porter, "'What Is Constructed Can Be Transformed'".
77. Since its official launch in 2002, the Gender Is My Agenda Campaign (GIMAC) has taken place bi-annually in advance of the AU summit of heads of state and government to engage AU member states on African women rights, issues, and concerns. Members of GIMAC include reliably progressive feminist organisations such as Senegal's Femmes Africa Solidarité (FAS), Uganda's Isis-Women's International Cross Cultural Exchange (Isis-WICCE), and Ghana's Abantu for Development.
78. Women's Situation Rooms—with minor variations—have been established during elections in countries such as Guinea-Bissau, Kenya, Liberia, Mali, Nigeria, Senegal, Sierra Leone, and Zimbabwe. For more information, *see* AU Commission, "Implementation of the Women, Peace, and Security Agenda in Africa".
79. AU Commission, "Implementation of the Women, Peace, and Security Agenda in Africa".
80. AU Commission, "Implementation of the Women, Peace, and Security Agenda in Africa", p. 42.
81. The Global Fund for Women reports that the platform has also enhanced women's skills and opportunities to resolve conflicts as they arise within the local community and armed forces. For more information, *see* Global Fund for Women, *Tipping Points: Economic and Political Empowerment*, October 2016.
82. Global Fund for Women, *Tipping Points.*
83. The Global Fund for Women anticipates that with targeted investment in a cohort of strong, well-connected activist grassroots groups, important outcomes would ensue such as increased engagement among communities to advocate for peace processes; improved livelihoods for women that increase economic and food security for their families or their communities; and increased women's and girls' participation and influence in peace processes.
84. Porter, "'What is Constructed Can be Transformed'".
85. *See* http://www.genderworks.org for more information.
86. Otitodun and Porter, "Gender and Peacebuilding".
87. "Gender fatigue" is described as a lack of enthusiasm for gender equality and gender-sensitive peacebuilding within national governments and even within development and peacebuilding institutions.
88. Scilla Elworthy, "Working for a World Without War", *The Ecologist*, 23 May 2017, http://www.theecologist.org/magazine/features/2988966/working_for_a_world_without_war.html (accessed 1 July 2017).
89. Elworthy, "Working for a World Without War".

90. The Tree of Life is a therapeutic process for adults and children that enables them to strengthen their relationships with their own history, their culture, and significant people in their lives, in ways that build their self-esteem.
91. The idea that there are specific values associated with masculinity and femininity is not universally agreed upon.
92. Heinecken, "Challenges Facing Women in Peacekeeping".

CHAPTER 19

The UN Peacebuilding Commission: Facts, Fictions, and Frustrations

Ejeviome Eloho Otobo

Every new institution grapples with the challenge of fulfilling expectations. Created in 2005 and inaugurated in 2006, the United Nations (UN) Peacebuilding Commission (PBC) is no exception. Performance expectations arise not only in relation to the stated objectives of institutions, but also from the presumptions of what various stakeholders think an institution ought to do. Where such stakeholders are very diverse, as in the case of the UN Peacebuilding Commission, it begs the question as to whose views should be regarded as the most valid in assessing the institution's performance: those of the members of the Commission, the country on its agenda, the relevant UN mission/country team, or independent experts?

The question of the extent to which the Peacebuilding Commission has fulfilled its stated objectives was the subject of a 2010 Review of the UN Peacebuilding Architecture. The review found that "the hopes that accompanied the 2005 resolutions [establishing the PBC in 2005] have yet to be realised",[1] but also noted that "[t]his is not to understate what has been accomplished, and certainly not to devalue the unfailing commitment shown by many dedicated Member State representatives, especially those with chairing responsibilities".[2] This represented a clear summons to action for the Peacebuilding Commission to work towards realising its full potential. Yet the subsequent 2015 Review of the UN Peacebuilding Architecture noted that "[F]ive years further on … those hopes have, if anything, further waned."[3] At the same time, the overarching finding of this ten-year review was "that the key task under the Charter, that of sustaining peace, remains critically underrecognised, underprioritised and underresourced globally and within the United Nations system."[4]

E.E. Otobo (✉)
Global Governance Institute, Brussels, Belgium

T. Karbo, K. Virk (eds.), *The Palgrave Handbook of Peacebuilding in Africa*, https://doi.org/10.1007/978-3-319-62202-6_19

Conducted five years apart, these two reviews of the UN peacebuilding architecture have shown the degree to which the performance of the Peacebuilding Commission—the main inter-governmental organ in this architecture—is critically dependent on several actors, and how it has been constrained by critical factors such as a lack of adequate financial resources. In this regard, carefully designed and sustained improvements in performance clearly hold the key to achieving the Commission's full institutional potential. Yet it would be hard to exaggerate the extent to which expectations about performance can, in fact, also be driven by the demands of stakeholders and by normative prescriptions.

As I have argued elsewhere, "the expectations of what [the] PBC should do to help advance peacebuilding in each country [on its agenda]"[5] was a major consideration for most governments that applied to be placed on this agenda. At the same time, as the relatively young field of peacebuilding has evolved, normative frameworks have also begun to shape the Commission's practices and expectations. Three such frameworks for peacebuilding have emerged over time in the literature. These are well-summarised by Canadian scholar Devon Curtis—in her introduction to the 2012 volume *Peacebuilding, Power, and Politics in Africa*, co-edited with Zimbabwean analyst Gwinyayi Dzinesa—as liberal peacebuilding, peacebuilding as stabilisation, and peacebuilding as social justice. Curtis notes:

> Although there are important areas of overlap between these positions, they rest on different conceptions of power and politics in Africa. Each of these views contains important normative assumptions about the nature of peace and about the identity and motivations of peace builders. They lead to different conclusions about the role of the state in peacebuilding, the type of economic policies best suited to recovery, the appropriate ways of encouraging societal reconciliation, and how best to ensure security.[6]

The experience of the UN Peacebuilding Commission confirms the insight that there are important areas of overlap in practice between these three normative frameworks for peacebuilding. Indeed, the Commission's engagement with the six countries on its agenda—Burundi, the Central African Republic (CAR), Guinea, Guinea-Bissau, Liberia, and Sierra Leone—shows that the key themes highlighted by each of the three frameworks are marked by considerable interlinkages. In this chapter, I seek to separate fact from fiction in the experience of the Peacebuilding Commission and, in so doing, shed important light on the results achieved, and challenges and constraints faced in the practice of peacebuilding. The chapter concludes by highlighting several key issues for the future orientation of the Commission.

Facts

The UN Peacebuilding Commission operates through three structures: (1) a standing Organisational Committee, which serves as a plenary bringing together 31 countries selected or elected, as relevant, from different categories including the UN Security Council, the Economic and Social Council (ECOSOC), the principal financial contributors to the UN system, the top troop-contributing countries, and the UN regional groups of member states; (2) Country-Specific Configurations (six as of 2017), with each configuration dedicated to a country on the agenda of the PBC;[7] and (3) a Working Group on Lessons Learned. The chair of the Organisational Committee is elected for a one-year term on a rotational basis from among the five UN regional groups. The chairs of the Country-Specific Configurations are elected for a one-year term, which is renewable for as long as the incumbent remains interested in serving in the position. The same practice holds for the chair of the Working Group on Lessons Learned.

Straddling of Security and Development Work Enables the Commission to Fulfil Its Mandate

The ability of the UN Peacebuilding Commission to provide support to countries on its agenda in ways that link security and development issues, is one of the important features and strengths of the commission in its design and actual performance. Indeed, "it is the only body that explicitly links the political, security and economic functions of the [United Nations]".[8] The Peacebuilding Commission has given practical effect to this advantage in two well-documented cases. First, in Sierra Leone, the Commission, in its initial phase of engagement with that country in 2006–2007, accepted the government's argument that the restoration of electric power supply was not only a national emergency, but also an important peacebuilding priority. This led the Commission to include energy-sector development among the initial five peacebuilding priority areas in the cooperation framework for Sierra Leone, adopted in December 2007. The other four areas were: youth employment and empowerment; consolidation of democracy and "good governance"; justice and security sector reform; and capacity-building, with the sub-regional dimensions of peacebuilding and cross-cutting issues (such as gender equality) to be considered in the analysis and the selection of commitments.[9] (On women, gender, and peacebuilding, see Porter in this volume.) An independent study, published by the New York University (NYU) Center on International Cooperation and the International Peace Institute (IPI), in April 2008, noted that: "the incorporation of energy as a priority in the framework highlights an important principle: specifically, that economic risk can be as significant a threat to peace as security or political risks. In this case, the PBC fostered negotiations among the relevant stakeholders to garner political support for the inclusion of energy—normally considered a medium-to-long-term development concern—in a framework of peace consolidation".[10] (See also Omeje in this volume.)

The second case involves Burundi. The effort of the first chair of the Commission's Burundi configuration, Norway's Johan Løvald, in helping to persuade the International Monetary Fund (IMF), in 2007, to lift its ban on the sixth review of Burundi's economic reform programme is usually seen as an example of the Commission's advocacy work. On closer examination, it can also be viewed as a striking illustration of how the Commission's work straddles security and development.[11] The Commission's démarche, through Løvald, took place in the context of what was referred to as the "triple obstacles"—perhaps more appropriately, the "triple threats"—to peace consolidation in Burundi at the time. These were the decision of the opposition to boycott parliament because of the disagreement between the main opposition parties and the Burundian government on the implementation of power-sharing principles contained in various peace accords; the withdrawal of the rebel National Forces of Liberation (FNL) from the joint verification and monitoring mechanism in July 2007; and the delay by the IMF in not concluding its sixth review of Burundi, without which donors withheld their budgetary support to the Burundian government. The chair of the Commission's Burundi configuration, Løvald, intervened in this context, to make the argument to the IMF that if the Fund did not complete the sixth review and thereby "enable the Government to deal decisively with the political and socio-economic situation", Burundi risked relapsing into conflict.[12] In so doing, Løvald thus recognised the link between the Fund's financial assistance and the political-security situation in the country.

Work in Resource Mobilisation Is Progressing Slowly But Steadily

One of the most difficult responsibilities entrusted to the UN Peacebuilding Commission is mobilising resources to support post-conflict peacebuilding. The nature and scope of the role that the Peacebuilding Commission is expected to play in this area have been bedevilled as much by the definition of the task as by operational details. The 2005 founding resolutions establishing the Commission confer the responsibility on the body by mandating it to "to bring together all relevant actors to *marshal* resources and to advise on and propose integrated strategies for post-conflict peacebuilding and recovery ... and to help to ensure predictable financing for early recovery activities".[13] The term "marshal", though, is imprecise and lacking in operational guidance.

The appropriate interpretation of the role of the Peacebuilding Commission here has to be the mobilising of financial and technical expertise and the harnessing of ongoing funding efforts, in support of peacebuilding priorities. Absent this element of prioritisation linked to peacebuilding, the Commission's resource mobilisation work otherwise begins to resemble traditional development assistance. This conception of the role of the Commission in resource mobilisation has validation in the 2010 review, which noted that: "The Commission's role is essentially one of advocacy, a relentless advocacy for the allocation of adequate resources to certain critical and urgent issues which, if left unaddressed or unfunded, have the potential to threaten peace".[14] The review also noted that "[t]he record as regards resource mobilisation is ... mixed" and called on the Commission to "[i]ntensify overall resource mobilisation efforts; ensure they are strongly attuned to development challenges with political implications."[15]

In response to the 2010 review, the Commission focussed its efforts on three aspects of resource mobilisation: (1) mobilising financial support through donors' roundtables for national development plans and for elections; (2) developing partnerships with international financial institutions (IFIs); and (3) promoting partnership with the private sector. The first aspect is discussed in detail later in the chapter, so I concentrate here on the latter two.

Developing and deepening partnerships with international financial institutions has ranked high on the agenda of the Peacebuilding Commission. This is because the Commission understands that these institutions—in particular, the World Bank—are major actors in most post-conflict countries. In this context, there is further recognition by the Commission that not all its efforts in resource mobilisation will lead to financial resources in terms of "money on the table"; rather that some of its efforts might result in complementary actions being undertaken by other key actors such as the IFIs. For example, in the 2010 Statement of Mutual Commitments for Peacebuilding in Liberia, the government pledged to "increase budgetary allocations for institutions central to security and the rule of law, including the Armed Forces of Liberia, Liberia National Police, Bureau of Immigration and Naturalization and Corrections."[16] Subsequently, a 2011 report on public expenditure review, jointly financed by the World Bank and the UN Partnership Trust Fund, recommended that the Liberian government should increase its budgetary allocations to the security sector from 4.9 per cent to 6 per cent of gross domestic product (GDP).[17] This recommendation was used to provide encouragement to the government to increase allocations to the security sector, even if the proposed target might take time to achieve.[18] (On Liberia, see also Omeje in this volume.) Similarly, in the Central African Republic, the World Bank and the UN Peacebuilding Fund "joined efforts to pay the salaries of civil servants from May through August 2014, contributing to reestablishment of core public services in the country."[19]

As it did in the case of IFIs, the Peacebuilding Commission also recognised the need to work with the private sector early on. I have provided elsewhere a narrative of the Commission's early efforts in articulating an orientation for its work with the private sector.[20] The new momentum for action in outreach to the private sector arose from the Commission's policy discussion in July 2012, centred on a paper titled, "Resource Mobilization for Peacebuilding Priorities: The Role of the Peacebuilding Commission".[21] This led to the convening in June 2013, in New York, of a high-level event jointly organised by the Peacebuilding Commission and the UN Global Compact (a voluntary corporate sustainability initiative)[22] on the theme "Business for Peacebuilding: The Role of [the] Private Sector". A major outcome of this event was the recognition that the individual Country-Specific Configurations should identify practical entry points for the Commission, in support of the efforts of the countries on the agenda—six, as of 2017—to develop their local private sectors; to build up their local systems to manage and use natural resources; and to attract responsible investment. Moreover, where private sector investment flows occur, the impact will show up not only in money, but also in the sharing of organisational and technological expertise that goes with it.

The Chairs of the Country-Specific Configurations Play an Important Role in the Commission's Work

Neither the founding resolutions establishing the UN Peacebuilding Commission, nor its rules of procedure, explicitly made provision for independent chairs of the Country-Specific Configurations, separate from the Commission's chair and vice-chairs. The Commission's rules of procedure simply state: "The Chair or the Vice-Chairs of the Commission shall preside over both the Organisational Committee and the country-specific meetings, unless the Organisational Committee decides otherwise."[23] Indeed, the first chair of the Burundi configuration, Norway's Johan Løvald, was selected for that position due to his status as a vice-chair of the Commission. However, the selection of the independent chairs for the other Country-Specific Configurations reflected a practical adaptation to the reality that as more countries came onto the agenda, it became impractical for the chair and the two vice-chairs of the Commission to serve simultaneously in those positions and also be assigned chairing responsibilities for the Country-Specific Configurations. That being said, there is no question that the Country-Specific Configurations occupy a central position in the work of the Commission.

As Bartjan Wegter, an adviser to his Dutch compatriot, Frank Majoor, the first chair of the Commission's Sierra Leone configuration, has noted: "The country-specific [configurations] of the PBC have proved to be the engine rooms where its peacebuilding mandate was given operational meaning."[24] If this is the case, the chair of the Country-Specific Configuration is the "chief engineer", and his/her work is of crucial importance in the work of the configuration. The roles of the chair can be summed up as advocate, resource mobiliser, and facilitator. These roles are directly derived from the key functions of the Commission itself: advocacy, resource mobilisation, and (fostering) coherence. Some of the key achievements of the Commission to date are attributable to how individual chairs of the Country-Specific Configurations have played each of these roles.

Thus, the first chair of the Commission's Liberia configuration, Jordan's Zeid Ra'ad Al Hussein, during his tenure from September 2010 to March 2012, championed the development of regional justice and security hubs aimed at extending state authority in the country. Writing on the occasion of the inauguration of the Gbarnga hub in February 2013—the first of five regional justice and security hubs—Liberia's Minister of Justice Christiana Tah, and the UN Assistant Secretary-General for Peacebuilding Support, Malaysia's Judy Cheng-Hopkins, jointly noted that: "each hub is designed to increase citizens' access to justice and security by co-locating police, courts, and immigration departments—creating, in effect, a 'one stop shop' for their services. The hubs will also enhance the government's efforts to extend the provision of these services from the capital to outlying and previously neglected areas of the country".[25] In addition to ensuring that the work on the second and third hubs is initiated, the successor chair of the configuration, Sweden's Staffan Tillander, intensified efforts to support the government's work on national reconciliation. (See Omeje in this volume.)

Meanwhile, the chair of the Commission's Guinea configuration, Luxembourg's Sylvie Lucas, has offered much encouragement for the political process in that country, in particular, by issuing statements at critical turning points, such as welcoming the accord of July 2013 among the political parties; encouraging the parties to conduct fair, peaceful, and transparent elections; and congratulating the people of Guinea for their peaceful participation in the September 2013 legislative elections.[26] These appeals are intended to convey an expression of international solidarity and support, and to calm the national political environment.

Political advocacy work is not a one-way street, though, with the chairs of the Country-Specific Configurations always offering only positive support for the efforts of the countries on the agenda. There have been important moments when the configuration chairs have had to deliver "tough messages" to the national governments. A striking illustration is provided by a May 2010 letter, written by the Brazilian chair of the Guinea-Bissau configuration, then Maria Luiza Ribeiro Viotti, to the country's minister of foreign affairs, Adelino Mano Queta, expressing the Commission's deep concern about the incident of April 2010, in which Guinea-Bissau's prime minister, Carlos Gomes, was briefly detained and the country's chief of armed forces, Admiral Zamora Induta, and other officers were illegally detained for some time thereafter.[27] The chair demanded assurances from the government of Guinea-Bissau that such actions would not occur in the future. The foreign minister, Queta, replied two weeks later, offering the needed assurances.[28] However, the political fragility in Guinea-Bissau was underlined by the fact that almost exactly two years after this incident, in April 2012, the military staged a coup to halt the second round of presidential elections. The chair of the Commission's country configuration, in that instance, similarly issued a statement condemning in the "strongest terms" the illegal seizure of power from the legitimate government of Guinea-Bissau.[29]

The chair of the Commission's Burundi configuration, Paul Seger of Switzerland, in his speech to the second sectoral conference on government priorities for poverty reduction, held in October 2013, recalled the outcome of the 2012 partner conference in Geneva, where Burundi succeeded in highlighting economic progress in the country; and noted that while the spirit of Geneva was still alive, the enthusiasm had somewhat faded. Positive developments in Burundi, including workshops in March and May 2013 on elections and on the return of opposition leaders respectively, have, to a certain extent, been thwarted by less positive developments, like the adoption of a new media law or the sense that political space in Burundi is, at times, restricted.[30] The new media law, adopted in June 2013, compelled journalists to reveal their information sources and forbade them from publishing stories deemed to undermine national security. In retrospect, these curbs on press freedom presaged part of the incumbent president, Pierre Nkurunziza's, design to extend his term in office beyond the two-term constitutional limit. The risk remained high that popular protests against Nkurunziza's third-term bid could morph into conflict and unravel peacebuilding efforts in the country. In July 2015, Nkurunziza won a controversial third term as president of Burundi. In 2017, the situation in the country remained perilous, with over 400,000 Burundian refugees and asylum seekers in neighbouring countries (including Tanzania, Rwanda, Uganda, and the Democratic Republic of the Congo [DRC]),[31] scores of opposition members imprisoned or in exile, and tens of thousands still internally displaced in Burundi.

Successive chairs of the Commission's Burundi configuration have led efforts in organising donor conferences in support of the country. As the New York-based Security Council Report noted: "The $655.6 million in funds pledged from international donors to Burundi in May [2007] would probably have been much lower if it had not been for the Commission, in particular the influence of Norway's Ambassador to the UN, Johan Løvald, who chairs the Commission's Burundi [configuration]."[32] In 2012, Switzerland's Paul Seger, the then chair of the Burundi configuration, also supported the government in organising a donor conference, held in October 2012 in Geneva, that resulted in pledges of $2.5 billion for Burundi's second poverty reduction strategy, covering the period 2013–2016. The then chair of the Commission's CAR configuration, Jan Grauls of Belgium, similarly supported the government in organising a partner roundtable in Brussels, in June 2011, to raise awareness about the funding needs of the country's second poverty reduction strategy, covering the period 2012–2016.

The fact that the chairs of various Country-Specific Configurations have organised, or co-sponsored, donor conferences in support of poverty reduction strategies shows that the Peacebuilding Commission's instruments are not in competition with such strategies, but are complementary to them. The Commission's instruments of engagement, which have evolved from the strategic peacebuilding framework to the statement on mutual peacebuilding commitments, are no more in competition with poverty reduction strategies than are the World Bank's country assistance strategies or the African Development Bank's (AfDB) country strategies. Indeed, where a country has already developed a peacebuilding-sensitive poverty reduction strategy or a "new deal" compact, the Commission's instrument of engagement is a brief statement of mutual commitments outlining areas of peacebuilding support and what the PBC intends to achieve in each agreed priority area.

To appreciate how difficult it is for a Country-Specific Configuration to function without a chair, one need look no further than the Commission's experience with the Central African Republic. The first chair of the CAR configuration, Belgium's Jan Grauls, resigned in June 2012. The configuration subsequently seemed rudderless until the election of his successor, Morocco's Mohammed Loulichki, in June 2014. The problem of lack of direction for a configuration, in the absence of a chair, was accentuated by the fact that the Country-Specific

Configurations do not, as yet, have an institutional position of vice-chair who could temporarily take over the position. Indeed, the failure of the 2010 review to recommend the creation of the position of a vice-chair for the Country-Specific Configurations was one of the unfulfilled expectations of that review. Whether the Peacebuilding Commission retains the system of Country-Specific Configurations or moves to a system of country meetings directly under the Organisational Committee, whoever leads the arrangement—chair or co-ordinator—will play an equally important role, especially during the transition phase of the Commission's engagement with a country before its exit.

Fictions

The Exclusion of Conflict Prevention from the Remit of the Commission Is an Important Limitation

The notion that the Peacebuilding Commission's remit excludes conflict prevention work is traceable to the UN Secretary-General, Ghana's Kofi Annan's, statement in his 2005 report, *In Larger Freedom*, that he did "not believe that such a body should have an early warning or monitoring function" in conflict situations.[33] The decision of the Secretary-General to excise the "early warning and monitoring function" from the Peacebuilding Commission, contrary to a 2004 recommendation of the UN High-Level Panel on Threats, Challenges, and Change,[34] though, was intended more to avoid giving a global role to the Commission—in particular, one that the Security Council already performs—than to preclude the Commission from performing that role at all in the countries on its agenda.

As Dutchman Bartjan Wegter has noted, "the PBC is aimed at preventing a relapse into conflict in states that have recently emerged from a period of internal strife ... it is an undisputed fact that activities aimed at building peace (reinforcing a given country's recovery and sustainable development) are instrumental to preventing conflict in the longer term".[35] Indeed, the strategic intent behind the creation of the Peacebuilding Commission was to enhance the international community's ability to prevent repeated relapse into conflict in many countries—a broad and multi-faceted task that requires the Commission to actively and effectively fulfil the functions set out in its founding resolutions. The real issue, then, is not so much that the Commission lacks the remit to undertake preventive work, but rather how to ensure that this work can contribute to preventing countries on its agenda from relapsing into conflict.

The Commission Is Dominated by the Permanent Members of the Security Council, Principal Donors of the UN system, and Largest Troop Contributors

The idea of creating one category for principal donors and another for troop-contributing countries in the Peacebuilding Commission's Organisational Committee has been described as a reward for "global good citizenship".[36]

The contrary view is that the UN's principal donors and its largest troop-contributing countries, along with the five permanent members (P-5) of the Security Council—the United States (US), Britain,[37] France, China, and Russia—dominate the Peacebuilding Commission.[38] (See Ugarte in this volume.) Although what "domination" in this context means is not usually explained, we can usefully examine the notion from three aspects: (1) that these three categories of countries (the P-5, the largest troop-contributing countries, and the principal donors) are taking a leading role by assuming responsibility of chairing the Commission's Country-Specific Configurations; (2) that they are actively engaged in the work of the Commission, including leading the efforts to generate initiatives; and (3) that they set the tone of peacebuilding in the countries on the Commission's agenda, because they make substantial contributions to finance peacebuilding, especially through the UN Peacebuilding Fund.

Using these criteria to assess the supposed domination by these three categories of countries shows that the notion of domination is a fiction. For example, none of the P-5 has taken on a chairing role in any of the Commission's three main structures: its Organisational Committee, its Country-Specific Configurations, or its Working Group on Lessons Learned. It is true that the chairs of the six Country-Specific Configurations have mostly been from major industrialised countries, including donors such as Norway, Sweden, the Netherlands, and Canada. However, not all are major donors, and this includes Belgium, which chaired the CAR configuration (2008–2012), and Luxembourg, which chairs the Guinea configuration (since 2011). Moreover, there have been a few chairs from countries in the global South as well—Brazil, for example, has chaired the Guinea-Bissau configuration since its inception in 2007, and Morocco currently chairs the CAR configuration (since 2014). Only one major troop-contributing country, Jordan, has assumed the chair of a Country-Specific Configuration (Liberia) and only one major troop-contributing country—Bangladesh—has been elected to chair the Commission's Organisational Committee in 2012. The major donor countries that have been elected to chair the Organisational Committee have done so because of the rotation to their regional group.

In terms of the generation of initiatives for advancing the work of the Peacebuilding Commission, the record similarly does not confirm the view of domination by the P-5, principal donors, and top troop-contributors. Indeed, many important initiatives that have emerged in the Commission—excluding those undertaken by the chairs of Country-Specific Configurations (highlighted earlier)—have emanated neither from the P-5 nor the major troop-contributing countries. The ideas of financing Commission field trips and working closely with the private sector, for example, were pushed by Japan during its tenure as chair of the Commission in 2007–2008; of strengthening relations with regional organisations and outreach to philanthropic organisations were pushed by Chile during its tenure as the chair in 2009; of enhancing relations with the AfDB was pushed by Rwanda during its term as chair in 2011; and of convening annual sessions of the Commission was pushed by Indonesia over a three-year period from 2010 to 2012.

Regarding financial contributions to the UN Peacebuilding Fund, as of December 2015, all the P-5 countries had contributed to the fund. But these contributions were relatively small, with the US having committed a mere $0.25 million for the period 2006–2019; France less than $3 million; China $8 million; and Russia $16 million; with only Britain having made a relatively substantial commitment of over $154 million through its Department for International Development (DFID). The highest contribution by a major troop-contributing country had been made by India ($4 million), with other major troop contributors having committed relatively small amounts, varying from $24,000 to $5,000, or not contributed at all.[39]

One final issue to consider—which minimises the possibility of domination by one group or another—is that the UN resolutions establishing the Peacebuilding Commission explicitly state that "the Commission shall act in all matters on the basis of consensus of its members"[40]—a very unusual stipulation for an inter-governmental body, but one that potentially limits the extent to which any member state can dominate the Commission.

The Results of the Commission's Work Should Always Be Tangible and Visible

As explained earlier, as the field of peacebuilding has evolved, the expectations of what the field should accomplish have grown, reflecting the fact that peacebuilding draws upon, and indeed, stands at the intersection of many disciplines. It should not come as a surprise that the work of the UN Peacebuilding Commission is marked by multiple expectations of what it should be. One such expectation is that the work of the Peacebuilding Commission must be tangible and visible. But one need look no further than the main remit of the Commission—advocacy, resource mobilisation, and coherence—to realise that some of its work will not show up as tangible—if "tangible" is defined as money and institution-building, the latter including, for example, the regional justice and security hubs in Liberia mentioned earlier. As an illustration, advocacy and support for training of soldiers to accept civilian control of the armed forces will show up in behavioural or attitudinal changes over time, but will not be tangible. (See Rashid in this volume.) The same is true when the Commission encourages and supports processes of national reconciliation.

Both the UN General Assembly and Security Council, in their resolutions on the 2015 Review of the UN Peacebuilding Architecture, have, furthermore, underlined the need for the Commission "to serve as a platform to convene all relevant actors within and outside the United Nations, including from Member States, national authorities, United Nations missions and country teams … in order to provide recommendations and information to improve recommendations."[41]

Frustrations

The Commission Does Not "Show Us the Money"

The expectation that the UN Peacebuilding Commission should be helping to mobilise resources for the countries on its agenda, beyond what the Peacebuilding Fund provides, is very high. As I have indicated elsewhere, "several representatives of the governments of countries on the agenda and Heads of UN missions have underlined that well-articulated peacebuilding strategies are meaningless if not adequately funded".[42] The Commission's role in mobilising resources goes beyond money, and that includes mobilising technical expertise from within and beyond its membership to tackle peacebuilding issues. More importantly, the disappointed expectations about the Commission's performance in this area can be attributed, in part, to the belief that it ought to mobilise financial resources for issues in the broader development agenda in a country and, in part, to the hope that these resource mobilisation efforts will yield financial resources for the in-country UN Multi-Donor Trust Fund.

The one country where the Commission's efforts in resource mobilisation have been noteworthy—as described earlier—is Burundi. There is risk, though, that the political crisis that has convulsed that country since 2015, precipitated by Pierre Nkurunziza's controversial, successful bid for a third presidential term, could potentially undermine the results of that modest effort, as the peacebuilding programmes that the financial resources supported could be damaged or destroyed.

The recognition that more financial resources are required for peacebuilding prompted the recommendation, made by the 2015 Review of the UN Peacebuilding Architecture, of "[P]roviding the [Peacebuilding] Fund annually with a symbolic 1 per cent of the value of the total United Nations budget for peace operations as core funding from assessed contributions [which] would help close the gap between mandates and programme resources."[43] This recommendation had not, however, been adopted at the time of writing.

The Commission Should Focus Not on "Hard" But "Soft" Issues in Peacebuilding

Given the expansive nature of peacebuilding, it should not come as a surprise that the UN Peacebuilding Commission's engagement in the countries on its agenda has spanned both so-called "hard" and "soft" issues. (See Omeje, and Richmond in this volume.) However, there is a growing belief that the Peacebuilding Commission is highly unlikely to make great impact on the hard issues—resource mobilisation, natural resource management, and support for institutional infrastructure. As such, the Commission should focus on soft issues such as reconciliation, transitional justice, support for inclusive political dialogue, and civil society engagement in peacebuilding. This debate harks back to the contending perspectives between the three normative frameworks, to the "tangible vs. intangible" controversy, and to the definition of peacebuilding itself. Yet the stress on soft issues is recognition that some of the Commission's impacts are reflected in intangibles, such as behavioural or attitudinal changes, that are not amenable to quantitative measurement. There is no easy way to resolve this dilemma of "soft vs. hard" issues. But it bears special emphasis that respecting the peacebuilding priorities proposed to the Commission by the country concerned will be a crucial determining factor in overcoming this tension.

Conclusion: The Future of the UN Peacebuilding Commission

The way that the UN Peacebuilding Commission manages three issues holds the key to its future success: the Commission's relations with the wider peacebuilding field, defined in terms of support for, and actions in, the countries on its agenda through appropriate institutional arrangements; its ability to contribute to financing peacebuilding priorities in these countries; and its relations with the UN Security Council. (See Ugarte in this volume.) It is easy enough to make the point that all these issues are "means to an end". That end is laying the foundation for sustainable peace and development, a process that can be long and arduous.

At one level, getting the Commission's processes right is fundamental to creating the impact that it seeks to achieve, and that most stakeholders expect the body to achieve. Hence, improving processes is essential. But improving the processes of the Commission concerns more than just the aforementioned issues; as the areas of frustration outlined in this chapter highlight, the scope of improvements required is large. In fact, making improvements in many of these areas will contribute significantly to the functioning and effectiveness of the Commission.

At a deeper level, there is a need to develop some commonly agreed criteria under the auspices of the Commission's Organisational Committee on how the body's impact should be measured. The lack of such criteria has led to conflicting assessments or judgements of the Commission's performance. As is the case in other disciplines and institutions, it is important that the guesswork be taken out of measuring the Commission's performance. If there is one contribution that can be made to improving the performance of the Commission, it is precisely to develop a common measurement of success.

In the final analysis, the future of the UN Peacebuilding Commission will ride on the commitment of its members to support the countries on its agenda; on the flexibility and adaptability of its working methods; on developing and strengthening partnerships that help it to deliver desired results; on agreements on how its impact should be measured; and on the willingness and sustained commitment of the countries on the agenda to pursue the policies and measures that enable them to overcome the legacy of conflict and fragility and lay the foundations for sustainable peace and development.

Notes

1. United Nations (UN), "Review of the United Nations Peacebuilding Architecture", UN Doc. A/64/868 and S/2010/393, 21 July 2010, p. 7.
2. UN, "Review of the United Nations Peacebuilding Architecture", p. 8.
3. UN, "Challenge of Sustaining Peace: Report of the Advisory Group of Experts on the Review of the Peacebuilding Architecture", UN Doc. A69/968 and S/2015/490, 30 June 2015, p. 8.
4. UN, "Challenge of Sustaining Peace", pp. 8–9.
5. Ejeviome Eloho Otobo, *Consolidating Peace in Africa: The Role of the United Nations Peacebuilding Commission* (Princeton: AMV Publishing Services, 2015), p. 117.
6. Devon Curtis, "Introduction: The Contested Politics of Peacebuilding in Africa", in Devon Curtis and Gwinyayi A. Dzinesa (eds.), *Peacebuilding, Power, and Politics in Africa* (Johannesburg: Wits University Press; and Athens: Ohio University Press, 2013), p. 9.
7. As of June 2017, the six countries were: Burundi, the Central African Republic (CAR), Guinea, Guinea-Bissau, Sierra Leone, and Liberia.
8. Center on International Cooperation (CIC) and International Peace Institute (IPI), *Taking Stock, Looking Forward: A Strategic Review of the Peacebuilding Commission*, independent study commissioned by the Permanent Mission of Denmark to the UN (New York, 2008), p. 28.
9. UN, "Sierra Leone Peacebuilding Cooperation Framework", UN Doc. PBC/2/SLE/1, 3 December 2007, pp. 4–8.
10. CIC and IPI, *Taking Stock, Looking Forward*, p. 3.
11. The CIC and IPI report, *Taking Stock, Looking Forward*, highlights this view of the work by the chair of the Commission's Burundi configuration; *see* pp. 2–3.
12. UN Peacebuilding Commission (PBC), "Report of the Fact-Finding Mission of the Chairman of the Burundi Specific Meeting of the Peacebuilding Commission to Burundi", 5–7 September 2007, p. 4.
13. UN General Assembly Resolution 60/180 (2005) and UN Security Council Resolution 1645 (2005), para. 2 (a, c), emphasis added.
14. UN, "Review of the United Nations Peacebuilding Architecture", p. 11.
15. UN, "Review of the United Nations Peacebuilding Architecture", pp. 13, 18.
16. UN, "Statement of Mutual Commitments for Peacebuilding in Liberia", UN Doc. A/PBC/4/LBR/1, 16 November 2010, p. 8.
17. Geopolicity, "Public Expenditure and Needs Assessment Review of the Security Sector in Liberia: Establishing a Sustainable security Sector in View of UNMIL Transition", Washington DC, 2011, p. 1.
18. This encouragement was provided in a letter addressed to Amara Konneh, Liberia's minister of finance, dated 21 February 2012 and jointly signed by the World Bank Country Manager and Officer-in-Charge of the UN Mission in Liberia (UNMIL), proposing that the Liberian government should increase its budget allocation to the security sector.
19. *See* UN, "Report of the Peacebuilding Commission on its Eighth Session", UN Doc. A/818 and S/2015/174, 11 March 2015, p. 5.
20. *See* Ejeviome Eloho Otobo, "Leading the Peacebuilding Commission: An Institutional History in the Making", Views from Practice no. 1/2013 (Brussels: Global Governance Institute, March 2013), pp. 7–9.

21. UN Peacebuilding Support Office, "Resource Mobilization for Peacebuilding Priorities: The Role of the Peacebuilding Commission", New York, 2012.
22. For more information, *see* https://www.unglobalcompact.org/ (accessed 28 November 2016).
23. *See* UN, "Provisional Rules of Procedure of the Peacebuilding Commission", UN Doc. PBC/1/OC/3/Rev.1, 5 December 2012, p. 1.
24. Bartjan Wegter, "Emerging from the Crib: The Difficult First Steps of the Newly Born UN Peacebuilding Commission", *International Organisation Law Review* 4, no. 2 (2008), pp. 343–345.
25. Christiana Tah and Judy Cheng-Hopkins, "Rebuilding Liberia, One Hub at a Time", *Mail and Guardian* (South Africa), 10 February 2013.
26. Statements issued by the chair of the Commission's Guinea configuration on 8 July 2013, 17 September 2013, and 24 October 2013.
27. Letter from the chair of the Commission's Guinea-Bissau configuration to Guinea-Bissau's minister of foreign affairs, dated 6 May 2010.
28. The reply from Guinea-Bissau's minister of foreign affairs was dated 21 May 2010.
29. Statement issued by the chair of the Commission's Guinea-Bissau configuration on 13 April 2012.
30. Statement of the chair of the Commission's Burundi configuration to the second sectoral conference devoted to governance, held in Bujumbura, Burundi, on 28 October 2013. The first sectoral conference, held in July 2013, had been devoted to infrastructure development.
31. UN High Commissioner for Refugees (UNHCR), "Burundi Situation", Regional Update, May 2017, http://reliefweb.int/sites/reliefweb.int/files/resources/UNHCR_0.pdf (accessed 9 August 2017).
32. Security Council Report, *Peacebuilding Commission*, Special Report no.2, 5 October 2007, p. 7.
33. UN, *In Larger Freedom: Towards Development, Security, and Human Rights for All*, Report of the UN Secretary-General, New York, 2005, para. 115.
34. *See* UN, "A More Secure World: Our Shared Responsibility", Report of the Secretary-General's High-Level Panel on Threats, Challenges and Change, UN Doc. A/59/565, 2 December 2004.
35. *See* Wegter, "Emerging from the Crib", pp. 345–346.
36. Mark Malloch-Brown, "Holmes Lecture: Can the UN Be Reformed?", presentation at the annual meeting of the Academic Council on the UN System (ACUNS), New York, 7 June 2007, p. 7.
37. Britain is used synonymously with the United Kingdom (UK) in this volume.
38. Funmi Olonisakin and Eka Ikpe, "The United Nations Peacebuilding Commission", in Curtis and Dzinesa, *Peacebuilding, Power, and Politics in Africa*, p. 149.
39. Data from the Multi-Partner Trust Fund Office, http://mptf.undp.org/factsheet/fund/PB000 (accessed 28 November 2016).
40. UN General Assembly Resolution A/60/180, operative para. 18.
41. *See* UN General Assembly Resolution A/70/263, 27 April 2016, and UN Security Council Resolution S/2282/2016, 27 April 2016, para. 4(d).
42. Otobo, "Leading the Peacebuilding Commission", p. 16.
43. UN, "Challenge of Sustaining Peace", p. 5.

CHAPTER 20

The Practice of Peacemaking and Peacebuilding in Somalia

Augustine Mahiga

Peacemaking typically comprises mediation processes that lead to negotiated agreements between conflicting parties. Once secured, peace has to be kept and consolidated through a combination of political, security, and civilian actions. In cases where peaceful negotiated settlements fail, peace enforcement can become necessary. This involves the application of coercive measures that may include sanctions and military force. Peacebuilding, on the other hand, can be viewed as a series of measures that cut across the processes of peacemaking, peacekeeping, and in particular, post-conflict peace consolidation, with a view towards sustaining the peace and reducing the risk of societies relapsing into conflict (see Omeje in this volume).[1] The United Nations (UN) Peacebuilding Commission, created in 2005, sought to define and institutionalise national capacities for the management of sustainable peace and development (see Otobo in this volume). Though even before the creation of the Peacebuilding Commission, the UN had engaged in a range of peacebuilding activities in various countries.[2] These past and current experiences have shown that there are activities within the processes of peacemaking and peacekeeping that can constitute peacebuilding measures. The experience in Somalia, in particular, with its history of protracted conflicts, has been demonstrative of how making, enforcing, and building peace are simultaneous processes that can become mutually reinforcing.

This chapter examines the interwoven processes of peacemaking and peacebuilding in Somalia over the past two decades and focuses, in particular, on the experience of the Somali peace process from 2010 to 2013, when I was the Special Representative of the UN Secretary-General for Somalia. This period was preceded by 15 failed peace initiatives since the collapse of the Siad Barre

A. Mahiga (✉)
Tanzania's Minister of Foreign Affairs and East African Cooperation, Dar es Salaam, Tanzania

T. Karbo, K. Virk (eds.), *The Palgrave Handbook of Peacebuilding in Africa*, https://doi.org/10.1007/978-3-319-62202-6_20

military regime in January 1991. The 16th initiative, discussed here, succeeded in ending a transition period that had begun with the Mbagathi Peace Process (2002–2004) under the auspices of the Intergovernmental Authority on Development (IGAD). The ending of that transition was marked by the adoption of an interim constitution, which Somalia had not had since 1969 (when the independence constitution was abolished by the military), and the formation of a new, inclusive, and representative clan-based parliament in August 2012; followed by the election of a new parliamentary speaker, Mohamed Osman Jawari, later in the same month and of a president, Hassan Sheikh Mohamud, in September 2012. The new Somali president subsequently nominated a prime minister, Abdi Farah Shirdon, who was approved by parliament and, together with the president, by November 2012 formed a new Somali federal government representing all major clans, minority ethnic groups, and women. With a more legitimate national outlook, the new government won national support as well as wider international recognition compared to the previous government.[3] The only faction that was not represented in the peace process and was not represented in the government was the al-Shabaab insurgent group. Since then Somalia has reached another milestone with a peaceful transfer of power that saw Abdullahi Mohamed Farmajo installed as president in 2017, albeit following a delayed and limited-franchise electoral process, with universal elections put off till 2021 (see Hirsch in this volume).

Liberal Peacebuilding in Somalia and Its Limitations

The bulk of scholarly work and discussions on peacebuilding relates to theoretical analysis and operational experiences of peacebuilding in post-conflict situations. Because Somalia is not yet fully free of conflict, and as such, not seen to be in an entirely post-conflict stage, the country's experience has tended to be left out or has received only cursory attention in these conversations. As Christopher Clapham has correctly pointed out: "In a volume on peacebuilding in Africa, Somalia lies at the bottom of the pile".[4] Indeed, the reality is that violent conflicts in some parts of Somalia have raged unabated since 1991, although there have been areas of exceptional stability such as the self-declared Republic of Somaliland and the semi-autonomous Puntland State of Somalia (see Richmond in this volume). In the rest of Somalia, there was no sustainable peace to keep or to build upon before 2012, when Somalia was commonly referred to as a "failed" or "failing" state. The country had no effective central government and was dominated by competing, localised, clan-based warlords who were not inclined to support national peacemaking or peacebuilding initiatives.

Furthermore, the practice of peacebuilding in post-conflict countries such as Sierra Leone, Burundi, and Liberia has been based on the assumptions of the founding United Nations Security Council and General Assembly resolutions that established the UN Peacebuilding Commission in December 2005.[5] (See Omeje, and Otobo in this volume.) A key purpose of the Commission is to, among other things, "bring together all relevant actors to marshal resources and to advise on and propose integrated strategies for post-conflict peacebuilding and recovery".[6] The Commission's mandate involves five activities: (1) initiatives to support long-term processes for consolidating peace, by addressing the root causes of violent conflicts; (2) measures aimed at preventing and reducing the risks of lapse or relapse into violent conflict; (3) assistance to governments of countries emerging from conflict, with priority given to strategies for socio-economic recovery, reintegration of former combatants, and return of refugees and internally displaced persons (IDPs); (4) re-focusing the attention of the international community after the initial media coverage in order to marshal resources for peacebuilding activities; and (5) building national capacities for reforming and managing security and political institutions for "good governance" and democratic dispensation.

Since the re-establishment of the UN Political Office for Somalia (UNPOS) in Mogadishu in January 2012, the formation of the new Somali government later in the same year, and especially the adoption of UN Security Council Resolution 2093 in March 2013,[7] state-building and peacebuilding have been included in the activities of the world organisation in Somalia, and in particular, in the mandate of the UN Assistance Mission in Somalia (UNSOM), which replaced UNPOS in June 2013.[8] Prior to that, the UN Peacebuilding Fund (part of the Peacebuilding Commission) had only given seed money to the UN Development Programme (UNDP) for police training activities in the semi-autonomous Puntland State of Somalia. As the Mbagathi transition period neared its end, the Peacebuilding Fund also gave UNPOS and UNDP financial support to complete the constitution-making process. The Peacebuilding Fund has since focused on mobilising resources for peacebuilding activities, in support of the Somali federal government, where there is relative peace. These activities have included creating administrative capacities, building the security and judiciary sectors, and creating conditions for social and economic reconstruction at district and regional levels.

The activities of the UN Peacebuilding Commission are based on the prevailing liberal assumptions and approaches of Western liberal democratic political systems and competitive market economies. The end of the Cold War by 1990 left these as the dominant global political and economic models. Indeed, in the absence of alternative models, the liberal approach has become the de facto approach to peacebuilding in most countries emerging from conflict. However, liberal peacebuilding has not necessarily brought peace, stability, and socio-economic transformation to the countries that have adopted it. For instance, while it has opened space for political pluralism, the denial of political participation to marginalised groups has persisted in cases, leading to political tensions that have on occasion erupted into violent conflict. Similarly, multiparty elections have not always been the panacea, and their outcomes have in cases resulted in violence and political crises. The liberal approach to peacebuilding thus has shortcomings that need to be addressed in order to make it more responsive to social needs and social justice, and more adaptive to the different contexts in countries emerging from conflict. (See also Richmond in this volume.)

Devon Curtis and Gwinyayi Dzinesa, in their 2012 book *Peacebuilding, Power, and Politics in Africa*, make three important observations that are relevant to the Somali experience. First, "[l]iberal peacebuilding is … both a normative agenda, as well as a framework for understanding … diverse [sectoral] activities and initiatives".[9] Second, liberal peacebuilding cannot have uniform application, as there are varied national as well as local causes and characteristics across conflicts. Third, peacebuilding is not necessarily the next stage of a linear progression after peacemaking and peacekeeping, but can be undertaken concurrently. As Curtis writes: "Activities to strengthen 'peace' can take place before, during, or after conflict. Likewise, 'peace' and 'war' may exist simultaneously in different parts of the same country".[10] These observations, especially the third, are particularly applicable to the situation in Somalia, where peacemaking and peacebuilding are taking place concurrently in some parts of the country as armed conflict against the al-Shabaab militant group rages in other parts.

Before examining other different approaches to peacemaking and peacebuilding in Somalia, it is useful thus to explore the historical context of state collapse that led to political anarchy in the country and necessitated various national, regional, and international peace initiatives.

Somalia: Background and Historical Context

Somalia Under Siad Barre, 1969–1991

The fall of Siad Barre's military government in 1991 was a classic consequence of the internal political stresses and tensions inherent in dictatorial regimes, one precipitated by the end of the Cold War rivalry between the United States (US)-led West and the Soviet Union in Africa. In October 1969, when Barre successfully staged a military coup, he inherited an irredentist agenda for a Greater Somalia from the deposed civilian government, which had sought to galvanise the country's historically deep-rooted clan divisions and to promote pan-Somali aspirations beyond its borders. Barre sought to use this populist ideology, with its appeal of pan-Somali nationalism, to stay in power.

Somali expansionism, however, went against the letter and spirit of the new Organisation of African Unity (OAU), created in May 1963, which upheld inherited colonial boundaries to avoid border disputes among the newly independent African states. The UN as well supported this African position. Nonetheless, Siad Barre exploited the strategic Cold War rivalry in the Horn of Africa between the US and the Soviet Union, to obtain military support from the Soviets to pursue his claims to the Ogaden region of Ethiopia. With the longest coastline (3,000 kilometres) in Africa, Somalia is situated in a strategically important location at the entrance of the Red Sea to the Suez Canal and close to the Middle East's oil resources. Ethiopia, under Haile Selassie, had been a strategic partner of the US since the 1950s. France, as a (former) colonial power in the region, had naval and land-based military in Djibouti, while Britain had a military presence in Kenya.[11] For the Soviet Union, which had no other presence in the Horn of Africa or the Indian Ocean region at the time, Somalia was a promising strategic outpost to counter the West's historical presence and influence in these regions.

Siad Barre embraced Marxism-Leninism, built a one-party state, and with the help of Soviet expertise and planners, tried to orient Somalia's predominantly pastoralist economy towards a centrally planned socialist economy. In return, the Soviet Union generously assisted Barre to build one of the biggest and best-equipped military establishments in sub-Saharan Africa at the time. This military machine gave Barre the confidence to invade the Ogaden region of Ethiopia in 1977. He tried to take further advantage of the political turmoil that enveloped Ethiopia at the time, following the fall of Selassie in 1974. Contrary to expectations, Barre's Ethiopian adventure turned into a military and political disaster. The Somali army was routed by the Ethiopians, with help from Cuban troops airlifted by the Soviet Union from Angola.

The Soviets had switched sides, having found a new, more ideologically committed ally in Ethiopia's Mengistu Haile Mariam, who had overthrown Selassie. In a dramatic turnabout, Barre turned to the US, which had just lost Ethiopia's partnership with the change of regime, and in 1977, expelled all Soviet personnel from their bases in Somalia. However, Somalia's strategic significance began declining as the Cold War neared its end by 1990. At the same time, following the Ogaden fiasco, Siad Barre's domestic support had been eroding.

Barre created a highly centralised political system in Somalia. He suspended the independence constitution, abolished clan-based political parties, and established a Marxist-Leninist vanguard party, though the ideological depth of the party and commitment of its cadres remained doubtful and superficial in a country without a working class or a significant peasantry. Notwithstanding the ban on clan-based political organisations, Barre's inner political circle and key advisors continued mainly to be from his Darood clan and sub-clans. His regime's achievements included the introduction of the Roman alphabet for writing the Somali language, the provision of secular education to boys and girls, and the launch of successful adult literacy campaigns. But these were overshadowed by human rights abuses, political patronage, and corruption in the state machinery and public life.[12] When the Barre regime fell in January 1991, the military and all other public institutions collapsed, with socialism having failed to take root or provide a durable basis for state-building. Somaliland broke away in May 1991,[13] while the rest of Somalia became a political void dominated by feuding clan-based warlords.

Warlords and Anarchy, 1991–1995

The collapse of Siad Barre's military regime left Somalia awash with weapons. Former military commanders formed rival clan-based militias and fought to control territory, with widespread looting. As lawlessness spread, traditional elders were marginalised and their authority curbed by warlords, who soon controlled up to ten different militias in Mogadishu and other major cities in southwestern Somalia. Neighbouring Ethiopia and Djibouti tried to broker agreements among warlords, but without lasting success. The competing clan-based warlords had no plan to restore national authority. Rather, they were mainly interested in maximising their own benefits from the crumbling national economy, extorting local economies, and looting public property. At the same time, during this period, Somalia—together with the rest of the Horn of Africa—was hit by a severe drought that led to severe famine, with devastating humanitarian consequences, and marked the beginning of UN involvement in the country.[14]

In April 1992, the United Nations Security Council established the first UN Operation in Somalia (UNOSOM I) to encourage a cessation of hostilities among the warlords and facilitate the delivery of humanitarian assistance.[15] But the mission arrived late, and with only 50 observers and 500 troops, was no match for the heavily armed militias of the warlords. It was unable even to move out of the Mogadishu airport. Meanwhile, the humanitarian situation continued to worsen. At the initiative of the United States, in December 1992, the Security Council authorised a more robust multilateral force, the Unified Task Force (UNITAF), comprising 30,000 troops led by the US, to secure the country for the delivery of humanitarian assistance. Thus confronted, the warlord controlling Mogadishu, Mohamed Farah Aideed, accepted the humanitarian mission on the understanding that he would remain in charge of the Somali capital and its environs. By the time its mandate expired in May 1993, the US-led task force had recorded some success in the delivery of humanitarian assistance.

UNITAF was replaced by the second UN Operation in Somalia (UNOSOM II)—established by the Security Council in March 1993—after a brief transition period. The 28,000-strong mission, backed up by a US Marines unit that had served with UNITAF, was mandated to create conditions for disarmament, political reconciliation, and the creation of a national government in Somalia. Furthermore, UNOSOM II was deployed under Chapter VII of the UN Charter of 1945, with the authority to use force if necessary,[16] and as such, represented an external attempt for the first time to enforce peace in Somalia. As expected, the Mogadishu warlords resisted the deployment of the mission with an aggressive media offensive and military skirmishes. The UN initially responded robustly.

However, following the downing of two US Marine helicopters and the death of 18 American soldiers in the "Black Hawk Down" incident of October 1993 (see Mzali in this volume), the peace enforcement objectives of UNOSOM II were aborted. The incident shattered the confidence of the UN mission and provoked an international public outcry, especially in the US which withdrew its Marines immediately and then pulled out completely from Somalia in March 1994.[17] (See Jonah, and Hirsch in this volume.) Meanwhile, the security situation continued to deteriorate, and the UN received no cooperation from the warlords. In these difficult and dangerous conditions, the UN was compelled to leave Somalia in March 1995 and moved its offices to Nairobi in neighbouring Kenya. Most of the diplomatic missions still in Somalia also left the country. Somalia was, in effect, abandoned and left to its own devices.

Local and Traditional Peacemaking and Peacebuilding Efforts in Somalia

"Governance Without Government": The Peacebuilding Role of Civil Society

The phrase "governance without government" is borrowed from political commentators writing on the role of civil society in peacebuilding initiatives in Somalia after 1995.[18] While warlords continued to hold sway at this time, their grip on communities was weakening. The period from 1995 to 2006 was characterised by informal governance arrangements at the local level, which involved various actors—such as business, neighbourhood watch groups, and civil society movements—and employed a combination of governance practices including customary law and Sharia courts. In their limited ways, they together provided a modicum of law and order in Somalia, and were able to deliver some social services to local communities.[19] This was a unique example of stand-alone approaches at the local level in the absence of a central authority in a country. Civil society organisations created local structures to manage and coordinate their respective mandates, in defiance of the warlords. The organisational capacities of these traditional and civil society groups created the foundation for a bottom-up approach to later peacemaking and peacebuilding initiatives in the process of ending the Somali transition by 2012.

The rise and vibrancy of civil society during this period can be partly attributed to the resilience of the Somali people in the face of adversity, as well as to a proactive approach towards Somalia by certain sections of the international community. In the absence of a functioning central government, some international actors, operating from neighbouring Kenya, provided direct support to Somali civil society. The European Commission, through Oxfam, and the US Agency for International Development (USAID), through CARE, provided capacity-building support to civil society organisations to strengthen organisational skills and to provide basic social services. Interpeace and Sweden's Life and Peace Institute (LPI) helped to create local civil society organisations in Mogadishu, Puntland, and Somaliland. Similarly, Islamic civil society and charitable organisations from Arabia, the Gulf States, and South Asia were also involved in assisting civil society and community-based organisations by providing social services, mainly in the education and public health sectors.

Somali civil society groups facilitated dialogue and reconciliation between and among social groups, including clan elders, clerics, women's groups, and business people. Two notable experiences of reconciliation happened during this period.

One was a "peace caravan", when elders from warring clans agreed to travel together, across various warlord-held territories, to a reconciliation conference. The other involved women's groups facilitating negotiations and successfully ending long-standing deadly communal clashes in Mogadishu.[20] Indeed, several women's groups were established during this period, some of which grew to become vibrant national organisations. These women's groups built national networks that are now engaged in advocacy work for women's empowerment, and have demonstrated an ability to provide leadership at both the local and national levels. Apart from participating in the delivery of community services, women then, as they are now, were active in demanding human rights and political participation, opposing gender-based violence. (See Porter in this volume.)

Traditional Systems

The traditional clan and kinship system in Somalia has been used for generations to address issues of reconciliation, to ensure the protection of families, to deliver justice, and to promote peace at the local level within clans and subclans. It is a community-level approach to peacebuilding, below the level of the state. This system has been operating in Somali society with remarkable success, facilitated by a common language, history, religion, and culture. The local traditional systems have been used for mediation and arbitration of local clan disputes over such issues as access to water and land. The informal traditional structure of using elders to enforce law and order to resolve disputes, and maintain peace within communities, predates the colonial era. The authority of the traditional elders was restricted at the height of warlordism, but their legitimacy and authority, rooted in historical claims, remained valid and respected.

Clan identity has acted like an "insurance policy" in Somalia, especially in times of adversity.[21] Its main limitation is that at a higher level of organisation, it needs an overriding authority to enforce the consensus reached at the community level; hence the need for institutionalising it at regional and national levels. In this regard, national peacebuilding approaches must consider the traditional grassroots approaches to promoting reconciliation and delivering justice. In the absence of fully functioning district and regional administrations, peacemaking and peacebuilding will continue to rely on these traditional mechanisms. Another notable shortcoming of the traditional approach is that it excludes women from participating in deliberations. In this context, it is encouraging to note that the provisional constitution of 2012 has incorporated provisions for women to participate in decision-making at all levels. It has also recognised and entrenched, where appropriate, the traditional approaches to peacemaking and peacebuilding.

The Union of Islamic Courts

The Union of Islamic Courts (UIC) began as a grassroots civil society movement, during the period of "governance without government", to address—

through the application of Sharia law—the insecurity and injustice perpetuated by the warlords. The UIC also worked closely with Islamic charities in the delivery of social services. As it gained popular support, the Union quickly spread from Mogadishu to other parts of south-central Somalia between 1995 and 2006. It eventually evolved into an umbrella organisation of different Sharia courts in various parts of south-central Somalia, with political and military capacities to challenge the excesses of the warlords. By 2006, the Mogadishu-based UIC was arguably the undisputed authority in south-central Somalia, seeking as it was to fill the vacuum created by the collapsed central state. The most prominent and popular role of the UIC was the delivery of justice through Sharia law, which brought law and order to supplant the intimidation, extortion, and violence of the warlords.

The leadership of the UIC also aimed to establish a national government as an alternative to the Transitional Federal Government (TFG) formed at the 2004 Mbagathi Peace Conference, but which had remained in exile in Nairobi for over two years. Encouraged by the rise of global Islamic fundamentalism in the Middle East, the UIC sought to form a caliphate in Somalia through its network of Sharia courts in the country. Through its governing council, the union proceeded to build a radical and powerful military wing that later came to be called al-Shabaab (meaning "The Youth").[22] The UIC did not exist long enough to establish its own version of political and governance institutions in the country, before it collapsed following the intervention of the Ethiopian military in Somalia in December 2006. Nonetheless, in its short life, the UIC succeeded in attracting diverse shades of Islamic groups to give its leadership political clout inside and outside the country. However, within the movement, there were radical and moderate elements who differed in their application of Sharia law, and in their relations with neighbouring countries. At the same time, the harsh application of Sharia law, with draconian punishments and reported, extensive human rights violations, caused divisions within the ranks of the UIC and resulted in mixed support for the courts domestically, and negative publicity internationally. The military wing of the UIC distinguished itself early as an uncompromising ideological group linked to al-Qaeda.[23]

Regional Initiatives

The League of Arab States, together with IGAD, attempted to initiate a political dialogue between the leadership of the Transitional Federal Government (in exile in Nairobi), and the leadership of the UIC. The two parties met in Khartoum, Sudan, in June 2006 and agreed to adopt the Khartoum Declaration, which called for a cessation of hostilities and power-sharing between them. But they were unable to agree on how to implement the declaration, and in particular on who should take the lead in the proposed power-sharing arrangement. The transitional federal leadership had won international recognition and felt that it should take the lead in the partnership, while the UIC had neither international nor regional recognition but was in control of a significant swath of territory inside Somalia, and had a sizable, powerful military force. This strategic advantage gave the UIC confidence to reject the power-sharing arrangement.

In anticipation of the Khartoum Declaration's implementation, IGAD meanwhile had requested authorisation from the UN Security Council to deploy its Peace Support Mission in Somalia (IGASOM) to facilitate that process. In December 2006, the Security Council—through Resolution 1725—authorised IGASOM to monitor progress in the peace dialogue between the two parties. The resolution also called upon the UIC "to cease any further military expansion and reject those with an extremist agenda or links to international terrorism".[24] The Council further warned that it would take measures against those blocking the peaceful dialogue, and against those seeking to overthrow by force the TFG and otherwise threaten regional stability. In the wake of this resolution, the UIC had no incentive to pursue further dialogue with the transitional federal leadership. The Khartoum talks collapsed, and IGASOM was never deployed.

Furthermore, relations between the UIC and neighbouring Ethiopia, which supported the TFG, became increasingly confrontational and strained. Ethiopia felt uncomfortable with a jihadist militant outfit with allegiance to international terrorist groups at its doorstep. Encouraged by the international community, Ethiopia sent a force into Somalia in December 2006 that dislodged the UIC and installed the TFG in Mogadishu, which for the previous two years had struggled to relocate to the capital without success. The radical al-Shabaab faction of the UIC continued its campaign against what it called foreign occupation by Ethiopia, while its moderate wing went into exile in Eritrea and regrouped as the Alliance for the Re-Liberation of Somalia (ARS). The Eritrean faction entered into negotiations with the TFG, under UN auspices, in Djibouti, and the two sides agreed to form a new coalition government under the Djibouti Agreement of 2008.[25] This new government continued to be known as Somalia's Transitional Federal Government and to retain the institutions contained in the Transitional Federal Charter of 2004.

Securing Space for Peacemaking and Peacebuilding in South-Central Somalia

As Ethiopian troops began to withdraw from Somalia, the African Union (AU) Peace and Security Council (PSC) decided to send immediately, for an initial six months, the African Mission in Somalia (AMISOM) to stabilise the security situation in the country. (On the African Peace and Security Architecture, see Kuwali in this volume.) In February 2007, the UN Security Council authorised the deployment of AMISOM with the following mandate: (1) to support dialogue and reconciliation initiatives in the country led by the transitional federal institutions; (2) to protect the transitional institutions and provide security for key infrastructures; (3) to build, reform, and train Somali forces; (4) to undertake the disarmament, demobilisation, and reintegration of militias and ex-combatants; and (5) to create the necessary security conditions for the provision of humanitarian assistance.[26] From the very outset, the AU expressed the hope that the mission would eventually evolve into a UN peacekeeping operation in Somalia to support long-term stabilisation and post-conflict peacebuilding. But this hope has continued to be unrealised, ostensibly because there is no peace to keep.

Initially, the AU followed an earlier IGAD recommendation intended for IGASOM that Somalia's neighbouring states should not contribute troops to AMISOM, and accepted troop offers from Uganda and Burundi. Other African countries were reluctant to send troops to Somalia because of the difficult security situation there, and the high costs involved in the absence of assured and predictable additional support. Ugandan President Yoweri Museveni argued that his willingness to send troops to Somalia was motivated by a commitment to the spirit of pan-Africanism instilled in him by the late Tanzanian president, Julius Nyerere, who had sent Tanzanian troops to assist Ugandans in liberating themselves from the dictatorship of Idi Amin in 1979. President Museveni further maintained that because Tanzania also then helped Uganda rebuild its security sector, Uganda was similarly willing not only to fight the al-Shabaab insurgents together with the Somali armed forces, but also to contribute to building the security capabilities of the Somali army and police.[27]

The AU and the UN have since 2011 allowed other African troops, including those from countries neighbouring Somalia such as Ethiopia and Kenya, to join the over 22,000-strong AMISOM to deal with the strong resistance from al-Shabaab. Since its early campaign against Ethiopian troops, al-Shabaab has incited Somali nationalism to oppose and fight all forms of foreign military presence in the country, including AMISOM. From the beginning, AMISOM was compelled to adopt a robust peace enforcement posture against al-Shabaab, which fought its troops as they landed in Mogadishu in 2007 while other al-Shabaab units regrouped and consolidated themselves in the rest of southwestern Somalia. When the leadership of the new transitional federal institutions was installed in Mogadishu, with the help of AMISOM, it occupied only a few blocks around Villa Somalia (the official presidential residence), which AMISOM had secured alongside the Mogadishu airport and the seaport for bringing in supplies vital to the mission.

Following the installation of the Transitional Federal Government in Mogadishu, it was deemed necessary to bring the peace process inside Somalia in order to give the Somali people ownership. A secure space for the planned meetings and conferences had to be created by AMISOM after al-Shabaab had been pushed out of Mogadishu in August 2011. The space created by AMISOM allowed the process of implementing the roadmap to end the transition in Somalia, to begin in Mogadishu in October 2011. AMISOM performed a localised peacekeeping function in Mogadishu to secure the city from asymmetrical warfare while pushing the front lines beyond Mogadishu with conventional warfare. The restored security in Mogadishu, albeit fragile, permitted the UN Political Office for Somalia to relocate back from Nairobi. The return of

UNPOS was inaugurated by the visit of the UN Secretary-General, South Korea's Ban Ki-moon, to Mogadishu in December 2011, the first such visit in nearly two decades. The AU and several foreign embassies have also since re-established their offices in Mogadishu.

The protection of civilians in the ongoing conflict against al-Shabaab has been a major challenge to AMISOM and to Somalia's armed forces. Warfare against terrorism in a heavily populated urban environment, with only basic conventional weapons without air support, claimed many civilian causalities in Mogadishu in the early part of the war. Though exact figures are hard to come by, according to Amnesty International, "About 6,000 civilians were reportedly killed in fighting in the capital Mogadishu and across southern and central Somalia in 2007 and more than 600,000 Somali civilians were internally displaced".[28] As AMISOM and Somalia's armed forces have gained an upper hand in conventional warfare in the urban and rural areas, al-Shabaab has resorted more and more too asymmetrical terrorist tactics against civilians, the armed forces, and government institutions. These tactics have continued to cause periodic havoc, mainly in Mogadishu. Observance of humanitarian and human rights law has become an integral part of AMISOM's mandate, the training of Somali forces, and battlefield practice. Significant improvements in operational activities have been recorded by AMISOM and Somalia's armed forces. Consequently, refugees and internally displaced persons, as well as persons from the diaspora, have been returning to some urban areas, mainly to Mogadishu, and to other parts of south-central Somalia. As of 2017, an estimated 1.5 million Somalis continued to be internally displaced and nearly 900,000 were refugees in neighbouring countries (including Kenya, Yemen, and Ethiopia).[29]

The Dynamics and Challenges of an Integrated Peacemaking and Peacebuilding Process

The Somali peace process was mediated and advanced through simultaneous peacemaking and peacebuilding processes that comprised: (1) broadening inclusiveness through clan, geographical, and political constituencies; (2) reconciling clan and personal institutional interests; (3) laying the foundations for institutional legitimacy and broad representation through the roadmap process that would pave the way for a new interim constitution, parliament, and government; and (4) interlinking and mutually reinforcing the various processes to bring the transitional period of governance to a successful conclusion.

As earlier mentioned, the 2008 Djibouti Agreement permitted the installation of a new Transitional Federal Government in Mogadishu and revived the Somali peace process, which had stalled since 2004. No sooner had the new government been established in Mogadishu than tension began to develop between President Sheikh Sherif Ahmed and then Prime Minister Omar Sharmake over issues related to the division of administrative responsibilities and the implementation of the transitional tasks outlined in the Federal Charter, especially the process of crafting a new constitution. In the end, Sharmake resigned in September 2010 and was replaced by Abdullahi Mohamed Farmajo. The Djibouti Agreement had provided for a reconciliation committee to address differences within the new government and to bring additional constituencies into the peace process, but President Sherif Ahmed argued that this would generate new political controversies that would divert attention and efforts away from fighting al-Shabaab.

The agreement had left out emerging actors such as the states of Puntland and Galmudug, as well as the Sufi group Ahlu Sunna Waljamaa, which was ideologically and militarily opposed to al-Shabaab and had, by 2010, brought under its control significant territory previously held by al-Shabaab. These additional actors not only were united in their opposition to al-Shabaab and keen to end the transition, but also added inclusivity to the peace process. But the leadership of the TFG was not interested in including political actors considered marginal to the peace process. The president and the new prime minister were opposed to the inclusion of political participants, while parliament and its speaker supported the inclusion of the additional actors. It took stern warnings from the UN Security Council in Nairobi in May 2011 to pressure the Somali government to become more inclusive at this new stage of the peace process ushered in by the Djibouti Agreement. Unlike at the Mbagathi Peace Conference, the warlords were no longer a factor to reckon with in this new peace process. Their influence, power, and militias had been degraded and discredited in most local communities. It was therefore not prudent to include them in the new political process. Somaliland, to the north, had all along stayed out of the peace process taking place in the south. It continued to pursue its own independence agenda, which it had declared since 1991.

Yet another set of challenges to the peacemaking process arose from within the transitional federal institutions. The appointment of a new prime minister acceptable to the president to replace Sharmake led to a new alliance between the two offices, one that created mistrust between the executive and the legislature, the latter led by Sheikh Hassan as speaker of parliament. The rivalry between President Sherif Ahmed and the speaker was institutional as well as personal. A particularly contentious issue was who among the two institutions should control the process of ending the transition, as parliament considered itself vested with more authority than the executive, according to the Transitional Federal Charter. Another contentious issue was whether the transitional period should be extended again, beyond August 2011, after the first extension of 2008 provided for in the Djibouti Agreement. At a personal level, Sheikh Hassan felt that the new prime minister, Abdullahi Mohamed Farmajo, was too close to President Sherif Ahmed, and that this closeness had tilted the political balance in favour of the president.

It was also widely speculated that the speaker had personal ambition to win the presidency. This competition virtually paralysed the federal institutions from the later part of 2010 through the first half of 2011. Puntland, as well as the international community, were also divided over the issue of whether the transitional period should be extended again, as none of the transitional tasks envisaged in the charter had been implemented. The tension and rivalry within the transitional federal institutions evidently adversely impacted the war efforts against al-Shabaab. Morale among the fighters was declining as the political leaders squabbled. Tension between the two leaders—the speaker and the president—was so high that they were not even on speaking terms. The situation reached the point that Sheikh Hassan was about to use his parliamentary powers to oust President Sherif Ahmed or form a parallel government in Mogadishu. Urgent action had to be taken to break the impasse and find a quick solution.

It was against this background that I, as the Special Representative of the UN Secretary-General, requested Uganda's president, Yoweri Museveni, to facilitate a political agreement between the two feuding Somali leaders. After long negotiations, the two reached a compromise and agreed to sign the Kampala Accord in June 2011. In the accord, Speaker Sheikh Hassan agreed for the extension of the transitional period for one year, which President Sherif Ahmed very much wanted, and in return the latter accepted the removal of Abdullahi Mohamed Farmajo as prime minister, which the speaker had demanded as a concession for another extension of the transition period. Later in the same month, a new prime minister, Abdiwelli Mohamed, was appointed from within the existing cabinet. He was widely respected for his integrity and competence, and turned out to be one of the most committed leaders to the roadmap to ending the transition. It was also agreed that priority tasks should be identified and implemented within the one-year extension period ending in August 2012. As these political challenges were being resolved, al-Shabaab intensified its offensive to defeat AMISOM and the nascent Somali forces, and to drive the federal institutions out of Mogadishu. After fierce tunnel and trench warfare for several weeks, AMISOM and the Somali forces prevailed over al-Shabaab, which eventually pulled out of Mogadishu in August 2011.

The Roadmap to End the Transition

The 2011 Kampala Accord paved the way for the launch and adoption of a roadmap to end the transition within 12 months. The roadmap was signed in September 2011 in Mogadishu by representatives of the key stakeholders of the transitional federal institutions (the executive and the legislature), Puntland, and Galmudug, as well as by representatives of the Sufi group Ahlu Sunna Waljamaa. This was the first time in almost two decades that a meeting to discuss the Somali peace process was held inside Somalia. The consultative process that led to the signing of the roadmap prioritised critical peacebuilding tasks essential for ending the transition. The selected tasks included drafting and adopting a provisional constitution. In August 2012, the draft constitution was adopted by a national constituent assembly of 600 delegates nominated by traditional elders from 68 major clans and sub-clans and drawn from across the country, including Somaliland.

As part of the process, the elders convened in Mogadishu, and their first task was to consult and agree among themselves on the authenticity of their claims as genuine representatives of their respective clans and sub-clans. Second, they had to agree on the process of nominating clan representatives to the national constituent assembly from six civil society focal groups consisting of religious leaders, business communities, women, professionals, youths, and the diaspora. In a country without a functioning road network, and widespread insecurity, bringing the elders to Mogadishu was a major logistical challenge. Equally challenging were the consultations that took place among the elders and their respective communities around the country to nominate representatives to the constituent assembly. In this process, the cell phone played a major role in long-distance communication. Air transport, although risky and expensive, was also the only reliable means of bringing the elders and the various delegates to Mogadishu. The costs of bringing all the delegates and maintaining them in Mogadishu were met by the UN as well as major partners such as the European Union (EU), the US, Britain, and Norway.

The drafting of the constitution was a long and contentious undertaking. An independent, federal constitution commission had been formed in 2006, comprising a cross-section of clan, gender, and professional individuals. It was assisted by constitutional experts from Somalia and other Islamic countries, as well as by additional international constitutional experts. The first draft was ready to be launched in 2010, but President Sherif Ahmed disowned it, criticising that it did not adequately reflect Somali culture and Islamic principles. Interestingly, then Prime Minister Sharmake had accepted the draft, and had approved its launch, but the launch had to be cancelled following the president's objection. In response, the drafting team was expanded to review the draft and to ensure that Sharia law principles and Somali customary practices were adequately incorporated. The draft also incorporated universal human rights principles including the participation of women in public institutions (see Porter in this volume). This draft constitution, as mentioned earlier, was overwhelmingly adopted in August 2012. A referendum, as foreseen in the Transitional Federal Charter, was not possible due to the prevailing insecurity in some parts of the country. The provisional constitution review process continued under the new federal parliament, and was expected to have been subjected to a referendum in 2016, based on the assumption that in the interim the security situation would have improved significantly enough to allow the referendum to take place.

A second priority task that had to be accomplished with the help of the traditional elders was the formation and reform of a new parliament. The members of the new parliament were to reflect a clan balance including minority clans consisting of non-Somali ethnic groups such as the Bantu and descendants of Arabs. The new parliament, consisting of 275 members, was half the size of the parliament formed under the Mbagathi Agreement. Nomination of the members to the new, smaller parliament was competitive and susceptible to manipulation, intimidation, and corruption. Women, in particular, were easy victims of the malpractices of the spoilers of this process, as tradition was prejudiced against them participating in public life. To minimise the negative impact of these practices, a technical selection committee was formed by the signatories to filter the nominees against agreed benchmarks of criminal records, human rights violations, intimidation, and corruption. The committee included women as well as ex-officio observers from the region and the international community. Some of the signatories, including President Sherif Ahmed, reneged on the role of the selection committee because the latter had disqualified some of their prospective supporters, such as former warlords. The members of the selection committee, including the Special Representative of the UN Secretary-General, were also subjected to intimidation, but refused to compromise. The committee excluded some of the notorious individuals from parliament, and succeeded in upholding women nominees to parliament against great odds. (On women, gender, and peacebuilding, see Porter in this volume.)

The speaker of the new parliament, Mohamed Osman Jawari, and the president of the new government, Hassan Sheikh Mohamud, were elected by secret ballot of the new parliament in an internationally televised process in August–September 2012. Women played a conspicuous role through watchdog groups in monitoring ballot boxes and foiling last-minute corrupt voting methods by some parliamentarians in choosing the speaker and the president. The women ensured not only that the process was free and fair, but also that the balloting remained secret, by collecting all cell phones from voters before votes were cast. The president then nominated the prime minister, Abdi Farah Shirdon, who later had to be approved by parliament, and together by November 2012 the two formed the cabinet of the new Somali federal government.

Another priority task identified to end the transition was the adoption of a national security stabilisation plan, which had been under preparation since 2010. It was finally adopted by presidential decree in 2012, as parliament had already dissolved itself due to internal bickering. The plan was prepared by a joint security committee created by the 2008 Djibouti Agreement and co-chaired by the Somali prime minister and the Special Representative of the UN Secretary-General for Somalia. The military and police forces had to be built from scratch, following the total collapse previously of the security sector and the proliferation of personal militias. There were several challenges within the new army. Payment for the new forces was unpredictable, discipline was low, and defections were high. Security sector reform (SSR) included building the justice and correctional sectors, promotion of human rights, protection and empowerment of women, as well as protection of children in armed conflict. There were five key elements to the national security stabilisation plan: (1) developing capacities in counter-terrorism, counter-insurgency, and combating transitional organised crime including piracy; (2) integrating into the national army and allied militias a comprehensive plan for disengaging former al-Shabaab combatants; (3) defining the roles and accountability of private security companies operating in Somalia; (4) institutionalising and enhancing the protection of civilians, in particular women, children, and minority groups, as well as addressing gender-based violence; and (5) introducing legislative mechanisms and procedures for democratic civilian oversight of security sector institutions to ensure democratic accountability, civilian political oversight, and leadership of the armed forces.

One of the measures the newly formed Somali government undertook to facilitate implementation of the plan was to request the UN Security Council to ease restrictions on the arms embargo imposed on Somalia since January 1992. A related challenge in building security has been that of mobilising resources for developing and reforming the new security sector institutions, especially the police and armed forces of Somalia, which have to be built while simultaneously engaged in fighting a war against al-Shabaab. Various partners from the region and the international community, including new partners like Turkey, have responded positively to Somalia's security needs as the al-Shabaab threat continues. Significant numbers of combatants disengaging from al-Shabaab need to be demobilised, and the Somali government, in partnership with AMISOM and support from the international community, has been working on a comprehensive plan for the disarmament, demobilisation, and reintegration (DDR) of the former combatants. The numbers of former combatants who have been successfully reintegrated remained low at the time of writing.

Conclusion

Peacemaking and peacebuilding activities, under the roadmap to end the transition in Somalia, took place inside the country only after Mogadishu had been made relatively safe following the withdrawal of al-Shabaab from the city in August 2011. Beyond the capital, meetings also took place in Garowe in Puntland and Galcayo in Galmudug to give a wider sense of national ownership of the process. The expanded inclusiveness of these peacemaking and peacebuilding activities brought new actors, as well as mainstream civil society groups, into the peace process. Civil society activism was part of peace processes in Somalia from the very beginning, even before the adoption of the roadmap, which civil society endorsed through various consultative processes. The pivotal players in the roadmap process were the traditional elders from the major clans and sub-clans. In the absence of direct elections due to the prevailing insecurity in the country, the elders brought needed legitimacy and representativeness to the roadmap process.

The role of women in the roadmap process deserves to be underscored. Women's activism in Somalia in support of peacemaking and peacebuilding began immediately after the collapse of the Siad Barre regime in 1991 and assumed prominence in the period of "governance without government" from 1995 to 2006. It acquired such a dynamism of its own as to become a process of self-empowerment. As the roadmap took off, women organised themselves and participated at every stage of the implementation process. They lobbied for 30 per cent representation of women in the new government and other public institutions, despite opposition from traditional elders and other conservative elements. Women's activism in the national constituent assembly succeeded in bringing significant numbers of women representatives into the new Somali parliament and federal government institutions. (See Porter in this volume.)

The process of ending the transition within 13 months by August 2012 was a major milestone in the Somali peace process. Several peace initiatives had been initiated before, but had stalled and failed. The success of the transition can be attributed to the greater inclusiveness of all the groups fatigued by the "unending transition", unity of purpose among clans yearning for peace, and increased civil society involvement in implementing the roadmap. The renewed interest and reengagement with Somalia by the international community has also been a major factor in encouraging and assisting the Somali peace process. This support has come as piracy off the coast of Somalia and international terrorism based in Somalia have emerged as new threats to international peace and security. The unremitting humanitarian crisis in Somalia, which reached a new height with the famine of 2011, brought wider international response and support to Somalia. New partners like Turkey responded positively and substantially, and have remained and broadened their support to Somalia to include reconstruction and investments in the social, infrastructure, and economic sectors.

Although al-Shabaab continues to lose ground in urban and rural areas in Somalia, the insurgent group has proved capable of prolonging the war through acts of terrorism and exporting violence to neighbouring countries. The Westgate attack of September 2013 in Kenya, previous attacks in Uganda, and several failed attempts in other parts of Eastern Africa have shown that al-Shabaab is a threat to the region beyond Somalia. While the military offensive by the Somali armed forces and AMISOM has continued, the Somali federal government has been extending peace overtures to some moderate elements of al-Shabaab. Although there are no significant breakthroughs as yet, the judicious combination of peace enforcement and dialogue could be the way forward in this long-standing conflict. The combined international efforts to combat piracy off the coast of Somalia, mainly through armed guards on commercial ships, have recorded significant reduction in attacks in the Indian Ocean. However, it is acknowledged by all concerned that a long-term durable solution to piracy must take place on land through support of a functioning government in Somalia that can restore the rule of law and security in the country and its territorial waters.

A few Somalis from neighbouring countries and the wider diaspora have been returning to Somalia, though exact figures are difficult to determine. These returnees are creating more demand on the already overstretched basic social services such as shelter, water, sanitation, and health facilities. Priority peacebuilding activities need to be delivered to these sectors to improve their absorptive capacity in some of the areas of return. The international community must continue to support the Somali government to improve credibility and legitimacy among its people. Following the signing of a tripartite agreement between the governments of Somalia and Kenya, and the UN High Commissioner for Refugees (UNHCR), in November 2013, to facilitate voluntary repatriation, some returnees may end up in areas from which they did not originate, as has already happened in Mogadishu. In some parts of the country, such as Jubaland, where there are already historical tensions over landownership among clans and ethnic groups, the situation may trigger new conflicts. These issues need to be factored into assisting and planning voluntary repatriation, to avert new tensions. A comprehensive peacebuilding strategy in Somalia will also have to include a voluntary, safe, and dignified return of refugees back to Somalia, as the process of peacemaking and peacebuilding in the country enters a new phase. Similarly, a durable peace in Somalia would be one of the solutions to the protracted refugee outflows from Somalia to various countries of the world, on all five continents.

I have noted in this chapter that the liberal approach to national-level peacebuilding in most post-conflict countries has become the de facto approach in the absence of other tested alternative approaches. I have also shown that peacemaking and the initial peacebuilding phase in Somalia, during the ending of the transition, were not only simultaneous but also mutually reinforcing processes. The peacebuilding tasks, as prioritised in the roadmap to ending the Somali transition, represent the preliminary and basic phase of creating the institutional infrastructure for subsequent peacebuilding activities in the ongoing state-building process in Somalia, covering political reconciliation, security, justice, and governance as well as socio-economic aspects. All these are happening as the war against the al-Shabaab insurgency continues; if this war can be successfully contained, it may lead to a peacekeeping phase, which will further facilitate and reinforce the ongoing peacebuilding initiatives and pave the way to full-fledged post-conflict peacebuilding.

Notes

1. For definitions of peacemaking, peace enforcement, and peacebuilding, *see* United Nations (UN), Department of Peacekeeping Operations, Department of Field Support, *United Nations Peacekeeping Operations: Principles and Guidelines* (New York, 2010).
2. On peacebuilding activities in Africa before the existence of the UN Peacebuilding Commission, *see* Ejeviome E. Otobo, "The UN Peacebuilding Architecture: African Countries as Early Beneficiaries", in Georg Lennkh and Irene Freudenschuss-Reichl (eds.), *Nachbar Afrika: Dimensionenen eines Kontinents* (Neighbour Africa: Dimensions of a Continent) (Vienna: Passagen Verlag, 2010).
3. The United States (US) recognised the new Somali federal government in 2013. Relations with the European Union (EU) and Japan have expanded, and more traditional and new partners have re-established diplomatic relations with the new government since 2012.
4. Christopher Clapham, "Peacebuilding Without a State: The Somali Experience", in Devon Curtis and Gwinyayi A. Dzinesa (eds.), *Peacebuilding, Power, and Politics in Africa* (Athens: Ohio University Press, 2013), p. 308.

5. UN General Assembly Resolution 60/80 and UN Security Council Resolution 1645, both adopted 20 December 2005.
6. UN General Assembly Resolution 60/80, para. 2(a).
7. UN Security Council Resolution 2093, adopted 6 March 2013.
8. UN Security Council Resolution 2102 (2013), adopted 2 May 2013, authorised the establishment of the UN Assistance Mission in Somalia (UNSOM) to replace the UN Political Office for Somalia (UNPOS), pursuant in particular to its previous Resolution 2093 (2013), adopted 6 March 2013.
9. Curtis, "Introduction: The Contested Politics of Peacebuilding in Africa", in Curtis and Dzinesa (eds.), *Peacebuilding, Power, and Politics in Africa*, p. 10.
10. Curtis, "Introduction", p. 7. *See also* Susanna Campbell, David Chandler, and Meera Sabaratnam (eds.), *A Liberal Peace? The Problems and Practices of Peacebuilding* (London and New York: Zed, 2011).
11. Britain is used synonymously with the United Kingdom (UK) in this volume.
12. *See* Peter Woodward, *Crisis in the Horn of Africa: Politics, Piracy, and the Threat of Terror* (London: Tauris, 2012).
13. Mark Bradbury, *African Issues: Becoming Somaliland* (Bloomington: Indiana University Press, 2008).
14. *See* John L. Hirsch and Robert B. Oakley, *Somalia and Operation Restore Hope: Reflections on Peacemaking and Peacekeeping* (Washington, DC: United States Institute of Peace, 1995), pp. 3–17.
15. UN Security Council Resolution 751, adopted 24 April 1992; Hirsch and Oakley, *Somalia and Operation Restore Hope.*
16. UN Security Council Resolution 814, adopted 26 March 1993; Kinfe Abraham, *Somalia Calling: The Crisis of Statehood, and the Quest for Peace* (Addis Ababa: Ethiopia International Institute for Peace and Development, 2002).
17. For details, *see* Mark Bowden, *Black Hawk Down: A Story of Modern War* (New York: Signet, 2001). Since the incident in Somalia, the US has avoided deploying its ground troops, directly or through the UN, in Africa. It has instead trained and financed operations through regional partners and organisations.
18. *See* Ken Menkhaus, "Governance Without Government in Somalia: Spoilers, State Building and the Politics of Coping", *International Security* 31, no. 3 (Winter 2006–2007), pp. 74–106.
19. Rachel Morrow, "Preventing Violent Conflict in Somalia: Traditional and Constitutional Opportunities", *Conflict Trends* no. 1 (2014), pp. 11–19.
20. Afyare Abdi Elmi, *Understanding the Somalia Conflagration: Identity, Political Islam, and Peacebuilding* (London: Pluto Press, 2010), pp. 28–47.
21. Abraham, *Somalia Calling*, pp. 117–118.
22. For a detailed analysis of the role of the Union of Islamic Courts (UIC) and the rise of al-Shabaab in south-central Somalia, *see* Stig Jarle Hansen, *Al Shabaab in Somalia: The History and Ideology of a Militant Islamic Group, 2005–2012* (Oxford: Oxford University Press, 2013).
23. Ken Menkhaus with Hassan Sheikh, Shanne Quinn, and Ibrahim Farah, "Somalia: Civil Society in a Collapsed State", in Thania Paffenholz (ed.), *Civil Society and Peacebuilding: A Critical Assessment* (Boulder, CO: Rienner, 2010), p. 323.
24. UN Security Council Resolution 1725, adopted 6 December 2006.
25. The 2008 Djibouti Agreement was facilitated by the Special Representative of the UN Secretary-General for Somalia, Ahmedou Ould-Abdallah of Mauritius,

and was endorsed by UN Security Council Resolution 1814 (2008), adopted 15 May 2008. It also extended the authority of the Transitional Federal Government (TFG) from August 2008 to August 2011.

26. UN Security Council Resolution 1744, adopted 20 February 2007.
27. Kenneth J. Menkhaus, "Somalia and Somaliland: Terrorism, Political Islam, and State Collapse", in Robert I. Rothberg (ed.), *Battling Terrorism in the Horn of Africa* (Washington, DC: Brookings Institution; and Somerville, MA: World Peace Foundation, 2005), pp. 23–47.
28. Amnesty International, *Routinely Targeted: Attacks on Civilians in Somalia* (London: Amnesty International, 2008), p. 2.
29. Office of the UN High Commissioner for Refugees (UNHCR), "Somalia Situation 2017: Supplementary Appeal, January–December 2017", May 2017, p. 6, http://www.unhcr.org/591ae0e17.pdf (accessed 10 August 2017).

PART VI

The Role of External Actors

CHAPTER 21

The UN and Africa's Regional Organisations: An Insider's Perspective

Margaret Vogt†

The establishment of an effective peace and security architecture for strengthening relations and collaboration between the United Nations (UN), the African Union (AU), and Africa's regional economic communities (RECs) has become increasingly imperative for peacekeeping initiatives on the continent. The Addis Ababa–based UN Economic Commission for Africa (UNECA), which has the largest institutional presence on the continent, and the UN country teams and regional offices that have been established to support the AU, have all sought to develop African capacity in the areas of governance and conflict prevention. UNECA and the rest of the UN family in Addis Ababa have also put in place thematic clusters consisting of UN agencies to share information and to coordinate their activities in support of the New Partnership for Africa's Development (NEPAD). However, these measures have centred mainly on socio-economic development issues, and from the point of view of peace and security, have been stop-gap in nature and remained inadequate. Both the UN Department of Peacekeeping Operations (DPKO) and the UN Department of Political Affairs (DPA) have established direct links with the AU Commission in

This chapter has been compiled by Dawn Nagar, a former Senior Researcher at the Centre for Conflict Resolution (CCR), Cape Town, South Africa. It draws on a paper presented by Margaret Vogt at a policy research seminar, hosted by the Centre in Stellenbosch, South Africa; and on a chapter by her in a previous CCR volume: Margaret Vogt, "The UN and Africa's Regional Organisations", in Adekeye Adebajo (ed.), *From Global Apartheid to Global Village: Africa and the United Nations* (Scottsville: University of KwaZulu-Natal Press, 2009), pp. 251–268.

M. Vogt†
Former Special Representative of the UN Secretary-General to the Central African Republic, Bangui, Central African Republic

†Deceased

T. Karbo, K. Virk (eds.), *The Palgrave Handbook of Peacebuilding in Africa*, https://doi.org/10.1007/978-3-319-62202-6_21

Addis Ababa, as well as with Africa's regional organisations. These two departments have the largest capacity to shoulder the responsibilities for continental peace and security, yet they are not Africa-based, but New York–based. The UN is, therefore, not adequately engaged in Africa's peacekeeping and peacebuilding processes. The world organisation needs to redefine its supporting role in peace and security in Africa through improved coordination, and in a manner that takes into account developments on the ground. The UN also needs to allow for greater flexibility and for adapting its approaches to, and strategies for, the successful resolution and prevention of conflict on the African continent.

In this chapter, I assess the effectiveness of the partnership between the UN and Africa's regional organisations. First, the chapter interrogates the issues that underpin the logic for the partnership. Second, the discussion expands on the rationale for having a partnership between Africa's regional organisations and the UN, assessing their respective peacemaking, peacekeeping, and peacebuilding processes of managing conflict. Third, the chapter provides a review of the work that has been initiated on peace and security, and critiques the partnership roles played by the UN and Africa's regional organisations. In so doing, it seeks to address two fundamental questions: What is the status of their relations in this partnership? And, how can the gaps identified within the partnership be dealt with more effectively? Finally, I provide some recommendations for Africa's future peace and security engagements with the world organisation.

A Framework for Enhancing Cooperation Between the AU and the UN

Between 2003 and 2008, the Malian chair of the AU Commission, Alpha Konaré, called for several dialogues with the UN that sought to address the structure and content of AU-UN relations. For example, a 2006 dialogue resulted in a memorandum of understanding (MOU) between the AU and the UN on enhancing their cooperation in capacity-building.[1] The MOU defined a framework for better coordination between the UN and Africa's regional organisations. It also urged that UN support should not be limited to peacekeeping.[2] Owing to the intrinsic nature of Africa's conflicts, which have causes that are deeply rooted in political and socio-economic issues, a multidimensional approach was deemed more fitting for managing peace and security interventions and for adequately addressing such challenges. Thus, in June 2007, the UN Security Council and the AU Peace and Security Council (PSC) met in Addis Ababa and institutionalised their relationship more firmly. This was reflected, for example, in the establishment of a joint AU-UN Hybrid Operation in Darfur (UNAMID) (see Gambari in this volume).

The AU Commission, under Konaré, developed a 15-year strategic plan, which provided a stronger focus on conflict resolution to assist the continent in achieving its development objectives. The main areas of cooperation included: (1) an annual joint consultative UN Security Council–AU Peace and Security Council meeting, (2) an AU-UN Joint Task Force, (3) desk-to-desk exchanges, and (4) capacity-building for mediation and electoral assistance. In addition to elaborating strategies for enhancing continental and regional capacities for conflict prevention, management, and resolution, the plan also stressed the importance of partnerships with the international community, particularly with the UN. The plan was predicated on Africa's sub-regional organisations underpinning the Commission's conflict management mechanisms, and outlined the UN's role of focusing on developing the capacities of Africa's sub-regional organisations. Konaré's 15-year strategic plan also placed particular emphasis on the willingness and openness of the AU and Africa's sub-regional bodies to learn from UN experiences, as well as to forge closer institutional linkages with the world body, in accordance with the spirit of the UN Charter of 1945. Thus, Konaré specified UN-AU engagement by expanding, and placing more emphasis on, consultation and greater reliance on the UN system. In honouring the partnership's call for greater UN involvement, former UN Secretary-General, Kofi Annan of Ghana, responded to the initiative by providing both human and material resources for peacekeeping interventions, and allowing for more personal engagement with the African Union, and with its chair, Konaré, in particular.

The new framework of the UN's relations with the AU is based on the premise that the two organisations need to cooperate more closely to promote international peace and security in a way that considers Africa's political and socio-economic developmental needs. The two organisations have committed themselves to developing capacities for conflict prevention, mediation, and resolution; for peacekeeping; and for peacebuilding, through joint activities, including periodic consultations between the senior officials of both organisations. The UN and the AU have also committed themselves to more collaboration on crime prevention; institution building; political and electoral matters; governance; human rights and the rule of law; food security; social, cultural, and health issues; and the environment. Within this new framework, the two organisations have furthered their commitment to align with, and to extend the support being provided to, NEPAD by the UN's organs. It was envisaged that the structure of the UN's representations to, and relations with, the AU would be realigned to reflect this new and expanded framework of collaboration. In this regard, it was expected that UN actors in Addis Ababa and New York would coordinate their programmes with the AU, and operate within a new framework providing greater synergy and streamlining the interface between the UN family in New York and the AU Commission in Addis Ababa, while avoiding overlap of initiatives and resources.

The UN liaison office in Addis Ababa, once viewed as a "post office", was extensively revamped into a full-fledged UN secretariat reflecting the different departments of the organisation in Addis Ababa. The AU and the UN made advances in peacekeeping partnerships, but mixed results were achieved, as seen, for example, in the AU Mission in Somalia (AMISOM) and the UN's role in support of AMISOM. (See Hirsch, and Mahiga in this volume.) While some analysts and practitioners in the field viewed AMISOM as a model of peacekeeping that should never be repeated, others were of the view that the mission could be seen as a model for the future. Similarly, the AU-UN Hybrid Operation in Darfur was considered to be a successful hybrid model by some analysts, while other practitioners underscored that UNAMID as a hybrid mission should also never be repeated as a peacekeeping model. (See also Gambari in this volume.)

Africa's Sub-regional Organisations

Africa's sub-regional organisations are of fundamental importance in conflict interventions. It is, therefore, imperative that sub-regional organisations play a key role on issues related to improving interventions, such as UNAMID. A sub-regional organisation must be clearly visible in a peacekeeping capacity. The logistical support, however, must be provided for by the United Nations, since this is the responsibility of the UN as the highest global body. The basic premise of the AU-UN partnership is to enhance subsidiarity and complementarity, based on studies (in which I was personally involved) conducted several years ago. The studies show that conflicts are more effectively managed when sub-regional actors and sub-regional states that are close to a conflict are more integrally involved in the management of that conflict. The framework of cooperation between the AU and the UN has also become a model for regional organisations in other parts of the world. For example, the UN has established a full-fledged office in Brussels that interacts effectively with its New York headquarters on a number of issues pertaining to peace and security, and development. The Brussels office is slightly more advanced than the AU's Addis Ababa–based PSC office. Similar structures have been put in place in Southeast Asia and in other sub-regional organisations where frameworks for cooperation with the UN have been established.

The AU's Addis Ababa office has been further enhanced with the appointment of an under-secretary-general, providing a UN presence for Africa. The elevated position has enabled the under-secretary-general more autonomy, and the capacity to speak with authority within the AU and with Africa's regional organisations. Capacities have also been put in place to support the AU in mission planning, as well as to provide support to the AU Commission in conflict prevention and humanitarian crises. Although initially some of the agencies did not want to be part of a coordinated approach with the AU, they eventually decided to join. Nevertheless, challenges still persist and hamper effective engagement between the UN and the AU.

The Need for Strategic Cooperation Between the AU and the UN

Some of the challenges identified within UNAMID (see Gambari in this volume), and the relationship between the UN and Africa's regional organisations on Mali (see Yates, and Adebajo in this volume), show that a strategic platform for open and frank dialogue between the AU and UN has been fundamentally lacking. If partnerships with regional organisations are to help expand the options available to the international community in addressing contemporary security challenges, then the UN must develop better mechanisms for consultation with these bodies. Joint meetings of the AU Peace and Security Council and the UN Security Council still require much work. Although attempts have been made by members of the PSC to develop a strategic relationship with the UN Security Council, such attempts have been resisted by some members of the Security Council who view these engagements as depriving the Security Council of some of its primary responsibility for the management of international peace and security. Initiatives to maintain international peace and security through regional arrangements and agencies are encouraged by the UN as defined in its Charter, specifically Chapter VIII, which provides clear parameters for regional peacekeeping initiatives.

Notably, the lessons of Somalia resulted in a distinct reluctance by non-African members of the UN Security Council, in particular, its five vote-wielding permanent members (P-5)—the United States (US), Russia, China, France, and Britain[3]—to agree to the deployment of their forces to Africa (see Hirsch in this volume). Furthermore, the perceived need for interventions in internal conflicts was informed by the international community's reluctance to intervene in conflict situations that were viewed as not yet "ripe for intervention", and where conditions on the ground mitigated against the useful deployment of UN peacekeeping forces: that is, in cases where there was no peace to be kept. These "lessons" are—in my view—flawed, and were partly responsible for the reluctance of the international community to act to prevent the Rwandan genocide in 1994, during which 800,000 people were slaughtered. These issues are fundamentally linked to resistance, partly because the UN Security Council wants to dictate or decide where it wants to expend its resources, and where it does not want to expend resources.

Key questions—such as who holds the "pen" in the UN Security Council for situations such as those in the Central African Republic (CAR) and in Somalia—need to be addressed. The reality is that peacekeeping is usually underpinned by some hard "horse-trading" within the Security Council, and members do not want to be pushed into interventions that they may not want to undertake, even though some crises may necessitate immediate intervention. Therefore, the AU and Africa's RECs must develop an effective strategy that deals with UN Security Council resistance, a strategy that Africa currently lacks (see Jonah, Gambari, and Ugarte in this volume).

The Central African Republic: Direct AU-UN Personal Engagement

The current African engagement with the UN is disorderly, partly owing to the manner in which African institutions are administered and conduct business. Even though African institutions have advanced peace and security structures in place, and the AU Commission has expanded its initiatives and efforts in this area, fundamental weaknesses remain. One such weakness is the lack of a strategic perspective by the AU itself, and by Africans themselves, in adopting a coherent approach to conflict interventions. In my position as Special Representative of the Secretary-General to the Central African Republic (2011–2013), my first port of call was the African Union office in Bangui, which became my core partner. Being a UN representative and also being a woman were helpful in building rapport in furtherance of engagement efforts and effective partnership. (On women, gender, and peacebuilding, see Porter in this volume.) Initiatives were undertaken in managing the CAR's protracted conflicts that were jointly orchestrated through consultation, which was not a norm in previous interventions.

My partnership with the AU representation was extremely important because it strengthened my capacity as the UN representative to adopt a more independent stance, and to withstand external pressures. It was a lot more difficult for the actors in the CAR conflict to disagree with a UN representative, even when they tried to do so through the "back door", largely owing to the strong partnership between the AU and the UN that was forged. Thus, it was not "just Margaret Vogt" that they were dealing with; neither was it just the UN that they were dealing with, but rather both the UN and the AU. For example, during the March 2013 coup in the CAR, some spectators pointed to the ousted president, François Bozizé, as being the source of the problem, and wanted the UN to support their view. However, the UN maintained its support for the African Union position of non-recognition of unconstitutional changes of government and, in so doing, with AU backing, a stronger collaborative effort was forged, and we were therefore more able to resist the push-back from opposing forces. Similar resistance came from opposing views from African sub-regional organisations, with some sub-regional heads of states wanting to derail the AU-UN attempts and accept the coup. However, the opposing forces could not overcome the strong collaboration of the AU and the UN in declaring the coup as unacceptable. The partnership forged between the AU and the UN during this experience also strengthened the two organisations' position of taking principled decisions on constitutional issues.

In moving forward, the AU Peace and Security Council must address the issue of proper strategic engagement, primarily among its own members and sub-regional bodies, but also between the AU and the UN. The current meetings between the AU and the UN have no basis in common understandings concerning situations on the ground. At joint meetings, AU representatives in New York are often not informed of AU decisions taken in Addis Ababa, owing to the lack of a strategic relationship among the African ambassadors in Addis Ababa and those in New York, as well as the African representation on the UN Security Council.

One of the cardinal points made in the strategic plan developed by Konaré, while he was at the AU Commission, concerned the differences in capacity and resources between the AU office in Addis Ababa and the AU office in New York. The AU Permanent Observer to the UN—Tete Antonio (since 2009)—had very limited resources. The office was poorly staffed and therefore unable to penetrate the UN infrastructure and impact UN activities. Whereas the UN was investing and expanding its presence in Addis Ababa, the AU was not replicating this effort in its presence in New York, and therefore the AU lacked the capacity to deal with issues effectively there. Very often, simply to obtain an effective interlocutor from the AU on an issue was difficult. For example, a telephone call made to the AU's Peace and Security Department (PSD) in Addis Ababa effectively meant calling El Ghassim Wane, the then director of the department, or Ramtane Lamamra, the then commissioner for peace and security at the African Union Commission. Failure to contact either meant no answer to any concern or question. The AU must be re-equipped to enhance African capacity to engage with the UN, and with other partners in the international community. The AU office in New York must be the secretariat of the African members of the UN Security Council.

African Representation on the UN Security Council

For Africa to be a strategic partner of the UN, it must have adequate representation on the Security Council. African members sitting on the Security Council must consider themselves as representatives of an African voice. Once elections are held, and endorsements are made, for African states to represent the continent on the UN Security Council, there is no further engagement between them and African leaders. The African Union thus has a major and a central role to play in determining that African states representing the continent on the UN Security Council implement a system whereby there is continuous engagement among those representing Africa, and there are consistent discussions to orchestrate the positions that best pertain to Africa's peace and security issues. The European Union (EU), France, Britain, and the United States have shown greater interest in African issues than have Africans themselves, and have been able to adopt positions in pursuit of their own parochial interests. Communication and direction from the AU office—for example, by way of a simple telephone call—to inform the Security Council about the African position on an issue being tabled, or to advise the Security Council on the direction that it should take on an issue pertaining to Africa, seems rarely to happen, if ever. Although the African Group meets in New York, it does not have a coherent strategy on how to approach the UN. Such weaknesses in the engagement by the AU, on behalf of its member states, need to be addressed.

Coordination Between the AU and Africa's Sub-Regional Organisations

Africa's peace and security mechanisms all call for a need to have their mandates endorsed by the UN Security Council. The world body should exercise this responsibility with care, and work closely with the peace and security structures of Africa's regional organisations. It is important that the UN embrace the normative evolution of conflict management in Africa and seek a structure to incorporate African norms within the international legal framework. The UN must set new ground rules to govern the practical application of these new norms. Africa's security mechanisms, for their part, should ensure clear and direct communication with the world body.

The UN has yet to forge proper links between itself and regional organisations to enable more effective support for conflict prevention, which is the most important task of the regional mechanisms. Very often, African actors intervene at much earlier stages of conflicts than the UN. Interventions being tabled on the agenda of the UN Security Council have often been delayed, owing to political horse-trading. The UN's Department of Political Affairs should thus seek to develop a wider menu of arrangements to allow closer interaction with African regional mechanisms, and enable the UN to work with these bodies in the early stages of conflicts.

The trend to reinforce the capacity of regional organisations to manage peace operations should be encouraged, as the UN did in Darfur with the establishment of the 26,000-strong UNAMID force in August 2007 (see Gambari in this volume). This is especially important in the early stages of interventions, when the African continent can act from a position of comparative advantage. African institutions can often put greater pressure on the parties in a conflict, and can speak with greater directness and authority (because they share much in common with the parties), all of which can diminish recourse to military intervention—often seen as "neo-colonial"—by external actors. In the case of Darfur, the UN insisted on the deployment of an international force to stop the crimes being committed against the civilian population (an estimated 200,000 people had perished in the region since 2003). The Sudanese government had resisted an operational and command role for the UN, arguing that a UN force would be a "Trojan horse" to be exploited by Western nations in pursuit of neo-colonial agendas in Sudan. China's influence on Sudan is said to have been important in convincing Khartoum to accept the UN force. (On Sudan and South Sudan, see also Deng in this volume.)

When the UN takes over responsibility for operations led by African actors, the management of such transfers must be carefully handled so as not to undermine the credibility or stature of regional arrangements. The UN should thus avoid the impression that it takes over missions whenever the region has failed. The objective should always be to see the transfers as a sharing of responsibility, as an incremental step in a broader international agenda, and as a means to develop African capacity as part of an expanded international UN capacity, both of which may be kept in reserve for use—as required—by the region or by the UN, separately or together. However, to ensure continued engagement of the world body in the management of operations led by regional actors, and to provide oversight of the implementation of mandates endorsed by the UN Security Council, the Council should insist that periodic reports be provided by regional organisations to allow for greater transparency, as well as to serve as a mechanism for reviewing progress of interventions undertaken by regional bodies. Such reports would enable coordinated efforts between Africa's RECs and the UN to become more effective, and would allow for timely transference of the management aspects of interventions to the UN.

Similar progress reports regarding the strategic UN partnership to the AU might also allow Africa's sub-regional organisations an opportunity to strengthen their engagement with the African Union. The relationship between the AU and Africa's RECs is otherwise leaning towards a crisis. On the one hand, Africa has strong sub-regional organisations such as the Economic Community of West African States (ECOWAS), the Intergovernmental Authority on Development (IGAD), and the Southern African Development Community (SADC), and these RECs have proven themselves as organisations that can assert a certain degree of independence and autonomy in the interventions that they undertake. (See, for example, Adebajo in this volume on ECOWAS in Mali.) However, there are also weaker RECs such as the Economic Community of Central African States (ECCAS), which could be described as an "organisation" in name only. The core problem for ECCAS concerns the competing interests among its member states to ascend to the status of "intervener" during regional conflicts, which impacts negatively on the development of peacekeeping interventions, as was the case during the crisis in the Central African Republic in 2013.

During the CAR crisis, however, ECCAS member states did at times unite, and were successful in their attempts to get rid of François Bozizé, the former dictator and army chief of staff who launched a coup in the Central African country that culminated in the overthrow of its president, Ange-Félix Patassé, in March 2003.[4] However, by and large, member states were highly divided and showed clear resentment towards external interventions in their region, particularly by the AU. For its part, the African Union, which is essentially responsible for overseeing peace and security efforts on the continent, must take greater ownership of its role in resolving regional conflicts. Given the huge divisions within ECCAS, the AU should take a lead role in addressing the conflicts in CAR.

Although ECCAS members strongly resented the AU's role in managing the 2013 conflict in the CAR, the threat of losing peace and security funding from the AU (a major source of funding for the member states in the sub-region) meant that they were forced, albeit reluctantly, into accepting the peacekeeping role of the AU. Any efforts at re-hatting the ECCAS force on the ground into an AU force, though, were seen as negative, and it became exceedingly difficult for the sub-regional organisation to comply with the AU's position. Although ECCAS accepted, in theory, the concept of re-hatting its military force into an AU force, it would have preferred being re-hatted into a UN force. It was also evident that it would have been very difficult for the UN Security Council to authorise another UN operation in the Central African Republic, unless France became the penholder for the CAR and approved such an intervention. During the CAR crisis, in August 2013, about 1,000 people flooded into the country's airport, where a "sit-in" took place by the residents of the capital city of Bangui. The Chadian soldiers wanted to intervene, but were blocked by French troops, since Chad was largely viewed as part of the problem, and therefore, was not in a position to play an impartial role that could bring stability to the CAR crisis. (See Yates in this volume.) Thus, the coordination of strategic partnerships between the AU and Africa's own subregional organisations is a priority.

In a similar situation in Sudan, the UN and the AU collaborated on a consolidated plan for strengthening the AU Mission in Sudan (AMIS) through a UN support package, and agreed to the transfer of AMIS to a UN peacekeeping operation. Owing to an early agreement reached by the 15-member AU Peace and Security Council, and the need to avoid a security vacuum in Darfur, the AU and the UN agreed to a three-step plan designed to enhance the size, mandate, and capacity of the AU and to allay Sudanese concerns about the transfer of AMIS to the UN. The plan consisted of two packages. The "light package", implemented in 2006, provided the AU with headquarters support for planning, logistics, and airlift. The subsequent "heavy package" allowed for deployment of about 17,000 new troops and 2,000 additional police personnel paid for by the UN; the required operational, communication, and logistical support to make the peacekeepers more effective in implementing an enhanced mandate; and command and control support, with UN personnel supporting the mission headquarters and cells, and managing the mission's finances and administration. This mission aimed to provide the UN with its first practical experience of a Chapter VIII operation and true burden-sharing with a regional organisation. But the UN must consider developing more flexible and innovative approaches in dealing with challenges to international peace and security efforts that fall outside the conventional framework within which it is more inclined to operate. Effective partnerships and closer working relationships with regional organisations may provide the world body with the appropriate mix of options.

While the UN and Africa's regional organisations realise that effective peacekeeping and peace support operations can be achieved by halting immediate threats to security—especially those posed by armed conflicts—these missions hardly address the root causes of conflicts. Experience from countries such as Somalia, Angola, and Liberia suggests that as soon as UN peacekeepers withdraw, conflicts re-erupt, owing to the international community's failure to maintain its focus on, and support for, addressing the root causes of conflicts through effective peacebuilding. The UN's Department of Political Affairs and the UN Development Programme's (UNDP) Bureau for Conflict Prevention and Reconstruction have quietly supported UN member states with expertise and resources, to help them to deal with conflicts at the local level. The creation of a Mediation Support Unit (MSU) in the UN Department of Political Affairs, in 2006, should serve as a mechanism to build a repository of lessons learned and offer more systematic support to UN mediators and mediation partners.[5] The UN has actively engaged in peacemaking as well as peacebuilding efforts in the Democratic Republic of the Congo (DRC), Burundi, and South Sudan, and has provided expertise to IGAD's mediation efforts on South Sudan. These mediation efforts have produced positive results, notably the 2005 Comprehensive Peace Agreement between the government of Sudan and the Sudan People's Liberation Movement/Army (SPLM/A) (see Deng in this volume). This deal was a landmark achievement for mediating Africa's protracted conflicts and ended the longest-running civil war in Africa (which lasted from 1956 to 1972, and from 1983 to 2005). In Darfur, the UN provided support to the AU-led negotiations in Abuja, Nigeria, which produced the Darfur Peace Agreement of 2005, an accord that, unfortunately, although backed by the government, was signed by only one of the major rebel groups (a faction of the SPLM/A). Officials from the UN's Department of Political Affairs and its Office for the Coordination of Humanitarian Affairs (OCHA) were also deployed in Juba to support the talks facilitated by the government of then Southern Sudan on the 20-year conflict in northern Uganda involving the Lord's Resistance Army (LRA).

Although much has been achieved in addressing the weaknesses of peacemaking generally, more needs to be done. The UN has established regional presences in Dakar, Senegal; Libreville, Gabon; and now in Ethiopia through its AU office in Addis Ababa. All these efforts have been made in an attempt by the UN to equip itself with a more robust capacity to better understand the root causes of conflict and to deal more effectively with them. Still, the Addis Ababa office needs to be a lot more robust; its political capacity needs to be enlarged. The Dakar office needs to become more capacitated as well. A central concern is that the situation in the Sahel is still facing an enormous knowledge gap. The objective of establishing the UN office in Dakar was to erect an "antenna" in West Africa to enable the UN to better understand the dynamics of regional security issues, with conflicts having become more regional than national. But the UN can be effective only if it works closely with ECOWAS and with partner organisations within the West African region. The same can be said of the Libreville office: the conflict in the CAR cannot be solved if there is no understanding of the national security dynamics in Chad, no understanding of what is happening in Darfur, and no processes in place to acquire a regional perspective.

Conclusion: Reflections on the Way Forward

The African countries that sit on the UN Security Council are working in isolated silos, as are their representatives. There is a lack of consciousness, a lack of sensitivity, and a lack of strategy among them. Meanwhile, the AU office in New York lacks effectiveness. Konaré's strategic plan envisaged an office that would be staffed by 16 professional officers to ensure that each AU department had adequate representation in New York. This plan was presented to the AU's membership, but the member states shot down the request, decreasing the proposed number of officers from 16 to three, owing to lack of funding. This reflects a lack of appreciation for what is needed—a strategic relationship between the AU and the UN. Proper appreciation of this fact would generate greater willingness among AU member states to invest in, and to pay for, peace and security matters out of their annual subscriptions to the continental body, to ensure its relevance. The way forward for AU member states is to begin to understand that they must provide the necessary resources to the continental body to support its peace and security architecture. Part and parcel of these efforts would be for the AU office in New York to become the secretariat of the African members of the UN Security Council. Much more needs to be done as well, if civil society is to encourage political actors to see the AU as a resource for the advancement of their own domestic political interests, and to pressure their governments to make this perspective a reality.

Notes

1. African Union (AU), "Enhancing UN-AU Cooperation: Framework for the Ten-Year Capacity Building Programme for the African Union", November 2006, http://www.au.int/en/organs/uno (accessed 1 March 2016).
2. *See* Security Council Report, "Working Together for Peace and Security in Africa: The Security Council and the AU Peace and Security Council", Special Research Report no. 2, 10 May 2011, http://www.securitycouncilreport.org/atf/cf/%7B65BFCF9B-6D27-4E9C-8CD3-CF6E4FF96FF9%7D/Research%20Report%20Working%20Together%20for%20Peace%20and%20Security%20in%20Africa%2010%20May%202011.pdf (accessed 23 December 2016).
3. Britain is used synonymously with the United Kingdom (UK) in this volume.
4. *See* François Bozizé, "Central African Republic (CAR)", http://www.globalsecurity.org/military/world/war/car-3.htm (accessed 5 November 2015).
5. *See* Centre for Conflict Resolution (CCR), *United Nations Mediation Experience in Africa*, Seminar Report no. 16 (Cape Town, 16–17 October 2006), http://www.ccr.org.za (accessed 9 August 2017).

CHAPTER 22

French Military Interventions in Africa

Douglas A. Yates

It was the fall of 2012, barely six months after François Hollande's arrival at the Elysée, and his popularity and credibility had plummeted. Layoffs were multiplying. Budget deficits were growing. Promises to tax the rich had been abandoned. Then, a few months later, Hollande went to war, and never came back. First Operation Serval in Mali (2013–2014), next Operation Sangaris in the Central African Republic (CAR) (2013–2016), then air strikes against the Syrian regime (2015), followed by participation in the international coalition against the Islamic State of Iraq and Syria (ISIS), Operation Barkhane (since 2014) in five countries in the Sahel, and finally, on the home front, Operation Sentinelle (2015), deploying soldiers over the national territory after jihadists had struck in Paris. Where did the prudent social democrat go? How did a man so moderate in expression, so temperate in action, suddenly transform into this man of war? It all looks like a little bit of history repeating.

French military interventionism in its former empire appears to be a consistent policy since decolonisation. Between 1960 and 2005, France launched some 46 military operations in its former African colonies in Africa.[1] According to one estimate, between 1945 and 2005, there were 122 African military interventions, of which ten were still active at the end of 2016.[2] Any list of major French military interventions in Africa is quite long, starting with the first one in Gabon (1964), and including in the post-Cold War era: Operation Noroit (Rwanda 1990–1993), Operation Verdier (Benin 1991), Operation Godoria (Djibouti 1991), Operation Baumier (Zaire 1991), Operation Addax (Angola 1992), Operation Simbleau (Sierra Leone 1992), Operation Iskoutir (Djibouti 1992–1993), Operation Oryx (Somalia 1992–1993), Operation

D.A. Yates (✉)
American Graduate School in Paris, Paris, France

T. Karbo, K. Virk (eds.), *The Palgrave Handbook of Peacebuilding in Africa*, https://doi.org/10.1007/978-3-319-62202-6_22

Balata (Cameroon 1994), Operation Amaryllis (Rwanda 1994), Operation Diapason (Yemen 1994), Operation Turquoise (Zaire/Rwanda 1994), Operation Azalée (Comoros 1995), Operation Almandin (the CAR 1996–1997), Operation Pelican (Congo-Brazzaville 1997), Operation Licorne (Côte d'Ivoire 2002), Operation Artemis (the Democratic Republic of the Congo [DRC] 2003), Operation EUFOR-Tchad (Chad 2007–2008), Operation Atalante (Djibouti 2008), and Operation Harmattan (Libya 2011)—to mention but a sample of the intervention operations, counter-insurgency missions, combat support operations, peacekeeping interpositions, peace security operations, and non-combatant evacuation operations conducted under the tricolour before Hollande. (See Adebajo in this volume.)

Operation Serval in Mali

The irony of the 2013 intervention in Mali was that President Hollande had never wanted this war. His position had been unvarying since his 2012 campaign promise that once he was president he would not intervene with French troops on Malian soil. He wanted to mark a clean break with *Françafrique*[3] and not be taxed with straying into neo-colonialism. Mostly he shunned military engagement, especially going it alone in the former French Sudan. The real solution in his eyes was above all diplomatic, not military. This was a matter of mobilising African armies under the aegis of the Economic Community of West African States (ECOWAS), or of the North Atlantic Treaty Organisation (NATO), the European Union (EU), and the United Nations (UN). It was a matter of reconstructing the Malian army and helping it re-conquer what jihadists had taken after a military coup had toppled the regime in Bamako.

The military option had been studied during the last days of President Nicolas Sarkozy, and had been rejected. Not a single French soldier would serve on the ground in an election year. Sarkozy had been busy running his presidential campaign when Touareg rebels in the north were joined by al-Qaeda in the Islamic Maghreb (AQIM) and Ansar al-Dine, combining their forces to declare the short-lived independent state of Azawad.

During the fall of 2012, Hollande buzzed like a pollinating bee from one international meeting to another, discussing the possibility of bilateral and multilateral operations, trying to achieve through diplomacy this mission impossible. From his first days in office he had obtained, on paper, the deployment of an ECOWAS mission, instruction of Mali's army by EU trainers, as well as support from the UN. In May 2013, he brought the Malian dossier before NATO. In September 2012, he organised a conference on the Mali crisis on the margins of the UN General Assembly meeting in New York. That same day, defence minister Jean-Yves Le Drian met with European leaders in Cyprus to mobilise them around the table. But Le Drian noticed the consternation of his European homologues, who wondered what this was all about, really. What did *they* have to do with francophone Africa? What were the *real* interests of France? Disenchantment and inaction had also set in on the part of the Africans. Nigeria, the regional hegemon in West Africa, was further preoccupied with its own domestic fight against Boko Haram. One French defence ministry official speaking anonymously told a journalist: "We understood very quickly that ECOWAS was incapable of doing anything whatsoever, that they did not have a kopeck, and that we were completely alone."[4] (See also Adebajo in this volume.)

But the situation north of the Niger river was degrading rapidly, which pushed Hollande to call upon his defence ministry, at that time preoccupied with the withdrawal of all French forces from Afghanistan. This retreat had been his highlighted military policy of the 2012 presidential campaign, a total withdrawal of French troops by the end of the year. The irony of the story is that while candidate Hollande had promised a complete military disengagement, once elected president Hollande decided to embark upon what was surely the most important mobilisation of French troops in half a century.

Jean-Yves Le Drian, barely installed at the ministry of defence, was seduced by the scenario of direct military intervention. He presented his hawkish ideas at the very first defence council, in May 2012, rejecting Sarkozy's strategy of confrontation that had privileged an indirect approach with the lowest possible visibility of French military presence. This strategy, Le Drian said, had not achieved its objectives. "The north of Mali has become a sanctuary for AQIM and its allies which threatens the entire sub-region and potentially our national territory." He warned the president "not to let AQIM establish a terrorist sanctuary beyond all control, like what Al Qaida had done in the Afghan tribal zones of Pakistan."[5]

Hollande was obsessed with speed, ordering his military advisor, General Benoît Puga, and his commander of the Joint Chiefs of Staff, Admiral Edouard Guillaud, to advance rapidly and quickly recapture visible symbols of victory, Gao and Timbuktu. These goals were accomplished in January 2013 with parachute drops of the 21st Marine Infantry Regiment—the first such operation since the 1978 battle of Kolwezi to liberate European hostages in the Katanga. Hollande flew to Mali in February 2013 to celebrate the "liberation" of Timbuktu and to harvest the first fruits of his military triumph. This was his first trip to sub-Saharan Africa, and landing on the tarmac in Bamako he uncharacteristically declared with sweating emotion: "I have just come to live the most important day of my political life."[6] After his speech, reminiscent of George W. Bush's 2003 victory speech after the capture of Baghdad, the war in Mali entered into a new, less romantic phase. French troop numbers had increased over January from 550 to 3,500 and then to an apogee of 5,200 pairs of boots on the ground.

"The president was very clear," said one ministry official, "that the objective was not only the re-conquest of Timbuktu and Gao."[7] Operation Serval started experiencing mission drift. It was now about eliminating high-value targets—that is, assassinating jihad leaders. Hollande ordered Rafale and Mirage jets to drop bombs on Adrar while the French army conducted a deadly "cleanup" operation in the rocks and caves of the Ifoghas mountains. Dozens of jihadists, including several high-value targets, were "neutralised" and numerous hidden logistical caches were discovered with tons of weapons and hundreds of litres of gasoline. The mountain combats were also deadly for French and Chadian soldiers, the largest contingents of the 6,300 African soldiers deployed (see Fig. 22.1). By April 2013, the bulk of this cleanup mission could be considered accomplished. Mali's territorial integrity had been restored. Jihadists had not been totally destroyed, but they had suffered major casualties, losing more than 400 fighters. And now they were dispersed. To provide Serval with a semblance of legitimate authority, elections were hastily orchestrated by France and won by Ibrahim Boubacar Keïta in August 2013. It was mission accomplished. The French army was satisfied. After its long indecisive military engagement in Afghanistan, its battlefield successes were now followed by presidential elections.

Unlike Libya, where the fall of Muammar Qaddafi had been followed by degeneration into chaos, the Mali mission was touted as a success. The RAND Corporation, for example, published a special report highlighting how it could serve as a lesson for American expeditionary forces in similar conflicts: "France fielded a relatively small force put together using small, scalable combined arms task organized units as basic building blocks and conducted a campaign that emphasized speed and manoeuvre over force protection. The French force, moreover, is for all intents and purposes regionally aligned, and it demonstrated the benefits that could accrue through its apparently effective operations among and with local and regional actors."[8]

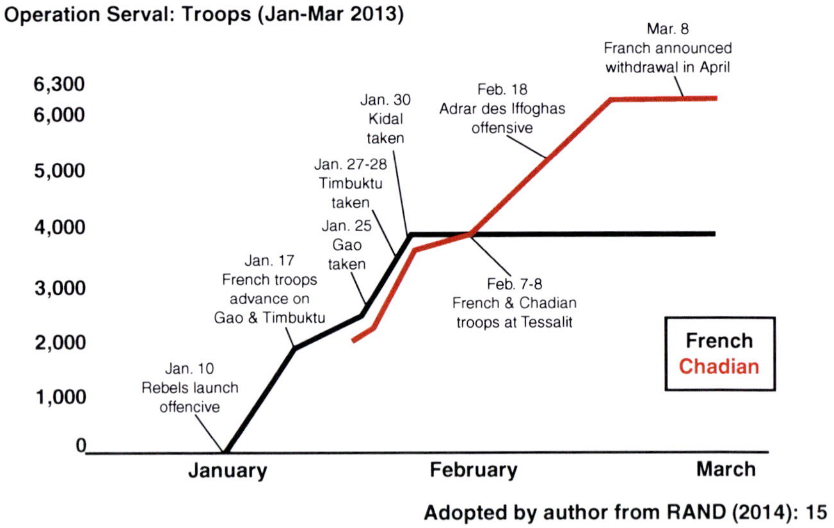

Fig. 22.1 Operation Serval Troops, January–March 2013. *Source*: Adopted from Michael Shurkin, *France's War in Mali: Lessons for Expeditionary Army* (Santa Monica, CA: RAND, 2014), p. 15

France officially ended Operation Serval in July 2014, replacing it with a broader regional counter-terrorism effort, Operation Barkhane, whose headquarters were in Chad, but whose focus remained on northern Mali. The total cost of Operation Serval was €650 million. To pay for this extra expense, Le Drian obtained an increase in the defence ministry budget.

"We are going to break apart those bastards as much as possible", Le Drian announced, leaving no one in his entourage with any doubts of his intentions. The order of the day was eradication. For the first time in decades, French soldiers in Africa were receiving orders to kill and to give no quarter, the equivalent of "search and destroy" orders given to American soldiers after the 2001 World Trade Centre bombing. When evaluating the United Nations Multidimensional Integrated Stabilisation Mission in Mali (MINUSMA), we might reflect on how this UN peacekeeping mission, meant to create and consolidate peace in Mali through Operation Barkhane, employed methods better described as "dirty war". (See also Adebajo in this volume.)

Operation Barkhane and the Sahel

Parallel to other official military operations, another kind of battle was silently being waged in the shadows of peacekeeping that involved secret services and special operations. These "special ops" are another kind of intervention. They surpass the traditional notions of war. Less visible, usually clandestine, aimed at eradicating those networks considered dangerous, killing the presumed enemies of France, they are run by the Service Action (SA) of the Directorate-General for External Security (DGSE)—the French equivalent of the United States (US) Central Intelligence Agency (CIA)—sometimes using conventional military commandos because they are complementary with traditional "opex" (external ops) military missions. Lines between clandestine and military action have become more blurred. New conflicts are prolonged under non-conventional forms faced with more elusive enemies. An ultra-secret list of names of persons to be eliminated unofficially by special ops is kept in the drawer of the president's office.[9] Hollande decided on the special operations by himself. He did not bask in their successes as he did for other, more conventional military adventures. Special ops are about killing people, not capturing them; difficult to define as peacekeeping; and hard to confess publicly. To speak in the clearest possible terms, these operations are political executions, assassinations, and murders.

A few hours after launching Operation Serval in January 2013, a restricted ad hoc defence meeting was held at the Elysée during which the president, surrounded by his defence minister Le Drian, General Puga, and Admiral Guillaud, formulated a policy to stop the advance of the terrorist rebels. "His orders were very clear", confessed Admiral Guillaud later. "The chiefs of staff received the order to kill, with rules of offensive engagement going well beyond mere legitimate defense: Any person suspected of setting foot in a forbidden zone could be targeted."[10] France had no forces in

Mali. But it did have some military assets close at hand: 250 soldiers in Senegal, 950 troops and Mirage 2000D fighters in Chad, and 450 soldiers in Côte d'Ivoire. "Finally, a Special Operations Forces (SOF) contingent possibly numbering as many as 400, with ISR [intelligence, surveillance, and reconnaissance aircraft] and helicopters, was in the region as part of a counterterrorism operation known as Operation Sabre, based in Ouagadougou, Burkina Faso."[11] A few hours later, on the back of the air raids, commandos from French special forces arrived from their base in Burkina Faso to stop the advance of jihadists at Sévaré, Konna, and Diabali, with two Gazelle attack helicopters. Within a few weeks, these forces had pushed back the rebels and destroyed their mountain sanctuaries. But they did not eradicate the terrorist threat in the Sahel. In the words of General Vincent Desportes, they won the battle, not the war: "From Afghanistan to CAR to Mali the major problem is one of 'permanence' and the syndrome which corresponds to it—the 'Sisyphus warrior' who every morning must re-conquer what he abandons during the night."[12] "In truth, the AQIM wake-up call was very hard in 2013", said one former DGSE agent. "We should have been fighting AQIM for years with more force and consistency. For twelve years we had seen this menace grow, observed its growing influence all over West Africa like a metastasis. But we were afraid to intervene. We had tried to help the governments of the concerned countries by training and surrounding them with special forces and presidential guards. The results were catastrophic, with runaway corruption and ineffective local armies. Worse, we paid ransom for hostages, which only reinforced the phenomenon."[13]

By the 1990s, French intelligence had identified the main terrorist leaders who later formed AQIM, including Mokhtar Belmokhtar (former head of the Armed Islamic Group of Algeria [GIA] known as the "Malborough Man" for his smuggling activities in the Sahel). The DGSE had given French authorities enough information to conduct a raid on his camp in 1999, but Gaullist president Jacques Chirac was paralysed by co-habitation with Socialist prime minister Lionel Jospin. So when faced by recalcitrant Algerian authorities who did not look favourably on any French operations in their Sahara, Chirac balked. "We could have eliminated Belmokhtar", said a former DGSE agent of the Service Action. "We could have eradicated AQIM as of that time, when they only represented some 200 persons. It was a serious mistake not to have taken care of them in those days."[14] The World Trade Centre bombings of 2001 reinforced the image of al-Qaeda in the eyes of these Salafist fighters like Abdelmalek Droukdel, Aberazak El Para, and Mokhtar Belmokhtar, who started confronting the US in 2002 after President George W. Bush launched the Pan Sahel Initiative. Algerian terrorists regularly took European hostages and held them for ransom, which, despite public denials, the French authorities regularly paid. Between 1998 and 2012, French intelligence sources estimate, the terrorists raised $100 million this way.[15] Strengthened by success, they pledged allegiance to Osama Bin Laden. By January 2007, they had changed their name to al-Qaeda in the Islamic Maghreb. Their designated enemy was France.

In 2008, France launched special operations in Mauritania with an assault on terrorists in a residential neighbourhood of Nouakchott, the capital. In reprisal, Mauritanian soldiers were killed in ambush in 2008. The French embassy was attacked by a suicide bomber in 2009. The DGSE started working more closely with Mauritania on a deadly campaign of "neutralisation" that resulted in the arrest or elimination of some 80 jihadists in three years.[16] Sarkozy decided to send special forces into the region as part of a secret task force code-named Operation Sabre, starting in Mauritania in 2009 and then venturing into northern Mali, Burkina Faso, and to a lesser degree Niger. In 2009, Abdelmalek Droukdel, the Algerian emir of AQIM, who had suffered repeated assault in his fiefdom, moved into the north of Mali and, with his lieutenants, principally Abou Zeid, multiplied hostage takings in order to raise money for his jihad. By 2008–2009, remembers one security agent for French uranium mining company Areva, "we had warned the French and local authorities that the menace was intensifying in northern Niger and that the risks of hostage taking [were] become greater in the region. They responded that we shouldn't be so dramatic, stop trying to ... [create] psychosis".[17]

Between 2009 and 2011, a series of highly publicised kidnappings in Mauritania, Mali, and Niger, including several employees taken from Areva's site at Arlit, Niger, resulted in several famous failed French attempts to liberate hostages. Then came the fall of the Qaddafi regime in the summer of 2011, and hundreds of Tuaregs who had been integrated in the Libyan armed forces came south with an arsenal of military materiel pillaged from the stocks of the Libyan dictator, including armoured transporters, four-wheel-drive vehicles with lance rockets, and portable ground-to-air missiles. They allied themselves with the National Movement for the Liberation of Azawad (MNLA). In 2013, Operation Serval was launched. But France was already at war. In addition to the estimated 600 to 1,000 jihadist combatants officially killed by Operation Serval, high-value targets were unofficially neutralised. According to sources close to the DGSE, between 2013 and mid-2014 more than 15 high-value targets were eliminated in Mali on the personal orders of François Hollande, a number confirmed by the DGSE's Marc Pimond: "Before we used to keep files on Al Qaida. Now we track them down and neutralize them."[18]

Operation Sangaris

After Operation Serval in Mali came Operation Sangaris in the Central African Republic. Seen by critics as an umpteenth military intervention by France in the CAR, Sangaris was Hollande's second adventure in sub-Saharan Africa, more daring in its brazen unilateralism, less fortunate in its results. France was haunted by its failure to stop Rwanda's genocide in 1994 and eager to save the CAR from an analogous outbreak of ethnic cleansing, yet this was another dark chapter in the longest scandal of the Fifth Republic, "inscribed in a global strategy of maintaining French domination over its African sphere of influence [*pré carré*], a brilliant example of the system of Françafrique".[19] (See Adebajo in this volume.) France has during each period of its history weighed upon the destiny of the CAR and its citizens, from the concessionary regimes of the colonial period that caused the death of around one-third of its population between 1880 and 1930,[20] to the false independence of Barthélémy Boganda and Andre Kolingba under the neo-colonial network of Jacques Foccart, through the tragic comedy of Emperor Jean-Bedel Bokassa,[21] and the civilianised military regimes of David Dacko, Ange-Félix Patassé, and François Bozizé, each brought to power by French-backed coups, each made, and each broken, by France. Under President François Bozizé, peace had been something of a relative notion. But events that occurred at the end of 2012 were about to plunge the country into bloody chaos.

A first attack occurred in November 2012, when four CAR soldiers were killed at Bako by an unidentified armed group. The real offensive began in December, with the taking of Ndélé, Sam-Ouandja, and Ouadda in the northeast of the country by guerrillas under the banner of the Union of Democratic Forces for Unity (UFDR) under the command of Michel Djotodia. As its name implies, the UFDR was a collection of armed groups from diverse horizons gathered around the word "democratic", if not the practice the word denotes. Djotodia had already been part of an earlier 2006 anti-Bozizé rebellion. In 2003, he had helped Bozizé stage his coup, but he had not shared in the spoils. Bozizé was a former general under Emperor Bokassa who had toppled his predecessor, Ange-Félix Patassé, himself a former Bokassa prime minister. Bozizé had legitimised his coup with fake presidential elections in 2005. His soldiers committed summary executions of hundreds of opponents that resulted in over 100,000 people fleeing into the bush.[22] This refugee crisis inspired a decade of rebellion in northern CAR. Deeply discontented by their poverty and marginalisation, northern guerrillas in Djotodia's UFDR attacked the principal cities of the north in 2006–2007: Birao, Sam-Ouandja, Ouanda Djallé, Ouadda, and Ndélé.

When viewed from Paris, this rebellion was disturbing because it threatened the uranium region of Bakouma, where French nuclear giant Areva was preparing to purchase Uramin, an obscure Canadian concessionaire. In December 2006, French soldiers launched an offensive alongside the Central African armed forces and an African expedition sent by ECOWAS—the Mission for the Consolidation of Peace in the Central African Republic (MICOPAX). In July 2007, Areva made its acquisition of Uramin. Bozizé, inspired by the example set by then–president of Niger Mamadou Tandja, who had engaged in hard bargaining with Areva over the price of uranium, declared the Uramin contract "irregular" and demanded a financial bonus before he would give his signature. Bozizé was received at the Elysée by Sarkozy.

The president-director general of Areva travelled to Bangui to sign the agreement. While the agreement remains confidential, a mention was made in the press about $40 million to be paid out over five years. No figure was given concerning the bonus clandestinely paid to Bozizé,[23] however—money that he ostensibly used to pay for his 2011 "re-election" campaign.

The French army installed for the long duration in this region, seen as strategic because of conflict in neighbouring Darfur as well as the chance it offered in 2007 to stop columns of Chadian rebels from toppling the regime of France's main regional military ally, Idriss Déby. In order not to find itself alone on the front line of combat in this hotspot of collapsing states, Sarkozy had called for help from his European allies. In January 2008, the European Union launched its force in Chad and the CAR (EUFOR Tchad/RCA) to protect Darfurian refugees in eastern Chad and inhabitants in the north threatened by the Ugandan Lord's Resistance Army (LRA) and the Sudanese Janjaweed. In March 2009, EUFOR Tchad/RCA handed over the torch to the United Nations Mission in the Central African Republic and Chad (MINURCAT). But President Déby immediately demanded the retreat of this UN force, saying his troops were sufficient to ensure by themselves protection of both the region's inhabitants and its refugees. Unwelcome, MINURCAT decided to withdraw in 2010, which left the country without any international peacekeeping force.

In 2011, while the world's attention was focused mainly on the events of the "Afro-Arab Spring", only a handful of country specialists noticed that "inter-religious violence erupted in Bangui on 31 May and 1 June. A mosque was burnt down by Christians, police shot at demonstrators and a curfew was imposed. Seven deaths were officially reported".[24] It was the beginning of new kind of sectarian conflict—Muslim-Christian inter-communal violence—that the CAR had not known before. (See also Vogt in this volume.) That same year, Areva discovered, much to its chagrin, that the Bakouma uranium mines were worthless and not exploitable, causing huge losses for the company.[25] The 2011 elections in the CAR were a farce, a spectacle of democratic electioneering. It was virtually impossible for opposition candidates to tour the country with the restrictions on free travel put in place by Bozizé. Seven opposition members resigned from the independent electoral commission to protest irregularities detected two days before the poll. Not only was Bozizé re-elected with two-thirds of the vote, but after opposition parties boycotted the second round of the legislative elections, his ruling party and its allies took an overwhelming majority of the votes.[26] Focusing on re-election and economic rents from extractive industries, Bozizé did not seem concerned about the failed peace process in the north.

Not only had his negligence enabled the infamous Lord's Resistance Army to establish itself solidly in the far eastern part of the country, it also had allowed rebels to build their forces, which would sweep down in 2012 to overthrow Bozizé. Troops under Michel Djotodia captured the town of Bria in December 2012, called for the first time "Séléka" troops, using the Sango word for "Alliance".[27] When he saw that his own armed forces were helpless (the rebels were better armed after a flood of weapons came from Libya), Bozizé turned to his allies, France and Chad. Idriss Déby dispatched a contingent of Chadian troops to the CAR to stop the Séléka advance. Now Bozizé found himself entirely dependent on his powerful neighbour, which demanded he enter into talks. For reasons that are still not clear, Hollande did nothing to save Bozizé: "Speaking generally", he said, "if we are present, it is not to protect a regime, but to protect our expatriates and our interests. Not to intervene in the domestic affairs of a country, in this case Central Africa. Those days are over."[28] On New Year's Eve, Bozizé found himself trapped in Bangui with rebel forces stopped ten kilometres outside the capital by ECOWAS forces (MICOPAX); abandoned by his traditional supporters, France and Chad; and forced to seek terms with his enemies. That was when he turned to South Africa, invoking a military cooperation accord with Pretoria (Tshwane), which sent 250 troops to protect him, significantly reducing Bozizé's dependency on sub-regional actors, Gabon and Chad, which convinced the parties to a temporary ceasefire in January 2013.

Bozizé accepted a national union government with Séléka rebels, who in quid pro quo demanded the removal of South African troops. Séléka rebels also chose as new prime minister a lawyer who had defended Emperor Bokassa in 1986–1987—defence minister Michel Djotodia. In March 2013, Djotodia asked Bozizé to step down, but Bozizé refused. Séléka rebels broke their ceasefire and started advancing on Bangui. Two columns of 2,000 soldiers each were driving straight to the capital. This time the ECOWAS forces (MICOPAX) did nothing to stop them, but instead left the way open to the rebels. Once at the gates of Bangui, they found themselves fighting the South African soldiers, who held on for nine hours before raising the white flag. On 24 March 2013, the presidential palace fell. Bozizé fled the country by helicopter to neighbouring Cameroon to regroup and launch his return to power.

Michel Djotodia briefly became president. ECOWAS recognised Djotodia and allowed his "election" by a national transitional council. During this period, Séléka forces started targeting Christians across the country, burning villages to the ground, killing their inhabitants, raping their women, and pillaging their homes. Conscious that the situation risked escaping them, French diplomats now started to mobilise, calling a strategy meeting at the Quai d'Orsay (foreign affairs ministry) in July 2013, at which Le Drian raised the spectre once more of a jihadist movement in the CAR akin to that in Afghanistan. Bozizé played up the same "Africanistan"[29] message, reproaching Djotodia of wanting to "Islamicise" the country. Like US President Bush, who embarked on an invasion of Iraq while his army was in Afghanistan, President Hollande prepared for a two-front war. History did not repeat itself, but from Mali to the CAR it rhymed.[30]

While exactions were carried out by Séléka rebels, now being joined by new irregulars, Christian communities threatened by this violence began to organise themselves into militia called "anti-Balaka" (anti-machete). Within their ranks were three kinds of actors: self-defence militia who called themselves anti-Balaka "originelles", opportunistic looters, and pro-Bozizé partisans—that is, his loyalists from the armed forces, gendarmes, and the police. By June, Bozizé's partisans had organised themselves in Yaoundé and Paris for a countercoup. (Following the outbreak of violence, the Séléka forces were dissolved by

President Djotodia. So members of the rebellion would thereafter be called "ex-Séléka".)

On the political front, the Bozizé clan tried to stigmatise "foreigners" and "Muslims" in their propaganda. In so doing, they instrumentalised religious differences for their political ends, contributing to the construction of religious antagonisms for ethnic cleansing, then civil war. For example, when the anti-Balaka militia attacked Fula in the region of Boali, ex-Séléka helped these Fula to take vengeance on the "Christians". The simplistic presentation of this violence as a combat between Christians and Muslims created a dynamic of self-fulfilling prophecy, transforming the war into one of inter-religious conflict. This fracture line between Christians/animists and Muslims was a new thing in Central Africa, which until then had rather seen people torn apart on ethno-regional considerations. Hollande, without any authorisation from the UN, started moving supplies from a French base in Toulon to Cameroon, on boats that were shipping materiel for the maritime Operation Corymbe (another mission aimed at protecting the Gulf of Guinea from piracy). Cameroon was the closest place from which French forces could bring new vehicles to the CAR. Realising now that France was on the verge of yet another military intervention in Africa, in December 2013, anti-Balaka troops, tele-commanded by the Bozizé clan, coordinated attacks on minority Muslim neighbourhoods in the capital, resulting in hundreds of deaths. That same day, the UN Security Council passed Resolution 2127, authorising the deployment of the new African-led International Support Mission to the Central African Republic (MISCA) to protect civilians.

Thus, given the green light to wage another peace war, Hollande and Le Drian launched Operation Sangaris with 1,600 soldiers (soon to be 2,000) in December 2013. This operation turned into a fiasco. French troops started disarming ex-Séléka soldiers without taking any precautions to protect the Muslim minorities living in the capital city. France effectively left Muslims at the mercy of the vengeful anti-Balaka militias. For by disarming only the ex-Séléka, they had left the Muslim communities of Bangui defenceless. "A mob started assaulting boutiques belonging to Muslim merchants and sacked and pillaged them. Then the owners chased them away with machetes. The French were already far away. So were the African forces of FOMAC [Central African Multinational Force]. Muslims had the impression of being deliberately disarmed by France in order to be delivered to their enemies."[31] Pro-Bozizé, anti-Balaka militia soon took control of the capital and started deploying men all around its hinterland, multiplying the number of their vengeful retributions. In one week they killed 600 people around the country, 400 in the capital alone.

In December 2013, seeing this anti-Muslim violence, Chadian "peacekeepers" at the Bangui airport opened fire on anti-Balaka protestors, after which other "Christian" militia attacked Chadian convoys, killing three of them. At this point, the MISCA commander ordered Chadian troops out of the capital. No longer able to protect Muslims in Bangui, Chad decided to evacuate. But they remained in the countryside, and now they were supporting the ex-Séléka rebels. Witnessing the anti-Muslim violence in the capital, Djotodia no longer felt protected. In January 2014, Catherine Samba-Panza became the first female president of the CAR. She was a French lawyer, trained at the University of Paris, who had worked for the insurance group Allianz and the Compagnie Française Gras Savoye. An assimilated Francophile whose candidacy was supported by Laurent Fabius, she had been named mayor of Bangui by Djotodia in May 2013. Her prime minister was another francophone technocrat who had worked for the BDEAC (*Banque de Développement des Etats de l'Afrique Centrale*), the regional central bank of the *Communauté Financière Africaine* (CFA) franc zone. Neither had been properly elected. Neither of them controlled any armed factions. Both were therefore defenceless, entirely dependent on France and Chad for their security.

By February 2014, the UN assistant secretary-general in charge of humanitarian affairs, Valérie Amos, declared that there remained fewer than 1,000 Muslims in Bangui out of an estimated 100,000 who had inhabited the capital before the crisis.[32] The Office of the UN High Commissioner for Refugees (UNHCR) estimated that 15,000 persons were blocked in 18 enclaves (notably Boda, Bouar, Bossangoa, and the PK-12 neighbourhood of Bangui), encircled by anti-Balaka militia; more than 700,000 persons were displaced within the country, including Bangui, where about 273,000 people were dispersed over 66 sites; while another 288,000 people had simply fled to neighbouring countries.[33] Clearly, Operation Sangaris was unable, with 2,000 men, to stop the ethnic cleansing. On the contrary, by the spring of 2014, they had to recognise that the operation had probably increased the level of violence. Gone were the days when a handful of parachutists could occupy the capital and restore a semblance of order. Moreover, the Chadian troops in MICOPAX had been no better at coming between the parties, giving the appearance of siding with ex-Séléka and the Muslims. Operation Sangaris had turned into an intervention gone too far.

No matter. The hawks at the Elysée continued with their game plan, advancing troops to the centre of the country, where the rebels had established their headquarters, fighting ex-Séléka forces at the end of May 2014. The rebels had by then tried to politically restructure themselves, nominating a joint command for their different armed groups. The anti-Balaka had organised themselves into two factions, both connected to the Bozizé clan, one directed by Bozizé's former minister of sports, the other by an engineer close to one of Bozizé's sisters. By June the African Union had organised talks between the parties. The official AU mediator, President Dénis Sassou-Nguesso, held talks in Brazzaville and tried to get the parties to sign a ceasefire agreement, while Le Drian travelled to the Central African Republic to start the process of setting up a war crimes tribunal. By now, France's new "Monsieur Afrique", the deputy from Britanny, found himself working with Sassou to get a ceasefire signed by mid-July, while combat continued with uncontrollable confrontations between ex-Séléka and anti-Balaka forces in a vicious cycle of ethnic, regional, and sectarian violence.

Concerned with the security problems, the humanitarian crisis, human rights violence, and political collapse in the Central African Republic as well as its regional implications, the UN Security Council adopted Resolution 2149 in April 2014, authorising the deployment of a new peacekeeping operation, the United Nations Multidimensional Integrated Stabilisation Mission in the Central African Republic (MINUSCA), with the protection of civilians as its utmost priority. The mission's mandate also included the provision of "support for the transition process, facilitating humanitarian assistance; promotion and protection of human rights, support for justice and the rule of law; and disarmament, demobilization, reintegration and repatriation processes."[34] It consolidated all of the other intervention forces—except the French—by September 2014. Concretely, the AU soldiers in MISCA remained in place but changed the colour of their helmets. The commander-in-chief of this peacekeeping operation was French general Frédéric Hingray, former commander of army intelligence and an alumnus of the Special Operations Command (COS)—that is, a special ops commando. The only real difference was that the new peacekeeping operation—with an increased strength of 10,000 troops and 1,820 police—incorporated non-African soldiers.

Following their custom, French forces remained entirely outside the command structure of the UN peacekeeping mission. That way Paris could maintain its operational autonomy and be able to weigh in heavily on the country's political situation.

Soon after MINUSCA came into effect, the new interim president, Catherine Samba-Panza, was accused in the French-language press of taking $10 million from Angola. She denied taking any money, rather claiming she had distributed it for diverse actions that she threatened to reveal. She had a list of names of beneficiaries. Bozizé's anti-Balaka took advantage of the situation and launched a destabilisation campaign. In the Muslim enclaves of the capital, protected by the French and UN forces, anti-Balaka militia attacked. Riots organised by pro-Bozizé partisans called for Samba-Panza's resignation. Meanwhile, ex-Séléka forces had split into three separate factions, which made it practically impossible to conduct peace talks, given that none of the three could sign any effective ceasefire agreement on behalf of the other two. During January 2015, talks were held secretly in Nairobi between ex-Séléka representatives who demanded that French forces in Sangaris be placed under the command of MINUSCA. The French refused. On 29 January, French helicopters attacked a column of ex-Séléka in four-wheel-drive vehicles who were accused of trying to disrupt the consultations. In February 2013, Sangaris forces, flanked by Moroccan blue helmets, attacked another ex-Séléka force. These attacks were a manner of reminding the rebels who it was that made decisions about peacekeeping command structures in Central Africa.

In April 2015, *The Guardian* newspaper revealed that soldiers of Operation Sangaris, as well as Chadian and Equatoguinean soldiers of MISCA, were accused of sexually abusing children between the ages of nine and 15 at the refugee camp at Bangui airport.[35] These soldiers, taking advantage of the hungry kids, exchanged food rations for sexual favours between December 2013 and June 2014. The testimony of six children, victims, and eyewitnesses was compiled into a report by UN officials on-site, and by July 2014, this report had been transmitted to the French defence ministry, which brought it to civil authorities in Paris for criminal charges. But it was not until the affair was leaked to the press nine months later that any criminal investigation was finally started.[36] Accusation of French soldiers raping refugee children was too close a reminder of the charges brought against French soldiers in Operation Turquoise in Rwanda in 1994. On that occasion, French troops who were supposed to be protecting victims of the Rwandan genocide exchanged food rations for sex with Tutsi girls. That matter has still never been tried in court. (See Akonor in this volume.)

The UN showed itself, like the Catholic Church, incapable of dealing with a sex scandal, as revealed by an independent report ordered by the organisation and rendered public in December 2015.[37] According to another, more recent UN report, around 30,000 cases of sexual violence were perpetrated in the CAR between January and October 2015, with 25 cases cited against MINUSCA peacekeepers. In March 2016, the American non-governmental organisation (NGO) AIDS-Free World provided the United Nations Children's Fund (UNICEF) with monstrous accusations that 13 soldiers from Operation Sangaris and five African soldiers from MISCA had tied up and stripped three girls in the middle of their military camp and then forced these children to have sexual relations with a dog. Each of the girls was then paid €8. The soldiers filmed the act and transmitted it by portable telephone, although the French ambassador to the UN denies that any French soldiers were involved in the video or that this zoophile event occurred in Central Africa.[38]

Conscious that these sexual-abuse accusations risked undermining his effort to manage elections and impose a pro-French president of the CAR, Le Drian flew into Bangui at the end of July 2015 to finalise preparations for the democratic transition. On 24 July, the constitutional council of the CAR rejected an appeal by Catherine Samba-Panza to delay the elections because over a quarter million refugees living in neighbouring countries, mostly Muslims, would be de facto excluded from participating in any vote. The last act of this French fiasco took place in January 2016 when Bozizé's former prime minister, Faustin-Archange Touadéra, was elected president of the CAR. The former math professor and rector of the University of Bangui was a total unknown before his victory over Patassé's former prime minister, Anicet-Georges Dologuélé. Touadéra imposed himself as the candidate of the Bozizé clan. His entourage contains one of Bozizé's maternal uncles and one of his nephews. Anti-Balaka militias have already promised to provide him with a presidential security force. So although French troops had not succeeded in stopping the combats or ethnic exactions, they did impose a political settlement. Ex-Séléka rebels—fragmented by internal dissent, limited by ceasefires signed on their behalf, harassed by French expeditionary forces that remain autonomous of the UN peacekeeping mission, and having toppled the "Françafrican" Bozizé in 2013—were forced to see him return to influence three years later.

Conclusion: The Challenge of French Overstretch

In addition to its military interventions in Mali and the Central African Republic, France was the first European country to join the American-led coalition striking the Islamic State of Iraq and Syria. In 2015, it launched Operation Sentinelle with 10,000 troops patrolling the streets in France. In 2016, Hollande had raised defence spending by €3.8 billion over four years and expanded its total ground forces from 66,000 to 77,000. "Our technical capacity is very good", says General Vincent Desportes, a critic of Sentinelle. "But clearly France is in no position to commit to any further adventure."[39] What Desportes is talking about is known as military overstretch. The question that is being asked by some military strategists in Paris is precisely whether or not France is overstretched.

Over three decades, France has cut its military budget in half, from 3 per cent of gross domestic product (GDP) in 1982 to 1.4 per cent in 2015,[40] professionalised its armed forces by getting rid of mandatory military service, and reduced its total number of troops from 350,000 to 120,000 over the same period. In 1977, France had 210 regiments; by 2015 it had only 79. "For decades, in defiance of the reality of this world and its threats, the state has left our armies to degrade to the point that they are henceforth incapable of meeting the requirements of security."[41] The contradiction between the diminishing size and budget of French forces and their overextension is the main concern that seems to have escaped the president, now mockingly called "François Homeland". Desportes blames French politicians for playing budget games with their toy soldiers: "Unable to rest the grandeur of France upon its economic power, military interventions are used to make it believed that the Grande nation continues to play an essential role in the affairs of the world."[42] Never have French armies been employed so much while going through such a rapid pauperisation and degradation of their capacities, he scolds.

In *The Rise and Fall of the Great Powers*, Yale political scientist Paul Kennedy argued that ascendancy of a great power over the long term correlates strongly with its resources and economic durability, and that military overstretch and relative decline are the consistent threat facing powers whose ambitions and security requirements are greater than their resource base can provide.[43] For almost a decade, France has reeled in the wake of the 2008–2009 global economic crisis. French peacekeeping missions under President Hollande—unexpected, surprising, daring, and very expensive in terms of finances and materiel—perhaps maintained France's image as a great power in the world system, and preserved its reputation as still able to project power on the African continent. But overextension to such a degree may result in French armed forces being unable to accomplish the goals of peacekeeping missions in Africa: protecting civilians, defeating terrorists, and preventing genocide. Overstretch might also leave France in a position so reduced that it will not be able to defend itself.

What are the effects of France's military engagement on security in the subcontinent? For governing elites, security appears to be about territorial sovereignty and the protection of patrimonial state largesse. For the majority of impoverished, underprivileged Africans, security is about basic livelihoods; access to farmland, human capital, employment, and wages; protection from violence; functional development infrastructures; and availability of essential services. This raises a dilemma for anyone who seeks to evaluate net security: Whose security matters?[44] In francophone Africa, French military engagement has tended to provide security for post-colonial territorial integrity, for governing elites and pro-French regimes in power, for French businesses and expatriate communities who continue to benefit from the larger context of cooperation. This neo-colonial approach to security has evolved since the Cold War ended to include humanitarian intervention and the doctrine of the responsibility to protect (R2P). Now it includes the "war on terror". But such mission creep dramatically overstretches French military capabilities, and it will prove difficult to sustain. For ordinary people who live in the Sahel, insecurity is greater now than during the Cold War. But for the client states in the Gulf of Guinea, they have their security protected by a France that is still willing to intervene militarily to preserve grandeur and its African sphere of influence.

Notes

1. Christopher Griffon, "French Military Interventions in Africa", paper presented at 48th annual meeting of the International Studies Association, Chicago, 28 February 2007.
2. Bruno Charbonneau, *France and the New Imperialism: Security Policy in Sub-Saharan Africa* (London: Routledge, 2016), p. 66 (*see* tab. 4.2, "French Military Interventions in Africa, 1945–2005").
3. François-Xavier Verschaeve, *La Françafrique: Le Plus Long Scandale de la République* (Paris: Stock, 1998), is the French-language classic.
4. David Revault d'Allonnes, *Les Guerres du Président* (Paris: Seuil, 2016), p. 34.
5. Revault d'Allonnes, *Les Guerres du Président*, p. 35.
6. "François Hollande à Bamako: 'Nous Serons à Vos Côtés'", *Le Monde*, 2 May 2013.
7. Revault d'Allonnes, *Les Guerres du Président*, p. 50.
8. Michael Shurkin, *France's War in Mali: Lessons for an Expeditionary Army* (Santa Monica, CA: RAND, 2014), p. xi.
9. Vincent Nouzille, *Les Tueurs de la République: Assassinats et Opérations Spéciales des Services Secrets* (Paris: Fayard, 2015), p. 7.
10. Jean-Christophe Notin, *La Guerre de la France au Mali* (Paris: Tallandier, 2014), p. 175.
11. Shurkin, *France's War in Mali*, pp. 6–7.
12. Vincent Desportes, *La Dernière Bataille de France: Lettre au Français Qui Croient Encore Être Defendus* (Paris: Gallimard, 2015), p. 31.
13. Nouzille, *Les Tueurs de la République*, pp. 382–383.
14. Nouzille, *Les Tueurs de la République*, p. 385.

15. Mériadec Raffray, "Les Rébellions Touarègues au Sahel", in *Les Cahiers du Retex* (Centre de Doctrine d'Emploi des Forces, January 2013), *cited in* Nouzille, *Les Tueurs de la République*, p. 389.
16. Notin, *La Guerre de la France au Mali*, p. 83.
17. Nouzille, *Les Tueurs de la République*, p. 394.
18. Christophe Cornevin, "DGSE, au Cœur de Nos Services Secrets", *Le Figaro*, 11 July 2014.
19. Yanis Thomas, *Centrafrique: Un Destin Volé—Histoire d'Une Domination Drançaise* (Paris: Agone, 2016), p. 2.
20. John Iliffe, *Les Africains* (Paris: Flammarion, 2007), p. 417.
21. Geraldine Faes and Stephen Smith, *Bokassa 1er Un Empereur Français* (Paris: Calmann-Lévy, 2000).
22. Human Rights Watch, *Etat d'Anarchie: Rébellions et Exactions Contre la Population Civile* (September 2007), pp. 38, 47.
23. International Crisis Group, "République Centrafricaine: Débloquer le Dialogue Politique Inclusif", *Briefing Afrique*, 9 December 2008, p. 4.
24. Andreas Mehler, "Central Africa," in *Africa Yearbook: Politics, Economy, and Society South of the Sahara in 2011* (Leiden: Brill, 2002), p. 222.
25. According to South Africa's *Mail & Guardian*, the huge losses from Areva's purchase of Uramin were actually used to cover up a gigantic operation of corruption of African National Congress (ANC) leaders during the presidency of Thabo Mbeki to obtain the market for the construction of nuclear reactors (worth tens of billions of dollars) before this plan was foiled by the election of Jacob Zuma. According to the French watchdog *Mediapart*, some of the retro-commissions paid for Sarkozy's 2007 election campaign. *See* R. Granvaud, *Areva en Afrique* (Paris: Agone, 2012), and articles by journalist Martine Orange at http://www.mediapart.fr.
26. Mehler, "Central Africa", p. 220.
27. Sango was one of the official languages, along with French, adopted by the coalition of armed movements. Concretely the Séléka were composed of Central Africans coming from the northeast regions of the country, notably the Bakaga and Bainguit-Bangoran, but Chadians and Sudanese.
28. "Centrafrique: La France N'a Pas à 'Protéger un Régime', Selon François Hollande", *Radio France International*, 28 December 2012.
29. Serge Michailof, *Africanistan: L'Afrique en Crise Va-t-Elle se Retrouver dans Nos Banlieues?* (Paris: Fayard, 2015), is the latest in a series of works drawing an analogy between the Sahel and Afghanistan. *See also* Marwan Bishra's English-language Al Jazeera episode of *Empire*: "Africanistan: The Scramble for Africa", http://www.blacklistednews.com/Africanistan_-The_New_Scramble_for_Africa/37040/0/38/38/Y/M.html (accessed 13 May 2016).
30. Usually attributed to Samuel Clemens, but there is no proven attribution.
31. Adrien Jaulmes, "Centrafrique: Les Soldats Français au Milieu des Haines à Bangui", *Le Figaro*, 9 December 2013.
32. "Il Reste Moins de Mille Musulmans à Bangui", *Le Figaro*, 7 March 2014.
33. UN High Commission for Refugees, "Le HCR Appelle à Protéger 15,000 Personnes Directement Menacées en République Centrafricaine", 25 February 2014.
34. *See* http://www.un.org/en/peacekeeping/missions/minusca (accessed 13 May 2016).

35. Sandra Laville, "UN Aid Worker Suspended for Leaking Report on Child Abuse by French Troops", *The Guardian*, 29 April 2015.
36. The French watchdog *Mediapart* made this report available in July 2015.
37. Marie Deschamps, Hassan B. Yallow, and Yasmin Sooka, *Report of an Independent Review on Sexual Exploitation and Abuse by International Peacekeeping Forces in the Central African Republic*, 17 December 2015.
38. Cyril Bensimon and Marie Bourreau, "Nouvelles Accusations de viols en RCA", *Le Monde*, 2 April 2016, p. 3.
39. "Aux Armes", *The Economist*, 7 May 2016, p. 20.
40. Martial Foucault, "Les Budgets de Défense en France, Entre Déni et Déclin", *Focus Stratégique* no. 36 (April 2012).
41. Desportes, *La Dernière Bataille de France*, p. 11.
42. Desportes, *La Dernière Bataille de France*, p. 27.
43. Paul Kennedy, *The Rise and Fall of the Great Powers: Economic Change and Military Conflict from 1500 to 2000* (New York: Random, 1988), pp. 438–439.
44. Kenneth Omeje, "Whose Security? The Global Security Debate and the African Paradox", in Jamila Abubakar, Kenneth Omeje, and Habu Galadima (eds.), *Conflict of Securities: Reflections on State and Human Security in Africa* (London: Adonis and Abbey, 2010), pp. 17–42.

CHAPTER 23

Britain's Role in Promoting Security Sector Reform in Sierra Leone

Ismail Rashid

Following the election of the New Labour government headed by Tony Blair in 1997, Britain became deeply invested in resolving the Sierra Leone conflict and reconstructing the country's state and economy.[1] It steadfastly supported the restoration of the democratically elected government of Ahmad Tejan Kabbah when a military junta attempted to supplant it in 1997. Britain deployed two military operations in 2000, which helped stabilise the United Nations Mission in Sierra Leone (UNAMSIL) and saved the 1999 Lomé peace agreement.[2] Its most crucial contribution to conflict resolution and peacebuilding in Sierra Leone, however, was in restructuring, retraining, and equipping the country's police, intelligence services, army, and defence ministry. The British-led and financed security sector reform (SSR) programmes have been regarded not only as crucial in stabilising the country since the end of its civil war in 2002, but also as successful models of post-conflict reform of security institutions.[3] (On peacebuilding in Sierra Leone, see also Omeje in this volume.)

Britain's contributions to tackling the security and developmental challenges faced by Sierra Leone in the past two decades have further been lauded as an exemplary achievement in the ethical, security-enhancing, and poverty-minimising Africa policy agenda of the New Labour government.[4] These contributions stand in stark contrast to Britain's other controversial foreign policy actions around the same period. Britain's involvement in the United States (US)–led "war on terror", after 11 September 2001, especially in the quagmire that followed the US-led invasion of Iraq in 2003, damaged its international prestige. The country's stance against the autocratic policies and actions of President Robert Mugabe and his Zimbabwe African National Union–Patriotic Front (ZANU-PF) regime also produced disastrous results. It hardened rather

I. Rashid (✉)
Department of History, Vassar College, Poughkeepsie, New York, United States

T. Karbo, K. Virk (eds.), *The Palgrave Handbook of Peacebuilding in Africa*, https://doi.org/10.1007/978-3-319-62202-6_23

than dislodged Mugabe's regime, pushed Zimbabwe's economy into a tailspin, and generated disapproval from several African countries. Thus, at a time when Britain's involvement in other conflict-affected zones around the world and in Africa was seriously questioned, its roles in Sierra Leone and Kosovo stood out as the only credible testaments to an "ethical" foreign policy whose shine was quickly fading.[5]

The timeliness and necessity of the British military interventions and their support for the reform of Sierra Leone's security institutions are incontrovertible. There is also not much doubt that they have helped ensure stability in the country over the past decade. The extent to which they have effected deep transformations in the security architecture of the country, however, remains unclear. Furthermore, the public appreciation of the British contributions should not obscure some of the difficulties inherent in the reform process. The fact that British resources, ideas, and expatriates largely drove the reform process generated considerable disaffection and lack of agency among Sierra Leoneans. In addition, although the reform process was premised on the paradigm that security and development are inextricably linked,[6] the British and Sierra Leone governments found it difficult at different points in their engagement to define clearly or establish the precise relationship between the two objectives.

It was the British secretary of state for international development, Clare Short, who popularised the idea of security sector reform in the Sierra Leone context, and insisted that it should be embedded within a security-development nexus.[7] While reform of the security sector in failing and conflict-affected states is now regarded as crucial to ensuring long-term stability, defining the nature of the sector has not been simple. It depends very much on whether one's approach is state-centric or human-centric. Narrow and state-centric definitions of the security sector tend to emphasise mainly institutions with authority to bear arms and use force for the protection of the state and society from domestic and foreign threats: the armed forces, police, paramilitary groups, and intelligence services. Legislatures, judiciaries, ministries, and statutory bodies that manage, control, and oversee these institutions are usually included in the definition. Also taken into consideration are liberation movements, guerrilla and insurgent groups, as well as private security agencies. Broader definitions of the sector, on the other hand, tend be more human-centric, and include all statutory and non-statutory bodies as well as civil society organisations tasked with oversight and the democratic governance of security institutions. Such definitions are also sensitive to the fact that security systems are not only national but also regional and global.[8] Although the reform process in Sierra Leone deftly navigated these different conceptions of the security sector, and endeavoured to include the broadest range of actors and institutions possible, its core programmes concentrated on reforming state-centric security agencies. This chapter focuses on British contributions to reforming state-centric security agencies, in particular the police, intelligence services, and army.

British Liberal Interventionism and Sierra Leone

Britain's relations with Sierra Leone extend as far back as 1787, when the Freetown peninsula became the site for the resettlement of Africans freed from enslavement in the Americas and Europe, and from captivity in slaving ships on the Atlantic Ocean. Sierra Leone became a Crown colony in 1808 and, after the addition of an extensive hinterland protectorate in 1896, remained under British rule until 1961. Throughout colonial rule, Freetown served as a strategic naval outpost for the British, who used its natural harbour for refuelling and restaging allied ships during the Second World War. British corporations—the Sierra Leone Selection Trust Company and the Sierra Leone Development Company—dominated the mining and export of diamonds and iron ore between the 1930s and 1970s. Although Britain received the permission of the Sierra Leone government to use the Freetown harbour during the Falklands War of 1982, military and economic relations between the two countries had declined considerably by the early 1990s. The country was therefore not on the radar of British politicians when its civil war started in 1990.

The election of Tony Blair's New Labour government in 1997, with its strong liberal-interventionist foreign policy agenda, led to the resuscitation of Britain's relations with Sierra Leone. The new British foreign secretary, Robin Cook, insisted that in contrast to the previous Conservative government, Britain's "foreign policy must have an ethical dimension and must support the demands of other people for democratic rights which we insist for ourselves".[9] This ideological reorientation produced a muscular approach to achieving British foreign policy goals. Consequently, Britain participated in five major wars and heightened its focus on anti-terrorism and global security.[10] The ethical and activist thrust of New Labour's foreign policy was also evident in Britain's overseas development agenda, especially towards sub-Saharan Africa, which Blair described as a "scar on the conscience of the word".[11] The region represented not only a developmental but also a security challenge. The British government repeatedly vowed to foster "good governance" and human rights, reduce debt and increase aid, and ensure security in Africa within the principles of internationalism, partnership, and mutuality. For Sierra Leone, Britain's ethical foreign policy and muscular liberal-interventionism translated into a willingness to expend substantial funds, as well as military force and technical assistance, to help resolve its conflict and rebuild its war-ravaged institutions.

Britain's re-engagement with Sierra Leone, however, started inauspiciously. Peter Penfold, newly appointed as Britain's high commissioner to Sierra Leone in 1997, began his diplomatic mission when the 1996 Abidjan peace agreement between the Sierra Leone government and the Revolutionary United Front (RUF) had collapsed. Citing tribalism and inadequate wages, a group of subaltern officers led by Captain John Paul Koroma forced the newly elected government of Ahmad Tejan Kabbah and thousands of Sierra Leoneans into exile in Guinea and other parts of the West African sub-region in 1997.[12] The coup-makers set up a junta, the Armed Forces Revolutionary

Council (AFRC), and then invited the RUF to join them in forming a people's army. The British government conveyed to the coup-makers that they would not be recognised and that the Kabbah government would remain the legitimate ruler of Sierra Leone. It backed this policy by financially supporting the upkeep and operations of the Kabbah government-in-exile in Conakry, Guinea.[13]

With strong British and African backing, Kabbah and his officials continued to participate in international forums like the United Nations (UN) General Assembly and the Commonwealth Summit. Britain used its position as a permanent member of the UN Security Council to advocate for robust international support for Sierra Leone. It also supported various agreements brokered by the Economic Community of West African States (ECOWAS) to ensure the peaceful restoration of the Kabbah government in Sierra Leone. The failure of these restoration plans eventually implicated the British government in what the British press labelled as the "arms-to-Africa" affair.[14] With the tacit support of Peter Penfold and senior officials of the British Foreign and Commonwealth Office, Kabbah signed a $10 million contract with Sandline International, a security outfit based in London, to provide arms, logistical support, and training for the pro-government Civil Defence Forces (CDF), and the Nigerian-led ECOWAS Ceasefire Monitoring Group (ECOMOG) forces, to oust the AFRC. In return, the Kabbah government promised diamond and other mineral mining concessions to Rakesh Saxena, an Indian businessman, who agreed to finance the Sandline operation. Though the Sandline arms arrived too late to make a difference in the Sierra Leone situation—the CDF and ECOMOG had pushed the AFRC out of Freetown in February 1998—this became a scandal in Britain.[15] And though parliament cleared the Labour government of wrongdoing, especially of violating the UN arms embargo on Sierra Leone, the Sandline Affair irreparably tarnished Penfold's reputation.[16]

Unlike the Sandline Affair, Britain's two military interventions in Sierra Leone in 2000 had more decisive impact on the situation on the ground. They were launched in response to the unravelling of the Lomé peace agreement, signed by the Sierra Leone government and RUF following the destructive AFRC-RUF invasion of Freetown in 1999. RUF combatants, opposed to the agreement, disarmed and kidnapped over 500 members of the United Nations Mission in Sierra Leone who were replacing ECOMOG troops in May 2000.[17] Meanwhile, remnants of the AFRC continued to terrorise civilians as well as the international peacekeepers on the outskirts of Freetown. In response to appeals from President Kabbah and Kofi Annan, the UN Secretary-General, Britain launched Operation Palliser in May 2000, its largest military deployment since the Falklands War of 1982. Its goals were to evacuate British and other European nationals as well as to shore up UNAMSIL.[18] Then in August 2000, Britain launched another intervention, Operation Barras, to rescue 11 British troops and their Sierra Leonean liaison officer who had been kidnapped by soldiers known as the West Side Boys on the outskirts of Freetown.[19]

In the wake of the Sandline debacle, and despite the high risks accompanying the direct military actions in Barras and Palliser, Britain had been compelled to act by not only idealist but also realist reasons. Sierra Leonean scholar Michael Kargbo comprehensively spells out the reasons for these operations as "the need to match foreign-policy pronouncements with actions; the obligations to safeguard British nationals and other interests; the prevention of a humanitarian catastrophe reminiscent of the January 1999 rebel invasion of Freetown; the defence of a democracy threatened by rebels with no political ideology; and the need to prevent the collapse of the biggest peacekeeping operation undertaken by the UN".[20] Despite its two robust military interventions in Sierra Leone, Britain, like the other permanent members of the UN Security Council, did not contribute any troops to UNAMSIL. However, Britain was the mission's strongest advocate in the Security Council.[21]

The British military interventions, coupled with defeats of recalcitrant RUF combatants by loyal Sierra Leonean government troops and Guinean armed forces, as well as the arrest and replacement of Foday Sankoh as leader of the RUF, saved the Lomé peace agreement. They also helped stabilise the security environment, and enabled UN peacekeepers to deploy throughout the country and to disarm the various combatant groups. The Sierra Leone government and its international partners, especially Britain, acquired the necessary space to focus on medium- as well as long-range projects of rebuilding the state, society, and economy. While UNAMSIL focused on establishing security and extending government control over the country, Britain and other international partners (the International Monetary Fund [IMF] and World Bank) worked mainly with the Sierra Leone government on two major long-range programmes: security sector reform and poverty reduction.[22] The partners tried to ground both programmes in the widely embraced paradigm that security and development are inextricably connected.

Like many other African countries facing fiscal problems, the production of a poverty reduction strategy paper (PRSP) by the Sierra Leone government was a fundamental requirement for debt relief and access to funds from sources underwritten by the IMF, the World Bank, the European Union (EU), and Britain. As the successor of the structural adjustment programmes (SAPs) of the 1980s and 1990s, the PRSP was expected to support the "continued implementation of sound economic policies to attain macroeconomic stability within the framework of good governance".[23] It was expected that programmes would be developed for post-war rehabilitation, provisions of basic services, and improvement of the living standards of the most vulnerable Sierra Leonean groups.[24] The lack of technical capacity meant that the process of outlining the programmes and priorities of the PRSP was done under the tutelage of the IMF and World Bank. Solidly ensconced within a neo-liberal capitalist framework that had been embraced by the British New Labour government, the interim PRSP (2001–2004) and first PRSP (2004–2007) were expected to ensure the continued liberalisation of markets, expansion of opportunities for private sector operators, and reduction of the country's debt burden.[25] All of the actors involved in the production of the PRSP, including Britain, insisted that provision of security for Sierra Leone should be one of its prime pillars. (See also Richmond in this volume.)

Britain concentrated considerable resources and personnel on the reform of the country's security (and justice) sector, namely the national intelligence services, the police, the army, and the judiciary. It cooperated with UNAMSIL on the ground in Sierra Leone to ensure that its security sector reform policies and programmes strengthened rather than weakened the mission. British engagement in the SSR process across Africa required the pooling of financial resources between Britain's Department for International Development (DFID), its Ministry of Defence, and its Foreign and Commonwealth Office into the African Conflict Prevention Pool (ACPP), the lion's share of which went to Sierra Leone between 2001 and 2004.[26] Unlike the PRSP, which had an overarching and globalised neo-liberal framework, the security sector programme in Sierra Leone had none. Instead, it unfolded in a piecemeal and compartmentalised fashion, with attempts at fashioning a coherent and strategic vision emerging only during the process.

The Security Sector Reform Process in Sierra Leone

The foundation for British engagement in security sector reform was laid in 1996 when the newly inaugurated Kabbah government solicited support from Britain for retraining the military and the police as well as strengthening civilian governance of security agencies. Britain funded the Commonwealth Police Development Task Force (CPDTF), which worked with UNAMSIL to assess the country's policing needs and to lead the reform of the Sierra Leone Police (SLP). It also dispatched military advisors to retrain loyal soldiers between 1997 and 1999; some of these advisors subsequently formed the core of the British Military Assistance Training Team (BMATT), which was later transformed into the International Military Assistance Training Team (IMATT) in 2001 following an agreement between DFID, headed by Clare Short, and the Sierra Leone government, for the overhauling of the country's security agencies.[27]

After the restoration of the Kabbah government in 1998, efforts to reform the various security institutions and develop a coherent national security strategy intensified. With the support of Britain, the Sierra Leone government undertook several studies and assessments. With Sierra Leone being essentially a pilot case, Britain's DFID and Ministry of Defence worked with the Sierra Leone government to implement the medium-term, comprehensive Sierra Leone Security Sector Reform Programme (SILSEP).[28] Britain funded a Ministry of Defence Advisory Team (MODAT) to reform the Sierra Leone Ministry of Defence and Office of National Security Advisor. MODAT subsequently recommended a more expansive process of reform and reorganisation of the defence ministry, intelligence services, and armed forces. With the work of the CPDTF in mind, the Sierra Leone government, with international assistance (from DFID, in particular), sought to develop a national security strategy.

This resulted in the production of a Sierra Leone national security paper in February 2000, which provided the basis for the establishment of a security sector review programme by President Kabbah.[29] The review programme entailed assessments of the threats facing the country as well as extensive consultations with government ministries and agencies, civil society organisations, scholars, and other stakeholders across the country. At the core of the post-war Sierra Leone security reform project was the challenge of ensuring not only the adequacy, efficiency, and accountability of security agencies, but also their functioning within a framework of democratic governance and subordination to civilian oversight.

Police Reforms: Creating a Force for Good

Between 1999 and 2003, Britain and UNAMSIL strongly supported the rebuilding and restructuring of the severely degraded Sierra Leone Police, which had lost about a third of its membership (from 9,317 to 6,600 personnel) to desertions and death during the decade-long civil war. Its infrastructure, including its buildings, vehicles, and communications equipment, had been damaged or destroyed. The Commonwealth Police Development Task Force, led by Keith Biddle, a retired British police officer with 38 years of experience, underlined a number of obvious characteristics about the post-war SLP: it was severely understaffed; it was perceived as corrupt, incompetent, aggressive, and unresponsive to local needs; its members were poorly remunerated; and the force was inadequately equipped, over-centralised, and unaccountable to the public.[30] The first outcome of the team's work was the development and launching of a police charter by the Kabbah government, which aimed at re-branding and re-establishing the SLP as the primary agency responsible for security in the country. The second was the provision by Britain's DFID of £25 million to the Commonwealth Community Safety and Security Project (CCSSP) to support the rebuilding and restructuring of the force. The third was the hiring of Biddle as inspector-general of the SLP by Kabbah from 1999 to 2003.

Biddle spearheaded the rebuilding of police stations and barracks, reinstatement of the police presence throughout the country, and restoration of confidence in the force. The strength of the force was raised from around 6,600 to 9,500 personnel. Uniforms, communications equipment, and over 700 vehicles were purchased. Biddle also oversaw the reorganisation of the force's operational, leadership, and management structure. The number of ranks was reduced and restructured from 21 to nine. Sixty senior officers of the SLP force were retrained at the Police Staff College, Bramshill, England, under Biddle's watch.[31] Rather than following the customary rules of seniority and political favouritism, he opened up promotion to younger and talented officers. Older officers, passed over for promotion in favour of their younger and more junior colleagues, resented these changes. So did officers whose ranks were eliminated and who themselves were demoted, like the sub-inspectors (designated sergeants) and sergeants (designated constables).[32]

Following the British model, greater emphasis was placed on accountability to civilians and community policing, an approach dubbed "local needs policing".[33] From 2004, local policing partnership boards, set up at each station, included concerned citizens who worked voluntarily with the police on preventing crime. In a controversial move, the Special Security Division (SSD), the hated paramilitary police unit created by Siaka Stevens, president of the repressive All People's Congress (APC), was retrained and designated the Operational Support Division (OSD). Ultimately, public opposition to the OSD was minimal, because of the heroic defence of Freetown by SSD officers in 1999. Less contentious and more popular was the upgrading of the Domestic Violence Unit to the Family Support Unit, with a broader role in investigating domestic violence, sexual offences, and cruelty against women and children.[34] (On women, gender, and peacebuilding, see Porter in this volume.)

The various reforms produced a Sierra Leone Police with better infrastructure and operational capability than before and during the war. It became more efficient and better managed, with commanders routinely conducting reviews of operations and performance of the force. Since 2002, it has better responded to, and managed, public-order events. The OSD has also demonstrated that it is an effective mobile force that can support other police units. There has been greater clarification of the roles of police, especially those of the senior echelon.[35] Overall, public perception of the force has improved slightly. The lines of communication between the various ranks have been shortened. In particular, the professional performance of the Sierra Leone Police during the 2007 and 2012 elections stands as a testimony of the positive impact of the reform process.

While the British-sponsored reforms improved the structure, operations, and initially the public perception of the SLP, the force continues to face serious management, operational, and image problems. First, despite being under the direct guidance and supervision of the government—the office of the vice-president rather than the internal affairs ministry—the force is still not subject to direct civilian oversight. The Sierra Leone Independent Police Complaints Board is expected to ensure greater accountability on the part of the force, but it was only recently launched, in 2015, and is not yet fully functional.[36] Second, even though numbers of police personnel have been steadily strengthened to almost 10,000, they and policing in general remain inadequate, even in the capital, Freetown, where the bulk of the force is still concentrated. The force finds it difficult to keep up with the growth of the various urban centres, and the increase in crime. Third, the remuneration and conditions of service for the police still remain inadequate, and remuneration has not kept up with inflation. Fourth, corruption remains rife among members of the force. Police officers still collect bribes, often in full view of the public, from operators of commercial vehicles. Demands for bribes and inconsistent application of the law continue to generate frequent friction between police and commercial transport operators, especially with the ubiquitous commercial bike-riders (*okada*) in the city. Misuse of police vehicles remains widespread.[37]

Justice Sector Reforms

Attempts to include the justice sector in the larger reform process met with much less success. In 2003, a justice sector task force, established after extensive consultations with various stakeholders, recommended a sector-wide approach to issues of policing and justice, rather than just an exclusive focus on the SLP. The group recommended improvements in the judiciary and prison systems, and in the systems and processes linking them.[38] Law and magistrate courts in Freetown, Bo, and Kenema were refurbished, and clerks and bailiffs were trained under a DFID-funded law-development project. From 2005, after the conclusion of the Commonwealth Community Safety and Security Project, the Justice Sector Development Programme (JSDP) was launched with the aim of sustaining broader legal and justice sector reform.[39] The JSDP's work has encompassed the police, judiciary, prisons, and internal affairs ministry. The JSDP has especially focused on supporting the partnership boards and the Family Support Unit, and improving police capacity to manage change, custody and detention, training, and investigations. The broadening of the scope of the SSR process intensified the competition between various governmental and non-governmental organisations (NGOs) for access to resources from Britain's DFID. Furthermore, the JSDP has faced stiff resistance from the judiciary, who see themselves as a separate branch of government rather than part of the security sector.

Intelligences Services: Identifying and Responding to National Threats

With substantial British financial input and personnel support, the intelligence services in the country were also organised and restructured. At the centre of the project was the enactment by the Sierra Leone parliament of the Sierra Leone National Security and Central Intelligence Act in 2002.[40] It established the National Security Council and a host of other national and local structures to collect, process, and act on information and developments deemed threatening to national security. Under the leadership of the president, the National Security Council brought together key ministries[41] and the heads of the police and military to fashion appropriate responses to national security threats. The act also created the Joint Intelligence Committee, comprising representatives from the Sierra Leone Police and the Republic of Sierra Leone Armed Forces (RSLAF). The Joint Intelligence Committee coordinated and processed information from the main security agencies as well as from provincial security committees (PROSECS) and district security committees (DISECS), bodies consisting of the most senior government officials, security commanders, and elected representatives at the different administrative levels.

At the heart of the national security architecture created by the act was the Office of National Security (ONS), which became the secretariat for the National Security Council. The head of the ONS, the national security coordinator, served as the principal advisor to the president on security matters. By

2007, the ONS had become the main body responsible not only for pulling together the leadership of the main security agencies, but also for improving the effectiveness and coordination of the security sector. The Office of National Security Advisor had been highly politicised before the war. Under the Sierra Leone Security Sector Reform Programme, the office became professionalised, with the holder expected to have the capacity to analyse threats, develop an overall security strategy, and undertake policy planning, integration, and coordination of the country's different security agencies and intelligence services.[42]

The National Security Act also established the Central Intelligence and Security Unit (CISU), headed by a director-general and staffed by civil servants, whose main purpose was to collect and analyze intelligence on internal and external activities that threatened the security of the country. As with the ONS, the Sierra Leone Security Sector Reform Programme also aimed to depoliticise the leadership and control structure of the CISU, and to ensure that it had adequate and trained staff who could undertake meaningful intelligence assessments and transmit them to the relevant decision-making structures.

The reform of the Sierra Leone intelligence architecture was not without criticism and problems. Joe Blell, the country's deputy minister of defence, criticised it as expensive and "too complex".[43] This may not have been an exaggeration, given that some of the key bodies do not meet as frequently as designated in the 2002 Sierra Leone National Security and Central Intelligence Act. Also, the equating of official positions in the military and civilian wings of the ministry caused resentment. Senior military officials did not like the fact that civilians with no military experience or extensive employment record were designated the equivalent of colonels, brigadiers, and generals.[44] This criticism, however, seems unwarranted, given that the civilian personnel drawn from various ministries to work in defence headquarters received extensive training in defence policy, administration, and procurement in Britain.[45]

Army and Defence Ministry: Building a Force to Serve the Nation

The rebuilding and reorganisation of the armed forces proved to be the most extensive, expensive, and time-consuming of the three facets of the Sierra Leone Security Sector Reform Programme. Between 1997 and 1999, the fate of the Sierra Leone army hung in balance as President Kabbah seriously contemplated its disbandment. Charles Margai, the minister of internal affairs, met with President Oscar Arias of Costa Rica at a conference—sponsored by the United Nations Development Programme (UNDP)—in 1998 in Arusha, Tanzania, to learn about Costa Rica's experience without a military force. Sierra Leonean general Maxwell Khobe, however, cautioned against the move to disband the army, arguing that it would be unwise to turn battle-tested veterans loose in a volatile and unstable environment. He also highlighted the heroic contributions of some Sierra Leonean soldiers during the war. Khobe recommended retraining, restructuring, and reducing the size of the military to around 5,000 personnel.[46] He died before the radical restructuring of the military began, and the task fell on the International Military Assistance Training Team. As in the case of the Sierra Leone Police, Kabbah asked for a British general to head the Sierra Leone army during the restructuring period, but the New Labour government declined the request and instead offered him a military advisor.[47]

Under the command of a British brigadier, the International Military Assistance Training Team consisted mainly of British officers, with some participation from the United States, Canada, Nigeria, Ghana, and other countries. Some of these British officers occupied the senior executive and advisory positions in the country's defence ministry and army until 2003, when Sierra Leoneans began to replace them. These officers usually had unfettered access to President Kabbah, who was also the defence minister. In rebuilding the rechristened Republic of Sierra Leone Armed Forces, IMATT officers followed the reports and recommendations of the British-funded Ministry of Defence Advisory Team, which had recommended the development of new recruitment criteria, new structures, new missions, and new military tasks. MODAT had also produced a military reintegration plan for the absorption of ex-combatants from the various warring factions, as per the Lomé Accord. Working with the UN-led disarmament, demobilisation, and reintegration (DDR) process, IMATT oversaw the screening, training, and absorption of nearly 2,500 former CDF, RUF, and renegade AFRC members into the new army.[48]

Under Operation Cheetah, IMATT retrained the Freetown military garrison to be a rapid reaction force with the capacity to deploy quickly and respond more effectively to security threats to the city. Other military units were retrained and deployed in particularly vulnerable areas, especially border points. With revised and newly developed training manuals, veteran soldiers were retrained on how to function in a democratic environment. By the time of the national elections of 2002, the new RSLAF had been sufficiently retrained and strategically deployed nationwide. By the start of 2003, new recruits who were expected to be the core of the new breed of soldiers had commenced training at Benguema.[49]

In 2001, IMATT set up a new institution, the Horton Military Staff Academy in Leicester in Western Area, for the training of junior and senior officers. As new blood was being injected into the reconstituted military, older and long-serving officers were retired, and by 2010 the military had essentially been downsized from around 15,000 personnel during the war to 10,500 in 2006 and around 8,500 in 2012. In the process, IMATT overhauled the command-and-control structures; administration, maintenance, and personnel management systems; and training regimes of the new army.[50]

As in the case of the Sierra Leone Police, the reconstituted military was extensively re-equipped, with new uniforms, vehicles, communications equipment, and armaments purchased. Seventy-five military Land Rovers, 25 military trucks, seven ambulances, and eight armoured vehicles were provided with the support of Britain's DFID.[51] Existing administrative and residential facilities were refurbished, and new ones were built. In the reorganisation and retraining of the Sierra Leone Police, IMATT has ensured that the Sierra Leone government and RSLAF maintain their commitment to the West African security architecture, though African participation in the team has been minimal.[52] It trained a company for (potential) deployment to the ECOWAS and African Union (AU) standby forces and other international peace support operations (see Kuwali, and Nagar in this volume). It is noteworthy that since 2007, Sierra Leone police and military officers have been deployed to support AU and UN peacekeeping operations in Haiti, Sudan, Somalia, Lebanon, and Nepal.[53]

The rebuilding of the army was preceded by the reorganisation of the Sierra Leone defence ministry by IMATT. The ministry was relocated from a small, decrepit building to the former Paramount Hotel on State Avenue, close to State House. The reformed ministry consisted of two parallel organisations, the Joint Force Command, headed by a military officer—the chief of defence staff; and the Joint Support Command, headed by a civil servant—a director-general in the ministry. Both heads were under the direction of the deputy minister of defence and the president, and were also placed under the command of IMATT. The creation of the joint commands minimised the ability of a single commander to mobilise troops and other resources for coups.

The British-sponsored reform of the Sierra Leone defence ministry and the army helped soldiers to gain a better understanding of their relationship vis-à-vis the government, other security agencies (in particular, the police), and the public. The overall condition and cohesion of the RSLAF has improved greatly since 2002. Soldiers are better trained and better disciplined, and their public standing has improved. The most concrete tests of the efficacy of the military reforms were the 2007 and 2012 national elections, when the army remained neutral in its posture and in the public's perception. In the 2007 elections, the RSLAF intervened only to support the Sierra Leone Police at their request and with the authorisation of the government to maintain public order at some polling stations.[54]

The favourable public perception of the Sierra Leone military generated by the reforms, however, should not belie recurrent tensions between British expatriates and Sierra Leoneans involved in the security sector reform process. Not all Sierra Leonean officers, some of whom were corrupt and unaccountable to anyone under previous governments, were open to reform of the military.[55] Even when Sierra Leonean solders accepted the necessity of the reforms, they had to contend with the reality that the British, who provided the bulk of funding and technical expertise, controlled the reform agenda, ideas, and programmes. This had several unfavourable consequences for Sierra Leoneans. The average tour of duty for many IMATT advisors was about a year, and given the fact that many had not functioned in a post-conflict West African environment, Sierra Leoneans had to adjust constantly to the shifts in ideas and styles of new advisors. Some of the ideas introduced by British and other foreign military experts had little or no applicability in the Sierra Leone context or smacked of "colonialism".[56] Sierra Leonean military officers, especially senior ones, deeply resented their subordination to IMATT officers of lesser ranks, the overbearing attitude of the expatriates, and the lack of appreciation of their expertise and knowledge of the local terrain.

Despite the public pronouncements of the British about partnership and local ownership of the reforms, several senior Sierra Leonean military officials felt disempowered and a lack of ownership of the SSR process.[57] They felt that President Kabbah and his ministers listened too much to IMATT officers and did not pay sufficient attention to the advice of Sierra Leonean officers. There was also resentment over the control of resources for the military. Until 2003, the director-general of the defence ministry, a civilian British expatriate, controlled the allocation of military resources. His military equivalent, the Sierra Leonean chief of defence staff, had no control over resources, and in many instances he had to be "cleared" by the British military advisor to the government to see President Kabbah.[58] Sierra Leonean officers also viewed IMATT's handling of certain aspects of the reform process as corrupt and lacking in transparency despite their posturing. While IMATT answered to Britain's DFID, it was not directly accountable to the Sierra Leone government.

Operation Pebu, the problem-plagued project for the construction of housing for soldiers in Kailahun, is frequently cited as an instance of IMATT corruption and disregard of Sierra Leonean expertise with disastrous consequences.[59] The decision by IMATT officers to use Sierra Leonean soldiers to construct single-room mud-brick houses at inflated costs generated much criticism, which subsequently affected the ability of the IMATT to raise sufficient funds for the revised construction project.[60] The decision to scrap the naval and air wings of the RSLAF, contrary to the advice of Sierra Leonean officers, is cited as another example. Questions still continue to be asked about the £4 million allocated for the resuscitations of these military wings and about the outcomes of the investigations conducted by the British defence ministry.[61] Senior officers also expressed dissatisfaction with the restructuring process, especially with the speed with which combatants from various warring groups were reintegrated into the army without attention to the official criteria laid out by the Sierra Leone parliament. The "hurried training" given to reintegrated ex-combatants has also been criticised.[62] Many of the reintegrated ex-combatants subsequently left or have been discharged from the military for acts of indiscipline. The manner in which some long-serving officers were involuntarily retired also created some lingering disaffection.[63]

Just as in the case of the Sierra Leone Police, all indications are that the British-sponsored SSR process has reformed but not transformed the character, funding, and management of the RSLAF. The force remains inadequately equipped and financed. Regular maintenance and fuelling of its donated vehicles have been problematic.[64] Adequate compensation also continues to be an issue, since at around 8,500 troops the RSLAF remains a major financial burden for the Sierra Leone government. The infrastructure of the military remains deficient. There is also lingering discontent over compensation, rice rations, fuel, decent billeting, promotions, and the ongoing downsizing of the force. The retrenchment of old soldiers has created hiccups and tensions in the reorganisation process. However, these problems have not yet produced any major security crisis.[65] More recently, issues of recruiting along ethnic lines and political interference, which were responsible for the deterioration of the force in the past, have resurfaced.

Analysing the Security Sector Reform Process and Outcomes

The Sandline Affair in 1997 may have embarrassed the New Labour government, but its military interventions in Sierra Leone in 2000 enhanced the prestige of British military forces. The interventions saved UNAMSIL from becoming another international peacekeeping disaster in Africa (after Somalia and Rwanda), and underlined Britain's global leadership. (On Somalia, see Hirsch, and Mahiga; and on Rwanda, see Gambari, in this volume.) For Tony Blair's New Labour government, British involvement in Sierra Leone stands out, alongside Kosovo, as the only vindication of its much-vaunted "ethical" foreign policy and of the efficacy of its liberal interventionism, which have been savaged by domestic and foreign critics.[66] The post-war rebuilding of the country, especially the reform of its security sector, enabled British government officials and security experts to gain valuable, concrete experience that was applied in other, similar contexts.

Involvement of the British government in the Sierra Leone SSR process also led to the modification of its approach to international development, leading to new strategies of pooling and allocating funds as well as establishing new rules of engagement with other countries (such as Clare Short's 2002 memorandum of understanding on relations between Britain and Sierra Leone); and to the opening up of new avenues of cooperation between governmental departments—Britain's DFID, Foreign and Commonwealth Office, and Ministry of Defence—in delivering international development assistance.[67] Ultimately, British involvement in the Sierra Leone SSR process brought concrete financial benefits to British expatriates, who were remunerated for providing expertise to governmental and non-governmental agencies; and to businesses that procured contracts to provide services, equipment, vehicles, armaments, and other materials in Sierra Leone.

Though premised on the paradigm that security and development are inextricably connected, the British and their Sierra Leone counterparts faced considerable challenge in defining "security" and "development", and in figuring the precise relationship between the two, especially within the relatively short duration of the SSR process.[68] In 1997, when Blair's New Labour government became actively engaged in Sierra Leone, there was no doubt about the importance and primacy of establishing security in Sierra Leone. This meant devoting significant resources to ending the war, saving lives, and ensuring the survival of a democratically constituted government. The establishment of security for the people and the government remained crucial until cessation of the war and the conclusion of the DDR process in 2002. By 2005, it was evident on the ground that the security situation in Sierra Leone had stabilised. British and Sierra Leonean perceptions as well as assessments of the importance of security began to diverge. The Kabbah government, which was being criticised for its lacklustre economic performance, had less interest in security sector reform. The British government, reeling from terrorist attacks in London in 2005, remained strongly focused on the issue and pushed constantly for nearly all the developmental challenges faced by the country to be defined as security threats.

Two crucial questions then arose regarding the security sector reform programme. First, did the British unnecessarily securitise the development of Sierra Leone, and generate vested local interests in the issue because they continued to devote resources to it? And second, did they overemphasise security at the expense of development? Mark White, the DFID regional security advisor in Sierra Leone between 2006 and 2010, without rejecting the link between development and security, highlights the difficulties of integrating the two processes effectively in Sierra Leone. Rather than conceiving of them as two sides of the same coin, White suggests that they should be conceived more as a "seesaw" or as "weighing scales" in which an equilibrium is desirable but which also requires recognition that support for one might sometimes need to outweigh support for the other.[69]

Beyond struggling to maintain the nexus and balance between security and development, the most significant impact of the British intervention in Sierra Leone may lie in the developmental trajectory into which its intervention locked the country. The trajectory raises the role of ideology and power in the SSR process. The process took place within a context in which there was very little room for alternate visions and programmes. General Khobe, who had initially floated the idea of retraining the Sierra Leone army, died before the process commenced, and ECOWAS had neither the resources, the inclination, nor the will to take on the task. Without its own resources, the Sierra Leone government became highly dependent on international donors, especially Britain, for budgetary support and implementation of the security sector reform process.[70] With the country lacking the resources to pursue or effectively assert its own alternative visions, programmes, or strategies, Sierra Leone's ownership of, and partnership in, the SSR process were necessarily circumscribed. History and vast disparity in power make it difficult not to interpret the post-war relationship between Britain and Sierra Leone as neocolonial. Sierra Leoneans are very much aware of this disparity in power, and of their dependency on foreign donors.[71] Necessity and pragmatism compelled them to be part of the post-war rebuilding process—and in several ways, they did come to own the outcomes of the process, whether the police, army, civil service, or various structures and equipment.

Conclusion

Looking back at the situation in 1997, the active engagement of Britain in the Sierra Leone security sector reform process contributed substantially to restoring peace and stability through the rebuilding of key state security institutions that had been severely degraded by misrule, coups, and war. The reconstituted and retrained military and police function much better now than in the pre-war era, despite the numerous challenges they face. They are now much more subordinated to (civilian) governmental authority and supervision, even if they still struggle with being accountable to civil society. Violent conflict and coups have been prevented so far. Three elections have been held, in 2002, 2007, and 2012, since the conclusion of the war, and the governments they have produced have been stable, even if still bedevilled by intractable problems. Against this background, a realist view would underline that the British and Sierra Leone governments mutually achieved some of their key objectives.

The reconstituted security institutions, however, continue to be plagued with problems similar to those that led to their degradation in the first place. Despite the constant scrutiny of international donors, and the efforts of the country's Anti-Corruption Commission (ACC), corruption remains prevalent in Sierra Leone. While the ACC has successfully indicted some corrupt senior governmental officials, others have utilised their political connections to escape serious penalties. Sierra Leonean scholar Jimmy Kandeh therefore cautions against "prematurely" celebrating Sierra Leone as a model of post-war rebuilding.[72] He underlines the fact that access to state institutions and resources remains a major source of elite enrichment, a "mode of accumulation", which he argues "is incommensurate with both democracy and development". In short, while Sierra Leonean society and politics, like the country's security institutions, have seen some significant changes since 2002, they have not been sufficiently transformed to prevent a potential return to the crisis of the 1980s and 1990s.

Notes

1. Britain is used synonymously with the United Kingdom (UK) in this volume.
2. Paul Williams, "Fighting for Freetown: British Military Intervention in Sierra Leone", *Contemporary Security Policy* 22, no. 3 (2001), pp. 140–168.
3. Daniel Bendix and Ruth Stanley, *Security Sector Reform in Africa: The Promise and Practice of a New Donor Approach* (Durban, South Africa: African Centre for the Constructive Resolution of Disputes [ACCORD], 2008); Michael Kargbo, "International Peacebuilding in Sierra Leone: The Case of the United Kingdom", in Tunde Zack-Williams (ed.), *When the State Fails: Studies in Intervention in Civil War* (London: Pluto, 2012), pp. 65–88.
4. Julia Gallagher, "Healing the Scar: Idealizing Britain in Africa, 1997–2007", *African Affairs* 108, no. 432 (2009), pp. 435–451; David Chandler, "Rhetoric Without Responsibility: The Attraction of 'Ethical' Foreign Policy", *British Journal of Politics and International Relations* 8, no. 3 (2006), pp. 331–350.
5. "The Ethics of Labour's Foreign Policy: Angels and Demons", *The Economist*, 10 September 2009.
6. Mark White, "The Security-Development Nexus in Sierra Leone", in Peter Albrecht and Paul Jackson (eds.), *Security Sector Reform in Sierra Leone, 1997–2007: Views from the Frontline* (Geneva: Geneva Centre for the Democratic Control of Armed Forces [DCAF], 2010), pp. 71–91.

7. Nicole Ball, *Spreading Good Practices in Security Sector Reform: Policy Options for the British Government* (London: Saferworld, 1998).
8. Heiner Hänggi, "Conceptualising Security Sector Reform and Reconstruction", in Alan Bryden and Heiner Hänggi (eds.), *Reform and Reconstruction of the Security Sector* (Münster: LIT Verlag, 2004), pp. 3–20; Adedeji Ebo, "The Role of Security Sector Reform in Sustainable Development: Donor Policy Trends and Challenges", *Conflict, Security, and Development* 7, no. 1 (2007), pp. 27–60; Michael Brzoska and David Law, "Security Sector Construction and Reform in Peace Support Operations", *International Peacekeeping* 13, no. 1 (2008), p. 6.
9. Robin Cook, "British Foreign Policy", 12 May 1997, http://www.fco.gov.uk/ (accessed 19 August 2013).
10. The British military interventions during this period were in Iraq (1998, 2003), Kosovo (1999), Sierra Leone (2000), and Afghanistan (2001).
11. *See* Tony Blair, "Speech to Labour Party Conference", *Guardian Unlimited*, 2 October 2001, http://www.theguardian.com/politics/2001/oct/02/labourconference.labour6 (accessed 14 February 2016); Department for International Development, *Eliminating World Poverty: A Challenge for the 21st Century*, white paper (London, 1997).
12. Peter Penfold implied that the attempt to start the British-assisted retraining of the military might have triggered the 1997 coup; Peter Penfold, *Atrocities, Diamonds, and Diplomacy: The Inside Story of the Conflict in Sierra Leone* (Barnsley, South Yorkshire: Pen and Sword, 2012), p. 15.
13. The British High Commissioner, Peter Penfold, had a budget of about £150,000 to rent premises, support governmental travels, and pay for programs for Sierra Leonean refugees. *See* Interview with Peter Penfold, conducted by Charles Cullimore, 10 July 2003, British Diplomatic Oral History Programme (BDOHP), http://www.chu.cam.ac.uk/media/uploads/files/Penfold.pdf (accessed 10 February 2016).
14. "UK Government Faces Sierra Leone Grilling", *BBC News*, 18 May 1998, http://news.bbc.co.uk/2/hi/special_report/1998/05/98/arms_to_africa_row/95823.stm (accessed 10 February 2016); *The Guardian*, "Foreign Office Savaged over Arms to Africa", http://www.theguardian.com/politics/1999/feb/09/foreignpolicy.politicalnews (accessed 10 February 2016).
15. Tim Spicer, *An Orthodox Soldier: Peace and War and the Sandline Affair* (Edinburgh: Mainstream, 1999).
16. After Kabbah's restoration, Penfold was crowned an honorary Paramount Chief, the second British to receive that honour. The first was H.R.H. Prince Phillip.
17. Funmi Olonisakin, *Peacekeeping in Sierra Leone: The Story of UNAMSIL* (Boulder, CO: Lynne Rienner, 2008).
18. David Keen, *Conflict & Collusion in Sierra Leone* (New York: Palgrave, 2005), p. 265.
19. Mats Utas and Magnus Jorgel, "The West Side Boys: Military Navigation in the Sierra Leone Civil War", *Journal of Modern African Studies* 46, no. 3 (2008), pp. 487–511.
20. Michael Kargbo, *British Foreign Policy and the Conflict in Sierra Leone* (Oxford: Peter Lang, 2006), p. 298.
21. However, British presence was evident in the leadership of the organisation with the appointment of Alan Doss, a British career United Nations (UN) official, who was the deputy special representative, deputy head of the United Nations

Mission in Sierra Leone (UNAMSIL), and UN Development Programme (UNDP) representative in Sierra Leone.

22. Peter Albrecht and Paul Jackson, *Security System Transformation in Sierra Leone, 1997–2007*, February 2009, http://www.ssrnet.net/documents/Publications/SierraLeoneBook/Security%20System%20Transformation%20in%Sierra%20leone,%201997-2007.pdf (accessed 13 August 2012).
23. International Monetary Fund (IMF), *The Interim Poverty Reduction Strategy Reduction Paper* (Freetown, 2001), p. 8, http://www.imf.org/External/NP/prsp/2001/sle/01/index.htm (accessed 18 September 2012).
24. The inter-ministerial council, tasked by the cabinet to oversee the preparation of the interim PRSP, involved the following ministries: Development and Economic Planning (chair); Finance; Justice and Attorney-General; Health and Sanitation; Agriculture, Forestry, and Marine Resources; Social Welfare, Gender, and Children's Affairs; Education, Youths, and Sports; Internal Affairs; Energy and Power; Local Government and Rural Development; Presidential Affairs; Labour and Industrial Relations; Social Security; Transport and Communication; and Lands, Housing, Country Planning, and Environment. The commissioner of the National Commission for Reconstruction, Resettlement, and Rehabilitation was also included in the inter-ministerial council. *See* IMF, *The Interim Poverty Reduction Strategy Reduction Paper*.
25. Barry Riddell, "Sierra Leone: Urban-Elite Bias, Atrocity, and Debt", *Review of African Political Economy* no. 103 (2005), pp. 115–133.
26. Jeremy Ginifer and Kaye Oliver, "Evaluation of the Conflict Prevention Pools", Country/Regional Case Study no. 3, Evaluation Report no. EV 647 (London: Department for International Development [DFID], March 2004).
27. Author interview with officials of the Sierra Leone Office of National Security, 25 July 2013.
28. Author interview with officials of the Sierra Leone Office of National Security, 25 July 2013.
29. Author interview with officials of the Sierra Leone Office of National Security, 25 July 2013.
30. *See* Sierra Leone Truth and Reconciliation Commission, *Witness to Truth: Report of the Sierra Leone Truth and Reconciliation Commission*, vol. 3A (Accra: Graphic Packaging Ltd. GCGL, 2004).
31. Maria R. Haberfeld and Ibrahim Cerrah, *Comparative Policing: The Struggle for Democratization* (London: Sage, 2008), p. 135.
32. Kadi Fakondo, "Reforming and Building Capacity of the Sierra Leone Police, 1999–2007", in Albrecht and Jackson, *Security Sector Reform in Sierra Leone*, pp. 161–169.
33. Brice Baker, "Sierra Leone Police Reform: The Role of the UK Government", paper prepared for the GRIPS (National Graduate Institute for Policy Studies) State-Building Workshop 2010, "Organizing Police Forces in Post-Conflict Peace-Support Operations", Washington, DC, 27–28 January 2010, http://www.google.com/url?sa=t&rct=j&q=&esrc=s&source=web&cd=1&ved=0CCIQFjAA&url=http%3A%2F%2Fwww3.grips.ac.jp%2F~pinc%2Fdata%2F10-06.pdf&ei=131eUKjaE6nX0QHazYC4AQ&usg=AFQjCNHCA8T62vn_S-WcV4QHyKMVUEGQxA (accessed 18 September 2012).
34. J.P. Chris Charley, "Arms Regulations: A Challenging Issue for the Police Force in Post War Law Enforcement Order", in Anatole Ayissi and Robin Edward

Poulton (eds.), *Bound to Cooperate: Conflict, Peace, and People in Sierra Leone* (Geneva: UN Institute for Disarmament Research [UNIDIR], 2006), pp. 73–84.
35. Albrecht and Jackson, *Security System Transformation in Sierra Leone.*
36. UNDP, "New Independent Police Complaints Board to 'Ensure Greater Accountability and Peace'", 20 October 2015, http://www.sl.undp.org/content/sierraleone/en/home/presscenter/pressreleases/2015/10/20/new-independent-police-complaints-board-to-ensure-greater-accountability-and-peace-.html (accessed 14 February 2016).
37. Albrecht and Jackson, *Security System Transformation in Sierra Leone.*
38. Anthony Howlett-Bolton, "Justice Sector Reform", in Albrecht and Jackson, *Security Sector Reform in Sierra Leone*, pp. 95–112.
39. Osman Gbla, "The Role of External Actors in Sierra Leone's Security Reform", in Zack-Williams, *When the State Fails*, pp. 117–144.
40. "The National Security and Central Intelligence Act 2002", Supplement to *Sierra Leone Gazette* 132, no. 42 (4 July 2002).
41. The ministries are Finance; Foreign Affairs; Internal Affairs; Information and Broadcasting; Defence; and Presidential Affairs.
42. Robert Ashington-Pickett, "Intelligence and Security Services Reconstruction", in Albrecht and Jackson, *Security Sector Reform in Sierra Leone*, pp. 19–36.
43. Albrecht and Jackson, *Security System Transformation in Sierra Leone.*
44. Author interviews with officials of the National Security Agency (NSA), officers of the International Military Assistance Training Team (IMATT), and senior military commanders of the Republic of Sierra Leone Armed Forces (RSLAF), who preferred to remain anonymous, August 2007.
45. Nearly all of these trained civilian personnel have since left defence headquarters and have been reassigned to other ministries. Author interview with officials of the Sierra Leone Office of National Security, 25 July 2013.
46. Osman Gbla, "Security Sector Reform in Sierra Leone", in Len le Roux and Yemane Kidane (eds.), *Challenges to Security Sector Reform in the Horn of Africa*, Monograph no. 135 (Pretoria: Institute for Security Studies [ISS], 2007), pp. 13–36.
47. Author interview with officials of the Sierra Leone Office of National Security, 25 July 2013.
48. Emmanuel B. Osho Coker, "Governance and Security Sector Reform", in Albrecht and Jackson, *Security Sector Reform in Sierra Leone*, pp. 109–118.
49. Author interviews with NSA officials, IMATT officers, and senior RSLAF military commanders, who preferred to remain anonymous, August 2007.
50. Alfred Nelson-Williams, "Restructuring the Republic of Sierra Leone Military Forces", in Albrecht and Jackson, *Security Sector Reform in Sierra Leone*, pp. 119–148.
51. Gbla, "The Role of External Actors", p. 133.
52. The total number of IMATT personnel has varied over the years. As of 2007, it stood at around 105, of which 88 were British, 11 were Canadian, two were Nigerian, three were American, and one was Jamaican. The tour of duty for the officer is normally six months, with some tours lasting up to a year. Among the Nigerians who have served with IMATT are Lieutenant-Colonel Okay, Major B.E. Oyefuga, Major J. Ataguba, and Staff Sergeant Direala.
53. *See* Brigadier Samuel Omar Williams, "DCDS: A Dawn in the RSLAF", *Sierra Media Express*, n.d., http://www.sierraexpressmedia.com/archives/37362

(accessed 23 September 2012). This article was culled from *Defender Magazine*, March 2012.
54. Author interviews with NSA officials, IMATT officers, and senior RSLAF military commanders, who preferred to remain anonymous, August 2007.
55. Author interview with officials of the Sierra Leone Office of National Security, 25 July 2013.
56. Author interview with officials of the Sierra Leone Office of National Security, 25 July 2013.
57. Author interviews with NSA officials, IMATT officers, and senior RSLAF military commanders, who preferred to remain anonymous, August 2007.
58. Author interview with officials of the Sierra Leone Office of National Security, 25 July 2013.
59. Nelson-Williams, "Restructuring the Republic of Sierra Leone Military Forces", p. 140.
60. Aldo Gaeta, "Operation Pebu and the Ministry of Defence", in Albrecht and Jackson, *Security Sector Reform in Sierra Leone*, pp. 59–69.
61. Author interview with officials of the Sierra Leone Office of National Security, 25 July 2013.
62. Gbla, "The Role of External Actors", p. 142.
63. *See* "Viewpoint, IMATT: A Problem to the Sierra Leone Armed Forces?", *Standard Times* (Freetown), 28 May 2008.
64. Author interviews with NSA officials, IMATT officers, and senior RSLAF military commanders, who preferred to remain anonymous, August 2007.
65. Guy Thompson, Angus Morris, Chris Goostrey, Peter Wilson, and Piet Biesheuvel, *Sierra Leone Security Sector Reform Programme III (SILSEP III): Output to Purpose Review* (London: DFID, September 2005). These problems still continue to plague the military; *see* Captain Ken Josiah, "The Defender: Voice of the Institution or Political Publication?", http://www.sierraexpress-media.com/archives/40126 (accessed 23 September 2012).
66. David Chandler, "Rhetoric Without Responsibility: The Attraction of 'Ethical' Foreign Policy", *British Journal of Politics and International Relations* 8, no. 3 (2006), pp. 331–350; Oliver Daddow and Jamie Gaskarth, *British Foreign Policy: The New Labour Years* (New York: Palgrave Macmillan, 2011); Andrew M. Dorman, *Blair's Successful War: British Military Intervention in Sierra Leone* (London: Ashgate, 2009), pp. 3–4.
67. Peter Albrecht and Paul Jackson, *Reconstructing Security After Conflict: Security Sector Reform in Sierra Leone* (New York: Palgrave Macmillan, 2011).
68. Lisa Denny, "Reducing Poverty with Teargas and Batons: The Security-Development in Sierra Leone", *African Affairs* 110, no. 439 (2011), pp. 275–294.
69. White, "The Security-Development Nexus in Sierra Leone".
70. *See* Samura Kamara, "Government Budget and Statement of Economic and Financial Policies for Financial Year 2011", http://www.mofed.gov.sl/speeches/Bud1.pdf (accessed 10 February 2016).
71. "Sierra Leone: Time to End Country's Dependency on Aid", *Concord Times* (Freetown), 17 May 2011, http://allafrica.com/stories/201105180198.html (accessed 23 September 2012).
72. Jimmy Kandeh, "Intervention and Peacebuilding in Sierra Leone", in Zack-Williams, *When the State Fails*, p. 89.

CHAPTER 24

South Asian Peacekeepers in Africa

Kudrat Virk

Eighteen American soldiers, deployed as part of the United Nations (UN)–authorised Unified Task Force (UNITAF) in Somalia, died in October 1993 in an incident in Mogadishu, made famous by the film *Black Hawk Dawn* (see Mzali in this volume). The loss of life was followed by a decision by the United States (US) to withdraw its forces from Somalia (see Hirsch in this volume). Twenty-four Pakistani peacekeepers were earlier killed—the largest loss of life suffered in a single day by "blue helmets" at the time[1]—also in Mogadishu in June 1993. However, Pakistani troops stayed in Somalia, holding up a crumbling UN mission in the country until its bitter end, and were, in fact, the last out in 1995,[2] heralding the rise of South Asian blue helmets in post–Cold War peacekeeping.

Since the resurgence of international peacekeeping at the turn of the twenty-first century, three South Asian countries—India, Pakistan, and Bangladesh—have been among the biggest contributors to UN peacekeeping missions (see Fig. 24.1). Nepal has also been a consistent and significant participant in peacekeeping under the UN flag, though its deployments, in line with the size of its armed forces, have been relatively smaller. For much of the decade from 2005 to 2015, India, Pakistan, and Bangladesh, in fact, dominated the top three positions on the leader board of UN troop-contributing countries. In mid-2015 Ethiopia broke into the podium ranks and has, since 2016, occupied pole position, as part of a broader upward trend in African contributions to peacekeeping (see Fig. 24.2). Other Asian countries have also sought to increase their peacekeeping commitments. China, notably, had 2,515 blue helmets deployed in June 2017 (see Table 24.2), up from less than 100 in 2000 and "more than the other permanent members of the UN Security Council combined."[3] Meanwhile, Indonesia, another member of this cohort of relatively

K. Virk (✉)
Centre for Conflict Resolution, Cape Town, South Africa

T. Karbo, K. Virk (eds.), *The Palgrave Handbook of Peacebuilding in Africa*, https://doi.org/10.1007/978-3-319-62202-6_24

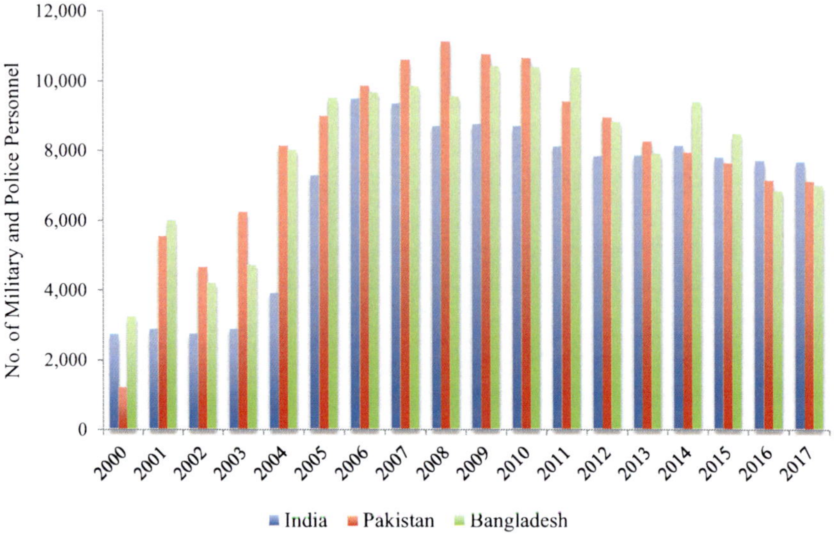

Fig. 24.1 Indian, Pakistani, and Bangladeshi contributions of uniformed personnel to UN peacekeeping, 2000–2017. *Source*: UN Peacekeeping, Troop and Police Contributors, http://www.un.org/en/peacekeeping/resources/statistics/contributors.shtml (accessed 12 June 2017 and 1 August 2017). *Note*: Based on year-end 2000–2016 and end-June 2017 data

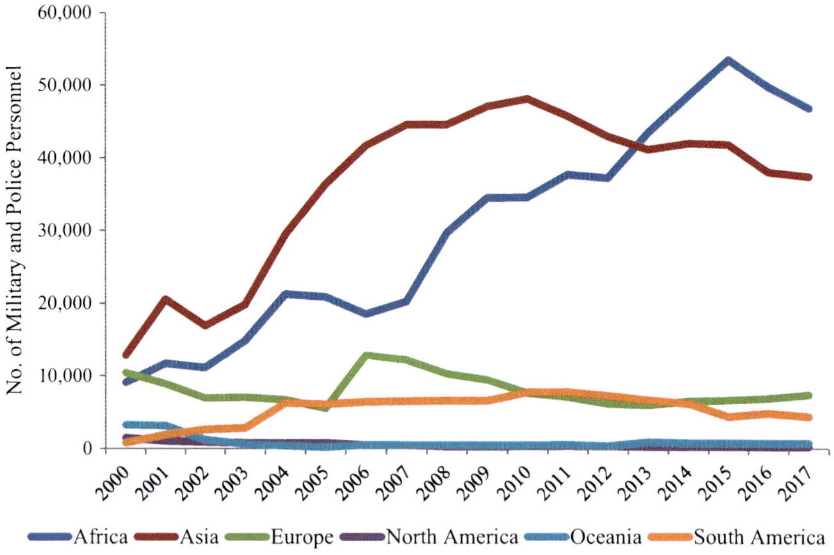

Fig. 24.2 Uniformed contributions to UN peacekeeping by continent, 2000–2017. *Source*: International Peace Institute Peacekeeping Database, Region-Level Data, http://www.providingforpeacekeeping.org/contributions (accessed 5 August 2017). *Note*: Based on year-end 2000–2016 and end-April 2017 data

new Asian and African peacekeepers, was seeking to break into the ranks of the UN top ten by 2019.[4] Even so, the South Asian trio of India, Pakistan, and Bangladesh remain major contributors to UN missions, close behind only Ethiopia in the rankings in June 2017, with a total of 21,812 blue helmets deployed between them (see Tables 24.1 and 24.2).

This chapter seeks to take a close look at the three South Asian "providers of peacekeepers"[5] in Africa, beginning with an overview of their peacekeeping

Table 24.1 Top ten military and police contributors to UN peacekeeping, June 2017

	Country	*Contingent troops*	*Experts on mission*	*Police*	*Staff officers*	*Total*	*Share of UN total (%)*
1.	Ethiopia	7,936	100	67	118	8,221	8
2.	India	6,755	67	760	94	7,676	8
3.	Pakistan	6,703	74	280	66	7,123	7
4.	Bangladesh	5,730	53	1,122	108	7,013	7
5.	Rwanda	5,048	32	1,049	74	6,203	6
6.	Nepal	4,336	55	708	103	5,202	5
7.	Egypt	2,043	74	879	64	3,060	3
8.	Burkina Faso	2,495	15	390	33	2,933	3
9.	Senegal	1,459	5	1,318	38	2,820	3
10.	Ghana	2,229	56	394	73	2,752	3
	Sub-total					53,003	55
	UN total					96,853	

Source: UN Peacekeeping, "Summary of Contributions to UN Peacekeeping by Country and Post", 30 June 2017, http://www.un.org/en/peacekeeping/contributors/2017/jun17_4.pdf (accessed 5 August 2017).

Table 24.2 Top ten Asian and African contributors to UN peacekeeping, June 2017

	Asia			*Africa*	
	Country	*Total*		*Country*	*Total*
1.	India	7,676	1.	Ethiopia	8,221
2.	Pakistan	7,123	2.	Rwanda	6,203
3.	Bangladesh	7,013	3.	Egypt	3,060
4.	Nepal	5,202	4.	Burkina Faso	2,933
5.	Indonesia	2,715	5.	Senegal	2,820
6.	China	2,515	6.	Ghana	2,752
7.	Jordan	1,012	7.	Tanzania	2,283
8.	Mongolia	947	8.	Nigeria	1,667
9.	Malaysia	876	9.	Morocco	1,607
10.	Cambodia	823	10.	South Africa	1,428
	Sub-total	35,902		**Sub-total**	32,974
	UN total	96,853		**UN total**	96,853
	Share of UN total	37%		**Share of UN total**	34%

Source: UN Peacekeeping, "Summary of Troop Contributing Countries by Ranking", 30 June 2017, http://www.un.org/en/peacekeeping/contributors/2017/jun17_2.pdf (accessed 1 August 2017).

footprint on the ground and situating the heavy focus on the continent in their contemporary UN deployment profiles. It then assesses the motivational sources of this peacekeeping activism, suggesting that they are located, not in Africa itself, but in their own particular national contexts, with the limited exception of India—the rising Asian economic power has a longer history of peacekeeping originally grounded, at least partly, in a spirit of Third World solidarity that has in the present day blended with a strategic interest in African affairs.[6] Finally, the chapter assesses the contribution of South Asian UN peacekeeping in Africa, as well as its accompanying challenges.

South Asia's Peacekeeping Footprint: Facts and "Boots on the Ground"

As C. Raja Mohan and Varun Vira, among others, have pointed out, the professional ability and capacity of South Asia's armed forces—particularly India and Pakistan—to participate in peacekeeping operations from the outset of independence is a colonial inheritance.[7] The institutional history of the modern Indian army dates back to the seventeenth and eighteenth centuries, when the British East India Company initially raised local troops at need, which were subsequently organised into regular units. It is worth noting that the first major Indian rebellion against colonial rule was sparked, in 1857, by an act of mutiny by Indian soldiers serving in the British East India Company's Bengal Army, and that the uprising was suppressed only with the support of other Indian troops. In fact, under British crown rule, Indian forces were used to maintain "peace and stability" in various parts of the Raj, including modern-day Afghanistan, Burma, and Tibet, and participated in expeditions as far afield as Egypt and the Sudan. Furthermore, Indian soldiers served in all the major theatres of both world wars, from the trenches on the Western Front during World War I to the battlefields of North Africa and Southeast Asia during World War II. By 1945, the pre-partition Indian army had grown from just under 194,400 men in 1939 to 2.5 million, becoming "the largest all-volunteer force the world had ever seen".[8] It is thus not altogether surprising that modern-day India and Pakistan—both heirs of the Raj, born of a brutal partition in 1947—had the capacity to deploy trained and equipped soldiers to overseas missions early on,[9] though Bangladesh, after its separation from Pakistan in 1971, had to build its military apparatus "virtually from … scratch" and made a different journey to peacekeeping.[10] Taken together, the armies of India, Pakistan, and Bangladesh currently have a combined strength of 2.1 million[11]—a veritable "military reservoir"[12] that in 2016 contributed over one-fifth of all UN peacekeepers.[13]

Of the South Asian trio, India was first out of the blocks, providing a 6,130-strong custodian force to facilitate the return of prisoners of war in Korea in 1953–1954.[14] Since then, over a span of six decades, about 180,000 Indian uniformed personnel have served in 44 missions on four continents under the UN flag.[15] Particularly in Africa, India has one of the longest, as well as one of the more consistent, records of providing blue helmets for peacekeeping operations. Prior to 1989, the continent hosted but two such missions: the United Nations Emergency Force (UNEF) in Egypt—the first ever armed UN peacekeeping mission; and the UN Operation in the Congo (ONUC)—the world organisation's largest, most complex, and most challenging deployment during the Cold War (see Jonah in this volume). India made major contributions to both, providing 13,185 personnel to UNEF I over a period of 11 years from 1956 to 1967; and 12,222 men to ONUC over four years from 1960 to 1964.[16] Remarkably, as Kabilan Krishnasamy also points out, New Delhi sustained its commitment to both missions, while battling China in 1962; and in the case of UNEF I, through war with Pakistan in 1965.[17]

In fact, India provided one of the largest national contingents to ONUC, and—in contrast to its present-day reluctance to support "muscular" peace enforcement operations—argued in favour of a greater remit to use force for the maintenance of law and order on the ground, sending a significant number of combat troops when the mission's mandate was strengthened by the UN Security Council.[18] Following on, the Indian contingent played a major role in preventing the secession of Katanga when the UN effectively went to war in the Congo in late 1961, with Captain Gurbachan Singh Salaria posthumously awarded the country's highest military award for courage under fire (the *Param Vir Chakra*)—the first and to date only Indian soldier to earn the award while serving as a blue helmet. Over the four years, 147 Indians—including 39 peacekeepers—lost their lives in the Congo, staying the course even as other countries (including Egypt, Guinea, and Morocco) withdrew and domestic opposition to the deployment grew.[19] After ONUC, UN and Indian peacekeepers returned to African soil only in 1989, with New Delhi providing uniformed personnel subsequently to most missions on the continent, starting with the UN Transition Assistance Group (UNTAG) in Namibia and the UN Angola Verification Mission (UNAVEM).[20]

ONUC also marked the beginning of Pakistan's peacekeeping career, both globally and in Africa, with Islamabad making a smaller contribution of about 800 personnel to the UN operation.[21] Akin to it, New Delhi's arch rival on the Indian sub-continent can claim nearly 60 years of international peacekeeping experience. However, during the Cold War, Pakistan's actual involvement in blue helmet operations was more modest: New Delhi participated in 11 UN missions, while Islamabad contributed to four.[22] This disparity owes, in large part, to differences in the overall orientation of the two neighbours' foreign policies in a bipolar world. While India mainly anchored its external engagements around Third World solidarity through a policy of non-alignment, Pakistan focused on building alliances with the major powers, particularly the US.[23] The take-away point is that UN peacekeeping became a priority for Islamabad only once the Cold War ended by 1990.[24] However, it has since emerged as one of the most reliable and consistent troop-contributing countries,[25] continually vying with India and Bangladesh—as well as Ethiopia since 2015—for the lead in UN rankings. Since 1960, more than 142,500 Pakistani troops have served in 41 UN missions, with some of the largest contingents deployed to operations in Africa, including Somalia, Liberia, Sierra Leone, and the Democratic Republic of the Congo (DRC).[26]

The emergence of Bangladesh—famously described, in 1971, by former US secretary of state Henry Kissinger as a "basket case"—as a top troop-contributing country to UN peacekeeping operations, is a yet more contemporary, and dramatic, phenomenon. The youngest of the South Asian trio, Bangladesh (formerly East Pakistan) came into existence only in 1971, after a bloody civil war that generated an influx of ten million refugees into neighbouring India, necessitating an armed "humanitarian intervention" by New Delhi that served as a midwife for its birth into nationhood. Seventeen years after its violent separation from Pakistan, Bangladesh deployed blue helmets for the first time only in 1988, as part of the UN Iran-Iraq Military Observer Group (UNIIMOG). The first deployments to Africa occurred in 1989, with the despatch of 59 military and police observers to UNTAG in Namibia.[27] In the space of less than three decades, more than 128,500 Bangladeshi troops have served in 54 missions in 40 countries.[28] In June 2017, there were 7,013 Bangladeshi peacekeepers participating in ten UN missions (of 16), with the largest contingents deployed in the DRC, Mali, and the Central African Republic (CAR) (see Table 24.3).

Table 24.3 Indian, Pakistani, and Bangladeshi contributions of uniformed personnel to UN peacekeeping in Africa, June 2017

Mission	*Mission total*	*India*	*Pakistan*	*Bangladesh*	*Trio total*	*Trio share of mission total (%)*
MONUSCO	18,571	3,697	3,486	1,907	9,090	49
UNAMID	16,673	0	2,272	686	2,958	18
UNMISS	13,424	2,413	7	846	3,266	24
MINUSMA	12,815	0	0	1,818	1,818	14
MINUSCA	12,349	0	1,136	1,019	2,155	17
UNISFA	4,536	5	0	0	5	0
UNMIL	742	1	73	2	76	10
MINURSO	228	3	14	27	44	19
Sub-total	79,338	6,119	6,988	6,305	19,412	24
UN total	96,853	7,676	7,123	7,013	21,812	23
Share of UN total	82%	80%	98%	90%	89%	

Source: UN Peacekeeping, Troop and Police Contributors, http://www.un.org/en/peacekeeping/resources/statistics/contributors.shtml (accessed 1 August 2017).

Notes: MONUSCO: UN Organisation Stabilisation Mission in the Democratic Republic of the Congo; UNAMID: AU-UN Hybrid Operation in Darfur; UNMISS: UN Mission in South Sudan; MINUSMA: UN Multi-Dimensional Integrated Stabilisation Mission in Mali; MINUSCA: UN Multi-Dimensional Integrated Stabilisation Mission in the Central African Republic; UNISFA: UN Interim Security Force for Abyei; UNMIL: UN Mission in Liberia; MINURSO: UN Mission for the Referendum in Western Sahara.

The UN Operation in Côte d'Ivoire (UNOCI) ended in June 2017, with military personnel having been withdrawn by April 2017.

Indeed, since the end of the Cold War in 1990, the vast majority of peacekeepers from the South Asian "big three" have been deployed in Africa, reflecting a broader shift in the geography of peacekeeping—the continent hosted over 80 per cent of the UN's deployments worldwide in 2016 (see also Ugarte in this volume).[29] In a small number of instances, the individual South Asian contribution has been token; for example, there were only five Indian uniformed personnel serving as part of the 4,536-strong UN Interim Security Force for Abyei (UNISFA) in June 2017 (see Table 24.3). However, overall, the size of South Asian deployments in some of the most complex missions in Africa has been far from insubstantial. For example, Pakistani troops—about 8,400 over three years—were the first to arrive as part of the UN Operation in Somalia (UNOSOM) in 1992 and the last to leave in 1995, covering the withdrawal of the rest of the national contingents, with 42 fatalities.[30] Notably, the three largest contingents in the UN Organisation Stabilisation Mission in the DRC (MONUSCO) are from the three South Asian countries, and together constituted nearly half of its force strength of 18,571 in June 2017 (see Table 24.3).

Motives for Blue Helmet Peacekeeping in Africa

The capacity to provide peacekeepers is but one element of the story of South Asian blue helmets on the continent. The greater puzzle is two-fold. First, why have the independent Indian sub-continent's governments been willing time and again to deploy their uniformed personnel far away from home in unfamiliar, and often hostile, environments in the post–Cold War period? Second, what accounts for the large number of South Asian "boots on the ground" under the UN flag in Africa, in particular? A common mono-causal explanation of why the trio of India, Pakistan, and Bangladesh have been such determined troop-contributing countries is problematic, because it cannot account for the variation in their peacekeeping profiles, nor capture the complexity of motivations that lie behind their individual dispositions to participate in UN missions.[31] To say, for example, that it is in their self-interest only begs a deeper exploration of the nature of their interest in peacekeeping in Africa. This intuitively would differ for a rising power such as India with a sense of "manifest destiny" on the world stage and for a smaller country such as next-door Bangladesh dwarfed by its far larger sub-continental neighbour in terms of nearly all power-political indicators. Despite their shared colonial past and geographic proximity to each other, the South Asian trio are very different states that have traversed distinct trajectories.

In a snapshot, India is a reasonably stable democracy with a rare coup-free history among developing countries, but Bangladesh's political development has been characterised by troubled civil-military relations, while Pakistan's internal dysfunction over the past decades has pushed it close to the brink of state failure. The differences in their material capabilities are no less significant.

India's economy ranked seventh in the world with a gross domestic product (GDP) of $2.3 trillion in 2016; Pakistan and Bangladesh placed 40th and 44th respectively.[32] Similarly, India's armed forces—about 1.3 million strong—dwarf those of Bangladesh, which number about 157,000.[33] Their national demands, expectations, and aspirations are not identical, and it would be oversimple to assume a constancy or consistency in their motives for peacekeeping across the three countries.

Furthermore, India has sustained a relatively consistent pattern of UN deployments since the 1950s, even as the country's external and internal circumstances, as well as the nature of peacekeeping, have evolved. With the notable exception of the Congo, UN missions during the Cold War were by and large based on the principles of host-state consent, neutrality, and non-use of force except in self-defence, and composed of either unarmed military observers or lightly armed troops who monitored an agreed peace. Since then, peacekeeping has grown in ambition and complexity, evolving into a far wider range of activities, with a number of UN missions more willing and able to use force and characterised by shades of peace enforcement[34]—the extent of change from tradition highlighted by the creation, in 2013, of a Force Intervention Brigade, under the aegis of MONUSCO, with the authority to carry out offensive operations against armed rebel groups in the DRC. Notwithstanding its oft-stated qualms about the use of force in peacekeeping theatres, India has participated "from Congo to Congo" in Africa.[35] Though "newer" contributors, Pakistan and Bangladesh have similarly increased their commitments in response to the growing and changing demands for UN peacekeepers over the past two decades. Against this backdrop, assuming a single set of reasons for the South Asian trio's, especially India's, present-day peacekeeping activism is counter-intuitive.

That said, there are a clutch of overarching reasons why the three South Asian neighbours have provided peacekeepers in such numbers for missions in Africa.[36] Broadly, they relate to an idealistic belief in, or principled commitment to, the purposes of the UN and of peacekeeping; a quest for influence and prestige; a desire for the financial and institutional benefits that accrue from UN deployments for their own national militaries; and, at least in the case of India, an interest in the prospects of Africa, as well as its own interests on the continent. The nature and relative salience of each factor are different in the case of each individual country. For Bangladesh, the financial rewards for its military—at the level of both the institution as well as individual soldiers—and the improved prospects for its own democracy that flow from the armed forces' participation in UN peacekeeping operations, are particularly significant factors. In the case of Pakistan, where the military is dominant, its quest for a positive self-image, as well as greater influence within the UN system, stand out from the rest as sources of motivation. India's "peacekeeping habit",[37] though more strongly rooted in a history of belief in the values and purposes of the UN's mission and Afro-Asian solidarity, has become increasingly shaped by its own self-interest, in particular the opportunity to wield greater influence on the world stage by occupying a permanent seat on the UN Security Council. Be this as it may, the key point is that very little of their reasoning, with the limited exception of India, is actually about Africa itself, even though this is where the majority of Indian, Bangladeshi, and Pakistani blue helmets are deployed. Though varied, their individual motivations are a function of their own national priorities and firmly rooted in their own national contexts. The place of Africa is, in other words, somewhat incidental in their peacekeeping portfolios.[38]

Idealism

For all three South Asian peacekeeping countries, their troop and police contributions can, to some extent, be interpreted as a concrete expression of their principled commitment to the promotion of international peace and security through the UN as the "primary peacekeeper": the constitutions of India, Pakistan, and Bangladesh specifically exhort the state to work towards this end. Pakistan's constitution, for example, encourages the government to "support the common interests of the peoples of Asia, Africa and Latin America, [and] promote international peace and security",[39] while Bangladesh's directs it to base its international relations on UN Charter principles and to "support oppressed peoples throughout the world waging a just struggle against imperialism, colonialism or racialism".[40] Not surprisingly, idealism as a rationale for their commitment to peacekeeping—globally and in Africa—is commonplace today in all three capitals. However, constitutional directives are not legally binding, but rather guidelines that leave plenty of room for the state, if it so chooses, to decide how to pursue the objective of international peace. Providing peacekeepers does not automatically follow, nor does contributing troops to hazardous missions in faraway Africa—participation in UN missions did not, for example, become a distinct feature of Pakistan's foreign policy for quite some time after independence.

The case of India is slightly different. The country's early and active participation in peacekeeping was driven by its first prime minister, Jawaharlal Nehru, and his liberal internationalist worldview and championing of the UN as a vehicle for peace, which has left an enduring impression on Indian foreign policy.[41] So much so that a small measure of criticism has emerged of New Delhi as "an absent-minded peacekeeper—deploying troops because it could and not because it needed to", following the UN flag wherever it went.[42] With respect to peacekeeping in Africa—India's deployments to UNEF and ONUC took place on his watch—Nehru's vision, shared by an influential decision-making elite including V.K. Krishna Menon, India's permanent representative to the UN from 1952 to 1962, was reinforced by a genuine commitment to Afro-Asian solidarity. For instance, India's purposeful contribution to the difficult UN Operation in the Congo was heavily premised on the idea of providing help to a fellow Third World country in a painful struggle towards stable statehood, with New Delhi having been vocal in its criticism of Belgian policy for leaving that country ill-prepared for independence.[43] Indeed, as Frank van Rooyen observes: "Some analysts believe that India continues to regard most of the recent African wars as attributable to the ongoing and destructive legacy of the colonial past."[44]

However, even during the Cold War era of Nehruvian foreign policy, India's commitment to the UN, which—in W. Pal Sidhu's words—it "has been trying to kick out of Kashmir" for years, has never been exclusively ideational[45]—the United Nations Military Observer Group in India and Pakistan (UNMOGIP), deployed since 1949, is one of the world organisation's oldest missions, much to India's annoyance.[46] It is what Krishnasamy has called the "paradox of India's peacekeeping" that New Delhi's penchant for peacekeeping in the "far abroad" is accompanied by an unequivocal rejection of UN involvement in its own backyard, "even if that presence involves a mere observer mission".[47] Furthermore, in the post–Cold War period, there has been a gradual de-emphasis on principles in the actual conduct of India's foreign relations, notwithstanding rhetoric, and a more realist-inspired outlook on South-South solidarity, which has trickled into its peacekeeping commitments in Africa. In contrast to the Congo in the 1960s, for example, India precipitously withdrew its 3,000-odd troops from the UN Mission in Sierra Leone (UNAMSIL) in 2000 for political and operational reasons, despite requests—including reportedly from then secretary-general of the Organisation of African Unity (OAU), Salim Ahmed Salim—to rethink its decision, placing a small question mark against the extent of its professed commitment to the continent.[48] (UNAMSIL faced several difficulties including attacks and hostage-taking by Sierra Leone rebels, some ill-equipped troop contingents, and internal problems within the mission's leadership under its Indian force commander, Vijay Jetley.)

It would be going too far to suggest that some measure of genuine principled vocation does not underlie the willingness of South Asian troops, and South Asian governments to commit them, to risk their lives to "save strangers"[49] in Africa. In the post–Cold War period, Somalia stands out in this respect. Also, as Ruchita Beri noted (writing in 2008), Sierra Leone "was the only UN peacekeeping operation where the Indian troops withdrew before the end of the mandate".[50] For the most part, all three—India, Pakistan, and Bangladesh—have demonstrated their staying power in the most complex missions on the continent, emulating and competing with each other to be "firsts among equals", and they continue to take enormous pride in their respective traditions of UN peacekeeping, which have become deeply ingrained and taken-for-granted in the political cultures of all three countries. Tellingly, in none of the three countries have peace operations under the UN flag—bar Somalia in the case of Pakistan, and Sierra Leone in the case of India—come under serious, leave aside critical, public scrutiny, and the blue helmet is a mark of respect. The point is that a principled commitment—more so to the UN than to Africa per se—is far from the whole story.

Image and Influence

As Rashed Zaman and Niloy Biswas write about Bangladesh: "Over the past two decades, a country usually associated with floods, natural disasters, and poverty, has been able to project a positive international image through its participation in United Nations ... peacekeeping operations."[51] This has, in fact, become an essential part of the country's international identity, as reflected in the utterances of its political leaders and military officials.[52] To quote Bangladeshi prime minister Sheikh Hasina: "Our participation in peacekeeping operations and in other multinational assignments has enhanced the image of Bangladesh in the world forum. Our active participation in peacekeeping missions in one way has upheld our commitment to peace and on the other way has strengthened our diplomatic ties with economically developed and militarily powerful nations."[53]

Similarly, as Inam-ur-Rahman Malik argues, UN peacekeeping contributions have provided an opportunity for Pakistan to project an image of itself as a "good international citizen" on the world stage.[54] It was, perhaps, not entirely accidental that Islamabad's commitment to peacekeeping began rising in the early to middle 1990s, after the lacklustre years of the Cold War, at a time when it was under military and economic sanctions.[55] Later on, Pakistan's peacekeeping profile was actively used by the military regime of President Pervez Musharraf, as it sought to gain legitimacy—both at home and abroad—and to rehabilitate the country in the international community following its nuclear tests of May 1998. According to Malik, a positive image, particularly with respect to peacekeeping, has also allowed Islamabad to "raise what it considers the unresolved issue of Kashmir, consistently and more effectively at the UN Security Council".[56] This strategy is based on the premise that a stronger and more positive presence within the UN might enable the country to garner greater support for its own causes, among which the Kashmir dispute unquestionably ranks first, and also reduce any leverage that India might gain from its own peacekeeping credentials at the world organisation,[57] where African countries constitute a majority. However, since the matter—dormant for the moment—rests primarily with the Security Council, it might be a stretch to see the "Kashmir factor" as a critical rationale for Pakistan's blue helmet engagements in Africa. Be this as it may, it only underscores how Africa itself is somewhat ancillary to Islamabad's peacekeeping agenda.

A quest for influence has similarly become a critical determinant of India's international engagements at large, but particularly its peacekeeping commitments in Africa, albeit with a view towards a different goal. Its past and present record of participation in blue helmet operations forms a major plank in the country's bid for a permanent seat on a reformed UN Security Council, based on the idea that "a country that has ambitions for great power status and aspires to a permanent seat in the UN Security Council ... cannot forego its associated responsibilities".[58] In order to achieve the goal, India needs broad support—including from African countries—for its candidature. Professing solidarity with Africa through peacekeeping is a key element of New Delhi's effort to "win friends and influence people" on the continent. For example, in the months before India eventually pulled out its troops from UNAMSIL, Indian policymakers—including then-foreign minister Jaswant Singh, while on a trip to Africa—repeatedly and publicly cited two reasons for staying the course in Sierra Leone, even as the UN mission crumbled: commitment to the UN and solidarity with Africa.[59] In this respect, New Delhi's principled commitment to Afro-Asian solidarity has, since its origins in the 1940s, become increasingly infused with a stronger element of self-interest.

Interests

It is hard to discern what specific interests, if any, Bangladesh has had for deploying its peacekeepers in large numbers to Africa, as distant and unfamiliar as the continent is. Not one African country counts among its major trade partners, although Dhaka has recently joined the exodus to the continent described by many as "the next growth frontier",[60] leasing or buying land for agricultural production in countries such as Uganda.[61] It is worth bearing in mind that Bangladesh is one of the world's most densely populated and poorest countries, with a population of 156 million crammed into an area far smaller than Ghana (which has a population of 27 million). However, these relatively small-scale activities have occurred only recently, and cannot be seen as a significant source of motivation for Dhaka's substantive participation in UN peacekeeping operations in Africa over the course of two decades. The case of Pakistan is more or less similar. Trade between Pakistan and Africa was less than $4 billion in 2015.[62] Though there is a growing Pakistani diaspora on the continent, there is little to suggest that this has increased Africa's importance on Islamabad's strategic radar. To borrow from van Rooyen, if Pakistan has significant strategic interests in Africa that have especially predisposed it to provide blue helmets for missions in countries such as Somalia, Liberia, Sierra Leone, and the DRC, they are rather cryptic.[63]

India presents a slightly different story.[64] The nature of its engagement with Africa has changed over the past two decades. A fast-rising economy with the world's second largest population (1.3 billion), India is a resource and economic opportunity-hungry giant, whereas Africa is a resource-rich region—home to about 10 per cent of the world's oil reserves, 40 per cent of its gold, and 80–90 per cent of chromium and platinum-group metals, as well as significant deposits of cobalt and uranium, among other substances. Trade between India and Africa is still modest but growing, having jumped from $9.6 billion in 2004–2005 to $71.5 billion in 2014–2015.[65] Meanwhile, investments in Africa by private Indian companies, such as the Tata Group, Vedanta Resources, and Bharti Airtel, now run into the billions. Side-by-side, there is a growing Indian diaspora on the continent, as recently brought to light by the evacuation of about 15,000 Indians from Libya in 2011. Furthermore, the Indian Ocean region is seen by New Delhi as part of India's proximate, strategic neighbourhood, and the growing menaces of piracy and terrorism in the Horn of Africa are additional factors for the continent's increased importance for India.[66]

In this respect, India has a broad-based interest in promoting sustainable peace and stability on the continent through its participation in peacekeeping. It also has a growing economic stake in a number of African countries that currently host UN peace operations, notably the DRC and South Sudan.[67] For example, the state-owned Oil and Natural Gas Corporation (ONGC) Videsh—one of the country's biggest overseas exploring companies—has a 25 per cent share in the Greater Nile Oil production and pipeline project straddling Sudan and South Sudan. India was one of the first countries to recognise South Sudan's independence in 2011, having earlier established a diplomatic presence in Juba in 2007. Prior to the outbreak of the current civil war in December 2013 in South Sudan, India had offered concessional lines of credit for development projects in that country, and was exploring the potential for engagement in its health and agriculture sectors. As of June 2017, there were 2,413 Indian uniformed personnel attached to the UN Mission in South Sudan (UNMISS) (see Table 24.3). (On Sudan and South Sudan, see Deng in this volume.) Similarly, India's economic interests in the DRC—a rich source of copper, tin, coltan, uranium, as well as industrial diamonds—where Indian peacekeepers have been deployed since 2003, have expanded rapidly, with New Delhi financing a number of power, water, transportation, and education projects in the country.[68] However, it remains far from clear whether the benefits to India have accrued from its diplomatic and economic support to these countries, or whether its peacekeepers have helped open the doors for business. Also, this hints at a concerted effort at linking "the objective of participating in peace operations with New Delhi's strategic interests"[69] that would be at some odds with a more commonplace assessment of the country as having lacked an all joined-up foreign policy.

Institution-Building

An important source of motivation for Bangladesh's troop contributions to UN missions lies in the consolidation of democracy at home. Zaman and Biswas note that participation in peacekeeping has provided an outward-facing role for Bangladesh's armed forces, where the assertion of civilian control over the military has been a challenge since independence.[70] The crucible of civil war that gave birth to the nation also helped forge a heavily politicised army, characterised by factionalism, that struggled to withdraw from politics. Independence was followed by a volatile period, characterised by coups and military rule interspersed by only brief periods of civilian government, until 1990–1991. Since the restoration of democracy, an uneasy civil-military truce has existed based on the idea that "participation in UN peacekeeping will reduce the desire of the Bangladesh armed forces to take over state power", albeit a fragile one.[71] The army, for example, "indirectly intervened" in the country's 2007 political crisis, though it subsequently also helped in the holding of parliamentary elections, thus playing an ambiguous and "deeply divisive" role.[72] Furthermore, UN deployments are seen not only to have had a relatively positive impact on Bangladesh's civil-military relations, but also to have aided the professionalisation and modernisation of the military to keep up with the requirements of peacekeeping, particularly after its experience in Rwanda, where the Bangladeshi contingent deployed to the UN Assistance Mission for Rwanda (UNAMIR) came under criticism for being ill-equipped and poorly prepared for the mission.[73]

For Bangladesh—a country with limited economic resources—participation in peacekeeping operations also helps to subsidise its armed forces. Between 2001 and 2010, Dhaka received nearly $1.3 billion in reimbursements from the UN for its troop contributions.[74] At the individual level, the financial benefits and opportunity for professional development offered by peacekeeping have been no less significant for sustaining Bangladeshi soldiers' interest in participation in UN missions.[75] The opportunities that UN missions provide for operational experience, which is critical for professional advancement, is an additional inducement. Indeed, the extra income, international exposure, as well as the opportunity for training and experience are not insignificant motives for UN peacekeeping across the three South Asian countries' armed forces; and not surprisingly, competition for deployment overseas as a blue helmet is believed to be intense within their respective armies.

In the case of Pakistan, given its internal makeup, the institutional benefits that the military itself derives—not unlike Bangladesh, but for different reasons—are an important part of the explanation for its UN deployments.[76] The military is one of the principal institutions in Pakistan, with more autonomy than any other state apparatus. Well-organised and well-resourced, the Pakistani armed forces are not just any other military; rather, the military is a bona fide policymaker that helps set the national security agenda, and as Malik argues, its participation in UN peacekeeping is not "a compulsion dictated by the political leadership. To the contrary, it is in the institutional interest of the military to support and contribute to UN peacekeeping efforts".[77] This interest is multifaceted. Over the years, the Pakistani military has come to see itself as an active contributor to socio-economic development at home, taking on the tasks of building infrastructure and providing active disaster management in a country vulnerable to natural disasters. Following on, it has tended to see participation in UN peacekeeping, which increasingly incorporates humanitarian, state-building, and peacebuilding activities, as an opportunity to gain, as well as share, experience. Also, exposure and access to modern warfare technology, practices, and processes—particularly through contact with European and Western militaries—on international deployments, are seen as essential to strengthening the Pakistani military as an institution.

However, unlike the case of Bangladesh, the extent to which participation in peacekeeping actually helps to subsidise the large armies of Pakistan and India is questionable. In 2017–2018, India's core defence budget (excluding expenditures such as military pensions) amounted to $40.6 billion, while Pakistan's defence spending was estimated to be $8.7 billion.[78] Against this, the compensation that Pakistan is estimated to earn from its participation in UN peacekeeping operations stands at about $220 million per year.[79] (Given their comparable troop contributions, the amount for India is unlikely to be dissimilar.) Although this is not insignificant, it is but "a few drops in the ocean"; to put it in comparative context, Pakistan received migrant remittances of $20.1 billion in 2014, while India received $72.2 billion in the same year.[80] Quite the country, both countries have in the recent past made the argument that they, in fact, subsidise UN peacekeeping, given the fact that there are, in practice, significant delays in receiving reimbursements from the world organisation and that compensation rates have more or less remained frozen for well over a decade, failing to keep up with the costs of living in both countries, while their own remunerations to their soldiers have increased.[81]

Achievements and Challenges: South Asia's Blue Helmets in Africa

Notwithstanding the predominance of rationales unrelated to the continent in particular, South Asia's contributions to peacekeeping in Africa have been significant and, on the whole, positive, and in which Indians, Pakistanis, as well as Bangladeshis can rightfully take a strong measure of pride. Their blue helmets have served—for the most part with distinction—in high-risk operations, "from Congo to Congo", and shown themselves to be reliable peacekeepers with "staying power" when others have withdrawn in the face of deteriorating security conditions, most notably in Somalia.[82] The case of India in Sierra Leone is an exception—though arguably one that proves the rule. That said, South Asia's peacekeeping record in Africa has not been wholly untarnished and deserves a closer, more critical scrutiny.

First, South Asia's blue helmets—particularly from Bangladesh—have on occasion come under criticism for being a case of "quantity over quality". The level of preparedness of Bangladeshi troops, in terms of training as well as equipment, was a particular concern during the 1990s.[83] For example, as mentioned earlier, Dhaka was one of the main contributors to the UN Assistance Mission in Rwanda, itself an under-resourced and poorly mandated mission. The Bangladeshi contingent, though, was particularly ill-equipped and ill-prepared for the daunting situation that it faced on the ground. UNAMIR's Canadian force commander, Roméo Dallaire, was particularly critical of these troops, and "issued letters to senior Bangladeshi army officers and UN headquarters concerning the consistent disregard of the Bangladeshi contingent to his order on protecting civilians in Rwanda", which had an adverse impact on the mission.[84] However, to be fair, such concerns have not been unique to the South Asian contingents (see also Gambari, and Adebajo in this volume). In

Sierra Leone, for example, notwithstanding the serious tensions that rose between Nigeria and India in UNAMSIL, a number of contingents lacked key basic equipment, with Indian troops reporting having to loan vehicles, as well as communication equipment, to these contingents, including those from Nigeria and Ghana.[85]

Furthermore, South Asian governments have been responsive to the lessons of peacekeeping generally, and from Africa in particular. Bangladesh, for example, in answer to the criticism that it endured through the 1990s for its failure to perform to standards, has since made significant investments in training its blue helmets, which has helped to increase the skills and professionalism of its troops. This has included the establishment of the Bangladesh Institute of Peace Support Operations Training (BIPSOT, set up as the Peacekeeping Operation Training Centre in 1999 but renamed in 2002), as well as increases in budgetary allocations for UN operations to enable Bangladesh to meet mission requirements, although equipment problems have persisted.[86] India, similarly, hosts a Centre for United Nations Peacekeeping (CUNPK), which has since 2005 hosted the Secretariat for the International Association of Peacekeeping Training Centres (IAPTC), while Pakistan's Centre for International Peace and Stability, inaugurated in 2013, has a dedicated Department of UN Peacekeeping Training. More African peacekeepers could train at these centres—both BIPSOT and CUNPK offer training for participants from abroad[87]—and best practices could be shared more effectively among South Asian and African peacekeeping personnel.

In response to demand, the South Asian countries have also increased their contributions of police personnel for UN missions, with India deploying the first all-female police contingent to Liberia in 2007, shortly followed by Bangladesh in Haiti in 2010. (Increasing the number of female police personnel remains a priority for the UN.) (See also Porter in this volume.) Both Bangladesh and India remained among the top contributors of police personnel to UN peacekeeping operations in June 2017 (see Fig. 24.3), though Pakistan had dropped in the ranks, its contributions having declined to 280 personnel from having been as high as 949 in December 2010.[88]

It is worth noting, too, that India and Pakistan have since their experiences in Somalia focused on securing local support in their areas of peacekeeping deployment. In the case of Islamabad, this "has become the cardinal building-block for Pakistan's military contingents in all post-Somalia peacekeeping deployments",[89] the majority of which (at the risk of repetition) are in Africa. Although not unique to them, humanitarian activities and civil projects to "win hearts and minds"—under the banner of civil-military cooperation (CIMIC)—have been an integral component of India's and Pakistan's participation in UN peacekeeping operations. For example, in Liberia and Sierra Leone, making road improvements and providing medicine and food, including from their own rations, have been seen as key to the success that the Pakistanis enjoyed in

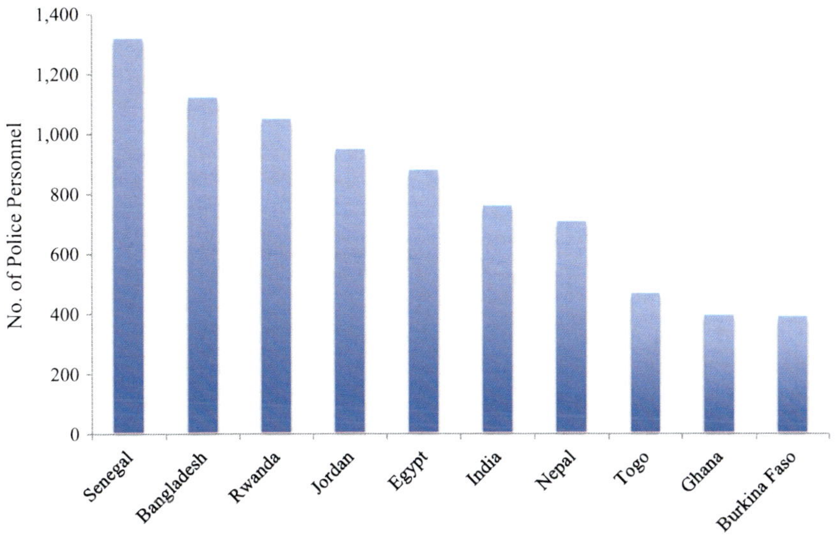

Fig. 24.3 Top ten police contributors to UN peacekeeping, June 2017. *Source*: UN Peacekeeping, "Summary of Contributions to UN Peacekeeping by Country and Post", 30 June 2017, http://www.un.org/en/peacekeeping/contributors/2017/jun17_4.pdf (accessed 5 August 2017)

peacekeeping missions in both African countries.[90] (On peacebuilding in Sierra Leone, see also Omeje, and Rashid in this volume.) India's deployment in Ethiopia-Eritrea included the undertaking of Operation Maitri (Friendship) to build relations with the local community, which involved digging water channels and wells; constructing veterinary camps; providing free medicines and medical treatment; repairing roads; and providing vocational training to locals.[91] Similar quick-impact projects have also been implemented by other African and Asian peacekeepers (for example, Rwanda and Thailand) in Sudan's Darfur region, in some cases using their own resources, in areas such as water and irrigation, and in so doing have helped to improve local livelihoods and address sources of conflict.[92]

However, relations between peacekeepers and local communities can be a challenge, as made clear in the case of the DRC, where South Asian troops struggled to interact with the people they were mandated to protect due, among other factors, to language and cultural barriers, resource constraints, and guidance on community engagement (though efforts have since been made to address some of these issues).[93] This was highlighted by the horrific case of the Kibua mass rapes in 2010. Over a period of four days, at least 387 civilians, including 300 women and 55 girls, were sexually assaulted; 923 houses looted; and 116 people abducted by a coalition of armed rebels in 13 villages in North Kivu,[94] with one of the villages about 30 kilometres from a MONUSCO base where Indian soldiers were deployed.[95] Among the conclusions reached by a subsequent UN fact-finding mission to the area was that limited interaction between local villagers and peacekeepers on patrols had "reduced the possibility of collecting timely information about their [villagers'] protection needs, as well as on the abuses by armed groups". However, the report also concluded that the Kibua peacekeepers' capacity was limited by a number of operational constraints, including "lack of military logistics, the inaccessibility of the telephone network, the poor road conditions, the insecurity in the region, long distances between villages and the remoteness of the area".[96] In this respect, the report also points to a larger difficulty with assessing the record of South Asian peacekeepers on deployments in Africa: the missions themselves are at times under-resourced and poorly mandated, and operate under constraints that amplify, if nothing else, the challenges faced by troops from distant places such as India, Pakistan, and Bangladesh. The 18,500-odd peacekeepers in MONUSCO, for example, are expected to cover an area roughly the size of Western Europe, with porous borders with nine countries.[97]

Second, there are deeper issues of accountability that have been raised by the recent activities of South Asian peacekeepers (as well as others) in Africa, particularly the DRC. In 2011, the Indian army launched a court of inquiry against 12 officers and 39 soldiers accused of sexual exploitation and abuse while serving as blue helmets in the DRC.[98] Allegations of corruption, smuggling, and exploitation, including illegal trade in gold, have also been made against Indian and Pakistani peacekeepers in the DRC, but these charges have been denied by the two countries and remain unproven. While the UN can investigate the crimes, it has no legal authority to hold the perpetrators properly accountable—it can only repatriate them and ban them from future missions under its flag. Peacekeepers, particularly military troops, have legal immunity from prosecution in the countries of their deployment; they remain under the exclusive jurisdiction of their own governments, which are required by the UN "to bring the full force of their legal sanctions to bear" and report back to it on the outcome.[99] However, there is no way of holding the troop-contributing countries accountable over the matter, and the UN is reluctant to press them on it. The UN cannot ensure enforcement; neither can the host countries. All three South Asian countries claim to have a zero-tolerance policy against sexual exploitation and abuse. It is also worth mentioning that almost no peacekeeping operation has been exempt from allegations of sexual exploitation and abuse by its blue helmets, and the South Asian trio are not, by any means, the only countries that have been implicated in the UN's sexual exploitation and abuse scandal. However, as Kate Grady points out: "Specific information about the personnel accused can be difficult to obtain from the UN, which refrains from officially and routinely identifying the nationality of those accused of SEA [sexual exploitation and abuse], due in part to the political weight wielded by troop-contributing countries (TCCs) in providing military and police personnel to missions in a context of shortages."[100] (See Akonor in this volume.)

Conclusion

Notwithstanding the shortcomings and the incidental and vested natures of their interests in providing "boots on the ground" to promote peace on the African continent, India, Pakistan, and Bangladesh—given their capacity to do so, and fairly rapidly—remain significant actors for the practice of peacekeeping on the continent. Africa's own capacities have grown, as made evident by the African Union (AU)–United Nations Hybrid Operation in Darfur (UNAMID) and the AU Mission in Somalia (AMISOM) (see Gambari, Hirsch, and Mahiga in this volume). African contributions to UN peacekeeping have also increased both in absolute numbers and as a percentage of overall share, rising from 29 per cent in 2008 to 38 per cent in 2016.[101] As mentioned earlier, since mid-2015, Ethiopia has emerged as the largest troop and police contributor to the world organisation's peacekeeping operations. Indeed, in June 2017, six of the top ten UN troop-contributing countries were African—Ethiopia, Rwanda, Egypt, Burkina Faso, Senegal, and Ghana—all major contributors with more than 2,500 personnel each deployed in the field (see Table 24.1). Even so, the UN's missions in Africa continue—at least for now—to rely on significant external contributions from South Asia, in particular, not least of all because of these countries' capacity, accompanied by their willingness, to contribute not only numbers but also specialised assets such as engineering units, field hospitals, and combat helicopters. As Garima Mohan points out, for instance: "The Indian deployment [in South Sudan] largely constitutes medical corps, engineering units, and supply corps, which have been crucial to running a mission in a new country with almost no existing infrastructure."[102]

However, the question then becomes about sustaining Indian, Pakistani, and Bangladeshi interest in providing peacekeepers and peacekeeping assets on the ground, over which African countries may have little say. The major troop-contributing countries, including the South Asian trio have been pushing for a greater say in decision-making about UN missions, "for more frequent and in-depth consultations with troop-contributing countries over specific missions to ensure their success and effectiveness".[103] Highlighting the importance of this matter for itself, India, as an elected member of the UN Security Council at the time, used its presidency of the body in August 2011 to host a thematic debate on peacekeeping, focusing in particular on the relationship with troop-contributing countries, and which included participation from Bangladesh and Pakistan. India, in particular, has pushed for the creation of a two-stage process that includes the troop-contributing countries in the formulation of mission mandates, while time and again pointing to the problems of unclear mandates and insufficient resources. The dilution of host-state consent—a key factor in India's decisions to contribute to UN missions—through the Council's greater recourse to Chapter VII, is becoming more of a concern by all accounts, as are changing attitudes to force, such as that reflected in the creation of the Force Intervention Brigade in the DRC.[104] For some, there has been growing evidence of India's ambivalence towards peacekeeping, underscored by a decision in 2010 to withdraw its helicopter contribution—a critical asset for the mission—from MONUSCO. However, the importance that New Delhi attaches to its bid for a permanent seat on the Security Council; the centrality of its peacekeeping credentials to its case; and the greater involvement by other rising powers, such as China, in peacekeeping activities, make it unlikely that India will forgo its activism in the near future. The point here is that the calculus can change for reasons not entirely down to African expectations and needs, and if it does, the issues raised for African countries are about where the continent will be if entirely without, or with fewer, South Asian blue-helmet resources.

Furthermore, as Africa builds its own continental peace and security architecture, including an African Standby Force (ASF) with rapid deployment capability (see Kuwali, and Nagar in this volume), and seeks to give substance to the vision of a new *Pax Africana* (see Introduction and Mazrui in this volume), another—arguably more important—set of questions enters into the picture. Can African regional organisations build new and innovative partnerships, under their own aegis (rather than that of the UN) with the South Asian peacekeeping countries, with a view both to learn from their collective experiences and to help meet shortfalls in African capacities? Looking beyond funding, what are the gaps (for instance, in terms of specialised assets, logistical support, strategic planning, or critical training) that these non-Western actors—by and large overlooked in the continental discourse on peace and security—can help bridge? Given its quest for greater power and influence globally, as well as its more specific interests in Africa, is India, in particular, able and willing to build on its tradition of South-South solidarity, and to consider partnering in peacekeeping with the AU and Africa's regional economic communities (RECs) outside the cover of a UN umbrella? Tackling such (as yet) unanswered questions and, in so doing, seeking to build South-South cooperation in relatively uncharted areas of peace and security, requires boldness and imagination all around.

Notes

1. Ramesh Thakur, "From Peacekeeping to Peace Enforcement: The UN Operation in Somalia", *The Journal of Modern African Studies* 32, no. 3 (1994), p. 396.
2. Inam-ur-Rahman Malik, "Pakistan", in Alex J. Bellamy and Paul D. Williams (eds.), *Providing Peacekeepers: The Politics, Challenges, and Future of United Nations Peacekeeping Contributions* (Oxford: Oxford University Press, 2013), p. 221.
3. Chin-Hao Huang, "Contributor Profile: The People's Republic of China", Providing for Peacekeeping, 27 April 2017, p. 1, http://www.providingforpeacekeeping.org/wp-content/uploads/2017/05/China-Chin-Hao-27Apr2017_FINAL.pdf (accessed 1 August 2017).

4. Sharon Wiharta, "Contributor Profile: Indonesia", Providing for Peacekeeping, 29 January 2016, http://providingforpeacekeeping.org/wp-content/uploads/2016/02/ipi-pub-ppp-Indonesia.pdf (accessed 1 August 2017).
5. This phrase is from Providing for Peacekeeping, a research project on United Nations (UN) peacekeeping operations, jointly hosted by the International Peace Institute (IPI), the Elliott School at George Washington University, and the Asia-Pacific Centre for the Responsibility to Protect at the University of Queensland. *See* http://www.providingforpeacekeeping.org (accessed 14 June 2017).
6. Kudrat Virk, "Deconstructing India's Peacekeeping Role in Africa", in Urvashi Aneja (ed.), *Asia with Africa: Opportunities and Challenges* (New Delhi: Observer Research Foundation, 2016), pp. 54–58.
7. C. Raja Mohan, "India and International Peace Operations", *SIPRI Insights on Peace and Security* no. 2013/3 (April 2013), pp. 1–3; C. Raja Mohan, "The Return of the Raj", *The American Interest* (May/June 2010), http://www.the-american-interest.com/article.cfm?piece=803 (accessed 22 August 2013); Varun Vira, "India and UN Peacekeeping: Declining Interest with Grave Implications", *Small Wars Journal*, 13 July 2012, http://smallwarsjournal.com/node/12949 (accessed 14 July 2012). *See* Indian Army, http://indianarmy.nic.in (accessed 20 August 2013).
8. Raja Mohan, "The Return of the Raj"; Indian Army.
9. Raja Mohan, "India and International Peace Operations", p. 3.
10. Rashed Uz Zaman and Niloy R. Biswas, "Bangladesh", in Bellamy and Williams, *Providing Peacekeepers*, pp. 183–184.
11. India's active armed forces comprise approximately 1,325,000 personnel (as of 2012), Pakistan's 643,800 (2014), and Bangladesh's 157,050 (2016). Data from Providing for Peacekeeping, Country Profiles, http://www.providingforpeacekeeping.org/profiles (accessed 14 June 2017).
12. Raja Mohan, "The Return of the Raj".
13. Based on monthly summaries of military and police contributions to UN missions from UN Peacekeeping, http://www.un.org/en/peacekeeping/resources/statistics/contributors.shtml (accessed 13 June 2017).
14. Dipankar Banerjee, "India", in Bellamy and Williams, *Providing Peacekeepers*, pp. 229–230.
15. Permanent Mission of India to the UN, "India and United Nations Peacekeeping and Peacebuilding", https://www.pminewyork.org/pages.php?id=1985 (accessed 14 June 2017).
16. Permanent Mission of India to the UN, "India and United Nations Peacekeeping and Peacebuilding".
17. Kabilan Krishnasamy, "The Paradox of India's Peacekeeping", *Contemporary South Asia* 12, no. 2 (2003), p. 266.
18. Alan Bullion, "India and UN Peacekeeping Operations", *International Peacekeeping* 4, no. 1 (1997), p. 101.
19. Permanent Mission of India to the UN, "India and United Nations Peacekeeping and Peacebuilding"; Frank van Rooyen, "Blue Helmets for Africa: India's Peacekeeping in Africa", Occasional Paper no. 60 (Johannesburg: South African Institute of International Affairs [SAIIA], May 2010), p. 8; Adekeye Adebajo, *UN Peacekeeping in Africa: From the Suez Crisis to the Sudan Conflicts* (Boulder, CO, and London: Lynne Rienner; and Johannesburg:

Fanele, 2011), p. 70; Bullion, "India and UN Peacekeeping Operations", pp. 101–102.
20. Van Rooyen, "Blue Helmets for Africa", p. 8.
21. Data from Pakistan Army, http://www.pakistanarmy.gov.pk (accessed 14 June 2017).
22. Alex J. Bellamy and Paul D. Williams, "Introduction: The Politics and Challenges of Providing Peacekeepers", in Bellamy and Williams, *Providing Peacekeepers*, p. 7.
23. Kabilan Krishnasamy, "'Recognition' for Third World Peacekeepers: India and Pakistan", *International Peacekeeping* 8, no. 4 (2001), pp. 56–57. *See* Bullion, "India and UN Peacekeeping Operations".
24. Bellamy and Williams, "Introduction", p. 7, n. 28; Malik, "Pakistan", p. 205.
25. Malik, "Pakistan", p. 221.
26. Data from Pakistan Army.
27. Zaman and Biswas, "Bangladesh", p. 184.
28. Data from Bangladesh Prime Minister's Office, Armed Forces Division, http://www.afd.gov.bd/index.php/un-peacekeeping/bangladesh-in-un-mission (accessed 14 June 2017).
29. UN Peacekeeping, "UN Missions Summary of Military and Police", 31 December 2016, http://www.un.org/en/peacekeeping/contributors/2016/dec16_6.pdf (accessed 14 June 2017).
30. Data from Pakistan Army.
31. On this point, *see* Bellamy and Williams, "Introduction"; Alex J. Bellamy and Paul D. Williams, "Explaining the National Politics of Peacekeeping Contributions", in Bellamy and Williams, *Providing Peacekeepers*, pp. 417–436.
32. Data from the World Bank, http://databank.worldbank.org/data/download/GDP.pdf (accessed 1 August 2017).
33. Data from Providing for Peacekeeping, Country Profiles.
34. *See generally* Alex J. Bellamy and Paul D. Williams, *Understanding Peacekeeping* (Cambridge: Polity, 2010); Marrack Goulding, "The Evolution of United Nations Peacekeeping", *International Affairs* 69, no. 3 (1993), pp. 451–464; Joachim A. Koops, Norrie MacQueen, Thierry Tardy, and Paul D. Williams (eds.), *The Oxford Handbook of United Nations Peacekeeping Operations* (Oxford: Oxford University Press, 2015).
35. Ruchita Beri, "India's Role in Keeping Peace in Africa", *Strategic Analysis* 32, no. 2 (2008), p. 203.
36. This and the rest of the section draw on research outputs of the Providing for Peacekeeping project, in particular: Banerjee, "India"; Malik, "Pakistan"; Zaman and Biswas, "Bangladesh".
37. Banerjee, "India", p. 227.
38. I make a similar argument in Virk, "Deconstructing India's Peacekeeping Role in Africa", pp. 54–58.
39. Constitution of the Islamic Republic of Pakistan, art. 40, http://www.pakistani.org/pakistan/constitution (accessed 25 August 2013).
40. Constitution of the People's Republic of Bangladesh, art. 25, http://www1.umn.edu/humanrts/research/bangladesh-constitution.pdf (accessed 25 August 2013).
41. Raja Mohan, "India and International Peace Operations", p. 2.
42. W. Pal Sidhu, "An Absent-Minded Peacekeeper, So Far", *Livemint*, 10 July 2011, http://www.livemint.com/Opinion/TOBPhkCEBZXNN3nyP5MoXK/An-absentminded-peacekeeper-so-far.html (accessed 15 August 2013).

43. Bullion, "India and UN Peacekeeping", p. 101.
44. Van Rooyen, "Blue Helmets for Africa", p. 6.
45. Sidhu, "An Absent-Minded Peacekeeper, So Far".
46. Malik, "Pakistan", p. 213.
47. Krishnasamy, "The Paradox of India's Peacekeeping", p. 277.
48. *See* Krishnasamy, "The Paradox of India's Peacekeeping", pp. 272–273. According to Krishnasamy, "India was determined to pull out of Sierra Leone, rather than going on record as having been downgraded from commanding the mission to an ordinary peacekeeper", suggesting that image was more important than on-the-ground need (p. 273). *See also* Banerjee, "India", pp. 233–236.
49. This phrase is from Nicholas J. Wheeler, *Saving Strangers: Humanitarian Intervention in International Society* (Oxford: Oxford University Press, 2000).
50. Beri, "India's Role in Keeping Peace in Africa", p. 208.
51. Zaman and Biswas, "Bangladesh", p. 183.
52. Zaman and Biswas, "Bangladesh", p. 195.
53. Speech by Bangladeshi prime minister Sheikh Hasina, Bangabandhu International Conference Centre, Dhaka, 29 May 2013. *See* Zaman and Biswas, "Bangladesh", p. 195.
54. Malik, "Pakistan", p. 210.
55. This and the rest of the paragraph draw on Malik, "Pakistan", pp. 209–214.
56. Malik, "Pakistan", p. 212. *See* Krishnasamy, "The Paradox of India's Peacekeeping", pp. 275–277.
57. Krishnasamy, "The Paradox of India's Peacekeeping", pp. 275–277.
58. Alan Bullion, "India", in David S. Sorenson and Pia Christina Woods (eds.), *The Politics of Peacekeeping in the Post–Cold War Era* (London and New York: Frank Cass, 2005), p. 202.
59. Kudrat Virk, "India and R2P's Burdens of Dissent and Accommodation", in Monica Serrano and Thomas G. Weiss (eds.), *The International Politics of Human Rights: Rallying to the R2P Cause?* (New York: Routledge, 2014), p. 135.
60. *See, for example*, "Africa Has Emerged as the Next Growth Frontier—Says Trade and Industry Minister, Rob Davies", 18 July 2012, http://www.gov.za/africa-has-emerged-next-growth-frontier-%E2%80%93-says-trade-and-industry-minister-rob-davies (accessed 18 June 2017).
61. Rashed Uz Zaman and Niloy Ranjan Biswas, "Contributor Profile: Bangladesh", Providing for Peacekeeping, 16 December 2016, http://www.providingforpeacekeeping.org/2014/04/03/contributor-profile-bangladesh (accessed 14 June 2017). *See* Anbarasan Ethirajan, "Bangladeshi Companies Launch Africa Farm Lease Plan", *BBC News*, 17 May 2011, http://www.bbc.com/news/world-south-asia-13428867 (accessed 18 June 2017).
62. Data from the Observatory of Economic Complexity, http://atlas.media.mit.edu/en/profile/country/pak/ (accessed 12 August 2017).
63. Van Rooyen, "Blue Helmets for Africa", p. 6. He writes thus, but of India's motives for peacekeeping in Africa: "What direct strategic purpose has been served by its participation in missions in African countries such as the Democratic Republic of Congo, Angola, Mozambique, Rwanda, Liberia and Sierra Leone, remains cryptic, and is therefore open to theorizing".
64. This paragraph and the next paragraph draw on Virk, "Deconstructing India's Peacekeeping Role in Africa".

65. Data from India's Ministry of Commerce and Industry, Department of Commerce, Export Import Data Bank, ver. 7.1—TRADESTAT, http://commerce.nic.in/eidb/default.asp (accessed 24 July 2016).
66. Ruchita Beri, "Evolving India-Africa Relations: Continuity and Change", Occasional Paper no. 76 (Johannesburg: SAIIA, February 2011), p. 12.
67. Sidhu, "An Absent-Minded Peacekeeper, So Far".
68. David Axe, "Why South Asia Loves Peacekeeping", *The Diplomat*, 20 December 2010, http://thediplomat.com/2010/12/20/why-south-asia-loves-peacekeeping (accessed 25 August 2013).
69. Sidhu, "An Absent-Minded Peacekeeper, So Far".
70. This paragraph and the next paragraph draw on Zaman and Biswas, "Bangladesh", especially pp. 193–203.
71. Zaman and Biswas, "Bangladesh", p. 201.
72. Zaman and Biswas, "Bangladesh", p. 201.
73. Zaman and Biswas, "Bangladesh", p. 199.
74. Zaman and Biswas, "Bangladesh", p. 195.
75. Zaman and Biswas, "Bangladesh", pp. 194–195.
76. This paragraph draws on Malik, "Pakistan", pp. 214–217.
77. Malik, "Pakistan", p. 215. *See also* Ayesha Siddiqa, *Military Inc.: Inside Pakistan's Military Economy* (London: Pluto, 2007).
78. Craig Caffrey, "Indian Defence Budget Increases by 5.6%", *Jane's 360*, 1 February 2017, http://www.janes.com/article/67382/indian-defence-budget-increases-by-5-6 (accessed 18 June 2017); Jon Grevat, "Pakistan Boosts Defence Spending for 2017–18", *Jane's 360*, 30 May 2017, http://www.janes.com/article/70892/pakistan-boosts-defence-spending-for-2017-18 (accessed 18 June 2017).
79. Inam-ur-Rahman Malik, "Contributor Profile: Pakistan", Providing for Peacekeeping, 25 June 2014, http://www.providingforpeacekeeping.org/2014/04/03/contributor-profile-pakistan (accessed 14 June 2017).
80. Malik, "Contributor Profile: Pakistan"; World Bank, *Migrant and Remittances Factbook 2016*, 3rd ed. (Washington, DC, 2016), p. 12.
81. Banerjee, "India", pp. 240–243; Malik, "Pakistan", pp. 218–220.
82. Malik, "Pakistan", p. 221.
83. Zaman and Biswas, "Bangladesh", p. 199.
84. Zaman and Biswas, "Bangladesh", pp. 185–186.
85. Banerjee, "India", p. 233. *See* Adebajo, *UN Peacekeeping in Africa*, pp. 148–152.
86. Zaman and Biswas, "Bangladesh", p. 199.
87. Zaman and Biswas, "Bangladesh", p. 192; Dipankar Banerjee, "South Asia: Contributors of Global Significance", in Donald C.F. Daniel, Patricia Taft, and Sharon Wiharta (eds.), *Peace Operations: Trends, Progress, and Prospects* (Washington, DC: Georgetown University Press, 2008), pp. 197–199.
88. UN Peacekeeping, "Summary of Contributions to UN Peacekeeping by Country and Post", 30 June 2017, http://www.un.org/en/peacekeeping/contributors/2017/jun17_4.pdf (accessed 6 August 2017).
89. Malik, "Pakistan", p. 221.
90. Malik, "Pakistan", pp. 221–222.
91. Beri, "India's Role in Keeping Peace in Africa", pp. 211–212.
92. I am grateful to Ibrahim Gambari, former Joint Special Representative of the AU-UN Hybrid Operation in Darfur (UNAMID), for this point.

93. Axe, "Why South Asia Loves Peacekeeping". In 2010, for example, the UN Organisation Stabilisation Mission in the Democratic Republic of the Congo (MONUSCO) introduced Community Liaison Assistants (CLAs) to facilitate information gathering and communication with local communities; several other missions, such as those in the Central African Republic (CAR) and South Sudan, have since followed suit.
94. MONUSCO and Office of the UN Commissioner for Human Rights (OHCHR), *Final Report of the Fact-Finding Missions of the United Nations Joint Human Rights Office into the Mass Rapes and Other Human Rights Violations Committed by a Coalition of Armed Groups Along the Kibua-Mpofi Axis in Walikale Territory, North Kivu, from 30 July to 2 August 2010*, July 2011, paras. 25, 30–31.
95. Security Council Report, "Democratic Republic of the Congo", Update Report no. 1, 3 September 2010, p. 1; MONUSCO, "Roger Meece on Kibua: 'We Are Shocked by This Large Scale Tragedy'", 13 September 2010, https://monusco.unmissions.org/en/roger-meece-kibua-we-are-shocked-large-scale-tragedy%E2%80%9D (accessed 21 June 2017).
96. MONUSCO and OHCHR, *Final Report*, paras. 47, 17.
97. *See, for example*, Danielle Shapiro, "Congo: UN Scrambles to Better Protect Civilians in Wake of Mass Rape", *Christian Science Monitor*, 13 November 2010, https://www.csmonitor.com/World/Africa/2010/1113/Congo-UN-scrambles-to-better-protect-civilians-in-wake-of-mass-rape (accessed 21 June 2017).
98. "Indian Army Probing Sexual Abuse Charges Against UN Peacekeepers in Congo", *NDTV*, 7 June 2011, http://www.ndtv.com/article/india/indian-army-probing-sexual-abuse-charges-against-un-peacekeepers-in-congo-110764 (accessed 26 August 2013).
99. "Who Will Watch the Watchmen?", *The Economist*, 29 May 2008, http://www.economist.com/node/11458241 (accessed 24 December 2016).
100. Kate Grady, "Sexual Exploitation and Abuse by UN Peacekeepers: A Threat to Impartiality", *International Peacekeeping* 17, no. 2 (2010), p. 219.
101. Richard Gowan and Megan Gleason, "UN Peacekeeping: The Next Five Years: A Report by the New York University Center on International Cooperation Commissioned by the Permanent Mission of Denmark to the United Nations", November 2012, p. 12, http://cic.es.its.nyu.edu/sites/default/files/cic_un_fiveyears.pdf (accessed 24 August 2013); Providing for Peacekeeping, "Breakdown of Peacekeepers Contributed by Region as of December 2016", http://www.providingforpeacekeeping.org/peacekeeping-data-graphs (accessed 21 June 2017).
102. Garima Mohan, "Modernizing India's Approach to Peacekeeping: The Case of South Sudan", 3 October 2016, http://carnegieindia.org/2016/10/03/modernizing-india-s-approach-to-peacekeeping-case-of-south-sudan-pub-64594 (accessed 1 August 2017).
103. Rohan Mukherjee and David M. Malone, "India and the UN Security Council: An Ambiguous Tale", *Economic and Political Weekly* 48, no. 29 (20 July 2013), p. 114.
104. Richard Gowan, "Diplomatic Fallout: Frustrations Mount for India at the UN", *World Politics Review*, 15 April 2013.

CHAPTER 25

Conclusion

Tony Karbo

As the collection of essays in this volume has shown, progress in the search for a "new" *Pax Africana* (see Mazrui in this volume) has significant implications for policy at the continental and regional levels in Africa. While the African Union (AU) has developed strong policy frameworks on collective security, implementation has lagged and been fraught with challenges, with the institutional arrangements and structures for translating policies into practice remaining weak. Based on the key issues discussed in this volume, ranging from conflict prevention, peacemaking, and peacekeeping to post-conflict reconstruction and development, several fundamental questions remain unanswered. Has the vision of a new *Pax Africana* been realised? What is the future of the philosophy of *Pax Africana*? Have the efforts at institutionalisation and consolidation of the AU contributed to building sustainable peace on the continent? Is the AU ready to confront new threats to peace and security in Africa?

The volume has explored in detail the concept of a new *Pax Africana* and ongoing endeavours to build a sustainable peace in Africa. Several contributing authors (see, for example, Richmond, and Hirsch in this volume) have presented arguments suggesting that the nature of the African state renders many of them ill-equipped to deal with conflict and build sustainable peace, even under international tutelage, because institutions are too weak to prevent violent conflict or to address the pervasive problems of inequality, poverty, and injustice. This being the case, it has been difficult to make progress on several fronts towards the realisation of a new *Pax Africana*. Even with a well-structured continental peace and security framework, many countries—individually and collectively—do not have the political will, nor the financial wherewithal, to address violence.

T. Karbo (✉)
N'Zarama Centre for Peacebuilding, Abidjan, Côte d'Ivoire

T. Karbo, K. Virk (eds.), *The Palgrave Handbook of Peacebuilding in Africa*, https://doi.org/10.1007/978-3-319-62202-6_25

Critical to sustaining the spirit of *Pax Africana* and building peace is a shift towards decisive structural change at all levels on the continent, from the AU level down to the grassroots level. This requires the construction of states that are responsive to the needs of many of their citizens, rather than a narrow group of parochial, neo-colonial interests. It requires the creation of states that can gain and use the support of their international partners for the development and promotion of human rights and justice for all, rather than for the self-enrichment of a small ruling elite. Such pursuit of self-enrichment has contributed to a persistent gap between rich and poor in Africa, while the continent's middle class remains small and fledgling. Inequality in African societies (see Richmond in this volume) today is perhaps the greatest threat to peace and security on the continent. Therefore, peacebuilding in Africa must, first and foremost, address problems arising from inequality, poverty, unemployment, marginalisation, and lack of inclusive development. To be effective and sustainable, peacebuilding activities must also include processes involving political reconciliation, transitional justice, rehabilitation and reintegration, and socio-economic development. In short, peacebuilding, to be transformative, must be carried out at all societal levels: political, economic, social, and cultural.

The essays in this volume have sought to unpack the multiple and complex challenges related to the realisation of a genuine, systematic, and functional institutional framework that will promote peace and build prosperous and sustainable communities in Africa. A general theme that runs across the volume is that Africa has taken bold steps in creating the legal and institutional frameworks that constitute the foundations for the realisation of the promise of a new *Pax Africana*. Since its creation in 2002, the African Union has made steady progress towards building peace and stability on the continent. The AU has now conducted several complex peacekeeping operations, for example, in Somalia since 2007 (see Hirsch, and Mahiga in this volume) and in Sudan's Darfur region in 2004–2007 (and thereafter in partnership with the United Nations [UN]), "most of them in contexts where the UN has been unable to deploy peacekeepers in a timely manner".[1] In this respect, the AU has represented a marked departure from its predecessor, the Organisation of African Unity (OAU), which did not have an established framework for such missions. However, as several chapters in this volume (see, for example, Kuwali, and Nagar) indicate, the AU faces major challenges related to the financing of, and logistical capacity for, complex peacekeeping operations, and remains dependent on partnerships with key external actors, such as the UN (see Vogt in this volume), to sustain its peace and security efforts. The African Union Mission in Sudan (AMIS), for instance, was restructured and merged into the AU-UN Hybrid Operation in Darfur (UNAMID)—the first such operation of its kind—in 2007 (see Gambari in this volume; on Sudan, see also Deng in this volume).

The challenges confronting the AU in its efforts to maintain peace and security in Africa are not entirely new. The regional organisation continues to be dependent on external actors for financial support of its operations, with several of its own member states failing to meet fully their obligations to the Union. For example, "the 2015 budget of US$522,121 million had a shortfall of

US$149,266 million, before the AU managed to collect another US$20 million from donors, before reducing the budget to $393,037 million".[2] Major external partners include Britain,[3] Germany, the Netherlands, Spain, Sweden, Canada, the United States (US), China, and Turkey, as well as organisations such as the European Union (EU) and the World Bank.[4] In 2016, member states were expected to contribute only about 40 per cent of the AU's total budget of $416.8 million, with the remainder to be sourced from its external donors.[5] As Malawian scholar Dan Kuwali puts it in this volume:

> If African states are unable or unwilling to mobilise resources for the continental peace and security agenda, and if the APSA [African Peace and Security Architecture] continues to take the reactive "fire brigade" approach to responding to conflicts on the continent, in the words of Nigerian scholar Adekeye Adebajo, "the elusive quest for *Pax Africana*, a peace that is protected and maintained by African institutions themselves, will remain endless".[6]

African countries must thus show greater commitment to, and political will for, supporting implementation of the AU's various programmes and initiatives through sustained financing. This is vital if concrete and sustainable solutions to the continent's peace and security challenges are to be found. In the absence of such support, the search for a new *Pax Africana* risks remaining no more than a weak slogan for solidarity and building consensus among African countries.

Africa's regional economic communities (RECs)—the building blocks of continental unity and integration—similarly face enormous challenges in their quest to build sustainable infrastructures for peace. Among the most daunting challenges facing the RECs are: weak regional and national institutions to coordinate policies and programmes for regional integration and security; inadequate human and institutional capacity to implement structural transformation; inadequate financial resources; simultaneous memberships to multiple regional and sub-regional organisations; and a lack of political will (see, for example, Nagar in this volume). These factors have all together contributed negatively to the implementation of peace and security programmes in Africa, and need greater and more concerted attention. The issue of adequate financing, in particular, cuts across the AU and Africa's RECs, and in this respect is one of the most pressing challenges in the search for African solutions to African problems. As important is the need for greater cooperation and collaboration between Africa's continental and regional organisations, with a view to working in tandem while using complementarities to build synergy in their collective endeavour towards a prosperous, peaceful, and secure continent.[7]

From Promise to Practice: The Continuing Search for a New *Pax Africana*

As has been highlighted in this volume, the AU has made strides in addressing the plethora of violent conflicts and attendant challenges facing Africa. This gives some reason to be cautiously optimistic about the future of a continent that can indeed give priority to the responsibility to protect (R2P) its own citizens (see Deng in this volume). Such cautious optimism is based, in large part, on the existence of legal and institutional frameworks—such as the AU Constitutive Act, the APSA, and institutions like the African Court on Human and Peoples' Rights (AfCHPR), among others—that provide a foundation for progress in key areas of conflict prevention, peacemaking, peacekeeping, peacebuilding, and post-conflict reconstruction. These frameworks can be built upon over time, as can be seen in the investments being made in the development of the Continental Early Warning System (CEWS)—one of the main pillars of the APSA, and a vital mechanism of conflict prevention.

Despite lofty conflict prevention aims and ideals, the AU has continued to fall short in the promotion of democracy and "good governance" on the continent. The gains of the 1990s and early 2000s seem to have been all but lost, with the late Kenyan scholar Ali Mazrui, for instance, noting that democracy in Africa remained in "intensive care" at the turn of the twenty-first century, despite efforts towards "resuscitating" it after its murder—he called it "democra-cide"—by African leaders and Westernised elites during the Cold War.[8] Recent evidence of this continued fragility of African democracy can be found in constitutional changes sought by African leaders to prolong their stays in power in countries such as the Democratic Republic of the Congo (DRC), Rwanda, and Uganda. In Rwanda, for example, President Paul Kagame has changed the constitution to remove term limits. In Burundi, President Pierre Nkurunziza's successful run for an unconstitutional third term has extended his hold on power, with violence continuing in the country. Meanwhile, Congolese president Joseph Kabila has used various reasons to hang on to power after the expiry of his mandate, with presidential elections scheduled for November 2016 postponed for two years.[9]

Furthermore, there is a lack of coordination among AU institutions on the modalities of implementing protocols and declarations, especially those concerned with conflict prevention, peacemaking, peacekeeping, and peacebuilding in Africa. Critics of the AU and the APSA have tended to argue that the problem lies in implementation, rather than in the content of the Union's protocols and agreements. Implementation of the AU's peace and security agenda has also experienced major setbacks including constitutional coups, and faced challenges from the existence of competing narratives and approaches to collective security on the continent. As well, the emphasis on conflict prevention remains weak, despite the existence of preventive mechanisms at the continental and regional levels. The result can be seen in the continuation of "old" conflicts (for example, the Ethiopia-Eritrea border conflict) and outbreaks of, or relapse into, fresh violence (such as in Burundi and the DRC). There is thus a clear and present need to focus more on prevention processes, and on supporting efforts to address the root causes of conflict, including "bad governance and weak state institutions that perpetuate poverty, inequality, marginalization and exclusion, as well as issues relating to state legitimacy and the rule of law".[10]

With the establishment of the African Peace and Security Architecture, the AU could respond more swiftly to conflicts on the continent. The continental security arrangement has also helped to shape Africa's peace and security relationships with key external actors, especially the UN. Nonetheless, African conflicts have become increasingly complex. Even though they have domestic origins, they have tended more and more to take on a regional character. Examples abound where this regional character has contributed to the protracted nature of conflicts on the continent. The situation in Somalia (see Hirsch, and Mahiga in this volume), for example, has drawn in countries such as Burundi, Ethiopia, Kenya, and Uganda, as well as Eritrea (which is believed to be providing support to the militant group al-Shabaab).[11] Similarly, the conflict in South Sudan (see Deng in this volume) has drawn in multiple actors including Kenya, Uganda, Ethiopia, and Sudan, with efforts to bring peace—mainly under the aegis of the Intergovernmental Authority on Development (IGAD)—further involving an array of international actors (such as the Troika, comprising the US, Britain, and Norway; and China, among others).[12] Such complicated conflicts clearly require multi-faceted approaches that involve a diverse range of actors at different levels (see, for example, Gambari, Hirsch, Mahiga, and Wamai in this volume). Almost 15 years on from its establishment in 2003,[13] the APSA's experience has highlighted these complexities, and at the same time provided the AU with the opportunity to reflect on the architecture through its Peace and Security Council (PSC). What is clear is that the APSA has to be seen within the wider, geo-political landscape of contemporary Africa. Peace and security on the continent need to be viewed within clusters—for example, instead of seeing the conflict in Burundi as isolated and concerning only Burundians, it should be seen in the context of the wider Great Lakes region, since it affects the countries of the region in terms of refugee flows and humanitarian action. Peace and security further need to be seen not only through the lens of geographic spaces, but also in terms of collaboration with external partners. Several chapters in this volume (see, for example, Jonah, Gambari, Vogt, Rashid, Yates, and Virk) point to the need for a more coordinated and multi-faceted approach to making, keeping, and building peace. The involvement of a multiplicity of actors, in turn, requires taking into consideration and carefully managing their different interests, as well as their often-varying approaches to peacekeeping and peacebuilding. Regional actors, for example, have short- and long-term interests that they seek to prioritise, but this can also complicate efforts to make, keep, and build sustainable peace.

In this context, it is also worth noting the importance of non-violent approaches to conflict management. Mediation as a form of conflict resolution offers parties in a conflict the opportunity to jointly come up with win-win outcomes. The Kenya National Dialogue and Reconciliation Process is a case in point, in which mediation was used to resolve the impasse during the country's 2007–2008 presidential election (see Wamai in this volume). It was also illustrative of the complex nature of politically charged mediation processes and of the challenges of peacemaking. A key challenge related to the involvement of a multiplicity of actors is coordinating and ensuring the inclusion of the varying interests of all the relevant parties. Having multiple processes ongoing simultaneously can jeopardise the entire peace process. Inclusivity is a *sine qua non* in mediation. The Kenyan example aptly illustrated how business, religious, and political leaders, as well as ordinary citizens, can come together to support the mediation process. The AU could borrow a leaf from the Kenyan experience in its efforts to broker peace in South Sudan, the Central African Republic (CAR), Libya, and Somalia, among other places.

Towards More Effective Peacebuilding in Africa

Arguably, the most effective way to achieve peace and security is to take seriously issues dealing with structural conflict prevention. Peacekeeping after the outbreak of violence cannot alone guarantee the peace. This can be seen in continuing conflicts across the continent (for example, Burundi, the DRC, Somalia, and South Sudan). Structural prevention efforts aimed at addressing the underlying causes and conditions of conflict and insecurity offer a much more robust means of building a sustainable peace. The APSA can be as effective as it ought to be only when its goals and objectives are geared towards a more proactive role and fully utilise the conflict prevention mechanisms that have already been developed, such as the Peace and Security Council and the Panel of the Wise. Structural conflict prevention also requires responsive, transparent, and accountable governance systems. Successful efforts in this regard could free up scarce resources allocated to support peacemaking and peacekeeping operations for use instead in post-conflict reconstruction as well as in other, more immediate preventive actions. In the final analysis, sustainable peace in Africa can only be achieved when structural inequalities are addressed and cultural violence is curbed.

The 2014 report of the chairperson of the AU Commission on structural conflict prevention, in particular, placed emphasis on "reinvigorating states in fragile situations in Africa".[14] The report provided an update on the follow-up steps taken by the AU Commission with respect to the finalisation of the Continental Structural Conflict Prevention Framework (CSCPF) of 2014 as a tool to facilitate a Commission-wide and coordinated approach to prevention, as well as the development of a Country Structural Vulnerability Assessment (CSVA) tool for the early identification of countries' structural vulnerability to conflict. It concluded with observations on the way forward. As the report also acknowledged:

> [T]he costs of managing conflict (whether in fielding peacekeeping operations, providing humanitarian relief, engaging in lengthy peace-making efforts or undertaking post-conflict reconstruction) are high. This lends further credence to the long-standing adage that "prevention is better than cure". Recognising that the human, financial and material costs of prevention are far less compared to the devastating consequences of armed violence, the AU and the Regional

> Economic Communities ... have, over the last two decades, developed policies and instruments aimed at preventing violent conflict on the continent, both operationally and structurally.[15]

There is awareness all around in the international community, including the UN and other development partners of the AU, of the huge costs of conflicts once they have broken out. Often, once violence breaks out, there is a need to manage this violence through peacekeeping operations, to provide humanitarian relief for internally displaced persons (IDPs) and refugees who flee across borders into neighbouring countries; or even simply to facilitate, or create the conditions necessary for reaching, a negotiated settlement, all of which are more costly than preventing conflict in the first place.[16] As the AU noted in a recent report: "The onerous nature of these missions is illustrated by the total cost of current operations which, for 2016, is estimated at $1.2 billion per year. AMISOM [the African Union Mission in Somalia] alone (with an approved strength of 22,126 uniformed personnel and 114 civilians) accounting for an estimated $900m per year."[17]

The Role of External Actors

External actors have a key role in supporting African-led peacemaking, peacekeeping, and peacebuilding efforts on the continent. For example, since the outbreak of violent conflict in South Sudan in December 2013, the UN, the EU, and the US have played important roles in efforts to resolve the crisis, and were instrumental in helping bring the belligerents together to negotiate the IGAD-mediated August 2015 Addis Ababa peace agreement, though this accord has since collapsed in the context of renewed fighting, highlighting the fragility of the process. On the ground, the United Nations Mission in South Sudan (UNMISS) has continued to monitor human rights violations and provide humanitarian assistance, while trying to support the implementation of the faltering Addis Ababa peace agreement. The Troika (comprising the US, Britain, and Norway) has also provided support to the ongoing peace process (including financial support), and imposed sanctions on perpetrators of violence. Other actors such as China and the EU have also been key players. Such international partnerships and support are required for sustainable peacebuilding in Africa.

Several chapters in this volume (see Deng, Hirsch, Jonah, Gambari, and Otobo) have highlighted the challenges facing the UN and the AU in conflict prevention, peacemaking, peacekeeping, and peacebuilding. Whereas some challenges differ from context to context, the fundamental issues of planning, logistics, and coordination remain the same. Successful joint activities in Sudan's Darfur region, Liberia, and Sierra Leone, where some form of cooperation between Africa's continental and regional organisations, and the UN, was forged, have been highlighted by several authors in this volume (see Jonah, Gambari, and Rashid) as pathways towards effective peacekeeping and peacebuilding. At issue, though, is the inter-agency or inter-departmental coordination of missions, with a view to planning and implementing a robust response to violent conflicts on the continent.

Sustainable peacebuilding requires effective partnerships to be forged between various parts of the UN system (such as its Department of Peacekeeping Operations [DPKO], its Peacebuilding Commission, and the United Nations Development Programme [UNDP]) on the one hand, and the AU and its institutions (such as the AU Commission, and Peace and Security Council) on the other. These partnerships must be coordinated sufficiently to be effective. This has been a challenge (see Vogt, and Mahiga in this volume), as in several cases actors within the same organisation do not communicate effectively with each other.

The UN, under its 1945 Charter, has the power and authority to intervene in situations of violent conflict, based on a Security Council resolution. Often, however, the UN is slow to act. A notable example is the genocide in Rwanda in 1994, which could have been prevented had the UN acted swiftly. The AU's predecessor, the OAU, was also apathetic and did not use the mandate of its new Mechanism for Conflict Prevention, Management, and Resolution to intervene in the Rwandan case. This example shows that political will is a decisive factor in building peace. Meanwhile, Africa has since become the "experimental laboratory" of UN peacekeeping operations. The UN Security Council has tended to use the AU to explore new avenues for the application of Chapters VII and VIII of the UN Charter (see Ugarte, Gambari, and Vogt in this volume). The UN and the AU can indeed work together to promote international peace and security, based on Chapter VIII, as demonstrated by the AU-UN Hybrid Operation in Darfur (see Gambari in this volume). This experiment could be replicated elsewhere.

Regarding the International Criminal Court (ICC), and its relevance to the protection of human rights and the accountability of perpetrators of human rights violations (see Nouwen in this volume), there are ongoing debates on the continent about proposals for African states to withdraw *en masse* from the ICC. The indicted sitting heads of state of Sudan and Kenya have been at the forefront of this crusade, arguing that the Court has mostly targeted Africans. (The charges against Kenya's Uhuru Kenyatta and his deputy, William Ruto, by the ICC have since been dropped.) In this context, perhaps a more sustainable solution to the problem of accountability is to use the African Court on Human and Peoples' Rights (see Akonor in this volume).

Since Donald Trump won the US presidential election in November 2016, the world has witnessed an increase in nationalistic and isolationist rhetoric from Washington. Politicians in Europe are also increasingly beating the nationalistic drum. The broader implications of these developments for Africa continue to unfold, and their true impact will not be known for some time. In the short term, however, Africa is likely to experience a decline in aid support due also to the poor economic performance of major donors in Europe (such as the EU, France, Germany, and Britain). With Britain engaged in negotiations to leave the EU ("Brexit"), a weak French economy, lack of a unified EU (most probably because of Brexit), and reduced spending across Europe and the US on development aid, peacekeeping in Africa will most likely become increasingly the burden of the AU. The AU has demonstrated, through its peacekeeping interventions in several situations (such as Somalia and Darfur), that it is up to the task when it comes to fielding personnel for combat and police action. The challenge, as has been articulated throughout this volume, is the financing of its operations. Unless the international community (led by the UN) steps in and acts to guarantee financing for such operations, the AU will continue to limp in its efforts to provide security on the continent.

* * *

Peacebuilding efforts in Africa are not new. For decades now, several African countries have been engulfed in violent conflict, with the UN, the AU, and Africa's regional economic communities having been at the forefront of trying to build peace in the affected countries. Many of these countries find themselves in complex politico-economic situations requiring sophisticated institutional arrangements and governance structures. Civil wars have undermined the lofty aspirations of countries and regional arrangements—in particular the AU—seeking to unite Africa politically and economically. The roots of the civil wars are complex, and so building sustainable peace requires multiple strategies and partnerships between regional and international organisations such as the UN and the AU. The solutions to these complex problems require bold, decisive, and innovative actions by the AU and its partners. The AU has put in place institutional structures and mechanisms to address problems of violence and post-conflict reconstruction and development, but faces challenges.

The key to successful peace and the integration of Africa is to facilitate rapid politico-economic and social recovery. While the AU has departments responsible for these tasks (for example, humanitarian affairs and post-conflict reconstruction and development), these are generally under-capacitated and need augmented resource allocation for both technical and material build-up. Sustainable peacebuilding requires support for political processes (see Omeje, Richmond, Porter, and Mahiga in this volume), economic processes (see Omeje in this volume), and cultural processes (see Deng in this volume). The roadmap to a peaceful and prosperous Africa has been drawn. Navigating the different bottlenecks and overcoming the challenges is work in progress. The aspirations of a politically and economically integrated Africa are noble. Africa's current leaders must continue to accept this responsibility and implement what they have set out as the graduated steps towards the realisation of an integrated Africa. This requires bold and courageous leadership. Regional leaders such as Nigeria, South Africa, Algeria, Angola, and Egypt must continue to take on this leadership role to make a united Africa a reality.

As Nigerian scholar Chris Ngwodo puts it: "No single African nation can compete with the economic power blocs of our time—the European Union, the United States, the emerging economies of China and India as well the latent union of South East Asian economies such as Singapore, Japan and

South Korea."[18] Ngwodo adds: "The whole point of regional integration is synergy—the amplification of human capital and economic potential. Regional integration means larger markets but more importantly it portends a larger, richer pool of human and intellectual capital, the prime currency of the twenty-first century world economy."[19] The founding fathers of pan-Africanism (Ghana's Kwame Nkrumah, Tanzania's Julius Nyerere, Ethiopia's Haile Selassie, Kenya's Jomo Kenyatta, and Ahmed Sékou Touré of Guinea, among others) rightly understood that Africa's only hope of advancement lay in dismantling the divisive boundaries imposed on the continent by European colonialists. Regional integration should continue the centuries-long relations of trade and culture. This is what *Pax Africana* should be all about: reinforcing natural connectors of peoples and cultures in Africa. These natural connectors provide the impetus for the new *Pax Africana*.

Notes

1. African Union (AU), "Securing Predictable and Sustainable Financing for Peace in Africa", August 2016, p. 2, http://www.peaceau.org/uploads/auhr-progress-report-final-020916-with-annexes.pdf (accessed 2 August 2017).
2. Peter Fabricius, "African Union Starts Putting Its Money Closer to Where Its Mouth Is", *Africa Sustainable Conservation News*, 12 February 2015, https://africasustainableconservation.com/2015/02/12/african-union-starts-putting-its-money-closer-to-where-its-mouth-is (accessed 30 June 2017).
3. Britain is used synonymously with the United Kingdom (UK) in this volume.
4. Mmanaledi Mataboge, "AU's Dependence on Cash from the West Still Rankles", *Mail & Guardian*, 12 June 2015, https://mg.co.za/article/2015-06-11-aus-dependence-on-cash-from-the-west-still-rankles (accessed 2 August 2017).
5. Centre for Conflict Resolution (CCR), *The African Union: Regional and Global Challenges*, Seminar Report no. 53 (Cape Town, August 2016), p. 24.
6. Adekeye Adebajo, "The Elusive Quest for Pax Africana Continues", *Business Day*, 27 January 2013.
7. AU Commission, "Agenda 2063 Framework Document", September 2015.
8. Ali Mazrui, "Who Killed Democracy in Africa? Clues of the Past, Concerns of the Future", *Development Policy Management Forum Network Bulletin* 9, no. 1 (2002), pp. 15–23.
9. CCR, *War and Peace in the Great Lakes Region*, Seminar Report no. 54 (Cape Town, October 2016). *See also* Gilbert M. Khadiagala (ed.), *War and Peace in Africa's Great Lakes Region* (New York: Palgrave, 2017).
10. AU Commission, "Agenda 2063 Framework Document", p. 65.
11. *See* Security Council Report, "Somalia-Eritrea Sanctions Committee Consultations", *What's In Blue*, 21 July 2017, http://www.whatsinblue.org/2017/07/somalia-eritrea-sanctions-committee-consultations.php (accessed 2 August 2017).
12. CCR, *Building Peace in South Sudan: Progress, Problems, and Prospects*, Seminar Report no. 57 (Cape Town, June 2017).
13. The 2002 Protocol Relating to the Establishment of the Peace and Security Council of the AU entered into force in December 2003.

14. AU Peace and Security Council, "Report of the Chairperson of the Commission on the Follow-Up to the Peace and Security Council Communiqué of 27 October 2014 on Structural Conflict Prevention", PSC/PR/2(D), 502nd Meeting, Addis Ababa, 29 April 2015, p. 1, http://www.peaceau.org/uploads/psc-502-cews-rpt-29-4-2015.pdf (accessed 1 December 2016 and 1 July 2017).
15. AU Peace and Security Council, "Report of the Chairperson of the Commission", p. 1.
16. AU Peace and Security Council, "Report of the Chairperson of the Commission", p. 1.
17. AU, "Securing Predictable and Sustainable Financing", p. 3.
18. Chris Ngwodo, "Pax Africana", 23 August 2005, http://nigeriaworld.com/articles/2005/aug/232.html (accessed 17 November 2016).
19. Ngwodo, "Pax Africana".

Notes on Contributors

Professor Adekeye Adebajo is Director of the Institute for Pan-African Thought and Conversation at the University of Johannesburg, South Africa. He was Executive Director of the Centre for Conflict Resolution (CCR) in Cape Town between 2003 and 2016. He served on United Nations (UN) missions in South Africa, Western Sahara, and Iraq; and is the author of six books on Africa's international relations, including on the UN; as well as a biography of Thabo Mbeki. Professor Adebajo is co-editor or editor of nine books on Africa's international relations. He obtained his doctorate from the University of Oxford in England, where he studied as a Rhodes Scholar.

Professor Kwame Akonor is Associate Professor of Political Science at Seton Hall University, New Jersey, in the United States (US), where he teaches international relations, human rights, and African political economy. He is also founding Director of the New York–based African Development Institute, a non-governmental think tank devoted to critical analyses of—and solutions to—the problems of development in Africa. Professor Akonor is a former president of the New York African(a) Studies Association (NYASA), a regional organisation that promotes the visibility and advancement of the African Studies discipline.

Ambassador Francis M. Deng, currently South Sudan's Roving Ambassador, was the country's first Permanent Representative to the United Nations. He also served as the UN Secretary-General's Special Advisor on the Prevention of Genocide and as the Representative of the UN Secretary-General on Internally Displaced Persons. He was Sudan's Ambassador to Canada, the Nordic countries, and the United States, and Minister of State for Foreign Affairs. Ambassador Deng also held a series of positions in leading think tanks and universities in the US. He graduated with an LL.B (honours) from the

T. Karbo, K. Virk (eds.), *The Palgrave Handbook of Peacebuilding in Africa*, https://doi.org/10.1007/978-3-319-62202-6

University of Khartoum in Sudan, and also holds an LL.M and a JSD from Yale Law School in the United States. He has authored and edited over 30 books in a wide variety of fields and written two novels.

Ambassador Ibrahim Gambari is Founder and Chairman of the Savannah Centre in Abuja, Nigeria. He was the Joint Special Representative of the African Union (AU)–United Nations Hybrid Operation in Darfur (UNAMID) from 2010 to 2012; Special Advisor on the International Compact with Iraq between 2007 and 2009; and UN Undersecretary-General for Political Affairs between 2005 and 2006. Ambassador Gambari was the first Undersecretary-General and Special Advisor to the UN Secretary-General on Africa (1999–2005). He was also the UN Secretary-General's Special Representative in Angola between 2002 and 2003, having previously served as his Special Envoy for Cyprus, Zimbabwe, and Myanmar. Before joining the UN Secretariat, he served as Foreign Minister of Nigeria between 1984 and 1985, and was his country's longest-serving Permanent Representative to the United Nations between 1990 and 1999. Ambassador Gambari obtained his doctorate from Columbia University in the United States, and his BA from the London School of Economics and Political Science (LSE). He was also a Research Fellow at the Brookings Institution in Washington, D.C., and is the author of several books and scholarly articles.

Ambassador John L. Hirsch is Senior Advisor at the International Peace Institute (IPI) in New York, United States, with a special focus on peace and security issues in Africa. Previously, he was Vice President and Acting Head of IPI's Africa Program between 1998 and 2005. From 2002 to 2011, he served as Director of the Occidental College United Nations Program in New York. Since 2000, Ambassador Hirsch has been an Adjunct Professor at Columbia University's School of International and Public Affairs (SIPA). His 32-year career in the US Foreign Service (1966–1998) included assignments at the United Nations, and in Africa and the Middle East. He was US Ambassador to Sierra Leone between 1995 and 1998; and served in Somalia as Political Advisor to the Commander of the Unified Task Force (UNITAF), General Robert Johnston, and as Deputy to President George H.W. Bush's Special Envoy, Ambassador Robert Oakley, in 1992–1993. He also served as Consul General in Johannesburg, South Africa, from 1990 to 1993 during that country's transition from apartheid to non-racial, multiparty democracy.

Ambassador James O.C. Jonah is a former United Nations Undersecretary-General for Political Affairs and holds a doctorate from the Massachusetts Institute of Technology (MIT) in Boston, United States. He is currently a Senior Fellow at the Ralph Bunche Institute for International Studies at the City University of New York (CUNY) Graduate Centre. In 2001, Ambassador Jonah won a Carnegie Scholar Grant to write his 2006 memoirs, *What Price the Survival of the United Nations? Memoirs of a Veteran International Civil*

Servant. Prior to this, he served his country, Sierra Leone, as Minister of Finance, Development, and Economic Planning; and as Permanent Representative of Sierra Leone to the United Nations.

Dr Tony Karbo is Co-Founder and Executive Director of N'Zarama Centre for Peacebuilding (NCP) based in Abidjan, Côte d'Ivoire. Previously, he was Executive Director of the Centre for Conflict Resolution in Cape Town, South Africa. Prior to joining CCR, he served as Director of the Karamoja Cluster Project at the University of Peace (UPEACE) Africa Programme in Kampala, Uganda, and as Managing Editor of the *Africa Peace and Conflict Journal* of the UPEACE Africa Programme. Dr Karbo has taught at universities across the Great Lakes region, the Horn of Africa, and in Eastern, Southern, and West Africa. He is a former Senior Lecturer at the Institute of Peace, Leadership, and Governance (IPLG) at Africa University, Zimbabwe. He has worked extensively in Africa with numerous organisations working in conflict zones, facilitating training in conflict resolution and peacebuilding; and monitoring and evaluating election processes and programmes. Dr Karbo is author of *Variations in Violent Conflicts in Africa: The Relative Influence of Political and Environmental Factors* (2008). He served as the Southern and Eastern Africa Representative for the Institute for Multi-Track Diplomacy (IMTD), a peacebuilding organisation based in Washington, D.C. He is a member of the Board of Trustees of the *Journal of Peacebuilding and Development*, and an Associate Director and Trainer of the South-North Center for Peacebuilding and Development. He holds a doctorate from the School of Conflict Analysis and Resolution at George Mason University, Virginia, in the United States.

Brigadier General (Professor) Dan Kuwali is an Extraordinary Professor at the Centre for Human Rights at the University of Pretoria; Distinguished Professor of Law at the University of Lilongwe, Malawi; Chief of Legal Services in the Malawi Defence Force; Fellow at the Harvard Kennedy School of Government in the United States; and Senior Fellow at the Canadian Centre for the Responsibility to Protect. Previously, he worked as a Research Fellow at the Danish Institute of International Legal Studies; Marie Curie Researcher at the Grotius Centre at Leiden University in the Netherlands; Guest Researcher at the Nordic Africa Institute in Uppsala, Sweden; Senior Researcher at the Centre for Conflict Resolution in Cape Town, South Africa; and Division Legal Advisor at the United Nations Organisation Mission in the Democratic Republic of the Congo (MONUC). He is co-editor of *By All Means Necessary: Protecting Civilians and Preventing Mass Atrocities in Africa* (2017) and *Africa and the Responsibility to Protect* (2014); and author of *Responsibility to Protect: Implementation of Article 4(h) Intervention* (2011), among other publications.

Ambassador Augustine Mahiga is Tanzania's Minister of Foreign Affairs and East African Cooperation. He was the Special Representative of the UN Secretary-General for Somalia and Head of the United Nations Political Office for Somalia (UNPOS) from 2010 to 2013. Prior to this, he was Tanzania's Permanent Representative to the UN in New York from 2003 to 2010, and Deputy Permanent Representative of Tanzania to the United Nations in Geneva from 1989 to 1992. Before joining the Tanzanian foreign service in 1983, Ambassador Mahiga worked in the President's Office as Acting Director-General and Director of Research and Training from 1977 to 1983. He also served in various capacities with the Office of the United Nations High Commissioner for Refugees (UNHCR), including as Chief of Mission to Liberia; Coordinator and Deputy Director of the humanitarian and refugee crisis in the Great Lakes region; and UNHCR Representative in India, Italy, Malta, the Holy See, and San Marino. Ambassador Mahiga holds a doctorate in philosophy and international relations from the University of Toronto, Canada.

Professor Ali A. Mazrui was Albert Schweitzer Professor in the Humanities and Director of the Institute of Global Cultural Studies at Binghamton University, State University of New York, in the United States. Previously, he was Head of the Political Science Department and Dean of the Faculty of Social Sciences at Makerere University in Uganda; and Director of the University of Michigan's Centre for Afro-American and African Studies. In 1986, Professor Mazrui wrote and narrated the influential nine-part documentary, *The Africans: A Triple Heritage*, which established his global reputation. The author of more than 30 books and hundreds of essays, he held a doctorate from the University of Oxford in England, and served in an advisory capacity to numerous organisations, including the United Nations. Professor Mazrui passed away in October 2014.

Mr Paul Mulindwa is a Senior Project Officer at the Centre for Conflict Resolution in Cape Town, South Africa. He previously served at the United Nations Population Fund (UNFPA), Minority Rights Group International, Amnesty International, and Rule of Law Association. He holds a master's degree from Makerere University in Uganda. His interests include human rights, conflict management, and peacebuilding.

Dr Ines Mzali is an Assistant Professor of English at Woosong University in Daejeon, South Korea. She specialised in African literature with a doctoral dissertation on resistance and negotiation in the representation of post-colonial conflict and violence in selected African novels. She believes in and practices an interdisciplinary approach through which artistic, political, and historical perspectives are in constant dialogue. She has since expanded the scope of her research to include film and documentary. Other research interests include the changing influence and perception of English as a first, second, and foreign language.

Dr Dawn Nagar is a former Senior Researcher at the Centre for Conflict Resolution in Cape Town, South Africa. She works on issues related to the political economy of regional integration in Africa; regional security; African politics; South Africa's foreign policy (mainly economic and security challenges); international organisations; and conflict resolution and mediation. She is co-editor of *Africa and the World: Bilateral and Multilateral International Diplomacy* (2018); *Region-Building in Africa: Political and Economic Challenges* (2016); and *Region-Building in Southern Africa: Progress, Problems and Prospects* (2012). She holds a doctorate in international relations from the University of the Witwatersrand (Wits), South Africa; and two master's degrees in philosophy and politics, from Nelson Mandela University (formerly the University of Port Elizabeth) and the University of Cape Town respectively.

Dr Sarah M.H. Nouwen is a Senior Lecturer in Law and a Co-Deputy Director of the Lauterpacht Centre for International Law at the University of Cambridge, and a Fellow of Pembroke College, Cambridge, in the United Kingdom (UK). She is the author of *Complementarity in the Line of Fire: The Catalysing Effect of the International Criminal Court in Uganda and Sudan* (2013). Dr Nouwen served as Senior Legal Advisor to the African Union High-Level Implementation Panel for Sudan, and as a consultant for the Netherlands Ministry of Foreign Affairs and the UK Department for International Development (DFID). She holds a PhD (Cantab) and LL.M (Utrecht) in international law, and an MPhil in international relations (Cantab).

Professor Kenneth Omeje is Senior Research Fellow at the John and Elnora Ferguson Centre for African Studies at the University of Bradford in the United Kingdom; and Research Fellow at the Centre for African Studies at the University of the Free State, Bloemfontein, in South Africa. He holds a doctorate in peace studies from the University of Bradford and an MA in peace and conflict studies from the European University Centre for Peace Studies in Stadtschlaining, Austria. Professor Omeje has more than 25 years of professional academic experience and has authored over 80 publications, including books, book chapters, contributions to international encyclopaedias, and articles in well-regarded journals.

Mr Ejeviome Eloho Otobo is currently a Non-Resident Senior Expert in Peacebuilding and Global Economic Policy at the Global Governance Institute in Brussels, Belgium. Previously, he held the position of Director and Deputy Head of the United Nations Peacebuilding Support Office (PBSO) at the UN Secretariat in New York, where he also acted as Assistant Secretary-General from February to August 2009.

Ms Antonia Porter is an independent consultant from the United Kingdom, currently based in Cape Town, South Africa. She has worked on conflict resolution issues with non-governmental organisations (NGOs) and think tanks based in South Africa, Mozambique, India, Nepal, the United States, and the UK for ten years. Her interest is in the use of mediation and dialogue, experiential methodologies, and multi-media and emerging technologies, to build peace at the grassroots and policymaking levels. Ms Porter has authored various book chapters on gender and peace, and co-edited a special issue of the journal *International Peacekeeping*. She has an MA in political science from the University of California, Berkeley, in the US; and a 1st class BA Honours degree from the University of Cambridge, England, with the Teape Prize.

Professor Ismail Rashid is Professor of History at Vassar College in New York, United States. Among his recent publications are *The West African Ebola Epidemic: Towards a Political Economy* (2017), co-edited with Ibrahim Abdullah; *The Paradoxes of History and Memory in Postcolonial Sierra Leone* (2013), co-edited with Sylvia Ojukutu-Macauley; and *West Africa's Security Challenges* (2004), co-edited with Adekeye Adebajo. He currently serves as Chair of the Advisory Board of the African Peacebuilding Network of the Social Science Research Council.

Professor Oliver P. Richmond is Professor of International Relations and Peace and Conflict Studies at the University of Manchester in the United Kingdom. He is also International Professor at the College of International Studies at Kyung Hee University, South Korea; and Visiting Professor at the University of Tromsø, Norway. His publications include *Peace Formation and Political Order in Conflict Affected Societies* (2016); *Failed Statebuilding* (2014); *Peace: A Very Short Introduction* (2014); *A Post-Liberal Peace* (2011); *Liberal Peace Transitions* (2009), with Jason Franks; *Peace in International Relations* (2008); and *The Transformation of Peace* (2005). He is editor of the Palgrave book series Rethinking Peace and Conflict Studies, and co-editor of the journal *Peacebuilding*.

Mr Oscar Siwali works at the Southern African Development and Reconstruction Agency (SADRA), a peacebuilding non-governmental organisation based in Cape Town, South Africa, with a focus on conflict transformation. He previously worked for many years at the Quaker Peace Centre and later the Centre for Conflict Resolution in Cape Town, where he was involved in training, facilitation, and mediation in local communities. Mr Siwali also conducted training workshops for various audiences, and undertook and provided technical assistance to partners and clients, including a range of organisations operating in the fields of conflict resolution, human rights, and HIV/AIDS. He is also an Election Conflict Resolution Panellist working with civil society and the Independent Electoral Commission (IEC) of South Africa.

Ambassador Bruno Stagno Ugarte is Deputy Executive Director of Human Rights Watch. Previously, he was Executive Director of Security Council Report (2011–2014); Foreign Minister of Costa Rica (2006–2010); Costa Rica's Ambassador to the United Nations (2002–2006); and Chief of Staff of the Foreign Ministry (1998–2000). He was elected President of the Assembly of States Parties of the International Criminal Court (ICC) (2005–2008) and of the Comprehensive Test Ban Treaty Article 14 Conferences (2007–2009). A graduate of Georgetown University, the Sorbonne, and Princeton University, he is author or editor of several publications, including *The UN Security Council in the 21st Century* (2015). He is an Officier de la Légion d'Honneur and a Visiting Professor at Sciences-Po in Paris, France.

Dr Kudrat Virk is Acting Executive Director of the Centre for Conflict Resolution in Cape Town, South Africa. She was previously Senior Researcher at the Centre for Conflict Resolution. She holds a doctorate in international relations from the University of Oxford in England. Most recently, Dr Virk is co-editor of *Foreign Policy in Post-Apartheid South Africa: Security, Diplomacy and Trade* (2018), with Adekeye Adebajo; and *The ACP Group and the EU Development Partnership: Beyond the North-South Debate* (2017), with Annita Montoute. She has contributed chapters on aspects of India's foreign policy to several volumes. Her work has also appeared in the journals *Global Responsibility to Protect* and *International Review of the Red Cross*. Dr Virk's research interests include the responsibility to protect (R2P) and humanitarian intervention; international peacekeeping and the protection of civilians; issues related to human rights, peace, and security; and emerging powers, in particular the BRICS countries (Brazil, Russia, India, China, and South Africa).

Ambassador Margaret Vogt was former Special Representative of the UN Secretary-General to the Central African Republic (CAR); and former Head of the United Nations Integrated Peacebuilding Support Office in the Central African Republic (BINUCA). Previously, she served as Deputy Director in the UN Department of Political Affairs; and as Acting Deputy Special Representative of the Secretary-General at the United Nations Political Office for Somalia. Ambassador Vogt was also Chef de Cabinet in the Office of the Chairperson of the African Union Commission in Addis Ababa. She consulted extensively for the Economic Community of West African States (ECOWAS); was the Director of the Africa Program at the International Peace Academy (now the International Peace Institute); and was an Associate Research Professor at the Nigerian Institute of International Affairs. She held a master's degree in international affairs from Columbia University, and edited or co-edited numerous publications including *Peacekeeping as a Security Strategy in Africa: Chad and Liberia as Case Studies* (1996); *Nigeria in International Peacekeeping, 1960–1992* (1993); and *The Liberian Crisis and ECOMOG: A Bold Attempt at Regional Peacekeeping* (1992). Ambassador Vogt passed away in September 2014.

Dr Njoki Wamai is a Post-Doctoral Research Associate at the Centre of Governance and Human Rights (CGHR), Department of Politics and International Studies, at the University of Cambridge, England. She completed her doctorate in politics and international studies at the University of Cambridge in 2016, where her thesis focused on the everyday politics of intervention during the period of International Criminal Court intervention in Kenya. She has previous degrees from the University of Nairobi and the African Leadership Centre (ALC) at King's College London. Dr Wamai is currently working on a book manuscript on the politics of the ICC intervention in Kenya at the everyday level.

Professor Douglas A. Yates is Professor of African Studies at the American Graduate School (AGS) in Paris; and Professor of Anglo-American Law at the University of Cergy-Pontoise, both in France. He has researched and written six books about Gabon, the oil industry, and French African policy, including *The Historical Dictionary of Gabon*, 4th edition (2018) and 3rd edition (2006); *The Scramble for African Oil* (2012); *The French Oil Industry and the Corps des Mines in Africa* (2009); and *The Rentier State in Africa: Oil-Rent Dependence and Neocolonialism in the Republic of Gabon* (1996).

Index[1]

[1] Note: Page numbers followed by 'n' refer to notes.

T. Karbo, K. Virk (eds.), *The Palgrave Handbook of Peacebuilding in Africa*, https://doi.org/10.1007/978-3-319-62202-6

B

C

H

N

O